NetBSD system operation and maintenance manuals

NetBSD System Manager's Manual
Volume 2 of 2
named(8) – zpool(8)

Title: NetBSD System Manager's Manual (Volume 2 of 2)
Subtitle: NetBSD system operation and maintenance manuals
Editor: Jeremy C. Reed
Publisher: Reed Media Services
Website: http://www.reedmedia.net/

Set ISBN 978-0-9790342-4-4
Volume 1 ISBN 978-0-9790342-5-1
Volume 2 ISBN 978-0-9790342-6-8

Contents

Preface

This is volume 2 of the NetBSD System Manager's Manual.

This two volume set contains a permuted index (in volume 1) and the definitive and official NetBSD system operation and maintenance manual from **ac** through **zpool**.

While this book is not officially published by NetBSD, it does contain the definitive documentation as maintained and distributed with the open source NetBSD operating system. It was compiled by Jeremy C. Reed, an active member of The NetBSD Foundation. Many documentation improvements from this book were *committed* into the official NetBSD source.

This set includes the section 8 manuals and a selection of section 1 manuals that also cover system maintenance procedures and commands. This book was published in May 2010 and reflects both NetBSD 5 and many features in the upcoming NetBSD 6.

This documentation was provided by a wide range of developers and projects. The many copyrights and licenses are included at the end of volume 2.

Historically, the System Manager's Manual (SMM) also included other system installation and administration documentation. Much of the original SMM and the Programmer's Supplementary Documents (PSD) and User's Supplementary Documents (USD), since published in print in 1994, have become stagnant and out-of-date or cover software or features no longer included with NetBSD. This printing does not include that unmaintained documentation. If you are interested in helping update this aged documentation, see the `src/share/doc/{smm,usd,psd}/` source files and contact the `netbsd-docs@NetBSD.org` mailing list. NetBSD also provides other open source books: *The NetBSD Guide*, *The pkgsrc Guide*, and *NetBSD Internals* (for developers).

Donations to NetBSD

The NetBSD Foundation is a non-profit organization that produces widely-used open source software. The Foundation has no regular source of income and relies on generous donations. The Foundation has U.S. Internal Revenue Code 501(c)(3) status. Please donate by visiting `http://www.NetBSD.org/donations/` or by emailing `finance-exec@NetBSD.org`.

A portion of the profits from this printed book will also be donated to The NetBSD Foundation.

Other books

The publisher of this printed book also provides other printed books, some available at Amazon, Barnes & Noble, and other book stores. Visit `http://reedmedia.net/` for more details.

History of Berkeley Unix by Jeremy C. Reed

The History of Berkeley Unix covers the origins of the Berkeley UNIX Software Tape, Second Berkeley Software Distribution, VMUnix, 4BSD and TCP/IP through the modern Berkeley Unix systems: NetBSD, FreeBSD, OpenBSD, DragonFlyBSD, and more. The book covers court cases, competition, influences on other Unix systems, licensing, and numerous other topics — based on interviews with many of the original contributors.

The Daemon, the Gnu, and the Penguin by Peter H. Salus

This book covers more than just a history of free and open source – it explores how free and open software is changing the world. Salus, a noted UNIX, open source, and Internet historian and author of *A Quarter Century of UNIX* and *Casting The Net* books, has interviewed well over a hundred key figures to document the history and background of BSD, Unix, Linux, and free and open source software. Foreword by Jon "maddog" Hall.

The Best of FreeBSD Basics by Dru Lavigne

Geared toward new users and also useful for experienced admins, The Best of FreeBSD Basics contains a lot of information relevant to all BSDs (and Unix). Dru Lavigne's book covers a wide range of topics with step-by-step directions, such as setting up a window manager, using FreeBSD on the desktop, upgrading ports, mounting filesystems, configuring ACLs, Unix fundamentals, using Wireshark, printing basics, NFS, DHCP services, checking system security, configuring SSH, setting up VPNs, and a lot more.

The pfSense Handbook by Christopher M. Buechler

The book covers the installation, configuration, and maintenance of pfSense, an open source, customized distribution of FreeBSD tailored for use as a firewall and router, entirely managed in an easy-to-use web interface. The book covers hardware, network designs, firewalling, packet filtering, network address translation, routing, WANs, traffic shaping, IPsec, PPTP, VPNs, load balancing, wireless access points, virtualization, CARP and redundancy, DHCP, DNS, and other various services and special purpose appliances. No FreeBSD knowledge is required to deploy and use pfSense.

The BSD Associate Study Guide

The beginning BSD Unix administration book covers the objectives for the BSD Certification Group's BSDA (BSD Associate) Certification focused for BSD Unix system administrators with light to moderate skills. The community-written, open source book covers generic *BSD administration and specific skills as necessary for NetBSD, FreeBSD, OpenBSD, and DragonFly.

Getting started with NetBSD by Jeremy C. Reed

This book quickly introduces NetBSD – from installation, standard setup, maintenance, standard system operations, and common use of NetBSD. It covers installation using sysinst, the first login, system startup, users and groups, networking setup and troubleshooting, DNS, system clock, software packages, pkgsrc (for easily installing software from source), email services, cron and scheduled tasks, log files, disks and file systems, custom kernels, updating NetBSD, security, performance monitoring and tuning, packet filtering, X11 and graphical interfaces, popular applications, multimedia, and printing.

BIND DNS Administration Reference Book

This book includes the authoritative reference of the configuration syntax and grammar plus the the usage and command-line arguments for the ISC BIND suite. The book is based on open source documentation included in the BIND source. It adds new content, examples, detailed indexing and cross-referencing for easy research and study.

Beginning DNSSEC

An introduction to signing, deploying, validating, maintaining, and troubleshooting signed DNS zones. Includes many real-world examples and it uses ISC BIND as the reference for the DNS server, DNS libraries, and related tools for implementing and testing DNSSEC. (Other software and tools are also introduced.) This book also introduces DNSSEC-enabled resolver functions so developers can take advantage of signed zones in their own code. While the main focus is signing DNS records, Beginning DNSSEC also covers securing communications between DNS servers.

DNSSEC Specifications

This DNSSEC Specifications book contains a compilation of DNS Security Extensions standards. This authoritative reference includes numerous examples, detailed descriptions, design background and decisions, and references.

The OpenBSD PF Packet Filter Book

This book introduces the features and capabilities of PF and its related tools with many examples and steps for configuring and using the packet filter, ALTQ, address translation, spamd and more on the OpenBSD, NetBSD, FreeBSD and DragonFly operating systems. The book includes ample cross-referencing and a detailed index for easy research and reading.

Manuals

named(8) - zpool(8)

NAME
named – Internet domain name server

SYNOPSIS
named [**–4**] [**–6**] [**–c** *config–file*] [**–d** *debug–level*] [**–E** *engine–name*] [**–f**] [**–g**] [**–m** *flag*] [**–n** *#cpus*]
[**–p** *port*] [**–s**] [**–S** *#max–socks*] [**–t** *directory*] [**–u** *user*] [**–v**] [**–V**] [**–x** *cache–file*]

DESCRIPTION
named is a Domain Name System (DNS) server, part of the BIND 9 distribution from ISC. For more information on the DNS, see RFCs 1033, 1034, and 1035.

When invoked without arguments, **named** will read the default configuration file */etc/named.conf*, read any initial data, and listen for queries.

OPTIONS
–4
Use IPv4 only even if the host machine is capable of IPv6. **–4** and **–6** are mutually exclusive.

–6
Use IPv6 only even if the host machine is capable of IPv4. **–4** and **–6** are mutually exclusive.

–c *config–file*
Use *config–file* as the configuration file instead of the default, */etc/named.conf*. To ensure that reloading the configuration file continues to work after the server has changed its working directory due to to a possible **directory** option in the configuration file, *config–file* should be an absolute pathname.

–d *debug–level*
Set the daemon's debug level to *debug–level*. Debugging traces from **named** become more verbose as the debug level increases.

–E *engine–name*
Use a crypto hardware (OpenSSL engine) for the crypto operations it supports, for instance re–signing with private keys from a secure key store. When compiled with PKCS#11 support *engine–name* defaults to pkcs11, the empty name resets it to no engine.

–f
Run the server in the foreground (i.e. do not daemonize).

–g
Run the server in the foreground and force all logging to *stderr*.

–m *flag*
Turn on memory usage debugging flags. Possible flags are *usage*, *trace*, *record*, *size*, and *mctx*. These correspond to the ISC_MEM_DEBUGXXXX flags described in *<isc/mem.h>*.

–n *#cpus*
Create *#cpus* worker threads to take advantage of multiple CPUs. If not specified, **named** will try to determine the number of CPUs present and create one thread per CPU. If it is unable to determine the number of CPUs, a single worker thread will be created.

–p *port*
Listen for queries on port *port*. If not specified, the default is port 53.

–s
Write memory usage statistics to *stdout* on exit.
Note: This option is mainly of interest to BIND 9 developers and may be removed or changed in a future release.

–S *#max–socks*
Allow **named** to use up to *#max–socks* sockets.
Warning: This option should be unnecessary for the vast majority of users. The use of this option could even be harmful because the specified value may exceed the limitation of the

underlying system API. It is therefore set only when the default configuration causes exhaustion of file descriptors and the operational environment is known to support the specified number of sockets. Note also that the actual maximum number is normally a little fewer than the specified value because **named** reserves some file descriptors for its internal use.

−t *directory*

Chroot to *directory* after processing the command line arguments, but before reading the configuration file.

> **Warning:** This option should be used in conjunction with the **−u** option, as chrooting a process running as root doesn't enhance security on most systems; the way **chroot(2)** is defined allows a process with root privileges to escape a chroot jail.

−u *user*

Setuid to *user* after completing privileged operations, such as creating sockets that listen on privileged ports.

> **Note:** On Linux, **named** uses the kernel's capability mechanism to drop all root privileges except the ability to **bind(2)** to a privileged port and set process resource limits. Unfortunately, this means that the **−u** option only works when **named** is run on kernel 2.2.18 or later, or kernel 2.3.99−pre3 or later, since previous kernels did not allow privileges to be retained after **setuid(2)**.

−v

Report the version number and exit.

−V

Report the version number and build options, and exit.

−x *cache−file*

Load data from *cache−file* into the cache of the default view.

> **Warning:** This option must not be used. It is only of interest to BIND 9 developers and may be removed or changed in a future release.

SIGNALS

In routine operation, signals should not be used to control the nameserver; **rndc** should be used instead.

SIGHUP

Force a reload of the server.

SIGINT, SIGTERM

Shut down the server.

The result of sending any other signals to the server is undefined.

CONFIGURATION

The **named** configuration file is too complex to describe in detail here. A complete description is provided in the BIND 9 Administrator Reference Manual.

named inherits the **umask** (file creation mode mask) from the parent process. If files created by **named**, such as journal files, need to have custom permissions, the **umask** should be set explicitly in the script used to start the **named** process.

FILES

/etc/named.conf

The default configuration file.

/var/run/named/named.pid

The default process−id file.

SEE ALSO

RFC 1033, RFC 1034, RFC 1035, **named−checkconf**(8), **named−checkzone**(8), **rndc**(8), **lwresd**(8), **named.conf**(5), BIND 9 Administrator Reference Manual.

AUTHOR

Internet Systems Consortium

COPYRIGHT

NAME

named–checkconf – named configuration file syntax checking tool

SYNOPSIS

named–checkconf [**–h**] [**–v**] [**–j**] [**–t** *directory*] {filename} [**–p**] [**–z**]

DESCRIPTION

named–checkconf checks the syntax, but not the semantics, of a named configuration file.

OPTIONS

–h

Print the usage summary and exit.

–t *directory*

Chroot to *directory* so that include directives in the configuration file are processed as if run by a similarly chrooted named.

–v

Print the version of the **named–checkconf** program and exit.

–p

Print out the *named.conf* and included files in canonical form if no errors were detected.

–z

Perform a test load of all master zones found in *named.conf*.

–j

When loading a zonefile read the journal if it exists.

filename

The name of the configuration file to be checked. If not specified, it defaults to */etc/named.conf*.

RETURN VALUES

named–checkconf returns an exit status of 1 if errors were detected and 0 otherwise.

SEE ALSO

named(8), **named–checkzone**(8), BIND 9 Administrator Reference Manual.

AUTHOR

Internet Systems Consortium

COPYRIGHT

Copyright © 2004, 2005, 2007, 2009 Internet Systems Consortium, Inc. ("ISC")
Copyright © 2000–2002 Internet Software Consortium.

NAME

named–checkzone, named–compilezone – zone file validity checking or converting tool

SYNOPSIS

named–checkzone [**–d**] [**–h**] [**–j**] [**–q**] [**–v**] [**–c** *class*] [**–f** *format*] [**–F** *format*] [**–i** *mode*] [**–k** *mode*]
[**–m** *mode*] [**–M** *mode*] [**–n** *mode*] [**–r** *mode*] [**–s** *style*] [**–S** *mode*] [**–t** *directory*]
[**–w** *directory*] [**–D**] [**–W** *mode*] {zonename} {filename}

named–compilezone [**–d**] [**–j**] [**–q**] [**–v**] [**–c** *class*] [**–C** *mode*] [**–f** *format*] [**–F** *format*] [**–i** *mode*]
[**–k** *mode*] [**–m** *mode*] [**–n** *mode*] [**–o** *filename*] [**–r** *mode*] [**–s** *style*] [**–t** *directory*]
[**–w** *directory*] [**–D**] [**–W** *mode*] {**–o** *filename*} {zonename} {filename}

DESCRIPTION

named–checkzone checks the syntax and integrity of a zone file. It performs the same checks as **named**
does when loading a zone. This makes **named–checkzone** useful for checking zone files before configuring
them into a name server.

named–compilezone is similar to **named–checkzone**, but it always dumps the zone contents to a specified
file in a specified format. Additionally, it applies stricter check levels by default, since the dump output will
be used as an actual zone file loaded by **named**. When manually specified otherwise, the check levels must
at least be as strict as those specified in the **named** configuration file.

OPTIONS

–d

Enable debugging.

–h

Print the usage summary and exit.

–q

Quiet mode – exit code only.

–v

Print the version of the **named–checkzone** program and exit.

–j

When loading the zone file read the journal if it exists.

–c *class*

Specify the class of the zone. If not specified, "IN" is assumed.

–i *mode*

Perform post–load zone integrity checks. Possible modes are **"full"** (default), **"full–sibling"**, **"local"**,
"local–sibling" and **"none"**.

Mode **"full"** checks that MX records refer to A or AAAA record (both in–zone and out–of–zone
hostnames). Mode **"local"** only checks MX records which refer to in–zone hostnames.

Mode **"full"** checks that SRV records refer to A or AAAA record (both in–zone and out–of–zone
hostnames). Mode **"local"** only checks SRV records which refer to in–zone hostnames.

Mode **"full"** checks that delegation NS records refer to A or AAAA record (both in–zone and
out–of–zone hostnames). It also checks that glue address records in the zone match those advertised
by the child. Mode **"local"** only checks NS records which refer to in–zone hostnames or that some
required glue exists, that is when the nameserver is in a child zone.

Mode **"full–sibling"** and **"local–sibling"** disable sibling glue checks but are otherwise the same as
"full" and **"local"** respectively.

Mode **"none"** disables the checks.

–f *format*

Specify the format of the zone file. Possible formats are **"text"** (default) and **"raw"**.

−F *format*

Specify the format of the output file specified. Possible formats are **"text"** (default) and **"raw"**. For **named–checkzone**, this does not cause any effects unless it dumps the zone contents.

−k *mode*

Perform **"check–names"** checks with the specified failure mode. Possible modes are **"fail"** (default for **named–compilezone**), **"warn"** (default for **named–checkzone**) and **"ignore"**.

−m *mode*

Specify whether MX records should be checked to see if they are addresses. Possible modes are **"fail"**, **"warn"** (default) and **"ignore"**.

−M *mode*

Check if a MX record refers to a CNAME. Possible modes are **"fail"**, **"warn"** (default) and **"ignore"**.

−n *mode*

Specify whether NS records should be checked to see if they are addresses. Possible modes are **"fail"** (default for **named–compilezone**), **"warn"** (default for **named–checkzone**) and **"ignore"**.

−o *filename*

Write zone output to *filename*. If *filename* is − then write to standard out. This is mandatory for **named–compilezone**.

−r *mode*

Check for records that are treated as different by DNSSEC but are semantically equal in plain DNS. Possible modes are **"fail"**, **"warn"** (default) and **"ignore"**.

−s *style*

Specify the style of the dumped zone file. Possible styles are **"full"** (default) and **"relative"**. The full format is most suitable for processing automatically by a separate script. On the other hand, the relative format is more human–readable and is thus suitable for editing by hand. For **named–checkzone** this does not cause any effects unless it dumps the zone contents. It also does not have any meaning if the output format is not text.

−S *mode*

Check if a SRV record refers to a CNAME. Possible modes are **"fail"**, **"warn"** (default) and **"ignore"**.

−t *directory*

Chroot to *directory* so that include directives in the configuration file are processed as if run by a similarly chrooted named.

−w *directory*

chdir to *directory* so that relative filenames in master file $INCLUDE directives work. This is similar to the directory clause in *named.conf*.

−D

Dump zone file in canonical format. This is always enabled for **named–compilezone**.

−W *mode*

Specify whether to check for non–terminal wildcards. Non–terminal wildcards are almost always the result of a failure to understand the wildcard matching algorithm (RFC 1034). Possible modes are **"warn"** (default) and **"ignore"**.

zonename

The domain name of the zone being checked.

filename

The name of the zone file.

NAMED–CHECKZONE(8)   BIND9   NAMED–CHECKZONE(8)

RETURN VALUES
  named–checkzone returns an exit status of 1 if errors were detected and 0 otherwise.

SEE ALSO
  named(8), **named–checkconf**(8), RFC 1035, BIND 9 Administrator Reference Manual.

AUTHOR
  Internet Systems Consortium

COPYRIGHT
  Copyright © 2004–2007, 2009 Internet Systems Consortium, Inc. ("ISC")
  Copyright © 2000–2002 Internet Software Consortium.

NAME

ncdcs — update the CRC & size in an IBM Network Station 1000 bootable

SYNOPSIS

ncdcs *infile* [*outfile*]

DESCRIPTION

The **ncdcs** utility adds the cyclic redundancy check and image size information to a bootable NetBSD image. The image must contain an NCD firmware header at the very beginning of its text segment.

HISTORY

The **ncdcs** utility came from the Linux IBM Network Station 1000 port by Jochen Roth.

NAME

ndbootd — Sun Network Disk (ND) Protocol server

SYNOPSIS

ndbootd [**-s** *boot2*] [**-i** *interface*] [**-w** *windowsize*] [**-d**] *boot1*

DESCRIPTION

ndbootd is a server which supports the Sun Network Disk (ND) Protocol. This protocol was designed by Sun before they designed NFS. ND simply makes the raw blocks of a disk available to network clients. Contrast this with the true namespace and file abstractions that NFS provides.

The only reason you're likely to encounter ND nowadays is if you have an old Sun 2 machine, like the 2/120 or 2/50. The Sun 2 PROMs can only use ND to boot over the network. (Later, the Sun 3 PROMs would use RARP and TFTP to boot over the network.)

ndbootd is a very simple ND server that only supports client reads for booting. It exports a disk that the clients consider to be /dev/ndp0 (ND public unit zero). The disk is available only to clients that are listed in /etc/ethers and have valid hostnames. (Sun 2 PROMs don't do RARP, but they do learn their IP address from the first ND response they receive from the server.)

boot1 is a file containing the mandatory first-stage network boot program, typically /usr/mdec/bootyy. The layout of the exported disk is:

- block 0: normally a Sun disklabel (but ignored by the PROM)
- blocks 1-15: the first-stage network boot program

With the **-s** *boot2* option, **ndbootd** will also make a second-stage network boot program available to clients, typically /usr/mdec/netboot. When *boot2* is a filename, that file is the single second-stage network boot program to be served to all clients.

When *boot2* is a directory name, typically /tftpboot, **ndbootd** finds a client's second-stage network boot program by turning its IP address into a filename in that directory, in the same manner later Sun 3 PROMs do when TFTPing (i.e., if a client has IP address 192.168.1.10, **ndbootd** expects to find /tftpboot/C0A8010A.SUN2).

When used in this last manner with an ND-aware first-stage boot program, **ndbootd** serves the same purpose in the Sun 2 netboot process as tftpd(8) serves in the Sun 3 netboot process.

Any second-stage network boot program always begins at block 16 of the exported disk, regardless of the length of the first-stage network boot program.

All first- and second-stage network boot programs must have all executable headers stripped off; they must be raw binary programs.

The remaining options are:

-i *interface*
> Only listen for ND clients on interface *interface*. Normally **ndbootd** listens for clients on the first non-loopback IP interface that is up and running.

-w *windowsize*
> This adjusts the window size of the ND protocol. This is the number of 1-kilobyte packets that can be transmitted before waiting for an acknowledgement. Defaults to 6.

-d
> Run in debug mode. Debugging output goes to standard error and the server will not fork.

FILES

    /etc/ethers
    /etc/hosts

SEE ALSO

    tftpd(8)

BUGS

Whether or not there is a second-stage network boot program, the exported disk appears to all clients to have infinite length. The content of all blocks not used by the first- or second-stage network boot programs is undefined. All client reads of undefined blocks are silently allowed by the server.

NAME

ndiscvt — convert Windows® NDIS drivers for use with NetBSD

SYNOPSIS

ndiscvt [-O] [-i *inffile*] [-n *devname*] [-o *outfile*] -s *sysfile*

DESCRIPTION

The **ndiscvt** utility transforms a Windows® NDIS driver into a data file which is used to build an ndis compatibility driver module. Windows® drivers consist of two main parts: a .SYS file, which contains the actual driver executable code, and an .INF file, which provides the Windows® installer with device identifier information and a list of driver-specific registry keys. The **ndiscvt** utility can convert these files into a header file that is compiled into if_ndis.c to create an object code module that can be linked into the NetBSD kernel.

The .INF file is typically required since only it contains device identification data such as PCI vendor and device IDs or PCMCIA indentifier strings. The .INF file may be optionally omitted however, in which case the **ndiscvt** utility will only perform the conversion of the .SYS file. This is useful for debugging purposes only.

OPTIONS

The options are as follows:

-i *inffile*   Open and parse the specified .INF file when performing conversion. The **ndiscvt** utility will parse this file and emit a device identification structure and registry key configuration structures which will be used by the ndis driver and ndisapi kernel subsystem. If this is omitted, **ndiscvt** will emit a dummy configuration structure only.

-n *devname*   Specify an alternate name for the network device/interface which will be created when the driver is instantiated. If you need to load more than one NDIS driver into your system (i.e., if you have two different network cards in your system which require NDIS driver support), each module you create must have a unique name. Device can not be larger than IFNAMSIZ. If no name is specified, the driver will use the default a default name ("ndis").

-O   Generate both an ndis_driver_data.h file and an ndis_driver.data.o file. The latter file will contain a copy of the Windows® .SYS driver image encoded as a NetBSD ELF object file (created with objcopy(1)). Turning the Windows® driver image directly into an object code file saves disk space and compilation time.

-o *outfile*   Specify the output file in which to place the resulting data. This can be any file pathname. If *outfile* is a single dash (' - '), the data will be written to the standard output. The if_ndis.c module expects to find the driver data in a file called ndis_driver_data.h, so it is recommended that this name be used.

-s *sysfile*   Open and parse the specified .SYS file. This file must contain a Windows® driver image. The **ndiscvt** utility will perform some manipulation of the sections within the executable file to make runtime linking within the kernel a little easier and then convert the image into a data array.

SEE ALSO
> ld(1), objcopy(1), ndis(4)

HISTORY
> The **ndiscvt** utility first appeared in FreeBSD 5.3.

AUTHORS
> The **ndiscvt** utility was written by Bill Paul ⟨wpaul@windriver.com⟩. The lex(1) and yacc(1) .INF file parser was written by Matthew Dodd ⟨mdodd@FreeBSD.org⟩.

NAME

ndp — control/diagnose IPv6 neighbor discovery protocol

SYNOPSIS

ndp [-nt] *hostname*
ndp [-nt] -a | -c | -p
ndp [-nt] -r
ndp [-nt] -H | -P | -R
ndp [-nt] -A *wait*
ndp [-nt] -d *hostname*
ndp [-nt] -f *filename*
ndp [-nt] -i *interface* [*expressions* ...]
ndp [-nt] -I [*interface* | delete]
ndp [-nt] -s *nodename etheraddr* [temp] [proxy]

DESCRIPTION

The **ndp** command manipulates the address mapping table used by the Neighbor Discovery Protocol (NDP).

-a   Dump the currently existing NDP entries. The following information will be printed:

    Neighbor   IPv6 address of the neighbor.

    Linklayer Address
           Linklayer address of the neighbor. It could be "(incomplete)" when the address is not available.

    Netif   Network interface associated with the neighbor cache entry.

    Expire   The time until expiry of the entry. The entry could become "permanent", in which case it will never expire.

    S   State of the neighbor cache entry, as a single letter:

N	Nostate
W	Waitdelete
I	Incomplete
R	Reachable
S	Stale
D	Delay
P	Probe
?	Unknown state (should never happen).

    Flags   Flags on the neighbor cache entry, in a single letter. They are: Router, proxy neighbor advertisement ("p"). The field could be followed by a decimal number, which means the number of NS probes the node has sent during the current state.

-A *wait*
    Repeat **-a** (dump NDP entries) every *wait* seconds.

-c   Erase all the NDP entries.

-d   Delete specified NDP entry.

-f   Parse the file specified by *filename*.

-H   Harmonize consistency between the routing table and the default router list; install the top entry of the list into the kernel routing table.

-I   Shows the default interface used as the default route when there is no default router.

-I *interface*
              Specifies the default *interface* to be used when there is no interface specified even though required.

-I delete
              The current default interface will be deleted from the kernel.

-i *interface* [*expressions* . . .]
              View ND information for the specified interface. If additional arguments *expressions* are given, **ndp** sets or clears the flags or variables for the interface as specified in the expression. Each expression should be separated by white spaces or tab characters. Possible expressions are as follows. Some of the expressions can begin with the special character '–', which means the flag specified in the expression should be cleared. Note that you need **--** before **-foo** in this case.

              nud   Turn on or off NUD (Neighbor Unreachability Detection) on the interface. NUD is usually turned on by default.

              accept_rtadv
                        Specify whether or not to accept Router Advertisement messages received on the *interface*. Note that the kernel does not accept Router Advertisement messages, even if the flag **accept_rtadv** is on, unless either the net.inet6.ip6.accept_rtadv variable is non-0, or the flag **override_rtadv** is on. This flag is set to 1 by default.

              override_rtadv
                        Specify whether or not to override the net.inet6.ip6.accept_rtadv variable. If the flag is on, then it will suffice to set the flag **accept_rtadv** to make the kernel accept Router Advertisement messages on the *interface*. This flag is set to 0 by default.

              prefer_source
                        Prefer addresses on the *interface* as candidates of the source address for outgoing packets. The default value of this flag is off. For more details about the entire algorithm of source address selection, see the IMPLEMENTATION file supplied with the KAME kit.

              disabled
                        Disable IPv6 operation on the interface. When disabled, the interface discards any IPv6 packets received on or being sent to the interface. In the sending case, an error of ENET-DOWN will be returned to the application. This flag is typically set automatically in the kernel as a result of a certain failure of Duplicate Address Detection. While the flag can be set or cleared by hand with the **ndp** command, it is not generally advisable to modify this flag manually.

              basereachable=(number)
                        Specify the BaseReachbleTimer on the interface in millisecond.

              retrans=(number)
                        Specify the RetransTimer on the interface in millisecond.

              curhlim=(number)
                        Specify the Cur Hop Limit on the interface.

-n   Do not try to resolve numeric addresses to hostnames.

-p   Show prefix list.

-P   Flush all the entries in the prefix list.

-r   Show default router list.

-R   Flush all the entries in the default router list.

-s Register an NDP entry for a node. The entry will be permanent unless the word `temp` is given in the command. If the word `proxy` is given, this system will act as a proxy NDP server, responding to requests for *hostname* even though the host address is not its own.

-t Print timestamp on each entry, making it possible to merge output with `tcpdump`(8). Most useful when used with **−A**.

RETURN VALUES

  The **ndp** command will exit with 0 on success, and non-zero on errors.

SEE ALSO

  `arp`(8)

HISTORY

  The **ndp** command first appeared in the WIDE Hydrangea IPv6 protocol stack kit.

NAME

    netgroup_mkdb — generate the netgroup database

SYNOPSIS

    netgroup_mkdb [**-o** *database*] [file]

DESCRIPTION

    netgroup_mkdb creates a db(3) database for the specified file. If no file is specified, then /etc/netgroup is used. This database is installed into /var/db/netgroup.db. The file must be in the correct format (see netgroup(5)).

    The options are as follows:

    -o *database*
        Put the output databases in the named file.

    The databases are used by the C library netgroup routines (see getnetgrent(3)).

    netgroup_mkdb exits zero on success, non-zero on failure.

FILES

    /var/db/netgroup.db   The current netgroup database
    /var/db/netgroup.db.tmp
                   A temporary file
    /etc/netgroup   The current netgroup file

SEE ALSO

    db(3), getnetgrent(3), netgroup(5)

BUGS

    Because **netgroup_mkdb** guarantees not to install a partial destination file it must build a temporary file in the same file system and if successful use rename(2) to install over the destination file.

    If **netgroup_mkdb** fails it will leave the previous version of the destination file intact.

NAME
newbtconf — multiple boot-up configurations

SYNOPSIS
newbtconf *new-conf-name* [*orig-conf-name*]
newbtconf init
newbtconf revert

DESCRIPTION
newbtconf is used to set up the system in such a way that the user is offered a selection of environments in which to boot the system up into. The most obvious application being for laptops to provide a network and non-network environment after a successful boot into multi-user mode.

Background
In order to accomplish this task, the files usually associated with establishing the current system's running configuration are replaced with symbolic links which are adjusted with each boot to point to the appropriate file for the desired run-time environment. This is accomplished by directing all of the symbolic links through a directory which itself is a symbolic link (/etc/etc.current), to the destination files. At each bootup, the selection made changes which directory /etc/etc.current points to.

Through doing this and reloading /etc/rc.conf in /etc/rc after the link has been established, the resulting run-time configuration is effectively controlled without the need to directly edit any files. The default boot-up environment is selected by manually directing which configuration directory /etc/etc.default points to. As opposed to /etc/etc.current (which is updated with every boot), /etc/etc.default is not automatically updated.

Getting Started
By default, NetBSD only has one boot-up configuration - that set in the file /etc/rc.conf. In order to initialize the system for operating in a manner which supports multiple boot configurations, **newbtconf** must be run with an argument of 'init'. This will create two symbolic links /etc/etc.current and /etc/etc.default to the directory /etc/etc.network. The following files are all moved into that directory and symbolic links put in their place, in /etc, pointing to /etc/etc.current/<filename>:

```
/etc/defaultdomain
/etc/fstab
/etc/ifconfig.*
/etc/inetd.conf
/etc/mrouted.conf
/etc/mygate
/etc/myname
/etc/netstart
/etc/nsswitch.conf
/etc/ntp.conf
/etc/rc.conf
/etc/rc.conf.d
/etc/resolv.conf
```

To test that this has been performed correctly, reboot your system into NetBSD. After the kernel has autoconfigured and tty flags have been set, a prompt should appear, preceded by the following like, looking like this:

```
[network]
Which configuration [network] ?
```

The []'s are used to indicate the default configuration, which can be selected by just pressing return. If there were other configurations available at this stage, you would have 30 seconds to enter that name and press **RETURN**.

Multiple Configurations

Once an initial configuration has been set up, we can proceed to set up further run time environments. This is done by invoking **newbtconf** with the name of the new configuration to be created. By default, this step will use the current configuration files as the basis for this setup unless a second parameter is given - that of the configuration to use as the basis for the new one. Upon completion, a new directory, /etc/etc.<newname>, will have been created, priming the directory with the appropriate files for editing. For example, if we do **newbtconf** *nonet network* it would create a directory named /etc/etc.nonet and copy all the files from /etc/etc.network into that directory. Upon rebooting, we should see:

```
[network] nonet
Which configuration [network] ?
```

To set up the system for booting into the "nonet" configuration, the files in /etc/etc.nonet need be edited.

If you wanted to make "nonet" the default configuration when booting, you would need delete the symbolic link /etc/etc.default and create a new symbolic link (with the same name) to /etc/etc.nonet. Booting up after having made such a change would result in the following being displayed:

```
network [nonet]
Which configuration [nonet] ?
```

No Network

Assuming that we performed the above command successfully, in order to successfully configure NetBSD to not configure interfaces (or generate no errors from attempting to do so), the following settings (at least) should be used in /etc/etc.nonet/rc.conf:

```
auto_ifconfig=NO
net_interfaces=NO
```

Of course other networking services, such as NTP, routed, etc, are all expected to be "NO". In general, the only setting that should be "YES" is syslogd, and perhaps cron (if your cron scripts don't need the network) or screenblank/wscons (if applicable). Other actions such as deleting any NFS mounts from /etc/etc.nonet/fstab would also need to be undertaken.

Reverting multiple boot configurations

Multiple boot configurations can be deactivated by running **newbtconf** with an argument of **revert**. All the symlinks mentioned above are then removed and the files they point to are copied to their default place. This effectively makes the currently selected configuration the only one active. The symbolic links /etc/etc.current and /etc/etc.default are also removed so upon rebooting no configuration selection menu is displayed. Note that the previously created configurations (in /etc/etc.<name>) are not removed.

FILES

/etc/etc.current	Symbolic link to current config directory.
/etc/etc.default	Symbolic link to default config directory.
/etc/defaultdomain	These files all become symbolic links.

```
/etc/fstab
/etc/ifconfig.*
/etc/inetd.conf
/etc/mrouted.conf
/etc/mygate
/etc/myname
/etc/netstart
/etc/nsswitch.conf
/etc/ntp.conf
/etc/rc.conf
/etc/rc.conf.d
/etc/resolv.conf
```

SEE ALSO

rc.conf(5), rc(8)

HISTORY

The **newbtconf** program first appeared in NetBSD 1.5.

AUTHORS

This shell script was written by Darren Reed ⟨darrenr@NetBSD.org⟩ with initial input from Matthew Green ⟨mrg@NetBSD.org⟩ on how to approach this problem.

BUGS

It presently does not display a count down timer whilst waiting for input to select which configuration and nor does it abort said timer when a key is first pressed.

The management of the overall collection of multiple configurations is much more manual than it ought to be. A general system configuration tool needs to be written to ease their management.

NAME

newdisk — Prepare a new disk to be usable for X680x0

SYNOPSIS

newdisk [**-vnfcp**] [**-m** *mboot*] *raw_device*

DESCRIPTION

newdisk prepares a new hard disk to be bootable from by X680x0. It should NOT be used for floppy disks.

It creates a disk mark for IOCS to determine the disk geometry, writes the primary boot program (mboot), and creates empty partition table. The option are as follows:

-v   Verbose mode.

-n   Dryrun mode. Nothing is written to the disk.

-f   Force. Usually, when **newdisk** detects existing disk mark, it aborts with some error messages. **-f** option prevents this behaviour.

-c   Check only. **newdisk** looks at the disk whether it is already marked.

-p   Do not create the partition table.

-m *mboot*
        Specifies the mboot program to be written.

FILES

/usr/mdec/mboot   The default primary boot program.

SEE ALSO

boot(8), installboot(8)

HISTORY

The **newdisk** utility first appeared in NetBSD 1.5.

AUTHORS

newdisk was written by MINOURA Makoto ⟨minoura@NetBSD.org⟩.

NAME

newfs — construct a new file system

SYNOPSIS

newfs [**-FINZ**] [**-a** *maxcontig*] [**-B** *byte-order*] [**-b** *block-size*] [**-d** *maxbsize*]
    [**-e** *maxbpg*] [**-f** *frag-size*] [**-g** *avgfilesize*] [**-h** *avgfpdir*]
    [**-i** *bytes-per-inode*] [**-m** *free-space*] [**-n** *inodes*]
    [**-O** *filesystem-format*] [**-o** *optimization*] [**-S** *sector-size*] [**-s** *size*]
    [**-T** *disk-type*] [**-v** *volname*] [**-V** *verbose*] *special*

DESCRIPTION

newfs is used to initialize and clear file systems before first use. Before running **newfs** the disk must be
labeled using disklabel(8). **newfs** builds a file system on the specified special device basing its defaults
on the information in the disk label. Typically the defaults are reasonable, however **newfs** has numerous
options to allow the defaults to be selectively overridden.

Options with numeric arguments may contain an optional (case-insensitive) suffix:

b   Bytes; causes no modification. (Default)
k   Kilo; multiply the argument by 1024.
m   Mega; multiply the argument by 1048576.
g   Giga; multiply the argument by 1073741824.
t   Tera; multiply the argument by 1099511627776.

The following options define the general layout policies.

-a *maxcontig*

This sets the obsolete maxcontig parameter.

-B *byte-order*

Specify the metadata byte order of the file system to be created. Valid byte orders are 'be' and
'le'. If no byte order is specified, the file system is created in host byte order.

-b *block-size*

The block size of the file system, in bytes. It must be a power of two. The smallest allowable
size is 4096 bytes. The default size depends upon the size of the file system:

file system size	block-size
< 20 MB	4 KB
< 1024 MB	8 KB
>= 1024 MB	16 KB

-d *maxbsize*

Set the maximum extent size to *maxbsize*.

-e *maxbpg*

This indicates the maximum number of blocks any single file can allocate out of a cylinder
group before it is forced to begin allocating blocks from another cylinder group. The default is
about one quarter of the total blocks in a cylinder group. See tunefs(8) for more details on
how to set this option.

-F   Create a file system image in *special*. The file system size needs to be specified with "**-s**
size". No attempts to use or update the disk label will be made.

-f *frag-size*

The fragment size of the file system in bytes. It must be a power of two ranging in value
between *block-size*/8 and *block-size*. The optimal *block-size:frag-size* ratio
is 8:1. Other ratios are possible, but are not recommended, and may produce unpredictable

results. The default size depends upon the size of the file system:

file system size	frag-size
< 20 MB	0.5 KB
< 1024 MB	1 KB
>= 1024 MB	2 KB

-g *avgfilesize*

>   The expected average file size for the file system.

-h *avgfpdir*

>   The expected average number of files per directory on the file system.

-I

>   Do not require that the file system type listed in the disk label is 4.2BSD or Apple UFS.

-i *bytes-per-inode*

>   This specifies the density of inodes in the file system. If fewer inodes are desired, a larger number should be used; to create more inodes a smaller number should be given. The default is to create an inode for every (4 * frag-size) bytes of data space:

file system size	bytes-per-inode
< 20 MB	2 KB
< 1024 MB	4 KB
>= 1024 MB	8 KB

-m *free-space*

>   The percentage of space reserved from normal users; the minimum free space threshold. The default value used is 5%. See tunefs(8) for more details on how to set this option.

-N

>   Causes the file system parameters to be printed out without really creating the file system.

-n *inodes*

>   This specifies the number of inodes for the filesystem. If both **-i** and **-n** are specified then **-n** takes precedence.

-O *filesystem-format*

>   Select the filesystem-format.
>
>   0   4.3BSD; This option is primarily used to build root file systems that can be understood by older boot ROMs.
>
>   1   FFSv1; normal fast-filesystem (default). This is also known as 'FFS', 'UFS', or 'UFS1'.
>
>   2   FFSv2; enhanced fast-filesystem (suited for more than 1 Terabyte capacity, access control lists). This is also known as 'UFS2'.
>
>   To create an LFS filesystem see newfs_lfs(8). To create a Linux ext2 filesystem see newfs_ext2fs(8).

-o *optimization*

>   Optimization preference; either "space" or "time". The file system can either be instructed to try to minimize the time spent allocating blocks, or to try to minimize the space fragmentation on the disk. If the value of minfree (see above) is less than 5%, the default is to optimize for space; if the value of minfree is greater than or equal to 5%, the default is to optimize for time. See tunefs(8) for more details on how to set this option.

-s *size*   The size of the file system in sectors. An 's' suffix will be interpreted as the number of sectors (the default). All other suffixes are interpreted as per other numeric arguments, except that the number is converted into sectors by dividing by the sector size (as specified by **-S** *secsize*) after suffix interpretation.

If no **−s** `size` is specified then the filesystem size defaults to that of the partition, or, if **−F** is specified, the existing file.

If `size` is negative the specified size is subtracted from the default size (reserving space at the end of the partition).

−T `disk-type`

Uses information for the specified disk from /etc/disktab instead of trying to get the information from the disk label.

−v `volname`

This specifies that an Apple UFS filesystem should be created with the given volume name.

−V `verbose`

This controls the amount of information written to stdout:

0   No output.

1   Overall size and cylinder group details.

2   A progress bar (dots ending at right hand margin).

3   The first few super-block backup sector numbers are displayed before the progress bar.

4   All the super-block backup sector numbers are displayed (no progress bar).

The default is 3. If **−N** is specified **newfs** stops before outputting the progress bar.

−Z   Pre-zeros the file system image created with **−F**. This is necessary if the image is to be used by vnd(4) (which doesn't support file systems with 'holes').

The following option overrides the standard sizes for the disk geometry. The default value is taken from the disk label. Changing this default is useful only when using **newfs** to build a file system whose raw image will eventually be used on a different type of disk than the one on which it is initially created (for example on a write-once disk). Note that changing this value from its default will make it impossible for fsck_ffs(8) to find the alternative superblocks if the standard superblock is lost.

−S `sector-size`

The size of a sector in bytes (almost never anything but 512). Defaults to 512.

NOTES

The file system is created with 'random' inode generation numbers to improve NFS security.

The owner and group IDs of the root node of the new file system are set to the effective UID and GID of the user initializing the file system.

For the **newfs** command to succeed, the disk label should first be updated such that the fstype field for the partition is set to 4.2BSD or Apple UFS, unless **−F** or **−I** is used.

To create and populate a filesystem image within a file use the makefs(8) utility.

The partition size is found using fstat(2), not by inspecting the disk label. The block size and fragment size will be written back to the disk label only if the last character of `special` references the same partition as the minor device number.

Unless **−F** is specified, `special` must be a raw device. This means that for example wd0a or /dev/rwd0a must be specified instead of /dev/wd0a.

SEE ALSO

fstat(2), disktab(5), fs(5), disklabel(8), diskpart(8), dumpfs(8), fsck_ffs(8), makefs(8), mount(8), mount_mfs(8), newfs_ext2fs(8), newfs_lfs(8), newfs_msdos(8), tunefs(8)

M. McKusick, W. Joy, S. Leffler, and R. Fabry, "A Fast File System for UNIX,", *ACM Transactions on Computer Systems 2*, 3, pp 181-197, August 1984, (reprinted in the BSD System Manager's Manual).

M. McKusick, "Enhancements to the fast filesystem to support multi-terabyte storage systems", *Proceedings of the BSD Conference 2003*, pp 79-90, September 2003.

HISTORY

The **newfs** command appeared in 4.2 BSD.

NAME
newfs_ext2fs — construct a new ext2 file system

SYNOPSIS
newfs_ext2fs [**-FINZ**] [**-b** *block-size*] [**-D** *inodesize*] [**-f** *frag-size*]
            [**-i** *bytes-per-inode*] [**-m** *free-space*] [**-n** *inodes*]
            [**-O** *filesystem-format*] [**-S** *sector-size*] [**-s** *size*] [**-V** *verbose*]
            [**-v** *volname*] *special*

DESCRIPTION
newfs_ext2fs is used to initialize and clear ext2 file systems before first use. Before running
newfs_ext2fs the disk must be labeled using disklabel(8). **newfs_ext2fs** builds a file system on
the specified special device basing its defaults on the information in the disk label. Typically the defaults are
reasonable, however **newfs_ext2fs** has numerous options to allow the defaults to be selectively overridden.

Options with numeric arguments may contain an optional (case-insensitive) suffix:

b	Bytes; causes no modification. (Default)
k	Kilo; multiply the argument by 1024.
m	Mega; multiply the argument by 1048576.
g	Giga; multiply the argument by 1073741824.

The following options define the general layout policies.

-b *block-size*
> The block size of the file system, in bytes. It must be a power of two. The smallest allowable
> size is 1024 bytes. The default size depends upon the size of the file system:
>
> | file system size | block-size |
> |---|---|
> | <= 512 MB | 1 KB |
> | > 512 MB | 4 KB |

-D *inodesize*
> Set the inode size. Defaults to 128, and can also be set to 256 for compatibility with ext4.

-F
> Create a file system image in *special*. The file system size needs to be specified with "**-s**
> *size*". No attempts to use or update the disk label will be made.

-f *frag-size*
> The fragment size of the file system in bytes. It must be the same with blocksize because the
> current ext2fs implementation doesn't support fragmentation.

-I
> Do not require that the file system type listed in the disk label is Linux Ext2.

-i *bytes-per-inode*
> This specifies the density of inodes in the file system. If fewer inodes are desired, a larger
> number should be used; to create more inodes a smaller number should be given.

-m *free-space*
> The percentage of space reserved from normal users; the minimum free space threshold. The
> default value used is 5%.

-N
> Causes the file system parameters to be printed out without really creating the file system.

-n *inodes*
> This specifies the number of inodes for the file system. If both **-i** and **-n** are specified then
> **-n** takes precedence. The default number of inodes is calculated from a number of blocks in
> the file system.

-O *filesystem-format*
>   Select the filesystem-format.
>> 0   GOOD_OLD_REV; this option is primarily used to build root file systems that can be understood by old or dumb firmwares for bootstrap. (default)
>> 1   DYNAMIC_REV; various extended (and sometimes incompatible) features are enabled (though not all features are supported on NetBSD). Currently only the following features are supported:

RESIZE	Prepare some reserved structures which enable future file system resizing.
FTYPE	Store file types in directory entries to improve performance.
SPARSESUPER	
	Prepare superblock backups for the fsck_ext2fs(8) utility on not all but sparse block groups.
LARGEFILE	Enable files larger than 2G bytes.

-s *size*   The size of the file system in sectors. An 's' suffix will be interpreted as the number of sectors (the default). All other suffixes are interpreted as per other numeric arguments, except that the number is converted into sectors by dividing by the sector size (as specified by **-S** *secsize*) after suffix interpretation.

>   If no **-s** *size* is specified then the filesystem size defaults to that of the partition, or, if **-F** is specified, the existing file.

>   If *size* is negative the specified size is subtracted from the default size (reserving space at the end of the partition).

-V *verbose*
>   This controls the amount of information written to stdout:
>> 0   No output.
>> 1   Overall size and cylinder group details.
>> 2   A progress bar (dots ending at right hand margin).
>> 3   The first few super-block backup sector numbers are displayed before the progress bar.
>> 4   All the super-block backup sector numbers are displayed (no progress bar).
>   The default is 3. If **-N** is specified **newfs_ext2fs** stops before outputting the progress bar.

-v *volname*
>   This specifies a volume name for the file system.

-Z   Pre-zeros the file system image created with **-F**. This is necessary if the image is to be used by vnd(4) (which doesn't support file systems with 'holes').

The following option overrides the standard sizes for the disk geometry. The default value is taken from the disk label. Changing this default is useful only when using **newfs_ext2fs** to build a file system whose raw image will eventually be used on a different type of disk than the one on which it is initially created (for example on a write-once disk). Note that changing this value from its default will make it impossible for fsck_ext2fs(8) to find the alternative superblocks if the standard superblock is lost.

-S *sector-size*
>   The size of a sector in bytes (almost never anything but 512). Defaults to 512.

NOTES
There is no option to specify the metadata byte order on the file system to be created because the native ext2 file system is always little endian even on big endian hosts.

The file system is created with 'random' inode generation numbers to improve NFS security.

The owner and group IDs of the root node and reserved blocks of the new file system are set to the effective UID and GID of the user initializing the file system.

For the **newfs_ext2fs** command to succeed, the disk label should first be updated such that the fstype field for the partition is set to Linux Ext2, unless **−F** or **−I** is used.

The partition size is found using fstat(2), not by inspecting the disk label. The block size and fragment size will be written back to the disk label only if the last character of *special* references the same partition as the minor device number.

SEE ALSO

fstat(2), disklabel(5), disktab(5), fs(5), disklabel(8), diskpart(8), fsck_ext2fs(8), mount(8), mount_ext2fs(8), newfs(8)

Remy Card, Theodore Ts'o, and Stephen Tweedie, "Design and Implementation of the Second Extended Filesystem", *The Proceedings of the First Dutch International Symposium on Linux*.

HISTORY

The **newfs_ext2fs** command first appeared in NetBSD 5.0.

AUTHORS

The **newfs_ext2fs** command was written by Izumi Tsutsui ⟨tsutsui@NetBSD.org⟩.

BUGS

The **newfs_ext2fs** command is still experimental and there are few sanity checks.

The **newfs_ext2fs** command doesn't have options to specify each REV1 file system feature independently.

The **newfs_ext2fs** command doesn't support the bad block list accounted by the bad blocks inode.

Many newer ext2 file system features (especially journaling) are not supported yet.

Some features in file systems created by the **newfs_ext2fs** command might not be recognized properly by the fsck_ext2fs(8) utility.

There is no native tool in the NetBSD distribution for resizing ext2 file systems yet.

NAME

newfs_lfs — construct a new LFS file system

SYNOPSIS

newfs_lfs [*newfs_lfs-options*] *special*

DESCRIPTION

newfs_lfs builds a log-structured file system on the specified special device basing its defaults on the information in the disk label. Before running **newfs_lfs** the disk must be labeled using disklabel(8), the proper fstype is 4.4LFS. Reasonable values for the fsize, bsize, and sgs fields are 1024, 8192, and 7 respectively.

The following options define the general layout policies.

-A   Attempt to compute the appropriate segment size using the formula *4 * bandwidth * access time*. The disk is tested for twenty seconds to discover its bandwidth and seek time.

-B *logical-segment-size*
             The logical segment size of the file system in bytes. If not specified, the segment size is computed by left-shifting the partition label's block size by the amount indicated in the partition table's segshift. If the disklabel indicates a zero block size or segment shift, a compile-time default segment size of 1M is used.

-b *block-size*
             The block size of the file system in bytes. If not specified, the block size is taken from the partition label, or if the partition label indicates 0, a compile-time default of 8K is used.

-F   Force creation of an LFS even on a partition labeled as another type. **newfs_lfs** will use compile-time default values for block and fragment size, and segment shift, unless these are overridden by command-line flags.

-f *fragment-size*
             The fragment size of the file system in bytes. If not specified, the fragment size is taken from the partition label, or if the partition label indicates 0, a compile-time default of 1K is used.

-I *interleave*
             Specify the interleave between segments. The default is zero.

-i   The size of an inode block, in bytes. The default is to use the same size as a fragment, or in a v1 filesystem, the same size as a data block.

-L   Create a log-structured file system (LFS). This is the default, and this option is provided for compatibility only.

-M *nsegs*   Specify *lfs_minfreeseg*, the number of segments left out of the amount allocated to user data. A higher number increases cleaner performance, while a lower number gives more usable space. The default is based on the size of the filesystem, either 5% of the total number of segments or 20 segments, whichever is larger.

-m *free space %*
             The percentage of space reserved from normal users; the minimum free space threshold. The default value used is 10%.

-N   Do not actually create the filesystem.

-O *offset*
             Start the first segment this many sectors from the beginning of the partition. The default is zero.

-R *nsegs*   Specify *lfs_resvseg*, the number of segments set aside for the exclusive use of the cleaner. A larger figure reduces the likelihood of running out of clean segments, but if *lfs_resvseg* is too close to *lfs_minfreeseg*, the cleaner will run without ceasing when the filesystem becomes close to full. The default is the larger of 15 or the quantity *lfs_minfreeseg* / 2 + 1 .

-r *ident*   For a v2 filesystem, specify the roll-forward identifier for the filesystem. This identifier, a 32-bit numeric quantity, should be different from that of any LFS that may previously have existed on the same disk. By default the identifier is chosen at random.

-s *size*   The size of the file system in sectors.

-v *version*
   Make a filesystem with the specified disk layout version. Valid options are 1 or 2 (the default). *Note*, however, that LFS version 1 is deprecated.

SEE ALSO
disktab(5), disklabel(8), diskpart(8), dumplfs(8)

M. Seltzer, K. Bostic, M. McKusick, and C. Staelin, "An Implementation of a Log-Structured File System for UNIX", *Proceedings of the Winter 1993 USENIX Conference*, pp. 315-331, January 25-29, 1993.

J. Matthews, D. Roselli, A. Costello, R. Wang, and T. Anderson, "Improving the Performance of Log-Structured File Systems with Adaptive Methods", *Proceedings of the Sixteenth ACM SOSP*, October 1997.

HISTORY
A **newlfs** command appeared in 4.4 BSD, and was renamed to **newfs_lfs** for NetBSD 1.4.

NAME

newfs_msdos — construct a new MS-DOS (FAT) file system

SYNOPSIS

newfs_msdos [**-N**] [**-@** *offset*] [**-B** *boot*] [**-C** *create-size*] [**-F** *FAT-type*]
            [**-I** *volid*] [**-L** *label*] [**-O** *OEM*] [**-S** *sector-size*] [**-a** *FAT-size*]
            [**-b** *block-size*] [**-c** *cluster-size*] [**-e** *dirents*] [**-f** *format*]
            [**-h** *heads*] [**-i** *info*] [**-k** *backup*] [**-m** *media*] [**-n** *FATs*] [**-o** *hidden*]
            [**-r** *reserved*] [**-s** *total*] [**-u** *track-size*] *special* [*disktype*]

DESCRIPTION

The **newfs_msdos** utility creates a FAT12, FAT16, or FAT32 file system on device or file named *special*, using disktab(5) entry *disktype* to determine geometry, if required.

The options are as follow:

-N   Don't create a file system: just print out parameters.

-@ *offset*
       Build the filesystem at the specified offset in bytes in the device or file. A suffix s, k, m, g (lower or upper case) appended to the offset specifies that the number is in sectors, kilobytes, megabytes or gigabytes, respectively.

-B *boot*
       Get bootstrap from file.

-C *create-size*
       Create the image file with the specified size. A suffix character appended to the size is interpreted as for the **-@** option. The file is created by truncating any existing file with the same name, seeking just before the required size and writing a single 0 byte. As a consequence, the space occupied on disk may be smaller than the size specified as a parameter.

-F *FAT-type*
       FAT type (one of 12, 16, or 32).

-I *volid*
       Volume ID.

-L *label*
       Volume label (up to 11 characters). The label should consist of only those characters permitted in regular DOS (8+3) filenames. The default is "NO_NAME".

-O *OEM*
       OEM string (up to 8 characters). The default is "NetBSD".

-S *sector-size*
       Number of bytes per sector. Acceptable values are powers of 2 in the range 512 through 32768.

-a *FAT-size*
       Number of sectors per FAT.

-b *block-size*
       File system block size (bytes per cluster). This should resolve to an acceptable number of sectors per cluster (see below).

-c *cluster-size*
       Sectors per cluster. Acceptable values are powers of 2 in the range 1 through 128. If the block or cluster size are not specified, the code uses a cluster between 512 bytes and 32K depending on the

filesystem size.

-e *dirents*
Number of root directory entries (FAT12 and FAT16 only).

-f *format*
Specify a standard (floppy disk) format. The standard formats are (capacities in kilobytes): 160, 180, 320, 360, 640, 720, 1200, 1232, 1440, 2880.

-h *heads*
Number of drive heads.

-i *info*
Location of the file system info sector (FAT32 only). A value of 0xffff signifies no info sector.

-k *backup*
Location of the backup boot sector (FAT32 only). A value of 0xffff signifies no backup sector.

-m *media*
Media descriptor (acceptable range 0xf0 to 0xff).

-n *FATs*
Number of FATs. Acceptable values are 1 to 16 inclusive. The default is 2.

-o *hidden*
Number of hidden sectors.

-r *reserved*
Number of reserved sectors.

-s *total*
File system size.

-u *track-size*
Number of sectors per track.

If **newfs_msdos** receives a SIGINFO signal (see the **status** argument for stty(1)), a line will be written to the standard error output indicating the name of the device currently being formatted, the sector number being written, and the total number of sectors to be written.

NOTES

If some parameters (e.g. size, number of sectors, etc.) are not specified through options or disktype, the program tries to generate them automatically. In particular, the size is determined as the device or file size minus the offset specified with the **-@** option. When the geometry is not available, it is assumed to be 63 sectors, 255 heads. The size is then rounded to become a multiple of the track size and avoid complaints by some filesystem code.

FAT file system parameters occupy a "Boot Sector BPB (BIOS Parameter Block)" in the first of the "reserved" sectors which precede the actual file system. For reference purposes, this structure is presented below.

```
struct bsbpb {
    u_int16_t  bps;          /* [-S] bytes per sector */
    u_int8_t   spc;          /* [-c] sectors per cluster */
    u_int16_t  res;          /* [-r] reserved sectors */
    u_int8_t   nft;          /* [-n] number of FATs */
    u_int16_t  rde;          /* [-e] root directory entries */
    u_int16_t  sec;          /* [-s] total sectors */
    u_int8_t   mid;          /* [-m] media descriptor */
```

```
        u_int16_t   spf;                /* [-a] sectors per FAT */
        u_int16_t   spt;                /* [-u] sectors per track */
        u_int16_t   hds;                /* [-h] drive heads */
        u_int32_t   hid;                /* [-o] hidden sectors */
        u_int32_t   bsec;               /* [-s] big total sectors */
};
/* FAT32 extensions */
struct bsxbpb {
        u_int32_t   bspf;               /* [-a] big sectors per FAT */
        u_int16_t   xflg;               /* control flags */
        u_int16_t   vers;               /* file system version */
        u_int32_t   rdcl;               /* root directory start cluster */
        u_int16_t   infs;               /* [-i] file system info sector */
        u_int16_t   bkbs;               /* [-k] backup boot sector */
};
```

EXAMPLES

```
        newfs_msdos /dev/rwd1a
```

Create a file system, using default parameters, on /dev/rwd1a.

```
        newfs_msdos -f 1440 -L foo /dev/rfd0a
```

Create a standard 1.44M file system, with volume label *foo*, on /dev/rfd0a. Create a 30MB image file, with the FAT partition starting 63 sectors within the image file:

```
        newfs_msdos -C 30M -@63s ./somefile
```

DIAGNOSTICS

Exit status is 0 on success and 1 on error.

SEE ALSO

disktab(5), disklabel(8), fdisk(8), newfs(8)

HISTORY

The **newfs_msdos** command first appeared in NetBSD 1.3.

AUTHORS

Robert Nordier ⟨rnordier@FreeBSD.org⟩.

NEWFS_SYSVBFS (8)   NetBSD   NEWFS_SYSVBFS (8)

NAME
    newfs_sysvbfs — construct a new System V Boot File System

SYNOPSIS
    newfs_sysvbfs [**-FZ**] [**-s** *sectors*] *special*

DESCRIPTION
    newfs_sysvbfs builds a System V boot file system on the specified special. If it is a device, the size information will be taken from the disk label and before running **newfs_sysvbfs** the disk must be labeled using disklabel(8); the proper fstype is "SysVBFS". Otherwise, the size must be specified on the command line.

    The following arguments are supported:

    -F   Create file system to a regular file.

    -s *sectors*
              Create file system with specified number of disk sectors.

    -z   Fill file with zeroes instead of creating a sparse file.

SEE ALSO
    disklabel(5), disktab(5), disklabel(8), diskpart(8)

HISTORY
    A **newfs_sysvbfs** command first appeared in NetBSD 4.0.

BUGS
    The sysvbfs support is still experimental and there are few sanity checks.

NAME

    newfs_udf — construct a new UDF file system

SYNOPSIS

    newfs_udf [**-cFM**] [**-L** *loglabel*] [**-P** *discid*] [**-S** *setlabel*] [**-s** *size*]
          [**-p** *percentage*] [**-t** *gmtoff*] [**-V** *max_udf*] [**-v** *min_udf*] *special*

DESCRIPTION

    The **newfs_udf** utility creates an UDF file system on device *special* suitable for the media currently inserted.

    The options are as follow:

    -c   Perform a crude surface check first to weed out disc faults on rewritable media.

    -F   Force file system construction on non-empty recordable media.

    -L *loglabel*
          Set the disc logical label to the specified *loglabel*.

    -P *discid*
          Set the phyisical disc label to the specified *discid*. For strict conformance and interchange, don't set this manually.

    -S *setlabel*
          Set the disc set label to the specified *setlabel*. For strict conformance and interchange, don't set this manually.

    -M   Disable metadata partition creation when selected UDF version or media dictates this. For strict conformance and interchange, don't disable this unless its causing problems.

    -s *size*
          Ignored for now.

    -p *percentage*
          Percentage of partition to be initially reserved for metadata on the Metadata partition. It defaults to 20 %.

    -t *gmtoff*
          Use the specified *gmtoff* as gmt time offset for recording times on the disc.

    -V *max_udf*
          Select *max_udf* as the maximum UDF version to be supported. For UDF version 2.50, use "0x250" or "2.50".

    -v *min_udf*
          Select *min_udf* as the minimum UDF version to be supported. For UDF version 2.01, use "0x201" or "2.01".

NOTES

    The UDF file system is defined for the entire optical medium. It can only function on the entire CD/DVD/BD so the raw partition has to be specified for read/write actions. For **newfs_udf** this means specifying the raw device with the raw partition, i.e. /dev/rcd0d or /dev/rcd0c.

    Some rewritable optical media needs to be formatted first before it can be used by UDF. This can be done using mmcformat(8).

The default UDF version is version 2.01.

EXAMPLES

```
newfs_udf -S "Encyclopedia" -L "volume 2" -P "copy-nr-1" /dev/rcd0d
```

Create a file system, using the specified names on the device `/dev/rcd0d` with the default UDF version.

```
dd if=/dev/zero of=bigdisk.2048.udf seek=9999999 count=1
vnconfig -c vnd0 bigdisk.2048.udf 2048/1/1/1
newfs_udf -L bigdisk /dev/rvnd0d
```

Create a 4.8 GiB sparse file and configure it using `vnconfig(8)` to be a 2048 sector size disc and create a new UDF file system on `/dev/rvnd0d`.

```
newfs_udf -L "My USB stick" /dev/rsd0d
```

Create a new UDF file system on the inserted USB stick using its "native" sectorsize of 512.

SEE ALSO

disktab(5), disklabel(8), mmcformat(8), newfs(8)

HISTORY

The **newfs_udf** command first appeared in NetBSD 5.0.

AUTHORS

Reinoud Zandijk ⟨reinoud@NetBSD.org⟩

NAME

newsyslog — maintain system log files to manageable sizes

SYNOPSIS

newsyslog [**-nrsvF**] [**-f** *config_file*] [file . . .]

DESCRIPTION

newsyslog is a program that should be scheduled to run periodically by cron(8). When it is executed it archives log files if necessary. If a log file is determined to require archiving, **newsyslog** rearranges the files so that "*logfile*" is empty, "*logfile* . 0" has the last period's logs in it, "*logfile* . 1" has the next to last period's logs in it and so on, up to a user-specified number of archived logs. Optionally the archived logs can be compressed to save space.

A log can be archived for three reasons:

1.   It is larger than the configured size (in kilobytes).

2.   A configured number of hours have elapsed since the log was last archived.

3.   The configured time for rotation of the log occurred within the last 60 minutes.

The granularity of **newsyslog** is dependent on how often it is scheduled to run by cron(8). It is recommended that **newsyslog** be run once hourly.

When starting up, **newsyslog** reads in a configuration file to determine which logs may potentially be archived. By default, this configuration file is /etc/newsyslog.conf. Each line of the file contains information about a particular log file that should be handled by **newsyslog**. Each line has six mandatory fields and three optional fields, with whitespace separating each field. Blank lines or lines beginning with "#" are ignored. The fields of the configuration file are as follows:

logfile_name
        Name of the system log file to be archived.

owner:group
        This optional field specifies the owner and group for the archive file. The ":" is essential, even if the *owner* or *group* field is left blank. The field may be numeric, or a name which is present in /etc/passwd or /etc/group. For backward compatibility, "." is usable in lieu of ":", however use of this feature is discouraged.

mode   Specify the mode of the log file and archives.

ngen   Specify the number of archive files to be kept besides the log file itself.

size   When the size of the log file reaches *size* kilobytes, the log file will be trimmed as described above. If this field is replaced by an asterisk ('*'), then the size of the log file is not taken into account when determining when to trim the log file.

when   The *when* field can consist of an interval, a specific time, or both. If the *when* field is an asterisk ('*') log rotation will depend only on the contents of the *size* field. Otherwise, the *when* field consists of an optional interval in hours, optionally followed by an '@'-sign and a time in a restricted ISO 8601 format or by an '$'-sign and a time specification for logfile rotation at a fixed time once per day, per week or per month.

        If a time is specified, the log file will only be trimmed if **newsyslog** is run within one hour of the specified time. If an interval is specified, the log file will be trimmed if that many hours have passed since the last rotation. When both a time and an interval are specified, the log will be trimmed if either condition is met.

There is no provision for specification of a timezone. There is little point in specifying an explicit minutes or seconds component in the current implementation, since the only comparison is 'within the hour'.

ISO 8601 restricted time format

The lead-in character for a restricted ISO 8601 time is an '@'-sign. The particular format of the time in restricted ISO 8601 is: [[[[[*cc*]*yy*]*mm*]*dd*][T[*hh*[*mm*[*ss*]]]]]. Optional date fields default to the appropriate component of the current date; optional time fields default to midnight; hence if today is January 22, 1999, the following date specifications are all equivalent:

```
'19990122T000000'
'990122T000000'
'0122T000000'
'22T000000'
'T000000'
'T0000'
'T00'
'22T'
'T'
''
```

Day, week and month time format

The lead-in character for day, week and month specification is a '$'-sign. The particular format of day, week and month specification is: [*Dhh*], [*Ww*[*Dhh*]] and [*Mdd*[*Dhh*]] respectively. Optional time fields default to midnight. The ranges for day and hour specifications are:

hh	hours, range 0 ... 23
w	day of week, range 0 ... 6, 0 = Sunday
dd	day of month, range 1 ... 31, or the letter *L* or *l* to specify the last day of the month.

Some examples:

$D0	rotate every night at midnight
$D23	rotate every day at 23:00 hr
$W0D23	
	rotate every week on Sunday at 23:00 hr
$W5D16	
	rotate every week on Friday at 16:00 hr
$MLD0	rotate at the last day of every month at midnight
$M5D6	rotate on every 5th day of month at 6:00 hr

flags This field specifies any special processing that is required. These flags are parsed in a case insensitive manner. Individual flags and their meanings:

- This flag means nothing - it is used as a spacer when no flags are set.

b The file is a binary file or is not in `syslogd`(8) format: the ASCII message which **newsyslog** inserts to indicate that the logs have been trimmed should not be included.

c Create an empty log file if none currently exists.

n No signal should be sent when the log is trimmed.

p The first historical log file (i.e. the historical log file with the suffix ".0") should not be compressed.

j   Archived log files should be compressed with bzip2(1) to save space.

z   Archived log files should be compressed with gzip(1) to save space.

path_to_pid_file

This optional field specifies the file name to read to find the daemon process id. If this field is missing, it defaults to the /var/run/syslogd.pid file. A signal of type *sigtype* is sent to the process id contained in this *path_to_pid_file* file. This field must start with '/' in order to be recognized properly.

sigtype

This optional field specifies the type of signal to be sent to the daemon process. This may be a numeric or symbolic value. By default a SIGHUP (hang-up) will be sent.

OPTIONS

The following options can be used with newsyslog:

-f *config_file*

Use *config_file* instead of /etc/newsyslog.conf as the configuration file.

-n   Do not trim the logs, but print out what would be done if this option were not specified: **-n** implies **-v**.

-r   Remove the restriction that **newsyslog** must be running as root. When running as a regular user, **newsyslog** will not be able to send a HUP signal to syslogd(8), so this option should be used only when debugging or trimming user generated logs.

-s   Do not signal daemon processes.

-v   Run in verbose mode. In this mode each action that is taken will be printed.

-F   Force trimming of the logs, even if the trim conditions have not been met. This option is useful for diagnosing system problems by providing you with fresh logs.

If additional command line arguments are given, **newsyslog** will only examine log files that match those arguments; otherwise, it will examine all files listed in the configuration file.

FILES

/etc/newsyslog.conf   **newsyslog** configuration file.

SEE ALSO

bzip2(1), gzip(1), syslog(3), syslogd(8)

NAME
nfsd — remote NFS server

SYNOPSIS
nfsd [-6rut] [-n *num_threads*]

DESCRIPTION
nfsd runs on a server machine to service NFS requests from client machines. At least one nfsd must be running for a machine to operate as a server.

Unless otherwise specified, four servers for UDP transport are started.

The following options are available:

-r   Register the NFS service with rpcbind(8) without creating any servers. This option can be used along with the -u or -t options to re-register NFS if the portmap server is restarted.

-n   Specifies how many server threads to create. The default is 4. A server should run enough threads to handle the maximum level of concurrency from its clients.

-6   Listen to IPv6 requests as well as IPv4 requests. If IPv6 support is not available, nfsd will silently continue and just use IPv4.

-t   Serve TCP NFS clients.

-u   Serve UDP NFS clients.

For example, "nfsd -t -u -n 6" serves UDP and TCP transports using six threads.

nfsd listens for service requests at the port indicated in the NFS server specification; see *Network File System Protocol Specification*, RFC 1094 and *NFS: Network File System Version 3 Protocol Specification*.

The nfsd utility exits 0 on success, and >0 if an error occurs.

SEE ALSO
nfsstat(1), nfssvc(2), mountd(8), rpcbind(8)

HISTORY
The nfsd utility first appeared in 4.4 BSD.

NAME
nis, **yp** — description of the NIS (formerly YP) subsystem

SYNOPSIS
ypbind [**-ypset**]
ypbind [**-ypsetme**]

ypset [**-h** *host*] [**-d** *domain*] *server*

yppoll [**-h** *host*] [**-d** *domain*] *mapname*

ypcat [**-kt**] [**-d** *domainname*] *mapname*
ypcat **-x**

ypmatch [**-kt**] [**-d** *domainname*] *key* . . . *mapname*
ypmatch **-x**

ypwhich [**-d** *domain*] [[**-t**] **-m** [*mname*] | *host*]
ypwhich **-x**

ypserv [**-d**] [**-x**]

yppush [**-d** *domainname*] [**-h** *hostname*] [**-v**] *mapname*

ypxfr [**-bcf**] [**-d** *domain*] [**-h** *host*] [**-s** *domain*] [**-C** *tid prog ipadd port*]
          mapname

ypinit **-m** [*domainname*]
ypinit **-s** *master_server* [*domainname*]

yptest

rpc.yppasswdd [**-noshell**] [**-nogecos**] [**-nopw**] [**-m** *arg1 arg2* . . .]

DESCRIPTION
The NIS subsystem allows network management of passwd and group file entries through the functions getpwent(3) and getgrent(3). NIS also provides hooks for other client programs, such as amd(8) and rpc.bootparamd(8), that can use NIS maps.

Password maps in standard YP are insecure, because the pw_passwd field is accessible by any user. A common solution to this is to generate a secure map (using "makedbm -s") which can only be accessed by a client bound to a privileged port. To activate the secure map, see the appropriate comment in /var/yp/Makefile.yp.

The NIS subsystem is conditionally started in /etc/rc. See the /etc/rc.conf file for configuration variables.

SEE ALSO
domainname(1), ypcat(1), ypmatch(1), ypwhich(1), ypclnt(3), group(5), hosts_access(5), nsswitch.conf(5), passwd(5), rc.conf(5), rc(8), ypbind(8), ypinit(8), yppoll(8), yppush(8), ypserv(8), ypset(8), yptest(8), ypxfr(8)

HISTORY
The NIS client subsystem was originally written by Theo de Raadt to be compatible with Sun's implementation. The NIS server suite was originally written by Mats O Jansson.

BUGS

If `ypbind`(8) cannot find a server, the system behaves the same way as Sun's code: it hangs.

The 'secure map' feature is not compatible with non-BSD implementations as found e.g. in Solaris.

NAME
nologin — politely refuse a login

SYNOPSIS
nologin

DESCRIPTION
nologin displays a message that an account is not available and returns a non-zero exit code. It is intended as a replacement shell field for accounts that have been disabled.

SEE ALSO
login(1)

HISTORY
The **nologin** command appeared in 4.4 BSD, a free re-implementation was contributed in NetBSD 1.5 by Hubert Feyrer to avoid bloat through the copyright comment.

NAME
nslookup — query Internet name servers interactively

SYNOPSIS
nslookup [**-option** . . .] [*host-to-find* | -[*server*]]

DESCRIPTION
nslookup is a program to query Internet domain name servers. **nslookup** has two modes: interactive and non-interactive. Interactive mode allows the user to query name servers for information about various hosts and domains or to print a list of hosts in a domain. Non-interactive mode is used to print just the name and requested information for a host or domain.

ARGUMENTS
Interactive mode is entered in the following cases:

1.   when no arguments are given (the default name server will be used),

2.   when the first argument is a hyphen ('-') and the second argument is the host name or Internet address of a name server.

Non-interactive mode is used when the name or Internet address of the host to be looked up is given as the first argument. The optional second argument specifies the host name or address of a name server.

The options listed under the "set" command below can be specified in the .nslookuprc file in the user's home directory if they are listed one per line. Options can also be specified on the command line if they precede the arguments and are prefixed with a hyphen. For example, to change the default query type to host information, and the initial timeout to 10 seconds, type:

>   nslookup –query=hinfo –timeout=10

INTERACTIVE COMMANDS
Commands may be interrupted at any time by typing a control-C. To exit, type a control-D (EOF) or type exit. The command line length must be less than 256 characters. To treat a built-in command as a host name, precede it with an escape character ('\'). *N.B.:* unrecognized command will be interpreted as a host name.

host [*server*]
>   Look up information for *host* using the current default server or using *server*, if specified. If *host* is an Internet address and the query type is A or PTR, the name of the host is returned. If *host* is a name and does not have a trailing period, the default domain name is appended to the name. (This behavior depends on the state of the **set** options **domain**, **srchlist**, **defname**, and **search**.)

>   To look up a host not in the current domain, append a period to the name.

server *domain*

lserver *domain*
>   Change the default server to *domain*; **lserver** uses the initial server to look up information about *domain*, while **server** uses the current default server. If an authoritative answer can't be found, the names of servers that might have the answer are returned.

root   Changes the default server to the server for the root of the domain name space. Currently, the host ns.internic.net is used. (This command is a synonym for "**lserver ns.internic.net**".) The name of the root server can be changed with the "**set root**" command.

finger [*name*] [**>** *filename*]

finger [*name*] [**>>** *filename*]

> Connects with the finger server on the current host. The current host is defined when a previous lookup for a host was successful and returned address information (see the "**set querytype**=A" command). The *name* is optional. **>** and **>>** can be used to redirect output in the usual manner.

ls [*option*] *domain* [**>** *filename*]

ls [*option*] *domain* [**>>** *filename*]

> List the information available for *domain*, optionally creating or appending to *filename*. The default output contains host names and their Internet addresses. *Option* can be one of the following:

> **-t** *querytype*
> > lists all records of the specified type (see *querytype* below).

> **-a** lists aliases of hosts in the domain; synonym for "**-t** CNAME".

> **-d** lists all records for the domain; synonym for "**-t** ANY".

> **-h** lists CPU and operating system information for the domain; synonym for "**-t** HINFO".

> **-s** lists well-known services of hosts in the domain; synonym for "**-t** WKS".

> When output is directed to a file, hash marks are printed for every 50 records received from the server.

view *filename*

> Sorts and lists the output of previous **ls** command(s) with more(1).

help

?   Prints a brief summary of commands.

exit Exits the program.

set *keyword*[=*value*]

> This command is used to change state information that affects the lookups. Valid keywords are:

> **all**   Prints the current values of the frequently-used options to **set**. Information about the current default server and host is also printed.

> **class**=*value*
> > Change the query class to one of:

> > IN   the Internet class

> > CHAOS   the Chaos class

> > HESIOD   the MIT Athena Hesiod class

> > ANY   wildcard (any of the above)

> > The class specifies the protocol group of the information.

> > (Default = IN; abbreviation = **cl**)

> [no]debug
> > Turn debugging mode on. A lot more information is printed about the packet sent to the server and the resulting answer.

(Default = **nodebug**; abbreviation = [**no**]**deb**)

[**no**]**d2**   Turn exhaustive debugging mode on. Essentially all fields of every packet are printed.

(Default = **nod2**)

domain=*name*

Change the default domain name to *name*. The default domain name is appended to a lookup request depending on the state of the **defname** and **search** options. The domain search list contains the parents of the default domain if it has at least two components in its name. For example, if the default domain is CC.Berkeley.EDU, the search list is CC.Berkeley.EDU and Berkeley.EDU. Use the "**set srchlist**" command to specify a different list. Use the "**set all**" command to display the list.

(Default = value from hostname(1), /etc/resolv.conf, or LOCALDOMAIN; abbreviation = **do**)

srchlist=*name1*/*name2*/ . . .

Change the default domain name to *name1* and the domain search list to *name1*, *name2*, etc. A maximum of 6 names separated by slashes ('/') can be specified. For example,

```
set srchlist=lcs.MIT.EDU/ai.MIT.EDU/MIT.EDU
```

sets the domain to lcs.MIT.EDU and the search list to the three names. This command overrides the default domain name and search list of the "**set domain**" command. Use the "**set all**" command to display the list.

(Default = value based on hostname(1), /etc/resolv.conf, or LOCALDOMAIN; abbreviation = **srchl**)

[**no**]**defname**

If set, append the default domain name to a single-component lookup request (i.e., one that does not contain a period).

(Default = **defname**; abbreviation = [**no**]**defname**)

[**no**]**search**

If the lookup request contains at least one period but *doesn't* end with a trailing period, append the domain names in the domain search list to the request until an answer is received.

(Default = **search**; abbreviation = [**no**]**sea**)

port=*value*

Change the default TCP/UDP name server port to *value*.

(Default = 53; abbreviation = **po**)

querytype=*value*

type=*value*

Change the type of information query to one of:

A   the host's Internet address.

CNAME   the canonical name for an alias.

HINFO	the host CPU and operating system type.
MINFO	the mailbox or mail list information.
MX	the mail exchanger.
NS	the name server for the named zone.
PTR	the host name if the query is an Internet address; otherwise, the pointer to other information.
SOA	the domain's "start-of-authority" information.
TXT	the text information.
UINFO	the user information.
WKS	the supported well-known services.

Other types (ANY, AXFR, MB, MD, MF, NULL) are described in the RFC-1035 document.

(Default = A; abbreviations = **q**, **ty**)

[no]recurse

Tell the name server to query other servers if it does not have the information.

(Default = **recurse**; abbreviation = **[no]rec**)

retry=*number*

Set the number of retries to *number*. When a reply to a request is not received within a certain amount of time (changed with "**set timeout**"), the timeout period is doubled and the request is resent. The retry value controls how many times a request is resent before giving up.

(Default = 4, abbreviation = **ret**)

root=*host*

Change the name of the root server to *host*. This affects the "**root**" command.

(Default = **ns.internic.net.**; abbreviation = **ro**)

timeout=*number*

Change the initial timeout interval for waiting for a reply to *number* seconds. Each retry doubles the timeout period.

(Default = 5 seconds; abbreviation = **ti**)

[no]vc   Always use a virtual circuit when sending requests to the server.

(Default = **novc**; abbreviation = **[no]v**)

[no]ignoretc

Ignore packet truncation errors.

(Default = **noignoretc**; abbreviation = **[no]ig**)

ENVIRONMENT

| HOSTALIASES | file containing host aliases |
| LOCALDOMAIN | overrides default domain |

FILES
>   /etc/resolv.conf   initial domain name and name server addresses
> $HOME/.nslookuprc   user's initial options
>   /usr/share/misc/nslookup.help   summary of commands

DIAGNOSTICS
>   If the lookup request was not successful, an error message is printed. Possible errors are:
>
>   Timed out
>   The server did not respond to a request after a certain amount of time (changed with "**set timeout**=*value*") and a certain number of retries (changed with "**set retry**=*value*").
>
>   No response from server
>   No name server is running on the server machine.
>
>   No records
>   The server does not have resource records of the current query type for the host, although the host name is valid. The query type is specified with the "**set querytype**" command.
>
>   Non-existent domain
>   The host or domain name does not exist.
>
>   Connection refused
>
>   Network is unreachable
>   The connection to the name or finger server could not be made at the current time. This error commonly occurs with **ls** and **finger** requests.
>
>   Server failure
>   The name server found an internal inconsistency in its database and could not return a valid answer.
>
>   Refused
>   The name server refused to service the request.
>
>   Format error
>   The name server found that the request packet was not in the proper format. It may indicate an error in **nslookup**.

SEE ALSO
>   resolver(3), resolv.conf(5), named(8)
>
>   P.V. Mockapetris, *Domain Names - Concepts and Facilities*, RFC 1034, Nov 1, 1987.
>
>   P.V. Mockapetris, *Domain Names - Implementation and Specification*, RFC 1035, Nov 1, 1987.

AUTHORS
>   Andrew Cherenson

NAME
ntalkd, talkd — remote user communication server

SYNOPSIS
ntalkd [-dl]

DESCRIPTION
ntalkd is the server that notifies a user that someone else wants to initiate a conversation. It acts as a repository of invitations, responding to requests by clients wishing to rendezvous to hold a conversation.

In normal operation, a client, the caller, initiates a rendezvous by sending a CTL_MSG to the server of type LOOK_UP (see <protocols/talkd.h>). This causes the server to search its invitation tables to check if an invitation currently exists for the caller (to speak to the callee specified in the message). If the lookup fails, the caller then sends an ANNOUNCE message causing the server to broadcast an announcement on the callee's login ports requesting contact.

When the callee responds, the local server uses the recorded invitation to respond with the appropriate rendezvous address and the caller and callee client programs establish a stream connection through which the conversation takes place.

OPTIONS
ntalkd supports the following options:

-d   The -d option turns on debugging logging.

-l   The -l option turns on accounting logging for ntalkd via the syslogd(8) service.

FILES
/usr/libexec/ntalkd

SEE ALSO
talk(1), write(1), syslog(3), syslogd(8)

HISTORY
The ntalkd command appeared in 4.3 BSD.

The original talkd program was coded improperly, in a machine and byte-order dependent fashion. When this was corrected, it required a protocol change, which necessitated a different daemon to handle it, thus ntalkd or "new" talk daemon. The old daemon has long since been removed, but the detritus remain.

NTP-KEYGEN(1)   Programmer's Manual   NTP-KEYGEN(1)

NAME

ntp-keygen – Create a NTP host key

SYNOPSIS

ntp-keygen [*–flag* [*value*]]... [*--opt-name* [[=|]*value*]]...

All arguments must be options.

DESCRIPTION

This manual page documents, briefly, the **ntp-keygen** command. If there is no new host key, look for an existing one. If one is not found, create it.

OPTIONS

–c *scheme*, **--certificate**=*scheme*
> certificate scheme.

> Just some descriptive text.

–d, **--debug-level**
> Increase output debug message level. This option may appear an unlimited number of times.

> Increase the debugging message output level.

–D *string*, **--set-debug-level**=*string*
> Set the output debug message level. This option may appear an unlimited number of times.

> Set the output debugging level. Can be supplied multiple times, but each overrides the previous value(s).

–e, **--id-key**
> Write identity keys.

> Just some descriptive text.

–G, **--gq-params**
> Generate GQ parameters and keys.

> Just some descriptive text.

–g, **--gq-keys**
> update GQ keys.

> Just some descriptive text.

–H, **--host-key**
> generate RSA host key.

> Just some descriptive text.

–I, **--iffkey**
> generate IFF parameters.

> Just some descriptive text.

–i, **--issuer-name**
> set issuer name.

> Just some descriptive text.

–M, **--md5key**
> generate MD5 keys.

Just some descriptive text.

−m *modulus*, **−−modulus**=*modulus*
> modulus. This option takes an integer number as its argument. The value of *modulus* is constrained to being:
> > in the range 256 through 2048

Just some descriptive text.

−P, **−−pvt-cert**
> generate PC private certificate.

Just some descriptive text.

−p *passwd*, **−−pvt-passwd**=*passwd*
> output private password.

Just some descriptive text.

−q *passwd*, **−−get-pvt-passwd**=*passwd*
> input private password.

Just some descriptive text.

−S *sign*, **−−sign-key**=*sign*
> generate sign key (RSA or DSA).

Just some descriptive text.

−s *host*, **−−subject-name**=*host*
> set subject name.

Just some descriptive text.

−T, **−−trusted-cert**
> trusted certificate (TC scheme).

Just some descriptive text.

−V *num*, **−−mv-params**=*num*
> generate <num> MV parameters. This option takes an integer number as its argument.

Just some descriptive text.

−v *num*, **−−mv-keys**=*num*
> update <num> MV keys. This option takes an integer number as its argument.

Just some descriptive text.

−?, **−−help**
> Display usage information and exit.

−!, **−−more-help**
> Extended usage information passed thru pager.

−> [*rcfile*], **−−save-opts**[=*rcfile*]
> Save the option state to *rcfile*. The default is the *last* configuration file listed in the **OPTION PRESETS** section, below.

−< *rcfile*, **−−load-opts**=*rcfile*, **−−no-load-opts**
> Load options from *rcfile*. The *no-load-opts* form will disable the loading of earlier RC/INI files. *--no-load-opts* is handled early, out of order.

−v [{*v*|*c*|*n*}], **−-version**[=*{v*|*c*|*n}*]
> Output version of program and exit. The default mode is 'v', a simple version. The 'c' mode will print copyright information and 'n' will print the full copyright notice.

OPTION PRESETS

> Any option that is not marked as *not presettable* may be preset by loading values from configuration ("RC" or ".INI") file(s) and values from environment variables named:
> **NTP_KEYGEN_<option-name>** or **NTP_KEYGEN**
> The environmental presets take precedence (are processed later than) the configuration files. The *homerc* files are "*$HOME*", and ".". If any of these are directories, then the file *.ntprc* is searched for within those directories.

AUTHOR

> David L. Mills and/or others
> Please send bug reports to: http://bugs.ntp.org, bugs@ntp.org

> see /usr/share/doc/html/ntp/copyright.html

> This manual page was *AutoGen*-erated from the **ntp-keygen** option definitions.

NAME

ntpd – NTP daemon program

SYNOPSIS

ntpd [–*flag* [*value*]]... [––*opt-name* [[=|]*value*]]...

All arguments must be options.

DESCRIPTION

This manual page documents, briefly, the **ntpd** command.

OPTIONS

–4, ––ipv4

Force IPv4 DNS name resolution. This option is a member of the ipv4 class of options.

Force DNS resolution of following host names on the command line to the IPv4 namespace.

–6, ––ipv6

Force IPv6 DNS name resolution. This option is a member of the ipv4 class of options.

Force DNS resolution of following host names on the command line to the IPv6 namespace.

–a, ––authreq

Require crypto authentication. This option must not appear in combination with any of the following options: authnoreq.

Require cryptographic authentication for broadcast client, multicast client and symmetric passive associations. This is the default.

–A, ––authnoreq

Do not require crypto authentication. This option must not appear in combination with any of the following options: authreq.

Do not require cryptographic authentication for broadcast client, multicast client and symmetric passive associations. This is almost never a good idea.

–b, ––bcastsync

Allow us to sync to broadcast servers.

–c *string*, ––configfile=*string*

configuration file name.

The name and path of the configuration file, /etc/ntp.conf by default.

–d, ––debug-level

Increase output debug message level. This option may appear an unlimited number of times.

Increase the debugging message output level.

–D *string*, ––set-debug-level=*string*

Set the output debug message level. This option may appear an unlimited number of times.

Set the output debugging level. Can be supplied multiple times, but each overrides the previous value(s).

–f *string*, ––driftfile=*string*

frequency drift file name.

The name and path of the frequency file, /etc/ntp.drift by default. This is the same operation as the driftfile driftfile configuration specification in the /etc/ntp.conf file.

–g, --panicgate
Allow the first adjustment to be Big.

Normally, ntpd exits with a message to the system log if the offset exceeds the panic threshold, which is 1000 s by default. This option allows the time to be set to any value without restriction; however, this can happen only once. If the threshold is exceeded after that, ntpd will exit with a message to the system log. This option can be used with the -q and -x options. See the tinker configuration file directive for other options.

–i *string*, **--jaildir=***string*
Jail directory.

Chroot the server to the directory jaildir This option also implies that the server attempts to drop root privileges at startup (otherwise, chroot gives very little additional security), and it is only available if the OS supports to run the server without full root privileges. You may need to also specify a -u option.

–I *iface*, **--interface=***iface*
Listen on interface. This option may appear an unlimited number of times.

–k *string*, **--keyfile=***string*
path to symmetric keys.

Specify the name and path of the symmetric key file. /etc/ntp.keys is the default. This is the same operation as the keys keyfile configuration file directive.

–l *string*, **--logfile=***string*
path to the log file.

Specify the name and path of the log file. The default is the system log file. This is the same operation as the logfile logfile configuration file directive.

–L, --novirtualips
Do not listen to virtual IPs.

Do not listen to virtual IPs. The default is to listen.

–M, --modifymmtimer
Modify Multimedia Timer (Windows only).

Set the Windows Multimedia Timer to highest resolution.

–n, --nofork
Do not fork.

–N, --nice
Run at high priority.

To the extent permitted by the operating system, run ntpd at the highest priority.

–p *string*, **--pidfile=***string*
path to the PID file.

Specify the name and path of the file used to record ntpd's process ID. This is the same operation as the pidfile pidfile configuration file directive.

−P *number*, **−−priority**=*number*
> Process priority. This option takes an integer number as its argument.

> To the extent permitted by the operating system, run ntpd at the specified sched_setscheduler(SCHED_FIFO) priority.

−q, **−−quit**
> Set the time and quit.

> ntpd will exit just after the first time the clock is set. This behavior mimics that of the ntpdate program, which is to be retired. The -g and -x options can be used with this option. Note: The kernel time discipline is disabled with this option.

−r *string*, **−−propagationdelay**=*string*
> Broadcast/propagation delay.

> Specify the default propagation delay from the broadcast/multicast server to this client. This is necessary only if the delay cannot be computed automatically by the protocol.

−U *number*, **−−updateinterval**=*number*
> interval in seconds between scans for new or dropped interfaces. This option takes an integer number as its argument.

> Give the time in seconds between two scans for new or dropped interfaces. For systems with routing socket support the scans will be performed shortly after the interface change has been detected by the system. Use 0 to disable scanning.

−s *string*, **−−statsdir**=*string*
> Statistics file location.

> Specify the directory path for files created by the statistics facility. This is the same operation as the statsdir statsdir configuration file directive.

−t *tkey*, **−−trustedkey**=*tkey*
> Trusted key number. This option may appear an unlimited number of times.

> Add a key number to the trusted key list.

−u *string*, **−−user**=*string*
> Run as userid (or userid:groupid).

> Specify a user, and optionally a group, to switch to. This option is only available if the OS supports to run the server without full root privileges. Currently, this option is supported under NetBSD (configure with --enable-clockctl) and Linux (configure with --enable-linuxcaps).

−v *nvar*, **−−var**=*nvar*
> make ARG an ntp variable (RW). This option may appear an unlimited number of times.

−V *ndvar*, **−−dvar**=*ndvar*
> make ARG an ntp variable (RW|DEF). This option may appear an unlimited number of times.

−x, **−−slew**
> Slew up to 600 seconds.

Normally, the time is slewed if the offset is less than the step threshold, which is 128 ms by default, and stepped if above the threshold. This option sets the threshold to 600 s, which is well within the accuracy window to set the clock manually. Note: Since the slew rate of typical Unix kernels is limited to 0.5 ms/s, each second of adjustment requires an amortization interval of 2000 s. Thus, an adjustment as much as 600 s will take almost 14 days to complete. This option can be used with the -g and -q options. See the tinker configuration file directive for other options. Note: The kernel time discipline is disabled with this option.

−?, −-help
> Display usage information and exit.

−!, −-more-help
> Extended usage information passed thru pager.

−v [{*v*|*c*|*n*}], **−-version**[=*{v*|*c*|*n}*]
> Output version of program and exit. The default mode is 'v', a simple version. The 'c' mode will print copyright information and 'n' will print the full copyright notice.

OPTION PRESETS

Any option that is not marked as *not presettable* may be preset by loading values from environment variables named:
> **NTPD_<option-name> or NTPD**

AUTHOR

David L. Mills and/or others
Please send bug reports to: http://bugs.ntp.org, bugs@ntp.org

see /usr/share/doc/html/ntp/copyright.html

This manual page was *AutoGen*-erated from the **ntpd** option definitions.

NAME

      `ntpdate` — set the date and time via NTP

SYNOPSIS

      `ntpdate` [`-bBdoqsuv`] [`-a` *key*] [`-e` *authdelay*] [`-k` *keyfile*] [`-o` *version*]
           [`-p` *samples*] [`-t` *timeout*] [*server ...*]

DESCRIPTION

      `ntpdate` sets the local date and time by polling the Network Time Protocol (NTP) server(s) given as the *server* arguments to determine the correct time. It must be run as root on the local host. A number of samples are obtained from each of the servers specified and a subset of the NTP clock filter and selection algorithms are applied to select the best of these. Note that the accuracy and reliability of **ntpdate** depends on the number of servers, the number of polls each time it is run and the interval between runs.

      `ntpdate` can be run manually as necessary to set the host clock, or it can be run from the host startup script to set the clock at boot time. This is useful in some cases to set the clock initially before starting the NTP daemon `ntpd`. It is also possible to run **ntpdate** from a `cron` script. However, it is important to note that **ntpdate** with contrived `cron` scripts is no substitute for the NTP daemon, which uses sophisticated algorithms to maximize accuracy and reliability while minimizing resource use. Finally, since **ntpdate** does not discipline the host clock frequency as does `ntpd`, the accuracy using **ntpdate** is limited.

      Time adjustments are made by **ntpdate** in one of two ways. If **ntpdate** determines the clock is in error more than 0.5 second it will simply step the time by calling the system `settimeofday`(2) routine. If the error is less than 0.5 seconds, it will slew the time by calling the system `adjtime`(2) routine. The latter technique is less disruptive and more accurate when the error is small, and works quite well when **ntpdate** is run by `cron` every hour or two.

      `ntpdate` will decline to set the date if an NTP server daemon (e.g., `ntpd`) is running on the same host. When running **ntpdate** on a regular basis from `cron` as an alternative to running a daemon, doing so once every hour or two will result in precise enough timekeeping to avoid stepping the clock.

      If NetInfo support is compiled into **ntpdate**, then the `server` argument is optional if **ntpdate** can find a time server in the NetInfo configuration for `ntpd`

COMMAND LINE OPTIONS

    `-a` *key*

           Enable the authentication function and specify the key identifier to be used for authentication as the argument *key* **ntpdate**. The keys and key identifiers must match in both the client and server key files. The default is to disable the authentication function.

    `-B`

           Force the time to always be slewed using the adjtime() system call, even if the measured offset is greater than +-128 ms. The default is to step the time using settimeofday() if the offset is greater than +-128 ms. Note that, if the offset is much greater than +-128 ms in this case, that it can take a long time (hours) to slew the clock to the correct value. During this time. the host should not be used to synchronize clients.

    `-b`

           Force the time to be stepped using the settimeofday() system call, rather than slewed (default) using the adjtime() system call. This option should be used when called from a startup file at boot time.

    `-d`

           Enable the debugging mode, in which **ntpdate** will go through all the steps, but not adjust the local clock. Information useful for general debugging will also be printed.

    `-e` *authdelay*

           Specify the processing delay to perform an authentication function as the value *authdelay* , in seconds and fraction (see `ntpd` for details). This number is usually small enough to be negligible for most purposes, though specifying a value may improve timekeeping on very slow CPU's.

-k *keyfile*

Specify the path for the authentication key file as the string *keyfile* The default is `/etc/ntp.keys`. This file should be in the format described in `ntpd`

-o *version*

Specify the NTP version for outgoing packets as the integer *version*, which can be 1 or 2. The default is 3. This allows **ntpdate** to be used with older NTP versions.

-p *samples*

Specify the number of samples to be acquired from each server as the integer *samples*, with values from 1 to 8 inclusive. The default is 4.

-q   Query only - don't set the clock.

-s   Divert logging output from the standard output (default) to the system `syslog` facility. This is designed primarily for convenience of `cron` scripts.

-t *timeout*

Specify the maximum time waiting for a server response as the value *timeout*, in seconds and fraction. The value is rounded to a multiple of 0.2 seconds. The default is 1 second, a value suitable for polling across a LAN.

-u   Direct **ntpdate** to use an unprivileged port for outgoing packets. This is most useful when behind a firewall that blocks incoming traffic to privileged ports, and you want to synchronise with hosts beyond the firewall. Note that the **-d** option always uses unprivileged ports.

-v   Be verbose. This option will cause **ntpdate** string to be logged.

FILES
   `/etc/ntp.keys` encryption keys used by **ntpdate**.

AUTHORS
   David L. Mills (mills@udel.edu)

BUGS
   The slew adjustment is actually 50% larger than the measured offset, since this (it is argued) will tend to keep a badly drifting clock more accurate. This is probably not a good idea and may cause a troubling hunt for some values of the kernel variables `tick` and `tickadj`.

NAME
ntpdc – vendor-specific NTP query program

SYNOPSIS
ntpdc [–*flag* [*value*]]... [--*opt-name* [[=|]*value*]]...
                [host ...]

DESCRIPTION
This manual page documents, briefly, the **ntpdc** command. The ntpdc utility program is used to query an NTP daemon about its current state and to request changes in that state. It uses NTP mode 7 control message formats described in the source code. The program may be run either in interactive mode or controlled using command line arguments. Extensive state and statistics information is available through the ntpdc interface. In addition, nearly all the configuration options which can be specified at startup using ntpd's configuration file may also be specified at run time using ntpdc.

OPTIONS
–4, --ipv4

Force IPv4 DNS name resolution. This option is a member of the ipv4 class of options.

Force DNS resolution of following host names on the command line to the IPv4 namespace.

–6, --ipv6

Force IPv6 DNS name resolution. This option is a member of the ipv4 class of options.

Force DNS resolution of following host names on the command line to the IPv6 namespace.

–c *cmd*, **--command**=*cmd*

run a command and exit. This option may appear an unlimited number of times.

The following argument is interpreted as an interactive format command and is added to the list of commands to be executed on the specified host(s).

–l, --listpeers

Print a list of the peers. This option must not appear in combination with any of the following options: command.

Print a list of the peers known to the server as well as a summary of their state. This is equivalent to the 'listpeers' interactive command.

–p, --peers

Print a list of the peers. This option must not appear in combination with any of the following options: command.

Print a list of the peers known to the server as well as a summary of their state. This is equivalent to the 'peers' interactive command.

–s, --showpeers

Show a list of the peers. This option must not appear in combination with any of the following options: command.

Print a list of the peers known to the server as well as a summary of their state. This is equivalent to the 'dmpeers' interactive command.

–i, --interactive

Force ntpq to operate in interactive mode. This option must not appear in combination with any of the following options: command, listpeers, peers, showpeers.

Force ntpq to operate in interactive mode. Prompts will be written to the standard output and commands read from the standard input.

–d, **––debug-level**
> Increase output debug message level. This option may appear an unlimited number of times.

> Increase the debugging message output level.

–D *string*, **––set-debug-level**=*string*
> Set the output debug message level. This option may appear an unlimited number of times.

> Set the output debugging level. Can be supplied multiple times, but each overrides the previous value(s).

–n, **––numeric**
> numeric host addresses.

> Output all host addresses in dotted-quad numeric format rather than converting to the canonical host names.

–?, **––help**
> Display usage information and exit.

–!, **––more-help**
> Extended usage information passed thru pager.

–> [*rcfile*], **––save-opts**[=*rcfile*]
> Save the option state to *rcfile*. The default is the *last* configuration file listed in the **OPTION PRESETS** section, below.

–< *rcfile*, **––load-opts**=*rcfile*, **––no-load-opts**
> Load options from *rcfile*. The *no-load-opts* form will disable the loading of earlier RC/INI files. *--no-load-opts* is handled early, out of order.

–v [{*v*|*c*|*n*}], **––version**[={*v*|*c*|*n*}]
> Output version of program and exit. The default mode is 'v', a simple version. The 'c' mode will print copyright information and 'n' will print the full copyright notice.

OPTION PRESETS
Any option that is not marked as *not presettable* may be preset by loading values from configuration ("RC" or ".INI") file(s) and values from environment variables named:
> **NTPDC_<option-name>** or **NTPDC**

The environmental presets take precedence (are processed later than) the configuration files. The *homerc* files are "*$HOME*", and ".". If any of these are directories, then the file *.ntprc* is searched for within those directories.

AUTHOR
David L. Mills and/or others
Please send bug reports to: http://bugs.ntp.org, bugs@ntp.org

see /usr/share/doc/html/ntp/copyright.html

This manual page was *AutoGen*-erated from the **ntpdc** option definitions.

NAME

ntpq – standard NTP query program

SYNOPSIS

ntpq [–*flag* [*value*]]... [--*opt-name* [[=|]*value*]]...
                    [host ...]

DESCRIPTION

This manual page documents, briefly, the **ntpq** command. The ntpq utility program is used to query NTP servers which implement the standard NTP mode 6 control message formats defined in Appendix B of the NTPv3 specification RFC1305, requesting information about current state and/or changes in that state. The same formats are used in NTPv4, although some of the variables have changed and new ones added. The description on this page is for the NTPv4 variables. The program may be run either in interactive mode or controlled using command line arguments. Requests to read and write arbitrary variables can be assembled, with raw and pretty-printed output options being available. The ntpq utility can also obtain and print a list of peers in a common format by sending multiple queries to the server.

If one or more request options is included on the command line when ntpq is executed, each of the requests will be sent to the NTP servers running on each of the hosts given as command line arguments, or on local-host by default. If no request options are given, ntpq will attempt to read commands from the standard input and execute these on the NTP server running on the first host given on the command line, again defaulting to localhost when no other host is specified. The ntpq utility will prompt for commands if the standard input is a terminal device.

The ntpq utility uses NTP mode 6 packets to communicate with the NTP server, and hence can be used to query any compatible server on the network which permits it. Note that since NTP is a UDP protocol this communication will be somewhat unreliable, especially over large distances in terms of network topology. The ntpq utility makes one attempt to retransmit requests, and will time requests out if the remote host is not heard from within a suitable timeout time.

Specifying a command line option other than or will cause the specified query (queries) to be sent to the indicated host(s) immediately. Otherwise, ntpq will attempt to read interactive format commands from the standard input. Interactive format commands consist of a keyword followed by zero to four arguments. Only enough characters of the full keyword to uniquely identify the command need be typed.

A number of interactive format commands are executed entirely within the ntpq utility itself and do not result in NTP mode 6 requests being sent to a server. These are described following.

? [command_keyword] A '?' by itself will print a list of all the command keywords known to this incarnation of ntpq. A followed by a command keyword will print function and usage information about the command. This command is probably a better source of information about ntpq than this manual page.

addvars

rmvars variable_name ...

clearvars The data carried by NTP mode 6 messages consists of a list of items of the form where the is ignored, and can be omitted, in requests to the server to read variables. The ntpq utility maintains an internal list in which data to be included in control messages can be assembled, and sent using the and commands described below. The command allows variables and their optional values to be added to the list. If more than one variable is to be added, the list should be comma-separated and not contain white space. The command can be used to remove individual variables from the list, while the command removes all variables from the list.

authenticate [yes | no] Normally ntpq does not authenticate requests unless they are write requests. The command causes ntpq to send authentication with all requests it makes. Authenticated requests causes some servers to handle requests slightly differently, and can occasionally melt the CPU in fuzzballs if you turn authentication on before doing a display. The command causes ntpq to display whether or not ntpq is currently autheinticating requests.

cooked Causes output from query commands to be "cooked", so that variables which are recognized by ntpq will have their values reformatted for human consumption. Variables which ntpq thinks should have a decodable value but didn't are marked with a trailing] With no argument, displays the current debug level. Otherwise, the debug level is changed to the indicated level.

delay milliseconds Specify a time interval to be added to timestamps included in requests which require authentication. This is used to enable (unreliable) server reconfiguration over long delay network paths or between machines whose clocks are unsynchronized. Actually the server does not now require timestamps in authenticated requests, so this command may be obsolete.

host hostname Set the host to which future queries will be sent. Hostname may be either a host name or a numeric address.

hostnames Cm yes | Cm no If is specified, host names are printed in information displays. If is specified, numeric addresses are printed instead. The default is unless modified using the command line switch.

keyid keyid This command allows the specification of a key number to be used to authenticate configuration requests. This must correspond to a key number the server has been configured to use for this purpose.

ntpversion [ ] Sets the NTP version number which ntpq claims in packets. Defaults to 3, Note that mode 6 control messages (and modes, for that matter) didn't exist in NTP version 1. There appear to be no servers left which demand version 1. With no argument, displays the current NTP version that will be used when communicating with servers.

quit Exit ntpq.

passwd This command prompts you to type in a password (which will not be echoed) which will be used to authenticate configuration requests. The password must correspond to the key configured for use by the NTP server for this purpose if such requests are to be successful.

raw Causes all output from query commands is printed as received from the remote server. The only formating/interpretation done on the data is to transform nonascii data into a printable (but barely understandable) form.

timeout Ar milliseconds Specify a timeout period for responses to server queries. The default is about 5000 milliseconds. Note that since ntpq retries each query once after a timeout, the total waiting time for a timeout will be twice the timeout value set.

OPTIONS
−4, −−ipv4
Force IPv4 DNS name resolution. This option is a member of the ipv4 class of options.

Force DNS resolution of following host names on the command line to the IPv4 namespace.

−6, −−ipv6
Force IPv6 DNS name resolution. This option is a member of the ipv4 class of options.

Force DNS resolution of following host names on the command line to the IPv6 namespace.

−c *cmd*, **−−command**=*cmd*
> run a command and exit. This option may appear an unlimited number of times.
>
> The following argument is interpreted as an interactive format command and is added to the list of commands to be executed on the specified host(s).

−d, **−−debug-level**
> Increase output debug message level. This option may appear an unlimited number of times.
>
> Increase the debugging message output level.

−D *string*, **−−set-debug-level**=*string*
> Set the output debug message level. This option may appear an unlimited number of times.
>
> Set the output debugging level. Can be supplied multiple times, but each overrides the previous value(s).

−p, **−−peers**
> Print a list of the peers. This option must not appear in combination with any of the following options: interactive.
>
> Print a list of the peers known to the server as well as a summary of their state. This is equivalent to the 'peers' interactive command.

−i, **−−interactive**
> Force ntpq to operate in interactive mode. This option must not appear in combination with any of the following options: command, peers.
>
> Force ntpq to operate in interactive mode. Prompts will be written to the standard output and commands read from the standard input.

−n, **−−numeric**
> numeric host addresses.
>
> Output all host addresses in dotted-quad numeric format rather than converting to the canonical host names.

−?, **−−help**
> Display usage information and exit.

−!, **−−more-help**
> Extended usage information passed thru pager.

−> [*rcfile*], **−−save-opts**[=*rcfile*]
> Save the option state to *rcfile*. The default is the *last* configuration file listed in the **OPTION PRESETS** section, below.

−< *rcfile*, **−−load-opts**=*rcfile*, **−−no-load-opts**
> Load options from *rcfile*. The *no-load-opts* form will disable the loading of earlier RC/INI files. *--no-load-opts* is handled early, out of order.

−v [{*v*|*c*|*n*}], **−−version**[=*{v*|*c*|*n}*]
> Output version of program and exit. The default mode is 'v', a simple version. The 'c' mode will print copyright information and 'n' will print the full copyright notice.

OPTION PRESETS

Any option that is not marked as *not presettable* may be preset by loading values from configuration ("RC" or ".INI") file(s) and values from environment variables named:

   NTPQ_<option-name> or **NTPQ**

The environmental presets take precedence (are processed later than) the configuration files. The *homerc* files are "*$HOME*", and ".". If any of these are directories, then the file *.ntprc* is searched for within those directories.

AUTHOR

David L. Mills and/or others
Please send bug reports to: http://bugs.ntp.org, bugs@ntp.org

see /usr/share/doc/html/ntp/copyright.html

This manual page was *AutoGen*-erated from the **ntpq** option definitions.

NAME
>   ntptime — read kernel time variables

SYNOPSIS
>   ntptime [-chr] [-e est_error] [-f frequency] [-m max_error] [-o offset]
>   [-s status] [-t time_constant]

DESCRIPTION
>   This program is useful only with special kernels described in the *A Kernel Model for Precision Timekeeping*
>   page in /usr/share/doc/html/ntp/kern.html. It reads and displays time-related kernel variables
>   using the ntp_gettime(2) system call. A similar display can be obtained using the **ntpdc** program and
>   kerninfo command.

OPTIONS
>   -c   Display the execution time of **ntptime** itself.
>
>   -e est_error
>   Specify estimated error, in microseconds.
>
>   -f frequency
>   Specify frequency offset, in parts per million.
>
>   -h   Display times in Unix timeval format. Default is NTP format.
>
>   -l   Specify the leap bits as a code from 0 to 3.
>
>   -m max_error
>   Display help information.
>
>   -o offset
>   Specify clock offset, in microseconds.
>
>   -r   Display Unix and NTP times in raw format.
>
>   -s status
>   Specify clock status, Better know what you are doing.
>
>   -t time_constant
>   Specify time constant, an integer in the range 0-4.

AUTHORS
>   David L. Mills (mills@udel.edu)

NAME
     `ntptrace` — trace a chain of NTP servers back to the primary source

SYNOPSIS
     `ntptrace` [`-vdn`] [`-r` *retries*] [`-t` *timeout*] [*server*]

DESCRIPTION
     `ntptrace` determines where a given Network Time Protocol (NTP) server gets its time from, and follows the chain of NTP servers back to their master time source. If given no arguments, it starts with `localhost`. Here is an example of the output from **ntptrace**:

% ntptrace
localhost: stratum 4, offset 0.0019529, synch distance 0.144135
server2ozo.com: stratum 2, offset 0.0124263, synch distance 0.115784
usndh.edu: stratum 1, offset 0.0019298, synch distance 0.011993, refid 'WWVB'

     On each line, the fields are (left to right): the host name, the host stratum, the time offset between that host and the local host (as measured by **ntptrace** ; this is why it is not always zero for `localhost`), the host synchronization distance, and (only for stratum-1 servers) the reference clock ID. All times are given in seconds. Note that the stratum is the server hop count to the primary source, while the synchronization distance is the estimated error relative to the primary source. These terms are precisely defined in RFC-1305.

OPTIONS
     `-d`   Turns on some debugging output.

     `-n`   Turns off the printing of host names; instead, host IP addresses are given. This may be useful if a nameserver is down.

     `-r` *retries*
          Sets the number of retransmission attempts for each host (default = 5).

     `-t` *timeout*
          Sets the retransmission timeout (in seconds) (default = 2).

     `-v`   Prints verbose information about the NTP servers.

AUTHORS
     David L. Mills (mills@udel.edu)

BUGS
     This program makes no attempt to improve accuracy by doing multiple samples.

NAME

ofctl — display the OpenPROM or OpenFirmware device tree

SYNOPSIS

ofctl [**-p**] [**-f** *file*] [*node*]

DESCRIPTION

ofctl provides an interface for displaying the OpenPROM or OpenFirmware device tree and node properties. The **ofctl** program is only installed on supported platforms.

Without any arguments, **ofctl** will dump the full tree. When given the name of a specific node, **ofctl** will display that node and its child nodes.

The options are as follows:

> **-f** *file*
>> On systems with OpenPROM, use *file* instead of the default /dev/openprom. On systems with OpenFirmware, use *file* instead of the default /dev/openfirm.
>
> **-p**   Display each node's properties.

FILES

/dev/openprom   The openprom device on systems with OpenPROM.

/dev/openfirm   The openfirm device on systems with OpenFirmware.

SEE ALSO

eeprom(8)

NAME
ofwboot, ofwboot.elf, ofwboot.xcf — Open Firmware boot command

SYNOPSIS
ofwboot

DESCRIPTION
Open Firmware is a FORTH-like command interpreter started by the BootROM after the power-on self test (POST). This command interpreter allows the user flexibility in choosing how their machine boots an operating system. NetBSD uses Open Firmware to initialize many of the devices in a system and uses it to load the primary bootloader, **ofwboot**.

The information in this man page should only serve as a guideline for users. Apple has made many revisions to Open Firmware, and the earlier versions had many problems and inconsistencies. You may find that a boot command that works on one model will not work on another.

In this man page, only one Open Firmware command will be described, **boot**, because it is used to pass arguments to **ofwboot**. The Open Firmware **boot** command takes up to three arguments:

boot [*boot-device* [*boot-file*]] [*options*]
boot-device   primary bootloader location
boot-file   kernel location
options   flags passed to the kernel (see below)

boot-device
The first argument, *boot-device*, actually designates the primary bootloader location and its name in the form:

        boot-device:[partition-num],[bootloader-filename]
A typical example, from a PowerBook (FireWire), is

        /pci@f2000000/mac-io@17/ata-4@1f000/@0:9,ofwboot.xcf
Note that colon (':') delimits the device to the left, and comma (',') separates the boot loader filename from the first part. For Open Firmware versions before 3, the primary bootloader is installed in partition "zero", and it is not necessary to specify the bootloader-filename. For Open Firmware version 3, you must specify the bootloader-filename.

Open Firmware stores aliases to common devices in NVRAM. In the example above, /pci@f2000000/mac-io@17/ata-4@1f000/@0 is the path on a PowerBook (FireWire) to the built-in ATA/100 hard drive. Use the **devalias** command in Open Firmware to print out a list of common device names on a particular model. The command above could then be simplified to:

        hd:9,ofwboot.xcf

boot-loader-file-name is usually **ofwboot.xcf**. (See also the **FILES** section for further discussion.)

If omitted, the Open Firmware variable *boot-device* is used.

boot-file
It may be necessary to specify the *boot-file* if Open Firmware does not know where to find the kernel. The default is to load the file named **netbsd** on partition "a" from the device used to load the primary bootloader.

For systems with Open Firmware versions less than 3 which are set up using **sysinst**, the *boot-file* argument is not necessary. Systems with Open Firmware version 3 may need to specify the *boot-file*.

The syntax is similar to the *boot-device* argument:
```
[boot-file-device:partition-num/][kernel-name]
```
This is a little different, since a kernel-name may be specified without listing a boot-file-device and partition-num. Additionally, a boot-file-device and partition-num may need to be specified, while using the default kernel-name.

If no kernel-name is specified, the primary bootloader will try to find kernels named either *netbsd* or *netbsd.gz* on the boot-device or (if specified) boot-file-device.

options

Possible options are:

-a   ask for the boot device
-s   single-user mode boot
-d   debug mode
exit   exit to Open Firmware after processing arguments

ENVIRONMENT

If set, the following Open Firmware variables will be used to determine which *boot-device* and *boot-file* Open Firmware should use when booting a system. If the user specifies arguments on the command line, these values are overridden.

boot-device   used as the first argument
boot-file   used as the second argument
auto-boot?   setting this variable to *false* will present the user with an Open Firmware command prompt after power-on reset. A value of *true* will automatically boot the system using the variables *boot-device* and *boot-file*. (This is not really related to the boot command, but is included for completeness.)

To restore these variables to their default values, use the **set-default** Open Firmware command:
set-default *boot-device*

FILES

The three files **ofwboot**, **ofwboot.elf**, and **ofwboot.xcf** are the same program, in different executable formats.

ofwboot   **ofwboot** is installed via *installboot*(8) on systems with Open Firmware versions less than 3. It is not necessary to specify this file name, as it is stored in a special location on the disk, partition "zero". For example, the following command might be used to boot from a SCSI device with ID 2: **0 >boot scsi-int/sd@2:0**.

ofwboot.xcf   **ofwboot.xcf** is in XCOFF format. This file is used on all Open Firmware 3 systems, and on Open Firmware systems prior to 3 when the bootloader is not installed in partition "zero", such as from an ISO-9660 format CD-ROM.

ofwboot.elf   **ofwboot.elf** is in *elf*(5) format and only functions on systems with Open Firmware version 3. To avoid confusion, all users should be using **ofwboot.xcf**, as **ofwboot.elf** offers no additional functionality. It is only included for historical reasons.

boot.fs   This 1.44 MB disk image contains everything necessary to boot and install NetBSD. It includes the partition "zero" bootloader (**ofwboot**), an INSTALL kernel (with limited device drivers), and the **sysinst** utility in a RAM disk. Since Open Firmware does not care what media files are loaded from, only whether they are supported and in the correct format, this disk image may be placed on media other than floppy disks, such as hard drives or Zip disks. Use *dd*(1) on Unix, or **DiskCopy** on MacOS 9.1 or later, or **suntar** on any MacOS version to copy this image onto the media.

netbsd   production kernel, using the GENERIC set of devices which supports almost all hardware
                         available for this platform.

netbsd_GENERIC_MD.gz
                         GENERIC kernel (the same as *netbsd*), with RAM disk and **sysinst** included.

macppccd.iso   bootable   CDROM   image   for   all   supported   systems.   Usually   located   at
                         `ftp://ftp.NetBSD.org/pub/NetBSD/iso/{RELEASE}/macppccd.iso`

EXAMPLES

Boot an Open Firmware 3 system, with *netbsd* installed on partition "a":

0 > boot hd:,ofwboot.xcf

Boot into single user mode:

0 > boot hd:,ofwboot.xcf netbsd -s

Boot from bootable CDROM with Open Firmware 3 or higher:

0 > boot cd:,\ofwboot.xcf netbsd.macppc

Boot from bootable CDROM (internal SCSI, id=3) of NetBSD 1.5 release with Open Firmware versions prior
to 3:

0 > boot scsi/sd@3:0,OFWBOOT.XCF NETBSD.MACPPC

Boot from floppy disk:

0 > boot fd:0

Boot from network, with bootps, `bootptab`(5), `tftpd`(8), and `nfsd`(8) server available:

0 > boot enet:0

Boot from network, but use internal root partition of second drive:

0 > boot enet:0 ultra1:0

Boot MacOS, looking for the first available bootable disk:

0 > boot hd:,\\:tbxi

Boot MacOS X residing on partition 10:

0 > boot hd:10,\\:tbxi

ERRORS

DEFAULT CATCH!, code=FF00300 at %SRR0: FF80AD38 %SRR1: 00001070
Could be "device not found" or I/O errors on the device. The numbers are just for example.

Can't LOAD from this device
Open Firmware found the device, but it is not supported by **load**.

0 > boot yy:0/netbsd
RESETing to change Configuration!
yy:0 doesn't exist, so Open Firmware ignores the string and uses the default parameters to boot MacOS; the
MacOS boot routine then clears some of the Open Firmware variables.

0 > boot ata/ata-disk@0:9 specified partition is not bootable
 ok
As it says.

0 > boot ata/ata-disk@0:0
>> NetBSD/macppc OpenFirmware Boot, Revision 1.3
>> (root@nazuha, Fri Jun 8 22:21:55 JST 2001)
no active package3337696/
and hangs: See the real-base part in the FAQ.

SEE ALSO
`installboot(8)`

```
INSTALL.html
http://www.NetBSD.org/ports/macppc/faq.html
http://www.NetBSD.org/docs/network/netboot/
```

STANDARDS
IEEE Std 1275-1994 ("Open Firmware")

BUGS
ofwboot can only boot from devices recognized by Open Firmware.

Early PowerMacintosh systems (particularly the 7500) seem to have problems with netbooting. Adding an arp entry at the tftp server with

```
        arp -s booting-host-name its-ethernet-address
```
may resolve this problem (see `arp(8)`).

0 > boot CLAIM failed
 ok
Once boot failed, successive boots may not be possible. You need to type **reset-all** or power-cycle to initialize Open Firmware.

NAME
omshell - OMAPI Command Shell

SYNOPSIS
omshell

DESCRIPTION
The OMAPI Command Shell, omshell, provides an interactive way to connect to, query, and possibly change, the ISC DHCP Server's state via OMAPI, the Object Management API. By using OMAPI and omshell, you do not have to stop, make changes, and then restart the DHCP server, but can make the changes while the server is running. Omshell provides a way of accessing OMAPI.

OMAPI is simply a communications mechanism that allows you to manipulate objects. In order to actually *use* omshell, you *must* understand what objects are available and how to use them. Documentation for OMAPI objects can be found in the documentation for the server that provides them - for example, in the **dhcpd(1)** manual page and the **dhclient(1)** manual page.

CONTRIBUTIONS
This software is free software. At various times its development has been underwritten by various organizations, including the ISC and Vixie Enterprises. The development of 3.0 has been funded almost entirely by Nominum, Inc.

At this point development is being shepherded by Ted Lemon, and hosted by the ISC, but the future of this project depends on you. If you have features you want, please consider implementing them.

LOCAL AND REMOTE OBJECTS
Throughout this document, there are references to local and remote objects. Local objects are ones created in omshell with the **new** command. Remote objects are ones on the server: leases, hosts, and groups that the DHCP server knows about. Local and remote objects are associated together to enable viewing and modification of object attributes. Also, new remote objects can be created to match local objects.

OPENING A CONNECTION
omshell is started from the command line. Once omshell is started, there are several commands that can be issued:

server *address*
> where address is the IP address of the DHCP server to connect to. If this is not specified, the default server is 127.0.0.1 (localhost).

port *number*
> where number is the port that OMAPI listens on. By default, this is 7911.

key *name secret*
> This specifies the TSIG key to use to authenticate the OMAPI transactions. *name* is the name of a key defined in *dhcpd.conf* with the **omapi-key** statement. The *secret* is the secret generated from **dnssec-keygen** or another key generation program.

connect
> This starts the OMAPI connection to the server as specified by the *server* statement.

CREATING LOCAL OBJECTS
Any object defined in OMAPI can be created, queried, and/or modified. The object types available to OMAPI are defined in **dhcpd(8)** and **dhclient**. When using omshell, objects are first defined locally, manipulated as desired, and then associated with an object on the server. Only one object can be manipulated at a time. To create a local object, use

new *object-type*
> *object-type* is one of group, host, or lease.

At this point, you now have an object that you can set properties on. For example, if a new lease object was created with *new lease*, any of a lease's attributes can be set as follows:

set *attribute-name = value*

Attribute names are defined in dhcpd(8) and **dhclient(8)**. Values should be quoted if they are strings. So, to set a lease's IP address, you would do the following:

set ip-address = 192.168.4.50

ASSOCIATING LOCAL AND REMOTE OBJECTS

At this point, you can query the server for information about this lease, by

open

Now, the local lease object you created and set the IP address for is associated with the corresponding lease object on the DHCP server. All of the lease attributes from the DHCP server are now also the attributes on the local object, and will be shown in omshell.

VIEWING A REMOTE OBJECT

To query a lease of address 192.168.4.50, and find out its attributes, after connecting to the server, take the following steps:

new lease

This creates a new local lease object.

set ip-address = 192.168.4.50

This sets the *local* object's IP address to be 192.168.4.50

open

Now, if a lease with that IP address exists, you will see all the information the DHCP server has about that particular lease. Any data that isn't readily printable text will show up in colon-separated hexadecimal values. In this example, output back from the server for the entire transaction might look like this:

```
> new "lease"
obj: lease
> set ip-address = 192.168.4.50
obj: lease
ip-address = c0:a8:04:32
> open
obj: lease
ip-address = c0:a8:04:32
state = 00:00:00:02
dhcp-client-identifier = 01:00:10:a4:b2:36:2c
client-hostname = "wendelina"
subnet = 00:00:00:06
pool = 00:00:00:07
hardware-address = 00:10:a4:b2:36:2c
hardware-type = 00:00:00:01
ends = dc:d9:0d:3b
starts = 5c:9f:04:3b
tstp = 00:00:00:00
tsfp = 00:00:00:00
cltt = 00:00:00:00
```

As you can see here, the IP address is represented in hexadecimal, as are the starting and ending times of the lease.

MODIFYING A REMOTE OBJECT

Attributes of remote objects are updated by using the **set** command as before, and then issuing an **update** command. The **set** command sets the attributes on the current local object, and the **update** command pushes those changes out to the server.

Continuing with the previous example, if a **set client-hostname = "something-else"** was issued, followed by an **update** command, the output would look about like this:

```
> set client-hostname = "something-else"
obj: lease
ip-address = c0:a8:04:32
state = 00:00:00:02
dhcp-client-identifier = 01:00:10:a4:b2:36:2c
client-hostname = "something-else"
subnet = 00:00:00:06
pool = 00:00:00:07
hardware-address = 00:10:a4:b2:36:2c
hardware-type = 00:00:00:01
ends = dc:d9:0d:3b
starts = 5c:9f:04:3b
tstp = 00:00:00:00
tsfp = 00:00:00:00
cltt = 00:00:00:00
> update
obj: lease
ip-address = c0:a8:04:32
state = 00:00:00:02
dhcp-client-identifier = 01:00:10:a4:b2:36:2c
client-hostname = "something-else"
subnet = 00:00:00:06
pool = 00:00:00:07
hardware-address = 00:10:a4:b2:36:2c
hardware-type = 00:00:00:01
ends = dc:d9:0d:3b
starts = 5c:9f:04:3b
tstp = 00:00:00:00
tsfp = 00:00:00:00
cltt = 00:00:00:00
```

NEW REMOTE OBJECTS

New remote objects are created much in the same way that existing server objects are modified. Create a local object using **new**, set the attributes as you'd wish them to be, and then create the remote object with the same properties by using

create

Now a new object exists on the DHCP server which matches the properties that you gave your local object. Objects created via OMAPI are saved into the dhcpd.leases file.

For example, if a new host with the IP address of 192.168.4.40 needs to be created it would be done as follows:

```
> new host
obj: host
> set name = "some-host"
obj: host
name = "some-host"
> set hardware-address = 00:80:c7:84:b1:94
obj: host
name = "some-host"
hardware-address = 00:80:c7:84:b1:94
> set hardware-type = 1
obj: host
name = "some-host"
hardware-address = 00:80:c7:84:b1:94
```

```
hardware-type = 1
> set ip-address = 192.168.4.40
obj: host
name = "some-host"
hardware-address = 00:80:c7:84:b1:94
hardware-type = 1
ip-address = c0:a8:04:28
> create
obj: host
name = "some-host"
hardware-address = 00:80:c7:84:b1:94
hardware-type = 00:00:00:01
ip-address = c0:a8:04:28
>
```

Your dhcpd.leases file would then have an entry like this in it:

```
host some-host {
  dynamic;
  hardware ethernet 00:80:c7:84:b1:94;
  fixed-address 192.168.4.40;
}
```

The *dynamic;* line is to denote that this host entry did not come from dhcpd.conf, but was created dynamically via OMAPI.

RESETTING ATTRIBUTES

If you want to remove an attribute from an object, you can do this with the **unset** command. Once you have unset an attribute, you must use the **update** command to update the remote object. So, if the host "some-host" from the previous example will not have a static IP address anymore, the commands in omshell would look like this:

```
obj: host
name = "some-host"
hardware-address = 00:80:c7:84:b1:94
hardware-type = 00:00:00:01
ip-address = c0:a8:04:28
> unset ip-address
obj: host
name = "some-host"
hardware-address = 00:80:c7:84:b1:94
hardware-type = 00:00:00:01
ip-address = <null>
>
```

REFRESHING OBJECTS

A local object may be refreshed with the current remote object properties using the **refresh** command. This is useful for object that change periodically, like leases, to see if they have been updated. This isn't particularly useful for hosts.

DELETING OBJECTS

Any remote object that can be created can also be destroyed. This is done by creating a new local object, setting attributes, associating the local and remote object using **open**, *and then using the* **remove** command. If the host "some-host" from before was created in error, this could be corrected as follows:

```
obj: host
name = "some-host"
```

```
          hardware-address = 00:80:c7:84:b1:94
          hardware-type = 00:00:00:01
          ip-address = c0:a8:04:28
          > remove
          obj: <null>
          >
```

HELP

The **help** command will print out all of the commands available in omshell, with some syntax pointers.

SEE ALSO

dhcpctl(3), omapi(3), dhcpd(8), dhclient(8), dhcpd.conf(5), dhclient.conf(5).

AUTHOR

omshell was written by Ted Lemon of Nominum, Inc. Information about Nominum and support contracts for DHCP and BIND can be found at **http://www.nominum.com. This preliminary documentation was** written by Wendy Verschoor of Nominum, Inc., while she was testing omshell.

NAME

oqmgr – old Postfix queue manager

SYNOPSIS

oqmgr [generic Postfix daemon options]

DESCRIPTION

The **oqmgr**(8) daemon awaits the arrival of incoming mail and arranges for its delivery via Postfix delivery processes. The actual mail routing strategy is delegated to the **trivial-rewrite**(8) daemon. This program expects to be run from the **master**(8) process manager.

Mail addressed to the local **double-bounce** address is logged and discarded. This stops potential loops caused by undeliverable bounce notifications.

MAIL QUEUES

The **oqmgr**(8) daemon maintains the following queues:

incoming

Inbound mail from the network, or mail picked up by the local **pickup**(8) agent from the **maildrop** directory.

active   Messages that the queue manager has opened for delivery. Only a limited number of messages is allowed to enter the **active** queue (leaky bucket strategy, for a fixed delivery rate).

deferred

Mail that could not be delivered upon the first attempt. The queue manager implements exponential backoff by doubling the time between delivery attempts.

corrupt

Unreadable or damaged queue files are moved here for inspection.

hold   Messages that are kept "on hold" are kept here until someone sets them free.

DELIVERY STATUS REPORTS

The **oqmgr**(8) daemon keeps an eye on per-message delivery status reports in the following directories. Each status report file has the same name as the corresponding message file:

bounce Per-recipient status information about why mail is bounced. These files are maintained by the **bounce**(8) daemon.

defer   Per-recipient status information about why mail is delayed. These files are maintained by the **defer**(8) daemon.

trace   Per-recipient status information as requested with the Postfix "**sendmail -v**" or "**sendmail -bv**" command. These files are maintained by the **trace**(8) daemon.

The **oqmgr**(8) daemon is responsible for asking the **bounce**(8), **defer**(8) or **trace**(8) daemons to send delivery reports.

STRATEGIES

The queue manager implements a variety of strategies for either opening queue files (input) or for message delivery (output).

leaky bucket

This strategy limits the number of messages in the **active** queue and prevents the queue manager from running out of memory under heavy load.

fairness

When the **active** queue has room, the queue manager takes one message from the **incoming** queue and one from the **deferred** queue. This prevents a large mail backlog from blocking the delivery of new mail.

slow start

This strategy eliminates "thundering herd" problems by slowly adjusting the number of parallel deliveries to the same destination.

round robin
> The queue manager sorts delivery requests by destination. Round-robin selection prevents one destination from dominating deliveries to other destinations.

exponential backoff
> Mail that cannot be delivered upon the first attempt is deferred. The time interval between delivery attempts is doubled after each attempt.

destination status cache
> The queue manager avoids unnecessary delivery attempts by maintaining a short-term, in-memory list of unreachable destinations.

TRIGGERS

On an idle system, the queue manager waits for the arrival of trigger events, or it waits for a timer to go off. A trigger is a one-byte message. Depending on the message received, the queue manager performs one of the following actions (the message is followed by the symbolic constant used internally by the software):

D (QMGR_REQ_SCAN_DEFERRED)
> Start a deferred queue scan. If a deferred queue scan is already in progress, that scan will be restarted as soon as it finishes.

I (QMGR_REQ_SCAN_INCOMING)
> Start an incoming queue scan. If an incoming queue scan is already in progress, that scan will be restarted as soon as it finishes.

A (QMGR_REQ_SCAN_ALL)
> Ignore deferred queue file time stamps. The request affects the next deferred queue scan.

F (QMGR_REQ_FLUSH_DEAD)
> Purge all information about dead transports and destinations.

W (TRIGGER_REQ_WAKEUP)
> Wakeup call, This is used by the master server to instantiate servers that should not go away forever. The action is to start an incoming queue scan.

The **oqmgr**(8) daemon reads an entire buffer worth of triggers. Multiple identical trigger requests are collapsed into one, and trigger requests are sorted so that **A** and **F** precede **D** and **I**. Thus, in order to force a deferred queue run, one would request **A F D**; in order to notify the queue manager of the arrival of new mail one would request **I**.

STANDARDS
RFC 3463 (Enhanced status codes)
RFC 3464 (Delivery status notifications)

SECURITY
The **oqmgr**(8) daemon is not security sensitive. It reads single-character messages from untrusted local users, and thus may be susceptible to denial of service attacks. The **oqmgr**(8) daemon does not talk to the outside world, and it can be run at fixed low privilege in a chrooted environment.

DIAGNOSTICS
Problems and transactions are logged to the **syslog**(8) daemon. Corrupted message files are saved to the **corrupt** queue for further inspection.

Depending on the setting of the **notify_classes** parameter, the postmaster is notified of bounces and of other trouble.

BUGS
A single queue manager process has to compete for disk access with multiple front-end processes such as **cleanup**(8). A sudden burst of inbound mail can negatively impact outbound delivery rates.

CONFIGURATION PARAMETERS
Changes to **main.cf** are not picked up automatically, as **oqmgr**(8) is a persistent process. Use the command "**postfix reload**" after a configuration change.

The text below provides only a parameter summary. See **postconf**(5) for more details including examples.

In the text below, *transport* is the first field in a **master.cf** entry.

COMPATIBILITY CONTROLS

Available before Postfix version 2.5:

allow_min_user (no)
> Allow a sender or recipient address to have '-' as the first character.

ACTIVE QUEUE CONTROLS

qmgr_clog_warn_time (300s)
> The minimal delay between warnings that a specific destination is clogging up the Postfix active queue.

qmgr_message_active_limit (20000)
> The maximal number of messages in the active queue.

qmgr_message_recipient_limit (20000)
> The maximal number of recipients held in memory by the Postfix queue manager, and the maximal size of the size of the short-term, in-memory "dead" destination status cache.

DELIVERY CONCURRENCY CONTROLS

qmgr_fudge_factor (100)
> Obsolete feature: the percentage of delivery resources that a busy mail system will use up for delivery of a large mailing list message.

initial_destination_concurrency (5)
> The initial per-destination concurrency level for parallel delivery to the same destination.

default_destination_concurrency_limit (20)
> The default maximal number of parallel deliveries to the same destination.

*transport*_**destination_concurrency_limit ($default_destination_concurrency_limit)**
> Idem, for delivery via the named message *transport*.

Available in Postfix version 2.5 and later:

*transport*_**initial_destination_concurrency ($initial_destination_concurrency)**
> Initial concurrency for delivery via the named message *transport*.

default_destination_concurrency_failed_cohort_limit (1)
> How many pseudo-cohorts must suffer connection or handshake failure before a specific destination is considered unavailable (and further delivery is suspended).

*transport*_**destination_concurrency_failed_cohort_limit**   **($default_destination_concurrency_failed_cohort_limit)**
> Idem, for delivery via the named message *transport*.

default_destination_concurrency_negative_feedback (1)
> The per-destination amount of delivery concurrency negative feedback, after a delivery completes with a connection or handshake failure.

*transport*_**destination_concurrency_negative_feedback**   **($default_destination_concurrency_negative_feedback)**
> Idem, for delivery via the named message *transport*.

default_destination_concurrency_positive_feedback (1)
> The per-destination amount of delivery concurrency positive feedback, after a delivery completes without connection or handshake failure.

*transport*_**destination_concurrency_positive_feedback**   **($default_destination_concurrency_positive_feedback)**
> Idem, for delivery via the named message *transport*.

destination_concurrency_feedback_debug (no)
    Make the queue manager's feedback algorithm verbose for performance analysis purposes.

RECIPIENT SCHEDULING CONTROLS
default_destination_recipient_limit (50)
    The default maximal number of recipients per message delivery.

*transport*_**destination_recipient_limit**
    Idem, for delivery via the named message *transport*.

OTHER RESOURCE AND RATE CONTROLS
minimal_backoff_time (300s)
    The minimal time between attempts to deliver a deferred message; prior to Postfix 2.4 the default
    value was 1000s.

maximal_backoff_time (4000s)
    The maximal time between attempts to deliver a deferred message.

maximal_queue_lifetime (5d)
    The maximal time a message is queued before it is sent back as undeliverable.

queue_run_delay (300s)
    The time between deferred queue scans by the queue manager; prior to Postfix 2.4 the default
    value was 1000s.

transport_retry_time (60s)
    The time between attempts by the Postfix queue manager to contact a malfunctioning message
    delivery transport.

Available in Postfix version 2.1 and later:

bounce_queue_lifetime (5d)
    The maximal time a bounce message is queued before it is considered undeliverable.

Available in Postfix version 2.5 and later:

default_destination_rate_delay (0s)
    The default amount of delay that is inserted between individual deliveries to the same destination;
    with per-destination recipient limit > 1, a destination is a domain, otherwise it is a recipient.

*transport*_**destination_rate_delay $default_destination_rate_delay**
    Idem, for delivery via the named message *transport*.

MISCELLANEOUS CONTROLS
config_directory (see 'postconf -d' output)
    The default location of the Postfix main.cf and master.cf configuration files.

defer_transports (empty)
    The names of message delivery transports that should not deliver mail unless someone issues
    "**sendmail -q**" or equivalent.

delay_logging_resolution_limit (2)
    The maximal number of digits after the decimal point when logging sub-second delay values.

helpful_warnings (yes)
    Log warnings about problematic configuration settings, and provide helpful suggestions.

ipc_timeout (3600s)
    The time limit for sending or receiving information over an internal communication channel.

process_id (read-only)
    The process ID of a Postfix command or daemon process.

process_name (read-only)
    The process name of a Postfix command or daemon process.

queue_directory (see 'postconf -d' output)
> The location of the Postfix top-level queue directory.

syslog_facility (mail)
> The syslog facility of Postfix logging.

syslog_name (see 'postconf -d' output)
> The mail system name that is prepended to the process name in syslog records, so that "smtpd" becomes, for example, "postfix/smtpd".

FILES
/var/spool/postfix/incoming, incoming queue
/var/spool/postfix/active, active queue
/var/spool/postfix/deferred, deferred queue
/var/spool/postfix/bounce, non-delivery status
/var/spool/postfix/defer, non-delivery status
/var/spool/postfix/trace, delivery status

SEE ALSO
trivial-rewrite(8), address routing
bounce(8), delivery status reports
postconf(5), configuration parameters
master(5), generic daemon options
master(8), process manager
syslogd(8), system logging

README FILES
Use "**postconf readme_directory**" or "**postconf html_directory**" to locate this information.
QSHAPE_README, Postfix queue analysis

LICENSE
The Secure Mailer license must be distributed with this software.

AUTHOR(S)
Wietse Venema
IBM T.J. Watson Research
P.O. Box 704
Yorktown Heights, NY 10598, USA

NAME
pac — printer/plotter accounting information

SYNOPSIS
pac [**-cmrs**] [**-P** *printer*] [**-p** *price*] [*name* ...]

DESCRIPTION
pac reads the printer/plotter accounting files, accumulating the number of pages (the usual case) or feet (for raster devices) of paper consumed by each user, and printing out how much each user consumed in pages or feet and dollars.

Options and operands available:

-P*printer*
    Accounting is done for the named printer. Normally, accounting is done for the default printer (site dependent) or the value of the environment variable PRINTER is used.

-c   flag causes the output to be sorted by cost; usually the output is sorted alphabetically by name.

-m   flag causes the host name to be ignored in the accounting file. This allows for a user on multiple machines to have all of his printing charges grouped together.

-p*price*   The value *price* is used for the cost in dollars instead of the default value of 0.02 or the price specified in /etc/printcap.

-r   Reverse the sorting order.

-s   Accounting information is summarized on the summary accounting file; this summarization is necessary since on a busy system, the accounting file can grow by several lines per day.

names   Statistics are only printed for user(s) *name*; usually, statistics are printed for every user who has used any paper.

OUTPUT FORMAT
pac formats the output into simple table, using four columns - number of feets or pages (column "pages/feet"), how many copies were made (column "runs"), total price for this print (column "price") and user login with host name (column "login" or "host name and login"). If argument *name* was not used and hence **pac** is printing information for all users, a summary line with print totals (runs, pages, price) is appended.

Note that **pac** on other system might print the price as price per copy.

FILES
/var/account/?acct raw accounting files
/var/account/?_sum summary accounting files
/etc/printcap   printer capability data base

SEE ALSO
printcap(5)

HISTORY
The **pac** command appeared in 4.0BSD.

BUGS
The relationship between the computed price and reality is as yet unknown.

NAME

pam — Pluggable Authentication Modules framework

DESCRIPTION

The Pluggable Authentication Modules (PAM) framework is a system of libraries that perform authentication tasks for services and applications. Applications that use the PAM API may have their authentication behavior configured by the system administrator though the use of the service's PAM configuration file.

PAM modules provide four classes of functionality:

account   Account verification services such as password expiration and access control.

auth   Authentication services. This usually takes the form of a challenge-response conversation. However, PAM can also support, with appropriate hardware support, biometric devices, smart-cards, and so forth.

password   Password (or, more generally, authentication token) change and update services.

session   Session management services. These are tasks that are performed before access to a service is granted and after access to a service is withdrawn. These may include updating activity logs or setting up and tearing down credential forwarding agents.

A primary feature of PAM is the notion of "stacking" different modules together to form a processing chain for the task. This allows fairly precise control over how a particular authentication task is performed, and under what conditions. PAM module configurations may also inherit stacks from other module configurations, providing some degree of centralized administration.

SEE ALSO

login(1), passwd(1), su(1), pam(3), pam.conf(5), pam_chroot(8), pam_deny(8), pam_echo(8), pam_exec(8), pam_ftpusers(8), pam_group(8), pam_guest(8), pam_krb5(8), pam_ksu(8), pam_lastlog(8), pam_login_access(8), pam_nologin(8), pam_permit(8), pam_radius(8), pam_rhosts(8), pam_rootok(8), pam_securetty(8), pam_self(8), pam_skey(8), pam_ssh(8), pam_unix(8)

HISTORY

The Pluggable Authentication Module framework was originally developed by SunSoft, described in DCE/OSF-RFC 86.0, and first deployed in Solaris 2.6. It was later incorporated into the X/Open Single Sign-On Service (XSSO) Pluggable Authentication Modules specifiation.

The Pluggable Authentication Module framework first appeared in NetBSD 3.0.

NAME
> **pam_afslog** — AFS credentials PAM module

SYNOPSIS
> [*service-name*] *module-type control-flag* pam_afslog [*arguments*]

DESCRIPTION
> The **pam_afslog** authentication service module for PAM provides functionality for only one PAM category: authentication (*module-type* of "auth").

> The **pam_sm_authenticate**() function does nothing and thus the module should be used with an *control-flag* of "optional".

> The value of the module comes from its **pam_sm_setcred**() function. If the *afslog* parameter is enabled in krb5.conf(5), then the module will take Kerberos 5 credentials from the cache created by pam_krb5(8) and convert them into AFS tokens, after first creating a PAG (Process Authentication Group) if necessary.

SEE ALSO
> kafs(3), pam.conf(5), pam(8), pam_krb5(8)

HISTORY
> The **pam_afslog** module was developed for NetBSD by Tyler C. Sarna. The **pam_afslog** module appeared in NetBSD 4.0.

NAME

pam_chroot — Chroot PAM module

SYNOPSIS

[*service-name*] *module-type control-flag* pam_chroot [*arguments*]

DESCRIPTION

The chroot service module for PAM chroots users into either a predetermined directory or one derived from their home directory. If a user's home directory as specified in the *passwd* structure returned by getpwnam(3) contains the string "/./", the portion of the directory name to the left of that string is used as the chroot directory, and the portion to the right will be the current working directory inside the chroot tree. Otherwise, the directories specified by the **dir** and **cwd** options (see below) are used.

also_root Do not hold user ID 0 exempt from the chroot requirement.

always Report a failure if a chroot directory could not be derived from the user's home directory, and the **dir** option was not specified.

cwd=*directory*
    Specify the directory to chdir(2) into after a successful chroot(2) call.

dir=*directory*
    Specify the chroot directory to use if one could not be derived from the user's home directory.

SEE ALSO

pam.conf(5), pam(8)

AUTHORS

The **pam_chroot** module and this manual page were developed for the FreeBSD Project by ThinkSec AS and NAI Labs, the Security Research Division of Network Associates, Inc. under DARPA/SPAWAR contract N66001-01-C-8035 ("CBOSS"), as part of the DARPA CHATS research program.

NAME

pam_deny — Deny PAM module

SYNOPSIS

[*service-name*] *module-type control-flag* pam_deny [*options*]

DESCRIPTION

The deny authentication service module for PAM provides functionality for all the PAM categories: authentication, account management, session management and password management. In terms of the *module-type* parameter, these are the "auth", "account", "session", and "password" features.

The Deny module will universally deny all requests. It is primarily of use during testing, and to "null-out" unwanted functionality.

The following options may be passed to the module:

debug   syslog(3) debugging information at LOG_DEBUG level.

no_warn suppress warning messages to the user. These messages include reasons why the user's authentication attempt was declined.

SEE ALSO

syslog(3), pam.conf(5), pam(8)

NAME

pam_echo — Echo PAM module

SYNOPSIS

[*service-name*] *module-type control-flag* pam_echo [*arguments*]

DESCRIPTION

The echo service module for PAM displays its arguments to the user, separated by spaces, using the current conversation function.

If the **%** character occurs anywhere in the arguments to **pam_echo**, it is assumed to introduce one of the following escape sequences:

%H   The name of the host on which the client runs (PAM_RHOST).

%s   The current service name (PAM_SERVICE).

%t   The name of the controlling tty (PAM_TTY).

%U   The applicant's user name (PAM_RUSER).

%u   The target account's user name (PAM_USER).

Any other two-character sequence beginning with **%** expands to the character following the **%** character.

SEE ALSO

pam.conf(5), pam(8)

AUTHORS

The **pam_echo** module and this manual page were developed for the FreeBSD Project by ThinkSec AS and NAI Labs, the Security Research Division of Network Associates, Inc. under DARPA/SPAWAR contract N66001-01-C-8035 ("CBOSS"), as part of the DARPA CHATS research program.

NAME

pam_exec — Exec PAM module

SYNOPSIS

[*service-name*] *module-type control-flag* pam_exec [*arguments*]

DESCRIPTION

The exec service module for PAM executes the program designated by its first argument, with its remaining arguments as command-line arguments. The child's environment is set to the current PAM environment list, as returned by pam_getenvlist(3). In addition, the following PAM items are exported as environment variables: PAM_RHOST, PAM_RUSER, PAM_SERVICE, PAM_TTY, and PAM_USER.

SEE ALSO

pam_get_item(3), pam.conf(5), pam(8)

AUTHORS

The **pam_exec** module and this manual page were developed for the FreeBSD Project by ThinkSec AS and NAI Labs, the Security Research Division of Network Associates, Inc. under DARPA/SPAWAR contract N66001-01-C-8035 ("CBOSS"), as part of the DARPA CHATS research program.

NAME

pam_ftpusers — ftpusers PAM module

SYNOPSIS

[*service-name*] *module-type control-flag* pam_ftpusers [*options*]

DESCRIPTION

The ftpusers service module for PAM provides functionality for only one PAM category: account management. In terms of the *module-type* parameter, this is the "account" feature.

Ftpusers Account Management Module

The ftpusers account management component (**pam_sm_acct_mgmt**()), succeeds if and only if the user is listed in /etc/ftpusers.

The following options may be passed to the authentication module:

debug   syslog(3) debugging information at LOG_DEBUG level.

no_warn   suppress warning messages to the user. These messages include reasons why the user's authentication attempt was declined.

disallow reverse the semantics; **pam_ftpusers** will succeed if and only if the user is not listed in /etc/ftpusers.

SEE ALSO

ftpusers(5), pam.conf(5), ftpd(8), pam(8)

AUTHORS

The **pam_ftpusers** module and this manual page were developed for the FreeBSD Project by ThinkSec AS and NAI Labs, the Security Research Division of Network Associates, Inc. under DARPA/SPAWAR contract N66001-01-C-8035 ("CBOSS"), as part of the DARPA CHATS research program.

BUGS

The current version of this module parses an older format of the ftpusers(5) file and should not be used. ftpd(8) will keep using its built-in ftpusers(5) parsing code until the parser code in the pam module is fixed.

NAME
pam_group — Group PAM module

SYNOPSIS
[*service-name*] *module-type control-flag* pam_group [*arguments*]

DESCRIPTION
The group service module for PAM accepts or rejects users based on their membership in a particular file group.

The following options may be passed to the **pam_group** module:

deny   Reverse the meaning of the test, i.e., reject the applicant if and only if he or she is a member of the specified group. This can be useful to exclude certain groups of users from certain services.

fail_safe   If the specified group does not exist, or has no members, act as if it does exist and the applicant is a member.

group=*groupname*
                Specify the name of the group to check. The default is "wheel".

root_only   Skip this module entirely if the target account is not the superuser account.

authenticate
                The user is asked to authenticate using his own password.

SEE ALSO
pam.conf(5), pam(8)

AUTHORS
The **pam_group** module and this manual page were developed for the FreeBSD Project by ThinkSec AS and NAI Labs, the Security Research Division of Network Associates, Inc. under DARPA/SPAWAR contract N66001-01-C-8035 ("CBOSS"), as part of the DARPA CHATS research program.

NAME

pam_guest — Guest PAM module

SYNOPSIS

[*service-name*] *module-type control-flag* pam_guest [*arguments*]

DESCRIPTION

The guest service module for PAM allows guest logins. If successful, the **pam_guest** module sets the PAM environment variable GUEST to the login name. The application can check this variable using pam_getenv(3) to differentiate guest logins from normal logins.

The following options may be passed to the **pam_guest** module:

guests=*list*   Comma-separated list of guest account names. The default is "guest". A typical value for ftpd(8) would be "anonymous,ftp".

nopass   Omits the password prompt if the target account is on the list of guest accounts.

pass_as_ruser   The password typed in by the user is exported as the PAM_RUSER item. This is useful for applications like ftpd(8) where guest users are encouraged to use their email address as password.

pass_is_user   Requires the guest user to type in the guest account name as password.

SEE ALSO

pam_get_item(3), pam_getenv(3), pam.conf(5), pam(8)

AUTHORS

The **pam_guest** module and this manual page were developed for the FreeBSD Project by ThinkSec AS and NAI Labs, the Security Research Division of Network Associates, Inc. under DARPA/SPAWAR contract N66001-01-C-8035 ("CBOSS"), as part of the DARPA CHATS research program.

NAME

pam_krb5 — Kerberos 5 PAM module

SYNOPSIS

[*service-name*] *module-type control-flag* pam_krb5 [*arguments*]

DESCRIPTION

The Kerberos 5 service module for PAM provides functionality for three PAM categories: authentication, account management, and password management. It also provides null functions for session management.

Kerberos 5 Authentication Module

The Kerberos 5 authentication component provides functions to verify the identity of a user (**pam_sm_authenticate**()) and to set user specific credentials (**pam_sm_setcred**()). **pam_sm_authenticate**() converts the supplied username into a Kerberos principal, by appending the default local realm name. It also supports usernames with explicit realm names. If a realm name is supplied, then upon a successful return, it changes the username by mapping the principal name into a local username (calling **krb5_aname_to_localname**()). This typically just means the realm name is stripped.

It prompts the user for a password and obtains a new Kerberos TGT for the principal. The TGT is verified by obtaining a service ticket for the local host.

When prompting for the current password, the authentication module will use the prompt "Password for <principal>:".

The **pam_sm_setcred**() function stores the newly acquired credentials in a credentials cache, and sets the environment variable KRB5CCNAME appropriately. The credentials cache should be destroyed by the user at logout with kdestroy(1).

The following options may be passed to the authentication module:

debug   syslog(3) debugging information at LOG_DEBUG level.

no_warn   suppress warning messages to the user. These messages include reasons why the user's authentication attempt was declined.

use_first_pass If the authentication module is not the first in the stack, and a previous module obtained the user's password, that password is used to authenticate the user. If this fails, the authentication module returns failure without prompting the user for a password. This option has no effect if the authentication module is the first in the stack, or if no previous modules obtained the user's password.

try_first_pass This option is similar to the **use_first_pass** option, except that if the previously obtained password fails, the user is prompted for another password.

renewable=*timeperiod*
                       Obtain renewable Kerberos credentials for the user. The renewable time can be specified, or it defaults to one month. Since spaces are not allowed in the pam configuration time, underscores are used to form parseable times (e.g., 1_month).

forwardable   Obtain forwardable Kerberos credentials for the user.

no_ccache   Do not save the obtained credentials in a credentials cache. This is a useful option if the authentication module is used for services such as ftp or pop, where the user would not be able to destroy them. [This is not a recommendation to use the module for those services.]

      ccache=*name*   Use *name* as the credentials cache. *name* must be in the form *type*:*residual*. The special tokens '%u', to designate the decimal UID of the user; and '%p', to designate the current process ID; can be used in *name*.

Kerberos 5 Account Management Module

The Kerberos 5 account management component provides a function to perform account management, **pam_sm_acct_mgmt**(). The function verifies that the authenticated principal is allowed to login to the local user account by calling **krb5_kuserok**() (which checks the user's .k5login file).

Kerberos 5 Password Management Module

The Kerberos 5 password management component provides a function to change passwords (**pam_sm_chauthtok**()). The username supplied (the user running the passwd(1) command, or the username given as an argument) is mapped into a Kerberos principal name, using the same technique as in the authentication module. Note that if a realm name was explicitly supplied during authentication, but not during a password change, the mapping done by the password management module may not result in the same principal as was used for authentication.

Unlike when changing a UNIX password, the password management module will allow any user to change any principal's password (if the user knows the principal's old password, of course). Also unlike UNIX, root is always prompted for the principal's old password.

The password management module uses the same heuristics as kpasswd(1) to determine how to contact the Kerberos password server.

The following options may be passed to the password management module:

      debug   syslog(3) debugging information at LOG_DEBUG level.

      use_first_pass If the password management module is not the first in the stack, and a previous module obtained the user's old password, that password is used to authenticate the user. If this fails, the password management module returns failure without prompting the user for the old password. If successful, the new password entered to the previous module is also used as the new Kerberos password. If the new password fails, the password management module returns failure without prompting the user for a new password.

      try_first_pass This option is similar to the **use_first_pass** option, except that if the previously obtained old or new passwords fail, the user is prompted for them.

Kerberos 5 Session Management Module

The Kerberos 5 session management component provides functions to initiate (**pam_sm_open_session**()) and terminate (**pam_sm_close_session**()) sessions. Since session management is not defined under Kerberos 5, both of these functions simply return success. They are provided only because of the naming conventions for PAM modules.

ENVIRONMENT

      KRB5CCNAME Location of the credentials cache.

FILES

      /tmp/krb5cc_*uid* default credentials cache (*uid* is the decimal UID of the user).
      $HOME/.k5login   file containing Kerberos principals that are allowed access.

SEE ALSO

      kdestroy(1), passwd(1), syslog(3), pam.conf(5), pam(8)

NOTES

Applications should not call **pam_authenticate**() more than once between calls to **pam_start**() and **pam_end**() when using the Kerberos 5 PAM module.

SECURITY CONSIDERATIONS

The **pam_krb5** module implements what is fundamentally a password authentication scheme. It does not use a Kerberos 5 exchange between client and server, but rather authenticates the password provided by the client against the Kerberos KDC. Therefore, care should be taken to only use this module over a secure session (secure TTY, encrypted session, etc.), otherwise the user's Kerberos 5 password could be compromised.

NAME
pam_ksu — Kerberos 5 SU PAM module

SYNOPSIS
[*service-name*] *module-type control-flag* pam_ksu [*options*]

DESCRIPTION
The Kerberos 5 SU authentication service module for PAM provides functionality for only one PAM category: authentication. In terms of the *module-type* parameter, this is the "auth" feature. The module is specifically designed to be used with the su(1) utility.

Kerberos 5 SU Authentication Module
The Kerberos 5 SU authentication component provides functions to verify the identity of a user (**pam_sm_authenticate**()), and determine whether or not the user is authorized to obtain the privileges of the target account. If the target account is "root", then the Kerberos 5 principal used for authentication and authorization will be the "root" instance of the current user, e.g. "user/root@REAL.M". Otherwise, the principal will simply be the current user's default principal, e.g. "user@REAL.M".

The user is prompted for a password if necessary. Authorization is performed by comparing the Kerberos 5 principal with those listed in the .k5login file in the target account's home directory (e.g. /root/.k5login for root).

The following options may be passed to the authentication module:

debug   syslog(3) debugging information at LOG_DEBUG level.

use_first_pass If the authentication module is not the first in the stack, and a previous module obtained the user's password, that password is used to authenticate the user. If this fails, the authentication module returns failure without prompting the user for a password. This option has no effect if the authentication module is the first in the stack, or if no previous modules obtained the user's password.

try_first_pass This option is similar to the **use_first_pass** option, except that if the previously obtained password fails, the user is prompted for another password.

SEE ALSO
su(1), syslog(3), pam.conf(5), pam(8)

NAME

    pam_lastlog — login accounting PAM module

SYNOPSIS

    [*service-name*] *module-type control-flag* pam_lastlog [*options*]

DESCRIPTION

    The login accounting service module for PAM provides functionality for only one PAM category: session management. In terms of the *module-type* parameter, this is the "session" feature.

    Login Accounting Session Management Module

        The login accounting session management component provides functions to initiate (**pam_sm_open_session**()) and terminate (**pam_sm_close_session**()) sessions. The **pam_sm_open_session**() function records the session in the utmp(5), utmpx(5), wtmp(5), wtmpx(5), lastlog(5), and lastlogx(5) databases. The **pam_sm_close_session**() function does nothing.

        The following options may be passed to the authentication module:

    debug   syslog(3) debugging information at LOG_DEBUG level.

    no_nested Don't update records or print messages if the user is "nested", i.e. logged in on the same tty on top of another user.

    no_warn   suppress warning messages to the user.

    no_fail   Ignore I/O failures.

SEE ALSO

    last(1), w(1), login(3), loginx(3), logout(3), logoutx(3), pam.conf(5), utmp(5), utmpx(5), lastlogin(8), pam(8)

AUTHORS

    The **pam_lastlog** module and this manual page were developed for the FreeBSD Project by ThinkSec AS and NAI Labs, the Security Research Division of Network Associates, Inc. under DARPA/SPAWAR contract N66001-01-C-8035 ("CBOSS"), as part of the DARPA CHATS research program.

NAME

pam_login_access — login.access PAM module

SYNOPSIS

[*service-name*] *module-type control-flag* pam_login_access [*options*]

DESCRIPTION

The login.access service module for PAM provides functionality for only one PAM category: account management. In terms of the *module-type* parameter, this is the "account" feature.

Login.access Account Management Module

The login.access account management component (**pam_sm_acct_mgmt**()), returns success if and only the user is allowed to log in on the specified tty (in the case of a local login) or from the specified remote host (in the case of a remote login), according to the restrictions listed in /etc/login.access.

SEE ALSO

login.access(5), pam.conf(5), pam(8)

AUTHORS

The login.access(5) access control scheme was designed and implemented by Wietse Venema.

The **pam_login_access** module and this manual page were developed for the FreeBSD Project by ThinkSec AS and NAI Labs, the Security Research Division of Network Associates, Inc. under DARPA/SPAWAR contract N66001-01-C-8035 ("CBOSS"), as part of the DARPA CHATS research program.

NAME
  pam_nologin — NoLogin PAM module

SYNOPSIS
  [*service-name*] *module-type control-flag* pam_nologin [*options*]

DESCRIPTION
  The NoLogin authentication service module for PAM provides functionality for only one PAM category:
  authentication. In terms of the *module-type* parameter, this is the "auth" feature. It also provides a null
  function for session management.

NoLogin Authentication Module
  The NoLogin authentication component (**pam_sm_authenticate**()), always returns success for the
  superuser, and returns success for all other users if the file /etc/nologin does not exist. If
  /etc/nologin does exist, then its contents are echoed to non-superusers before failure is returned. If a
  "nologin" capability is specified in login.conf(5), then the file thus specified is used instead. This usually defaults to /etc/nologin.

  The following options may be passed to the authentication module:

  debug   syslog(3) debugging information at LOG_DEBUG level.

  no_warn suppress warning messages to the user. These messages include reasons why the user's authenti-
                  cation attempt was declined.

SEE ALSO
  syslog(3), login.conf(5), pam.conf(5), nologin(8), pam(8)

NAME

pam_permit — Promiscuous PAM module

SYNOPSIS

[*service-name*] *module-type control-flag* pam_permit [*options*]

DESCRIPTION

The Promiscuous authentication service module for PAM provides functionality for all the PAM categories: authentication, account management, session management and password management. In terms of the *module-type* parameter, these are the "auth", "account", "session", and "password" features.

The Promiscuous module will universally allow all requests. It is primarily of use during testing, and to silence "noisy" PAM-enabled applications.

The following options may be passed to the module:

debug syslog(3) debugging information at LOG_DEBUG level.

SEE ALSO

syslog(3), pam.conf(5), pam(8)

NAME
   pam_radius — RADIUS PAM module

SYNOPSIS
   [*service-name*] *module-type control-flag* pam_radius [*options*]

DESCRIPTION
   The RADIUS service module for PAM provides authentication services based upon the RADIUS (Remote Authentication Dial In User Service) protocol.

   The **pam_radius** module accepts these optional parameters:

   use_first_pass
               causes **pam_radius** to use a previously entered password instead of prompting for a new one. If no password has been entered then authentication fails.

   try_first_pass
               causes **pam_radius** to use a previously entered password, if one is available. If no password has been entered, **pam_radius** prompts for one as usual.

   echo_pass
               causes echoing to be left on if **pam_radius** prompts for a password.

   conf=*pathname*
               specifies a non-standard location for the RADIUS client configuration file (normally located in /etc/radius.conf).

   nas_id=*identifier*
               specifies a NAS identifier to send instead of the hostname.

   template_user=*username*
               specifies a user whose passwd(5) entry will be used as a template to create the session environment if the supplied username does not exist in the local password database. The user will be authenticated with the supplied username and password, but his credentials to the system will be presented as the ones for *username*, i.e., his login class, home directory, resource limits, etc. will be set to ones defined for *username*.

               If this option is omitted, and there is no username in the system databases equal to the supplied one (as determined by call to getpwnam(3)), the authentication will fail.

   nas_ipaddr[=*address*]
               specifies a NAS IP address to be sent. If option is present, but there is no value provided then IP address corresponding to the current hostname will be used.

FILES
   /etc/radius.conf The standard RADIUS client configuration file for **pam_radius**

SEE ALSO
   passwd(5), radius.conf(5), pam(8)

HISTORY
   The **pam_radius** module first appeared in FreeBSD 3.1. The **pam_radius** manual page first appeared in FreeBSD 3.3.

AUTHORS

The **pam_radius** manual page was written by Andrzej Bialecki ⟨abial@FreeBSD.org⟩.

The **pam_radius** module was written by John D. Polstra ⟨jdp@FreeBSD.org⟩.

NAME

   pam_rhosts — rhosts PAM module

SYNOPSIS

   [*service-name*] *module-type control-flag* pam_rhosts [*options*]

DESCRIPTION

   The rhosts authentication service module for PAM provides functionality for only one PAM category: authentication. In terms of the *module-type* parameter, this is the "auth" feature.

   Rhosts Authentication Module

   The Rhosts authentication component (**pam_sm_authenticate**()), returns success if and only if the target user's UID is not 0 and the remote host and user are listed in /etc/hosts.equiv or in the target user's ~/.rhosts.

   The following options may be passed to the authentication module:

   debug   syslog(3) debugging information at LOG_DEBUG level.

   no_warn   suppress warning messages to the user. These messages include reasons why the user's authentication attempt was declined.

   allow_root   do not automatically fail if the target user's UID is 0.

SEE ALSO

   hosts.equiv(5), pam.conf(5), pam(8)

AUTHORS

   The **pam_rhosts** module and this manual page were developed for the FreeBSD Project by ThinkSec AS and NAI Labs, the Security Research Division of Network Associates, Inc. under DARPA/SPAWAR contract N66001-01-C-8035 ("CBOSS"), as part of the DARPA CHATS research program.

NAME

pam_rootok — RootOK PAM module

SYNOPSIS

[*service-name*] *module-type control-flag* pam_rootok [*options*]

DESCRIPTION

The RootOK authentication service module for PAM provides functionality for only one PAM category: authentication. In terms of the *module-type* parameter, this is the "auth" feature. It also provides a null function for session management.

RootOK Authentication Module

The RootOK authentication component (**pam_sm_authenticate**()), always returns success for the superuser; i.e., if getuid(2) returns 0.

The following options may be passed to the authentication module:

debug   syslog(3) debugging information at LOG_DEBUG level.

no_warn suppress warning messages to the user. These messages include reasons why the user's authentication attempt was declined.

SEE ALSO

getuid(2), pam.conf(5), pam(8)

NAME
   pam_securetty — SecureTTY PAM module

SYNOPSIS
   [*service-name*] *module-type control-flag* pam_securetty [*options*]

DESCRIPTION
   The SecureTTY service module for PAM provides functionality for only one PAM category: account management. In terms of the *module-type* parameter, this is the "account" feature. It also provides null functions for authentication and session management.

SecureTTY Account Management Module
   The SecureTTY account management component (**pam_sm_acct_mgmt**()), returns failure if the user is attempting to authenticate as superuser, and the process is attached to an insecure TTY. In all other cases, the module returns success.

   A TTY is considered secure if it is listed in /etc/ttys and has the TTY_SECURE flag set.

   The following options may be passed to the authentication module:

   debug   syslog(3) debugging information at LOG_DEBUG level.

   no_warn   suppress warning messages to the user. These messages include reasons why the user's authentication attempt was declined.

SEE ALSO
   getttynam(3), syslog(3), pam.conf(5), ttys(5), pam(8)

NAME

pam_self — Self PAM module

SYNOPSIS

[service-name] module-type control-flag pam_self *[options]*

DESCRIPTION

The Self authentication service module for PAM provides functionality for only one PAM category: authentication. In terms of the *module-type* parameter, this is the "auth" feature.

Self Authentication Module

The Self authentication component (**pam_sm_authenticate**()), returns success if and only if the target user's user ID is identical with the current real user ID. If the current real user ID is zero, authentication will fail, unless the **allow_root** option was specified.

The following options may be passed to the authentication module:

debug   syslog(3) debugging information at LOG_DEBUG level.

no_warn   suppress warning messages to the user. These messages include reasons why the user's authentication attempt was declined.

allow_root do not automatically fail if the current real user ID is 0.

SEE ALSO

getuid(2), pam.conf(5), pam(8)

AUTHORS

The **pam_self** module and this manual page were developed for the FreeBSD Project by ThinkSec AS and NAI Labs, the Security Research Division of Network Associates, Inc. under DARPA/SPAWAR contract N66001-01-C-8035 ("CBOSS"), as part of the DARPA CHATS research program.

NAME
pam_skey — S/Key PAM module

SYNOPSIS
[*service-name*] *module-type control-flag* pam_skey [*options*]

DESCRIPTION
The *S/Key* service module for PAM provides authentication services based on the *S/Key* One Time Password (OTP) authentication system.

The **pam_skey** module has no optional parameters.

FILES
/etc/skeykeys database of information for the S/Key system.

SEE ALSO
skey(1), skeyinit(1), pam(8)

NAME

pam_ssh — authentication and session management with SSH private keys

SYNOPSIS

[*service-name*] *module-type control-flag* pam_ssh [*options*]

DESCRIPTION

The SSH authentication service module for PAM provides functionality for two PAM categories: authentication and session management. In terms of the *module-type* parameter, they are the "auth" and "session" features.

SSH Authentication Module

The SSH authentication component provides a function to verify the identity of a user (**pam_sm_authenticate**()), by prompting the user for a passphrase and verifying that it can decrypt the target user's SSH key using that passphrase.

The following options may be passed to the authentication module:

use_first_pass If the authentication module is not the first in the stack, and a previous module obtained the user's password, that password is used to authenticate the user. If this fails, the authentication module returns failure without prompting the user for a password. This option has no effect if the authentication module is the first in the stack, or if no previous modules obtained the user's password.

try_first_pass This option is similar to the **use_first_pass** option, except that if the previously obtained password fails, the user is prompted for another password.

SSH Session Management Module

The SSH session management component provides functions to initiate (**pam_sm_open_session**()) and terminate (**pam_sm_close_session**()) sessions. The **pam_sm_open_session**() function starts an SSH agent, passing it any private keys it decrypted during the authentication phase, and sets the environment variables the agent specifies. The **pam_sm_close_session**() function kills the previously started SSH agent by sending it a SIGTERM.

The following options may be passed to the session management module:

want_agent Start an agent even if no keys were decrypted during the authentication phase.

FILES

$HOME/.ssh/identity   SSH1 RSA key
$HOME/.ssh/id_rsa   SSH2 RSA key
$HOME/.ssh/id_dsa   SSH2 DSA key

SEE ALSO

ssh-agent(1), pam.conf(5), pam(8)

AUTHORS

The **pam_ssh** module was originally written by Andrew J. Korty ⟨ajk@iu.edu⟩. The current implementation was developed for the FreeBSD Project by ThinkSec AS and NAI Labs, the Security Research Division of Network Associates, Inc. under DARPA/SPAWAR contract N66001-01-C-8035 ("CBOSS"), as part of the DARPA CHATS research program. This manual page was written by Mark R V Murray ⟨markm@FreeBSD.org⟩.

SECURITY CONSIDERATIONS

The **pam_ssh** module implements what is fundamentally a password authentication scheme. Care should be taken to only use this module over a secure session (secure TTY, encrypted session, etc.), otherwise the user's SSH passphrase could be compromised.

Additional consideration should be given to the use of **pam_ssh**. Users often assume that file permissions are sufficient to protect their SSH keys, and thus use weak or no passphrases. Since the system administrator has no effective means of enforcing SSH passphrase quality, this has the potential to expose the system to security risks.

NAME

pam_unix — UNIX PAM module

SYNOPSIS

[*service-name*] *module-type control-flag* pam_unix [*options*]

DESCRIPTION

The UNIX authentication service module for PAM provides functionality for two PAM categories: authentication and account management. In terms of the *module-type* parameter, they are the "auth" and "account" features. It also provides a null function for session management.

UNIX **Authentication Module**

The UNIX authentication component provides functions to verify the identity of a user (**pam_sm_authenticate**()), which obtains the relevant passwd(5) entry. It prompts the user for a password and verifies that this is correct with crypt(3).

The following options may be passed to the authentication module:

debug   syslog(3) debugging information at LOG_DEBUG level.

use_first_pass If the authentication module is not the first in the stack, and a previous module obtained the user's password, that password is used to authenticate the user. If this fails, the authentication module returns failure without prompting the user for a password. This option has no effect if the authentication module is the first in the stack, or if no previous modules obtained the user's password.

try_first_pass This option is similar to the **use_first_pass** option, except that if the previously obtained password fails, the user is prompted for another password.

auth_as_self   This option will require the user to authenticate himself as the user given by getlogin(2), not as the account they are attempting to access. This is primarily for services like su(1), where the user's ability to retype their own password might be deemed sufficient.

nullok   If the password database has no password for the entity being authenticated, then this option will forgo password prompting, and silently allow authentication to succeed.

UNIX **Account Management Module**

The UNIX account management component provides a function to perform account management, **pam_sm_acct_mgmt**(). The function verifies that the authenticated user is allowed to login to the local user account by checking the password expiry date.

The following options may be passed to the management module:

debug   syslog(3) debugging information at LOG_DEBUG level.

UNIX **Password Management Module**

The UNIX password management component provides a function to perform account management, **pam_sm_chauthtok**(). The function changes the user's password.

The following options may be passed to the password module:

debug   syslog(3) debugging information at LOG_DEBUG level.

no_warn   suppress warning messages to the user. These messages include reasons why the user's authentication attempt was declined.

passwd_db=*name* Change the user's password only the specified password database. Valid password database names are:

files   local password file

nis   NIS password database

FILES

    `/etc/master.passwd` default UNIX password database.

SEE ALSO

    passwd(1), getlogin(2), crypt(3), getpwent(3), syslog(3), nsswitch.conf(5), passwd(5), nis(8), pam(8)

NAME

paxctl — list and modify PaX flags associated with an ELF program

SYNOPSIS

paxctl *flags program* . . .

DESCRIPTION

The **paxctl** utility is used to list and manipulate PaX flags associated with an ELF program. The PaX flags signify to the loader the privilege protections to be applied to mapped memory pages, and fuller explanations of the specific protections can be found in the security(8) manpage.

Each flag can be prefixed either with a "+" or a "-" sign to add or remove the flag, respectively.

The following flags are available:

a   Explicitly disable PaX ASLR (Address Space Layout Randomization) for *program*.

A   Explicitly enable PaX ASLR for *program*.

g   Explicitly disable PaX Segvguard for *program*.

G   Explicitly enable PaX Segvguard for *program*.

m   Explicitly disable PaX MPROTECT (mprotect(2) restrictions) for *program*.

M   Explicitly enable PaX MPROTECT (mprotect(2) restrictions) for *program*.

To view existing flags on a file, execute **paxctl** without any flags.

SEE ALSO

mprotect(2), sysctl(3), options(4), elf(5), security(8), sysctl(8), fileassoc(9)

HISTORY

The **paxctl** utility first appeared in NetBSD 4.0.

The **paxctl** utility is modeled after a tool of the same name available for Linux from the PaX prcject.

AUTHORS

Elad Efrat ⟨elad@NetBSD.org⟩
Christos Zoulas ⟨christos@NetBSD.org⟩

BUGS

The **paxctl** utility currently uses elf(5) "note" sections to mark executables as PaX Segvguard enabled. This will be done using fileassoc(9) in the future so that we can control who does the marking and not altering the binary file signature.

NAME

    pbsdboot — load and boot NetBSD/hpcmips kernel from Windows CE

SYNOPSIS

    pbsdboot.exe

DESCRIPTION

    pbsdboot is a program runs on Windows CE. It loads and executes the specified NetBSD/netbsd kernel.

    The menu options (for **pbsdboot** itself) are as follows:

    kernel   Select Kernel Path.

    Frame buffer   Select Frame Buffer type.

    Option   option for pass kernel.

    The options for NetBSD kernel are as follows:

    −d   break into the kernel debugger.

    −m   use miniroot in memory.

    −s   single user mode.

    −h   use serial console.check also serial port on.and connect your terminal with 9600bps,8bit,non-parity,VT100 mode.

    −a   ask for name:kernel ask root/dump device,filesystem.

    −b=DEV

           change boot device to DEV(wd0,sd0,nfs,etc)

FILES

    `/msdos/pbsdboot.exe` You will find this program Windows CE readable disk partition.

SEE ALSO

    `reboot`(2)

HISTORY

    The **pbsdboot** utility first appeared in NetBSD 1.5.

BUGS

    pbsdboot reads the entire kernel image at once, and requires enough free area on the main memory.

NAME

    pcictl — a program to manipulate the PCI bus

SYNOPSIS

    pcictl *pcibus command* [*arg* [...]]

DESCRIPTION

    pcictl allows a user or system administrator to access various resources on a PCI bus.

    The following commands are available:

    list [**-n**] [**-b** *bus*] [**-d** *device*] [**-f** *function*]

    List the devices in the PCI domain, either as names or, if **-n** is given, as numbers. The bus, device, and function numbers may be specified by flags. If the bus is not specified, it defaults to the bus number of the PCI bus specified on the command line. Any other locator not specified defaults to a wildcard, or may be explicitly wildcarded by specifying "any".

    dump [**-b** *bus*] **-d** *device* [**-f** *function*]

    Dump the PCI configuration space for the specified device located at the specified bus, device, and function. If the bus is not specified, it defaults to the bus number of the PCI bus specified on the command line. If the function is not specified, it defaults to 0.

FILES

    /dev/pci* - PCI bus device nodes

SEE ALSO

    pci(3), pci(4), drvctl(8)

HISTORY

    The **pcictl** command first appeared in NetBSD 1.6.

NAME
pdisk — Apple partition table editor

SYNOPSIS
pdisk [-acdfhilLrv] [--abbr] [--compute_size] [--debug] [--fname] [--help]
       [--interactive] [--list device] [--logical] [--readonly] [--version]
       [device ...]

DESCRIPTION
pdisk is a menu driven program which partitions disks using the standard Apple disk partitioning scheme described in "Inside Macintosh: Devices". It does not support the Intel/DOS partitioning scheme supported by fdisk(8).

Supported options are:

-a
--abbr   Abbreviate the partition types shown in the partition list.

-c
--compute_size   Causes pdisk to always ignore the device size listed in the partition table and compute the device size by other means.

-d
--debug   Turns on debugging. Doesn't add that much output, but does add a new command 'x' to the editing commands that accesses an eclectic bunch of undocumented functionality.

-f
--fname   Show HFS volume names instead of partition name when available.

-h
--help   Prints a short help message.

-i
--interactive   Causes pdisk to go into an interactive mode similar to the MacOS version of the program.

-l
--list device   List the partition tables for the specified devices.

-L
--logical   Show partition limits in logical blocks. Default is physical blocks.

-r
--readonly   Prevents pdisk from writing to the device.

-v
--version   Prints the version number of pdisk.

Editing Partition Tables
An argument which is simply the name of a device indicates that pdisk should edit the partition table of that device.

The current top level editing commands are:

        C   (create with type also specified)
        c   create new partition
        d   delete a partition
        h   command help
        i   initialize partition map
        n   (re)name a partition
        P   (print ordered by base address)
        p   print the partition table

q   quit editing (don't save changes)
r   reorder partition entry in map
s   change size of partition map
t   change the type of an existing partition
w   write the partition table

Commands which take arguments prompt for each argument in turn. You can also type any number of the arguments separated by spaces and those prompts will be skipped. The only exception to typeahead are the confirmation prompts on the **i** and **w** commands, since if we expect you to confirm the decision, we shouldn't undermine that by allowing you to be precipitate about it.

Partitions are always specified by their number, which is the index of the partition entry in the partition map. Most of the commands will change the index numbers of all partitions after the affected partition. You are advised to print the table as frequently as necessary.

The **c** (create new partition) command is the only one with complicated arguments. The first argument is the base address (in blocks) of the partition. Besides a raw number, you can also specify a partition number followed by the letter 'p' to indicate that the first block of the new partition should be the same as the first block of that existing free space partition. The second argument is the length of the partition in blocks. This can be a raw number or can be a partition number followed by the letter 'p' to use the size of that partition or can be a number followed by 'k', 'm', or 'g' to indicate the size in kilobytes, megabytes, or gigabytes respectively. (These are powers of 1024, of course, not powers of 1000.) The third argument is the name of the partition. This can be a single word without quotes, or a string surrounded by single or double quotes. The type of the created partition will be Apple_UNIX_SVR2, which is the correct type for use with NetBSD. This command will prompt for the unix filesystem slice to set in the Block Zero Block bits.

The **C** command is similar to the **c** command, with the addition of a partition type argument after the other arguments. Choosing a type of Apple_UNIX_SVR2 will prompt for the unix filesystem slice to set in the Block Zero Block bits.

The **i** (initalize) command prompts for the size of the device.

The **n** (name) command allows the name of a partition to be changed. Note that the various "Apple_Driver" partitions depend on the name field for proper functioning. We are not aware of any other partition types with this limitation.

The **r** (reorder) command allows the index number of partitions to be changed. The index numbers are constrained to be a contiguous sequence.

The **t** (change partition type) command allows the type of a partition to be changed. Changing the type to Apple_UNIX_SVR2 will prompt for the unix filesystem slice to set in the Block Zero Block bits.

The **w** (write) command writes the partition map out. In order to use the new partition map you must reboot.

SEE ALSO
        fdisk(8), newfs(8)

HISTORY
        The **pdisk** utility was originally developed for MkLinux.

AUTHORS
        Eryk Vershen

BUGS
        Some people believe there should really be just one disk partitioning utility.

Filesystem volume names are out of place in a partition utility. This utility supports HFS volume names, but not volume names of any other filesystem types.

The **--logical** option has not been heavily tested.

pdisk will first try to use lseek(2) with SEEK_END to compute the size of the device. If this fails, it will try a binary search using lseek(2) and read(2) to find the end of the device. This has been observed to fail on some raw disk devices. As a workaround, try using the block device instead. **pdisk** should probably read the disklabel using the DIOCGDINFO ioctl(2) to get the device size instead.

NAME

    pfctl — control the packet filter (PF) and network address translation (NAT) device

SYNOPSIS

    pfctl [**-AdeghmNnOqRrvz**] [**-a** *anchor*] [**-D** *macro= value*] [**-F** *modifier*] [**-f** *file*]
        [**-i** *interface*] [**-K** *host | network*] [**-k** *host | network*] [**-o** *level*]
        [**-p** *device*] [**-s** *modifier*] [**-t** *table* **-T** *command* [*address* ...]]
        [**-x** *level*]

DESCRIPTION

    The **pfctl** utility communicates with the packet filter device using the ioctl interface described in pf(4). It allows ruleset and parameter configuration and retrieval of status information from the packet filter.

    Packet filtering restricts the types of packets that pass through network interfaces entering or leaving the host based on filter rules as described in pf.conf(5). The packet filter can also replace addresses and ports of packets. Replacing source addresses and ports of outgoing packets is called NAT (Network Address Translation) and is used to connect an internal network (usually reserved address space) to an external one (the Internet) by making all connections to external hosts appear to come from the gateway. Replacing destination addresses and ports of incoming packets is used to redirect connections to different hosts and/or ports. A combination of both translations, bidirectional NAT, is also supported. Translation rules are described in pf.conf(5).

    When the variable *pf* is set to YES in rc.conf(5), the rule file specified with the variable *pf_rules* is loaded automatically by the rc(8) scripts and the packet filter is enabled.

    The packet filter does not itself forward packets between interfaces. Forwarding can be enabled by setting the sysctl(8) variables *net.inet.ip.forwarding* and/or *net.inet6.ip6.forwarding* to 1. Set them permanently in /etc/sysctl.conf.

    The **pfctl** utility provides several commands. The options are as follows:

    -A   Load only the queue rules present in the rule file. Other rules and options are ignored.

    -a *anchor*

        Apply flags **-f**, **-F**, and **-s** only to the rules in the specified *anchor*. In addition to the main ruleset, **pfctl** can load and manipulate additional rulesets by name, called anchors. The main ruleset is the default anchor.

        Anchors are referenced by name and may be nested, with the various components of the anchor path separated by '/' characters, similar to how file system hierarchies are laid out. The last component of the anchor path is where ruleset operations are performed.

        Evaluation of *anchor* rules from the main ruleset is described in pf.conf(5).

        For example, the following will show all filter rules (see the **-s** flag below) inside the anchor "authpf/smith(1234)", which would have been created for user "smith" by authpf(8), PID 1234:

            `# pfctl -a "authpf/smith(1234)" -s rules`

        Private tables can also be put inside anchors, either by having table statements in the pf.conf(5) file that is loaded in the anchor, or by using regular table commands, as in:

            `# pfctl -a foo/bar -t mytable -T add 1.2.3.4 5.6.7.8`

        When a rule referring to a table is loaded in an anchor, the rule will use the private table if one is defined, and then fall back to the table defined in the main ruleset, if there is one. This is similar to C rules for variable scope. It is possible to create distinct tables with the same name in the global ruleset and in an anchor, but this is often bad design and a warning will be issued in that case.

By default, recursive inline printing of anchors applies only to unnamed anchors specified inline in the ruleset. If the anchor name is terminated with a '*' character, the **-s** flag will recursively print all anchors in a brace delimited block. For example the following will print the "authpf" ruleset recursively:

```
# pfctl -a 'authpf/*' -sr
```

To print the main ruleset recursively, specify only '*' as the anchor name:

```
# pfctl -a '*' -sr
```

-D *macro=value*
: Define *macro* to be set to *value* on the command line. Overrides the definition of *macro* in the ruleset.

-d
: Disable the packet filter.

-e
: Enable the packet filter.

-F *modifier*
: Flush the filter parameters specified by *modifier* (may be abbreviated):

-F nat	Flush the NAT rules.
-F queue	Flush the queue rules.
-F rules	Flush the filter rules.
-F states	Flush the state table (NAT and filter).
-F Sources	Flush the source tracking table.
-F info	Flush the filter information (statistics that are not bound to rules).
-F Tables	Flush the tables.
-F osfp	Flush the passive operating system fingerprints.
-F all	Flush all of the above.

-f *file*
: Load the rules contained in *file*. This *file* may contain macros, tables, options, and normalization, queueing, translation, and filtering rules. With the exception of macros and tables, the statements must appear in that order.

-g
: Include output helpful for debugging.

-h
: Help.

-i *interface*
: Restrict the operation to the given *interface*.

-K *host | network*
: Kill all of the source tracking entries originating from the specified *host* or *network*. A second **-K** *host* or **-K** *network* option may be specified, which will kill all the source tracking entries from the first host/network to the second.

-k *host | network*
: Kill all of the state entries originating from the specified *host* or *network*. A second **-k** *host* or **-k** *network* option may be specified, which will kill all the state entries from the first host/network to the second. For example, to kill all of the state entries originating from "host":

```
# pfctl -k host
```

To kill all of the state entries from "host1" to "host2":

```
# pfctl -k host1 -k host2
```

To kill all states originating from 192.168.1.0/24 to 172.16.0.0/16:

```
# pfctl -k 192.168.1.0/24 -k 172.16.0.0/16
```

A network prefix length of 0 can be used as a wildcard. To kill all states with the target "host2":

```
# pfctl -k 0.0.0.0/0 -k host2
```

-m   Merge in explicitly given options without resetting those which are omitted. Allows single options to be modified without disturbing the others:

```
# echo "set loginterface fxp0" | pfctl -mf -
```

-N   Load only the NAT rules present in the rule file. Other rules and options are ignored.

-n   Do not actually load rules, just parse them.

-O   Load only the options present in the rule file. Other rules and options are ignored.

-o *level*
          Control the ruleset optimizer, overriding any rule file settings.

> **-o none**   Disable the ruleset optimizer.
> **-o basic**   Enable basic ruleset optimizations. This is the default behaviour.
> **-o profile**   Enable basic ruleset optimizations with profiling.

For further information on the ruleset optimizer, see pf.conf(5).

-p *device*
          Use the device file *device* instead of the default /dev/pf.

-q   Only print errors and warnings.

-R   Load only the filter rules present in the rule file. Other rules and options are ignored.

-r   Perform reverse DNS lookups on states when displaying them.

-s *modifier*
          Show the filter parameters specified by *modifier* (may be abbreviated):

> **-s nat**   Show the currently loaded NAT rules.
> **-s queue**   Show the currently loaded queue rules. When used together with **-v**, per-queue statistics are also shown. When used together with **-v -v**, **pfctl** will loop and show updated queue statistics every five seconds, including measured bandwidth and packets per second.
> **-s rules**   Show the currently loaded filter rules. When used together with **-v**, the per-rule statistics (number of evaluations, packets and bytes) are also shown. Note that the "skip step" optimization done automatically by the kernel will skip evaluation of rules where possible. Packets passed statefully are counted in the rule that created the state (even though the rule isn't evaluated more than once for the entire connection).
> **-s Anchors**   Show the currently loaded anchors directly attached to the main ruleset. If **-a** *anchor* is specified as well, the anchors loaded directly below the given *anchor* are shown instead. If **-v** is specified, all anchors attached under the target anchor will be displayed recursively.
> **-s states**   Show the contents of the state table.
> **-s Sources**   Show the contents of the source tracking table.
> **-s info**   Show filter information (statistics and counters). When used together with **-v**, source tracking statistics are also shown.

-s labels	Show per-rule statistics (label, evaluations, packets total, bytes total, packets in, bytes in, packets out, bytes out) of filter rules with labels, useful for accounting.
-s timeouts	Show the current global timeouts.
-s memory	Show the current pool memory hard limits.
-s Tables	Show the list of tables.
-s osfp	Show the list of operating system fingerprints.
-s Interfaces	

Show the list of interfaces and interface drivers available to PF. When used together with **-v**, it additionally lists which interfaces have skip rules activated. When used together with **-vv**, interface statistics are also shown. **-i** can be used to select an interface or a group of interfaces.

-s all	Show all of the above, except for the lists of interfaces and operating system fingerprints.

-T *command* [*address* . . .]

Specify the *command* (may be abbreviated) to apply to the table. Commands include:

-T kill	Kill a table.
-T flush	Flush all addresses of a table.
-T add	Add one or more addresses in a table. Automatically create a nonexisting table.
-T delete	Delete one or more addresses from a table.
-T expire *number*	

Delete addresses which had their statistics cleared more than *number* seconds ago. For entries which have never had their statistics cleared, *number* refers to the time they were added to the table.

-T replace	Replace the addresses of the table. Automatically create a nonexisting table.
-T show	Show the content (addresses) of a table.
-T test	Test if the given addresses match a table.
-T zero	Clear all the statistics of a table.
-T load	Load only the table definitions from pf.conf(5). This is used in conjunction with the **-f** flag, as in:

```
# pfctl -Tl -f pf.conf
```

For the **add**, **delete**, **replace**, and **test** commands, the list of addresses can be specified either directly on the command line and/or in an unformatted text file, using the **-f** flag. Comments starting with a '#' are allowed in the text file. With these commands, the **-v** flag can also be used once or twice, in which case **pfctl** will print the detailed result of the operation for each individual address, prefixed by one of the following letters:

A	The address/network has been added.
C	The address/network has been changed (negated).
D	The address/network has been deleted.
M	The address matches (**test** operation only).
X	The address/network is duplicated and therefore ignored.
Y	The address/network cannot be added/deleted due to conflicting '!' attributes.
Z	The address/network has been cleared (statistics).

Each table maintains a set of counters that can be retrieved using the **-v** flag of **pfctl**. For example, the following commands define a wide open firewall which will keep track of packets going to or coming from the OpenBSD FTP server. The following commands configure the firewall and send 10 pings to the FTP server:

```
# printf "table <test> { ftp.NetBSD.org }\n \
    pass out to <test>\n" | pfctl -f-
```

```
                    # ping -qc10 ftp.NetBSD.org
```

We can now use the table **show** command to output, for each address and packet direction, the number of packets and bytes that are being passed or blocked by rules referencing the table. The time at which the current accounting started is also shown with the "Cleared" line.

```
         # pfctl -t test -vTshow
            129.128.5.191
               Cleared:          Thu Feb 13 18:55:18 2003
               In/Block:         [ Packets: 0            Bytes: 0            ]
               In/Pass:          [ Packets: 10           Bytes: 840          ]
               Out/Block:        [ Packets: 0            Bytes: 0            ]
               Out/Pass:         [ Packets: 10           Bytes: 840          ]
```

Similarly, it is possible to view global information about the tables by using the **−v** modifier twice and the **−s Tables** command. This will display the number of addresses on each table, the number of rules which reference the table, and the global packet statistics for the whole table:

```
         # pfctl -vvsTables
         --a-r-  test
               Addresses:        1
               Cleared:          Thu Feb 13 18:55:18 2003
               References:       [ Anchors: 0            Rules: 1            ]
               Evaluations:      [ NoMatch: 3496         Match: 1            ]
               In/Block:         [ Packets: 0            Bytes: 0            ]
               In/Pass:          [ Packets: 10           Bytes: 840          ]
               In/XPass:         [ Packets: 0            Bytes: 0            ]
               Out/Block:        [ Packets: 0            Bytes: 0            ]
               Out/Pass:         [ Packets: 10           Bytes: 840          ]
               Out/XPass:        [ Packets: 0            Bytes: 0            ]
```

As we can see here, only one packet – the initial ping request – matched the table, but all packets passing as the result of the state are correctly accounted for. Reloading the table(s) or ruleset will not affect packet accounting in any way. The two "XPass" counters are incremented instead of the "Pass" counters when a "stateful" packet is passed but doesn't match the table anymore. This will happen in our example if someone flushes the table while the ping(8) command is running.

When used with a single **−v**, **pfctl** will only display the first line containing the table flags and name. The flags are defined as follows:

c   For constant tables, which cannot be altered outside pf.conf(5).
p   For persistent tables, which don't get automatically killed when no rules refer to them.
a   For tables which are part of the *active* tableset. Tables without this flag do not really exist, cannot contain addresses, and are only listed if the **−g** flag is given.
i   For tables which are part of the *inactive* tableset. This flag can only be witnessed briefly during the loading of pf.conf(5).
r   For tables which are referenced (used) by rules.
h   This flag is set when a table in the main ruleset is hidden by one or more tables of the same name from anchors attached below it.

−t *table*
          Specify the name of the table.

−v   Produce more verbose output. A second use of **−v** will produce even more verbose output including ruleset warnings. See the previous section for its effect on table commands.

-x *level*

    Set the debug *level* (may be abbreviated) to one of the following:

    -x none   Don't generate debug messages.

    -x urgent   Generate debug messages only for serious errors.

    -x misc   Generate debug messages for various errors.

    -x loud   Generate debug messages for common conditions.

-z   Clear per-rule statistics.

FILES

    /etc/pf.conf Packet filter rules file.

    /etc/pf.os   Passive operating system fingerprint database.

SEE ALSO

    pf(4), pf.conf(5), pf.os(5), rc.conf(5), authpf(8), ftp-proxy(8), rc(8), sysctl(8)

HISTORY

    The **pfctl** program and the pf(4) filter mechanism first appeared in OpenBSD 3.0 and later in NetBSD 3.0.

NAME

pflogd — packet filter logging daemon

SYNOPSIS

pflogd [**-Dx**] [**-d** *delay*] [**-f** *filename*] [**-i** *interface*] [**-p** *pidfile*]
    [**-s** *snaplen*] [*expression*]

DESCRIPTION

pflogd is a background daemon which reads packets logged by pf(4) to a pflog(4) interface, normally pflog0, and writes the packets to a logfile (normally /var/log/pflog) in tcpdump(8) binary format. These logs can be reviewed later using the **-r** option of tcpdump(8), hopefully offline in case there are bugs in the packet parsing code of tcpdump(8).

pflogd closes and then re-opens the log file when it receives SIGHUP, permitting newsyslog(8) to rotate logfiles automatically. SIGALRM causes **pflogd** to flush the current logfile buffers to the disk, thus making the most recent logs available. The buffers are also flushed every *delay* seconds.

If the log file contains data after a restart or a SIGHUP, new logs are appended to the existing file. If the existing log file was created with a different snaplen, **pflogd** temporarily uses the old snaplen to keep the log file consistent.

pflogd tries to preserve the integrity of the log file against I/O errors. Furthermore, integrity of an existing log file is verified before appending. If there is an invalid log file or an I/O error, the log file is moved out of the way and a new one is created. If a new file cannot be created, logging is suspended until a SIGHUP or a SIGALRM is received.

The options are as follows:

-D   Debugging mode. **pflogd** does not disassociate from the controlling terminal.

-d *delay*
    Time in seconds to delay between automatic flushes of the file. This may be specified with a value between 5 and 3600 seconds. If not specified, the default is 60 seconds.

-f *filename*
    Log output filename. Default is /var/log/pflog.

-i *interface*
    Specifies the pflog(4) interface to use. By default, **pflogd** will use *pflog0*.

-p *pidfile*
    Writes a file containing the process ID of the program. The file name has the form /var/run/pidname.pid. If the option is not given, *pidfile* defaults to pflogd.

-s *snaplen*
    Analyze at most the first *snaplen* bytes of data from each packet rather than the default of 116. The default of 116 is adequate for IP, ICMP, TCP, and UDP headers but may truncate protocol information for other protocols. Other file parsers may desire a higher snaplen.

-x   Check the integrity of an existing log file, and return.

expression
    Selects which packets will be dumped, using the regular language of tcpdump(8).

FILES

`/var/run/pflogd.pid` Process ID of the currently running **pflogd**.
`/var/log/pflog`   Default log file.

EXAMPLES

Log specific tcp packets to a different log file with a large snaplen (useful with a log-all rule to dump complete sessions):

```
# pflogd -s 1600 -f suspicious.log port 80 and host evilhost
```

Log from another `pflog`(4) interface, excluding specific packets:

```
# pflogd -i pflog3 -f network3.log "not (tcp and port 23)"
```

Display binary logs:

```
# tcpdump -n -e -ttt -r /var/log/pflog
```

Display the logs in real time (this does not interfere with the operation of **pflogd**):

```
# tcpdump -n -e -ttt -i pflog0
```

Tcpdump has been extended to be able to filter on the pfloghdr structure defined in ⟨*net/if_pflog.h*⟩. Tcpdump can restrict the output to packets logged on a specified interface, a rule number, a reason, a direction, an IP family or an action.

ip	Address family equals IPv4.
ip6	Address family equals IPv6.
ifname kue0	Interface name equals "kue0".
on kue0	Interface name equals "kue0".
ruleset authpf	Ruleset name equals "authpf".
rulenum 10	Rule number equals 10.
reason match	Reason equals match. Also accepts "bad-offset", "fragment", "bad-timestamp", "short", "normalize", "memory", "congestion", "ip-option", "proto-cksum", "state-mismatch", "state-insert", "state-limit", "src-limit", and "synproxy".
action pass	Action equals pass. Also accepts "block".
inbound	The direction was inbound.
outbound	The direction was outbound.

Display the logs in real time of inbound packets that were blocked on the wi0 interface:

```
# tcpdump -n -e -ttt -i pflog0 inbound and action block and on wi0
```

SEE ALSO

`pcap`(3), `pf`(4), `pflog`(4), `pf.conf`(5), `newsyslog`(8), `tcpdump`(8)

HISTORY

The **pflogd** command appeared in OpenBSD 3.0 and later in NetBSD 3.0.

AUTHORS

pflogd was written by Can Erkin Acar ⟨canacar@openbsd.org⟩.

NAME
pfs — save and restore information for NAT and state tables

SYNOPSIS
pfs [**-v**] **-l**
pfs [**-bv**] **-R** *filename*
pfs [**-bv**] **-r** *filename*
pfs [**-v**] **-u**
pfs [**-bv**] **-W** *filename*
pfs [**-bv**] **-w** *filename*

DESCRIPTION
The **pfs** command allows state information created for NAT entries and rules using "keep state" to be locked (modification prevented) and then saved to disk, allowing for the system to experience a reboot, followed by the restoration of that information, resulting in connections not being interrupted.

OPTIONS

-b   The information are read or stored using binary format. The default format is a readable ASCII format, similar to `pfctl.conf` syntax.

-l   Lock state tables in the kernel.

-R *filename*   Restore information from *filename* and load it into the kernel. The state tables are locked at the beginning of this operation and unlocked once complete.

-r *filename*   Read information in from *filename* and load it into the kernel. This requires the state tables to have already been locked and does not change the lock once complete.

-u   Unlock state tables in the kernel.

-v   Provide a verbose description of what's being done.

-W *filename*   Write information from the kernel out to *filename*. The state tables are locked at the beginning of this operation and unlocked once complete.

-w *filename*   Write information from the kernel out to *filename*. This requires the state tables to have already been locked and does not change the lock once complete.

FILES
`/dev/pf`

SEE ALSO
`pf(4)`

NAME

pickup – Postfix local mail pickup

SYNOPSIS

pickup [generic Postfix daemon options]

DESCRIPTION

The **pickup**(8) daemon waits for hints that new mail has been dropped into the **maildrop** directory, and feeds it into the **cleanup**(8) daemon. Ill-formatted files are deleted without notifying the originator. This program expects to be run from the **master**(8) process manager.

STANDARDS

None. The **pickup**(8) daemon does not interact with the outside world.

SECURITY

The **pickup**(8) daemon is moderately security sensitive. It runs with fixed low privilege and can run in a chrooted environment. However, the program reads files from potentially hostile users. The **pickup**(8) daemon opens no files for writing, is careful about what files it opens for reading, and does not actually touch any data that is sent to its public service endpoint.

DIAGNOSTICS

Problems and transactions are logged to **syslogd**(8).

BUGS

The **pickup**(8) daemon copies mail from file to the **cleanup**(8) daemon. It could avoid message copying overhead by sending a file descriptor instead of file data, but then the already complex **cleanup**(8) daemon would have to deal with unfiltered user data.

CONFIGURATION PARAMETERS

As the **pickup**(8) daemon is a relatively long-running process, up to an hour may pass before a **main.cf** change takes effect. Use the command "**postfix reload**" command to speed up a change.

The text below provides only a parameter summary. See **postconf**(5) for more details including examples.

CONTENT INSPECTION CONTROLS

content_filter (empty)

The name of a mail delivery transport that filters mail after it is queued.

receive_override_options (empty)

Enable or disable recipient validation, built-in content filtering, or address mapping.

MISCELLANEOUS CONTROLS

config_directory (see 'postconf -d' output)

The default location of the Postfix main.cf and master.cf configuration files.

ipc_timeout (3600s)

The time limit for sending or receiving information over an internal communication channel.

line_length_limit (2048)

Upon input, long lines are chopped up into pieces of at most this length; upon delivery, long lines are reconstructed.

max_idle (100s)

The maximum amount of time that an idle Postfix daemon process waits for an incoming connection before terminating voluntarily.

max_use (100)

The maximal number of incoming connections that a Postfix daemon process will service before terminating voluntarily.

process_id (read-only)

The process ID of a Postfix command or daemon process.

process_name (read-only)
    The process name of a Postfix command or daemon process.

queue_directory (see 'postconf -d' output)
    The location of the Postfix top-level queue directory.

syslog_facility (mail)
    The syslog facility of Postfix logging.

syslog_name (see 'postconf -d' output)
    The mail system name that is prepended to the process name in syslog records, so that "smtpd" becomes, for example, "postfix/smtpd".

SEE ALSO

cleanup(8), message canonicalization
sendmail(1), Sendmail-compatible interface
postdrop(1), mail posting agent
postconf(5), configuration parameters
master(5), generic daemon options
master(8), process manager
syslogd(8), system logging

LICENSE

The Secure Mailer license must be distributed with this software.

AUTHOR(S)

Wietse Venema
IBM T.J. Watson Research
P.O. Box 704
Yorktown Heights, NY 10598, USA

NAME

ping — send ICMP ECHO_REQUEST packets to network hosts

SYNOPSIS

ping [-adDfLnoPqQrRv] [-c count] [-E policy] [-g gateway] [-h host]
[-i interval] [-I srcaddr] [-l preload] [-p pattern] [-s packetsize]
[-t tos] [-T ttl] [-w deadline] host

DESCRIPTION

ping uses the ICMP protocol's mandatory ECHO_REQUEST datagram to elicit an ICMP ECHO_RESPONSE from a host or gateway. ECHO_REQUEST datagrams ("pings") have an IP and ICMP header, followed by a "struct timeval" and then an arbitrary number of "pad" bytes used to fill out the packet. The options are as follows:

-a   Emit an audible beep (by sending an ascii BEL character to the standard error output) after each non-duplicate response is received. This is disabled for flood pings as it would probably cause temporary insanity.

-c count
      Stop after sending (and waiting the specified delay to receive) count ECHO_RESPONSE packets.

-d   Set the SO_DEBUG option on the socket being used.

-D   Set the Don't Fragment bit in the IP header. This can be used to determine the path MTU.

-E policy
      Use IPsec policy specification string policy for packets. For the format of specification string, please refer ipsec_set_policy(3). Please note that this option is same as -P in KAME/FreeBSD and KAME/BSDI (as -P was already occupied in NetBSD).

-f   Flood ping. Outputs packets as fast as they come back or one hundred times per second, whichever is more. For every ECHO_REQUEST sent a period "." is printed, while for every ECHO_REPLY received a backspace is printed. This provides a rapid display of how many packets are being dropped. Only the super-user may use this option. *This can be very hard on a network and should be used with caution.*

-g gateway
      Use Loose Source Routing to send the ECHO_REQUEST packets via gateway.

-i interval
      Wait interval seconds *between sending each packet*. The default is to wait for one second between each packet, except when the -f option is used the wait interval is 0.01 seconds.

-I srcaddr
      Set the source IP address to srcaddr which can be a hostname or an IP number. For multicast datagrams, it also specifies the outgoing interface.

-h host
      is an alternate way of specifying the target host instead of as the last argument.

-l preload
      If preload is specified, ping sends that many packets as fast as possible before falling into its normal mode of behavior. Only the super-user may use this option.

-L   Disable loopback when sending to multicast destinations, so the transmitting host doesn't see the ICMP requests.

-n   Numeric output only. No attempt will be made to look up symbolic names for host addresses.

-o   Exit successfully after receiving one reply packet.

-p *pattern*
        You may specify up to 16 "pad" bytes to fill out the packet you send. This is useful for diagnosing data-dependent problems in a network. For example, "-p ff" will cause the sent packet to be filled with all ones.

-P   Use a pseudo-random sequence for the data instead of the default, fixed sequence of incrementing 8-bit integers. This is useful to foil compression on PPP and other links.

-q   Quiet output. Nothing is displayed except the summary lines at startup time and when finished.

-Q   Do not display responses such as Network Unreachable ICMP messages concerning the ECHO_REQUESTs sent.

-r   Bypass the normal routing tables and send directly to a host on an attached network. If the host is not on a directly-attached network, an error is returned. This option can be used to ping a local host through an interface that has no route through it (e.g., after the interface was dropped by routed(8)).

-R   Record Route. Includes the RECORD_ROUTE option in the ECHO_REQUEST packet and displays the route buffer on returned packets. This should show the path to the target host and back, which is especially useful in the case of asymmetric routing. Note that the IP header is only large enough for nine such addresses, and only seven when using the **-g** option. This is why it was necessary to invent traceroute(8). Many hosts ignore or discard this option.

-s *packetsize*
        Specifies the number of data bytes to be sent. The default is 56, which translates into 64 ICMP data bytes when combined with the 8 bytes of ICMP header data. The maximum allowed value is 65467 bytes.

-T *ttl*
        Use the specified time-to-live.

-t *tos*
        Use the specified hexadecimal type of service.

-v   Verbose output. ICMP packets other than ECHO_RESPONSE that are received are listed.

-w *deadline*
        Specifies a timeout, in seconds, before ping exits regardless of how many packets have been sent or received.

When using **ping** for fault isolation, it should first be run on the local host, to verify that the local network interface is up and running. Then, hosts and gateways further and further away should be "pinged".

Round-trip times and packet loss statistics are computed. If duplicate packets are received, they are not included in the packet loss calculation, although the round trip time of these packets is used in calculating the minimum/average/maximum round-trip time numbers.

When the specified number of packets have been sent (and received) or if the program is terminated with a SIGINT, a brief summary is displayed. The summary information can be displayed while **ping** is running by sending it a SIGINFO signal (see the "status" argument for stty(1) for more information).

ping continually sends one datagram per second, and prints one line of output for every ECHO_RESPONSE returned. On a trusted system with IP Security Options enabled, if the network idiom is not MONO, **ping** also prints a second line containing the hexadecimal representation of the IP security option in the ECHO_RESPONSE. If the **-c** count option is given, only that number of requests is sent. No output is produced if there is no response. Round-trip times and packet loss statistics are computed. If duplicate packets are received, they are not included in the packet loss calculation, although the round trip time of these packets is used in calculating the minimum/average/maximum round-trip time numbers. When the specified number of packets have been sent (and received) or if the program is terminated with an interrupt (SIGINT), a brief summary is displayed. When not using the **−f** (flood) option, the first interrupt, usually generated by control-C or DEL, causes **ping** to wait for its outstanding requests to return. It will wait no longer than the longest round trip time encountered by previous, successful pings. The second interrupt stops ping immediately.

This program is intended for use in network testing, measurement and management. Because of the load it can impose on the network, it is unwise to use **ping** during normal operations or from automated scripts.

ICMP PACKET DETAILS

An IP header without options is 20 bytes. An ICMP ECHO_REQUEST packet contains an additional 8 bytes worth of ICMP header followed by an arbitrary amount of data. When a *packetsize* is given, this indicated the size of this extra piece of data (the default is 56). Thus the amount of data received inside of an IP packet of type ICMP ECHO_REPLY will always be 8 bytes more than the requested data space (the ICMP header).

If the data space is at least eight bytes large, **ping** uses the first eight bytes of this space to include a timestamp to compute round trip times. If less than eight bytes of pad are specified, no round trip times are given.

DUPLICATE AND DAMAGED PACKETS

ping will report duplicate and damaged packets. Duplicate packets should never occur, and seem to be caused by inappropriate link-level retransmissions. Duplicates may occur in many situations and are rarely (if ever) a good sign, although the presence of low levels of duplicates may not always be cause for alarm.

Damaged packets are obviously serious cause for alarm and often indicate broken hardware somewhere in the **ping** packet's path (in the network or in the hosts).

TRYING DIFFERENT DATA PATTERNS

The (inter)network layer should never treat packets differently depending on the data contained in the data portion. Unfortunately, data-dependent problems have been known to sneak into networks and remain undetected for long periods of time. In many cases the particular pattern that will have problems is something that doesn't have sufficient "transitions", such as all ones or all zeros, or a pattern right at the edge, such as almost all zeros. It isn't necessarily enough to specify a data pattern of all zeros (for example) on the command line because the pattern that is of interest is at the data link level, and the relationship between what you type and what the controllers transmit can be complicated.

This means that if you have a data-dependent problem you will probably have to do a lot of testing to find it. If you are lucky, you may manage to find a file that either can't be sent across your network or that takes much longer to transfer than other similar length files. You can then examine this file for repeated patterns that you can test using the **−p** option of **ping**.

TTL DETAILS

The TTL value of an IP packet represents the maximum number of IP routers that the packet can go through before being thrown away. In current practice you can expect each router in the Internet to decrement the TTL field by exactly one.

The TCP/IP specification states that the TTL field for TCP packets should be set to 60, but many systems use smaller values (4.3 BSD uses 30, 4.2 BSD used 15).

The maximum possible value of this field is 255, and most UNIX systems set the TTL field of ICMP ECHO_REQUEST packets to 255. This is why you will find you can "ping" some hosts, but not reach them with telnet(1) or ftp(1).

In normal operation ping prints the ttl value from the packet it receives. When a remote system receives a ping packet, it can do one of three things with the TTL field in its response:

• Not change it; this is what Berkeley UNIX systems did before the 4.3 BSD–Tahoe release. In this case the TTL value in the received packet will be 255 minus the number of routers in the round-trip path.

• Set it to 255; this is what current Berkeley UNIX systems do. In this case the TTL value in the received packet will be 255 minus the number of routers in the path *from* the remote system *to* the **ping**ing host.

• Set it to some other value. Some machines use the same value for ICMP packets that they use for TCP packets, for example either 30 or 60. Others may use completely wild values.

EXIT STATUS

ping returns 0 on success (the host is alive), and non-zero if the arguments are incorrect or the host is not responding.

SEE ALSO

netstat(1), icmp(4), inet(4), ip(4), ifconfig(8), routed(8), spray(8), traceroute(8)

HISTORY

The **ping** command appeared in 4.3 BSD. IPsec support was added by WIDE/KAME project.

BUGS

Flood pinging is not recommended in general, and flood pinging a broadcast or multicast address should only be done under very controlled conditions.

The **ping** program has evolved differently under different operating systems, and in some cases the same flag performs a different function under different operating systems. The −t flag conflicts with FreeBSD. The −a, −c, −i, −I, −l, −p, −P, −s, and −t flags conflict with **Solaris**.

Some hosts and gateways ignore the RECORD_ROUTE option.

The maximum IP header length is too small for options like RECORD_ROUTE to be completely useful. There's not much that that can be done about this, however.

NAME

ping6 — send ICMPv6 ECHO_REQUEST packets to network hosts

SYNOPSIS

ping6 [**−dfHmnNqRtvwW**] [**−a** *addrtype*] [**−b** *bufsiz*] [**−c** *count*] [**−g** *gateway*]
[**−h** *hoplimit*] [**−I** *interface*] [**−i** *wait*] [**−l** *preload*] [**−p** *pattern*]
[**−P** *policy*] [**−S** *sourceaddr*] [**−s** *packetsize*] [*hops* . . .] *host*

DESCRIPTION

ping6 uses the ICMPv6 protocol's mandatory ICMP6_ECHO_REQUEST datagram to elicit an
ICMP6_ECHO_REPLY from a host or gateway. ICMP6_ECHO_REQUEST datagrams ("pings") have an IPv6
header, and ICMPv6 header formatted as documented in RFC 2463. The options are as follows:

−a *addrtype*
Generate ICMPv6 Node Information Node Addresses query, rather than echo-request. *addrtype*
must be a string constructed of the following characters.

a   requests unicast addresses from all of the responder's interfaces. If the character is omitted,
only those addresses which belong to the interface which has the responder's address are
requests.

c   requests responder's IPv4-compatible and IPv4-mapped addresses.

g   requests responder's global-scope addresses.

s   requests responder's site-local addresses.

l   requests responder's link-local addresses.

A   requests responder's anycast addresses. Without this character, the responder will return
unicast addresses only. With this character, the responder will return anycast addresses
only. Note that the specification does not specify how to get responder's anycast addresses.
This is an experimental option.

−b *bufsiz*
Set socket buffer size.

−c *count*
Stop after sending (and receiving) *count* ECHO_RESPONSE packets.

−d   Set the SO_DEBUG option on the socket being used.

−f   Flood ping. Outputs packets as fast as they come back or one hundred times per second, whichever
is more. For every ECHO_REQUEST sent a period "." is printed, while for every ECHO_REPLY
received a backspace is printed. This provides a rapid display of how many packets are being
dropped. Only the super-user may use this option. *This can be very hard on a network and should
be used with caution.*

−g *gateway*
Specifies to use *gateway* as the next hop to the destination. The gateway must be a neighbor of
the sending node.

−H   Specifies to try reverse-lookup of IPv6 addresses. The **ping6** command does not try reverse-
lookup unless the option is specified.

−h *hoplimit*
Set the IPv6 hoplimit.

−I *interface*
Source packets with the given interface address. This flag applies if the ping destination is a multicast address, or link-local/site-local unicast address.

-i *wait*

Wait *wait* seconds *between sending each packet*. The default is to wait for one second between each packet. This option is incompatible with the **-f** option.

-l *preload*

If *preload* is specified, **ping6** sends that many packets as fast as possible before falling into its normal mode of behavior. Only the super-user may use this option.

-m

By default, **ping6** asks the kernel to fragment packets to fit into the minimum IPv6 MTU. **-m** will suppress the behavior in the following two levels: when the option is specified once, the behavior will be disabled for unicast packets. When the option is specified more than once, it will be disabled for both unicast and multicast packets.

-n

Numeric output only. No attempt will be made to lookup symbolic names from addresses in the reply.

-N

Probe node information multicast group (ff02::2:xxxx:xxxx). *host* must be string host-name of the target (must not be a numeric IPv6 address). Node information multicast group will be computed based on given *host*, and will be used as the final destination. Since node information multicast group is a link-local multicast group, outgoing interface needs to be specified by **-I** option.

-p *pattern*

You may specify up to 16 "pad" bytes to fill out the packet you send. This is useful for diagnosing data-dependent problems in a network. For example, "-p ff" will cause the sent packet to be filled with all ones.

-P *policy*

policy specifies IPsec policy to be used for the probe.

-q

Quiet output. Nothing is displayed except the summary lines at startup time and when finished.

-R

Make the kernel believe that the target *host* (or the first *hop* if you specify *hops*) is reachable, by injecting upper-layer reachability confirmation hint. The option is meaningful only if the target *host* (or the first hop) is a neighbor.

-S *sourceaddr*

Specifies the source address of request packets. The source address must be one of the unicast addresses of the sending node, and must be numeric.

-s *packetsize*

Specifies the number of data bytes to be sent. The default is 56, which translates into 64 ICMP data bytes when combined with the 8 bytes of ICMP header data. You may need to specify **-b** as well to extend socket buffer size.

-t

Generate ICMPv6 Node Information supported query types query, rather than echo-request. **-s** has no effect if **-t** is specified.

-v

Verbose output. ICMP packets other than ECHO_RESPONSE that are received are listed.

-w

Generate ICMPv6 Node Information DNS Name query, rather than echo-request. **-s** has no effect if **-w** is specified.

-W

Same as **-w**, but with old packet format based on 03 draft. This option is present for backward compatibility. **-s** has no effect if **-w** is specified.

hops IPv6 addresses for intermediate nodes, which will be put into type 0 routing header.

host   IPv6 address of the final destination node.

When using **ping6** for fault isolation, it should first be run on the local host, to verify that the local network interface is up and running. Then, hosts and gateways further and further away should be "pinged". Round-trip times and packet loss statistics are computed. If duplicate packets are received, they are not included in the packet loss calculation, although the round trip time of these packets is used in calculating the round-trip time statistics. When the specified number of packets have been sent (and received) or if the program is terminated with a SIGINT, a brief summary is displayed, showing the number of packets sent and received, and the minimum, maximum, mean, and standard deviation of the round-trip times.

This program is intended for use in network testing, measurement and management. Because of the load it can impose on the network, it is unwise to use **ping6** during normal operations or from automated scripts.

DUPLICATE AND DAMAGED PACKETS
ping6 will report duplicate and damaged packets. Duplicate packets should never occur when pinging a unicast address, and seem to be caused by inappropriate link-level retransmissions. Duplicates may occur in many situations and are rarely (if ever) a good sign, although the presence of low levels of duplicates may not always be cause for alarm. Duplicates are expected when pinging a multicast address, since they are not really duplicates but replies from different hosts to the same request.

Damaged packets are obviously serious cause for alarm and often indicate broken hardware somewhere in the **ping6** packet's path (in the network or in the hosts).

TRYING DIFFERENT DATA PATTERNS
The (inter)network layer should never treat packets differently depending on the data contained in the data portion. Unfortunately, data-dependent problems have been known to sneak into networks and remain unde-tected for long periods of time. In many cases the particular pattern that will have problems is something that does not have sufficient "transitions", such as all ones or all zeros, or a pattern right at the edge, such as almost all zeros. It is not necessarily enough to specify a data pattern of all zeros (for example) on the com-mand line because the pattern that is of interest is at the data link level, and the relationship between what you type and what the controllers transmit can be complicated.

This means that if you have a data-dependent problem you will probably have to do a lot of testing to find it. If you are lucky, you may manage to find a file that either cannot be sent across your network or that takes much longer to transfer than other similar length files. You can then examine this file for repeated patterns that you can test using the **-p** option of **ping6**.

EXIT STATUS
ping6 exits with 0 on success (the host is alive), and non-zero if the arguments are incorrect or the host is not responding.

EXAMPLES
Normally, **ping6** works just like ping(8) would work; the following will send ICMPv6 echo request to dst.foo.com.

```
ping6 -n dst.foo.com
```

The following will probe hostnames for all nodes on the network link attached to wi0 interface. The address ff02::1 is named the link-local all-node multicast address, and the packet would reach every node on the network link.

```
ping6 -w ff02::1%wi0
```

The following will probe addresses assigned to the destination node, dst.foo.com.

```
ping6 -a agl dst.foo.com
```

SEE ALSO

netstat(1), icmp6(4), inet6(4), ip6(4), ifconfig(8), ping(8), routed(8), traceroute(8), traceroute6(8)

A. Conta and S. Deering, *Internet Control Message Protocol (ICMPv6) for the Internet Protocol Version 6 (IPv6) Specification*, RFC 2463, December 1998.

Matt Crawford, *IPv6 Node Information Queries*, draft-ietf-ipngwg-icmp-name-lookups-09.txt, May 2002, work in progress material.

HISTORY

The ping(8) command appeared in 4.3 BSD. The **ping6** command with IPv6 support first appeared in the WIDE Hydrangea IPv6 protocol stack kit.

BUGS

ping6 is intentionally separate from ping(8).

NAME
pipe – Postfix delivery to external command

SYNOPSIS
pipe [generic Postfix daemon options] command_attributes...

DESCRIPTION
The **pipe**(8) daemon processes requests from the Postfix queue manager to deliver messages to external commands. This program expects to be run from the **master**(8) process manager.

Message attributes such as sender address, recipient address and next-hop host name can be specified as command-line macros that are expanded before the external command is executed.

The **pipe**(8) daemon updates queue files and marks recipients as finished, or it informs the queue manager that delivery should be tried again at a later time. Delivery status reports are sent to the **bounce**(8), **defer**(8) or **trace**(8) daemon as appropriate.

SINGLE-RECIPIENT DELIVERY
Some destinations cannot handle more than one recipient per delivery request. Examples are pagers or fax machines. In addition, multi-recipient delivery is undesirable when prepending a **Delivered-to:** or **X-Original-To:** message header.

To prevent Postfix from sending multiple recipients per delivery request, specify

    *transport*_**destination_recipient_limit = 1**

in the Postfix **main.cf** file, where *transport* is the name in the first column of the Postfix **master.cf** entry for the pipe-based delivery transport.

COMMAND ATTRIBUTE SYNTAX
The external command attributes are given in the **master.cf** file at the end of a service definition. The syntax is as follows:

chroot=*pathname* (optional)
> Change the process root directory and working directory to the named directory. This happens before switching to the privileges specified with the **user** attribute, and before executing the optional **directory=***pathname* directive. Delivery is deferred in case of failure.
>
> This feature is available as of Postfix 2.3.

directory=*pathname* (optional)
> Change to the named directory before executing the external command. The directory must be accessible for the user specified with the **user** attribute (see below). The default working directory is **$queue_directory**. Delivery is deferred in case of failure.
>
> This feature is available as of Postfix 2.2.

eol=*string* (optional, default: \n)
> The output record delimiter. Typically one would use either \r\n or \n. The usual C-style backslash escape sequences are recognized: \a \b \f \n \r \t \v *ddd* (up to three octal digits) and \\.

flags=BDFORXhqu.> (optional)
> Optional message processing flags. By default, a message is copied unchanged.

    B   Append a blank line at the end of each message. This is required by some mail user agents that recognize "**From** " lines only when preceded by a blank line.

    D   Prepend a "**Delivered-To:** *recipient*" message header with the envelope recipient address. Note: for this to work, the *transport*_**destination_recipient_limit** must be 1 (see SINGLE-RECIPIENT DELIVERY above for details).

The **D** flag also enforces loop detection (Postfix 2.5 and later): if a message already contains a **Delivered-To:** header with the same recipient address, then the message is returned as undeliverable. The address comparison is case insensitive.

This feature is available as of Postfix 2.0.

F   Prepend a "**From** *sender time_stamp*" envelope header to the message content. This is expected by, for example, **UUCP** software.

O   Prepend an "**X-Original-To:** *recipient*" message header with the recipient address as given to Postfix. Note: for this to work, the *transport*_**destination_recipient_limit** must be 1 (see SINGLE-RECIPIENT DELIVERY above for details).

This feature is available as of Postfix 2.0.

R   Prepend a **Return-Path:** message header with the envelope sender address.

X   Indicate that the external command performs final delivery. This flag affects the status reported in "success" DSN (delivery status notification) messages, and changes it from "relayed" into "delivered".

This feature is available as of Postfix 2.5.

h   Fold the command-line **$original_recipient** and **$recipient** address domain part (text to the right of the right-most @ character) to lower case; fold the entire command-line **$domain** and **$nexthop** host or domain information to lower case. This is recommended for delivery via **UUCP**.

q   Quote white space and other special characters in the command-line **$sender**, **$original_recipient** and **$recipient** address localparts (text to the left of the right-most @ character), according to an 8-bit transparent version of RFC 822. This is recommended for delivery via **UUCP** or **BSMTP**.

The result is compatible with the address parsing of command-line recipients by the Postfix **sendmail**(1) mail submission command.

The **q** flag affects only entire addresses, not the partial address information from the **$user**, **$extension** or **$mailbox** command-line macros.

u   Fold the command-line **$original_recipient** and **$recipient** address localpart (text to the left of the right-most @ character) to lower case. This is recommended for delivery via **UUCP**.

.   Prepend "**.**" to lines starting with "**.**". This is needed by, for example, **BSMTP** software.

>   Prepend "**>**" to lines starting with "**From** ". This is expected by, for example, **UUCP** software.

null_sender=*replacement* (default: MAILER-DAEMON)
    Replace the null sender address (typically used for delivery status notifications) with the specified text when expanding the **$sender** command-line macro, and when generating a From_ or Return-Path: message header.

If the null sender replacement text is a non-empty string then it is affected by the **q** flag for address quoting in command-line arguments.

The null sender replacement text may be empty; this form is recommended for content filters that feed mail back into Postfix. The empty sender address is not affected by the **q** flag for address quoting in command-line arguments.

Caution: a null sender address is easily mis-parsed by naive software. For example, when the **pipe**(8) daemon executes a command such as:

Wrong: command -f$sender -- $recipient

the command will mis-parse the -f option value when the sender address is a null string. For correct parsing, specify **$sender** as an argument by itself:

Right: command -f $sender -- $recipient

This feature is available as of Postfix 2.3.

size=*size_limit* (optional)

Don't deliver messages that exceed this size limit (in bytes); return them to the sender instead.

user=*username* (required)

user=*username*:*groupname*

Execute the external command with the rights of the specified *username*. The software refuses to execute commands with root privileges, or with the privileges of the mail system owner. If *groupname* is specified, the corresponding group ID is used instead of the group ID of *username*.

argv=*command*... (required)

The command to be executed. This must be specified as the last command attribute. The command is executed directly, i.e. without interpretation of shell meta characters by a shell command interpreter.

In the command argument vector, the following macros are recognized and replaced with corresponding information from the Postfix queue manager delivery request.

In addition to the form ${*name*}, the forms $*name* and $(*name*) are also recognized. Specify **$$** where a single **$** is wanted.

${client_address}

This macro expands to the remote client network address.

This feature is available as of Postfix 2.2.

${client_helo}

This macro expands to the remote client HELO command parameter.

This feature is available as of Postfix 2.2.

${client_hostname}

This macro expands to the remote client hostname.

This feature is available as of Postfix 2.2.

${client_port}

This macro expands to the remote client TCP port number.

This feature is available as of Postfix 2.5.

${client_protocol}

This macro expands to the remote client protocol.

This feature is available as of Postfix 2.2.

${domain}

This macro expands to the domain portion of the recipient address. For example, with an address *user+foo@domain* the domain is *domain*.

This information is modified by the **h** flag for case folding.

This feature is available as of Postfix 2.5.

${extension}
This macro expands to the extension part of a recipient address. For example, with an address *user+foo@domain* the extension is *foo*.

A command-line argument that contains **${extension}** expands into as many command-line arguments as there are recipients.

This information is modified by the **u** flag for case folding.

${mailbox}
This macro expands to the complete local part of a recipient address. For example, with an address *user+foo@domain* the mailbox is *user+foo*.

A command-line argument that contains **${mailbox}** expands to as many command-line arguments as there are recipients.

This information is modified by the **u** flag for case folding.

${nexthop}
This macro expands to the next-hop hostname.

This information is modified by the **h** flag for case folding.

${original_recipient}
This macro expands to the complete recipient address before any address rewriting or aliasing.

A command-line argument that contains **${original_recipient}** expands to as many command-line arguments as there are recipients.

This information is modified by the **hqu** flags for quoting and case folding.

This feature is available as of Postfix 2.5.

${recipient}
This macro expands to the complete recipient address.

A command-line argument that contains **${recipient}** expands to as many command-line arguments as there are recipients.

This information is modified by the **hqu** flags for quoting and case folding.

${sasl_method}
This macro expands to the name of the SASL authentication mechanism in the AUTH command when the Postfix SMTP server received the message.

This feature is available as of Postfix 2.2.

${sasl_sender}
This macro expands to the SASL sender name (i.e. the original submitter as per RFC 4954) in the MAIL FROM command when the Postfix SMTP server received the message.

This feature is available as of Postfix 2.2.

${sasl_username}

> This macro expands to the SASL user name in the AUTH command when the Postfix SMTP server received the message.
>
> This feature is available as of Postfix 2.2.

${sender}

> This macro expands to the envelope sender address. By default, the null sender address expands to MAILER-DAEMON; this can be changed with the **null_sender** attribute, as described above.
>
> This information is modified by the **q** flag for quoting.

${size} This macro expands to Postfix's idea of the message size, which is an approximation of the size of the message as delivered.

${user}

> This macro expands to the username part of a recipient address. For example, with an address *user+foo@domain* the username part is *user*.
>
> A command-line argument that contains **${user}** expands into as many command-line arguments as there are recipients.
>
> This information is modified by the **u** flag for case folding.

STANDARDS
RFC 3463 (Enhanced status codes)

DIAGNOSTICS
Command exit status codes are expected to follow the conventions defined in **<sysexits.h>**. Exit status 0 means normal successful completion.

Postfix version 2.3 and later support RFC 3463-style enhanced status codes. If a command terminates with a non-zero exit status, and the command output begins with an enhanced status code, this status code takes precedence over the non-zero exit status.

Problems and transactions are logged to **syslogd**(8). Corrupted message files are marked so that the queue manager can move them to the **corrupt** queue for further inspection.

SECURITY
This program needs a dual personality 1) to access the private Postfix queue and IPC mechanisms, and 2) to execute external commands as the specified user. It is therefore security sensitive.

CONFIGURATION PARAMETERS
Changes to **main.cf** are picked up automatically as **pipe**(8) processes run for only a limited amount of time. Use the command "**postfix reload**" to speed up a change.

The text below provides only a parameter summary. See **postconf**(5) for more details including examples.

RESOURCE AND RATE CONTROLS
In the text below, *transport* is the first field in a **master.cf** entry.

*transport*_**destination_concurrency_limit ($default_destination_concurrency_limit)**

> Limit the number of parallel deliveries to the same destination, for delivery via the named *transport*. The limit is enforced by the Postfix queue manager.

*transport*_**destination_recipient_limit ($default_destination_recipient_limit)**

> Limit the number of recipients per message delivery, for delivery via the named *transport*. The limit is enforced by the Postfix queue manager.

*transport*_**time_limit ($command_time_limit)**
> Limit the time for delivery to external command, for delivery via the named *transport*. The limit is enforced by the pipe delivery agent.
>
> Postfix 2.4 and later support a suffix that specifies the time unit: s (seconds), m (minutes), h (hours), d (days), w (weeks). The default time unit is seconds.

MISCELLANEOUS CONTROLS

config_directory (see 'postconf -d' output)
> The default location of the Postfix main.cf and master.cf configuration files.

daemon_timeout (18000s)
> How much time a Postfix daemon process may take to handle a request before it is terminated by a built-in watchdog timer.

delay_logging_resolution_limit (2)
> The maximal number of digits after the decimal point when logging sub-second delay values.

export_environment (see 'postconf -d' output)
> The list of environment variables that a Postfix process will export to non-Postfix processes.

ipc_timeout (3600s)
> The time limit for sending or receiving information over an internal communication channel.

mail_owner (postfix)
> The UNIX system account that owns the Postfix queue and most Postfix daemon processes.

max_idle (100s)
> The maximum amount of time that an idle Postfix daemon process waits for an incoming connection before terminating voluntarily.

max_use (100)
> The maximal number of incoming connections that a Postfix daemon process will service before terminating voluntarily.

process_id (read-only)
> The process ID of a Postfix command or daemon process.

process_name (read-only)
> The process name of a Postfix command or daemon process.

queue_directory (see 'postconf -d' output)
> The location of the Postfix top-level queue directory.

recipient_delimiter (empty)
> The separator between user names and address extensions (user+foo).

syslog_facility (mail)
> The syslog facility of Postfix logging.

syslog_name (see 'postconf -d' output)
> The mail system name that is prepended to the process name in syslog records, so that "smtpd" becomes, for example, "postfix/smtpd".

SEE ALSO
> qmgr(8), queue manager
> bounce(8), delivery status reports
> postconf(5), configuration parameters
> master(5), generic daemon options
> master(8), process manager
> syslogd(8), system logging

LICENSE

The Secure Mailer license must be distributed with this software.

AUTHOR(S)

Wietse Venema
IBM T.J. Watson Research
P.O. Box 704
Yorktown Heights, NY 10598, USA

NAME

pkg_add — a utility for installing and upgrading software package distributions

SYNOPSIS

pkg_add [**-AfILnRUuVv**] [**-K** *pkg_dbdir*] [**-m** *machine*] [**-P** *destdir*] [**-p** *prefix*]
    [**-W** *viewbase*] [**-w** *view*] *file* . . .
    [[ftp|http]://[*user*][:*password*]@]*host*[:*port*][/*path/*]*pkg-name* . . .

DESCRIPTION

The **pkg_add** command is used to extract and upgrade packages that have been previously created with the pkg_create(1) command. Packages are prepared collections of pre-built binaries, documentation, configurations, installation instructions and/or other files. **pkg_add** can recursively install other packages that the current package depends on or requires from both local disk and via FTP or HTTP.

WARNING

Since the **pkg_add** *command may execute scripts or programs contained within a package file, your system may be susceptible to "Trojan horses" or other subtle attacks from miscreants who create dangerous package files.*

You are advised to verify the competence and identity of those who provide installable package files. For extra protection, use the digital signatures provided where possible (see the pkg_install.conf(5)*), or, failing that, use* tar(1) *to extract the package file, and inspect its contents and scripts to ensure it poses no danger to your system's integrity. Pay particular attention to any* +INSTALL *or* +DEINSTALL *files, and inspect the* +CONTENTS *file for* **@cwd**, **@mode** *(check for setuid),* **@dirrm**, **@exec**, *and* **@unexec** *directives, and/or use the* pkg_info(1) *command to examine the package file.*

OPTIONS

The following command line arguments are supported:

pkg-name [. . .]
    The named packages are installed. **pkg_add** will first try to use *pkg-name* as full URL or path name without any wildcard processing. If that fails, **pkg_add** will try to match packages using wildcard processing. If that fails as well and *pkg-name* does not contain any /, the entries of the PKG_PATH variable are searched using the wildcard processing rules.

-A   Mark package as installed automatically, as dependency of another package. You can use
        pkg_admin set automatic=YES
    to mark packages this way after installation, and
        pkg_admin unset automatic
    to remove the mark. If you **pkg_add** a package without specifying **-A** after it had already been automatically installed, the mark is removed.

-f   Force installation to proceed even if prerequisite packages are not installed or the install script fails. Although **pkg_add** will still try to find and auto-install missing prerequisite packages, a failure to find one will not be fatal. This flag also overrides the fatal error when the operating system or architecture the package was built on differ from that of the host.

-I   If an installation script exists for a given package, do not execute it.

-K *pkg_dbdir*
    Override the value of the PKG_DBDIR configuration option with the value *pkg_dbdir*.

-L   Don't add the package to any views after installation.

 -m Override the machine architecture returned by uname with *machine*.

 -n Don't actually install a package, just report the steps that would be taken if it was.

 -P *destdir*
   Prefix all file and directory names with *destdir*. For packages without install scripts this has the same behavior as using chroot(8).

 -p *prefix*
   Override the prefix stored in the package with *prefix*.

 -R Do not record the installation of a package. This implies **-I**. This means that you cannot deinstall it later, so only use this option if you know what you are doing!

 -U Replace an already installed version from a package. Implies **-u**.

 -u If the package that's being installed is already installed, an update is performed. Installed dependent packages are updated recursively, if they are too old to fulfill the dependencies of the to-be-installed version. See below for a more detailed description of the process.

 -V Print version number and exit.

 -v Turn on verbose output.

 -W *viewbase*
   Passed down to pkg_view(1) for managed views.

 -w *view*
   Passed down to pkg_view(1) for managed views.

One or more *pkg-name* arguments may be specified, each being either a file containing the package (these usually ending with the ".tgz" suffix) or a URL pointing at a file available on an ftp or web site. Thus you may extract files directly from their anonymous ftp or WWW locations (e.g., **pkg_add** ftp://ftp.NetBSD.org/pub/pkgsrc/packages/NetBSD/i386/3.1_2007Q2/shells/bash-3.2.9.tgz or **pkg_add** http://www.example.org/packages/screen-4.0.tbz). Note: For ftp transfers, if you wish to use *passive mode* ftp in such transfers, set the variable *FTP_PASSIVE_MODE* to some value in your environment. Otherwise, the more standard ACTIVE mode may be used. If **pkg_add** consistently fails to fetch a package from a site known to work, it may be because you have a firewall that demands the usage of *passive mode* ftp.

TECHNICAL DETAILS

 pkg_add extracts each package's meta data (including the "packing list") to memory and then runs through the following sequence to fully extract the contents of the package:

  1. A check is made to determine if the package or another version of it is already recorded as installed. If it is, installation is terminated if the **-u** or **-U** options are not given.

    If the same version is installed and **-U** is not given, it is marked as manually installed and process stops. If the **-u** option is given, it's assumed the package should be replaced by the new version instead. Before doing so, all packages that depend on the pkg being upgraded are checked if they also work with the new version. If that test is not successful, the dependent packages are updated first. The replacing is then prepared by moving an existing +REQUIRED_BY file aside (if it exists), and running pkg_delete(1) on the installed package. Installation then proceeds as if the package was not installed, and restores the +REQUIRED_BY file afterwards.

  2. The package build information is extracted from the +BUILD_INFO file and compared against the result of uname(3). If the operating system or architecture of the package differ from that of the host, installation is aborted. This behavior is overridable with the **-f** flag.

3. The package build information from +BUILD_INFO is then checked for USE_ABI_DEPENDS=NO (or IGNORE_RECOMMENDED). If the package was built with ABI dependency recommendations ignored, a warning will be issued.

4. A check is made to determine if the package conflicts (from **@pkgcfl** directives, see pkg_create(1)) with an already recorded as installed package or if an installed package conflicts with the package. If it is, installation is terminated.

5. The file list of the package is compared to the file lists of the installed packages. If there is any overlap, the installation is terminated.

6. All package dependencies (from **@pkgdep** directives, see pkg_create(1)) are read from the packing list. If any of these required packages are not currently installed, an attempt is made to find and install it; if the missing package cannot be found or installed, the installation is terminated.

7. If the package contains an *install* script, it is executed with the following arguments:

    pkg-name   The name of the package being installed.

    PRE-INSTALL   Keyword denoting that the script is to perform any actions needed before the package is installed.

    If the *install* script exits with a non-zero status code, the installation is terminated.

8. The files from the file list are extracted to the chosen prefix.

9. If an *install* script exists for the package, it is executed with the following arguments:

    pkg_name   The name of the package being installed.

    POST-INSTALL Keyword denoting that the script is to perform any actions needed after the package has been installed.

10. After installation is complete, a copy of the packing list, *deinstall* script, description, and display files are copied into <PKG_DBDIR>/<pkg-name> for subsequent possible use by pkg_delete(1). Any package dependencies are recorded in the other packages' +REQUIRED_BY file.

11. If the package is a depoted package, then add it to the registered by calling pkg_view(1) accordingly.

12. Finally, if we were upgrading a package, any +REQUIRED_BY file that was moved aside before upgrading was started is now moved back into place.

The *install* script is called with the environment variable PKG_PREFIX set to the installation prefix (see the **-p** option above). This allows a package author to write a script that reliably performs some action on the directory where the package is installed, even if the user might change it with the **-p** flag to **pkg_add**. The scripts are also called with the PKG_METADATA_DIR environment variable set to the location of the +* meta-data files, and with the PKG_REFCOUNT_DBDIR environment variable set to the location of the package reference counts database directory. If the **-P** flag was given to **pkg_add**, PKG_DESTDIR will be set to *destdir*. Additionally, PKG_METADATA_DIR and PKG_REFCOUNT_DBDIR are prefixed with *destdir*.

ENVIRONMENT

See pkg_install.conf(5) for options, that can also be specified using the environment. Packages using views are also affected by the environment variables documented for pkg_view(1).

EXAMPLES

In all cases, **pkg_add** will try to install binary packages listed in dependencies list.

You can specify a compiled binary package explicitly on the command line.

```
# pkg_add /usr/pkgsrc/packages/All/tcsh-6.14.00.tgz
```

If you omit the version number, **pkg_add** will install the latest version available. With **-v**, **pkg_add** emits more messages to terminal.

```
# pkg_add -v /usr/pkgsrc/packages/All/unzip
```

You can grab a compiled binary package from remote location by specifying a URL. The base URL can also be provided by the configuration variable, PKG_PATH.

```
# pkg_add -v ftp://ftp.NetBSD.org/pub/pkgsrc/packages/NetBSD/i386/3.1_2007Q2
```

```
# export PKG_PATH=ftp://ftp.NetBSD.org/pub/pkgsrc/packages/NetBSD/i386/3.1_2
# pkg_add -v firefox
```

SEE ALSO

pkg_admin(1), pkg_create(1), pkg_delete(1), pkg_info(1), pkg_install.conf(5), pkgsrc(7)

AUTHORS

Jordan Hubbard
> Initial work and ongoing development.

John Kohl
> NetBSD refinements.

Hubert Feyrer
> NetBSD wildcard dependency processing, pkgdb, upgrading, etc.

Thomas Klausner
> HTTP support.

Joerg Sonnenberger
> Rewrote most of the code base to work without external commands.

BUGS

Package upgrading needs a lot more work to be really universal.

Sure to be others.

NAME

pkg_admin — perform various administrative tasks to the pkg system

SYNOPSIS

pkg_admin [**-bqSVv**] [**-C** *config*] [**-d** *lsdir*] [**-K** *pkg_dbdir*] [**-s** *sfx_pattern*]
        command [args ...]

DESCRIPTION

This command performs various administrative tasks around the NetBSD Packages System.

OPTIONS

The following command-line options are supported:

-b   Print only the base names when matching package names for **lsall** and **lsbest**.

-C *config*
      Read the configuration file from *config* instead of the system default.

-d *lsdir*
      Set *lsdir* as the path to the directory in which to find matching package names for **lsall** and
      lsbest.

-K *pkg_dbdir*
      Override the value of the PKG_DBDIR configuration option with the value *pkg_dbdir*.

-q   Perform checks in a quiet manner. In normal operation, **pkg_admin** prints a '.' to standard output to indicate progress. This option suppresses this progress indicator.

-S   Set the shell glob pattern for package suffixes when matching package names for **lsall** and
      lsbest to be the null suffix.

-s *sfx_pattern*
      Set the shell glob pattern for package suffixes when matching package names for **lsall** and
      lsbest. The default pattern is ".t[bg]z".

-V   Print version number and exit.

-v   Be more verbose.

The following commands are supported:

add *pkg* . . .
      For each listed package, write the absolute pathnames of the files listed in its +CONTENTS file together with the package they belong to into the package database. This should be used only by pkg_view(1).

audit [**-es**] [**-t** *type*] [*pkg*] ...
      Check the listed installed packages for vulnerabilities. If no package is given, check all installed packages. If **-e** is given, also include end-of-life information. If **-s** is given, check the signature of the pkg-vulnerabilities file before using it. **-t** restricts the reported vulnerabilities to type *type*.

audit-pkg [**-es**] [**-t** *type*] [*pkg*] ...
      Like **audit**, but check only the given package names or patterns.

audit-batch [**-es**] [**-t** *type*] [*pkg-list*] ...
      Like **audit-pkg**, but read the package names or patterns one per line from the given files.

audit-history [**-s**] [**-t** *type*] [*pkgbase*] ...
> Print all vulnerabilities for the given base package names.

check [*pkg* ...]
> Use this command to check the files belonging to some or all of the packages installed on the local machine against the checksum which was recorded in the +CONTENTS files at package installation time. Symbolic links also have their integrity checked against the recorded value at package installation time. If no additional argument is given, the files of all installed packages are checked, else only the named packages will be checked (wildcards can be used here, see pkg_info(1)).
>
> The packages' +CONTENTS files will be parsed and the checksum will be checked for every file found. A warning message is printed if the expected checksum differs from the checksum of the file on disk. Symbolic links are also checked, ensuring that the targets on disk are the same as the contents recorded at package installation time.

check-license *condition*
> Check if *condition* can be fulfilled with the currently set of accepted licenses. Prints either yes or no to stdout if the condition can be parsed, otherwise it exits with error.

check-pkg-vulnerabilities [**-s**] *file*
> Check format and hashes in the pkg-vulnerabilities file *file*. If **-s** is given, also check the embedded signature.

check-signature *file* ...
> Reports if *file* is a correctly signed package.

check-single-license *license*
> Check if *license* is a valid license name and if it is in the set of acceptable licenses. Prints either yes or no to stdout if the condition can be parsed, otherwise it exits with error.

config-var *variable*
> Print the current value of *variable* as used after parsing the configuration file.

delete *pkg* ...
> For each listed package, remove all file entries in the package database that belong to the package. This should be used only by pkg_view(1).

dump
> Dump the contents of the package database, similar to **pkg_info -F**. Columns are printed for the key field used in the pkgdb - the filename -, and the data field - the package the file belongs to.

fetch-pkg-vulnerabilities [**-su**]
> Fetch a new pkg-vulnerabilities file, check the format and if **-s** is given the signature. If all checks are passed, write it to pkgdb. If **-u** is given, the fetch is conditional and the file transfer is only done if the remote version is newer than the one in pkgdb.

findbest *pattern* ...
> Search the entries of PKG_PATH for packages matching *pattern*. Print the URL of the best matching package to stdout for each pattern. If a pattern is not matched, it is skipped and the command will return a failure.

lsall */dir/pkgpattern*

lsbest */dir/pkgpattern*
> List all/best package matching pattern in the given directory /dir. If the **-d** flag is given, then that directory path overrides /dir. Can be used to work around limitations of /bin/sh and other filename globbing mechanisms. This option implements matching of pkg-wildcards against arbitrary files and directories, useful mainly in the build system itself. See pkg_info(1) for a description of the pattern.

Example:

```
yui# cd /usr/pkgsrc/packages/i386ELF/All/
yui# ls unzip*
unzip-5.40.tgz   unzip-5.41.tgz
yui# pkg_admin lsall 'unzip*'
/usr/pkgsrc/packages/i386ELF/All/unzip-5.40.tgz
/usr/pkgsrc/packages/i386ELF/All/unzip-5.41.tgz
yui# pkg_admin lsall 'unzip≥5.40'
/usr/pkgsrc/packages/i386ELF/All/unzip-5.40.tgz
/usr/pkgsrc/packages/i386ELF/All/unzip-5.41.tgz
yui# pkg_admin lsall 'unzip≥5.41'
/usr/pkgsrc/packages/i386ELF/All/unzip-5.41.tgz
yui# pkg_admin lsbest 'unzip≥5.40'
/usr/pkgsrc/packages/i386ELF/All/unzip-5.41.tgz
yui# pkg_admin lsall /usr/pkgsrc/packages/i386ELF/All/'{mit,unproven}-pthread*
/usr/pkgsrc/packages/i386ELF/All/mit-pthreads-1.60b6.tgz
/usr/pkgsrc/packages/i386ELF/All/unproven-pthreads-0.15.tgz
```

pmatch *pattern pkg*

Returns true if *pkg* matches *pattern*, otherwise returns false.

rebuild

Rebuild the package database mapping from scratch. This option is only intended for recovery after system crashes during package installation and removal.

rebuild-tree

Rebuild the +REQUIRED_BY files from scratch by reresolving all dependencies.

This option is intended to be used for fixing inconsistencies between the records of depending and depended-on packages, such as can arise by the use of **pkg_delete −f**.

set *variable=value pkg* ...

Set variable with information about the installed package. Use **unset** to remove a variable.

Packages that are not installed directly by the user but pulled in as dependencies are marked by setting "automatic=YES".

gpg-sign-package pkg spkg

Sign the binary package *pkg* using GPG and write the result to *spkg*.

x509-sign-package pkg spkg key cert

Sign the binary package *pkg* using the key *key* and the certificate *cert*, using *spkg* as output file.

unset *variable pkg* ...

Remove an installation variable.

ENVIRONMENT

See pkg_install.conf(5) for options, that can also be specified using the environment.

FILES

```
/var/db/pkg/pkgdb.byfile.db
/var/db/pkg/<pkg>/+CONTENTS
```

SEE ALSO

    pkg_add(1), pkg_create(1), pkg_delete(1), pkg_info(1), pkg_view(1), pkg_install.conf(5), pkgsrc(7)

HISTORY

    The **pkg_admin** command first appeared in NetBSD 1.4.

AUTHORS

    The **pkg_admin** command was written by Hubert Feyrer.

NAME

pkg_create — a utility for creating software package distributions

SYNOPSIS

pkg_create [**-ElOUVv**] [**-B** *build-info-file*] [**-b** *build-version-file*] [**-C** *cpkgs*]
          [**-D** *displayfile*] [**-F** *compression*] [**-g** *group*] [**-I** *realprefix*]
          [**-i** *iscript*] [**-K** *pkg_dbdir*] [**-k** *dscript*] [**-n** *preserve-file*]
          [**-P** *dpkgs*] [**-T** *buildpkgs*] [**-p** *prefix*] [**-S** *size-all-file*]
          [**-s** *size-pkg-file*] [**-t** *template*] [**-u** *owner*] **-c** *comment*
          -d *description* **-f** *packlist pkg-name*

DESCRIPTION

The **pkg_create** command is used to create packages that will subsequently be fed to one of the package extraction/info utilities. The input description and command line arguments for the creation of a package are not really meant to be human-generated, though it is easy enough to do so. It is more expected that you will use a front-end tool for the job rather than muddling through it yourself. Nonetheless, a short description of the input syntax is included in this document.

OPTIONS

The following command line options are supported:

-B *build-info-file*

    Install the file *build-info-file* so that users of binary packages can see what make(1) definitions were used to control the build when creating the binary package. This allows various build definitions to be retained in a binary package and viewed wherever it is installed, using pkg_info(1).

-b *build-version-file*

    Install the file *build-version-file* so that users of binary packages can see what versions of the files used to control the build were used when creating the binary package. This allows some fine-grained version control information to be retained in a binary package and viewed wherever it is installed, using pkg_info(1).

-C *cpkgs*

    Set the initial package conflict list to *cpkgs*. This is assumed to be a whitespace separated list of package names and is meant as a convenient shorthand for specifying multiple **@pkgcfl** directives in the packing list (see PACKING LIST DETAILS section below).

-c *[-]desc*

    Fetch package (one line description) from file *desc* or, if preceded by **-**, the argument itself. This string should also give some idea of which version of the product (if any) the package represents.

-D *displayfile*

    Display the file after installing the package. Useful for things like legal notices on almost-free software, etc.

-d *[-]desc*

    Fetch long description for package from file *desc* or, if preceded by **-**, the argument itself.

-E   Add an empty views file to the package.

-F *compression*

    Use *compression* as compression algorithm. This overrides the heuristic to guess the compression type from the output name. Currently supported values are bzip2, gzip, none and xz.

-f *packlist*
> Fetch (packing list) for package from the file *packlist* or **stdin** if *packlist* is a − (dash).

-g *group*
> Make *group* the default group ownership instead of extracting it from the file system.

-I *realprefix*
> Provide the real prefix, as opposed to the staging prefix, for use in staged installations of packages.

-i *iscript*
> Set *iscript* to be the install procedure for the package. This can be any executable program (or shell script). It will be invoked automatically when the package is later installed.

-K *pkg_dbdir*
> Override the value of the PKG_DBDIR configuration option with the value *pkg_dbdir*.

-k *dscript*
> Set *dscript* to be the de-install procedure for the package. This can be any executable program (or shell script). It will be invoked automatically when the package is later (if ever) de-installed.

-l
> Check that any symbolic links which are to be placed in the package are relative to the current prefix. This means using unlink(2) and symlink(2) to remove and re-link any symbolic links which are targeted at full path names.

-n *preserve-file*
> The file is used to denote that the package should not be deleted. This is intended for use where the deletion of packages may present a bootstrap problem.

-O
> Go into a (packing list only) mode. This is used to do (fake pkg_add) operations when a package is installed. In such cases, it is necessary to know what the final, adjusted packing list will look like.

-P *dpkgs*
> Set the initial package dependency list to *dpkgs*. This is assumed to be a whitespace separated list of package names and is meant as a convenient shorthand for specifying multiple **@pkgdep** directives in the packing list (see PACKING LIST DETAILS section below). In addition, the exact versions of the packages referred to in the *dpkgs* list will be added to the packing list in the form of **@blddep** directives.

-T *buildpkgs*
> The exact versions of the packages referred to in the *buildpkgs* list will be added to the packing list in the form of **@blddep** directives. This directives are stored after those created by the **-P** option. *buildpkgs* is assumed to be a whitespace separated list of package names.

-p *prefix*
> Set *prefix* as the initial directory (base) to start from in selecting files for the package.

-S *size-all-file*
> Store the given file for later querying with the pkg_info(1) **-S** flag. The file is expected to contain the size (in bytes) of all files of this package plus any required packages added up and stored as a ASCII string, terminated by a newline.

-s *size-pkg-file*
> Store the given file for later querying with the pkg_info(1) **-s** flag. The file is expected to contain the size (in bytes) of all files of this package added up and stored as a ASCII string, terminated by a newline.

-t *template*

Use *template* as the input to mktemp(3). By default, this is the string /tmp/instmp.XXXXXX, but it may be necessary to override it in the situation where space in your /tmp directory is limited. Be sure to leave some number of 'X' characters for mktemp(3) to fill in with a unique ID.

-U   Do not update the package file database with any file information.

-u *owner*

Make *owner* the default owner instead of extracting it from the file system.

-V   Print version number and exit.

-v   Turn on verbose output.

PACKING LIST DETAILS

The (packing list) format (see **-f**) is fairly simple, being nothing more than a single column of filenames to include in the package. However, since absolute pathnames are generally a bad idea for a package that could be installed potentially anywhere, there is another method of specifying where things are supposed to go and, optionally, what ownership and mode information they should be installed with. This is done by embedding specialized command sequences in the packing list. Briefly described, these sequences are:

@cwd *directory*

Set the internal directory pointer to point to *directory*. All subsequent filenames will be assumed relative to this directory. Note: **@cd** is also an alias for this command.

@src *directory*

This command is supported for compatibility only. It was formerly used to override **@cwd** during package creation.

@exec *command*

Execute *command* as part of the unpacking process. If *command* contains any of the following sequences somewhere in it, they will be expanded inline. For the following examples, assume that **@cwd** is set to /usr/local and the last extracted file was bin/emacs.

%F   Expands to the last filename extracted (as specified), in the example case bin/emacs

%D   Expand to the current directory prefix, as set with **@cwd**, in the example case /usr/local.

%B   Expand to the (basename) of the fully qualified filename, that is the current directory prefix, plus the last filespec, minus the trailing filename. In the example case, that would be /usr/local/bin.

%f   Expand to the (filename) part of the fully qualified name, or the converse of **%B**, being in the example case, emacs.

@unexec *command*

Execute *command* as part of the deinstallation process. Expansion of special **%** sequences is the same as for **@exec**. This command is not executed during the package add, as **@exec** is, but rather when the package is deleted. This is useful for deleting links and other ancillary files that were created as a result of adding the package, but not directly known to the package's table of contents (and hence not automatically removable). The advantage of using **@unexec** over a deinstallation script is that you can use the (special sequence expansion) to get at files regardless of where they've been potentially redirected (see **-p**).

@mode *mode*

Set default permission for all subsequently extracted files to *mode*. Format is the same as that used by the **chmod** command (well, considering that it's later handed off to it, that's no surprise). Use without an arg to set back to default (extraction) permissions.

@option *option*

    Set internal package options, the only currently supported one being *preserve*, which tells pkg_add to move any existing files out of the way, preserving the previous contents (which are also resurrected on pkg_delete, so caveat emptor).

@owner *user*

    Set default ownership for all subsequently extracted files to *user*. Use without an arg to set back to default (extraction) ownership.

@group *group*

    Set default group ownership for all subsequently extracted files to *group*. Use without an arg to set back to default (extraction) group ownership.

@comment *string*

    Embed a comment in the packing list. Useful in trying to document some particularly hairy sequence that may trip someone up later.

@ignore

    Used internally to tell extraction to ignore the next file (don't copy it anywhere), as it's used for some special purpose.

@name *name*

    Set the name of the package. This is mandatory and is usually put at the top. This name is potentially different than the name of the file it came in, and is used when keeping track of the package for later deinstallation. Note that **pkg_create** will derive this field from the *pkg-name* and add it automatically if none is given.

@pkgdir *name*

    Declare directory *name* as managed. If it does not exist at installation time, it is created. If this directory is no longer referenced by packages and the last file or directory in it is deleted, the directory is removed as well.

@dirrm *name*

    This command is supported for compatibility only. If directory *name* exists, it will be deleted at deinstall time.

@display *name*

    Declare *name* as the file to be displayed at install time (see **-D** above).

@pkgdep *pkgname*

    Declare a dependency on the *pkgname* package. The *pkgname* package must be installed before this package may be installed, and this package must be deinstalled before the *pkgname* package is deinstalled. Multiple **@pkgdep** directives may be used if the package depends on multiple other packages.

@blddep *pkgname*

    Declare that this package was built with the exact version of *pkgname* (since the **@pkgdep** directive may contain wildcards or relational package version information).

@pkgcfl *pkgcflname*

    Declare a conflict with the *pkgcflname* package, as the two packages contain references to the same files, and so cannot co-exist on the same system.

ENVIRONMENT

    See pkg_install.conf(5) for options, that can also be specified using the environment.

SEE ALSO

    pkg_add(1), pkg_admin(1), pkg_delete(1), pkg_info(1), pkg_install.conf(5) pkgsrc(7)

HISTORY

    The **pkg_create** command first appeared in FreeBSD.

AUTHORS

    Jordan Hubbard

        most of the work

    John Kohl

        refined it for NetBSD

    Hubert Feyrer

        NetBSD wildcard dependency processing, pkgdb, pkg size recording etc.

NAME
   pkg_delete — a utility for deleting previously installed software package distributions

SYNOPSIS
   pkg_delete [**-ADFfkNnORrVv**] [**-K** *pkg_dbdir*] [**-P** *destdir*] [**-p** *prefix*] *pkg-name*
      . . .

DESCRIPTION
   The **pkg_delete** command is used to delete packages that have been previously installed with the
   pkg_add(1) command. The given packages are sorted, so that the dependencies needed by a package are
   deleted after the package. Before any action is executed, **pkg_delete** checks for packages that are marked
   as **preserved** or have depending packages left. If the **-k** flag is given, preserved packages are skipped
   and not removed. Unless the **-f** flag is given, **pkg_delete** stops on the first error.

WARNING
   Since the **pkg_delete** *command may execute scripts or programs provided by a package file, your system
   may be susceptible to "Trojan horses" or other subtle attacks from miscreants who create dangerous package files.*

   *You are advised to verify the competence and identity of those who provide installable package files. For
   extra protection, examine all the package control files in the package record directory*
   <PKG_DBDIR>/<pkg-name>/). *Pay particular attention to any* +INSTALL *or* +DEINSTALL *files, and
   inspect the* +CONTENTS *file for* **@cwd**, **@mode** *(check for setuid),* **@dirrm**, **@exec**, *and* **@unexec** *directives, and/or use the* pkg_info(1) *command to examine the installed package control files.*

OPTIONS
   The following command line options are supported:

   pkg-name . . .
                   The named packages are deinstalled, wildcards can be used, see pkg_info(1). If no version is
                   given, the one currently installed will be removed. If the **-F** flag is given, one or more (absolute)
                   filenames may be specified and the package database will be consulted for the package to which
                   the given file belongs. These packages are then deinstalled.

   -A   Recursively remove all automatically installed packages that were needed by the given packages
                   and are no longer required. Does not remove manually installed packages; see also the **-R** flag.

   -D   If a deinstallation script exists for a given package, do not execute it.

   -F   Any *pkg-name* given will be interpreted as pathname which is subsequently transformed in a
                   (real) package name via the package database. That way, packages can be deleted by giving a file-
                   name instead of the package-name.

   -f   Force removal of the package, even if a dependency is recorded or the deinstall script fails. This
                   might break the package database; see pkg_admin(1) on how to repair it.

   -ff   Force removal of the package, even if the package is marked as a **preserved** package. Note that
                   this is a dangerous operation. See also the **-k** option.

   -K *pkg_dbdir*
                   Override the value of the PKG_DBDIR configuration option with the value *pkg_dbdir*.

   -k   Silently skip all packages that are marked as **preserved**.

   -N   Remove the package's registration and its entries from the package database, but leave the files
                   installed. Don't run any deinstall scripts or **@unexec** lines either.

-n   Don't actually deinstall a package, just report the steps that would be taken.

-O   Only delete the package's entries from the package database; do not touch the package or its files itself.

-P *destdir*
       Prefix all file and directory names with *destdir*. For packages without install scripts this has the same behavior as using chroot(8).

-p *prefix*
       Set *prefix* as the directory in which to delete files from any installed packages which do not explicitly set theirs. For most packages, the prefix will be set automatically to the installed location by pkg_add(1).

-R   Recursively remove all packages that were needed by the given packages and are no longer required. This option overrides the **-A** flag.

-r   Recursively remove all packages that require one of the packages given.

-V   Print version number and exit.

-v   Turn on verbose output.

TECHNICAL DETAILS

pkg_delete does pretty much what it says. It examines installed package records in `<PKG_DBDIR>/<pkg-name>`, deletes the package contents, and finally removes the package records.

If a package is required by other installed packages, **pkg_delete** will list those dependent packages and refuse to delete the package (unless the **-f** option is given).

If a package has been marked as a **preserved** package, it will not be able to be deleted (unless more than one occurrence of the **-f** option is given).

If a filename is given instead of a package name, the package of which the given file belongs to can be deleted if the **-F** flag is given. The filename needs to be absolute, see the output produced by the pkg_info(1) **-aF** command.

If a **deinstall** script exists for the package, it is executed before and after any files are removed. It is this script's responsibility to clean up any additional messy details around the package's installation, since all **pkg_delete** knows how to do is delete the files created in the original distribution. The **deinstall** script is called as:
     deinstall ⟨*pkg-name*⟩ *VIEW-DEINSTALL*
before removing the package from a view, and as:
     deinstall ⟨*pkg-name*⟩ *DEINSTALL*
before deleting all files and as:
     deinstall ⟨*pkg-name*⟩ *POST-DEINSTALL*
after deleting them. Passing the keywords *VIEW-DEINSTALL*, *DEINSTALL*, and *POST-DEINSTALL* lets you potentially write only one program/script that handles all aspects of installation and deletion.

All scripts are called with the environment variable PKG_PREFIX set to the installation prefix (see the **-p** option above). This allows a package author to write a script that reliably performs some action on the directory where the package is installed, even if the user might have changed it by specifying the **-p** option when running **pkg_delete** or pkg_add(1). The scripts are also called with the PKG_METADATA_DIR environment variable set to the location of the +* meta-data files, and with the PKG_REFCOUNT_D3DIR environment variable set to the location of the package reference counts database directory. If the **-P** flag was given to **pkg_delete**, PKG_DESTDIR will be set to *destdir*.

ENVIRONMENT

See `pkg_install.conf`(5) for options, that can also be specified using the environment.

SEE ALSO

`pkg_add`(1), `pkg_admin`(1), `pkg_create`(1), `pkg_info`(1), `pkg_install.conf`(5) `pkgsrc`(7)

AUTHORS

Jordan Hubbard
        most of the work
John Kohl
        refined it for NetBSD
Hubert Feyrer
        NetBSD wildcard dependency processing, pkgdb, recursive "down" delete, etc.
Joerg Sonnenberger
        Rewrote most of the code to compute correct order of deinstallation and to improve error handling.

NAME

    pkg_info — a utility for displaying information on software packages

SYNOPSIS

    pkg_info [**-BbcDdFfhIikLmNnpqRrSsVvX**] [**-e** *package*] [**-E** *package*]
           [**-K** *pkg_dbdir*] [**-l** *prefix*] *pkg-name* . . .
    pkg_info [**-a** | **-u**] [flags]
    pkg_info [**-Q** *variable*] *pkg-name* . . .

DESCRIPTION

    The **pkg_info** command is used to dump out information for packages, which may be either packed up in files or already installed on the system with the pkg_create(1) command.

    The *pkg-name* may be the name of an installed package (with our without version), a pattern matching several installed packages (see the **PACKAGE WILDCARDS** section for a description of possible patterns), the pathname to a binary package, a filename belonging to an installed package (if **-F** is also given), or a URL to an ftp-available package.

    The following command-line options are supported:

    -a   Show information for all currently installed packages. See also **-u**.

    -B   Show some of the important definitions used when building the binary package (the "Build information") for each package. Additionally, any installation information variables (lowercase) can be queried, too. In particular, *automatic* tells if a package was installed automatically as a dependency of another package.

    -b   Show the NetBSD RCS Id strings from the files used in the construction of the binary package (the "Build version") for each package. These files are the package Makefile, any patch files, any checksum files, and the packing list file.

    -c   Show the one-line comment field for each package.

    -D   Show the install-message file (if any) for each package.

    -d   Show the long-description field for each package.

    -E *pkg-name*
           This option allows you to test for the existence of a given package. If a package identified by *pkg-name* is currently installed, return code is 0, otherwise 1. The name of the best matching package found installed is printed to stdout unless turned off using the **-q** option. *pkg-name* can contain wildcards (see the **PACKAGE WILDCARDS** section below).

    -e *pkg-name*
           This option allows you to test for the existence of a given package. If a package identified by *pkg-name* is currently installed, return code is 0, otherwise 1. The names of any package(s) found installed are printed to stdout unless turned off using the **-q** option. *pkg-name* can contain wildcards (see the **PACKAGE WILDCARDS** section below).

    -F   Interpret any pkg-name given as filename, and translate it to a package name using the package database. This can be used to query information on a per-file basis, e.g. in conjunction with the **-e** flag to find out which package a file belongs to.

    -f   Show the packing list instructions for each package.

    -I   Show the index entry for each package.

-i   Show the install script (if any) for each package.

-K *pkg_dbdir*

Override the value of the PKG_DBDIR configuration option with the value *pkg_dbdir*.

-k   Show the de-install script (if any) for each package.

-L   Show the files within each package. This is different from just viewing the packing list, since full pathnames for everything are generated. Files that were created dynamically during installation of the package are not listed.

-l *str*

Prefix each information category header (see **-q**) shown with *str*. This is primarily of use to front-end programs that want to request a lot of different information fields at once for a package, but don't necessary want the output intermingled in such a way that they can't organize it. This lets you add a special token to the start of each field.

-m   Show the mtree file (if any) for each package.

-N   Show which packages each package was built with (exact dependencies), if any.

-n   Show which packages each package needs (depends upon), if any.

-p   Show the installation prefix for each package.

-Q   Show the definition of *variable* from the build information for each package. An empty string is returned if no such variable definition is found for the package(s).

-q   Be "quiet" in emitting report headers and such, just dump the raw info (basically, assume a non-human reading).

-R   For each package, show the packages that require it.

-r   For each package, show the packages that require it. Continue recursively to show all dependents.

-S   Show the size of this package and all the packages it requires, in bytes.

-s   Show the size of this package in bytes. The size is calculated by adding up the size of each file of the package.

-u   Show information for all user-installed packages. Automatically installed packages (as dependencies of other packages) are not displayed. See also **-a**.

-V   Print version number and exit.

-v   Turn on verbose output.

-X   Print summary information for each package. The summary format is described in pkg_summary(5). Its primary use is to contain all information about the contents of a (remote) binary package repository needed by package managing software.

TECHNICAL DETAILS

Package info is either extracted from package files named on the command line, or from already installed package information in <PKG_DBDIR>/<pkg-name>.

A filename can be given instead of a (installed) package name to query information on the package this file belongs to. This filename is then resolved to a package name using the package database. For this translation to take place, the **-F** flag must be given. The filename must be absolute, compare the output of pkg_info **-aF**.

PACKAGE WILDCARDS

In the places where a package name/version is expected, e.g. for the **−e** switch, several forms can be used. Either use a package name with or without version, or specify a package wildcard that gets matched against all installed packages.

Package wildcards use `fnmatch(3)`. In addition, `csh(1)` style {,} alternates have been implemented. Package version numbers can also be matched in a relational manner using the ≥, ≤, >, and < operators. For example, `pkg_info -e 'name≥1.3'` will match versions 1.3 and later of the `name` package. Additionally, ranges can be defined by giving a lower bound with > or ≥ and an upper bound with < or ≤. The lower bound has to come first. For example, `pkg_info -e 'name≥1.3<2.0'` will match versions 1.3 (inclusive) to 2.0 (exclusive) of package `name`.

The collating sequence of the various package version numbers is unusual, but strives to be consistent. The magic string "alpha" equates to `alpha version` and sorts before a beta version. The magic string "beta" equates to `beta version` and sorts before a release candidate. The magic string "rc" equates to `release candidate` and sorts before a release. The magic string "pre", short for "pre-release", is a synonym for "rc". For example, `name-1.3rc3` will sort before `name-1.3` and after `name-1.2.9`. Similarly `name-1.3alpha2` will sort before `name-1.3beta1` and they both sort before `name-1.3rc1`. In addition, alphabetic characters sort in the same place as their numeric counterparts, so that `name-1.2e` has the same sorting value as `name-1.2.5` The magic string "pl" equates to a `patch level` and has the same value as a dot in the dewey-decimal ordering schemes, as does the underscore '_'.

ENVIRONMENT

See `pkg_install.conf(5)` for options, that can also be specified using the environment.

SEE ALSO

`pkg_add(1)`, `pkg_admin(1)`, `pkg_create(1)`, `pkg_delete(1)`, `pkg_install.conf(5)`
`pkgsrc(7)`

AUTHORS

Jordan Hubbard
    most of the work
John Kohl
    refined it for NetBSD
Hubert Feyrer
    NetBSD wildcard dependency processing, pkgdb, depends displaying, pkg size display etc.

NAME

postalias – Postfix alias database maintenance

SYNOPSIS

postalias [**-Nfinoprsvw**] [**-c** *config_dir*] [**-d** *key*] [**-q** *key*]
    [*file_type:*]*file_name* ...

DESCRIPTION

The **postalias**(1) command creates or queries one or more Postfix alias databases, or updates an existing one. The input and output file formats are expected to be compatible with Sendmail version 8, and are expected to be suitable for the use as NIS alias maps.

If the result files do not exist they will be created with the same group and other read permissions as their source file.

While a database update is in progress, signal delivery is postponed, and an exclusive, advisory, lock is placed on the entire database, in order to avoid surprises in spectator processes.

The format of Postfix alias input files is described in **aliases**(5).

By default the lookup key is mapped to lowercase to make the lookups case insensitive; as of Postfix 2.3 this case folding happens only with tables whose lookup keys are fixed-case strings such as btree:, dbm: or hash:. With earlier versions, the lookup key is folded even with tables where a lookup field can match both upper and lower case text, such as regexp: and pcre:. This resulted in loss of information with $*number* substitutions.

Options:

-c *config_dir*

Read the **main.cf** configuration file in the named directory instead of the default configuration directory.

-d *key*   Search the specified maps for *key* and remove one entry per map. The exit status is zero when the requested information was found.

If a key value of - is specified, the program reads key values from the standard input stream. The exit status is zero when at least one of the requested keys was found.

-f   Do not fold the lookup key to lower case while creating or querying a table.

With Postfix version 2.3 and later, this option has no effect for regular expression tables. There, case folding is controlled by appending a flag to a pattern.

-i   Incremental mode. Read entries from standard input and do not truncate an existing database. By default, **postalias**(1) creates a new database from the entries in *file_name*.

-N   Include the terminating null character that terminates lookup keys and values. By default, **postalias**(1) does whatever is the default for the host operating system.

-n   Don't include the terminating null character that terminates lookup keys and values. By default, **postalias**(1) does whatever is the default for the host operating system.

-o   Do not release root privileges when processing a non-root input file. By default, **postalias**(1) drops root privileges and runs as the source file owner instead.

-p   Do not inherit the file access permissions from the input file when creating a new file. Instead, create a new file with default access permissions (mode 0644).

-q *key*   Search the specified maps for *key* and write the first value found to the standard output stream. The exit status is zero when the requested information was found.

If a key value of - is specified, the program reads key values from the standard input stream and writes one line of *key: value* output for each key that was found. The exit status is zero when at least one of the requested keys was found.

-r   When updating a table, do not complain about attempts to update existing entries, and make those updates anyway.

-s   Retrieve all database elements, and write one line of *key: value* output for each element. The elements are printed in database order, which is not necessarily the same as the original input order. This feature is available in Postfix version 2.2 and later, and is not available for all database types.

-v   Enable verbose logging for debugging purposes. Multiple **-v** options make the software increasingly verbose.

-w   When updating a table, do not complain about attempts to update existing entries, and ignore those attempts.

Arguments:

file_type

The database type. To find out what types are supported, use the "**postconf -m**" command.

The **postalias**(1) command can query any supported file type, but it can create only the following file types:

btree   The output is a btree file, named *file_name***.db**. This is available on systems with support for **db** databases.

cdb   The output is one file named *file_name***.cdb**. This is available on systems with support for **cdb** databases.

dbm   The output consists of two files, named *file_name***.pag** and *file_name***.dir**. This is available on systems with support for **dbm** databases.

hash   The output is a hashed file, named *file_name***.db**. This is available on systems with support for **db** databases.

sdbm   The output consists of two files, named *file_name***.pag** and *file_name***.dir**. This is available on systems with support for **sdbm** databases.

When no *file_type* is specified, the software uses the database type specified via the **default_database_type** configuration parameter. The default value for this parameter depends on the host environment.

file_name

The name of the alias database source file when creating a database.

DIAGNOSTICS

Problems are logged to the standard error stream and to **syslogd**(8). No output means that no problems were detected. Duplicate entries are skipped and are flagged with a warning.

postalias(1) terminates with zero exit status in case of success (including successful "**postalias -q**" lookup) and terminates with non-zero exit status in case of failure.

ENVIRONMENT

MAIL_CONFIG

Directory with Postfix configuration files.

MAIL_VERBOSE

Enable verbose logging for debugging purposes.

CONFIGURATION PARAMETERS

The following **main.cf** parameters are especially relevant to this program.

The text below provides only a parameter summary. See **postconf**(5) for more details including examples.

alias_database (see 'postconf -d' output)
> The alias databases for **local**(8) delivery that are updated with "**newaliases**" or with "**sendmail -bi**".

config_directory (see 'postconf -d' output)
> The default location of the Postfix main.cf and master.cf configuration files.

berkeley_db_create_buffer_size (16777216)
> The per-table I/O buffer size for programs that create Berkeley DB hash or btree tables.

berkeley_db_read_buffer_size (131072)
> The per-table I/O buffer size for programs that read Berkeley DB hash or btree tables.

default_database_type (see 'postconf -d' output)
> The default database type for use in **newaliases**(1), **postalias**(1) and **postmap**(1) commands.

syslog_facility (mail)
> The syslog facility of Postfix logging.

syslog_name (see 'postconf -d' output)
> The mail system name that is prepended to the process name in syslog records, so that "smtpd" becomes, for example, "postfix/smtpd".

STANDARDS
RFC 822 (ARPA Internet Text Messages)

SEE ALSO
aliases(5), format of alias database input file.
local(8), Postfix local delivery agent.
postconf(1), supported database types
postconf(5), configuration parameters
postmap(1), create/update/query lookup tables
newaliases(1), Sendmail compatibility interface.
syslogd(8), system logging

README FILES
Use "**postconf readme_directory**" or "**postconf html_directory**" to locate this information.
DATABASE_README, Postfix lookup table overview

LICENSE
The Secure Mailer license must be distributed with this software.

AUTHOR(S)
Wietse Venema
IBM T.J. Watson Research
P.O. Box 704
Yorktown Heights, NY 10598, USA

NAME

postcat – show Postfix queue file contents

SYNOPSIS

postcat [**-oqv**] [**-c** *config_dir*] [*files...*]

DESCRIPTION

The **postcat**(1) command prints the contents of the named *files* in human-readable form. The files are expected to be in Postfix queue file format. If no *files* are specified on the command line, the program reads from standard input.

Options:

-c *config_dir*

The **main.cf** configuration file is in the named directory instead of the default configuration directory.

-o   Print the queue file offset of each record.

-q   Search the Postfix queue for the named *files* instead of taking the names literally.

Available in Postfix version 2.0 and later.

-v   Enable verbose logging for debugging purposes. Multiple **-v** options make the software increasingly verbose.

DIAGNOSTICS

Problems are reported to the standard error stream.

ENVIRONMENT

MAIL_CONFIG

Directory with Postfix configuration files.

CONFIGURATION PARAMETERS

The following **main.cf** parameters are especially relevant to this program.

The text below provides only a parameter summary. See **postconf**(5) for more details including examples.

config_directory (see 'postconf -d' output)

The default location of the Postfix main.cf and master.cf configuration files.

queue_directory (see 'postconf -d' output)

The location of the Postfix top-level queue directory.

FILES

/var/spool/postfix, Postfix queue directory

SEE ALSO

postconf(5), Postfix configuration

LICENSE

The Secure Mailer license must be distributed with this software.

AUTHOR(S)

Wietse Venema
IBM T.J. Watson Research
P.O. Box 704
Yorktown Heights, NY 10598, USA

NAME

postconf – Postfix configuration utility

SYNOPSIS

postconf [**-dhnv**] [**-c** *config_dir*] [*parameter ...*]

postconf [**-aAmlv**] [**-c** *config_dir*]

postconf [**-ev**] [**-c** *config_dir*] [*parameter=value ...*]

postconf [**-#v**] [**-c** *config_dir*] [*parameter ...*]

postconf [**-btv**] [**-c** *config_dir*] [*template_file*]

DESCRIPTION

The **postconf**(1) command displays the actual values of configuration parameters, changes configuration parameter values, or displays other configuration information about the Postfix mail system.

Options:

-a   List the available SASL server plug-in types. The SASL plug-in type is selected with the **smtpd_sasl_type** configuration parameter by specifying one of the names listed below.

        cyrus   This server plug-in is available when Postfix is built with Cyrus SASL support.

        dovecot
            This server plug-in uses the Dovecot authentication server, and is available when Postfix is built with any form of SASL support.

        This feature is available with Postfix 2.3 and later.

-A   List the available SASL client plug-in types. The SASL plug-in type is selected with the **smtp_sasl_type** or **lmtp_sasl_type** configuration parameters by specifying one of the names listed below.

        cyrus   This client plug-in is available when Postfix is built with Cyrus SASL support.

        This feature is available with Postfix 2.3 and later.

-b [*template_file*]
        Display the message text that appears at the beginning of delivery status notification (DSN) messages, with $**name** expressions replaced by actual values. To override the built-in message text, specify a template file at the end of the command line, or specify a template file in main.cf with the **bounce_template_file** parameter. To force selection of the built-in message text templates, specify an empty template file name (in shell language: "").

        This feature is available with Postfix 2.3 and later.

-c *config_dir*
        The **main.cf** configuration file is in the named directory instead of the default configuration directory.

-d   Print default parameter settings instead of actual settings.

-e   Edit the **main.cf** configuration file. The file is copied to a temporary file then renamed into place. Parameters and values are specified on the command line. Use quotes in order to protect shell metacharacters and whitespace.

-h   Show parameter values only, not the "name = " label that normally precedes the value.

-l   List the names of all supported mailbox locking methods. Postfix supports the following methods:

        flock   A kernel-based advisory locking method for local files only. This locking method is available on systems with a BSD compatible library.

fcntl   A kernel-based advisory locking method for local and remote files.

dotlock

       An application-level locking method. An application locks a file named *filename* by creating a file named *filename*.**lock**. The application is expected to remove its own lock file, as well as stale lock files that were left behind after abnormal termination.

-m   List the names of all supported lookup table types. In Postfix configuration files, lookup tables are specified as *type:name*, where *type* is one of the types listed below. The table *name* syntax depends on the lookup table type as described in the DATABASE_README document.

btree   A sorted, balanced tree structure. This is available on systems with support for Berkeley DB databases.

cdb   A read-optimized structure with no support for incremental updates. This is available on systems with support for CDB databases.

cidr   A table that associates values with Classless Inter-Domain Routing (CIDR) patterns. This is described in **cidr_table**(5).

dbm   An indexed file type based on hashing. This is available on systems with support for DBM databases.

environ

       The UNIX process environment array. The lookup key is the variable name. Originally implemented for testing, someone may find this useful someday.

hash   An indexed file type based on hashing. This is available on systems with support for Berkeley DB databases.

ldap (read-only)

       Perform lookups using the LDAP protocol. This is described in **ldap_table**(5).

mysql (read-only)

       Perform lookups using the MYSQL protocol. This is described in **mysql_table**(5).

pcre (read-only)

       A lookup table based on Perl Compatible Regular Expressions. The file format is described in **pcre_table**(5).

pgsql (read-only)

       Perform lookups using the PostgreSQL protocol. This is described in **pgsql_table**(5).

proxy (read-only)

       A lookup table that is implemented via the Postfix **proxymap**(8) service. The table name syntax is *type:name*.

regexp (read-only)

       A lookup table based on regular expressions. The file format is described in **regexp_table**(5).

sdbm   An indexed file type based on hashing. This is available on systems with support for SDBM databases.

static (read-only)

       A table that always returns its name as lookup result. For example, **static:foobar** always returns the string **foobar** as lookup result.

tcp (read-only)

       Perform lookups using a simple request-reply protocol that is described in **tcp_table**(5). This feature is not included with the stable Postfix release.

unix (read-only)

       A limited way to query the UNIX authentication database. The following tables are implemented:

unix:passwd.byname
> The table is the UNIX password database. The key is a login name. The result is a password file entry in **passwd**(5) format.

unix:group.byname
> The table is the UNIX group database. The key is a group name. The result is a group file entry in **group**(5) format.

Other table types may exist depending on how Postfix was built.

-n   Print parameter settings that are not left at their built-in default value, because they are explicitly specified in main.cf.

-t [*template_file*]
> Display the templates for delivery status notification (DSN) messages. To override the built-in templates, specify a template file at the end of the command line, or specify a template file in main.cf with the **bounce_template_file** parameter. To force selection of the built-in templates, specify an empty template file name (in shell language: "").

> This feature is available with Postfix 2.3 and later.

-v   Enable verbose logging for debugging purposes. Multiple **-v** options make the software increasingly verbose.

-#   Edit the **main.cf** configuration file. The file is copied to a temporary file then renamed into place. The parameters specified on the command line are commented-out, so that they revert to their default values. Specify a list of parameter names, not name=value pairs. There is no **postconf** command to perform the reverse operation.

> This feature is available with Postfix 2.6 and later.

DIAGNOSTICS
Problems are reported to the standard error stream.

ENVIRONMENT
MAIL_CONFIG
> Directory with Postfix configuration files.

CONFIGURATION PARAMETERS
The following **main.cf** parameters are especially relevant to this program.

The text below provides only a parameter summary. See **postconf**(5) for more details including examples.

config_directory (see 'postconf -d' output)
> The default location of the Postfix main.cf and master.cf configuration files.

bounce_template_file (empty)
> Pathname of a configuration file with bounce message templates.

FILES
/etc/postfix/main.cf, Postfix configuration parameters

SEE ALSO
bounce(5), bounce template file format
postconf(5), configuration parameters

README FILES
Use "**postconf readme_directory**" or "**postconf html_directory**" to locate this information.
DATABASE_README, Postfix lookup table overview

LICENSE
The Secure Mailer license must be distributed with this software.

AUTHOR(S)
Wietse Venema
IBM T.J. Watson Research
P.O. Box 704
Yorktown Heights, NY 10598, USA

NAME

postdrop – Postfix mail posting utility

SYNOPSIS

postdrop [-**rv**] [-**c** *config_dir*]

DESCRIPTION

The **postdrop**(1) command creates a file in the **maildrop** directory and copies its standard input to the file.

Options:

-**c** *config_dir*
> The **main.cf** configuration file is in the named directory instead of the default configuration directory. See also the MAIL_CONFIG environment setting below.

-**r**
> Use a Postfix-internal protocol for reading the message from standard input, and for reporting status information on standard output. This is currently the only supported method.

-**v**
> Enable verbose logging for debugging purposes. Multiple -**v** options make the software increasingly verbose. As of Postfix 2.3, this option is available for the super-user only.

SECURITY

The command is designed to run with set-group ID privileges, so that it can write to the **maildrop** queue directory and so that it can connect to Postfix daemon processes.

DIAGNOSTICS

Fatal errors: malformed input, I/O error, out of memory. Problems are logged to **syslogd**(8) and to the standard error stream. When the input is incomplete, or when the process receives a HUP, INT, QUIT or TERM signal, the queue file is deleted.

ENVIRONMENT

MAIL_CONFIG
> Directory with the **main.cf** file. In order to avoid exploitation of set-group ID privileges, a non-standard directory is allowed only if:
> - The name is listed in the standard **main.cf** file with the **alternate_config_directories** configuration parameter.
> - The command is invoked by the super-user.

CONFIGURATION PARAMETERS

The following **main.cf** parameters are especially relevant to this program. The text below provides only a parameter summary. See **postconf**(5) for more details including examples.

alternate_config_directories (empty)
> A list of non-default Postfix configuration directories that may be specified with "-c config_directory" on the command line, or via the MAIL_CONFIG environment parameter.

config_directory (see 'postconf -d' output)
> The default location of the Postfix main.cf and master.cf configuration files.

import_environment (see 'postconf -d' output)
> The list of environment parameters that a Postfix process will import from a non-Postfix parent process.

queue_directory (see 'postconf -d' output)
> The location of the Postfix top-level queue directory.

syslog_facility (mail)
> The syslog facility of Postfix logging.

syslog_name (see 'postconf -d' output)
> The mail system name that is prepended to the process name in syslog records, so that "smtpd" becomes, for example, "postfix/smtpd".

trigger_timeout (10s)
> The time limit for sending a trigger to a Postfix daemon (for example, the **pickup**(8) or **qmgr**(8) daemon).

Available in Postfix version 2.2 and later:

authorized_submit_users (static:anyone)
> List of users who are authorized to submit mail with the **sendmail**(1) command (and with the privileged **postdrop**(1) helper command).

FILES
/var/spool/postfix/maildrop, maildrop queue

SEE ALSO
sendmail(1), compatibility interface
postconf(5), configuration parameters
syslogd(8), system logging

LICENSE
The Secure Mailer license must be distributed with this software.

AUTHOR(S)
Wietse Venema
IBM T.J. Watson Research
P.O. Box 704
Yorktown Heights, NY 10598, USA

NAME
postfix – Postfix control program

SYNOPSIS
postfix [**-Dv**] [**-c** *config_dir*] *command*

DESCRIPTION
This command is reserved for the superuser. To submit mail, use the Postfix **sendmail**(1) command.

The **postfix**(1) command controls the operation of the Postfix mail system: start or stop the **master**(8) daemon, do a health check, and other maintenance.

By default, the **postfix**(1) command sets up a standardized environment and runs the **postfix-script** shell script to do the actual work.

However, when support for multiple Postfix instances is configured, **postfix**(1) executes the command specified with the **multi_instance_wrapper** configuration parameter. This command will execute the *command* for each applicable Postfix instance.

The following commands are implemented:

check   Warn about bad directory/file ownership or permissions, and create missing directories.

start   Start the Postfix mail system. This also runs the configuration check described above.

stop   Stop the Postfix mail system in an orderly fashion. If possible, running processes are allowed to terminate at their earliest convenience.

Note: in order to refresh the Postfix mail system after a configuration change, do not use the **start** and **stop** commands in succession. Use the **reload** command instead.

abort   Stop the Postfix mail system abruptly. Running processes are signaled to stop immediately.

flush   Force delivery: attempt to deliver every message in the deferred mail queue. Normally, attempts to deliver delayed mail happen at regular intervals, the interval doubling after each failed attempt.

Warning: flushing undeliverable mail frequently will result in poor delivery performance of all other mail.

reload   Re-read configuration files. Running processes terminate at their earliest convenience.

status   Indicate if the Postfix mail system is currently running.

set-permissions [*name=value* ...]
Set the ownership and permissions of Postfix related files and directories, as specified in the **postfix-files** file.

Specify *name=value* to override and update specific main.cf configuration parameters. Use this, for example, to change the **mail_owner** or **setgid_group** setting for an already installed Postfix system.

This feature is available in Postfix 2.1 and later. With Postfix 2.0 and earlier, use "**$config_directory/post-install set-permissions**".

upgrade-configuration [*name=value* ...]
Update the **main.cf** and **master.cf** files with information that Postfix needs in order to run: add or update services, and add or update configuration parameter settings.

Specify *name=value* to override and update specific main.cf configuration parameters.

This feature is available in Postfix 2.1 and later. With Postfix 2.0 and earlier, use

"**$config_directory/post-install upgrade-configuration**".

The following options are implemented:

-c *config_dir*

Read the **main.cf** and **master.cf** configuration files in the named directory instead of the default configuration directory. Use this to distinguish between multiple Postfix instances on the same host.

With Postfix 2.6 and later, this option forces the postfix(1) command to operate on the specified Postfix instance only. This behavior is inherited by postfix(1) commands that run as a descendant of the current process.

-D (with **postfix start** only)

Run each Postfix daemon under control of a debugger as specified via the **debugger_command** configuration parameter.

-v

Enable verbose logging for debugging purposes. Multiple **-v** options make the software increasingly verbose.

ENVIRONMENT

The **postfix**(1) command exports the following environment variables before executing the **postfix-script** file:

MAIL_CONFIG

This is set when the -c command-line option is present.

With Postfix 2.6 and later, this environment variable forces the postfix(1) command to operate on the specified Postfix instance only. This behavior is inherited by postfix(1) commands that run as a descendant of the current process.

MAIL_VERBOSE

This is set when the -v command-line option is present.

MAIL_DEBUG

This is set when the -D command-line option is present.

CONFIGURATION PARAMETERS

The following **main.cf** configuration parameters are exported as environment variables with the same names:

command_directory (see 'postconf -d' output)

The location of all postfix administrative commands.

daemon_directory (see 'postconf -d' output)

The directory with Postfix support programs and daemon programs.

config_directory (see 'postconf -d' output)

The default location of the Postfix main.cf and master.cf configuration files.

queue_directory (see 'postconf -d' output)

The location of the Postfix top-level queue directory.

mail_owner (postfix)

The UNIX system account that owns the Postfix queue and most Postfix daemon processes.

setgid_group (postdrop)

The group ownership of set-gid Postfix commands and of group-writable Postfix directories.

sendmail_path (see 'postconf -d' output)

A Sendmail compatibility feature that specifies the location of the Postfix **sendmail**(1) command.

newaliases_path (see 'postconf -d' output)

Sendmail compatibility feature that specifies the location of the **newaliases**(1) command.

mailq_path (see 'postconf -d' output)
Sendmail compatibility feature that specifies where the Postfix **mailq**(1) command is installed.

html_directory (see 'postconf -d' output)
The location of Postfix HTML files that describe how to build, configure or operate a specific Postfix subsystem or feature.

manpage_directory (see 'postconf -d' output)
Where the Postfix manual pages are installed.

readme_directory (see 'postconf -d' output)
The location of Postfix README files that describe how to build, configure or operate a specific Postfix subsystem or feature.

Available in Postfix version 2.5 and later:

data_directory (see 'postconf -d' output)
The directory with Postfix-writable data files (for example: caches, pseudo-random numbers).

Other configuration parameters:

config_directory (see 'postconf -d' output)
The default location of the Postfix main.cf and master.cf configuration files.

import_environment (see 'postconf -d' output)
The list of environment parameters that a Postfix process will import from a non-Postfix parent process.

syslog_facility (mail)
The syslog facility of Postfix logging.

syslog_name (see 'postconf -d' output)
The mail system name that is prepended to the process name in syslog records, so that "smtpd" becomes, for example, "postfix/smtpd".

Available in Postfix version 2.6 and later:

multi_instance_directories (empty)
An optional list of non-default Postfix configuration directories; these directories belong to additional Postfix instances that share the Postfix executable files and documentation with the default Postfix instance, and that are started, stopped, etc., together with the default Postfix instance.

multi_instance_wrapper (empty)
The pathname of a multi-instance manager command that the **postfix**(1) command invokes when the multi_instance_directories parameter value is non-empty.

multi_instance_group (empty)
The optional instance group name of this Postfix instance.

multi_instance_name (empty)
The optional instance name of this Postfix instance.

multi_instance_enable (no)
Allow this Postfix instance to be started, stopped, etc., by a multi-instance manager.

FILES

Prior to Postfix version 2.6, all of the following files were in **$config_directory**. Some files are now in **$daemon_directory** so that they can be shared among multiple instances that run the same Postfix version.

Use the command "**postconf config_directory**" or "**postconf daemon_directory**" to expand the names into their actual values.

$config_directory/main.cf, Postfix configuration parameters
$config_directory/master.cf, Postfix daemon processes
$daemon_directory/postfix-files, file/directory permissions

$daemon_directory/postfix-script, administrative commands
$daemon_directory/post-install, post-installation configuration

SEE ALSO

Commands:
postalias(1), create/update/query alias database
postcat(1), examine Postfix queue file
postconf(1), Postfix configuration utility
postfix(1), Postfix control program
postkick(1), trigger Postfix daemon
postlock(1), Postfix-compatible locking
postlog(1), Postfix-compatible logging
postmap(1), Postfix lookup table manager
postmulti(1), Postfix multi-instance manager
postqueue(1), Postfix mail queue control
postsuper(1), Postfix housekeeping
mailq(1), Sendmail compatibility interface
newaliases(1), Sendmail compatibility interface
sendmail(1), Sendmail compatibility interface

Postfix configuration:
bounce(5), Postfix bounce message templates
master(5), Postfix master.cf file syntax
postconf(5), Postfix main.cf file syntax
postfix-wrapper(5), Postfix multi-instance API

Table-driven mechanisms:
access(5), Postfix SMTP access control table
aliases(5), Postfix alias database
canonical(5), Postfix input address rewriting
generic(5), Postfix output address rewriting
header_checks(5), body_checks(5), Postfix content inspection
relocated(5), Users that have moved
transport(5), Postfix routing table
virtual(5), Postfix virtual aliasing

Table lookup mechanisms:
cidr_table(5), Associate CIDR pattern with value
ldap_table(5), Postfix LDAP client
mysql_table(5), Postfix MYSQL client
nisplus_table(5), Postfix NIS+ client
pcre_table(5), Associate PCRE pattern with value
pgsql_table(5), Postfix PostgreSQL client
regexp_table(5), Associate POSIX regexp pattern with value
tcp_table(5), Postfix client-server table lookup

Daemon processes:
anvil(8), Postfix connection/rate limiting
bounce(8), defer(8), trace(8), Delivery status reports
cleanup(8), canonicalize and enqueue message
discard(8), Postfix discard delivery agent
error(8), Postfix error delivery agent
flush(8), Postfix fast ETRN service
local(8), Postfix local delivery agent
master(8), Postfix master daemon

oqmgr(8), old Postfix queue manager
pickup(8), Postfix local mail pickup
pipe(8), deliver mail to non-Postfix command
proxymap(8), Postfix lookup table proxy server
qmgr(8), Postfix queue manager
qmqpd(8), Postfix QMQP server
scache(8), Postfix connection cache manager
showq(8), list Postfix mail queue
smtp(8), lmtp(8), Postfix SMTP+LMTP client
smtpd(8), Postfix SMTP server
spawn(8), run non-Postfix server
tlsmgr(8), Postfix TLS cache and randomness manager
trivial-rewrite(8), Postfix address rewriting
verify(8), Postfix address verification
virtual(8), Postfix virtual delivery agent

Other:
syslogd(8), system logging

README FILES

Use "**postconf readme_directory**" or "**postconf html_directory**" to locate this information.
OVERVIEW, overview of Postfix commands and processes
BASIC_CONFIGURATION_README, Postfix basic configuration
ADDRESS_REWRITING_README, Postfix address rewriting
SMTPD_ACCESS_README, SMTP relay/access control
CONTENT_INSPECTION_README, Postfix content inspection
QSHAPE_README, Postfix queue analysis

LICENSE

The Secure Mailer license must be distributed with this software.

AUTHOR(S)

Wietse Venema
IBM T.J. Watson Research
P.O. Box 704
Yorktown Heights, NY 10598, USA

TLS support by:
Lutz Jaenicke
Brandenburg University of Technology
Cottbus, Germany

Victor Duchovni
Morgan Stanley

SASL support originally by:
Till Franke
SuSE Rhein/Main AG
65760 Eschborn, Germany

LMTP support originally by:
Philip A. Prindeville
Mirapoint, Inc.
USA.

Amos Gouaux

University of Texas at Dallas
P.O. Box 830688, MC34
Richardson, TX 75083, USA

IPv6 support originally by:
Mark Huizer, Eindhoven University, The Netherlands
Jun-ichiro 'itojun' Hagino, KAME project, Japan
The Linux PLD project
Dean Strik, Eindhoven University, The Netherlands

NAME

   postinstall — check and fix installation after system upgrades

SYNOPSIS

   postinstall [**-a** *arch*] [**-d** *destdir*] [**-m** *machine*]
                [**-s** {*srcdir* | *tgzdir* | *tgzfile*}] *operation* [*item* [...]]

DESCRIPTION

   The **postinstall** utility performs post-installation checks and/or fixes on a system's configuration files.
   It is especially useful after system upgrades, e.g. after updating from NetBSD 1.6.2 to NetBSD 2.0. The items
   to check or fix are divided in two groups: enabled by default and disabled by default. The latter are items
   that are dangerous for some reason, for example because they remove files which may be still in use. If no
   items are provided, the default checks or fixes are applied. Those which are disabled by default must be
   provided explicitly.

   Supported options:

   -a *arch*   MACHINE_ARCH. Defaults to machine of the host operating system.

   -d *destdir*   Destination directory to check. Defaults to /.

   -m *machine*   MACHINE. Defaults to machine of the host operating system.

   -s {*srcdir* | *tgzdir* | *tgzfile*}
                   The location of the reference files, or the NetBSD source files used to create the
                   reference files. This may be specified in one of three ways:

                   -s *srcdir*   The top level directory of the NetBSD source tree. By default
                                   this is /usr/src.

                   -s *tgzdir*   A directory in which reference files have been extracted from
                                   a binary distribution of NetBSD. The files that are distributed
                                   in the "etc.tgz" set file must be present. The files that are
                                   distributed in the "xetc.tgz" set file are optional.

                   -s *tgzfile*   The location of a set file (or "tgz file") such as "etc.tgz"
                                   or "xetc.tgz" from a binary distribution of NetBSD. Each
                                   set file is a compressed archive containing reference files,
                                   which will be extracted to the temproot directory. Multi-
                                   ple **-s** options may be used to specify multiple set files. The
                                   "etc.tgz" set file must be specified. The "xetc.tgz" set
                                   file is optional.

   The *operation* argument may be one of:

   check   Perform post-installation checks on items.

   diff [diff(1) options]
             Similar to **check**, but also show the differences between the files.

   fix   Apply fixes that **check** determines need to be applied. Not all items can be automati-
             cally fixed by **postinstall**, and in some cases an error will be reported, after which
             manual intervention will be required.

             Conflicts between existing files in the target file system and new files from the NetBSD
             distribution are resolved by replacing the existing file with the new file; there is no
             attempt to merge the files. See etcupdate(8) for an alternative update method that is
             able to merge files.

       help   Display a short help.

       list   List available *items*, showing if they are enabled or disabled by default.

       usage   Same as **help**.

EXIT STATUS

The **postinstall** utility exits 0 on success, and >0 if an error occurs or a problem was found.

SEE ALSO

etcupdate(8)

HISTORY

The **postinstall** utility first appeared in NetBSD 1.6.

In NetBSD 4.0, the **−s** *tgzfile* option was added.

In NetBSD 5.0, the ability to specify multiple colon-separated files with a single **−s** option was deprecated.

NAME
postkick – kick a Postfix service

SYNOPSIS
postkick [**-c** *config_dir*] [**-v**] *class service request*

DESCRIPTION
The **postkick**(1) command sends *request* to the specified *service* over a local transport channel. This command makes Postfix private IPC accessible for use in, for example, shell scripts.

Options:

-c *config_dir*
> Read the **main.cf** configuration file in the named directory instead of the default configuration directory.

-v
> Enable verbose logging for debugging purposes. Multiple **-v** options make the software increasingly verbose.

Arguments:

class
> Name of a class of local transport channel endpoints, either **public** (accessible by any local user) or **private** (administrative access only).

service The name of a local transport endpoint within the named class.

request A string. The list of valid requests is service-specific.

DIAGNOSTICS
Problems and transactions are logged to the standard error stream.

ENVIRONMENT
MAIL_CONFIG
> Directory with Postfix configuration files.

MAIL_VERBOSE
> Enable verbose logging for debugging purposes.

CONFIGURATION PARAMETERS
The following **main.cf** parameters are especially relevant to this program. The text below provides only a parameter summary. See **postconf**(5) for more details including examples.

config_directory (see 'postconf -d' output)
> The default location of the Postfix main.cf and master.cf configuration files.

application_event_drain_time (100s)
> How long the **postkick**(1) command waits for a request to enter the server's input buffer before giving up.

queue_directory (see 'postconf -d' output)
> The location of the Postfix top-level queue directory.

FILES
/var/spool/postfix/private, private class endpoints
/var/spool/postfix/public, public class endpoints

SEE ALSO
qmgr(8), queue manager trigger protocol
pickup(8), local pickup daemon
postconf(5), configuration parameters

LICENSE
The Secure Mailer license must be distributed with this software.

POSTKICK(1)

AUTHOR(S)
Wietse Venema
IBM T.J. Watson Research
P.O. Box 704
Yorktown Heights, NY 10598, USA

NAME

postlock – lock mail folder and execute command

SYNOPSIS

postlock [**-c** *config_dir*] [**-l** *lock_style*]
    [**-v**] *file command...*

DESCRIPTION

The **postlock**(1) command locks *file* for exclusive access, and executes *command*. The locking method is compatible with the Postfix UNIX-style local delivery agent.

Options:

-c *config_dir*
    Read the **main.cf** configuration file in the named directory instead of the default configuration directory.

-l *lock_style*
    Override the locking method specified via the **mailbox_delivery_lock** configuration parameter (see below).

-v   Enable verbose logging for debugging purposes. Multiple **-v** options make the software increasingly verbose.

Arguments:

file   A mailbox file. The user should have read/write permission.

command...
    The command to execute while *file* is locked for exclusive access. The command is executed directly, i.e. without interpretation by a shell command interpreter.

DIAGNOSTICS

The result status is 75 (EX_TEMPFAIL) when **postlock**(1) could not perform the requested operation. Otherwise, the exit status is the exit status from the command.

BUGS

With remote file systems, the ability to acquire a lock does not necessarily eliminate access conflicts. Avoid file access by processes running on different machines.

ENVIRONMENT

MAIL_CONFIG

Directory with Postfix configuration files.

MAIL_VERBOSE

Enable verbose logging for debugging purposes.

CONFIGURATION PARAMETERS

The following **main.cf** parameters are especially relevant to this program. The text below provides only a parameter summary. See **postconf**(5) for more details including examples.

LOCKING CONTROLS

deliver_lock_attempts (20)

The maximal number of attempts to acquire an exclusive lock on a mailbox file or **bounce**(8) logfile.

deliver_lock_delay (1s)

The time between attempts to acquire an exclusive lock on a mailbox file or **bounce**(8) logfile.

stale_lock_time (500s)

The time after which a stale exclusive mailbox lockfile is removed.

mailbox_delivery_lock (see 'postconf -d' output)

How to lock a UNIX-style **local**(8) mailbox before attempting delivery.

RESOURCE AND RATE CONTROLS

fork_attempts (5)

> The maximal number of attempts to fork() a child process.

fork_delay (1s)

> The delay between attempts to fork() a child process.

MISCELLANEOUS CONTROLS

config_directory (see 'postconf -d' output)

> The default location of the Postfix main.cf and master.cf configuration files.

SEE ALSO

postconf(5), configuration parameters

LICENSE

The Secure Mailer license must be distributed with this software.

AUTHOR(S)

Wietse Venema
IBM T.J. Watson Research
P.O. Box 704
Yorktown Heights, NY 10598, USA

NAME
postlog – Postfix-compatible logging utility

SYNOPSIS
postlog [**-iv**] [**-c** *config_dir*] [**-p** *priority*] [**-t** *tag*] [*text...*]

DESCRIPTION
The **postlog**(1) command implements a Postfix-compatible logging interface for use in, for example, shell scripts.

By default, **postlog**(1) logs the *text* given on the command line as one record. If no *text* is specified on the command line, **postlog**(1) reads from standard input and logs each input line as one record.

Logging is sent to **syslogd**(8); when the standard error stream is connected to a terminal, logging is sent there as well.

The following options are implemented:

-c *config_dir*
> Read the **main.cf** configuration file in the named directory instead of the default configuration directory.

-i
> Include the process ID in the logging tag.

-p *priority*
> Specifies the logging severity: **info** (default), **warn**, **error**, **fatal**, or **panic**.

-t *tag*
> Specifies the logging tag, that is, the identifying name that appears at the beginning of each logging record. A default tag is used when none is specified.

-v
> Enable verbose logging for debugging purposes. Multiple **-v** options make the software increasingly verbose.

ENVIRONMENT
MAIL_CONFIG
> Directory with the **main.cf** file.

CONFIGURATION PARAMETERS
The following **main.cf** parameters are especially relevant to this program.

The text below provides only a parameter summary. See **postconf**(5) for more details including examples.

config_directory (see 'postconf -d' output)
> The default location of the Postfix main.cf and master.cf configuration files.

syslog_facility (mail)
> The syslog facility of Postfix logging.

syslog_name (see 'postconf -d' output)
> The mail system name that is prepended to the process name in syslog records, so that "smtpd" becomes, for example, "postfix/smtpd".

SEE ALSO
postconf(5), configuration parameters
syslogd(8), syslog daemon

LICENSE
The Secure Mailer license must be distributed with this software.

AUTHOR(S)
Wietse Venema
IBM T.J. Watson Research
P.O. Box 704

Yorktown Heights, NY 10598, USA

NAME
postmap – Postfix lookup table management

SYNOPSIS
postmap [**-Nbfhimnoprsvw**] [**-c** *config_dir*] [**-d** *key*] [**-q** *key*]
    [*file_type*:]*file_name* ...

DESCRIPTION
The **postmap**(1) command creates or queries one or more Postfix lookup tables, or updates an existing one. The input and output file formats are expected to be compatible with:

    makemap *file_type file_name* < *file_name*

If the result files do not exist they will be created with the same group and other read permissions as their source file.

While the table update is in progress, signal delivery is postponed, and an exclusive, advisory, lock is placed on the entire table, in order to avoid surprises in spectator processes.

INPUT FILE FORMAT
The format of a lookup table input file is as follows:

- A table entry has the form

    key whitespace *value*

- Empty lines and whitespace-only lines are ignored, as are lines whose first non-whitespace character is a '#'.

- A logical line starts with non-whitespace text. A line that starts with whitespace continues a logical line.

The *key* and *value* are processed as is, except that surrounding white space is stripped off. Unlike with Postfix alias databases, quotes cannot be used to protect lookup keys that contain special characters such as '#' or whitespace.

By default the lookup key is mapped to lowercase to make the lookups case insensitive; as of Postfix 2.3 this case folding happens only with tables whose lookup keys are fixed-case strings such as btree:, dbm: or hash:. With earlier versions, the lookup key is folded even with tables where a lookup field can match both upper and lower case text, such as regexp: and pcre:. This resulted in loss of information with $*number* substitutions.

COMMAND-LINE ARGUMENTS
-b   Enable message body query mode. When reading lookup keys from standard input with "**-q -**", process the input as if it is an email message in RFC 2822 format. Each line of body content becomes one lookup key.

    By default, the **-b** option starts generating lookup keys at the first non-header line, and stops when the end of the message is reached. To simulate **body_checks**(5) processing, enable MIME parsing with **-m**. With this, the **-b** option generates no body-style lookup keys for attachment MIME headers and for attached message/* headers.

    This feature is available in Postfix version 2.6 and later.

-c *config_dir*
    Read the **main.cf** configuration file in the named directory instead of the default configuration directory.

-d *key*   Search the specified maps for *key* and remove one entry per map. The exit status is zero when the requested information was found.

1

If a key value of - is specified, the program reads key values from the standard input stream. The exit status is zero when at least one of the requested keys was found.

-f   Do not fold the lookup key to lower case while creating or querying a table.

With Postfix version 2.3 and later, this option has no effect for regular expression tables. There, case folding is controlled by appending a flag to a pattern.

-h   Enable message header query mode. When reading lookup keys from standard input with "**-q** -", process the input as if it is an email message in RFC 2822 format. Each logical header line becomes one lookup key. A multi-line header becomes one lookup key with one or more embedded newline characters.

By default, the **-h** option generates lookup keys until the first non-header line is reached. To simulate **header_checks**(5) processing, enable MIME parsing with **-m**. With this, the **-h** option also generates header-style lookup keys for attachment MIME headers and for attached message/* headers.

This feature is available in Postfix version 2.6 and later.

-i   Incremental mode. Read entries from standard input and do not truncate an existing database. By default, **postmap**(1) creates a new database from the entries in **file_name**.

-m   Enable MIME parsing with "**-b**" and "**-h**".

This feature is available in Postfix version 2.6 and later.

-N   Include the terminating null character that terminates lookup keys and values. By default, **postmap**(1) does whatever is the default for the host operating system.

-n   Don't include the terminating null character that terminates lookup keys and values. By default, **postmap**(1) does whatever is the default for the host operating system.

-o   Do not release root privileges when processing a non-root input file. By default, **postmap**(1) drops root privileges and runs as the source file owner instead.

-p   Do not inherit the file access permissions from the input file when creating a new file. Instead, create a new file with default access permissions (mode 0644).

-q *key* Search the specified maps for *key* and write the first value found to the standard output stream. The exit status is zero when the requested information was found.

If a key value of - is specified, the program reads key values from the standard input stream and writes one line of *key value* output for each key that was found. The exit status is zero when at least one of the requested keys was found.

-r   When updating a table, do not complain about attempts to update existing entries, and make those updates anyway.

-s   Retrieve all database elements, and write one line of *key value* output for each element. The elements are printed in database order, which is not necessarily the same as the original input order.

This feature is available in Postfix version 2.2 and later, and is not available for all database types.

-v   Enable verbose logging for debugging purposes. Multiple **-v** options make the software increasingly verbose.

-w   When updating a table, do not complain about attempts to update existing entries, and ignore those attempts.

Arguments:

file_type
> The database type. To find out what types are supported, use the "**postconf -m**" command.
>
> The **postmap**(1) command can query any supported file type, but it can create only the following file types:
>
> **btree**   The output file is a btree file, named *file_name*.**db**. This is available on systems with support for **db** databases.
>
> **cdb**   The output consists of one file, named *file_name*.**cdb**. This is available on systems with support for **cdb** databases.
>
> **dbm**   The output consists of two files, named *file_name*.**pag** and *file_name*.**dir**. This is available on systems with support for **dbm** databases.
>
> **hash**   The output file is a hashed file, named *file_name*.**db**. This is available on systems with support for **db** databases.
>
> **sdbm**   The output consists of two files, named *file_name*.**pag** and *file_name*.**dir**. This is available on systems with support for **sdbm** databases.
>
> When no *file_type* is specified, the software uses the database type specified via the **default_database_type** configuration parameter.

file_name
> The name of the lookup table source file when rebuilding a database.

DIAGNOSTICS
Problems are logged to the standard error stream and to **syslogd**(8). No output means that no problems were detected. Duplicate entries are skipped and are flagged with a warning.

postmap(1) terminates with zero exit status in case of success (including successful "**postmap -q**" lookup) and terminates with non-zero exit status in case of failure.

ENVIRONMENT
MAIL_CONFIG
> Directory with Postfix configuration files.

MAIL_VERBOSE
> Enable verbose logging for debugging purposes.

CONFIGURATION PARAMETERS
The following **main.cf** parameters are especially relevant to this program. The text below provides only a parameter summary. See **postconf**(5) for more details including examples.

berkeley_db_create_buffer_size (16777216)
> The per-table I/O buffer size for programs that create Berkeley DB hash or btree tables.

berkeley_db_read_buffer_size (131072)
> The per-table I/O buffer size for programs that read Berkeley DB hash or btree tables.

config_directory (see 'postconf -d' output)
> The default location of the Postfix main.cf and master.cf configuration files.

default_database_type (see 'postconf -d' output)
> The default database type for use in **newaliases**(1), **postalias**(1) and **postmap**(1) commands.

syslog_facility (mail)
> The syslog facility of Postfix logging.

syslog_name (see 'postconf -d' output)
> The mail system name that is prepended to the process name in syslog records, so that "smtpd" becomes, for example, "postfix/smtpd".

3

POSTMAP(1)   POSTMAP(1)

SEE ALSO
> postalias(1), create/update/query alias database
> postconf(1), supported database types
> postconf(5), configuration parameters
> syslogd(8), system logging

README FILES
> Use "**postconf readme_directory**" or "**postconf html_directory**" to locate this information.
> DATABASE_README, Postfix lookup table overview

LICENSE
> The Secure Mailer license must be distributed with this software.

AUTHOR(S)
> Wietse Venema
> IBM T.J. Watson Research
> P.O. Box 704
> Yorktown Heights, NY 10598, USA

NAME
>   postmulti – Postfix multi-instance manager

SYNOPSIS
>   **postmulti -l** [-**aRv**] [-**g** *group*] [-**i** *name*]
>
>   **postmulti -p** [-**av**] [-**g** *group*] [-**i** *name*] *command...*
>
>   **postmulti -x** [-**aRv**] [-**g** *group*] [-**i** *name*] *command...*
>
>   **postmulti -e init** [-**v**]
>
>   **postmulti -e create** [-**av**] [-**g** *group*] [-**i** *name*] [-**G** *group*] [-**I** *name*] [*param=value ...*]
>
>   **postmulti -e import** [-**av**] [-**g** *group*] [-**i** *name*] [-**G** *group*] [-**I** *name*] [**config_directory=**/*path*]
>
>   **postmulti -e destroy** [-**v**] -**i** *name*
>
>   **postmulti -e deport** [-**v**] -**i** *name*
>
>   **postmulti -e enable** [-**v**] -**i** *name*
>
>   **postmulti -e disable** [-**v**] -**i** *name*
>
>   **postmulti -e assign** [-**v**] -**i** *name* [-**I** *name*] [-**G** *group*]

DESCRIPTION
>   The **postmulti**(1) command allows a Postfix administrator to manage multiple Postfix instances on a single host.
>
>   **postmulti**(1) implements two fundamental modes of operation. In **iterator** mode, it executes the same command for multiple Postfix instances. In **life-cycle management** mode, it adds or deletes one instance, or changes the multi-instance status of one instance.
>
>   Each mode of operation has its own command syntax. For this reason, each mode is documented in separate sections below.

BACKGROUND
>   A multi-instance configuration consists of one primary Postfix instance, and one or more secondary instances whose configuration directory pathnames are recorded in the primary instance's main.cf file. Postfix instances share program files and documentation, but have their own configuration, queue and data directories.
>
>   Currently, only the default Postfix instance can be used as primary instance in a multi-instance configuration. The **postmulti**(1) command does not currently support a **-c** option to select an alternative primary instance, and exits with a fatal error if the **MAIL_CONFIG** environment variable is set to a non-default configuration directory.
>
>   See the MULTI_INSTANCE_README tutorial for a more detailed discussion of multi-instance management with **postmulti**(1).

ITERATOR MODE
>   In iterator mode, **postmulti** performs the same operation on all Postfix instances in turn.
>
>   If multi-instance support is not enabled, the requested command is performed just for the primary instance.
>
>   Iterator mode implements the following command options:

Instance selection

    -a   Perform the operation on all instances. This is the default.

    -g *group*

            Perform the operation only for members of the named *group*.

    -i *name* Perform the operation only for the instance with the specified *name*. You can specify either the instance name or the absolute pathname of the instance's configuration directory. Specify "-" to select the primary Postfix instance.

    -R   Reverse the iteration order. This may be appropriate when updating a multi-instance system, where "sink" instances are started before "source" instances.

            This option cannot be used with **-p**.

List mode

    -l   List Postfix instances with their instance name, instance group name, enable/disable status and configuration directory.

Postfix-wrapper mode

    -p   Invoke **postfix(1)** to execute the specified *command*. This option implements the **postfix-wrapper**(5) interface.

        •   With "start"-like commands, "postfix check" is executed for instances that are not enabled. The full list of commands is specified with the postmulti_start_commands parameter.

        •   With "stop"-like commands, the iteration order is reversed, and disabled instances are skipped. The full list of commands is specified with the postmulti_stop_commands parameter.

        •   With "reload" and other commands that require a started instance, disabled instances are skipped. The full list of commands is specified with the postmulti_control_commands parameter.

        •   With "status" and other commands that don't require a started instance, the command is executed for all instances.

            The **-p** option can also be used interactively to start/stop/etc. a named instance or instance group. For example, to start just the instances in the group "msa", invoke **postmulti**(1) as follows:

                # postmulti -g msa -p start

Command mode

    -x   Execute the specified *command* for all Postfix instances. The command runs with appropriate environment settings for MAIL_CONFIG, command_directory, daemon_directory, config_directory, queue_directory, data_directory, multi_instance_name, multi_instance_group and multi_instance_enable.

Other options

    -v   Enable verbose logging for debugging purposes. Multiple **-v** options make the software increasingly verbose.

LIFE-CYCLE MANAGEMENT MODE

    With the **-e** option **postmulti**(1) can be used to add or delete a Postfix instance, and to manage the multi-instance status of an existing instance.

    The following options are implemented:

Existing instance selection

    -a   When creating or importing an instance, place the new instance at the front of the secondary instance list.

-g *group*

> When creating or importing an instance, place the new instance before the first secondary instance that is a member of the specified group.

-i *name*   When creating or importing an instance, place the new instance before the matching secondary instance.

> With other life-cycle operations, apply the operation to the named existing instance. Specify "-" to select the primary Postfix instance.

New or existing instance name assignment

-I *name*

> Assign the specified instance *name* to an existing instance, newly-created instance, or imported instance. Instance names other than "-" (which makes the instance "nameless") must start with "postfix-". This restriction reduces the likelihood of name collisions with system files.

-G *group*

> Assign the specified *group* name to an existing instance or to a newly created or imported instance.

Instance creation/deletion/status change

-e *action*

> "Edit" managed instances. The following actions are supported:

> **init**   This command is required before **postmulti**(1) can be used to manage Postfix instances. The "postmulti -e init" command updates the primary instance's main.cf file by setting:

>> multi_instance_wrapper =
>>> ${command_directory}/postmulti -p --
>> multi_instance_enable = yes

> You can set these by other means if you prefer.

> **create**   Create a new Postfix instance and add it to the multi_instance_directories parameter of the primary instance. The "**-I** *name*" option is recommended to give the instance a short name that is used to construct default values for the private directories of the new instance. The "**-G** *group*" option may be specified to assign the instance to a group, otherwise, the new instance is not a member of any groups.

> The new instance main.cf is the stock main.cf with the parameters that specify the locations of shared files cloned from the primary instance. For "nameless" instances, you should manually adjust "syslog_name" to yield a unique "logtag" starting with "postfix-" that will uniquely identify the instance in the mail logs. It is simpler to assign the instance a short name with the "**-I** *name*" option.

> Optional "name=value" arguments specify the instance config_directory, queue_directory and data_directory. For example:

>> # postmulti -I postfix-mumble \
>>> -G mygroup -e create \
>>> config_directory=/my/config/dir \
>>> queue_directory=/my/queue/dir \
>>> data_directory=/my/data/dir

> If any of these pathnames is not supplied, the program attempts to generate the pathname by taking the corresponding primary instance pathname, and by replacing the last pathname component by the value of the **-I** option.

> If the instance configuration directory already exists, and contains both a main.cf and master.cf file, **create** will "import" the instance as-is. For existing instances, **create** and **import** are identical.

import   Import an existing instance into the list of instances managed by the **postmulti**(1) multi-instance manager. This adds the instance to the multi_instance_directories list of the primary instance. If the "**-I** *name*" option is provided it specifies the new name for the instance and is used to define a default location for the instance configuration directory (as with **create** above). The "**-G** *group*" option may be used to assign the instance to a group. Add a "**config_directory=***/path*" argument to override a default pathname based on "**-I** *name*".

destroy

Destroy a secondary Postfix instance. To be a candidate for destruction an instance must be disabled, stopped and its queue must not contain any messages. Attempts to destroy the primary Postfix instance trigger a fatal error, without destroying the instance.

The instance is removed from the primary instance main.cf file's alternate_config_directories parameter and its data, queue and configuration directories are cleaned of files and directories created by the Postfix system. The main.cf and master.cf files are removed from the configuration directory even if they have been modified since initial creation. Finally, the instance is "deported" from the list of managed instances.

If other files are present in instance private directories, the directories may not be fully removed, a warning is logged to alert the administrator. It is expected that an instance built using "fresh" directories via the **create** action will be fully removed by the **destroy** action (if first disabled). If the instance configuration and queue directories are populated with additional files (access and rewriting tables, chroot jail content, etc.) the instance directories will not be fully removed.

The **destroy** action triggers potentially dangerous file removal operations. Make sure the instance's data, queue and configuration directories are set correctly and do not contain any valuable files.

deport   Deport a secondary instance from the list of managed instances. This deletes the instance configuration directory from the primary instance's multi_instance_directories list, but does not remove any files or directories.

assign   Assign a new instance name or a new group name to the selected instance. Use "**-G** -" to specify "no group" and "**-I** -" to specify "no name". If you choose to make an instance "nameless", set a suitable syslog_name in the corresponding main.cf file.

enable   Mark the selected instance as enabled. This just sets the multi_instance_enable parameter to "yes" in the instance's main.cf file.

disable   Mark the selected instance as disabled. This means that the instance will not be started etc. with "postfix start", "postmulti -p start" and so on. The instance can still be started etc. with "postfix -c config-directory start".

Other options

-v   Enable verbose logging for debugging purposes. Multiple **-v** options make the software increasingly verbose.

ENVIRONMENT

The **postmulti**(1) command exports the following environment variables before executing the requested *command* for a given instance:

MAIL_VERBOSE

This is set when the -v command-line option is present.

MAIL_CONFIG

The location of the configuration directory of the instance.

CONFIGURATION PARAMETERS

config_directory (see 'postconf -d' output)

The default location of the Postfix main.cf and master.cf configuration files.

daemon_directory (see 'postconf -d' output)

The directory with Postfix support programs and daemon programs.

import_environment (see 'postconf -d' output)

The list of environment parameters that a Postfix process will import from a non-Postfix parent process.

multi_instance_directories (empty)

An optional list of non-default Postfix configuration directories; these directories belong to additional Postfix instances that share the Postfix executable files and documentation with the default Postfix instance, and that are started, stopped, etc., together with the default Postfix instance.

multi_instance_group (empty)

The optional instance group name of this Postfix instance.

multi_instance_name (empty)

The optional instance name of this Postfix instance.

multi_instance_enable (no)

Allow this Postfix instance to be started, stopped, etc., by a multi-instance manager.

postmulti_start_commands (start)

The **postfix**(1) commands that the **postmulti**(1) instance manager treats as "start" commands.

postmulti_stop_commands (see 'postconf -d' output)

The **postfix**(1) commands that the **postmulti**(1) instance manager treats as "stop" commands.

postmulti_control_commands (reload flush)

The **postfix**(1) commands that the **postmulti**(1) instance manager treats as "control" commands, that operate on running instances.

syslog_facility (mail)

The syslog facility of Postfix logging.

syslog_name (see 'postconf -d' output)

The mail system name that is prepended to the process name in syslog records, so that "smtpd" becomes, for example, "postfix/smtpd".

FILES

$daemon_directory/main.cf, stock configuration file
$daemon_directory/master.cf, stock configuration file
$daemon_directory/postmulti-script, life-cycle helper program

SEE ALSO

postfix(1), Postfix control program
postfix-wrapper(5), Postfix multi-instance API

README FILES

Use "**postconf readme_directory**" or "**postconf html_directory**" to locate this information.
MULTI_INSTANCE_README, Postfix multi-instance management

HISTORY

The **postmulti**(1) command was introduced with Postfix version 2.6.

LICENSE

The Secure Mailer license must be distributed with this software.

AUTHOR(S)

Victor Duchovni
Morgan Stanley

Wietse Venema
IBM T.J. Watson Research
P.O. Box 704
Yorktown Heights, NY 10598, USA

NAME

postqueue – Postfix queue control

SYNOPSIS

postqueue [-v] [-c *config_dir*] **-f**
postqueue [-v] [-c *config_dir*] **-i** *queue_id*
postqueue [-v] [-c *config_dir*] **-p**
postqueue [-v] [-c *config_dir*] **-s** *site*

DESCRIPTION

The **postqueue**(1) command implements the Postfix user interface for queue management. It implements operations that are traditionally available via the **sendmail**(1) command. See the **postsuper**(1) command for queue operations that require super-user privileges such as deleting a message from the queue or changing the status of a message.

The following options are recognized:

-c *config_dir*

The **main.cf** configuration file is in the named directory instead of the default configuration directory. See also the MAIL_CONFIG environment setting below.

-f   Flush the queue: attempt to deliver all queued mail.

This option implements the traditional "**sendmail -q**" command, by contacting the Postfix **qmgr**(8) daemon.

Warning: flushing undeliverable mail frequently will result in poor delivery performance of all other mail.

-i *queue_id*

Schedule immediate delivery of deferred mail with the specified queue ID.

This option implements the traditional **sendmail -qI** command, by contacting the **flush**(8) server.

This feature is available with Postfix version 2.4 and later.

-p   Produce a traditional sendmail-style queue listing. This option implements the traditional **mailq** command, by contacting the Postfix **showq**(8) daemon.

Each queue entry shows the queue file ID, message size, arrival time, sender, and the recipients that still need to be delivered. If mail could not be delivered upon the last attempt, the reason for failure is shown. This mode of operation is implemented by executing the **postqueue**(1) command. The queue ID string is followed by an optional status character:

*   The message is in the **active** queue, i.e. the message is selected for delivery.

!   The message is in the **hold** queue, i.e. no further delivery attempt will be made until the mail is taken off hold.

-s *site*   Schedule immediate delivery of all mail that is queued for the named *site*. A numerical site must be specified as a valid RFC 2821 address literal enclosed in [], just like in email addresses. The site must be eligible for the "fast flush" service. See **flush**(8) for more information about the "fast flush" service.

This option implements the traditional "**sendmail -qR***site*" command, by contacting the Postfix **flush**(8) daemon.

-v   Enable verbose logging for debugging purposes. Multiple **-v** options make the software increasingly verbose. As of Postfix 2.3, this option is available for the super-user only.

SECURITY

This program is designed to run with set-group ID privileges, so that it can connect to Postfix daemon processes.

DIAGNOSTICS

Problems are logged to **syslogd**(8) and to the standard error stream.

ENVIRONMENT

MAIL_CONFIG

Directory with the **main.cf** file. In order to avoid exploitation of set-group ID privileges, a non-standard directory is allowed only if:

- The name is listed in the standard **main.cf** file with the **alternate_config_directories** configuration parameter.

- The command is invoked by the super-user.

CONFIGURATION PARAMETERS

The following **main.cf** parameters are especially relevant to this program. The text below provides only a parameter summary. See **postconf**(5) for more details including examples.

alternate_config_directories (empty)

A list of non-default Postfix configuration directories that may be specified with "-c config_directory" on the command line, or via the MAIL_CONFIG environment parameter.

config_directory (see 'postconf -d' output)

The default location of the Postfix main.cf and master.cf configuration files.

command_directory (see 'postconf -d' output)

The location of all postfix administrative commands.

fast_flush_domains ($relay_domains)

Optional list of destinations that are eligible for per-destination logfiles with mail that is queued to those destinations.

import_environment (see 'postconf -d' output)

The list of environment parameters that a Postfix process will import from a non-Postfix parent process.

queue_directory (see 'postconf -d' output)

The location of the Postfix top-level queue directory.

syslog_facility (mail)

The syslog facility of Postfix logging.

syslog_name (see 'postconf -d' output)

The mail system name that is prepended to the process name in syslog records, so that "smtpd" becomes, for example, "postfix/smtpd".

trigger_timeout (10s)

The time limit for sending a trigger to a Postfix daemon (for example, the **pickup**(8) or **qmgr**(8) daemon).

Available in Postfix version 2.2 and later:

authorized_flush_users (static:anyone)

List of users who are authorized to flush the queue.

authorized_mailq_users (static:anyone)

List of users who are authorized to view the queue.

FILES

/var/spool/postfix, mail queue

SEE ALSO

    qmgr(8), queue manager
    showq(8), list mail queue
    flush(8), fast flush service
    sendmail(1), Sendmail-compatible user interface
    postsuper(1), privileged queue operations

README FILES

    Use "**postconf readme_directory**" or "**postconf html_directory**" to locate this information.
    ETRN_README, Postfix ETRN howto

LICENSE

    The Secure Mailer license must be distributed with this software.

HISTORY

    The postqueue command was introduced with Postfix version 1.1.

AUTHOR(S)

    Wietse Venema
    IBM T.J. Watson Research
    P.O. Box 704
    Yorktown Heights, NY 10598, USA

NAME

postsuper – Postfix superintendent

SYNOPSIS

postsuper [-psv] [-c *config_dir*] [-d *queue_id*]
    [-h *queue_id*] [-H *queue_id*]
    [-r *queue_id*] [*directory* ...]

DESCRIPTION

The **postsuper**(1) command does maintenance jobs on the Postfix queue. Use of the command is restricted to the superuser. See the **postqueue**(1) command for unprivileged queue operations such as listing or flushing the mail queue.

By default, **postsuper**(1) performs the operations requested with the **-s** and **-p** command-line options on all Postfix queue directories - this includes the **incoming**, **active** and **deferred** directories with mail files and the **bounce**, **defer**, **trace** and **flush** directories with log files.

Options:

-c *config_dir*

The **main.cf** configuration file is in the named directory instead of the default configuration directory. See also the MAIL_CONFIG environment setting below.

-d *queue_id*

Delete one message with the named queue ID from the named mail queue(s) (default: **hold**, **incoming**, **active** and **deferred**).

If a *queue_id* of - is specified, the program reads queue IDs from standard input. For example, to delete all mail with exactly one recipient **user@example.com**:

```
mailq | tail +2 | grep -v '^ *(' | awk 'BEGIN { RS = "" }
    # $7=sender, $8=recipient1, $9=recipient2
    { if ($8 == "user@example.com" && $9 == "")
        print $1 }
' | tr -d '*!' | postsuper -d -
```

Specify "**-d ALL**" to remove all messages; for example, specify "**-d ALL deferred**" to delete all mail in the **deferred** queue. As a safety measure, the word **ALL** must be specified in upper case.

Warning: Postfix queue IDs are reused. There is a very small possibility that postsuper deletes the wrong message file when it is executed while the Postfix mail system is delivering mail.

The scenario is as follows:

1)   The Postfix queue manager deletes the message that **postsuper**(1) is asked to delete, because Postfix is finished with the message (it is delivered, or it is returned to the sender).

2)   New mail arrives, and the new message is given the same queue ID as the message that **postsuper**(1) is supposed to delete. The probability for reusing a deleted queue ID is about 1 in 2**15 (the number of different microsecond values that the system clock can distinguish within a second).

3)   **postsuper**(1) deletes the new message, instead of the old message that it should have deleted.

-h *queue_id*

Put mail "on hold" so that no attempt is made to deliver it. Move one message with the named queue ID from the named mail queue(s) (default: **incoming**, **active** and **deferred**) to the **hold** queue.

If a *queue_id* of **-** is specified, the program reads queue IDs from standard input.

Specify "**-h ALL**" to hold all messages; for example, specify "**-h ALL deferred**" to hold all mail in the **deferred** queue. As a safety measure, the word **ALL** must be specified in upper case.

Note: while mail is "on hold" it will not expire when its time in the queue exceeds the **maximal_queue_lifetime** or **bounce_queue_lifetime** setting. It becomes subject to expiration after it is released from "hold".

This feature is available in Postfix 2.0 and later.

-H *queue_id*
    Release mail that was put "on hold". Move one message with the named queue ID from the named mail queue(s) (default: **hold**) to the **deferred** queue.

    If a *queue_id* of **-** is specified, the program reads queue IDs from standard input.

    Note: specify "**postsuper -r**" to release mail that was kept on hold for a significant fraction of **$maximal_queue_lifetime** or **$bounce_queue_lifetime**, or longer.

    Specify "**-H ALL**" to release all mail that is "on hold". As a safety measure, the word **ALL** must be specified in upper case.

    This feature is available in Postfix 2.0 and later.

-p   Purge old temporary files that are left over after system or software crashes.

-r *queue_id*
    Requeue the message with the named queue ID from the named mail queue(s) (default: **hold**, **incoming**, **active** and **deferred**). To requeue multiple messages, specify multiple **-r** command-line options.

    Alternatively, if a *queue_id* of **-** is specified, the program reads queue IDs from standard input.

    Specify "**-r ALL**" to requeue all messages. As a safety measure, the word **ALL** must be specified in upper case.

    A requeued message is moved to the **maildrop** queue, from where it is copied by the **pickup**(8) and **cleanup**(8) daemons to a new queue file. In many respects its handling differs from that of a new local submission.

    •   The message is not subjected to the smtpd_milters or non_smtpd_milters settings. When mail has passed through an external content filter, this would produce incorrect results with Milter applications that depend on original SMTP connection state information.

    •   The message is subjected again to mail address rewriting and substitution. This is useful when rewriting rules or virtual mappings have changed.

        The address rewriting context (local or remote) is the same as when the message was received.

    •   The message is subjected to the same content_filter settings (if any) as used for new local mail submissions. This is useful when content_filter settings have changed.

Warning: Postfix queue IDs are reused. There is a very small possibility that **postsuper**(1) requeues the wrong message file when it is executed while the Postfix mail system is running, but no harm should be done.

2

This feature is available in Postfix 1.1 and later.

-s   Structure check and structure repair. This should be done once before Postfix startup.

- Rename files whose name does not match the message file inode number. This operation is necessary after restoring a mail queue from a different machine, or from backup media.

- Move queue files that are in the wrong place in the file system hierarchy and remove sub-directories that are no longer needed. File position rearrangements are necessary after a change in the **hash_queue_names** and/or **hash_queue_depth** configuration parameters.

-v   Enable verbose logging for debugging purposes. Multiple **-v** options make the software increasingly verbose.

DIAGNOSTICS

Problems are reported to the standard error stream and to **syslogd**(8).

postsuper(1) reports the number of messages deleted with **-d**, the number of messages requeued with **-r**, and the number of messages whose queue file name was fixed with **-s**. The report is written to the standard error stream and to **syslogd**(8).

ENVIRONMENT

MAIL_CONFIG
Directory with the **main.cf** file.

BUGS

Mail that is not sanitized by Postfix (i.e. mail in the **maildrop** queue) cannot be placed "on hold".

CONFIGURATION PARAMETERS

The following **main.cf** parameters are especially relevant to this program. The text below provides only a parameter summary. See **postconf**(5) for more details including examples.

config_directory (see 'postconf -d' output)
The default location of the Postfix main.cf and master.cf configuration files.

hash_queue_depth (1)
The number of subdirectory levels for queue directories listed with the hash_queue_names parameter.

hash_queue_names (deferred, defer)
The names of queue directories that are split across multiple subdirectory levels.

queue_directory (see 'postconf -d' output)
The location of the Postfix top-level queue directory.

syslog_facility (mail)
The syslog facility of Postfix logging.

syslog_name (see 'postconf -d' output)
The mail system name that is prepended to the process name in syslog records, so that "smtpd" becomes, for example, "postfix/smtpd".

SEE ALSO

sendmail(1), Sendmail-compatible user interface
postqueue(1), unprivileged queue operations

LICENSE

The Secure Mailer license must be distributed with this software.

AUTHOR(S)

Wietse Venema
IBM T.J. Watson Research
P.O. Box 704
Yorktown Heights, NY 10598, USA

NAME

powerd — power management daemon for sysmon

SYNOPSIS

powerd [**-d**]

DESCRIPTION

powerd acts upon power management events posted by the kernel's power management facility. When events are posted, **powerd** translates the event into a script name and a list of arguments. **powerd** then runs the script in order to implement the power management policy defined by the system administrator.

powerd supports the following option:

-d   Enable debugging mode. Verbose messages will be sent to stderr and **powerd** will stay in the foreground of the controlling terminal.

CONFIGURATION SCRIPTS

All configuration of **powerd** is encapsulated into scripts that are run when power management events occur. The daemon will look for the scripts from the directory /etc/powerd/scripts.

Configuration scripts are run synchronously; **powerd** will start the script and wait for its completion before it handles the next event.

Configuration scripts are called with different arguments, depending on the script class. These classes are described in the following sections.

POWER SWITCH SCRIPTS

Power switch scripts are called when a state change event occurs on a power switch device. Power switch scripts are called with two arguments: the device with which the event is associated, and the event type.

The following power switch script names are defined:

power_button   This script is called when an event occurs on a power button device.

reset_button   This script is called when an event occurs on a reset button device.

sleep_button   This script is called when an event occurs on a sleep button device.

lid_switch   This script is called when an event occurs on a lid switch device.

acadapter   This script is called when an online or offline event occurs on an AC adapter device.

hotkey_button   This script is called when an event occurs on a hotkey button device.

The following events are defined for power switch devices:

pressed   The button was pressed, the lid was closed, or the AC adapter was connected.

released   The button was released, the lid was opened, or the AC adapter was disconnected. Note that power and sleep button devices usually do not post this type of event.

The following is an example of how a power button script might be invoked when a power button is pressed by the operator:

```
/etc/powerd/scripts/power_button acpibut0 pressed
```

ENVSYS SCRIPTS

envsys(4) scripts are called when a condition was triggered in a sensor. These scripts are called with three arguments: the device associated, the event type, and the sensor's name. The **sensor_drive** and the **sensor_battery** scripts uses a fourth argument: state description.

The following envsys script names are defined:

sensor_battery	This script is called when an event occurs on a battery sensor (Wh/Ah/Battery state).
sensor_drive	This script is called when an event occurs on a drive sensor.
sensor_fan	This script is called when an event occurs on a fan sensor.
sensor_indicator	This script is called when an event ocurrs on a indicator/integer sensor.
sensor_power	This script is called when an event occurs on a power sensor (W/Ampere).
sensor_resistance	This script is called when an event occurs on a resistance sensor (Ohm).
sensor_temperature	This script is called when an event occurs on a temperature sensor.
sensor_voltage	This script is called when an event occurs on a voltage sensor.

The following events are defined for fan, indicator, power, resistance, temperature, and voltage sensors:

critical	A critical condition was triggered.
critical-under	A critical under condition was triggered.
critical-over	A critical over condition was triggered.
warning-under	A warning under condition was triggered.
warning-over	A warning over condition was triggered.

The following event is defined for all scripts, but it is only sent if any of the previous events has been previously sent:

normal	A normal state/capacity/condition was triggered.

The following events are defined only for battery sensors:

user-capacity	Capacity dropped below the limit set by the user.
low-power	System is running in low power. This implies that the AC adapter is disconnected and all batteries are in critical or low capacity. The script shutdowns the system gracefully by default.

The following events are defined for drive and battery sensors:

state-changed	The state of the sensor has been changed and it is not in the normal state.

The following is an example of how a temperature sensor script might be invoked when a critical over condition is triggered:

```
/etc/powerd/scripts/sensor_temperature lm0 critical-over "CPU Temp"
```

SEE ALSO
acpi(4), acpiacad(4), acpibut(4), acpilid(4), envsys(4), i386/apm(4)

HISTORY
powerd first appeared in NetBSD 2.0. Support to handle envsys(4) events appeared in NetBSD 5.0.

AUTHORS
powerd was written by Jason R. Thorpe ⟨thorpej@wasabisystems.com⟩ and contributed by Wasabi Systems, Inc.
Juan Romero Pardines added support to handle envsys(4) events.

BUGS

Due to its synchronous nature **powerd** cannot be trusted to handle events within a certain time.

NAME

pppd – Point-to-Point Protocol Daemon

SYNOPSIS

pppd [*options*]

DESCRIPTION

PPP is the protocol used for establishing internet links over dial-up modems, DSL connections, and many other types of point-to-point links. The *pppd* daemon works together with the kernel PPP driver to establish and maintain a PPP link with another system (called the *peer*) and to negotiate Internet Protocol (IP) addresses for each end of the link. Pppd can also authenticate the peer and/or supply authentication information to the peer. PPP can be used with other network protocols besides IP, but such use is becoming increasingly rare.

FREQUENTLY USED OPTIONS

ttyname

Use the serial port called *ttyname* to communicate with the peer. If *ttyname* does not begin with a slash (/), the string "/dev/" is prepended to *ttyname* to form the name of the device to open. If no device name is given, or if the name of the terminal connected to the standard input is given, pppd will use that terminal, and will not fork to put itself in the background. A value for this option from a privileged source cannot be overridden by a non-privileged user.

speed   An option that is a decimal number is taken as the desired baud rate for the serial device. On systems such as 4.4BSD and NetBSD, any speed can be specified. Other systems (e.g. Linux, SunOS) only support the commonly-used baud rates.

asyncmap *map*

This option sets the Async-Control-Character-Map (ACCM) for this end of the link. The ACCM is a set of 32 bits, one for each of the ASCII control characters with values from 0 to 31, where a 1 bit indicates that the corresponding control character should not be used in PPP packets sent to this system. The map is encoded as a hexadecimal number (without a leading 0x) where the least significant bit (00000001) represents character 0 and the most significant bit (80000000) represents character 31. Pppd will ask the peer to send these characters as a 2-byte escape sequence. If multiple *asyncmap* options are given, the values are ORed together. If no *asyncmap* option is given, the default is zero, so pppd will ask the peer not to escape any control characters. To escape transmitted characters, use the *escape* option.

auth   Require the peer to authenticate itself before allowing network packets to be sent or received. This option is the default if the system has a default route. If neither this option nor the *noauth* option is specified, pppd will only allow the peer to use IP addresses to which the system does not already have a route.

call *name*

Read additional options from the file /etc/ppp/peers/*name*. This file may contain privileged options, such as *noauth*, even if pppd is not being run by root. The *name* string may not begin with / or include .. as a pathname component. The format of the options file is described below.

connect *script*

Usually there is something which needs to be done to prepare the link before the PPP protocol can be started; for instance, with a dial-up modem, commands need to be sent to the modem to dial the appropriate phone number. This option specifies an command for pppd to execute (by passing it to a shell) before attempting to start PPP negotiation. The chat (8) program is often useful here, as it provides a way to send arbitrary strings to a modem and respond to received characters. A value for this option from a privileged source cannot be overridden by a non-privileged user.

crtscts   Specifies that pppd should set the serial port to use hardware flow control using the RTS and CTS signals in the RS-232 interface. If neither the *crtscts*, the *nocrtscts*, the *cdtrcts* nor the *nocdtrcts* option is given, the hardware flow control setting for the serial port is left unchanged. Some serial ports (such as Macintosh serial ports) lack a true RTS output. Such serial ports use this mode to implement unidirectional flow control. The serial port will suspend transmission when requested by the modem (via CTS) but will be unable to request the modem to stop sending to the computer. This mode retains the ability to use DTR as a modem control line.

defaultroute

Add a default route to the system routing tables, using the peer as the gateway, when IPCP negotiation is successfully completed. This entry is removed when the PPP connection is broken. This option is privileged if the *nodefaultroute* option has been specified.

disconnect *script*

Execute the command specified by *script*, by passing it to a shell, after pppd has terminated the link. This command could, for example, issue commands to the modem to cause it to hang up if hardware modem control signals were not available. The disconnect script is not run if the modem has already hung up. A value for this option from a privileged source cannot be overridden by a non-privileged user.

escape *xx,yy,...*

Specifies that certain characters should be escaped on transmission (regardless of whether the peer requests them to be escaped with its async control character map). The characters to be escaped are specified as a list of hex numbers separated by commas. Note that almost any character can be specified for the *escape* option, unlike the *asyncmap* option which only allows control characters to be specified. The characters which may not be escaped are those with hex values 0x20 - 0x3f or 0x5e.

file *name*

Read options from file *name* (the format is described below). The file must be readable by the user who has invoked pppd.

init *script*

Execute the command specified by *script*, by passing it to a shell, to initialize the serial line. This script would typically use the chat(8) program to configure the modem to enable auto answer. A value for this option from a privileged source cannot be overridden by a non-privileged user.

lock   Specifies that pppd should create a UUCP-style lock file for the serial device to ensure exclusive access to the device. By default, pppd will not create a lock file.

mru *n* Set the MRU [Maximum Receive Unit] value to *n*. Pppd will ask the peer to send packets of no more than *n* bytes. The value of *n* must be between 128 and 16384; the default is 1500. A value of 296 works well on very slow links (40 bytes for TCP/IP header + 256 bytes of data). Note that for the IPv6 protocol, the MRU must be at least 1280.

mtu *n* Set the MTU [Maximum Transmit Unit] value to *n*. Unless the peer requests a smaller value via MRU negotiation, pppd will request that the kernel networking code send data packets of no more than *n* bytes through the PPP network interface. Note that for the IPv6 protocol, the MTU must be at least 1280.

passive Enables the "passive" option in the LCP. With this option, pppd will attempt to initiate a connection; if no reply is received from the peer, pppd will then just wait passively for a valid LCP packet from the peer, instead of exiting, as it would without this option.

OPTIONS

<local_IP_address>:*<remote_IP_address>*

Set the local and/or remote interface IP addresses. Either one may be omitted. The IP addresses can be specified with a host name or in decimal dot notation (e.g. 150.234.56.78). The default local address is the (first) IP address of the hostname of the system (unless the *noipdefault* option is given). The remote address will be obtained from the peer if not specified in any option. Thus, in simple cases, this option is not required. If a local and/or remote IP address is specified with this option, pppd will not accept a different value from the peer in the IPCP negotiation, unless the *ipcp−accept−local* and/or *ipcp−accept−remote* options are given, respectively.

ipv6 *<local_interface_identifier>,<remote_interface_identifier>*

Set the local and/or remote 64-bit interface identifier. Either one may be omitted. The identifier must be specified in standard ascii notation of IPv6 addresses (e.g. ::dead:beef). If the *ipv6cp−use−ipaddr* option is given, the local identifier is the local IPv4 address (see above). On systems which supports a unique persistent id, such as EUI−48 derived from the Ethernet MAC address, *ipv6cp−use−persistent* option can be used to replace the *ipv6 <local>,<remote>* option. Otherwise the identifier is randomized.

active−filter−in *filter−expression*

active−filter−out *filter−expression*

Specifies an incoming and outgoing packet filter to be applied to data packets to determine which packets are to be regarded as link activity, and therefore reset the idle timer, or cause the link to be brought up in demand-dialing mode. This option is useful in conjunction with the **idle** option if there are packets being sent or received regularly over the link (for example, routing information packets) which would otherwise prevent the link from ever appearing to be idle. The *filter−expression* syntax is as described for tcpdump(8), except that qualifiers which are inappropriate for a PPP link, such as **ether** and **arp**, are not permitted. Generally the filter expression should be enclosed in single-quotes to prevent whitespace in the expression from being interpreted by the shell. This option is currently only available under NetBSD, and then only if both the kernel and pppd were compiled with PPP_FILTER defined.

allow−ip *address(es)*

Allow peers to use the given IP address or subnet without authenticating themselves. The parameter is parsed as for each element of the list of allowed IP addresses in the secrets files (see the AUTHENTICATION section below).

allow−number *number*

Allow peers to connect from the given telephone number. A trailing '*' character will match all numbers beginning with the leading part.

bsdcomp *nr,nt*

Request that the peer compress packets that it sends, using the BSD-Compress scheme, with a maximum code size of *nr* bits, and agree to compress packets sent to the peer with a maximum code size of *nt* bits. If *nt* is not specified, it defaults to the value given for *nr*. Values in the range 9 to 15 may be used for *nr* and *nt*; larger values give better compression but consume more kernel memory for compression dictionaries. Alternatively, a value of 0 for *nr* or *nt* disables compression in the corresponding direction. Use *nobsdcomp* or *bsdcomp 0* to disable BSD-Compress compression entirely.

callback *phone_number*

Request a call-back to the *phone-number*. This only works if the peer is speaking the Call Back Configuration Protocol. Don't put this into the main options file if you sometimes connect to servers that don't support it.

cdtrcts Use a non-standard hardware flow control (i.e. DTR/CTS) to control the flow of data on the serial port. If neither the *crtscts*, the *nocrtscts*, the *cdtrcts* nor the *nocdtrcts* option is given, the hardware flow control setting for the serial port is left unchanged. Some serial ports (such as Macintosh serial ports) lack a true RTS output. Such serial ports use this mode to implement true bi-directional flow control. The sacrifice is that this flow control mode does not permit using DTR as a modem control line.

chap−interval *n*

If this option is given, pppd will rechallenge the peer every *n* seconds.

chap−max−challenge *n*

Set the maximum number of CHAP challenge transmissions to *n* (default 10).

chap–restart *n*

> Set the CHAP restart interval (retransmission timeout for challenges) to *n* seconds (default 3).

child–timeout *n*

> When exiting, wait for up to *n* seconds for any child processes (such as the command specified with the **pty** command) to exit before exiting. At the end of the timeout, pppd will send a SIGTERM signal to any remaining child processes and exit. A value of 0 means no timeout, that is, pppd will wait until all child processes have exited.

connect–delay *n*

> Wait for up to *n* milliseconds after the connect script finishes for a valid PPP packet from the peer. At the end of this time, or when a valid PPP packet is received from the peer, pppd will commence negotiation by sending its first LCP packet. The default value is 1000 (1 second). This wait period only applies if the **connect** or **pty** option is used.

debug   Enables connection debugging facilities. If this option is given, pppd will log the contents of all control packets sent or received in a readable form. The packets are logged through syslog with facility *daemon* and level *debug*. This information can be directed to a file by setting up /etc/syslog.conf appropriately (see syslog.conf(5)).

default–asyncmap

> Disable asyncmap negotiation, forcing all control characters to be escaped for both the transmit and the receive direction.

default–mru

> Disable MRU [Maximum Receive Unit] negotiation. With this option, pppd will use the default MRU value of 1500 bytes for both the transmit and receive direction.

deflate *nr,nt*

> Request that the peer compress packets that it sends, using the Deflate scheme, with a maximum window size of $2^{**}nr$ bytes, and agree to compress packets sent to the peer with a maximum window size of $2^{**}nt$ bytes. If *nt* is not specified, it defaults to the value given for *nr*. Values in the range 9 to 15 may be used for *nr* and *nt*; larger values give better compression but consume more kernel memory for compression dictionaries. Alternatively, a value of 0 for *nr* or *nt* disables compression in the corresponding direction. Use *nodeflate* or *deflate 0* to disable Deflate compression entirely. (Note: pppd requests Deflate compression in preference to BSD-Compress if the peer can do either.)

demand

> Initiate the link only on demand, i.e. when data traffic is present. With this option, the remote IP address must be specified by the user on the command line or in an options file. Pppd will initially configure the interface and enable it for IP traffic without connecting to the peer. When traffic is available, pppd will connect to the peer and perform negotiation, authentication, etc. When this is completed, pppd will commence passing data packets (i.e., IP packets) across the link.
>
> The *demand* option implies the *persist* option. If this behavior is not desired, use the *nopersist* option after the *demand* option. The *idle* and *holdoff* options are also useful in conjunction with the *demand* option.

domain *d*

> Append the domain name *d* to the local host name for authentication purposes. For example, if gethostname() returns the name porsche, but the fully qualified domain name is porsche.Quotron.COM, you could specify *domain Quotron.COM*. Pppd would then use the name *porsche.Quotron.COM* for looking up secrets in the secrets file, and as the default name to send to the peer when authenticating itself to the peer. This option is privileged.

dryrun   With the **dryrun** option, pppd will print out all the option values which have been set and then exit, after parsing the command line and options files and checking the option values, but before initiating the link. The option values are logged at level info, and also printed to standard output unless the device on standard output is the device that pppd would be using to communicate with

4

the peer.

dump   With the **dump** option, pppd will print out all the option values which have been set. This option
is like the **dryrun** option except that pppd proceeds as normal rather than exiting.

endpoint <*epdisc*>
Sets the endpoint discriminator sent by the local machine to the peer during multilink negotiation
to <*epdisc*>. The default is to use the MAC address of the first ethernet interface on the system, if
any, otherwise the IPv4 address corresponding to the hostname, if any, provided it is not in the
multicast or locally-assigned IP address ranges, or the localhost address. The endpoint discriminator can be the string **null** or of the form *type:value*, where type is a decimal number or one of the
strings **local**, **IP**, **MAC**, **magic**, or **phone**. The value is an IP address in dotted-decimal notation
for the **IP** type, or a string of bytes in hexadecimal, separated by periods or colons for the other
types. For the MAC type, the value may also be the name of an ethernet or similar network interface. This option is currently only available under Linux.

eap-interval *n*
If this option is given and pppd authenticates the peer with EAP (i.e., is the server), pppd will
restart EAP authentication every *n* seconds. For EAP SRP-SHA1, see also the **srp-interval**
option, which enables lightweight rechallenge.

eap-max-rreq *n*
Set the maximum number of EAP Requests to which pppd will respond (as a client) without hear-
ing EAP Success or Failure. (Default is 20.)

eap-max-sreq *n*
Set the maximum number of EAP Requests that pppd will issue (as a server) while attempting
authentication. (Default is 10.)

eap-restart *n*
Set the retransmit timeout for EAP Requests when acting as a server (authenticator). (Default is 3
seconds.)

eap-timeout *n*
Set the maximum time to wait for the peer to send an EAP Request when acting as a client
(authenticatee). (Default is 20 seconds.)

hide-password
When logging the contents of PAP packets, this option causes pppd to exclude the password string
from the log. This is the default.

holdoff *n*
Specifies how many seconds to wait before re-initiating the link after it terminates. This option
only has any effect if the *persist* or *demand* option is used. The holdoff period is not applied if the
link was terminated because it was idle.

idle *n*   Specifies that pppd should disconnect if the link is idle for *n* seconds. The link is idle when no
data packets (i.e. IP packets) are being sent or received. Note: it is not advisable to use this option
with the *persist* option without the *demand* option. If the **active-filter-in** and/or **active-fil-
ter-out** options are given, data packets which are rejected by the specified activity filter also count
as the link being idle.

ipcp-accept-local
With this option, pppd will accept the peer's idea of our local IP address, even if the local IP
address was specified in an option.

ipcp-accept-remote
With this option, pppd will accept the peer's idea of its (remote) IP address, even if the remote IP
address was specified in an option.

ipcp−max−configure *n*
> Set the maximum number of IPCP configure-request transmissions to *n* (default 10).

ipcp−max−failure *n*
> Set the maximum number of IPCP configure-NAKs returned before starting to send configure-Rejects instead to *n* (default 10).

ipcp−max−terminate *n*
> Set the maximum number of IPCP terminate-request transmissions to *n* (default 3).

ipcp−restart *n*
> Set the IPCP restart interval (retransmission timeout) to *n* seconds (default 3).

ipparam *string*
> Provides an extra parameter to the ip−up, ip−pre−up and ip−down scripts. If this option is given, the *string* supplied is given as the 6th parameter to those scripts.

+ipv6   Enable IPv6CP negotiation and IPv6 communication. It needs to be explicitly specified if you want IPv6CP.

−ipv6   Disable IPv6CP negotiation and IPv6 communication.

ipv6cp−accept−local
> With this option, pppd will accept the peer's idea of our local IPv6 address, even if the local IPv6 address was specified in an option.

ipv6cp−use−ipaddr
> Use the local IPv4 address as the local interface address.

ipv6cp−use−persistent
> Use uniquely-available persistent value for link local address (Solaris 2 only).

ipv6cp−max−configure *n*
> Set the maximum number of IPv6CP configure-request transmissions to *n* (default 10).

ipv6cp−max−failure *n*
> Set the maximum number of IPv6CP configure-NAKs returned before starting to send configure-Rejects instead to *n* (default 10).

ipv6cp−max−terminate *n*
> Set the maximum number of IPv6CP terminate-request transmissions to *n* (default 3).

ipv6cp−restart *n*
> Set the IPv6CP restart interval (retransmission timeout) to *n* seconds (default 3).

ipx   Enable the IPXCP and IPX protocols. This option is presently only supported under Linux, and only if your kernel has been configured to include IPX support.

ipx−network *n*
> Set the IPX network number in the IPXCP configure request frame to *n*, a hexadecimal number (without a leading 0x). There is no valid default. If this option is not specified, the network number is obtained from the peer. If the peer does not have the network number, the IPX protocol will not be started.

ipx−node *n:m*
> Set the IPX node numbers. The two node numbers are separated from each other with a colon character. The first number *n* is the local node number. The second number *m* is the peer's node number. Each node number is a hexadecimal number, at most 10 digits long. The node numbers on the ipx−network must be unique. There is no valid default. If this option is not specified then the node numbers are obtained from the peer.

ipx−router−name *<string>*
> Set the name of the router. This is a string and is sent to the peer as information data.

ipx–routing *n*

> Set the routing protocol to be received by this option. More than one instance of *ipx–routing* may be specified. The *'none'* option (0) may be specified as the only instance of ipx–routing. The values may be *0* for *NONE*, *2* for *RIP/SAP*, and *4* for *NLSP*.

ipxcp–accept–local

> Accept the peer's NAK for the node number specified in the ipx–node option. If a node number was specified, and non-zero, the default is to insist that the value be used. If you include this option then you will permit the peer to override the entry of the node number.

ipxcp–accept–network

> Accept the peer's NAK for the network number specified in the ipx–network option. If a network number was specified, and non-zero, the default is to insist that the value be used. If you include this option then you will permit the peer to override the entry of the node number.

ipxcp–accept–remote

> Use the peer's network number specified in the configure request frame. If a node number was specified for the peer and this option was not specified, the peer will be forced to use the value which you have specified.

ipxcp–max–configure *n*

> Set the maximum number of IPXCP configure request frames which the system will send to *n*. The default is 10.

ipxcp–max–failure *n*

> Set the maximum number of IPXCP NAK frames which the local system will send before it rejects the options. The default value is 3.

ipxcp–max–terminate *n*

> Set the maximum number of IPXCP terminate request frames before the local system considers that the peer is not listening to them. The default value is 3.

kdebug *n*

> Enable debugging code in the kernel-level PPP driver. The argument values depend on the specific kernel driver, but in general a value of 1 will enable general kernel debug messages. (Note that these messages are usually only useful for debugging the kernel driver itself.) For the Linux 2.2.x kernel driver, the value is a sum of bits: 1 to enable general debug messages, 2 to request that the contents of received packets be printed, and 4 to request that the contents of transmitted packets be printed. On most systems, messages printed by the kernel are logged by syslogd(8) to a file as directed in the /etc/syslog.conf configuration file.

ktune   Enables pppd to alter kernel settings as appropriate. Under Linux, pppd will enable IP forwarding (i.e. set /proc/sys/net/ipv4/ip_forward to 1) if the *proxyarp* option is used, and will enable the dynamic IP address option (i.e. set /proc/sys/net/ipv4/ip_dynaddr to 1) in demand mode if the local address changes.

lcp–echo–failure *n*

> If this option is given, pppd will presume the peer to be dead if *n* LCP echo–requests are sent without receiving a valid LCP echo–reply. If this happens, pppd will terminate the connection. Use of this option requires a non-zero value for the *lcp–echo–interval* parameter. This option can be used to enable pppd to terminate after the physical connection has been broken (e.g., the modem has hung up) in situations where no hardware modem control lines are available.

lcp–echo–interval *n*

> If this option is given, pppd will send an LCP echo–request frame to the peer every *n* seconds. Normally the peer should respond to the echo–request by sending an echo–reply. This option can be used with the *lcp–echo–failure* option to detect that the peer is no longer connected.

lcp–max–configure *n*

> Set the maximum number of LCP configure-request transmissions to *n* (default 10).

lcp–max–failure *n*
> Set the maximum number of LCP configure-NAKs returned before starting to send configure-Rejects instead to *n* (default 10).

lcp–max–terminate *n*
> Set the maximum number of LCP terminate-request transmissions to *n* (default 3).

lcp–restart *n*
> Set the LCP restart interval (retransmission timeout) to *n* seconds (default 3).

linkname *name*
> Sets the logical name of the link to *name*. Pppd will create a file named **ppp–***name***.pid** in /var/run (or /etc/ppp on some systems) containing its process ID. This can be useful in determining which instance of pppd is responsible for the link to a given peer system. This is a privileged option.

local   Don't use the modem control lines. With this option, pppd will ignore the state of the CD (Carrier Detect) signal from the modem and will not change the state of the DTR (Data Terminal Ready) signal. This is the opposite of the **modem** option.

logfd *n*   Send log messages to file descriptor *n*. Pppd will send log messages to at most one file or file descriptor (as well as sending the log messages to syslog), so this option and the **logfile** option are mutually exclusive. The default is for pppd to send log messages to stdout (file descriptor 1), unless the serial port is already open on stdout.

logfile *filename*
> Append log messages to the file *filename* (as well as sending the log messages to syslog). The file is opened with the privileges of the user who invoked pppd, in append mode.

login   Use the system password database for authenticating the peer using PAP, and record the user in the system wtmp file. Note that the peer must have an entry in the /etc/ppp/pap–secrets file as well as the system password database to be allowed access.

maxconnect *n*
> Terminate the connection when it has been available for network traffic for *n* seconds (i.e. *n* seconds after the first network control protocol comes up).

maxfail *n*
> Terminate after *n* consecutive failed connection attempts. A value of 0 means no limit. The default value is 10.

modem
> Use the modem control lines. This option is the default. With this option, pppd will wait for the CD (Carrier Detect) signal from the modem to be asserted when opening the serial device (unless a connect script is specified), and it will drop the DTR (Data Terminal Ready) signal briefly when the connection is terminated and before executing the connect script. On Ultrix, this option implies hardware flow control, as for the *crtscts* option. This is the opposite of the **local** option.

mp   Enables the use of PPP multilink; this is an alias for the 'multilink' option. This option is currently only available under Linux.

mppe–stateful
> Allow MPPE to use stateful mode. Stateless mode is still attempted first. The default is to disallow stateful mode.

mpshortseq
> Enables the use of short (12-bit) sequence numbers in multilink headers, as opposed to 24-bit sequence numbers. This option is only available under Linux, and only has any effect if multilink is enabled (see the multilink option).

mrru *n*   Sets the Maximum Reconstructed Receive Unit to *n*. The MRRU is the maximum size for a received packet on a multilink bundle, and is analogous to the MRU for the individual links. This option is currently only available under Linux, and only has any effect if multilink is enabled (see the multilink option).

ms–dns *<addr>*
>   If pppd is acting as a server for Microsoft Windows clients, this option allows pppd to supply one
>   or two DNS (Domain Name Server) addresses to the clients. The first instance of this option spec-
>   ifies the primary DNS address; the second instance (if given) specifies the secondary DNS address.
>   (This option was present in some older versions of pppd under the name **dns–addr**.)

ms–wins *<addr>*
>   If pppd is acting as a server for Microsoft Windows or "Samba" clients, this option allows pppd to
>   supply one or two WINS (Windows Internet Name Services) server addresses to the clients. The
>   first instance of this option specifies the primary WINS address; the second instance (if given)
>   specifies the secondary WINS address.

multilink
>   Enables the use of the PPP multilink protocol. If the peer also supports multilink, then this link
>   can become part of a bundle between the local system and the peer. If there is an existing bundle
>   to the peer, pppd will join this link to that bundle, otherwise pppd will create a new bundle. See
>   the MULTILINK section below. This option is currently only available under Linux.

name *name*
>   Set the name of the local system for authentication purposes to *name*. This is a privileged option.
>   With this option, pppd will use lines in the secrets files which have *name* as the second field when
>   looking for a secret to use in authenticating the peer. In addition, unless overridden with the *user*
>   option, *name* will be used as the name to send to the peer when authenticating the local system to
>   the peer. (Note that pppd does not append the domain name to *name*.)

noaccomp
>   Disable Address/Control compression in both directions (send and receive).

noauth Do not require the peer to authenticate itself. This option is privileged.

nobsdcomp
>   Disables BSD-Compress compression; **pppd** will not request or agree to compress packets using
>   the BSD-Compress scheme.

noccp   Disable CCP (Compression Control Protocol) negotiation. This option should only be required if
>   the peer is buggy and gets confused by requests from pppd for CCP negotiation.

nocrtscts
>   Disable hardware flow control (i.e. RTS/CTS) on the serial port. If neither the *crtscts* nor the
>   *nocrtscts* nor the *cdtrcts* nor the *nocdtrcts* option is given, the hardware flow control setting for the
>   serial port is left unchanged.

nocdtrcts
>   This option is a synonym for *nocrtscts*. Either of these options will disable both forms of hardware
>   flow control.

nodefaultroute
>   Disable the *defaultroute* option. The system administrator who wishes to prevent users from creat-
>   ing default routes with pppd can do so by placing this option in the /etc/ppp/options file.

nodeflate
>   Disables Deflate compression; pppd will not request or agree to compress packets using the
>   Deflate scheme.

nodetach
>   Don't detach from the controlling terminal. Without this option, if a serial device other than the
>   terminal on the standard input is specified, pppd will fork to become a background process.

noendpoint
>   Disables pppd from sending an endpoint discriminator to the peer or accepting one from the peer
>   (see the MULTILINK section below). This option should only be required if the peer is buggy.

noip   Disable IPCP negotiation and IP communication. This option should only be required if the peer is buggy and gets confused by requests from pppd for IPCP negotiation.

noipv6 An alias for **-ipv6.**

noipdefault

Disables the default behavior when no local IP address is specified, which is to determine (if possible) the local IP address from the hostname. With this option, the peer will have to supply the local IP address during IPCP negotiation (unless it specified explicitly on the command line or in an options file).

noipx   Disable the IPXCP and IPX protocols. This option should only be required if the peer is buggy and gets confused by requests from pppd for IPXCP negotiation.

noktune

Opposite of the *ktune* option; disables pppd from changing system settings.

nolock Opposite of the *lock* option; specifies that pppd should not create a UUCP-style lock file for the serial device. This option is privileged.

nolog   Do not send log messages to a file or file descriptor. This option cancels the **logfd** and **logfile** options.

nomagic

Disable magic number negotiation. With this option, pppd cannot detect a looped-back line. This option should only be needed if the peer is buggy.

nomp   Disables the use of PPP multilink. This option is currently only available under Linux.

nomppe

Disables MPPE (Microsoft Point to Point Encryption). This is the default.

nomppe–40

Disable 40-bit encryption with MPPE.

nomppe–128

Disable 128-bit encryption with MPPE.

nomppe–stateful

Disable MPPE stateful mode. This is the default.

nompshortseq

Disables the use of short (12-bit) sequence numbers in the PPP multilink protocol, forcing the use of 24-bit sequence numbers. This option is currently only available under Linux, and only has any effect if multilink is enabled.

nomultilink

Disables the use of PPP multilink. This option is currently only available under Linux.

nopcomp

Disable protocol field compression negotiation in both the receive and the transmit direction.

nopersist

Exit once a connection has been made and terminated. This is the default unless the *persist* or *demand* option has been specified.

nopredictor1

Do not accept or agree to Predictor–1 compression.

noproxyarp

Disable the *proxyarp* option. The system administrator who wishes to prevent users from creating proxy ARP entries with pppd can do so by placing this option in the /etc/ppp/options file.

notty   Normally, pppd requires a terminal device. With this option, pppd will allocate itself a pseudo-tty master/slave pair and use the slave as its terminal device. Pppd will create a child process to act as a 'character shunt' to transfer characters between the pseudo-tty master and its standard input and output. Thus pppd will transmit characters on its standard output and receive characters on its standard input even if they are not terminal devices. This option increases the latency and CPU overhead of transferring data over the ppp interface as all of the characters sent and received must flow through the character shunt process. An explicit device name may not be given if this option is used.

novj   Disable Van Jacobson style TCP/IP header compression in both the transmit and the receive direction.

novjccomp

Disable the connection-ID compression option in Van Jacobson style TCP/IP header compression. With this option, pppd will not omit the connection-ID byte from Van Jacobson compressed TCP/IP headers, nor ask the peer to do so.

papcrypt

Indicates that all secrets in the /etc/ppp/pap–secrets file which are used for checking the identity of the peer are encrypted, and thus pppd should not accept a password which, before encryption, is identical to the secret from the /etc/ppp/pap–secrets file.

pap–max–authreq *n*

Set the maximum number of PAP authenticate-request transmissions to *n* (default 10).

pap–restart *n*

Set the PAP restart interval (retransmission timeout) to *n* seconds (default 3).

pap–timeout *n*

Set the maximum time that pppd will wait for the peer to authenticate itself with PAP to *n* seconds (0 means no limit).

pass–filter–in *filter–expression*

pass–filter–out *filter–expression*

Specifies an incoming and outgoing packet filter to applied to data packets being sent or received to determine which packets should be allowed to pass. Packets which are rejected by the filter are silently discarded. This option can be used to prevent specific network daemons (such as routed) using up link bandwidth, or to provide a basic firewall capability. The *filter–expression* syntax is as described for tcpdump(8), except that qualifiers which are inappropriate for a PPP link, such as **ether** and **arp**, are not permitted. Generally the filter expression should be enclosed in single-quotes to prevent whitespace in the expression from being interpreted by the shell. This option is currently only available under NetBSD, and then only if both the kernel and pppd were compiled with PPP_FILTER defined.

password *password–string*

Specifies the password to use for authenticating to the peer. Use of this option is discouraged, as the password is likely to be visible to other users on the system (for example, by using ps(1)).

persist   Do not exit after a connection is terminated; instead try to reopen the connection. The **maxfail** option still has an effect on persistent connections.

plugin *filename*

Load the shared library object file *filename* as a plugin. This is a privileged option. If *filename* does not contain a slash (/), pppd will look in the **/usr/lib/pppd/***version* directory for the plugin, where *version* is the version number of pppd (for example, 2.4.2).

predictor1

Request that the peer compress frames that it sends using Predictor-1 compression, and agree to compress transmitted frames with Predictor-1 if requested. This option has no effect unless the kernel driver supports Predictor-1 compression.

privgroup *group–name*

Allows members of group *group–name* to use privileged options. This is a privileged option. Use of this option requires care as there is no guarantee that members of *group–name* cannot use pppd to become root themselves. Consider it equivalent to putting the members of *group−name* in the kmem or disk group.

proxyarp

Add an entry to this system's ARP [Address Resolution Protocol] table with the IP address of the peer and the Ethernet address of this system. This will have the effect of making the peer appear to other systems to be on the local ethernet.

pty *script*

Specifies that the command *script* is to be used to communicate rather than a specific terminal device. Pppd will allocate itself a pseudo-tty master/slave pair and use the slave as its terminal device. The *script* will be run in a child process with the pseudo-tty master as its standard input and output. An explicit device name may not be given if this option is used. (Note: if the *record* option is used in conjunction with the *pty* option, the child process will have pipes on its standard input and output.)

receive−all

With this option, pppd will accept all control characters from the peer, including those marked in the receive asyncmap. Without this option, pppd will discard those characters as specified in RFC1662. This option should only be needed if the peer is buggy.

record *filename*

Specifies that pppd should record all characters sent and received to a file named *filename*. This file is opened in append mode, using the user's user-ID and permissions. This option is implemented using a pseudo-tty and a process to transfer characters between the pseudo-tty and the real serial device, so it will increase the latency and CPU overhead of transferring data over the ppp interface. The characters are stored in a tagged format with timestamps, which can be displayed in readable form using the pppdump(8) program.

remotename *name*

Set the assumed name of the remote system for authentication purposes to *name*.

remotenumber *number*

Set the assumed telephone number of the remote system for authentication purposes to *number*.

refuse−chap

With this option, pppd will not agree to authenticate itself to the peer using CHAP.

refuse−mschap

With this option, pppd will not agree to authenticate itself to the peer using MS−CHAP.

refuse−mschap−v2

With this option, pppd will not agree to authenticate itself to the peer using MS−CHAPv2.

refuse−eap

With this option, pppd will not agree to authenticate itself to the peer using EAP.

refuse−pap

With this option, pppd will not agree to authenticate itself to the peer using PAP.

require−chap

Require the peer to authenticate itself using CHAP [Challenge Handshake Authentication Protocol] authentication.

require−mppe

Require the use of MPPE (Microsoft Point to Point Encryption). This option disables all other compression types. This option enables both 40-bit and 128-bit encryption. In order for MPPE to successfully come up, you must have authenticated with either MS−CHAP or MS−CHAPv2. This option is presently only supported under Linux, and only if your kernel has been configured to include MPPE support.

require–mppe–40
> Require the use of MPPE, with 40-bit encryption.

require–mppe–128
> Require the use of MPPE, with 128-bit encryption.

require–mschap
> Require the peer to authenticate itself using MS–CHAP [Microsoft Challenge Handshake Authentication Protocol] authentication.

require–mschap–v2
> Require the peer to authenticate itself using MS–CHAPv2 [Microsoft Challenge Handshake Authentication Protocol, Version 2] authentication.

require–eap
> Require the peer to authenticate itself using EAP [Extensible Authentication Protocol] authentication.

require–pap
> Require the peer to authenticate itself using PAP [Password Authentication Protocol] authentication.

show–password
> When logging the contents of PAP packets, this option causes pppd to show the password string in the log message.

silent   With this option, pppd will not transmit LCP packets to initiate a connection until a valid LCP packet is received from the peer (as for the 'passive' option with ancient versions of pppd).

srp–interval *n*
> If this parameter is given and pppd uses EAP SRP–SHA1 to authenticate the peer (i.e., is the server), then pppd will use the optional lightweight SRP rechallenge mechanism at intervals of *n* seconds. This option is faster than **eap–interval** reauthentication because it uses a hash–based mechanism and does not derive a new session key.

srp–pn–secret *string*
> Set the long-term pseudonym-generating secret for the server. This value is optional and if set, needs to be known at the server (authenticator) side only, and should be different for each server (or poll of identical servers). It is used along with the current date to generate a key to encrypt and decrypt the client's identity contained in the pseudonym.

srp–use–pseudonym
> When operating as an EAP SRP–SHA1 client, attempt to use the pseudonym stored in ~/.ppp_psuedonym first as the identity, and save in this file any pseudonym offered by the peer during authentication.

sync   Use synchronous HDLC serial encoding instead of asynchronous. The device used by pppd with this option must have sync support. Currently supports Microgate SyncLink adapters under Linux and FreeBSD 2.2.8 and later.

unit *num*
> Sets the ppp unit number (for a ppp0 or ppp1 etc interface name) for outbound connections.

updetach
> With this option, pppd will detach from its controlling terminal once it has successfully established the ppp connection (to the point where the first network control protocol, usually the IP control protocol, has come up).

usehostname
> Enforce the use of the hostname (with domain name appended, if given) as the name of the local system for authentication purposes (overrides the *name* option). This option is not normally needed since the *name* option is privileged.

usepeerdns
> Ask the peer for up to 2 DNS server addresses. The addresses supplied by the peer (if any) are passed to the /etc/ppp/ip–up script in the environment variables DNS1 and DNS2, and the environment variable USEPEERDNS will be set to 1. In addition, pppd will create an /etc/ppp/resolv.conf file containing one or two nameserver lines with the address(es) supplied by the peer.

user *name*
> Sets the name used for authenticating the local system to the peer to *name*.

vj–max–slots *n*
> Sets the number of connection slots to be used by the Van Jacobson TCP/IP header compression and decompression code to *n*, which must be between 2 and 16 (inclusive).

welcome *script*
> Run the executable or shell command specified by *script* before initiating PPP negotiation, after the connect script (if any) has completed. A value for this option from a privileged source cannot be overridden by a non-privileged user.

xonxoff
> Use software flow control (i.e. XON/XOFF) to control the flow of data on the serial port.

OPTIONS FILES

Options can be taken from files as well as the command line. Pppd reads options from the files /etc/ppp/options, ˜/.ppprc and /etc/ppp/options.*ttyname* (in that order) before processing the options on the command line. (In fact, the command-line options are scanned to find the terminal name before the options.*ttyname* file is read.) In forming the name of the options.*ttyname* file, the initial /dev/ is removed from the terminal name, and any remaining / characters are replaced with dots.

An options file is parsed into a series of words, delimited by whitespace. Whitespace can be included in a word by enclosing the word in double-quotes ("). A backslash (\) quotes the following character. A hash (#) starts a comment, which continues until the end of the line. There is no restriction on using the *file* or *call* options within an options file.

SECURITY

pppd provides system administrators with sufficient access control that PPP access to a server machine can be provided to legitimate users without fear of compromising the security of the server or the network it's on. This control is provided through restrictions on which IP addresses the peer may use, based on its authenticated identity (if any), and through restrictions on which options a non-privileged user may use. Several of pppd's options are privileged, in particular those which permit potentially insecure configurations; these options are only accepted in files which are under the control of the system administrator, or if pppd is being run by root.

The default behaviour of pppd is to allow an unauthenticated peer to use a given IP address only if the system does not already have a route to that IP address. For example, a system with a permanent connection to the wider internet will normally have a default route, and thus all peers will have to authenticate themselves in order to set up a connection. On such a system, the *auth* option is the default. On the other hand, a system where the PPP link is the only connection to the internet will not normally have a default route, so the peer will be able to use almost any IP address without authenticating itself.

As indicated above, some security-sensitive options are privileged, which means that they may not be used by an ordinary non-privileged user running a setuid-root pppd, either on the command line, in the user's ˜/.ppprc file, or in an options file read using the *file* option. Privileged options may be used in /etc/ppp/options file or in an options file read using the *call* option. If pppd is being run by the root user, privileged options can be used without restriction.

When opening the device, pppd uses either the invoking user's user ID or the root UID (that is, 0), depending on whether the device name was specified by the user or the system administrator. If the device name comes from a privileged source, that is, /etc/ppp/options or an options file read using the *call* option, pppd uses full root privileges when opening the device. Thus, by creating an appropriate file under /etc/ppp/peers, the system administrator can allow users to establish a ppp connection via a device which they would not normally have permission to access. Otherwise pppd uses the invoking user's real UID when opening the device.

AUTHENTICATION

Authentication is the process whereby one peer convinces the other of its identity. This involves the first peer sending its name to the other, together with some kind of secret information which could only come from the genuine authorized user of that name. In such an exchange, we will call the first peer the "client" and the other the "server". The client has a name by which it identifies itself to the server, and the server also has a name by which it identifies itself to the client. Generally the genuine client shares some secret (or password) with the server, and authenticates itself by proving that it knows that secret. Very often, the names used for authentication correspond to the internet hostnames of the peers, but this is not essential.

At present, pppd supports three authentication protocols: the Password Authentication Protocol (PAP), Challenge Handshake Authentication Protocol (CHAP), and Extensible Authentication Protocol (EAP). PAP involves the client sending its name and a cleartext password to the server to authenticate itself. In contrast, the server initiates the CHAP authentication exchange by sending a challenge to the client (the challenge packet includes the server's name). The client must respond with a response which includes its name plus a hash value derived from the shared secret and the challenge, in order to prove that it knows the secret. EAP supports CHAP-style authentication, and also includes the SRP-SHA1 mechanism, which is resistant to dictionary-based attacks and does not require a cleartext password on the server side.

The PPP protocol, being symmetrical, allows both peers to require the other to authenticate itself. In that case, two separate and independent authentication exchanges will occur. The two exchanges could use different authentication protocols, and in principle, different names could be used in the two exchanges.

The default behaviour of pppd is to agree to authenticate if requested, and to not require authentication from the peer. However, pppd will not agree to authenticate itself with a particular protocol if it has no secrets which could be used to do so.

Pppd stores secrets for use in authentication in secrets files (/etc/ppp/pap-secrets for PAP, /etc/ppp/chap-secrets for CHAP, MS-CHAP, MS-CHAPv2, and EAP MD5-Challenge, and /etc/ppp/srp-secrets for EAP SRP-SHA1). All secrets files have the same format. The secrets files can contain secrets for pppd to use in authenticating itself to other systems, as well as secrets for pppd to use when authenticating other systems to itself.

Each line in a secrets file contains one secret. A given secret is specific to a particular combination of client and server - it can only be used by that client to authenticate itself to that server. Thus each line in a secrets file has at least 3 fields: the name of the client, the name of the server, and the secret. These fields may be followed by a list of the IP addresses that the specified client may use when connecting to the specified server.

A secrets file is parsed into words as for a options file, so the client name, server name and secrets fields must each be one word, with any embedded spaces or other special characters quoted or escaped. Note that case is significant in the client and server names and in the secret.

If the secret starts with an '@', what follows is assumed to be the name of a file from which to read the secret. A "*" as the client or server name matches any name. When selecting a secret, pppd takes the best match, i.e. the match with the fewest wildcards.

Any following words on the same line are taken to be a list of acceptable IP addresses for that client. If there are only 3 words on the line, or if the first word is "-", then all IP addresses are disallowed. To allow any address, use "*". A word starting with "!" indicates that the specified address is *not* acceptable. An address may be followed by "/" and a number n, to indicate a whole subnet, i.e. all addresses which have the same value in the most significant n bits. In this form, the address may be followed by a plus sign ("+") to indicate that one address from the subnet is authorized, based on the ppp network interface unit number in use. In this case, the host part of the address will be set to the unit number plus one.

Thus a secrets file contains both secrets for use in authenticating other hosts, plus secrets which we use for authenticating ourselves to others. When pppd is authenticating the peer (checking the peer's identity), it chooses a secret with the peer's name in the first field and the name of the local system in the second field.

The name of the local system defaults to the hostname, with the domain name appended if the *domain* option is used. This default can be overridden with the *name* option, except when the *usehostname* option is used. (For EAP SRP–SHA1, see the srp–entry(8) utility for generating proper validator entries to be used in the "secret" field.)

When pppd is choosing a secret to use in authenticating itself to the peer, it first determines what name it is going to use to identify itself to the peer. This name can be specified by the user with the *user* option. If this option is not used, the name defaults to the name of the local system, determined as described in the previous paragraph. Then pppd looks for a secret with this name in the first field and the peer's name in the second field. Pppd will know the name of the peer if CHAP or EAP authentication is being used, because the peer will have sent it in the challenge packet. However, if PAP is being used, pppd will have to determine the peer's name from the options specified by the user. The user can specify the peer's name directly with the *remotename* option. Otherwise, if the remote IP address was specified by a name (rather than in numeric form), that name will be used as the peer's name. Failing that, pppd will use the null string as the peer's name.

When authenticating the peer with PAP, the supplied password is first compared with the secret from the secrets file. If the password doesn't match the secret, the password is encrypted using crypt() and checked against the secret again. Thus secrets for authenticating the peer can be stored in encrypted form if desired. If the *papcrypt* option is given, the first (unencrypted) comparison is omitted, for better security.

Furthermore, if the *login* option was specified, the username and password are also checked against the system password database. Thus, the system administrator can set up the pap–secrets file to allow PPP access only to certain users, and to restrict the set of IP addresses that each user can use. Typically, when using the *login* option, the secret in /etc/ppp/pap–secrets would be "", which will match any password supplied by the peer. This avoids the need to have the same secret in two places.

Authentication must be satisfactorily completed before IPCP (or any other Network Control Protocol) can be started. If the peer is required to authenticate itself, and fails to do so, pppd will terminated the link (by closing LCP). If IPCP negotiates an unacceptable IP address for the remote host, IPCP will be closed. IP packets can only be sent or received when IPCP is open.

In some cases it is desirable to allow some hosts which can't authenticate themselves to connect and use one of a restricted set of IP addresses, even when the local host generally requires authentication. If the peer refuses to authenticate itself when requested, pppd takes that as equivalent to authenticating with PAP using the empty string for the username and password. Thus, by adding a line to the pap–secrets file which specifies the empty string for the client and password, it is possible to allow restricted access to hosts which refuse to authenticate themselves.

ROUTING

When IPCP negotiation is completed successfully, pppd will inform the kernel of the local and remote IP addresses for the ppp interface. This is sufficient to create a host route to the remote end of the link, which will enable the peers to exchange IP packets. Communication with other machines generally requires further modification to routing tables and/or ARP (Address Resolution Protocol) tables. In most cases the *defaultroute* and/or *proxyarp* options are sufficient for this, but in some cases further intervention is required. The /etc/ppp/ip–up script can be used for this.

Sometimes it is desirable to add a default route through the remote host, as in the case of a machine whose only connection to the Internet is through the ppp interface. The *defaultroute* option causes pppd to create such a default route when IPCP comes up, and delete it when the link is terminated.

In some cases it is desirable to use proxy ARP, for example on a server machine connected to a LAN, in order to allow other hosts to communicate with the remote host. The *proxyarp* option causes pppd to look for a network interface on the same subnet as the remote host (an interface supporting broadcast and ARP, which is up and not a point-to-point or loopback interface). If found, pppd creates a permanent, published ARP entry with the IP address of the remote host and the hardware address of the network interface found.

When the *demand* option is used, the interface IP addresses have already been set at the point when IPCP comes up. If pppd has not been able to negotiate the same addresses that it used to configure the interface (for example when the peer is an ISP that uses dynamic IP address assignment), pppd has to change the interface IP addresses to the negotiated addresses. This may disrupt existing connections, and the use of demand dialing with peers that do dynamic IP address assignment is not recommended.

MULTILINK

Multilink PPP provides the capability to combine two or more PPP links between a pair of machines into a single 'bundle', which appears as a single virtual PPP link which has the combined bandwidth of the individual links. Currently, multilink PPP is only supported under Linux.

Pppd detects that the link it is controlling is connected to the same peer as another link using the peer's endpoint discriminator and the authenticated identity of the peer (if it authenticates itself). The endpoint discriminator is a block of data which is hopefully unique for each peer. Several types of data can be used, including locally-assigned strings of bytes, IP addresses, MAC addresses, randomly strings of bytes, or E–164 phone numbers. The endpoint discriminator sent to the peer by pppd can be set using the endpoint option.

In some circumstances the peer may send no endpoint discriminator or a non-unique value. The bundle option adds an extra string which is added to the peer's endpoint discriminator and authenticated identity when matching up links to be joined together in a bundle. The bundle option can also be used to allow the establishment of multiple bundles between the local system and the peer. Pppd uses a TDB database in /var/run/pppd2.tdb to match up links.

Assuming that multilink is enabled and the peer is willing to negotiate multilink, then when pppd is invoked to bring up the first link to the peer, it will detect that no other link is connected to the peer and create a new bundle, that is, another ppp network interface unit. When another pppd is invoked to bring up another link to the peer, it will detect the existing bundle and join its link to it.

If the first link terminates (for example, because of a hangup or a received LCP terminate-request) the bundle is not destroyed unless there are no other links remaining in the bundle. Rather than exiting, the first pppd keeps running after its link terminates, until all the links in the bundle have terminated. If the first pppd receives a SIGTERM or SIGINT signal, it will destroy the bundle and send a SIGHUP to the pppd processes for each of the links in the bundle. If the first pppd receives a SIGHUP signal, it will terminate its link but not the bundle.

Note: demand mode is not currently supported with multilink.

EXAMPLES

The following examples assume that the /etc/ppp/options file contains the *auth* option (as in the default /etc/ppp/options file in the ppp distribution).

Probably the most common use of pppd is to dial out to an ISP. This can be done with a command such as

    pppd call isp

where the /etc/ppp/peers/isp file is set up by the system administrator to contain something like this:

    ttyS0 19200 crtscts
    connect '/usr/sbin/chat −v −f /etc/ppp/chat−isp'
    noauth

In this example, we are using chat to dial the ISP's modem and go through any log on sequence required. The /etc/ppp/chat−isp file contains the script used by chat; it could for example contain something like this:

    ABORT "NO CARRIER"
    ABORT "NO DIALTONE"
    ABORT "ERROR"
    ABORT "NO ANSWER"
    ABORT "BUSY"
    ABORT "Username/Password Incorrect"
    "" "at"
    OK "at&d0&c1"
    OK "atdt2468135"
    "name:" "^Umyuserid"

> "word:" "\qmypassword"
> "ispts" "\q^Uppp"
> "~-^Uppp-~"

See the chat(8) man page for details of chat scripts.

Pppd can also be used to provide a dial-in ppp service for users. If the users already have login accounts, the simplest way to set up the ppp service is to let the users log in to their accounts and run pppd (installed setuid-root) with a command such as

> pppd proxyarp

To allow a user to use the PPP facilities, you need to allocate an IP address for that user's machine and create an entry in /etc/ppp/pap–secrets, /etc/ppp/chap–secrets, or /etc/ppp/srp–secrets (depending on which authentication method the PPP implementation on the user's machine supports), so that the user's machine can authenticate itself. For example, if Joe has a machine called "joespc" that is to be allowed to dial in to the machine called "server" and use the IP address joespc.my.net, you would add an entry like this to /etc/ppp/pap–secrets or /etc/ppp/chap–secrets:

> joespc   server   "joe's secret"   joespc.my.net

(See srp–entry(8) for a means to generate the server's entry when SRP–SHA1 is in use.) Alternatively, you can create a username called (for example) "ppp", whose login shell is pppd and whose home directory is /etc/ppp. Options to be used when pppd is run this way can be put in /etc/ppp/.ppprc.

If your serial connection is any more complicated than a piece of wire, you may need to arrange for some control characters to be escaped. In particular, it is often useful to escape XON (^Q) and XOFF (^S), using *asyncmap a0000*. If the path includes a telnet, you probably should escape ^] as well (*asyncmap 200a0000*). If the path includes an rlogin, you will need to use the *escape ff* option on the end which is running the rlogin client, since many rlogin implementations are not transparent; they will remove the sequence [0xff, 0xff, 0x73, 0x73, followed by any 8 bytes] from the stream.

DIAGNOSTICS

Messages are sent to the syslog daemon using facility LOG_DAEMON. (This can be overridden by recompiling pppd with the macro LOG_PPP defined as the desired facility.) See the syslog(8) documentation for details of where the syslog daemon will write the messages. On most systems, the syslog daemon uses the /etc/syslog.conf file to specify the destination(s) for syslog messages. You may need to edit that file to suit.

The *debug* option causes the contents of all control packets sent or received to be logged, that is, all LCP, PAP, CHAP, EAP, or IPCP packets. This can be useful if the PPP negotiation does not succeed or if authentication fails. If debugging is enabled at compile time, the *debug* option also causes other debugging messages to be logged.

Debugging can also be enabled or disabled by sending a SIGUSR1 signal to the pppd process. This signal acts as a toggle.

EXIT STATUS

The exit status of pppd is set to indicate whether any error was detected, or the reason for the link being terminated. The values used are:

0   Pppd has detached, or otherwise the connection was successfully established and terminated at the peer's request.

1   An immediately fatal error of some kind occurred, such as an essential system call failing, or running out of virtual memory.

2   An error was detected in processing the options given, such as two mutually exclusive options being used.

3   Pppd is not setuid-root and the invoking user is not root.

4   The kernel does not support PPP, for example, the PPP kernel driver is not included or cannot be loaded.

5   Pppd terminated because it was sent a SIGINT, SIGTERM or SIGHUP signal.

6   The serial port could not be locked.

7   The serial port could not be opened.

8   The connect script failed (returned a non-zero exit status).

9   The command specified as the argument to the *pty* option could not be run.

10   The PPP negotiation failed, that is, it didn't reach the point where at least one network protocol (e.g. IP) was running.

11   The peer system failed (or refused) to authenticate itself.

12   The link was established successfully and terminated because it was idle.

13   The link was established successfully and terminated because the connect time limit was reached.

14   Callback was negotiated and an incoming call should arrive shortly.

15   The link was terminated because the peer is not responding to echo requests.

16   The link was terminated by the modem hanging up.

17   The PPP negotiation failed because serial loopback was detected.

18   The init script failed (returned a non-zero exit status).

19   We failed to authenticate ourselves to the peer.

SCRIPTS

Pppd invokes scripts at various stages in its processing which can be used to perform site-specific ancillary processing. These scripts are usually shell scripts, but could be executable code files instead. Pppd does not wait for the scripts to finish (except for the ip-pre-up script). The scripts are executed as root (with the real and effective user-id set to 0), so that they can do things such as update routing tables or run privileged daemons. Be careful that the contents of these scripts do not compromise your system's security. Pppd runs the scripts with standard input, output and error redirected to /dev/null, and with an environment that is empty except for some environment variables that give information about the link. The environment variables that pppd sets are:

DEVICE
        The name of the serial tty device being used.

IFNAME
        The name of the network interface being used.

IPLOCAL
        The IP address for the local end of the link. This is only set when IPCP has come up.

IPREMOTE
        The IP address for the remote end of the link. This is only set when IPCP has come up.

PEERNAME
        The authenticated name of the peer. This is only set if the peer authenticates itself.

SPEED
        The baud rate of the tty device.

ORIG_UID
        The real user-id of the user who invoked pppd.

PPPLOGNAME
        The username of the real user-id that invoked pppd. This is always set.

For the ip-down and auth-down scripts, pppd also sets the following variables giving statistics for the connection:

CONNECT_TIME
>   The number of seconds from when the PPP negotiation started until the connection was terminated.

BYTES_SENT
>   The number of bytes sent (at the level of the serial port) during the connection.

BYTES_RCVD
>   The number of bytes received (at the level of the serial port) during the connection.

LINKNAME
>   The logical name of the link, set with the *linkname* option.

DNS1   If the peer supplies DNS server addresses, this variable is set to the first DNS server address supplied.

DNS2   If the peer supplies DNS server addresses, this variable is set to the second DNS server address supplied.

Pppd invokes the following scripts, if they exist. It is not an error if they don't exist.

/etc/ppp/auth-up
>   A program or script which is executed after the remote system successfully authenticates itself. It is executed with the parameters
>
>   *interface-name peer-name user-name tty-device speed*
>
>   Note that this script is not executed if the peer doesn't authenticate itself, for example when the *noauth* option is used.

/etc/ppp/auth-down
>   A program or script which is executed when the link goes down, if /etc/ppp/auth-up was previously executed. It is executed in the same manner with the same parameters as /etc/ppp/auth-up.

/etc/ppp/ip-pre-up
>   A program or script which is executed just before the ppp network interface is brought up. It is executed with the same parameters as the ip-up script (below). At this point the interface exists and has IP addresses assigned but is still down. This can be used to add firewall rules before any IP traffic can pass through the interface. Pppd will wait for this script to finish before bringing the interface up, so this script should run quickly.

/etc/ppp/ip-up
>   A program or script which is executed when the link is available for sending and receiving IP packets (that is, IPCP has come up). It is executed with the parameters
>
>   *interface-name tty-device speed local-IP-address remote-IP-address ipparam*

/etc/ppp/ip-down
>   A program or script which is executed when the link is no longer available for sending and receiving IP packets. This script can be used for undoing the effects of the /etc/ppp/ip-up and /etc/ppp/ip-pre-up scripts. It is invoked in the same manner and with the same parameters as the ip-up script.

/etc/ppp/ipv6-up
>   Like /etc/ppp/ip-up, except that it is executed when the link is available for sending and receiving IPv6 packets. It is executed with the parameters
>
>   *interface-name tty-device speed local-link-local-address remote-link-local-address ipparam*

/etc/ppp/ipv6-down
>   Similar to /etc/ppp/ip-down, but it is executed when IPv6 packets can no longer be transmitted on the link. It is executed with the same parameters as the ipv6-up script.

/etc/ppp/ipx–up

A program or script which is executed when the link is available for sending and receiving IPX packets (that is, IPXCP has come up). It is executed with the parameters

*interface–name   tty–device   speed   network–number   local–IPX–node–address
remote–IPX–node–address   local–IPX–routing–protocol   remote–IPX–routing–protocol
local–IPX–router–name remote–IPX–router–name ipparam pppd–pid*

The local–IPX–routing–protocol and remote–IPX–routing–protocol field may be one of the following:

NONE   to indicate that there is no routing protocol
RIP   to indicate that RIP/SAP should be used
NLSP   to indicate that Novell NLSP should be used
RIP NLSP to indicate that both RIP/SAP and NLSP should be used

/etc/ppp/ipx–down

A program or script which is executed when the link is no longer available for sending and receiving IPX packets. This script can be used for undoing the effects of the /etc/ppp/ipx–up script. It is invoked in the same manner and with the same parameters as the ipx–up script.

FILES

/var/run/ppp*n*.pid (BSD or Linux), **/etc/ppp/ppp*n*.pid** (others)

Process-ID for pppd process on ppp interface unit *n*.

/var/run/ppp-*name*.pid (BSD or Linux),

/etc/ppp/ppp-*name*.pid (others) Process-ID for pppd process for logical link *name* (see the *linkname* option).

/var/run/pppd2.tdb

Database containing information about pppd processes, interfaces and links, used for matching links to bundles in multilink operation. May be examined by external programs to obtain information about running pppd instances, the interfaces and devices they are using, IP address assignments, etc. **/etc/ppp/pap–secrets** Usernames, passwords and IP addresses for PAP authentication. This file should be owned by root and not readable or writable by any other user. Pppd will log a warning if this is not the case.

/etc/ppp/chap–secrets

Names, secrets and IP addresses for CHAP/MS–CHAP/MS–CHAPv2 authentication. As for /etc/ppp/pap–secrets, this file should be owned by root and not readable or writable by any other user. Pppd will log a warning if this is not the case.

/etc/ppp/srp–secrets

Names, secrets, and IP addresses for EAP authentication. As for /etc/ppp/pap–secrets, this file should be owned by root and not readable or writable by any other user. Pppd will log a warning if this is not the case.

˜/.ppp_pseudonym

Saved client-side SRP–SHA1 pseudonym. See the *srp–use–pseudonym* option for details.

/etc/ppp/options

System default options for pppd, read before user default options or command-line options.

˜/.ppprc

User default options, read before /etc/ppp/options.*ttyname*.

/etc/ppp/options.*ttyname*

System default options for the serial port being used, read after ˜/.ppprc. In forming the *ttyname* part of this filename, an initial /dev/ is stripped from the port name (if present), and any slashes in the remaining part are converted to dots.

/etc/ppp/peers

A directory containing options files which may contain privileged options, even if pppd was invoked by a user other than root. The system administrator can create options files in this directory to permit non-privileged users to dial out without requiring the peer to authenticate, but only to certain trusted peers.

SEE ALSO

chat(8), **pppstats**(8)

RFC1144

Jacobson, V. *Compressing TCP/IP headers for low-speed serial links.* February 1990.

RFC1321

Rivest, R. *The MD5 Message-Digest Algorithm.* April 1992.

RFC1332

McGregor, G. *PPP Internet Protocol Control Protocol (IPCP).* May 1992.

RFC1334

Lloyd, B.; Simpson, W.A. *PPP authentication protocols.* October 1992.

RFC1661

Simpson, W.A. *The Point-to-Point Protocol (PPP).* July 1994.

RFC1662

Simpson, W.A. *PPP in HDLC-like Framing.* July 1994.

RFC2284

Blunk, L.; Vollbrecht, J., *PPP Extensible Authentication Protocol (EAP).* March 1998.

RFC2472

Haskin, D. *IP Version 6 over PPP* December 1998.

RFC2945

Wu, T., *The SRP Authentication and Key Exchange System* September 2000.

draft−ietf−pppext−eap−srp−03.txt

Carlson, J.; et al., *EAP SRP−SHA1 Authentication Protocol.* July 2001.

NOTES

Some limited degree of control can be exercised over a running pppd process by sending it a signal from the list below.

SIGINT, SIGTERM

These signals cause pppd to terminate the link (by closing LCP), restore the serial device settings, and exit. If a connector or disconnector process is currently running, pppd will send the same signal to its process group, so as to terminate the connector or disconnector process.

SIGHUP

This signal causes pppd to terminate the link, restore the serial device settings, and close the serial device. If the *persist* or *demand* option has been specified, pppd will try to reopen the serial device and start another connection (after the holdoff period). Otherwise pppd will exit. If this signal is received during the holdoff period, it causes pppd to end the holdoff period immediately. If a connector or disconnector process is running, pppd will send the same signal to its process group.

SIGUSR1

This signal toggles the state of the *debug* option.

SIGUSR2

This signal causes pppd to renegotiate compression. This can be useful to re-enable compression after it has been disabled as a result of a fatal decompression error. (Fatal decompression errors generally indicate a bug in one or other implementation.)

AUTHORS

Paul Mackerras (paulus@samba.org), based on earlier work by Drew Perkins, Brad Clements, Karl Fox, Greg Christy, and Brad Parker.

COPYRIGHT

Pppd is copyrighted and made available under conditions which provide that it may be copied and used in source or binary forms provided that the conditions listed below are met. Portions of pppd are covered by the following copyright notices:

The copyright notices contain the following statements.

Redistribution and use in source and binary forms, with or without modification, are permitted provided that the following conditions are met:

1. Redistributions of source code must retain the above copyright
   notice, this list of conditions and the following disclaimer.

2. Redistributions in binary form must reproduce the above copyright
   notice, this list of conditions and the following disclaimer in
   the documentation and/or other materials provided with the
   distribution.

3. The name "Carnegie Mellon University" must not be used to
   endorse or promote products derived from this software without
   prior written permission. For permission or any legal
   details, please contact
     Office of Technology Transfer
     Carnegie Mellon University
     5000 Forbes Avenue
     Pittsburgh, PA 15213-3890
     (412) 268-4387, fax: (412) 268-7395
     tech-transfer@andrew.cmu.edu

3b. The name(s) of the authors of this software must not be used to
    endorse or promote products derived from this software without
    prior written permission.

4. Redistributions of any form whatsoever must retain the following
   acknowledgments:
   "This product includes software developed by Computing Services
   at Carnegie Mellon University (http://www.cmu.edu/computing/)."
   "This product includes software developed by Paul Mackerras
   <paulus@samba.org>".
   "This product includes software developed by Pedro Roque Marques
   <pedro_m@yahoo.com>".
   "This product includes software developed by Tommi Komulainen
   <Tommi.Komulainen@iki.fi>".

CARNEGIE MELLON UNIVERSITY DISCLAIMS ALL WARRANTIES WITH REGARD TO THIS SOFTWARE, INCLUDING ALL IMPLIED WARRANTIES OF MERCHANTABILITY AND FITNESS,

IN NO EVENT SHALL CARNEGIE MELLON UNIVERSITY BE LIABLE FOR ANY SPECIAL, INDI-RECT OR CONSEQUENTIAL DAMAGES OR ANY DAMAGES WHATSOEVER RESULTING FROM LOSS OF USE, DATA OR PROFITS, WHETHER IN AN ACTION OF CONTRACT, NEGLIGENCE OR OTHER TORTIOUS ACTION, ARISING OUT OF OR IN CONNECTION WITH THE USE OR PER-FORMANCE OF THIS SOFTWARE.

THE AUTHORS OF THIS SOFTWARE DISCLAIM ALL WARRANTIES WITH REGARD TO THIS SOFTWARE, INCLUDING ALL IMPLIED WARRANTIES OF MERCHANTABILITY AND FITNESS, IN NO EVENT SHALL THE AUTHORS BE LIABLE FOR ANY SPECIAL, INDIRECT OR CONSE-QUENTIAL DAMAGES OR ANY DAMAGES WHATSOEVER RESULTING FROM LOSS OF USE, DATA OR PROFITS, WHETHER IN AN ACTION OF CONTRACT, NEGLIGENCE OR OTHER TOR-TIOUS ACTION, ARISING OUT OF OR IN CONNECTION WITH THE USE OR PERFORMANCE OF THIS SOFTWARE.

NAME
pppdump – convert PPP record file to readable format

SYNOPSIS
pppdump [**–h** | **–p** [**–d**]] [**–r**] [**–m** *mru*] [*file ...*]

DESCRIPTION
The **pppdump** utility converts the files written using the *record* option of **pppd** into a human-readable format. If one or more filenames are specified, **pppdump** will read each in turn; otherwise it will read its standard input. In each case the result is written to standard output.

The options are as follows:

–h   Prints the bytes sent and received in hexadecimal. If neither this option nor the **–p** option is specified, the bytes are printed as the characters themselves, with non-printing and non-ASCII characters printed as escape sequences.

–p   Collects the bytes sent and received into PPP packets, interpreting the async HDLC framing and escape characters and checking the FCS (frame check sequence) of each packet. The packets are printed as hex values and as characters (non-printable characters are printed as '.').

–d   With the **–p** option, this option causes **pppdump** to decompress packets which have been compressed with the BSD-Compress or Deflate methods.

–r   Reverses the direction indicators, so that 'sent' is printed for bytes or packets received, and 'rcvd' is printed for bytes or packets sent.

–m *mru*
       Use *mru* as the MRU (maximum receive unit) for both directions of the link when checking for over-length PPP packets (with the **–p** option).

SEE ALSO
pppd(8)

NAME

pppoectl, ipppctl — display or set parameters for an pppoe or isdn ppp (ippp) interface

SYNOPSIS

pppoectl [**-v**] *ifname* [*parameter*[=*value*]] [. . .]

ipppctl [**-v**] *ifname* [*parameter*[=*value*]] [. . .]

pppoectl -e *ethernet-ifname* [**-s** *service-name*]
            [**-a** *access-concentrator-name*] [**-d**] [**-n** *1* | *2*] *ifname*

pppoectl -f *config-file ifname* [. . .]

DESCRIPTION

There are two basic modes of operation: configuring security related parameters and attaching a PPPoE interface to its ethernet interface, optionally passing in additional parameters for the PPPoE encapsulation.

The later usage is indicated by the presence of the **-e** option, which takes the name of the ethernet interface as its argument.

-e   specifies the ethernet interface used to communicate with the access concentrator (typically via a DSL modem).

-a   specifies the name of the access concentrator.

-s   specifies the name of the service connected to.

-d   dump the current connection state information (this parameter is typically used alone, for informational purposes, not during interface configuration).

-n *1* | *2*
            print the IP address of the primary or secondary DNS name server for this PPP connection. This is only available if DNS query is enabled, see *query-dns*.

-f   parse *config-file* for *parameter*[=*value*] pairs, one per line, as if they had been specified on the command line. This allows the password to be not passed as a command line argument. Unless escaped by \, comments starting with # to the end of the current line are ignored.

Typically, not both the access concentrator name and the service name are specified.

The ippp(4) or the pppoe(4) drivers require a number of additional arguments or optional parameters besides the settings that can be adjusted with ifconfig(8). These are things like authentication protocol parameters, but also other tunable configuration variables. The **pppoectl** utility can be used to display the current settings, or adjust these parameters as required.

For whatever intent **pppoectl** is being called, at least the parameter *ifname* needs to be specified, naming the interface for which the settings are to be performed or displayed. Use ifconfig(8) or netstat(1) to see which interfaces are available.

If no other parameter is given, **pppoectl** will just list the current settings for *ifname* and exit. The reported settings include the current PPP phase the interface is in, which can be one of the names *dead*, *establish*, *authenticate*, *network*, or *terminate*. If an authentication protocol is configured for the interface, the name of the protocol to be used, as well as the system name to be used or expected will be displayed, plus any possible options to the authentication protocol if applicable. Note that the authentication secrets (sometimes also called *keys*) are not being returned by the underlying system call, and are thus not displayed.

If any additional parameter is supplied, superuser privileges are required, and the command works in set mode. This is normally done quietly, unless the option **-v** is also enabled, which will cause a final printout of the settings as described above once all other actions have been taken. Use of this mode will be rejected if the interface is currently in any other phase than *dead*. Note that you can force an interface into *dead* phase by calling `ifconfig`(8) with the parameter `down`.

The currently supported parameters include:

authproto=protoname
Set both his and my authentication protocol to *protoname*. The protocol name can be one of `chap`, `pap`, or `none`. In the latter case, the use of an authentication protocol will be turned off for the named interface. This has the side-effect of clearing the other authentication-related parameters for this interface as well (i. e., system name and authentication secret will be forgotten).

myauthproto=protoname
Same as above, but only for my end of the link. I.e., this is the protocol when remote is authenticator, and I am the peer required to authenticate.

hisauthproto=protoname
Same as above, but only for his end of the link.

myauthname=name
Set my system name for the authentication protocol.

hisauthname=name
Set his system name for the authentication protocol. For CHAP, this will only be used as a hint, causing a warning message if remote did supply a different name. For PAP, it's the name remote must use to authenticate himself (in connection with his secret).

myauthsecret=secret
Set my secret (key, password) for use in the authentication phase. For CHAP, this will be used to compute the response hash value, based on remote's challenge. For PAP, it will be transmitted as plaintext together with the system name. Don't forget to quote the secrets from the shell if they contain shell metacharacters (or whitespace).

myauthkey=secret
Same as above.

hisauthsecret=secret
Same as above, to be used if we are authenticator and the remote peer needs to authenticate.

hisauthkey=secret
Same as above.

callin
Require remote to authenticate himself only when he's calling in, but not when we are caller. This is required for some peers that do not implement the authentication protocols symmetrically (like Ascend routers, for example).

always
The opposite of *callin*. Require remote to always authenticate, regardless of which side is placing the call. This is the default, and will not be explicitly displayed in `list` mode.

norechallenge
Only meaningful with CHAP. Do not re-challenge peer once the initial CHAP handshake was successful. Used to work around broken peer implementations that can't grok being re-challenged once the connection is up.

rechallenge
With CHAP, send re-challenges at random intervals while the connection is in network phase. (The intervals are currently in the range of 300 through approximately 800 seconds.) This is the default, and will not be explicitly displayed in `list` mode.

idle-timeout=idle-seconds   For services that are charged by connection time the interface can optionally disconnect after a configured idle time. If set to 0, this feature is disabled. Note: for ISDN devices, it is preferable to use the isdnd(8) based timeout mechanism, as isdnd can predict the next charging unit for ISDN connections and optimize the timeout with this information.

lcp-timeout=timeout-value   Allows to change the value of the LCP timeout. The default value of the LCP timeout is currently set to 1 second. The timeout-value must be specified in milliseconds.

max-noreceive=sec   Sets the number of seconds after last reception of data from the peer before the line state is probed by sending LCP echo requests. The *sec* interval is not used verbatim, the first echo request might be delayed upto 10 seconds after the configured interval.

max-alive-missed=count   Sets the number of unanswered LCP echo requests that we will tolerate before considering a connection to be dead. LCP echo requests are sent in 10 seconds interval after the configured *max-noreceive* interval has passed with no data received from the peer.

max-auth-failure=count   Since some ISPs disable accounts after too many unsuccessful authentication attempts, there is a maximum number of authentication failures before we will stop retrying without manual intervention. Manual intervention is either changing the authentication data (name, password) or setting the maximum retry count. If *count* is set to *0* this feature is disabled.

clear-auth-failure   If an authentication failure has been caused by remote problems and you want to retry connecting using unchanged local settings, this command can be used to reset the failure count to zero.

query-dns=flags   During PPP protocol negotiation we can query the peer for addresses of two name servers. If `flags` is *1* only the first server address will be requested, if `flags` is *2* the second will be requested. Setting `flags` to *3* queries both.

            The result of the negotiation can be retrieved with the **−n** option.

EXAMPLES

```
# ipppctl ippp0
ippp0: phase=dead
        myauthproto=chap myauthname="uriah"
        hisauthproto=chap hisauthname="ifb-gw" norechallenge
        lcp timeout: 3.000 s
```

Display the settings for ippp0. The interface is currently in *dead* phase, i.e. the LCP layer is down, and no traffic is possible. Both ends of the connection use the CHAP protocol, my end tells remote the system name uriah, and remote is expected to authenticate by the name ifb-gw. Once the initial CHAP handshake was successful, no further CHAP challenges will be transmitted. There are supposedly some known CHAP secrets for both ends of the link which are not being shown.

```
# ipppctl ippp0 \
        authproto=chap \
        myauthname=uriah myauthsecret='some secret' \
        hisauthname=ifb-gw hisauthsecret='another' \
```

```
        norechallenge
```

A possible call to **pppoectl** that could have been used to bring the interface into the state shown by the previous example.

The following example is the complete sequence of commands to bring a PPPoE connection up:

```
# Need ethernet interface UP (or it won't send any packets)
ifconfig ne0 up

# Let pppoe0 use ne0 as its ethernet interface
pppoectl -e ne0 pppoe0

# Configure authentication
pppoectl pppoe0 \
  myauthproto=pap \
  myauthname=XXXXX \
  myauthsecret=YYYYY \
  hisauthproto=none

# Configure the pppoe0 interface itself.  These addresses are magic,
# meaning we don't care about either address and let the remote
# ppp choose them.
ifconfig pppoe0 0.0.0.0 0.0.0.1 netmask 0xffffffff up
```

SEE ALSO

netstat(1), ippp(4), pppoe(4), ifconfig(8), ifwatchd(8)

B. Lloyd and W. Simpson, *PPP Authentication Protocols*, RFC 1334.

W. Simpson, Editor, *The Point-to-Point Protocol (PPP)*, RFC 1661.

W. Simpson, *PPP Challenge Handshake Authentication Protocol (CHAP)*, RFC 1994.

L. Mamakos, K. Lidl, J. Evarts, D. Carrel, D. Simone, and R. Wheeler, *A Method for Transmitting PPP Over Ethernet (PPPoE)*, RFC 2516.

HISTORY

The **pppoectl** utility is based on the **spppcontrol** utility which appeared in FreeBSD 3.0.

AUTHORS

The program was written by Jörg Wunsch, Dresden, and modified for PPPoE support by Martin Husemann.

NAME
pppstats, slstats – print PPP/SLIP statistics

SYNOPSIS
pppstats, slstats [−a] [−v] [−r] [−z] [−c <*count*>] [−w <*secs*>] [*interface*]

DESCRIPTION
The **pppstats** or **slstats** utility reports PPP or SLIP related statistics at regular intervals for the specified PPP/SLIP interface. If the interface is unspecified, **pppstats** will default to ppp0 and **slstats** will default to sl0. The display is split horizontally into input and output sections containing columns of statistics describing the properties and volume of packets received and transmitted by the interface.

The options are as follows:

−a   Display absolute values rather than deltas. With this option, all reports show statistics for the time since the link was initiated. Without this option, the second and subsequent reports show statistics for the time since the last report.

−c *count*
      Repeat the display *count* times. If this option is not specified, the default repeat count is 1 if the −w option is not specified, otherwise infinity.

−r   Display additional statistics summarizing the compression ratio achieved by the packet compression algorithm in use.

−v   Display additional statistics relating to the performance of the Van Jacobson TCP header compression algorithm.

−w *wait*
      Pause *wait* seconds between each display. If this option is not specified, the default interval is 5 seconds.

−z   Instead of the standard display, show statistics indicating the performance of the packet compression algorithm in use.

The following fields are printed on the input side when the −z option is not used:

IN   The total number of bytes received by this interface.

PACK   The total number of packets received by this interface.

VJCOMP
      The number of header-compressed TCP packets received by this interface.

VJUNC
      The number of header-uncompressed TCP packets received by this interface. Not reported when the −r option is specified.

VJERR
      The number of corrupted or bogus header-compressed TCP packets received by this interface. Not reported when the −r option is specified.

VJTOSS
      The number of VJ header-compressed TCP packets dropped on reception by this interface because of preceding errors. Only reported when the −v option is specified.

NON-VJ
      The total number of non-TCP packets received by this interface. Only reported when the −v option is specified.

RATIO
      The compression ratio achieved for received packets by the packet compression scheme in use, defined as the uncompressed size divided by the compressed size. Only reported when the −r option is specified.

UBYTE

> The total number of bytes received, after decompression of compressed packets. Only reported when the **−r** option is specified.

The following fields are printed on the output side:

OUT   The total number of bytes transmitted from this interface.

PACK   The total number of packets transmitted from this interface.

VJCOMP

> The number of TCP packets transmitted from this interface with VJ-compressed TCP headers.

VJUNC

> The number of TCP packets transmitted from this interface with VJ-uncompressed TCP headers. Not reported when the **−r** option is specified.

NON-VJ

> The total number of non-TCP packets transmitted from this interface. Not reported when the **−r** option is specified.

VJSRCH

> The number of searches for the cached header entry for a VJ header compressed TCP packet. Only reported when the **−v** option is specified.

VJMISS

> The number of failed searches for the cached header entry for a VJ header compressed TCP packet. Only reported when the **−v** option is specified.

RATIO

> The compression ratio achieved for transmitted packets by the packet compression scheme in use, defined as the size before compression divided by the compressed size. Only reported when the **−r** option is specified.

UBYTE

> The total number of bytes to be transmitted, before packet compression is applied. Only reported when the **−r** option is specified.

When the **−z** option is specified, **pppstats** instead displays the following fields, relating to the packet compression algorithm currently in use. This option is not supported by **slstats** and it always displays zeros. If packet compression is not in use, these fields will all display zeroes. The fields displayed on the input side are:

COMPRESSED BYTE

> The number of bytes of compressed packets received.

COMPRESSED PACK

> The number of compressed packets received.

INCOMPRESSIBLE BYTE

> The number of bytes of incompressible packets (that is, those which were transmitted in uncompressed form) received.

INCOMPRESSIBLE PACK

> The number of incompressible packets received.

COMP RATIO

> The recent compression ratio for incoming packets, defined as the uncompressed size divided by the compressed size (including both compressible and incompressible packets).

The fields displayed on the output side are:

COMPRESSED BYTE

> The number of bytes of compressed packets transmitted.

COMPRESSED PACK
>The number of compressed packets transmitted.

INCOMPRESSIBLE BYTE
>The number of bytes of incompressible packets transmitted (that is, those which were transmitted in uncompressed form).

INCOMPRESSIBLE PACK
>The number of incompressible packets transmitted.

COMP RATIO
>The recent compression ratio for outgoing packets.

SEE ALSO
>pppd(8), slattach(8)

NAME

proxymap – Postfix lookup table proxy server

SYNOPSIS

proxymap [generic Postfix daemon options]

DESCRIPTION

The **proxymap**(8) server provides read-only or read-write table lookup service to Postfix processes. These services are implemented with distinct service names: **proxymap** and **proxywrite**, respectively. The purpose of these services is:

- To overcome chroot restrictions. For example, a chrooted SMTP server needs access to the system passwd file in order to reject mail for non-existent local addresses, but it is not practical to maintain a copy of the passwd file in the chroot jail. The solution:

  local_recipient_maps =
      proxy:unix:passwd.byname $alias_maps

- To consolidate the number of open lookup tables by sharing one open table among multiple processes. For example, making mysql connections from every Postfix daemon process results in "too many connections" errors. The solution:

  virtual_alias_maps =
      proxy:mysql:/etc/postfix/virtual_alias.cf

  The total number of connections is limited by the number of proxymap server processes.

- To provide single-updater functionality for lookup tables that do not reliably support multiple writers (i.e. all file-based tables).

The **proxymap**(8) server implements the following requests:

open *maptype:mapname flags*

Open the table with type *maptype* and name *mapname*, as controlled by *flags*. The reply includes the *maptype* dependent flags (to distinguish a fixed string table from a regular expression table).

lookup *maptype:mapname flags key*

Look up the data stored under the requested key. The reply is the request completion status code and the lookup result value. The *maptype:mapname* and *flags* are the same as with the **open** request.

update *maptype:mapname flags key value*

Update the data stored under the requested key. The reply is the request completion status code. The *maptype:mapname* and *flags* are the same as with the **open** request.

To implement single-updater maps, specify a process limit of 1 in the master.cf file entry for the **proxywrite** service.

This request is supported in Postfix 2.5 and later.

delete *maptype:mapname flags key*

Delete the data stored under the requested key. The reply is the request completion status code. The *maptype:mapname* and *flags* are the same as with the **open** request.

This request is supported in Postfix 2.5 and later.

The request completion status is one of OK, RETRY, NOKEY (lookup failed because the key was not found), BAD (malformed request) or DENY (the table is not approved for proxy read or update access).

There is no **close** command, nor are tables implicitly closed when a client disconnects. The purpose is to share tables among multiple client processes.

SERVER PROCESS MANAGEMENT

proxymap(8) servers run under control by the Postfix master(8) server. Each server can handle multiple simultaneous connections. When all servers are busy while a client connects, the master(8) creates a new proxymap(8) server process, provided that the process limit is not exceeded. Each server terminates after serving at least $max_use clients or after $max_idle seconds of idle time.

SECURITY

The proxymap(8) server opens only tables that are approved via the proxy_read_maps or proxy_write_maps configuration parameters, does not talk to users, and can run at fixed low privilege, chrooted or not. However, running the proxymap server chrooted severely limits usability, because it can open only chrooted tables.

The proxymap(8) server is not a trusted daemon process, and must not be used to look up sensitive information such as user or group IDs, mailbox file/directory names or external commands.

In Postfix version 2.2 and later, the proxymap client recognizes requests to access a table for security-sensitive purposes, and opens the table directly. This allows the same main.cf setting to be used by sensitive and non-sensitive processes.

Postfix-writable data files should be stored under a dedicated directory that is writable only by the Postfix mail system, such as the Postfix-owned data_directory.

In particular, Postfix-writable files should never exist in root-owned directories. That would open up a particular type of security hole where ownership of a file or directory does not match the provider of its content.

DIAGNOSTICS

Problems and transactions are logged to syslogd(8).

BUGS

The proxymap(8) server provides service to multiple clients, and must therefore not be used for tables that have high-latency lookups.

The proxymap(8) read-write service does not explicitly close lookup tables (even if it did, this could not be relied on, because the process may be terminated between table updates). The read-write service should therefore not be used with tables that leave persistent storage in an inconsistent state between updates (for example, CDB). Tables that support "sync on update" should be safe (for example, Berkeley DB) as should tables that are implemented by a real DBMS.

CONFIGURATION PARAMETERS

On busy mail systems a long time may pass before proxymap(8) relevant changes to main.cf are picked up. Use the command "postfix reload" to speed up a change.

The text below provides only a parameter summary. See postconf(5) for more details including examples.

config_directory (see 'postconf -d' output)
>   The default location of the Postfix main.cf and master.cf configuration files.

data_directory (see 'postconf -d' output)
>   The directory with Postfix-writable data files (for example: caches, pseudo-random numbers).

daemon_timeout (18000s)
>   How much time a Postfix daemon process may take to handle a request before it is terminated by a built-in watchdog timer.

ipc_timeout (3600s)
>   The time limit for sending or receiving information over an internal communication channel.

2

max_idle (100s)
> The maximum amount of time that an idle Postfix daemon process waits for an incoming connection before terminating voluntarily.

max_use (100)
> The maximal number of incoming connections that a Postfix daemon process will service before terminating voluntarily.

process_id (read-only)
> The process ID of a Postfix command or daemon process.

process_name (read-only)
> The process name of a Postfix command or daemon process.

proxy_read_maps (see 'postconf -d' output)
> The lookup tables that the **proxymap**(8) server is allowed to access for the read-only service.

Available in Postfix 2.5 and later:

data_directory (see 'postconf -d' output)
> The directory with Postfix-writable data files (for example: caches, pseudo-random numbers).

proxy_write_maps (see 'postconf -d' output)
> The lookup tables that the **proxymap**(8) server is allowed to access for the read-write service.

SEE ALSO
postconf(5), configuration parameters
master(5), generic daemon options

README FILES
Use "**postconf readme_directory**" or "**postconf html_directory**" to locate this information.
DATABASE_README, Postfix lookup table overview

LICENSE
The Secure Mailer license must be distributed with this software.

HISTORY
The proxymap service was introduced with Postfix 2.0.

AUTHOR(S)
Wietse Venema
IBM T.J. Watson Research
P.O. Box 704
Yorktown Heights, NY 10598, USA

NAME

    psrset — control processor sets

SYNOPSIS

    psrset [*setid* . . .]
    psrset -a *setid cpuid* . . .
    psrset -b *setid pid* . . .
    psrset -c [*cpuid* . . .]
    psrset -d *setid*
    psrset -e *setid command*
    psrset -i [*setid* . . .]
    psrset -p
    psrset -r *cpuid* . . .
    psrset -u *pid* . . .

DESCRIPTION

    The **psrset** command can be used to control and inspect processor sets.

    The system always contains at least one processor set: the default set. The default set must contain at least one online processor (CPU) at all times.

    Available options:

    -a   Assign one or more processors (CPUs) to the set *setid*. In the current implementation, a CPU may only be present in one set. CPU IDs are as reported and used by the cpuctl(8) command.

    -b   Bind one or more processes to the set *setid*. All LWPs within the processes will be affected. Bindings are inherited when new LWPs or processes are forked. However, setting a new binding on a parent process does not affect the bindings of its existing child processes.

    -c   Create a new processor set. If successful, the ID of the new set will be printed. If a list of CPU IDs is provided, those CPUs will be assigned to the set upon creation. Otherwise, the set will be created empty.

    -d   Delete the processor set specified by *setid*. Any LWPs bound to the set will be re-bound to the default processor set.

    -e   Execute a command within the processor set specified by *setid*.

    -i   List all processor sets. For each set, print the member CPUs. If **psrset** is run without any options, it behaves as if **-i** were given.

    -p   List all CPUs. For each CPU, print the associated processor set.

    -r   Remove a CPU from its current set, and return it back to the default processor set.

    -u   Bind the specified processes to the system default processor set.

SEE ALSO

    pset(3), cpuctl(8), schedctl(8)

HISTORY

    The **psrset** command first appeared in NetBSD 5.0.

NAME
    pstat — display system data structures

SYNOPSIS
    pstat [**-T** | **-f** | **-s** | **-t** | **-v**] [**-ghkmn**] [**-M** *core*] [**-N** *system*]

DESCRIPTION
    pstat displays open file entry, swap space utilization, terminal state, and vnode data structures. If *corefile* is given, the information is sought there, otherwise in /dev/kmem. The required namelist is taken from /netbsd unless *system* is specified.

    The following options are available:

    -T   Prints the number of used and free slots for open files, used vnodes, and swap space. This option is useful for checking to see how large system tables become if the system is under heavy load.

    -f   Print the open file table with these headings:

        LOC   The core location of this table entry.

        TYPE   The type of object the file table entry points to.

        FLG   Miscellaneous state variables encoded thus:

            R   open for reading
            W   open for writing
            A   open for appending
            S   shared lock present
            X   exclusive lock present
            I   signal pgrp when data ready

        CNT   Number of processes that know this open file.

        MSG   Number of messages outstanding for this file.

        DATA   The location of the vnode table entry or socket structure for this file.

        USE   Number of active users of this open file.

        IFLG   Value of internal flags.

        OFFSET
            The file offset (see lseek(2)).

    -g   The **-g** option uses (1024 * 1024 * 1024) byte blocks instead of the default 512 byte.

    -h   Use humanize_number(3) to display (swap) sizes.

    -k   Use 1K-byte blocks.

    -m   The **-m** option uses (1024 * 1024) byte blocks instead of the default 512 byte.

    -n   Print devices by major/minor number rather than by name.

    -s   Print information about swap space usage on all the swap areas compiled into the kernel. The first column is the device name of the partition. The next column is the total space available in the partition. The *Used* column indicates the total blocks used so far; the *Available* column indicates how much space is remaining on each partition. The *Capacity* reports the percentage of space used.

If more than one partition is configured into the system, totals for all of the statistics will be reported in the final line of the report.

-t   Print table for terminals with these headings:

LINE   Physical device name.

RAW   Number of characters in raw input queue.

CAN   Number of characters in canonicalized input queue.

OUT   Number of characters in output queue.

HWT   High water mark for output.

LWT   Low water mark for output.

COL   Calculated column position of terminal.

STATE   Miscellaneous state variables encoded thus:

T	delay timeout in progress
O	open
F	outq has been flushed during DMA
C	carrier is on
B	busy doing output
A	process is awaiting output
X	open for exclusive use
S	output stopped
K	further input blocked
Y	tty in async I/O mode
D	state for lowercase '\' work
E	within a \ . . . / for **PRTRUB**
L	next character is literal
P	retyping suspended input (**PENDIN**)
N	counting tab width, ignore FLUSHO
>	tty used for dialout

SESS   Session for which this is controlling terminal.

PGID   Current foreground process group associated with this terminal.

DISC   Line discipline; `term` for **TTYDISC** (see `termios(4)`), `tab` for **TABLDISC** (see `tb(4)`), `slip` for **SLIPDISC** (see `sl(4)`), `ppp` for **PPPDISC** (see `ppp(4)`), `strip` for **STRIPDISC** (see `strip(4)`), `hdlc` for **HDLCDISC**.

-v   Print the active vnodes. Each group of vnodes corresponding to a particular filesystem is preceded by a two line header. The first line consists of the following:

*** MOUNT *fstype from* `on` *on fsflags*

where *fstype* is one of *adosfs, afs, cd9660, fdesc, ffs, ext2fs, kernfs, lfs, lofs, mfs, msdos, nfs, null, procfs, umap, union*; *from* is the filesystem mounted from; *on* is the directory the filesystem is mounted on; and *fsflags* is a list of optional flags applied to the mount (see `mount(8)`). The second line is a header for the individual fields, the first part of which are fixed, and the second part are filesystem type specific. The headers common to all vnodes are:

ADDR   Location of this vnode.

TYP   File type.

VFLAG   A list of letters representing vnode flags:

R	VROOT root of its file system.
T	VTEXT pure text prototype.
S	VSYSTEM vnode being used by kernel.
I	VISTTY vnode is a tty.
E	VEXECMAP vnode has PROT_EXEC mappings.
L	VXLOCK locked to change underlying type.
W	VXWANT process is waiting for vnode.
B	VBWAIT waiting for output to complete.
A	VALIASED vnode has an alias.
D	VDIROP lfs vnode involved in directory op.
Y	VLAYER vnode is on layer filesystem.
O	VONWORKLST vnode is on syncer work-list.

USE   The number of references to this vnode.

HOLD   The number of I/O buffers held by this vnode.

TAG   The type of underlying data.

NPAGE   The number of pages in this vnode.

FILEID   The vnode fileid. In the case of *ffs* or *ext2fs* this is the inode number.

IFLAG   Miscellaneous filesystem specific state variables encoded thus:

For ffs, lfs or ext2fs:

A	access time must be corrected
C	changed time must be corrected
U	update time (fs(5)) must be corrected
M	contains modifications
a	has been accessed
R	has a rename in progress
S	shared lock applied
E	exclusive lock applied
c	is being cleaned (LFS)
D	directory operation in progress (LFS)
s	blocks to be freed in free count

For nfs:

W	waiting for I/O buffer flush to complete
P	I/O buffers being flushed
M	locally modified data exists
E	an earlier write failed
A	special file accessed
U	special file updated
C	special file times changed

SIZ/RDEV
              Number of bytes in an ordinary file, or major and minor device of special file.

ENVIRONMENT

BLOCKSIZE If the environment variable BLOCKSIZE is set, and the **−k** option is not specified, the block counts will be displayed in units of that size block.

FILES

/netbsd	namelist
/dev/kmem	default source of tables

SEE ALSO

ps(1), systat(1), vmstat(1), stat(2), fs(5), iostat(8)

K. Thompson, *UNIX Implementation.*

HISTORY

The **pstat** command appeared in 4.0BSD.

BUGS

Swap statistics are reported for all swap partitions compiled into the kernel, regardless of whether those partitions are being used.

Does not understand NFS swap servers.

NAME
>   pvchange – change attributes of a physical volume

SYNOPSIS
>   **pvchange** [--addtag Tag] [−A|--autobackup y|n] [−d|--debug] [--deltag Tag] [−h|−?|--help] [−t|--test]
>   [−v|--verbose] [−a|--all] [−x|--allocatable y|n] [−u|--uuid] [PhysicalVolumePath...]

DESCRIPTION
>   pvchange allows you to change the allocation permissions of one or more physical volumes.

OPTIONS
>   See **lvm** for common options.
>
>   −a, --all
>   If PhysicalVolumePath is not specified on the command line all physical volumes are searched for
>   and used.
>
>   −u, --uuid
>   Generate new random UUID for specified physical volumes.
>
>   −x, --allocatable y|n
>   Enable or disable allocation of physical extents on this physical volume.

Example
>   "pvchange -x n /dev/sdk1" disallows the allocation of physical extents on this physical volume (possibly
>   because of disk errors, or because it will be removed after freeing it.

SEE ALSO
>   **lvm**(8), **pvcreate**(8)

NAME

       pvck – check physical volume metadata

SYNOPSIS

       pvck [**–d**|**--debug**] [**–h**|**--help**] [**–v**|**--verbose**] [**--labelsector**] *PhysicalVolume* [*PhysicalVolume...*]

DESCRIPTION

       pvck checks physical volume LVM metadata for consistency.

OPTIONS

       See **lvm** for common options.

       --labelsector sector

             By default, 4 sectors of **PhysicalVolume** are scanned for an LVM label, starting at sector 0. This parameter allows you to specify a different starting sector for the scan and is useful for recovery situations. For example, suppose the partition table is corrupted or lost on /dev/sda, but you suspect there was an LVM partition at approximately 100 MB. This area of the disk may be scanned by using the **--labelsector** parameter with a value of 204800 (100 * 1024 * 1024 / 512 = 204800):

             pvck --labelsector 204800 /dev/sda

             Note that a script can be used with **--labelsector** to automate the process of finding LVM labels.

SEE ALSO

       lvm(8), **pvcreate**(8), **pvscan**(8) **vgck**(8)

NAME
        pvcreate – initialize a disk or partition for use by LVM

SYNOPSIS
        pvcreate [−d|−−debug] [−f[f]|−−force [−−force]] [−y|−−yes] [−h|−−help] [−t|−−test] [−v|−−verbose]
        [−−labelsector]   [−M|−−metadatatype*type*]   [−−metadatacopies#*copies*]   [−−metadatasize*size*]
        [−−restorefile*file*] [−−setphysicalvolumesize*size*] [−u|−−uuid*uuid*] [−−version] [−Z|−−zero*y|n*] *Physi-
        calVolume* [*PhysicalVolume*...]

DESCRIPTION
        pvcreate initializes *PhysicalVolume* for later use by the Logical Volume Manager (LVM). Each *Physi-
        calVolume* can be a disk partition, whole disk, meta device, or loopback file. For DOS disk partitions, the
        partition id should be set to 0x8e using **fdisk**(8), **cfdisk**(8), or a equivalent. For **whole disk devices only**
        the partition table must be erased, which will effectively destroy all data on that disk. This can be done by
        zeroing the first sector with:

        dd if=/dev/zero of=*PhysicalVolume* **bs=512 count=1**

        Continue with **vgcreate**(8) to create a new volume group on *PhysicalVolume*, or **vgextend**(8) to add *Physi-
        calVolume* to an existing volume group.

OPTIONS
        See **lvm**(8) for common options.

        −f, −−force
                Force the creation without any confirmation. You can not recreate (reinitialize) a physical volume
                belonging to an existing volume group. In an emergency you can override this behaviour with -ff.

        −u, −−uuid uuid
                Specify the uuid for the device. Without this option, **pvcreate** generates a random uuid. All of
                your physical volumes must have unique uuids. You need to use this option before restoring a
                backup of LVM metadata onto a replacement device - see **vgcfgrestore**(8).

        −y, −−yes
                Answer yes to all questions.

        −Z, −−zero y|n
                Whether or not the first 4 sectors (2048 bytes) of the device should be wiped. If this option is not
                given, the default is to wipe these sectors unless either or both of the --restorefile or --uuid options
                were specified.

NEW METADATA OPTIONS
        LVM2 introduces a new format for storing metadata on disk. This new format is more efficient and
        resilient than the format the original version of LVM used and offers the advanced user greater flexibility
        and control.

        The new format may be selected on the command line with **-M2** or by setting **format = "lvm2"** in the
        global section of **lvm.conf**. Each physical volume in the same volume group must use the same format, but
        different volume groups on a machine may use different formats simultaneously: the tools can handle both
        formats. Additional formats can be added as shared libraries.

        Additional tools for manipulating the locations and sizes of metadata areas will be written in due course.
        Use the verbose/debug options on the tools to see where the metadata areas are placed.

        −−metadatasize size
                The approximate amount of space to be set aside for each metadata area. (The size you specify
                may get rounded.)

−−metadatacopies copies

> The number of metadata areas to set aside on each PV. Currently this can be 0, 1 or 2. If set to 2, two copies of the volume group metadata are held on the PV, one at the front of the PV and one at the end. If set to 1 (the default), one copy is kept at the front of the PV (starting in the 5th sector). If set to 0, no copies are kept on this PV - you might wish to use this with VGs containing large numbers of PVs. But if you do this and then later use **vgsplit** you must ensure that each VG is still going to have a suitable number of copies of the metadata after the split!

−−restorefile file

> In conjunction with **--uuid**, this extracts the location and size of the data on the PV from the file (produced by **vgcfgbackup**) and ensures that the metadata that the program produces is consistent with the contents of the file i.e. the physical extents will be in the same place and not get overwritten by new metadata. This provides a mechanism to upgrade the metadata format or to add/remove metadata areas. Use with care. See also **vgconvert**(8).

−−labelsector sector

> By default the PV is labelled with an LVM2 identifier in its second sector (sector 1). This lets you use a different sector near the start of the disk (between 0 and 3 inclusive - see LABEL_SCAN_SECTORS in the source). Use with care.

−−setphysicalvolumesize size

> Overrides the automatically-detected size of the PV. Use with care.

Example

Initialize partition #4 on the third SCSI disk and the entire fifth SCSI disk for later use by LVM:

pvcreate /dev/sdc4 /dev/sde

SEE ALSO

lvm(8), **vgcreate**(8), **vgextend**(8), **lvcreate**(8), **cfdisk**(8), **fdisk**(8), **losetup**(8), **mdadm**(8), **vgcfgrestore**(8), **vgconvert**(8)

NAME
pvcsif — configure ATM PVC sub interfaces

SYNOPSIS
pvcsif *interface* [**-s**]
pvcsif -a

DESCRIPTION
pvcsif creates a sub interface for an ATM PVC. A sub interface pvc(4) is dynamically created. The created interface is bound to *interface* but at this point no VC is assigned. To assign a VC, pvctxctl(8) should be used later.

A PVC sub interface is intended to use an ATM PVC as an alternative serial connection, and to be allocated per PVC basis. A PVC sub interface looks as a point-to-point interface and is multicast capable, as opposed to the NBMA (NonBroadcast Multiple Access) model that requires a MARS server. A point-to-point interface is useful to run MBone or protocols requiring multicast, such as RSVP and IPv6, over a PVC WAN connection.

Note that a sub interface is not a full-fledged interface but just an indirect reference to the real interface.

The options are as follows:

-s   For use with a shell, it prints the created interface name.

-a   Lists the existing sub interfaces.

SEE ALSO
en(4), pvc(4), ifconfig(8), pvctxctl(8)

BUGS
Currently, there is no way to remove a sub interface.

NAME
pvctxctl — display or control ATM PVC transmitter parameters

SYNOPSIS
pvctxctl *interface* [[vpi:]*vci*]
pvctxctl *interface* [vpi:]*vci* [**-n**] [**-b** *max-bandwidth*] [**-j** [vpi:]*vci*] [**-p** *pcr*]

DESCRIPTION
pvctxctl displays or controls the shaper parameters of an ATM VC. When a shaper value is specified, **pvctxctl** sets a shaper to an ATM VC. **pvctxctl** works for a PVC sub interface pvc(4) as well as a real ATM interface en(4).

For a real ATM interface, the specified VC should be assigned beforehand by route(8).

For a sub interface, **pvctxctl** assigns the specified VC to the sub interface. If another VC is already assigned to the sub interface, the old VC is invalidated.

Availability of shapers, the number of hardware shaper channels, and accuracy of shaping are all device dependent. For example, ENI Midway chip has 8 shaper channels but the driver reserves one for non-shaping VCs.

The options are as follows:

interface
             The *interface* parameter is a string of the form "name unit", for example, "en0".

[vpi:]*vci*   The VC number to which the shaper is assigned. When the VPI number is omitted, VPI number 0 is assumed. For example, to assign a shaper to VPI=0 and VCI=201, the following forms can be used: "201", "0xc9", "0:201", "0:0xc9".

-b *max-bandwidth*
             The PCR parameter can be specified also in "bits per second". The rate is the rate of AAL5 frame and the PCR is calculated by the following form:

                      PCR = max-bandwidth / 8 / 48

             "K" and "M" can be used as a short hand of "000" and "000000" respectively. For example, "45M" means "45Mbps" or PCR value "117187".

-j [vpi:]*vci*
             The join parameter is intended for VP shaping. The VC shaper channel is shared with the existing VC, which means the sum of the cell rates never exceeds the maximum PCR among the shared VCs. On the other hand, when the shaper channel is not shared, the sum of the cell rates could be the sum of the PCRs.

             For example, if two VCs (say 201 and 202) share a 45Mbps VP, use:

                      # pvctxctl en0 201 -b 45M
                      # pvctxctl en0 202 -b 45M -j 201

-n   This parameter is only for a sub interface. Use NULL encapsulation instead of LLC/SNAP.

-p *pcr*   The PCR (Peak Cell Rate) parameter specifies the peak cell rate in "cells per second". If PCR value "0" is specified, no shaper is assigned, which means cells are sent at full-speed of the link. If PCR value "-1" is specified, the corresponding VC is invalidated.

SEE ALSO

en(4), ifconfig(8), pvcsif(8), route(8)

BUGS

A real ATM interface and a sub interface require different sequences to set a shaper. For example, to assign a 45Mbps shaper to VC 201 (0xc9) of en0:

```
# ifconfig en0 10.0.0.1
# route add -iface 10.0.0.2 -link en0:3.0.0.c9
# pvctxctl en0 0xc9 -b 45M
```

For a shadow interface,

```
# pvcsif en0                            # creates pvc0
# ifconfig pvc0 10.0.0.1 10.0.0.2
# pvctxctl pvc0 201 -b 45M
```

NAME
pvdisplay – display attributes of a physical volume

SYNOPSIS
pvdisplay [–c|––colon] [–d|––debug] [–h|–?|––help] [–s|––short] [–v[v]|––verbose [––verbose]] Physical VolumePath [PhysicalVolumePath...]

DESCRIPTION
pvdisplay allows you to see the attributes of one or more physical volumes like size, physical extent size, space used for the volume group descriptor area and so on.

pvs (8) is an alternative that provides the same information in the style of **ps** (1).

OPTIONS
See **lvm** for common options.

–c, ––colon

> Generate colon separated output for easier parsing in scripts or programs. N.B. **pvs** (8) provides considerably more control over the output.

> The values are:

> * physical volume device name
> * volume group name
> * physical volume size in kilobytes
> * internal physical volume number (obsolete)
> * physical volume status
> * physical volume (not) allocatable
> * current number of logical volumes on this physical volume
> * physical extent size in kilobytes
> * total number of physical extents
> * free number of physical extents
> * allocated number of physical extents

–s, ––short

> Only display the size of the given physical volumes.

–m, ––maps

> Display the mapping of physical extents to logical volumes and logical extents.

SEE ALSO
lvm(8), **pvcreate**(8), **lvcreate**(8), **vgcreate**(8)

NAME

pvmove – move physical extents

SYNOPSIS

pvmove [--abort] [--alloc AllocationPolicy] [-b|--background] [-d|--debug] [-h|--help] [-i|--interval
Seconds] [-v|--verbose] [-n|--name LogicalVolume] [SourcePhysicalVolume[:PE[-PE]...] [Destination-
PhysicalVolume[:PE[-PE]...]...]]

DESCRIPTION

pvmove allows you to move the allocated physical extents (PEs) on *SourcePhysicalVolume* to one or more
other physical volumes (PVs). You can optionally specify a source *LogicalVolume* in which case only
extents used by that LV will be moved to free (or specified) extents on *DestinationPhysicalVolume*(s). If no
DestinationPhysicalVolume is specified, the normal allocation rules for the volume group are used.

If **pvmove** gets interrupted for any reason (e.g. the machine crashes) then run **pvmove** again without any
PhysicalVolume arguments to restart any moves that were in progress from the last checkpoint. Alternatively use **pvmove --abort** at any time to abort them at the last checkpoint.

You can run more than one pvmove at once provided they are moving data off different SourcePhysicalVol-
umes, but additional pvmoves will ignore any logical volumes already in the process of being changed, so
some data might not get moved.

pvmove works as follows:

1. A temporary 'pvmove' logical volume is created to store details of all the data movements required.

2. Every logical volume in the volume group is searched for contiguous data that need moving according to
the command line arguments. For each piece of data found, a new segment is added to the end of the
pvmove LV. This segment takes the form of a temporary mirror to copy the data from the original location
to a newly-allocated location. The original LV is updated to use the new temporary mirror segment in the
pvmove LV instead of accessing the data directly.

3. The volume group metadata is updated on disk.

4. The first segment of the pvmove logical volume is activated and starts to mirror the first part of the data.
Only one segment is mirrored at once as this is usually more efficient.

5. A daemon repeatedly checks progress at the specified time interval. When it detects that the first temporary mirror is in-sync, it breaks that mirror so that only the new location for that data gets used and writes a
checkpoint into the volume group metadata on disk. Then it activates the mirror for the next segment of the
pvmove LV.

6. When there are no more segments left to be mirrored, the temporary logical volume is removed and the
volume group metadata is updated so that the logical volumes reflect the new data locations.

Note that this new process cannot support the original LVM1 type of on-disk metadata. Metadata can be
converted using **vgconvert**(8).

OPTIONS

--*abort*
    Abort any moves in progress.

-*b*, --*background*
    Run the daemon in the background.

       −i, −−interval Seconds
             Report progress as a percentage at regular intervals.

       −n, −−name LogicalVolume
             Move only the extents belonging to *LogicalVolume* from *SourcePhysicalVolume* instead of all allo-
             cated extents to the destination physical volume(s).

EXAMPLES
       To move all logical extents of any logical volumes on **/dev/hda4** to free physical extents elsewhere in the
       volume group, giving verbose runtime information, use:

           pvmove -v /dev/hda4

SEE ALSO
       lvm(8), **vgconvert**(8)

NAME
pvremove – remove a physical volume

SYNOPSIS
pvremove [−d|−−**debug**] [−**f**[f]|−−**force** [−−**force**]] [−h|−−help] [−t|−−**test**] [−v[v]|−−**verbose** [−−**ver-
bose**]] [−y|−−**yes**] *PhysicalVolume* [*PhysicalVolume*...]

DESCRIPTION
pvremove wipes the label on a device so that LVM will no longer recognise it as a physical volume.

OPTIONS
See **lvm** for common options.

SEE ALSO
lvm(8), **pvcreate**(8), **pvdisplay**(8)

NAME
pvresize – resize a disk or partition in use by LVM2

SYNOPSIS
pvresize [**–d|--debug**] [**–h|--help**] [**–t|--test**] [**–v|--verbose**] [**--setphysicalvolumesize**size] *PhysicalVolume* [*PhysicalVolume*...]

DESCRIPTION
pvresize resizes *PhysicalVolume* which may already be in a volume group and have active logical volumes allocated on it.

OPTIONS
See **lvm**(8) for common options.

--setphysicalvolumesize size
> Overrides the automatically-detected size of the PV. Use with care, or prior to reducing the physical size of the device.

EXAMPLES
Expand the PV on /dev/sda1 after enlarging the partition with fdisk:

pvresize /dev/sda1

Shrink the PV on /dev/sda1 prior to shrinking the partition with fdisk (ensure that the PV size is appropriate for your intended new partition size):

pvresize --setphysicalvolumesize 40G /dev/sda1

RESTRICTIONS
pvresize will refuse to shrink *PhysicalVolume* if it has allocated extents after where its new end would be. In the future, it should relocate these elsewhere in the volume group if there is sufficient free space, like **pvmove** does.

pvresize won't currently work correctly on LVM1 volumes or PVs with extra metadata areas.

SEE ALSO
lvm(8), **pvmove**(8), **lvresize**(8), **fdisk**(8)

NAME

pvs – report information about physical volumes

SYNOPSIS

pvs [--aligned] [-d|--debug] [-h|-?|--help] [--ignorelockingfailure] [--nameprefixes] [--noheadings]
[--nosuffix] [-o|--options [+]Field[,Field]] [-O|--sort [+|-]Key1[,[+|-]Key2[,...]]] [--rows] [--seg-
ments] [--separator Separator] [--unbuffered] [--units hsbkmgtHKMGT] [--unquoted] [-v|--verbose]
[--version] [PhysicalVolume [PhysicalVolume...]]

DESCRIPTION

pvs produces formatted output about physical volumes.

OPTIONS

See **lvm** for common options.

--aligned

Use with --separator to align the output columns.

--nameprefixes

Add an "LVM2_" prefix plus the field name to the output. Useful with --noheadings to produce a
list of field=value pairs that can be used to set environment variables (for example, in **udev (7)**
rules).

--noheadings

Suppress the headings line that is normally the first line of output. Useful if grepping the output.

--nosuffix

Suppress the suffix on output sizes. Use with --units (except h and H) if processing the output.

-o, --options

Comma-separated ordered list of columns. Precede the list with '+' to append to the default selection of columns. Column names are: pv_fmt, pv_uuid, pv_size, dev_size, pv_free, pv_used,
pv_name, pv_attr, pv_pe_count, pv_pe_alloc_count, pv_tags, pvseg_start, pvseg_size, pe_start,
pv_mda_count, pv_mda_free, and pv_mda_size. With --segments, any "pvseg_" prefixes are
optional; otherwise any "pv_" prefixes are optional. Columns mentioned in **vgs (8)** can also be
chosen. The pv_attr bits are: (a)llocatable and e(x)ported. Use -o help to view the full list of fields
available.

--segments

Produces one line of output for each contiguous allocation of space on each Physical Volume,
showing the start (pvseg_start) and length (pvseg_size) in units of physical extents.

-O, --sort

Comma-separated ordered list of columns to sort by. Replaces the default selection. Precede any
column with - for a reverse sort on that column.

--rows

Output columns as rows.

--separator Separator

String to use to separate each column. Useful if grepping the output.

--unbuffered

Produce output immediately without sorting or aligning the columns properly.

--units hsbkmgtHKMGT

All sizes are output in these units: (h)uman-readable, (s)ectors, (b)ytes, (k)ilobytes, (m)egabytes,
(g)igabytes, (t)erabytes. Capitalise to use multiples of 1000 (S.I.) instead of 1024. Can also specify custom (u)nits e.g. --units 3M

--unquoted

When used with --nameprefixes, output values in the field=value pairs are not quoted.

SEE ALSO
        lvm(8), **pvdisplay**(8), **lvs**(8), **vgs**(8)

NAME
pvscan – scan all disks for physical volumes

SYNOPSIS
pvscan [−d|−−**debug**] [−e|−−exported] [−h|−−help] [−−ignorelockingfailure] [−n|−−**novolumegroup**] [−s|−−short] [−u|−−uuid] [−**v**[**v**]|−−**verbose** [−−**verbose**]]

DESCRIPTION
pvscan scans all supported LVM block devices in the system for physical volumes.

OPTIONS
See **lvm** for common options.

−e, −−**exported**
> Only show physical volumes belonging to exported volume groups.

−n, −−**novolumegroup**
> Only show physical volumes not belonging to any volume group.

−s, −−**short**
> Short listing format.

−u, −−**uuid**
> Show UUIDs (Uniform Unique Identifiers) in addition to device special names.

SEE ALSO
lvm(8), **pvcreate**(8), **pvdisplay**(8)

NAME
pwd_mkdb — generate the password databases

SYNOPSIS
pwd_mkdb [**-BLpsvw**] [**-c** *cachesize*] [**-d** *directory*] [**-u** *username*] [**-V** *version*]
        file

DESCRIPTION
pwd_mkdb creates db(3) style secure and insecure databases for the specified file. These databases are then installed into "/etc/spwd.db" and "/etc/pwd.db" respectively. The file is installed into "/etc/master.passwd". The file must be in the correct format (see passwd(5)). It is important to note that the format used in this system is different from the historic Version 7 style format.

The options are as follows:

-B   Store data in big-endian format (see also **-L**).

-c *cachesize*
        Specify the size of the memory cache in megabytes used by the hashing library. On systems with a large user base, a small cache size can lead to prohibitively long database file rebuild times. As a rough guide, the memory usage of **pwd_mkdb** in megabytes will be a little bit more than twice the figure specified here. If unspecified, this value will be calculated based on the size of the input file up to a maximum of 8 megabytes.

-d *directory*
        Change the root directory of the generated files from "/" to *directory*.

-L   Store data in little-endian format (see also **-B**).

-p   Create a Version 7 style password file and install it into "/etc/passwd".

-s   Update the secure database only. This is useful when only encrypted passwords have changed. This option negates the effect of any **-p** option.

-u *name*
        Don't re-build the database files, but instead modify or add entries for the specified user only. This option may only be used when the line number and user name in the password file have not changed, or when adding a new user from the last line in the password file.

-V *version*
        Upgrade or downgrade databases to the numbered version. Version 0 is the old format (up to and including NetBSD 5.0) with the 4 byte time fields and version 1 is the new format with the 8 byte time fields (greater than NetBSD 5.0). NetBSD 5.0 cannot read version 1 databases. All versions above NetBSD 5.0 can read and write both version 0 and version 1 databases. By default the databases stay in the version they were before the command was run.

-v   Mention when a version change occurs.

-w   Print a warning if the system is using old style databases.

The two databases differ in that the secure version contains the user's encrypted password and the insecure version has an asterisk ("*").

The databases are used by the C library password routines (see getpwent(3)).

EXIT STATUS
pwd_mkdb exits zero on success, non-zero on failure.

FILES

/etc/master.passwd	The current password file.
/etc/passwd	A Version 7 format password file.
/etc/pwd.db	The insecure password database file.
/etc/pwd.db.tmp	A temporary file.
/etc/spwd.db	The secure password database file.
/etc/spwd.db.tmp	A temporary file.

SEE ALSO

chpass(1), passwd(1), pwhash(1), db(3), getpwent(3), pw_mkdb(3), passwd(5), useradd(8), userdel(8), usermod(8), vipw(8)

COMPATIBILITY

Previous versions of the system had a program similar to **pwd_mkdb** which built *dbm* style databases for the password file but depended on the calling programs to install them. The program was renamed in order that previous users of the program not be surprised by the changes in functionality.

BUGS

Because of the necessity for atomic update of the password files, **pwd_mkdb** uses rename(2) to install them. This, however, requires that the file specified on the command line live on the same file system as the "/etc" directory.

There are the obvious races with multiple people running **pwd_mkdb** on different password files at the same time. The front-ends to chpass(1), passwd(1), useradd(8), userdel(8), usermod(8), and vipw(8) handle the locking necessary to avoid this problem.

The database files are copied when the **−u** option is used. Real locking would make this unnecessary.

Although the DB format is endian-transparent, the data stored in the DB is not. Also, the format doesn't lend itself to insertion or removal of records from arbitrary locations in the password file. This is difficult to fix without breaking compatibility.

Using the **−u** option on a system where multiple users share the same UID can have unexpected results.

NAME

     pxeboot — network boot NetBSD/i386 through a PXE BIOS extension

DESCRIPTION

     pxeboot is a NetBSD boot program running on top of a PXE BIOS extension which is provided by the motherboard or a plug-in network adapter, in accordance with the Intel Preboot eXecution Environement (PXE) specification.

     This manual page assumes the **pxeboot** program has been configured via installboot(8) to use a boot.cfg(5) file. For historical reasons boot.cfg(5) is NOT loaded by default. See **EXAMPLES** for how to enable it.

     Network booting a system through PXE is a two-stage process:

1.   The PXE BIOS issues a DHCP request and fetches the NetBSD **pxeboot** program using TFTP.

2.   The NetBSD **pxeboot** program takes control. It immediately issues another DHCP request to get the name of a boot.cfg(5) file to load, using "boot.cfg" by default. If the boot config file is not found, or if the supplied file appears not to be a boot configuration file, the file is skipped. Otherwise it is loaded and obeyed as described in boot.cfg(5). If a boot configuration is not loaded, the user has the option to enter a limited version of the standard interactive boot mode by pressing a key within five seconds. After this time, or after the user's **boot** command, another DHCP request is issued and the kernel filename returned by the DHCP reply, using "netbsd" by default, is loaded. To read the kernel file, the NFS (version 2) or TFTP protocols can be used.

     The DHCP request issued by the NetBSD **pxeboot** program has the following special parameters:

Bootfile name
> is set to "boot.cfg" during the first request, and then to the *filename* argument on the **boot** command line typed in by the user (can be empty), using "netbsd" in the non-interactive case.

DHCP Vendor class identifier tag
> is set to "NetBSD:i386:libsa".

     The DHCP server can use these fields (i.e. the DHCP vendor class identifier tag and the requested file name, possibly supplied by the user's command line input to the **pxeboot** program) to distinguish between the various originators of requests (PXE BIOS, first and second **pxeboot** stage, NetBSD kernel), and to alter its behaviour. For example, this can be used to support alternative NetBSD installations on one machine.

     In addition to the standard network interface configuration, the following fields in the DHCP reply are interpreted:

Bootfile name
> specifies the protocol to be used, and the filename of the boot config or NetBSD kernel to be booted, separated by a colon. Available protocols are "nfs" and "tftp". The boot config or kernel filename part is interpreted relatively to the NFS root directory (see the *Root path* reply field below) or the TFTP server's root directory (which might be a subdirectory within the TFTP server's filesystem, depending on the implementation), respectively. If the *Bootfile name* field replied by the DHCP server does not contain a colon, it is ignored, and the *filename* typed in at the **pxeboot** command line prompt (or the "netbsd" default, see the section about the *Bootfile name* field in the DHCP request above) is used. If no protocol was specified, "nfs" is assumed.

Next server
> is used as the location of the tftp server.

Swap server
> can be used to override the "server IP address" if NFS is used to access the kernel. This matches the behaviour of the NetBSD kernel to access its root file system on NFS. This way, different TFTP and

NFS servers can be communicated to the DHCP client (it is actually a deficiency of the DHCP protocol to provide a "root path" field but no corresponding IP address).

Root path
>   is used as path to be mounted in the NFS case to access the kernel file, matching the NetBSD kernel's behaviour.

The commands accepted in interactive mode are:

boot [*device*:] [*filename*] [**-1234abcdmqsvxz**]
>   Boot NetBSD. See **boot** in boct(8) for full details.

help
>   Print an overview about commands and arguments.

quit
>   Leave the **pxeboot** program.

By default the output from **pxeboot** and from the booted kernel will go to the system's BIOS console. This can be changed to be one of the serial ports by using **installboot** to modify the boot options contained in the pxeboot_ia32.bin file.

FILES
/usr/mdec/pxeboot_ia32.bin

EXAMPLES
To enable boot.cfg(5) support in the **pxeboot** program:

```
installboot -e -o bootconf pxeboot_ia32.bin
```

The first /etc/dhcpd.conf example shows a simple configuration which just loads "boct.cfg" and "netbsd" from the client's NFS root directory, using the defaults for protocol and kernel filename. Similar setups should be possible with any BOOTP/DHCP server.

```
host myhost {
    hardware ethernet 00:00:00:00:00:00;
    fixed-address myhost;
    option host-name "myhost";
    filename "pxeboot_ia32.bin";
    option swap-server mynfsserver;
    option root-path "/export/myhost";
}
```

The following /etc/dhcpd.conf entry sets loads the boot config and kernel over tftp. This can be used, for example, for installing machines by using an install kernel.

```
host myhost {
    hardware ethernet 00:00:0C:00:00:00;
    fixed-address myhost;
    option host-name "myhost";
    next-server mytftpserver;

    # This section allows dhcpd to respond with different answers
    # for the different tftp requests for the bootloader and kernel.
    if substring (option vendor-class-identifier, 0, 20)
      = "PXEClient:Arch:00000" {
        filename "pxeboot_ia32.bin";
```

```
        } elsif substring (option vendor-class-identifier, 0, 17)
        = "NetBSD:i386:libsa" {
          if filename = "boot.cfg" {
              filename "tftp:boot.cfg";
          } else if filename = "netbsd" {
              filename "tftp:netbsd-INSTALL.gz";
          }
        }
      }
```

The following /etc/dhcpd.conf entry shows how different system installations can be booted depending on the user's input on the **pxeboot** command line.

```
host myhost {
    hardware ethernet 00:00:00:00:00:00;
    fixed-address myhost;
    option host-name "myhost";
    next-server mytftpserver;
    if substring (option vendor-class-identifier, 0, 9) = "PXEClient" {
        filename "pxeboot_ia32.bin";
    } elsif filename = "boot.cfg" {
        filename "tftp:boot.cfg";
    } elsif filename = "tftp" {
        filename "tftp:netbsd.myhost";
    } else {
        option swap-server mynfsserver;
        option root-path "/export/myhost";
        if filename = "generic" {
            filename "nfs:gennetbsd";
        } else {
            filename "nfs:netbsd";
        }
    }
}
```

The TFTP server is supplied using the *next-server* directive. The NFS server for the root file system is *mynfsserver*. The *swap-server:root-path* is only used in the NFS case and by the NetBSD kernel to mount the root file system.

SEE ALSO

boot.cfg(5), boot(8), dhcpd(8), diskless(8), installboot(8)

Intel Corporation, *Preboot Execution Environment (PXE) Specification*, Version 2.1, September 20, 1999.

HISTORY

The NetBSD/i386 **pxeboot** command first appeared in NetBSD 1.6.

BUGS

If an error is encountered while reading the NetBSD kernel file or if its file format wasn't recognized, it is impossible to retry the operation because the PXE network stack is already removed from the system RAM.

You need the **pxeboot** from an i386 build to boot an i386 kernel, and that from an amd64 build to boot an amd64 kernel.

NAME

qmgr – Postfix queue manager

SYNOPSIS

qmgr [generic Postfix daemon options]

DESCRIPTION

The **qmgr**(8) daemon awaits the arrival of incoming mail and arranges for its delivery via Postfix delivery processes. The actual mail routing strategy is delegated to the **trivial-rewrite**(8) daemon. This program expects to be run from the **master**(8) process manager.

Mail addressed to the local **double-bounce** address is logged and discarded. This stops potential loops caused by undeliverable bounce notifications.

MAIL QUEUES

The **qmgr**(8) daemon maintains the following queues:

incoming

Inbound mail from the network, or mail picked up by the local **pickup**(8) daemon from the **maildrop** directory.

active Messages that the queue manager has opened for delivery. Only a limited number of messages is allowed to enter the **active** queue (leaky bucket strategy, for a fixed delivery rate).

deferred

Mail that could not be delivered upon the first attempt. The queue manager implements exponential backoff by doubling the time between delivery attempts.

corrupt

Unreadable or damaged queue files are moved here for inspection.

hold Messages that are kept "on hold" are kept here until someone sets them free.

DELIVERY STATUS REPORTS

The **qmgr**(8) daemon keeps an eye on per-message delivery status reports in the following directories. Each status report file has the same name as the corresponding message file:

bounce Per-recipient status information about why mail is bounced. These files are maintained by the **bounce**(8) daemon.

defer Per-recipient status information about why mail is delayed. These files are maintained by the **defer**(8) daemon.

trace Per-recipient status information as requested with the Postfix "**sendmail -v**" or "**sendmail -bv**" command. These files are maintained by the **trace**(8) daemon.

The **qmgr**(8) daemon is responsible for asking the **bounce**(8), **defer**(8) or **trace**(8) daemons to send delivery reports.

STRATEGIES

The queue manager implements a variety of strategies for either opening queue files (input) or for message delivery (output).

leaky bucket

This strategy limits the number of messages in the **active** queue and prevents the queue manager from running out of memory under heavy load.

fairness

When the **active** queue has room, the queue manager takes one message from the **incoming** queue and one from the **deferred** queue. This prevents a large mail backlog from blocking the delivery of new mail.

slow start

This strategy eliminates "thundering herd" problems by slowly adjusting the number of parallel deliveries to the same destination.

round robin
> The queue manager sorts delivery requests by destination. Round-robin selection prevents one destination from dominating deliveries to other destinations.

exponential backoff
> Mail that cannot be delivered upon the first attempt is deferred. The time interval between delivery attempts is doubled after each attempt.

destination status cache
> The queue manager avoids unnecessary delivery attempts by maintaining a short-term, in-memory list of unreachable destinations.

preemptive message scheduling
> The queue manager attempts to minimize the average per-recipient delay while still preserving the correct per-message delays, using a sophisticated preemptive message scheduling.

TRIGGERS

On an idle system, the queue manager waits for the arrival of trigger events, or it waits for a timer to go off. A trigger is a one-byte message. Depending on the message received, the queue manager performs one of the following actions (the message is followed by the symbolic constant used internally by the software):

D (QMGR_REQ_SCAN_DEFERRED)
> Start a deferred queue scan. If a deferred queue scan is already in progress, that scan will be restarted as soon as it finishes.

I (QMGR_REQ_SCAN_INCOMING)
> Start an incoming queue scan. If an incoming queue scan is already in progress, that scan will be restarted as soon as it finishes.

A (QMGR_REQ_SCAN_ALL)
> Ignore deferred queue file time stamps. The request affects the next deferred queue scan.

F (QMGR_REQ_FLUSH_DEAD)
> Purge all information about dead transports and destinations.

W (TRIGGER_REQ_WAKEUP)
> Wakeup call, This is used by the master server to instantiate servers that should not go away forever. The action is to start an incoming queue scan.

The **qmgr**(8) daemon reads an entire buffer worth of triggers. Multiple identical trigger requests are collapsed into one, and trigger requests are sorted so that **A** and **F** precede **D** and **I**. Thus, in order to force a deferred queue run, one would request **A F D**; in order to notify the queue manager of the arrival of new mail one would request **I**.

STANDARDS
> RFC 3463 (Enhanced status codes)
> RFC 3464 (Delivery status notifications)

SECURITY
> The **qmgr**(8) daemon is not security sensitive. It reads single-character messages from untrusted local users, and thus may be susceptible to denial of service attacks. The **qmgr**(8) daemon does not talk to the outside world, and it can be run at fixed low privilege in a chrooted environment.

DIAGNOSTICS
> Problems and transactions are logged to the syslog daemon. Corrupted message files are saved to the **corrupt** queue for further inspection.
>
> Depending on the setting of the **notify_classes** parameter, the postmaster is notified of bounces and of other trouble.

BUGS
> A single queue manager process has to compete for disk access with multiple front-end processes such as **cleanup**(8). A sudden burst of inbound mail can negatively impact outbound delivery rates.

CONFIGURATION PARAMETERS

Changes to **main.cf** are not picked up automatically as **qmgr**(8) is a persistent process. Use the "**postfix reload**" command after a configuration change.

The text below provides only a parameter summary. See **postconf**(5) for more details including examples.

In the text below, *transport* is the first field in a **master.cf** entry.

COMPATIBILITY CONTROLS

Available before Postfix version 2.5:

allow_min_user (no)
> Allow a sender or recipient address to have '-' as the first character.

ACTIVE QUEUE CONTROLS

qmgr_clog_warn_time (300s)
> The minimal delay between warnings that a specific destination is clogging up the Postfix active queue.

qmgr_message_active_limit (20000)
> The maximal number of messages in the active queue.

qmgr_message_recipient_limit (20000)
> The maximal number of recipients held in memory by the Postfix queue manager, and the maximal size of the size of the short-term, in-memory "dead" destination status cache.

qmgr_message_recipient_minimum (10)
> The minimal number of in-memory recipients for any message.

default_recipient_limit (20000)
> The default per-transport upper limit on the number of in-memory recipients.

*transport*_**recipient_limit ($default_recipient_limit)**
> Idem, for delivery via the named message *transport*.

default_extra_recipient_limit (1000)
> The default value for the extra per-transport limit imposed on the number of in-memory recipients.

*transport*_**extra_recipient_limit ($default_extra_recipient_limit)**
> Idem, for delivery via the named message *transport*.

Available in Postfix version 2.4 and later:

default_recipient_refill_limit (100)
> The default per-transport limit on the number of recipients refilled at once.

*transport*_**recipient_refill_limit ($default_recipient_refill_limit)**
> Idem, for delivery via the named message *transport*.

default_recipient_refill_delay (5s)
> The default per-transport maximum delay between recipients refills.

*transport*_**recipient_refill_delay ($default_recipient_refill_delay)**
> Idem, for delivery via the named message *transport*.

DELIVERY CONCURRENCY CONTROLS

initial_destination_concurrency (5)
> The initial per-destination concurrency level for parallel delivery to the same destination.

default_destination_concurrency_limit (20)
> The default maximal number of parallel deliveries to the same destination.

*transport*_**destination_concurrency_limit ($default_destination_concurrency_limit)**
> Idem, for delivery via the named message *transport*.

Available in Postfix version 2.5 and later:

*transport*_**initial_destination_concurrency ($initial_destination_concurrency)**
> Initial concurrency for delivery via the named message *transport*.

default_destination_concurrency_failed_cohort_limit (1)
> How many pseudo-cohorts must suffer connection or handshake failure before a specific destination is considered unavailable (and further delivery is suspended).

*transport*_**destination_concurrency_failed_cohort_limit**   **($default_destination_concurrency_failed_cohort_limit)**
> Idem, for delivery via the named message *transport*.

default_destination_concurrency_negative_feedback (1)
> The per-destination amount of delivery concurrency negative feedback, after a delivery completes with a connection or handshake failure.

*transport*_**destination_concurrency_negative_feedback**   **($default_destination_concurrency_negative_feedback)**
> Idem, for delivery via the named message *transport*.

default_destination_concurrency_positive_feedback (1)
> The per-destination amount of delivery concurrency positive feedback, after a delivery completes without connection or handshake failure.

*transport*_**destination_concurrency_positive_feedback**   **($default_destination_concurrency_positive_feedback)**
> Idem, for delivery via the named message *transport*.

destination_concurrency_feedback_debug (no)
> Make the queue manager's feedback algorithm verbose for performance analysis purposes.

RECIPIENT SCHEDULING CONTROLS
default_destination_recipient_limit (50)
> The default maximal number of recipients per message delivery.

*transport*_**destination_recipient_limit ($default_destination_recipient_limit)**
> Idem, for delivery via the named message *transport*.

MESSAGE SCHEDULING CONTROLS
default_delivery_slot_cost (5)
> How often the Postfix queue manager's scheduler is allowed to preempt delivery of one message with another.

*transport*_**delivery_slot_cost ($default_delivery_slot_cost)**
> Idem, for delivery via the named message *transport*.

default_minimum_delivery_slots (3)
> How many recipients a message must have in order to invoke the Postfix queue manager's scheduling algorithm at all.

*transport*_**minimum_delivery_slots ($default_minimum_delivery_slots)**
> Idem, for delivery via the named message *transport*.

default_delivery_slot_discount (50)
> The default value for transport-specific _delivery_slot_discount settings.

*transport*_**delivery_slot_discount ($default_delivery_slot_discount)**
> Idem, for delivery via the named message *transport*.

default_delivery_slot_loan (3)
> The default value for transport-specific _delivery_slot_loan settings.

*transport*_**delivery_slot_loan ($default_delivery_slot_loan)**
> Idem, for delivery via the named message *transport*.

OTHER RESOURCE AND RATE CONTROLS

minimal_backoff_time (300s)

> The minimal time between attempts to deliver a deferred message; prior to Postfix 2.4 the default value was 1000s.

maximal_backoff_time (4000s)

> The maximal time between attempts to deliver a deferred message.

maximal_queue_lifetime (5d)

> The maximal time a message is queued before it is sent back as undeliverable.

queue_run_delay (300s)

> The time between deferred queue scans by the queue manager; prior to Postfix 2.4 the default value was 1000s.

transport_retry_time (60s)

> The time between attempts by the Postfix queue manager to contact a malfunctioning message delivery transport.

Available in Postfix version 2.1 and later:

bounce_queue_lifetime (5d)

> The maximal time a bounce message is queued before it is considered undeliverable.

Available in Postfix version 2.5 and later:

default_destination_rate_delay (0s)

> The default amount of delay that is inserted between individual deliveries to the same destination; with per-destination recipient limit > 1, a destination is a domain, otherwise it is a recipient.

*transport*_destination_rate_delay $default_destination_rate_delay

> Idem, for delivery via the named message *transport*.

MISCELLANEOUS CONTROLS

config_directory (see 'postconf -d' output)

> The default location of the Postfix main.cf and master.cf configuration files.

defer_transports (empty)

> The names of message delivery transports that should not deliver mail unless someone issues "**sendmail -q**" or equivalent.

delay_logging_resolution_limit (2)

> The maximal number of digits after the decimal point when logging sub-second delay values.

helpful_warnings (yes)

> Log warnings about problematic configuration settings, and provide helpful suggestions.

ipc_timeout (3600s)

> The time limit for sending or receiving information over an internal communication channel.

process_id (read-only)

> The process ID of a Postfix command or daemon process.

process_name (read-only)

> The process name of a Postfix command or daemon process.

queue_directory (see 'postconf -d' output)

> The location of the Postfix top-level queue directory.

syslog_facility (mail)

> The syslog facility of Postfix logging.

syslog_name (see 'postconf -d' output)

> The mail system name that is prepended to the process name in syslog records, so that "smtpd" becomes, for example, "postfix/smtpd".

FILES

/var/spool/postfix/incoming, incoming queue
/var/spool/postfix/active, active queue
/var/spool/postfix/deferred, deferred queue
/var/spool/postfix/bounce, non-delivery status
/var/spool/postfix/defer, non-delivery status
/var/spool/postfix/trace, delivery status

SEE ALSO

trivial-rewrite(8), address routing
bounce(8), delivery status reports
postconf(5), configuration parameters
master(5), generic daemon options
master(8), process manager
syslogd(8), system logging

README FILES

Use "**postconf readme_directory**" or "**postconf html_directory**" to locate this information.
SCHEDULER_README, scheduling algorithm
QSHAPE_README, Postfix queue analysis

LICENSE

The Secure Mailer license must be distributed with this software.

AUTHOR(S)

Wietse Venema
IBM T.J. Watson Research
P.O. Box 704
Yorktown Heights, NY 10598, USA

Preemptive scheduler enhancements:
Patrik Rak
Modra 6
155 00, Prague, Czech Republic

NAME

quot — display disk space occupied by each user

SYNOPSIS

quot [**-acfhknv**] [*filesystem* ...]

DESCRIPTION

quot is used to gather statistics about the disk usage for each local user.

The following options are available:

-a   Include statistics for all mounted filesystems.

-c   Display three columns containing number of blocks per file, number of files in this category, and aggregate total of blocks in files with this or lower size.

-f   For each user, display count of files and space occupied.

-h   Estimate the number of blocks in each file based on its size. Despite that this doesn't give the correct results (it doesn't account for the holes in files), this option isn't any faster and thus is discouraged.

-k   By default, all sizes are reported in 512-byte block counts. The **-k** options causes the numbers to be reported in kilobyte counts.

-n   Given a list of inodes (plus some optional data on each line) in the standard input, for each file print out the owner (plus the remainder of the input line). This is traditionally used in the pipe:

               ncheck filesystem | sort +0n | quot -n filesystem

           to get a report of files and their owners.

-v   In addition to the default output, display the number of files not accessed within 30, 60 and 90 days.

ENVIRONMENT

BLOCKSIZE If the environment variable BLOCKSIZE is set, and the **-k** option is not specified, the block counts will be displayed in units of that size block.

SEE ALSO

df(1), quota(1), getbsize(3), getmntinfo(3), fstab(5), mount(8)

NAME
quotacheck — filesystem quota consistency checker

SYNOPSIS
quotacheck [-gquv] *filesystem* . . .
quotacheck [-gquv] [-l *maxparallel*] -a

DESCRIPTION
quotacheck examines each filesystem, builds a table of current disk usage, and compares this table against that recorded in the disk quota file for the filesystem. If any inconsistencies are detected, both the quota file and the current system copy of the incorrect quotas are updated (the latter only occurs if an active filesystem is checked). By default both user and group quotas are checked.

Available options:

-a   If the **-a** flag is supplied in place of any filesystem names, **quotacheck** will check all the filesystems indicated in /etc/fstab to be read-write with disk quotas. By default only the types of quotas listed in /etc/fstab are checked. See also **-l**.

-g   Only group quotas listed in /etc/fstab are to be checked. See also **-u**.

-l *maxparallel*
        Limit the number of parallel checks to the number specified in the following argument. By default, the limit is the number of disks, running one process per disk. If a smaller limit is given, the disks are checked round-robin, one file system at a time. This option is only valid with **-a**.

-q   **quotacheck** runs more quickly, particularly on systems with sparse user id usage, but fails to correct quotas for users [groups] not in the system user [group] database, and owning no files on the filesystem, if the quota file incorrectly believes that they do.

-u   Only user quotas listed in /etc/fstab are to be checked. See also **-g**.

-v   **quotacheck** is more verbose, and reports corrected discrepancies between the calculated and recorded disk quotas.

Specifying both **-g** and **-u** is equivalent to the default. Parallel passes are run on the filesystems required, using the pass numbers in /etc/fstab in an identical fashion to fsck(8).

Normally **quotacheck** operates silently.

quotacheck expects each filesystem to be checked to have a quota files named quota.user and quota.group which are located at the root of the associated file system. These defaults may be overridden in /etc/fstab. If a file is not present, **quotacheck** will create it.

quotacheck is normally run at boot time from the /etc/rc file, see rc(8), before enabling disk quotas with quotaon(8).

quotacheck accesses the raw device in calculating the actual disk usage for each user. Thus, the filesystems checked should be quiescent while **quotacheck** is running.

If **quotacheck** receives a SIGINFO signal (see the **status** argument for stty(1)), a line will be written to the standard error output indicating the name of the device currently being checked and progress information.

FILES
quota.user   at the filesystem root with user quotas
quota.group   at the filesystem root with group quotas

`/etc/fstab`   default filesystems

SEE ALSO
quota(1), quotactl(2), fstab(5), edquota(8), fsck(8), quotaon(8), repquota(8)

HISTORY
The **quotacheck** command appeared in 4.2 BSD.

NAME

quotaon, quotaoff — turn filesystem quotas on and off

SYNOPSIS

quotaon [-g] [-u] [-v] *filesystem* . . .
quotaon [-g] [-u] [-v] -a
quotaoff [-g] [-u] [-v] *filesystem* . . .
quotaoff [-g] [-u] [-v] -a

DESCRIPTION

quotaon announces to the system that disk quotas should be enabled on one or more filesystems. quotaoff announces to the system that the specified filesystems should have any disk quotas turned off. The filesystems specified must have entries in /etc/fstab and be mounted. quotaon expects each filesystem to have quota files named quota.user and quota.group which are located at the root of the associated file system. These defaults may be overridden in /etc/fstab. By default both user and group quotas are enabled.

Available options:

-a   If the -a flag is supplied in place of any filesystem names, quotaon/quotaoff will enable/disable all the filesystems indicated in /etc/fstab to be read-write with disk quotas. By default only the types of quotas listed in /etc/fstab are enabled.

-g   Only group quotas listed in /etc/fstab should be enabled/disabled.

-u   Only user quotas listed in /etc/fstab should be enabled/disabled.

-v   Causes quotaon and quotaoff to print a message for each filesystem where quotas are turned on or off.

Specifying both -g and -u is equivalent to the default.

FILES

quota.user   at the filesystem root with user quotas
quota.group   at the filesystem root with group quotas
/etc/fstab   filesystem table

SEE ALSO

quota(1), quotactl(2), fstab(5), edquota(8), quotacheck(8), repquota(8)

HISTORY

The quotaon command appeared in 4.2 BSD.

NAME

racoon — IKE (ISAKMP/Oakley) key management daemon

SYNOPSIS

racoon [**-46BdFLVv**] [**-f** *configfile*] [**-l** *logfile*] [**-P** *isakmp-natt-port*]
[**-p** *isakmp-port*]

DESCRIPTION

racoon speaks the IKE (ISAKMP/Oakley) key management protocol, to establish security associations with other hosts. The SPD (Security Policy Database) in the kernel usually triggers **racoon**. **racoon** usually sends all informational messages, warnings and error messages to syslogd(8) with the facility LOG_DAEMON and the priority LOG_INFO. Debugging messages are sent with the priority LOG_DEBUG. You should configure syslog.conf(5) appropriately to see these messages.

-4

-6   Specify the default address family for the sockets.

-B   Install SA(s) from the file which is specified in racoon.conf(5).

-d   Increase the debug level. Multiple **-d** arguments will increase the debug level even more.

-F   Run **racoon** in the foreground.

-f *configfile*
       Use *configfile* as the configuration file instead of the default.

-L   Include *file_name:line_number:function_name* in all messages.

-l *logfile*
       Use *logfile* as the logging file instead of syslogd(8).

-P *isakmp-natt-port*
       Use *isakmp-natt-port* for NAT-Traversal port-floating. The default is 4500.

-p *isakmp-port*
       Listen to the ISAKMP key exchange on port *isakmp-port* instead of the default port number, 500.

-V   Print racoon version and compilation options and exit.

-v   This flag causes the packet dump be more verbose, with higher debugging level.

racoon assumes the presence of the kernel random number device rnd(4) at /dev/urandom.

RETURN VALUES

The command exits with 0 on success, and non-zero on errors.

FILES

/etc/racoon.conf default configuration file.

SEE ALSO

ipsec(4), racoon.conf(5), syslog.conf(5), setkey(8), syslogd(8)

HISTORY

The **racoon** command first appeared in the "YIPS" Yokogawa IPsec implementation.

SECURITY CONSIDERATIONS

The use of IKE phase 1 aggressive mode is not recommended, as described in
`http://www.kb.cert.org/vuls/id/886601`.

NAME
racoonctl — racoon administrative control tool

SYNOPSIS
racoonctl [opts] reload-config
racoonctl [opts] show-schedule
racoonctl [opts] show-sa [isakmp|esp|ah|ipsec]
racoonctl [opts] get-sa-cert [inet|inet6] *src dst*
racoonctl [opts] flush-sa [isakmp|esp|ah|ipsec]
racoonctl [opts] delete-sa *saopts*
racoonctl [opts] establish-sa [**-w**] [**-n** *remoteconf*] [**-u** *identity*] *saopts*
racoonctl [opts] vpn-connect [**-u** *identity*] *vpn_gateway*
racoonctl [opts] vpn-disconnect *vpn_gateway*
racoonctl [opts] show-event
racoonctl [opts] logout-user *login*

DESCRIPTION
racoonctl is used to control racoon(8) operation, if ipsec-tools was configured with adminport support. Communication between **racoonctl** and racoon(8) is done through a UNIX socket. By changing the default mode and ownership of the socket, you can allow non-root users to alter racoon(8) behavior, so do that with caution.

The following general options are available:

-d   Debug mode. Hexdump sent admin port commands.

-l   Increase verbosity. Mainly for show-sa command.

-s *socket*
           Specify unix socket name used to connecting racoon.

The following commands are available:

reload-config
           This should cause racoon(8) to reload its configuration file.

show-schedule
           Unknown command.

show-sa [isakmp|esp|ah|ipsec]
           Dump the SA: All the SAs if no SA class is provided, or either ISAKMP SAs, IPsec ESP SAs, IPsec AH SAs, or all IPsec SAs. Use **-l** to increase verbosity.

get-sa-cert [inet|inet6] *src dst*
           Output the raw certificate that was used to authenticate the phase 1 matching *src* and *dst*.

flush-sa [isakmp|esp|ah|ipsec]
           is used to flush all SAs if no SA class is provided, or a class of SAs, either ISAKMP SAs, IPsec ESP SAs, IPsec AH SAs, or all IPsec SAs.

establish-sa [**-w**] [**-n** *remoteconf*] [**-u** *username*] *saopts*
           Establish an SA, either an ISAKMP SA, IPsec ESP SA, or IPsec AH SA. The optional **-u** *username* can be used when establishing an ISAKMP SA while hybrid auth is in use. The exact remote block to use can be specified with **-n** *remoteconf*. **racoonctl** will prompt you for the password associated with *username* and these credentials will be used in the Xauth exchange.

Specifying **-w** will make racoonctl wait until the SA is actually established or an error occurs.

saopts has the following format:

isakmp {inet|inet6} *src dst*

{esp|ah} {inet|inet6} *src/prefixlen/port dst/prefixlen/port*
{icmp|tcp|udp|gre|any}

vpn-connect [**-u** *username*] *vpn_gateway*
>   This is a particular case of the previous command. It will establish an ISAKMP SA with *vpn_gateway*.

delete-sa *saopts*
>   Delete an SA, either an ISAKMP SA, IPsec ESP SA, or IPsec AH SA.

vpn-disconnect *vpn_gateway*
>   This is a particular case of the previous command. It will kill all SAs associated with *vpn_gateway*.

show-event
>   Listen for all events reported by racoon(8).

logout-user *login*
>   Delete all SA established on behalf of the Xauth user *login*.

Command shortcuts are available:

rc	reload-config
ss	show-sa
sc	show-schedule
fs	flush-sa
ds	delete-sa
es	establish-sa
vc	vpn-connect
vd	vpn-disconnect
se	show-event
lu	logout-user

RETURN VALUES
>   The command should exit with 0 on success, and non-zero on errors.

FILES
>   /var/racoon/racoon.sock or
>   /var/run/racoon.sock   racoon(8) control socket.

SEE ALSO
>   ipsec(4), racoon(8)

HISTORY
>   Once was **kmpstat** in the KAME project. It turned into **racoonctl** but remained undocumented for a while. Emmanuel Dreyfus ⟨manu@NetBSD.org⟩ wrote this man page.

NAME

    raidctl — configuration utility for the RAIDframe disk driver

SYNOPSIS

    raidctl [**-v**] **-a** *component dev*
    raidctl [**-v**] **-A** [yes | no | root] *dev*
    raidctl [**-v**] **-B** *dev*
    raidctl [**-v**] **-c** *config_file dev*
    raidctl [**-v**] **-C** *config_file dev*
    raidctl [**-v**] **-f** *component dev*
    raidctl [**-v**] **-F** *component dev*
    raidctl [**-v**] **-g** *component dev*
    raidctl [**-v**] **-G** *dev*
    raidctl [**-v**] **-i** *dev*
    raidctl [**-v**] **-I** *serial_number dev*
    raidctl [**-v**] **-m** *dev*
    raidctl [**-v**] **-M** [yes | no | set *params*] *dev*
    raidctl [**-v**] **-p** *dev*
    raidctl [**-v**] **-P** *dev*
    raidctl [**-v**] **-r** *component dev*
    raidctl [**-v**] **-R** *component dev*
    raidctl [**-v**] **-s** *dev*
    raidctl [**-v**] **-S** *dev*
    raidctl [**-v**] **-u** *dev*

DESCRIPTION

    raidctl is the user-land control program for raid(4), the RAIDframe disk device. **raidctl** is primarily used to dynamically configure and unconfigure RAIDframe disk devices. For more information about the RAIDframe disk device, see raid(4).

    This document assumes the reader has at least rudimentary knowledge of RAID and RAID concepts.

    The command-line options for **raidctl** are as follows:

-a *component dev*

    Add *component* as a hot spare for the device *dev*. Component labels (which identify the location of a given component within a particular RAID set) are automatically added to the hot spare after it has been used and are not required for *component* before it is used.

-A yes *dev*

    Make the RAID set auto-configurable. The RAID set will be automatically configured at boot *before* the root file system is mounted. Note that all components of the set must be of type RAID in the disklabel.

-A no *dev*

    Turn off auto-configuration for the RAID set.

-A root *dev*

    Make the RAID set auto-configurable, and also mark the set as being eligible to be the root partition. A RAID set configured this way will *override* the use of the boot disk as the root device. All components of the set must be of type RAID in the disklabel. Note that only certain architectures (currently alpha, i386, pmax, sparc, sparc64, and vax) support booting a kernel directly from a RAID set.

-B *dev*

    Initiate a copyback of reconstructed data from a spare disk to its original disk. This is performed after a component has failed, and the failed drive has been reconstructed onto a spare drive.

-c *config_file dev*

    Configure the RAIDframe device *dev* according to the configuration given in *config_file*. A description of the contents of *config_file* is given later.

-C *config_file dev*

    As for **-c**, but forces the configuration to take place. Fatal errors due to uninitialized components are ignored. This is required the first time a RAID set is configured.

-f *component dev*

    This marks the specified *component* as having failed, but does not initiate a reconstruction of that component.

-F *component dev*

    Fails the specified *component* of the device, and immediately begin a reconstruction of the failed disk onto an available hot spare. This is one of the mechanisms used to start the reconstruction process if a component does have a hardware failure.

-g *component dev*

    Get the component label for the specified component.

-G *dev*

    Generate the configuration of the RAIDframe device in a format suitable for use with the **-c** or **-C** options.

-i *dev*

    Initialize the RAID device. In particular, (re-)write the parity on the selected device. This *MUST* be done for *all* RAID sets before the RAID device is labeled and before file systems are created on the RAID device.

-I *serial_number dev*

    Initialize the component labels on each component of the device. *serial_number* is used as one of the keys in determining whether a particular set of components belong to the same RAID set. While not strictly enforced, different serial numbers should be used for different RAID sets. This step *MUST* be performed when a new RAID set is created.

-m *dev*

    Display status information about the parity map on the RAID set, if any. If used with **-v** then the current contents of the parity map will be output (in hexadecimal format) as well.

-M yes *dev*

    Enable the use of a parity map on the RAID set; this is the default, and greatly reduces the time taken to check parity after unclean shutdowns at the cost of some very slight overhead during normal operation. Changes to this setting will take effect the next time the set is configured. Note that RAID-0 sets, having no parity, will not use a parity map in any case.

-M no *dev*

    Disable the use of a parity map on the RAID set; doing this is not recommended. This will take effect the next time the set is configured.

-M set *cooldown tickms regions dev*

    Alter the parameters of the parity map; parameters to leave unchanged can be given as 0, and trailing zeroes may be omitted. The RAID set is divided into *regions* regions; each region is marked dirty for at most *cooldown* intervals of *tickms* milliseconds each after a write to it, and at least *cooldown* − 1 such intervals. Changes to *regions* take effect the next time is configured, while changes to the other parameters are applied immediately. The default parameters are expected to be reasonable for most workloads.

-p *dev*

Check the status of the parity on the RAID set. Displays a status message, and returns successfully if the parity is up-to-date.

-P *dev*

Check the status of the parity on the RAID set, and initialize (re-write) the parity if the parity is not known to be up-to-date. This is normally used after a system crash (and before a fsck(8)) to ensure the integrity of the parity.

-r *component dev*

Remove the spare disk specified by *component* from the set of available spare components.

-R *component dev*

Fails the specified *component*, if necessary, and immediately begins a reconstruction back to *component*. This is useful for reconstructing back onto a component after it has been replaced following a failure.

-s *dev*

Display the status of the RAIDframe device for each of the components and spares.

-S *dev*

Check the status of parity re-writing, component reconstruction, and component copyback. The output indicates the amount of progress achieved in each of these areas.

-u *dev*

Unconfigure the RAIDframe device. This does not remove any component labels or change any configuration settings (e.g. auto-configuration settings) for the RAID set.

-v

Be more verbose. For operations such as reconstructions, parity re-writing, and copybacks, provide a progress indicator.

The device used by **raidctl** is specified by *dev*. *dev* may be either the full name of the device, e.g., /dev/rraid0d, for the i386 architecture, or /dev/rraid0c for many others, or just simply raid0 (for /dev/rraid0[cd]). It is recommended that the partitions used to represent the RAID device are not used for file systems.

Configuration file

The format of the configuration file is complex, and only an abbreviated treatment is given here. In the configuration files, a '#' indicates the beginning of a comment.

There are 4 required sections of a configuration file, and 2 optional sections. Each section begins with a 'START', followed by the section name, and the configuration parameters associated with that section. The first section is the 'array' section, and it specifies the number of rows, columns, and spare disks in the RAID set. For example:

```
START array
1 3 0
```

indicates an array with 1 row, 3 columns, and 0 spare disks. Note that although multi-dimensional arrays may be specified, they are *NOT* supported in the driver.

The second section, the 'disks' section, specifies the actual components of the device. For example:

```
START disks
/dev/sd0e
/dev/sd1e
```

```
/dev/sd2e
```

specifies the three component disks to be used in the RAID device. If any of the specified drives cannot be found when the RAID device is configured, then they will be marked as 'failed', and the system will operate in degraded mode. Note that it is *imperative* that the order of the components in the configuration file does not change between configurations of a RAID device. Changing the order of the components will result in data loss if the set is configured with the −C option. In normal circumstances, the RAID set will not configure if only −c is specified, and the components are out-of-order.

The next section, which is the 'spare' section, is optional, and, if present, specifies the devices to be used as 'hot spares' — devices which are on-line, but are not actively used by the RAID driver unless one of the main components fail. A simple 'spare' section might be:

```
START spare
/dev/sd3e
```

for a configuration with a single spare component. If no spare drives are to be used in the configuration, then the 'spare' section may be omitted.

The next section is the 'layout' section. This section describes the general layout parameters for the RAID device, and provides such information as sectors per stripe unit, stripe units per parity unit, stripe units per reconstruction unit, and the parity configuration to use. This section might look like:

```
START layout
# sectPerSU SUsPerParityUnit SUsPerReconUnit RAID_level
32 1 1 5
```

The sectors per stripe unit specifies, in blocks, the interleave factor; i.e., the number of contiguous sectors to be written to each component for a single stripe. Appropriate selection of this value (32 in this example) is the subject of much research in RAID architectures. The stripe units per parity unit and stripe units per reconstruction unit are normally each set to 1. While certain values above 1 are permitted, a discussion of valid values and the consequences of using anything other than 1 are outside the scope of this document. The last value in this section (5 in this example) indicates the parity configuration desired. Valid entries include:

0 RAID level 0. No parity, only simple striping.

1 RAID level 1. Mirroring. The parity is the mirror.

4 RAID level 4. Striping across components, with parity stored on the last component.

5 RAID level 5. Striping across components, parity distributed across all components.

There are other valid entries here, including those for Even-Odd parity, RAID level 5 with rotated sparing, Chained declustering, and Interleaved declustering, but as of this writing the code for those parity operations has not been tested with NetBSD.

The next required section is the 'queue' section. This is most often specified as:

```
START queue
fifo 100
```

where the queuing method is specified as fifo (first-in, first-out), and the size of the per-component queue is limited to 100 requests. Other queuing methods may also be specified, but a discussion of them is beyond the scope of this document.

The final section, the 'debug' section, is optional. For more details on this the reader is referred to the RAIDframe documentation discussed in the **HISTORY** section.

See **EXAMPLES** for a more complete configuration file example.

FILES
    /dev/{,r}raid* **raid** device special files.

EXAMPLES
It is highly recommended that before using the RAID driver for real file systems that the system administrator(s) become quite familiar with the use of **raidctl**, and that they understand how the component reconstruction process works. The examples in this section will focus on configuring a number of different RAID sets of varying degrees of redundancy. By working through these examples, administrators should be able to develop a good feel for how to configure a RAID set, and how to initiate reconstruction of failed components.

In the following examples 'raid0' will be used to denote the RAID device. Depending on the architecture, /dev/rraid0c or /dev/rraid0d may be used in place of raid0.

Initialization and Configuration
The initial step in configuring a RAID set is to identify the components that will be used in the RAID set. All components should be the same size. Each component should have a disklabel type of FS_RAID, and a typical disklabel entry for a RAID component might look like:

        f: 1800000 200495   RAID   # (Cyl. 405*- 4041*)

While FS_BSDFFS will also work as the component type, the type FS_RAID is preferred for RAIDframe use, as it is required for features such as auto-configuration. As part of the initial configuration of each RAID set, each component will be given a 'component label'. A 'component label' contains important information about the component, including a user-specified serial number, the row and column of that component in the RAID set, the redundancy level of the RAID set, a 'modification counter', and whether the parity information (if any) on that component is known to be correct. Component labels are an integral part of the RAID set, since they are used to ensure that components are configured in the correct order, and used to keep track of other vital information about the RAID set. Component labels are also required for the auto-detection and auto-configuration of RAID sets at boot time. For a component label to be considered valid, that particular component label must be in agreement with the other component labels in the set. For example, the serial number, 'modification counter', number of rows and number of columns must all be in agreement. If any of these are different, then the component is not considered to be part of the set. See raid(4) for more information about component labels.

Once the components have been identified, and the disks have appropriate labels, **raidctl** is then used to configure the raid(4) device. To configure the device, a configuration file which looks something like:

        START array
        # numRow numCol numSpare
        1 3 1

        START disks
        /dev/sd1e
        /dev/sd2e
        /dev/sd3e

        START spare
        /dev/sd4e

        START layout
        # sectPerSU SUsPerParityUnit SUsPerReconUnit RAID_level_5

```
32 1 1 5

START queue
fifo 100
```

is created in a file. The above configuration file specifies a RAID 5 set consisting of the components /dev/sd1e, /dev/sd2e, and /dev/sd3e, with /dev/sd4e available as a 'hot spare' in case one of the three main drives should fail. A RAID 0 set would be specified in a similar way:

```
START array
# numRow numCol numSpare
1 4 0

START disks
/dev/sd10e
/dev/sd11e
/dev/sd12e
/dev/sd13e

START layout
# sectPerSU SUsPerParityUnit SUsPerReconUnit RAID_level_0
64 1 1 0

START queue
fifo 100
```

In this case, devices /dev/sd10e, /dev/sd11e, /dev/sd12e, and /dev/sd13e are the components that make up this RAID set. Note that there are no hot spares for a RAID 0 set, since there is no way to recover data if any of the components fail.

For a RAID 1 (mirror) set, the following configuration might be used:

```
START array
# numRow numCol numSpare
1 2 0

START disks
/dev/sd20e
/dev/sd21e

START layout
# sectPerSU SUsPerParityUnit SUsPerReconUnit RAID_level_1
128 1 1 1

START queue
fifo 100
```

In this case, /dev/sd20e and /dev/sd21e are the two components of the mirror set. While no hot spares have been specified in this configuration, they easily could be, just as they were specified in the RAID 5 case above. Note as well that RAID 1 sets are currently limited to only 2 components. At present, n-way mirroring is not possible.

The first time a RAID set is configured, the −C option must be used:

```
raidctl -C raid0.conf raid0
```

where `raid0.conf` is the name of the RAID configuration file. The `-C` forces the configuration to succeed, even if any of the component labels are incorrect. The `-C` option should not be used lightly in situations other than initial configurations, as if the system is refusing to configure a RAID set, there is probably a very good reason for it. After the initial configuration is done (and appropriate component labels are added with the `-I` option) then raid0 can be configured normally with:

```
raidctl -c raid0.conf raid0
```

When the RAID set is configured for the first time, it is necessary to initialize the component labels, and to initialize the parity on the RAID set. Initializing the component labels is done with:

```
raidctl -I 112341 raid0
```

where '112341' is a user-specified serial number for the RAID set. This initialization step is *required* for all RAID sets. As well, using different serial numbers between RAID sets is *strongly encouraged*, as using the same serial number for all RAID sets will only serve to decrease the usefulness of the component label checking.

Initializing the RAID set is done via the `-i` option. This initialization *MUST* be done for *all* RAID sets, since among other things it verifies that the parity (if any) on the RAID set is correct. Since this initialization may be quite time-consuming, the `-v` option may be also used in conjunction with `-i`:

```
raidctl -iv raid0
```

This will give more verbose output on the status of the initialization:

```
Initiating re-write of parity
Parity Re-write status:
  10% |****                                      | ETA:    06:03 /
```

The output provides a 'Percent Complete' in both a numeric and graphical format, as well as an estimated time to completion of the operation.

Since it is the parity that provides the 'redundancy' part of RAID, it is critical that the parity is correct as much as possible. If the parity is not correct, then there is no guarantee that data will not be lost if a component fails.

Once the parity is known to be correct, it is then safe to perform `disklabel`(8), `newfs`(8), or `fsck`(8) on the device or its file systems, and then to mount the file systems for use.

Under certain circumstances (e.g., the additional component has not arrived, or data is being migrated off of a disk destined to become a component) it may be desirable to configure a RAID 1 set with only a single component. This can be achieved by using the word "absent" to indicate that a particular component is not present. In the following:

```
START array
# numRow numCol numSpare
1 2 0

START disks
absent
/dev/sd0e

START layout
# sectPerSU SUsPerParityUnit SUsPerReconUnit RAID_level_1
128 1 1 1
```

```
START queue
fifo 100
```

/dev/sd0e is the real component, and will be the second disk of a RAID 1 set. The first component is simply marked as being absent. Configuration (using **-C** and **-I** *12345* as above) proceeds normally, but initialization of the RAID set will have to wait until all physical components are present. After configuration, this set can be used normally, but will be operating in degraded mode. Once a second physical component is obtained, it can be hot-added, the existing data mirrored, and normal operation resumed.

The size of the resulting RAID set will depend on the number of data components in the set. Space is automatically reserved for the component labels, and the actual amount of space used for data on a component will be rounded down to the largest possible multiple of the sectors per stripe unit (sectPerSU) value. Thus, the amount of space provided by the RAID set will be less than the sum of the size of the components.

Maintenance of the RAID set

After the parity has been initialized for the first time, the command:

```
raidctl -p raid0
```

can be used to check the current status of the parity. To check the parity and rebuild it necessary (for example, after an unclean shutdown) the command:

```
raidctl -P raid0
```

is used. Note that re-writing the parity can be done while other operations on the RAID set are taking place (e.g., while doing a fsck(8) on a file system on the RAID set). However: for maximum effectiveness of the RAID set, the parity should be known to be correct before any data on the set is modified.

To see how the RAID set is doing, the following command can be used to show the RAID set's status:

```
raidctl -s raid0
```

The output will look something like:

```
Components:
           /dev/sd1e: optimal
           /dev/sd2e: optimal
           /dev/sd3e: optimal
Spares:
           /dev/sd4e: spare
Component label for /dev/sd1e:
   Row: 0 Column: 0 Num Rows: 1 Num Columns: 3
   Version: 2 Serial Number: 13432 Mod Counter: 65
   Clean: No Status: 0
   sectPerSU: 32 SUsPerPU: 1 SUsPerRU: 1
   RAID Level: 5  blocksize: 512 numBlocks: 1799936
   Autoconfig: No
   Last configured as: raid0
Component label for /dev/sd2e:
   Row: 0 Column: 1 Num Rows: 1 Num Columns: 3
   Version: 2 Serial Number: 13432 Mod Counter: 65
   Clean: No Status: 0
   sectPerSU: 32 SUsPerPU: 1 SUsPerRU: 1
   RAID Level: 5  blocksize: 512 numBlocks: 1799936
   Autoconfig: No
   Last configured as: raid0
Component label for /dev/sd3e:
```

```
           Row: 0 Column: 2 Num Rows: 1 Num Columns: 3
           Version: 2 Serial Number: 13432 Mod Counter: 65
           Clean: No Status: 0
           sectPerSU: 32 SUsPerPU: 1 SUsPerRU: 1
           RAID Level: 5  blocksize: 512 numBlocks: 1799936
           Autoconfig: No
           Last configured as: raid0
   Parity status: clean
   Reconstruction is 100% complete.
   Parity Re-write is 100% complete.
   Copyback is 100% complete.
```

This indicates that all is well with the RAID set. Of importance here are the component lines which read 'optimal', and the 'Parity status' line. 'Parity status: clean' indicates that the parity is up-to-date for this RAID set, whether or not the RAID set is in redundant or degraded mode. 'Parity status: DIRTY' indicates that it is not known if the parity information is consistent with the data, and that the parity information needs to be checked. Note that if there are file systems open on the RAID set, the individual components will not be 'clean' but the set as a whole can still be clean.

To check the component label of /dev/sd1e, the following is used:

```
   raidctl -g /dev/sd1e raid0
```

The output of this command will look something like:

```
   Component label for /dev/sd1e:
       Row: 0 Column: 0 Num Rows: 1 Num Columns: 3
       Version: 2 Serial Number: 13432 Mod Counter: 65
       Clean: No Status: 0
       sectPerSU: 32 SUsPerPU: 1 SUsPerRU: 1
       RAID Level: 5  blocksize: 512 numBlocks: 1799936
       Autoconfig: No
       Last configured as: raid0
```

Dealing with Component Failures

If for some reason (perhaps to test reconstruction) it is necessary to pretend a drive has failed, the following will perform that function:

```
   raidctl -f /dev/sd2e raid0
```

The system will then be performing all operations in degraded mode, where missing data is re-computed from existing data and the parity. In this case, obtaining the status of raid0 will return (in part):

```
   Components:
               /dev/sd1e: optimal
               /dev/sd2e: failed
               /dev/sd3e: optimal
   Spares:
               /dev/sd4e: spare
```

Note that with the use of −f a reconstruction has not been started. To both fail the disk and start a reconstruction, the −F option must be used:

```
   raidctl -F /dev/sd2e raid0
```

The −f option may be used first, and then the −F option used later, on the same disk, if desired. Immediately after the reconstruction is started, the status will report:

```
        Components:
                  /dev/sd1e: optimal
                  /dev/sd2e: reconstructing
                  /dev/sd3e: optimal
        Spares:
                  /dev/sd4e: used_spare
        [...]
        Parity status: clean
        Reconstruction is 10% complete.
        Parity Re-write is 100% complete.
        Copyback is 100% complete.
```

This indicates that a reconstruction is in progress. To find out how the reconstruction is progressing the **−S** option may be used. This will indicate the progress in terms of the percentage of the reconstruction that is completed. When the reconstruction is finished the **−s** option will show:

```
        Components:
                  /dev/sd1e: optimal
                  /dev/sd2e: spared
                  /dev/sd3e: optimal
        Spares:
                  /dev/sd4e: used_spare
        [...]
        Parity status: clean
        Reconstruction is 100% complete.
        Parity Re-write is 100% complete.
        Copyback is 100% complete.
```

At this point there are at least two options. First, if /dev/sd2e is known to be good (i.e., the failure was either caused by **−f** or **−F**, or the failed disk was replaced), then a copyback of the data can be initiated with the **−B** option. In this example, this would copy the entire contents of /dev/sd4e to /dev/sd2e. Once the copyback procedure is complete, the status of the device would be (in part):

```
        Components:
                  /dev/sd1e: optimal
                  /dev/sd2e: optimal
                  /dev/sd3e: optimal
        Spares:
                  /dev/sd4e: spare
```

and the system is back to normal operation.

The second option after the reconstruction is to simply use /dev/sd4e in place of /dev/sd2e in the configuration file. For example, the configuration file (in part) might now look like:

```
START array
1 3 0

START disks
/dev/sd1e
/dev/sd4e
/dev/sd3e
```

This can be done as /dev/sd4e is completely interchangeable with /dev/sd2e at this point. Note that extreme care must be taken when changing the order of the drives in a configuration. This is one of the few instances where the devices and/or their orderings can be changed without loss of data! In general, the ordering of components in a configuration file should *never* be changed.

If a component fails and there are no hot spares available on-line, the status of the RAID set might (in part) look like:

```
Components:
          /dev/sd1e: optimal
          /dev/sd2e: failed
          /dev/sd3e: optimal
No spares.
```

In this case there are a number of options. The first option is to add a hot spare using:

```
raidctl -a /dev/sd4e raid0
```

After the hot add, the status would then be:

```
Components:
          /dev/sd1e: optimal
          /dev/sd2e: failed
          /dev/sd3e: optimal
Spares:
          /dev/sd4e: spare
```

Reconstruction could then take place using **-F** as describe above.

A second option is to rebuild directly onto /dev/sd2e. Once the disk containing /dev/sd2e has been replaced, one can simply use:

```
raidctl -R /dev/sd2e raid0
```

to rebuild the /dev/sd2e component. As the rebuilding is in progress, the status will be:

```
Components:
          /dev/sd1e: optimal
          /dev/sd2e: reconstructing
          /dev/sd3e: optimal
No spares.
```

and when completed, will be:

```
Components:
          /dev/sd1e: optimal
          /dev/sd2e: optimal
          /dev/sd3e: optimal
No spares.
```

In circumstances where a particular component is completely unavailable after a reboot, a special component name will be used to indicate the missing component. For example:

```
Components:
          /dev/sd2e: optimal
         component1: failed
No spares.
```

indicates that the second component of this RAID set was not detected at all by the auto-configuration code. The name 'component1' can be used anywhere a normal component name would be used. For example, to add a hot spare to the above set, and rebuild to that hot spare, the following could be done:

```
raidctl -a /dev/sd3e raid0
raidctl -F component1 raid0
```

at which point the data missing from 'component1' would be reconstructed onto /dev/sd3e.

When more than one component is marked as 'failed' due to a non-component hardware failure (e.g., loss of power to two components, adapter problems, termination problems, or cabling issues) it is quite possible to recover the data on the RAID set. The first thing to be aware of is that the first disk to fail will almost certainly be out-of-sync with the remainder of the array. If any IO was performed between the time the first component is considered 'failed' and when the second component is considered 'failed', then the first component to fail will *not* contain correct data, and should be ignored. When the second component is marked as failed, however, the RAID device will (currently) panic the system. At this point the data on the RAID set (not including the first failed component) is still self consistent, and will be in no worse state of repair than had the power gone out in the middle of a write to a file system on a non-RAID device. The problem, however, is that the component labels may now have 3 different 'modification counters' (one value on the first component that failed, one value on the second component that failed, and a third value on the remaining components). In such a situation, the RAID set will not autoconfigure, and can only be forcibly re-configured with the −C option. To recover the RAID set, one must first remedy whatever physical problem caused the multiple-component failure. After that is done, the RAID set can be restored by forcibly configuring the raid set *without* the component that failed first. For example, if /dev/sd1e and /dev/sd2e fail (in that order) in a RAID set of the following configuration:

```
START array
1 4 0

START disks
/dev/sd1e
/dev/sd2e
/dev/sd3e
/dev/sd4e

START layout
# sectPerSU SUsPerParityUnit SUsPerReconUnit RAID_level_5
64 1 1 5

START queue
fifo 100
```

then the following configuration (say "recover_raid0.conf")

```
START array
1 4 0

START disks
absent
/dev/sd2e
/dev/sd3e
/dev/sd4e

START layout
# sectPerSU SUsPerParityUnit SUsPerReconUnit RAID_level_5
64 1 1 5
```

```
START queue
fifo 100
```

can be used with

```
raidctl -C recover_raid0.conf raid0
```

to force the configuration of raid0. A

```
raidctl -I 12345 raid0
```

will be required in order to synchronize the component labels. At this point the file systems on the RAID set can then be checked and corrected. To complete the re-construction of the RAID set, /dev/sd1e is simply hot-added back into the array, and reconstructed as described earlier.

RAID on RAID

RAID sets can be layered to create more complex and much larger RAID sets. A RAID 0 set, for example, could be constructed from four RAID 5 sets. The following configuration file shows such a setup:

```
START array
# numRow numCol numSpare
1 4 0

START disks
/dev/raid1e
/dev/raid2e
/dev/raid3e
/dev/raid4e

START layout
# sectPerSU SUsPerParityUnit SUsPerReconUnit RAID_level_0
128 1 1 0

START queue
fifo 100
```

A similar configuration file might be used for a RAID 0 set constructed from components on RAID 1 sets. In such a configuration, the mirroring provides a high degree of redundancy, while the striping provides additional speed benefits.

Auto-configuration and Root on RAID

RAID sets can also be auto-configured at boot. To make a set auto-configurable, simply prepare the RAID set as above, and then do a:

```
raidctl -A yes raid0
```

to turn on auto-configuration for that set. To turn off auto-configuration, use:

```
raidctl -A no raid0
```

RAID sets which are auto-configurable will be configured before the root file system is mounted. These RAID sets are thus available for use as a root file system, or for any other file system. A primary advantage of using the auto-configuration is that RAID components become more independent of the disks they reside on. For example, SCSI ID's can change, but auto-configured sets will always be configured correctly, even if the SCSI ID's of the component disks have become scrambled.

Having a system's root file system (/) on a RAID set is also allowed, with the 'a' partition of such a RAID set being used for /. To use raid0a as the root file system, simply use:

```
raidctl -A root raid0
```

To return raid0a to be just an auto-configuring set simply use the **-A** *yes* arguments.

Note that kernels can only be directly read from RAID 1 components on architectures that support that (currently alpha, i386, pmax, sparc, sparc64, and vax). On those architectures, the FS_RAID file system is recognized by the bootblocks, and will properly load the kernel directly from a RAID 1 component. For other architectures, or to support the root file system on other RAID sets, some other mechanism must be used to get a kernel booting. For example, a small partition containing only the secondary boot-blocks and an alternate kernel (or two) could be used. Once a kernel is booting however, and an auto-configuring RAID set is found that is eligible to be root, then that RAID set will be auto-configured and used as the root device. If two or more RAID sets claim to be root devices, then the user will be prompted to select the root device. At this time, RAID 0, 1, 4, and 5 sets are all supported as root devices.

A typical RAID 1 setup with root on RAID might be as follows:

1.   wd0a - a small partition, which contains a complete, bootable, basic NetBSD installation.

2.   wd1a - also contains a complete, bootable, basic NetBSD installation.

3.   wd0e and wd1e - a RAID 1 set, raid0, used for the root file system.

4.   wd0f and wd1f - a RAID 1 set, raid1, which will be used only for swap space.

5.   wd0g and wd1g - a RAID 1 set, raid2, used for /usr, /home, or other data, if desired.

6.   wd0h and wd1h - a RAID 1 set, raid3, if desired.

RAID sets raid0, raid1, and raid2 are all marked as auto-configurable. raid0 is marked as being a root file system. When new kernels are installed, the kernel is not only copied to /, but also to wd0a and wd1a. The kernel on wd0a is required, since that is the kernel the system boots from. The kernel on wd1a is also required, since that will be the kernel used should wd0 fail. The important point here is to have redundant copies of the kernel available, in the event that one of the drives fail.

There is no requirement that the root file system be on the same disk as the kernel. For example, obtaining the kernel from wd0a, and using sd0e and sd1e for raid0, and the root file system, is fine. It *is* critical, however, that there be multiple kernels available, in the event of media failure.

Multi-layered RAID devices (such as a RAID 0 set made up of RAID 1 sets) are *not* supported as root devices or auto-configurable devices at this point. (Multi-layered RAID devices *are* supported in general, however, as mentioned earlier.) Note that in order to enable component auto-detection and auto-configuration of RAID devices, the line:

```
options      RAID_AUTOCONFIG
```

must be in the kernel configuration file. See raid(4) for more details.

Swapping on RAID

A RAID device can be used as a swap device. In order to ensure that a RAID device used as a swap device is correctly unconfigured when the system is shutdown or rebooted, it is recommended that the line

```
swapoff=YES
```

be added to /etc/rc.conf.

Unconfiguration

The final operation performed by **raidctl** is to unconfigure a raid(4) device. This is accomplished via a simple:

```
raidctl -u raid0
```

at which point the device is ready to be reconfigured.

Performance Tuning

Selection of the various parameter values which result in the best performance can be quite tricky, and often requires a bit of trial-and-error to get those values most appropriate for a given system. A whole range of factors come into play, including:

1. Types of components (e.g., SCSI vs. IDE) and their bandwidth

2. Types of controller cards and their bandwidth

3. Distribution of components among controllers

4. IO bandwidth

5. file system access patterns

6. CPU speed

As with most performance tuning, benchmarking under real-life loads may be the only way to measure expected performance. Understanding some of the underlying technology is also useful in tuning. The goal of this section is to provide pointers to those parameters which may make significant differences in performance.

For a RAID 1 set, a SectPerSU value of 64 or 128 is typically sufficient. Since data in a RAID 1 set is arranged in a linear fashion on each component, selecting an appropriate stripe size is somewhat less critical than it is for a RAID 5 set. However: a stripe size that is too small will cause large IO's to be broken up into a number of smaller ones, hurting performance. At the same time, a large stripe size may cause problems with concurrent accesses to stripes, which may also affect performance. Thus values in the range of 32 to 128 are often the most effective.

Tuning RAID 5 sets is trickier. In the best case, IO is presented to the RAID set one stripe at a time. Since the entire stripe is available at the beginning of the IO, the parity of that stripe can be calculated before the stripe is written, and then the stripe data and parity can be written in parallel. When the amount of data being written is less than a full stripe worth, the 'small write' problem occurs. Since a 'small write' means only a portion of the stripe on the components is going to change, the data (and parity) on the components must be updated slightly differently. First, the 'old parity' and 'old data' must be read from the components. Then the new parity is constructed, using the new data to be written, and the old data and old parity. Finally, the new data and new parity are written. All this extra data shuffling results in a serious loss of performance, and is typically 2 to 4 times slower than a full stripe write (or read). To combat this problem in the real world, it may be useful to ensure that stripe sizes are small enough that a 'large IO' from the system will use exactly one large stripe write. As is seen later, there are some file system dependencies which may come into play here as well.

Since the size of a 'large IO' is often (currently) only 32K or 64K, on a 5-drive RAID 5 set it may be desirable to select a SectPerSU value of 16 blocks (8K) or 32 blocks (16K). Since there are 4 data sectors per stripe, the maximum data per stripe is 64 blocks (32K) or 128 blocks (64K). Again, empirical measurement will provide the best indicators of which values will yield better performance.

The parameters used for the file system are also critical to good performance. For newfs(8), for example, increasing the block size to 32K or 64K may improve performance dramatically. As well, changing the cylinders-per-group parameter from 16 to 32 or higher is often not only necessary for larger file systems, but may also have positive performance implications.

Summary

Despite the length of this man-page, configuring a RAID set is a relatively straight-forward process. All that needs to be done is the following steps:

1. Use `disklabel`(8) to create the components (of type RAID).

2. Construct a RAID configuration file: e.g., `raid0.conf`

3. Configure the RAID set with:

   ```
   raidctl -C raid0.conf raid0
   ```

4. Initialize the component labels with:

   ```
   raidctl -I 123456 raid0
   ```

5. Initialize other important parts of the set with:

   ```
   raidctl -i raid0
   ```

6. Get the default label for the RAID set:

   ```
   disklabel raid0 > /tmp/label
   ```

7. Edit the label:

   ```
   vi /tmp/label
   ```

8. Put the new label on the RAID set:

   ```
   disklabel -R -r raid0 /tmp/label
   ```

9. Create the file system:

   ```
   newfs /dev/rraid0e
   ```

10. Mount the file system:

    ```
    mount /dev/raid0e /mnt
    ```

11. Use:

    ```
    raidctl -c raid0.conf raid0
    ```

    To re-configure the RAID set the next time it is needed, or put `raid0.conf` into `/etc` where it will automatically be started by the `/etc/rc.d` scripts.

SEE ALSO

`ccd`(4), `raid`(4), `rc`(8)

HISTORY

RAIDframe is a framework for rapid prototyping of RAID structures developed by the folks at the Parallel Data Laboratory at Carnegie Mellon University (CMU). A more complete description of the internals and functionality of RAIDframe is found in the paper "RAIDframe: A Rapid Prototyping Tool for RAID Systems", by William V. Courtright II, Garth Gibson, Mark Holland, LeAnn Neal Reilly, and Jim Zelenka, and published by the Parallel Data Laboratory of Carnegie Mellon University.

The **raidctl** command first appeared as a program in CMU's RAIDframe v1.1 distribution. This version of **raidctl** is a complete re-write, and first appeared in NetBSD 1.4.

WARNINGS

Certain RAID levels (1, 4, 5, 6, and others) can protect against some data loss due to component failure. However the loss of two components of a RAID 4 or 5 system, or the loss of a single component of a RAID 0 system will result in the entire file system being lost. RAID is *NOT* a substitute for good backup practices.

Recomputation of parity *MUST* be performed whenever there is a chance that it may have been compromised. This includes after system crashes, or before a RAID device has been used for the first time. Failure to keep parity correct will be catastrophic should a component ever fail — it is better to use RAID 0 and get the additional space and speed, than it is to use parity, but not keep the parity correct. At least with RAID 0 there is no perception of increased data security.

BUGS

Hot-spare removal is currently not available.

NAME
rarpd — Reverse ARP Daemon

SYNOPSIS
rarpd [**-adfl**] [*interface* [. . .]]

DESCRIPTION
rarpd services Reverse ARP requests on the Ethernet connected to *interface*. Upon receiving a request, **rarpd** maps the target hardware address to an IP address via its name, which must be present in both the ethers(5) and hosts(5) databases. If a host does not exist in both databases the translation cannot proceed and a reply will not be sent.

In normal operation, **rarpd** forks a copy of itself and runs in the background. Anomalies and errors are reported via syslog(3).

OPTIONS
-a   Listen on all the Ethernets attached to the system. If ' **-a**' is omitted, an interface must be specified.

-d   Run in debug mode, with all the output to stderr. This option implies the **-f** option.

-f   Run in the foreground.

-l   Log all requests to syslog.

FILES
/etc/ethers
/etc/hosts

SEE ALSO
bpf(4)

Finlayson, R., Mann, T., Mogul, J.C., and Theimer, M., A Reverse Address Resolution Protocol, RFC 903.

AUTHORS
Craig Leres (leres@ee.lbl.gov) and Steven McCanne (mccanne@ee.lbl.gov). Lawrence Berkeley Laboratory, University of California, Berkeley, CA.

NAME

rbootd — HP remote boot server

SYNOPSIS

rbootd [-ad] [-i *interface*] [config_file]

DESCRIPTION

The **rbootd** utility services boot requests from Hewlett-Packard workstations over a local area network. All boot files must reside in the boot file directory; further, if a client supplies path information in its boot request, it will be silently stripped away before processing. By default, **rbootd** only responds to requests from machines listed in its configuration file. If the client doesn't supply a file name (HP700 series machines don't), the first one listed for this machine will be supplied.

The options are as follows:

-a   Respond to boot requests from any machine. The configuration file is ignored if this option is specified.

-d   Run **rbootd** in debug mode. Packets sent and received are displayed to the terminal.

-i *interface*
            Service boot requests on specified interface. If unspecified, **rbootd** searches the system interface list for the lowest numbered, configured "up" interface (excluding loopback). Ties are broken by choosing the earliest match.

Specifying *config_file* on the command line causes **rbootd** to use a different configuration file from the default.

The configuration file is a text file where each line describes a particular machine. A line must start with a machine's Ethernet address followed by an optional list of boot file names. An Ethernet address is specified in hexadecimal with each of its six octets separated by a colon. The boot file names come from the boot file directory. The ethernet address and boot file(s) must be separated by white-space and/or comma characters. A pound sign causes the remainder of a line to be ignored.

Here is a sample configuration file:

```
#
# ethernet addr     boot file(s)              comments
#
08:00:09:0:66:ad    SYSHPBSD                  # snake (4.3BSD)
08:00:09:0:59:5b                              # vandy (anything)
8::9:1:C6:75        SYSHPBSD,SYSHPUX          # jaguar (either)
```

rbootd logs status and error messages via syslog(3). A startup message is always logged, and in the case of fatal errors (or deadly signals) a message is logged announcing the server's termination. In general, a non-fatal error is handled by ignoring the event that caused it (e.g. an invalid Ethernet address in the config file causes that line to be invalidated).

The following signals have the specified effect when sent to the server process using the kill(1) command:

                SIGHUP   Drop all active connections and reconfigure.

                SIGUSR1   Turn on debugging, do nothing if already on.

                SIGUSR2   Turn off debugging, do nothing if already off.

FILES

`/dev/bpf`	packet-filter device
`/etc/rbootd.conf`	configuration file
`/tmp/rbootd.dbg`	debug output
`/usr/mdec/rbootd`	directory containing boot files
`/var/run/rbootd.pid`	process id

SEE ALSO

kill(1), socket(2), signal(3), syslog(3), rmp(4)

BUGS

If multiple servers are started on the same interface, each will receive and respond to the same boot packets.

NAME

rc, rc.local, rc.shutdown, rc.d/ — startup and shutdown scripts

SYNOPSIS

rc
rc.local
rc.shutdown
rc.d/

DESCRIPTION

rc is the command script which controls the startup of various services, and is invoked by init(8) as part of the process of entering the automatic reboot to multi-user startup, or after the single user mode shell has exited. If init(8) is starting the automatic reboot process, **rc** is invoked with the argument of 'autoboot'.

rc.local is a command script to which local boot-time actions can be added. It is (nearly) the last thing invoked by **rc** during a normal boot.

rc.shutdown is the command script which shuts down various services, and is invoked by shutdown(8) as part of the process of shutting down the system.

rc.d/ is the directory which contains various sh(1) scripts, one for each service, which are called by **rc** at startup, **rc.shutdown** at shutdown, and as necessary during system operation to stop, start, restart, reload, or otherwise control the service.

Operation of rc

1. Source /etc/rc.subr to load various rc.subr(8) shell functions to use.

2. If autobooting, set **autoboot=yes** and enable a flag (**rc_fast=yes**), which prevents the **rc.d** scripts from performing the check for already running processes (thus speeding up the boot process). This **rc_fast=yes** speedup won't occur when **rc** is started up after exiting the single-user shell.

3. Invoke rcorder(8) to order the files in /etc/rc.d/ that do not have a "nostart" keyword (refer to rcorder(8)'s **−s** flag), and assigns the result to a variable.

4. Calls each script in turn using **run_rc_script**() (from rc.subr(8)), which sets $1 to 'start', and sources the script in a subshell. If the script has a '.sh' suffix then it is sourced directly into the current shell.

5. The output from the above steps is sent to a post-processor. If **rc_silent** is false, then the post-processor displays the output. If **rc_silent** is true, then the post-processor invokes the command specified in *rc_silent_cmd* once for each line, without otherwise displaying the output. Useful values for *rc_silent_cmd* include ":" to display nothing at all, and "twiddle" to display a spinning symbol on the console. Regardless of the value of **rc_silent**, the post-processor saves the output in /var/run/rc.log.

Operation of rc.shutdown

1. Source /etc/rc.subr to load various rc.subr(8) shell functions to use.

2. Invoke rcorder(8) to order the files in /etc/rc.d/ that have a "shutdown" keyword (refer to rcorder(8)'s **−k** flag), reverses that order, and assigns the result to a variable.

3. Calls each script in turn using **run_rc_script**() (from rc.subr(8)), which sets $1 to 'stop', and sources the script in a subshell. If the script has a '.sh' suffix then it is sourced directly into the current shell.

Contents of rc.d/

    `rc.d/` is located in `/etc/rc.d`. The following file naming conventions are currently used in **`rc.d/`**:

`ALLUPPERCASE`   Scripts that are 'placeholders' to ensure that certain operations are performed before others. In order of startup, these are:

    `NETWORKING`   Ensure basic network services are running, including general network configuration (`network`) and `dhclient`.

    `SERVERS`   Ensure basic services (such as `NETWORKING`, `ppp`, `syslogd`, and `kdc`) exist for services that start early (such as `named`), because they're required by `DAEMON` below.

    `DAEMON`   Before all general purpose daemons such as `dhcpd`, `lpd`, and `ntpd`.

    `LOGIN`   Before user login services (`inetd`, `telnetd`, `rshd`, `sshd`, and `xdm`), as well as before services which might run commands as users (`cron`, `postfix`, and `sendmail`).

`foo.sh`   Scripts that are to be sourced into the current shell rather than a subshell have a '`.sh`' suffix. Extreme care must be taken in using this, as the startup sequence will terminate if the script does. `/etc/rc.d/bootconf.sh` uses this behaviour to allow the user to select a different configuration (including `/etc/rc.conf`) early in the boot.

`bar`   Scripts that are sourced in a subshell. The boot does not stop if such a script terminates with a non-zero status, but a script can stop the boot if necessary by invoking the **`stop_boot`**() function (from `rc.subr`(8)).

Each script should contain `rcorder`(8) keywords, especially an appropriate "PROVIDE" entry.

The scripts are expected to support at least the following arguments:

start   Start the service. This should check that the service is to be started as specified by `rc.conf`(5). Also checks if the service is already running and refuses to start if it is. This latter check is not performed by standard NetBSD scripts if the system is starting directly to multi-user mode, to speed up the boot process.

stop   If the service is to be started as specified by `rc.conf`(5), stop the service. This should check that the service is running and complain if it's not.

restart   Perform a **stop** then a **start**.

status   If the script starts a process (rather than performing a one-off operation), show the status of the process. Otherwise it's not necessary to support this argument. Defaults to displaying the process ID of the program (if running).

poll   If the script starts a process (rather than performing a one-off operation), wait for the command to exit. Otherwise it's not necessary to support this argument.

rcvar   Display which `rc.conf`(5) variables are used to control the startup of the service (if any).

Other arguments (such as 'reload', 'dumpdb', etc) can be added if necessary.

The argument may have one of the following prefixes to alter its operation:

fast   Skip the check for an existing running process. Sets **rc_fast=yes**.

force   Skips the rc.conf(5) check, ignores a failure result from any of the prerequisite checks, executes the command, and always returns a zero exit status. Sets **rc_force=yes**.

one   Skips the rc.conf(5) check, but performs all other prerequisite tests.

In order to simplify scripts, the **run_rc_command**() function from rc.subr(8) may be used.

FILES

/etc/rc	Startup script called by init(8).
/etc/rc.d/	Directory containing control scripts for each service.
/etc/rc.local	Local startup script.
/etc/rc.shutdown	Shutdown script called by shutdown(8).
/etc/rc.subr	Contains rc.subr(8) functions used by various scripts.
/etc/rc.conf	System startup configuration file.
/var/run/rc.log	Log file created by **rc**.

SEE ALSO

rc.conf(5), init(8), rc.subr(8), rcorder(8), reboot(8), shutdown(8)

Luke Mewburn, "The Design and Implementation of the NetBSD rc.d system", *Proceedings of the FREENIX Track: 2001 USENIX Annual Technical Conference, USENIX Association*, June 25-30, 2001.

HISTORY

The **rc** command appeared in 4.0BSD. The /etc/rc.d support was implemented in NetBSD 1.5 by Luke Mewburn ⟨lukem@NetBSD.org⟩. The post-processor, support for *rc_silent*, and saving output to a file, was implemented in NetBSD 6.0 by Alan Barrett.

NAME

rc.subr — functions used by system shell scripts

SYNOPSIS

. /etc/rc.subr

backup_file *action file current backup*

checkyesno *var*

check_pidfile *pidfile procname* [*interpreter*]

check_process *procname* [*interpreter*]

err *exitval message*

load_rc_config *command*

load_rc_config_var *command var*

mount_critical_filesystems *type*

no_rc_postprocess *command* [*arguments*]

print_rc_metadata *string*

print_rc_normal *string*

rc_usage *command* [. . .]

reverse_list *item* [. . .]

run_rc_command *argument* [*parameters*]

run_rc_script *file argument*

stop_boot

twiddle

wait_for_pids [*pid* [. . .]]

warn *message*

yesno_to_truefalse *var*

DESCRIPTION

rc.subr contains commonly used shell script functions which are used by various scripts such as rc(8), and the periodic system services which are controlled by daily.conf(5), monthly.conf(5), security.conf(5), and weekly.conf(5).

The **rc.subr** functions are accessed by sourcing /etc/rc.subr into the current shell.

The following shell functions are available:

backup_file *action file current backup*

Make a backup copy of *file* into *current*. If the rc.conf(5) variable **backup_uses_rcs** is 'YES', use rcs(1) to archive the previous version of *current*, otherwise save the previous version of *current* as *backup*.

action may be one of the following:

add   `file` is now being backed up by or possibly re-entered into this backup mechanism. `current` is created, and if necessary, the `rcs`(1) files are created as well.

update   `file` has changed and needs to be backed up. If `current` exists, it is copied to `backup` or checked into `rcs`(1) (if the repository file is old), and then `file` is copied to `current`.

remove   `file` is no longer being tracked by this backup mechanism. If `rcs`(1) is being used, an empty file is checked in and `current` is removed, otherwise `current` is moved to `backup`.

checkyesno `var`
> Return 0 if `var` is defined to 'YES', 'TRUE', 'ON', or '1'. Return 1 if `var` is defined to 'NO', 'FALSE', 'OFF', or '0'. Otherwise, warn that `var` is not set correctly. The values are case insensitive.
>
> Note that the warning message shown by this function when `var` is not set references a manual page where the user can find more information. Its name is picked up from the **rcvar_manpage** variable.

check_pidfile `pidfile procname` [`interpreter`]
> Parses the first word of the first line of `pidfile` for a PID, and ensures that the process with that PID is running and its first argument matches `procname`. Prints the matching PID if successful, otherwise nothing. If `interpreter` is provided, parse the first line of `procname`, ensure that the line is of the form
>
>   #! interpreter [...]
>
> and use `interpreter` with its optional arguments and `procname` appended as the process string to search for.

check_process `procname` [`interpreter`]
> Prints the PIDs of any processes that are running with a first argument that matches `procname`. `interpreter` is handled as per **check_pidfile**.

err `exitval message`
> Display an error message to *stderr*, log it to the system log using `logger`(1), and **exit** with an exit value of `exitval`. The error message consists of the script name (from **$0**), followed by ": ERROR: ", and then `message`.

load_rc_config `command`
> Source in the `rc.conf`(5) configuration files for `command`. First, `/etc/rc.conf` is sourced if it has not yet been read in. Then, `/etc/rc.conf.d/command` is sourced if it is an existing file. The latter may also contain other variable assignments to override **run_rc_command** arguments defined by the calling script, to provide an easy mechanism for an administrator to override the behaviour of a given `rc.d`(8) script without requiring the editing of that script.

load_rc_config_var `command var`
> Read the `rc.conf`(5) variable `var` for `command` and set in the current shell, using **load_rc_config** in a sub-shell to prevent unwanted side effects from other variable assignments.

mount_critical_filesystems `type`
> Go through a list of critical file systems, as found in the `rc.conf`(5) variable **critical_filesystems_**`type`, mounting each one that is not currently mounted.

no_rc_postprocess `command` [`arguments`]
> Execute the specified command with the specified arguments, in such a way that its output bypasses the post-processor that `rc`(8) uses for most commands. This implies that the output will not appear in the `/var/run/rc.log` file, and will appear on the console regardless of the value of *rc_silent*. This is expected to be useful for interactive commands, and this mechanism is automatically used by **run_rc_command** when a script contains the `rcorder`(8) keyword "interactive".

If invoked from a context that does not appear to be under the control of rc(8), then the command is executed without special treatment.

print_rc_metadata *string*

Print the specified *string* in such a way that it should be handled as meta-data by the rc(8) post-processor. If invoked from a context that does not appear to be under the control of rc(8), then the *string* is discarded.

Any rc.d(8) script may invoke this function with an argument that begins with "note:", followed by one line of arbitrary text; the text will be logged by rc(8) but will not be displayed on the console.

The use of arguments that do not begin with "note:" is reserved for internal use by rc(8) and **rc.subr**.

print_rc_normal *string*

Print the specified *string* in such a way that it should be handled as normal output by the rc(8) post-processor. If invoked from a context that does not appear to be under the control of rc(8), then the *string* is printed to standard output.

Ths intent is that a script that is run via the **no_rc_postprocess**() function (so its output would ordinarily be invisible to the post-processor) can nevertheless arrange for the post-processor to see things printed with **print_rc_normal**.()

rc_usage *command* [. . .]

Print a usage message for **$0**, with *commands* being the list of valid arguments prefixed by "[fast|force|one]".

reverse_list *item* [. . .]

Print the list of *items* in reverse order.

run_rc_command *argument* [*parameter* . . .]

Run the *argument* method for the current rc.d(8) script, based on the settings of various shell variables. **run_rc_command** is extremely flexible, and allows fully functional rc.d(8) scripts to be implemented in a small amount of shell code. The optional set of parameters is passed verbatim to the command, but not to its pre/post hooks.

argument is searched for in the list of supported commands, which may be one of:

start	Start the service. This should check that the service is to be started as specified by rc.conf(5). Also checks if the service is already running and refuses to start if it is. This latter check is not performed by standard NetBSD scripts if the system is starting directly to multi-user mode, to speed up the boot process.
stop	If the service is to be started as specified by rc.conf(5), stop the service. This should check that the service is running and complain if it's not.
restart	Perform a **stop** then a **start**. Defaults to displaying the process ID of the program (if running).
rcvar	Display which rc.conf(5) variables are used to control the startup of the service (if any).

If **pidfile** or **procname** is set, also support:

poll	Wait for the command to exit.
status	Show the status of the process.

Other supported commands are listed in the optional variable **extra_commands**.

argument may have one of the following prefixes which alters its operation:

fast   Skip the check for an existing running process, and sets **rc_fast=YES**.

force   Skip the checks for **rcvar** being set to yes, and sets **rc_force=YES**. This ignores *argument*_**precmd** returning non-zero, and ignores any of the **required_*** tests failing, and always returns a zero exit status.

one   Skip the checks for **rcvar** being set to yes, but performs all the other prerequisite tests.

run_rc_command uses the following shell variables to control its behaviour. Unless otherwise stated, these are optional.

name   The name of this script. This is not optional.

rcvar   The value of **rcvar** is checked with **checkyesno** to determine if this method should be run.

rcvar_manpage
     The manual page containing information about **rcvar**. It will be part of the warning message shown when **rcvar** is undefined. Defaults to `rc.conf(5)`.

command   Full path to the command. Not required if *argument*_**cmd** is defined for each supported keyword.

command_args
     Optional arguments and/or shell directives for **command**.

command_interpreter
     command is started with
          `#! command_interpreter [...]`
     which results in its ps(1) command being
          `command_interpreter [...] command`
     so use that string to find the PID(s) of the running command rather than `command`.

extra_commands
     Extra commands/keywords/arguments supported.

pidfile   Path to pid file. Used to determine the PID(s) of the running command. If **pidfile** is set, use
          `check_pidfile $pidfile $procname`
     to find the PID. Otherwise, if **command** is set, use
          `check_process $procname`
     to find the PID.

procname   Process name to check for. Defaults to the value of **command**.

required_dirs
     Check for the existence of the listed directories before running the default start method.

required_files
     Check for the readability of the listed files before running the default start method.

required_vars
     Perform **checkyesno** on each of the list variables before running the default start method.

${name}_chdir
> Directory to **cd** to before running **command**, if **${name}_chroot** is not provided.

${name}_chroot
> Directory to chroot(8) to before running **command**. Only supported after /usr is mounted.

${name}_env
> List of additional or modified environment variables to set when starting **command**.

${name}_flags
> Arguments to call **command** with. This is usually set in rc.conf(5), and not in the rc.d(8) script. The environment variable 'flags' can be used to override this.

${name}_nice
> nice(1) level to run **command** as. Only supported after /usr is mounted.

${name}_user
> User to run **command** as, using chroot(8). if **${name}_chroot** is set, otherwise uses su(1). Only supported after /usr is mounted.

${name}_group
> Group to run the chrooted **command** as.

${name}_groups
> Comma separated list of supplementary groups to run the chrooted **command** with.

*argument_***cmd**
> Shell commands which override the default method for *argument*.

*argument_***precmd**
> Shell commands to run just before running *argument_***cmd** or the default method for *argument*. If this returns a non-zero exit code, the main method is not performed. If the default method is being executed, this check is performed after the **required_*** checks and process (non-)existence checks.

*argument_***postcmd**
> Shell commands to run if running *argument_***cmd** or the default method for *argument* returned a zero exit code.

sig_stop Signal to send the processes to stop in the default **stop** method. Defaults to SIGTERM.

sig_reload Signal to send the processes to reload in the default **reload** method. Defaults to SIGHUP.

For a given method *argument*, if *argument_***cmd** is not defined, then a default method is provided by **run_rc_command**:

Argument	Default method
start	If **command** is not running and **checkyesno** **rcvar** succeeds, start **command**.
stop	Determine the PIDs of **command** with **check_pidfile** or **check_process** (as appropriate), **kill** **sig_stop** those PIDs, and run **wait_for_pids** on those PIDs.

reload	Similar to **stop**, except that it uses **sig_reload** instead, and doesn't run **wait_for_pids**.
restart	Runs the **stop** method, then the **start** method.
status	Show the PID of **command**, or some other script specific status operation.
poll	Wait for **command** to exit.
rcvar	Display which rc.conf(5) variable is used (if any). This method always works, even if the appropriate rc.conf(5) variable is set to 'NO'.

The following variables are available to the methods (such as *argument*_**cmd**) as well as after **run_rc_command** has completed:

rc_arg	Argument provided to **run_rc_command**, after fast and force processing has been performed.
rc_flags	Flags to start the default command with. Defaults to **${name}_flags**, unless overridden by the environment variable 'flags'. This variable may be changed by the *argument*_**precmd** method.
rc_pid	PID of **command** (if appropriate).
rc_fast	Not empty if "fast" prefix was used.
rc_force	Not empty if "force" prefix was used.

run_rc_script *file argument*

Start the script *file* with an argument of *argument*, and handle the return value from the script.

Various shell variables are unset before *file* is started:

> **name**, **command**, **command_args**, **command_interpreter**, **extra_commands**, **pidfile**, **rcvar**, **required_dirs**, **required_files**, **required_vars**, *argument*_**cmd**, *argument*_**precmd**. *argument*_**postcmd**.

The startup behaviour of *file* depends upon the following checks:

1. If *file* ends in .sh, it is sourced into the current shell.

2. If *file* appears to be a backup or scratch file (e.g., with a suffix of '~', '#', '.OLD', or '.orig'), ignore it.

3. If *file* is not executable, ignore it.

4. If the rc.conf(5) variable **rc_fast_and_loose** is empty, source *file* in a sub shell, otherwise source *file* into the current shell.

5. If *file* contains the rcorder(8) keyword "interactive", then the command is executed using **no_rc_postprocess**.

stop_boot

Prevent booting to multiuser mode. If the **autoboot** variable is 'yes', then a **SIGTERM** signal is sent to the parent process (which is assumed to be rc(8)). Otherwise, the shell exits with status 1.

twiddle

Display one of the characters '/, -, \, |', followed by a backspace. Repeated calls to this function will create the appearance of a spinning symbol, as a different character is displayed on each call. Output is to /dev/tty, so this function may be useful even inside a script whose output has been redirected.

wait_for_pids [*pid* [. . .]]
> Wait until all of the provided *pids* don't exist any more, printing the list of outstanding *pids* every two seconds.

warn *message*
> Display a warning message to *stderr* and log it to the system log using logger(1). The warning message consists of the script name (from **$0**), followed by ": WARNING: ", and then *message*.

yesno_to_truefalse *var*
> Change the value of the specified variable from any of the forms acceptable to the **checkyesno** function, to "true" or "false".

FILES
> /etc/rc.subr The **rc.subr** file resides in /etc.

SEE ALSO
> rc.conf(5), rc(8)

HISTORY
> **rc.subr** appeared in NetBSD 1.3. The rc.d(8) support functions appeared in NetBSD 1.5. Support for the rc(8) post-processor appeared in NetBSD 6.0.

NAME

rcorder — print a dependency ordering of interdependent files

SYNOPSIS

rcorder [-k *keep*] [-s *skip*] *file* . . .

DESCRIPTION

rcorder is designed to print out a dependency ordering of a set of interdependent files. Typically it is used to find an execution sequence for a set of shell scripts in which certain files must be executed before others.

Each file passed to rcorder should be annotated with special lines (which look like comments to the shell) which indicate the dependencies the files have upon certain points in the sequence, known as "conditions", and which indicate, for each file, which "conditions" may be expected to be filled by that file.

Within each file, a block containing a series of "REQUIRE", "PROVIDE", "BEFORE" and "KEYWORD" lines should appear. The format of the lines is rigid. Each line must begin with a single "#", followed by a single space, followed by "PROVIDE:", "REQUIRE:", "BEFORE:", or "KEYWORD:". No deviation is permitted. Each dependency line is then followed by a series of conditions, separated by whitespace. Multiple "PROVIDE", "REQUIRE", "BEFORE" and "KEYWORD" lines may appear, but all such lines must appear in a sequence without any intervening lines, as once a line that does not follow the format is reached, parsing stops.

The options are as follows:

-k   Add the specified keyword to the "keep list". If any -k option is given, only those files containing the matching keyword are listed.

-s   Add the specified keyword to the "skip list". If any -s option is given, files containing the matching keyword are not listed.

An example block follows:

```
# REQUIRE: networking syslog
# REQUIRE: usr
# PROVIDE: dns nscd
```

This block states that the file in which it appears depends upon the "networking", "syslog", and "usr" conditions, and provides the "dns" and "nscd" conditions.

A file may contain zero "PROVIDE" lines, in which case it provides no conditions, and may contain zero "REQUIRE" lines, in which case it has no dependencies. A file containing no "PROVIDE", "REQUIRE", or "BEFORE" lines may be output at an arbitrary position in the dependency ordering.

There must be at least one file with no dependencies in the set of arguments passed to rcorder in order for it to find a starting place in the dependency ordering.

DIAGNOSTICS

rcorder may print one of the following error messages and exit with a non-zero status if it encounters an error while processing the file list.

Requirement %s has no providers, aborting. No file has a "PROVIDE" line corresponding to a condition present in a "REQUIRE" line in another file.

Circular dependency on provision %s, aborting. A set of files has a circular dependency which was detected while processing the stated condition.

      Circular dependency on file %s, aborting. A set of files has a circular dependency which was detected while processing the stated file.

SEE ALSO
    `rc`(8)

HISTORY
    The **rcorder** program first appeared in NetBSD 1.5.

AUTHORS
    Written by Perry E. Metzger ⟨perry@piermont.com⟩ and Matthew R. Green ⟨mrg@eterna.com.au⟩.

NAME

rdate — set the system's date from a remote host

SYNOPSIS

rdate [**-psa**] *host*

DESCRIPTION

rdate displays and sets the local date and time from the host name or address given as the argument. It uses the RFC 868 protocol which is usually implemented as a built-in service of inetd(8).

Available options:

-p   Do not set, just print the remote time

-s   Do not print the time.

-a   Use the adjtime(2) call to gradually skew the local time to the remote time rather than just hopping.

FILES

/var/log/wtmp A record of date resets and time changes.

SEE ALSO

adjtime(2), gettimeofday(2), utmp(5), inetd(8)

NAME
reboot, **poweroff**, **halt** — restarting, powering down and stopping the system

SYNOPSIS
halt [**-dlnpq**]
poweroff [**-dlnq**]
reboot [**-dlnq**] [*arg* . . .]

DESCRIPTION
The **poweroff**, **halt** and **reboot** utilities flush the file system cache to disk, send all running processes a SIGTERM, wait for up to 30 seconds for them to die, send a SIGKILL to the survivors and, respectively, power down, halt or restart the system. The action is logged, including entering a shutdown record into the login accounting file and sending a message via syslog(3).

The options are as follows:

-d   Create a dump before halting or restarting. This option is useful for debugging system dump procedures or capturing the state of a corrupted or misbehaving system.

-l   Suppress sending a message via syslog(3) before halting or restarting.

-n   Do not flush the file system cache. This option should be used with extreme caution. It can be used if a disk or the processor is on fire.

-p   Attempt to powerdown the system. If the powerdown fails, or the system does not support software powerdown, the system will halt. This option is only valid for **halt**.

-q   Do not give processes a chance to shut down before halting or restarting. This option should not normally be used.

If there are any arguments passed to **reboot** they are concatenated with spaces and passed as *bootstr* to the reboot(2) system call. The string is passed to the firmware on platforms that support it.

Normally, the shutdown(8) utility is used when the system needs to be halted or restarted, giving users advance warning of their impending doom.

SEE ALSO
reboot(2), syslog(3), utmp(5), boot(8), init(8), rescue(8), shutdown(8), sync(8)

HISTORY
A **reboot** command appeared in Version 6 AT&T UNIX.

The **poweroff** command first appeared in NetBSD 1.5.

CAVEATS
Once the command has begun its work, stopping it before it completes will probably result in a system so crippled it must be physically reset. To prevent premature termination, the command blocks many signals early in its execution. However, nothing can defend against deliberate attempts to evade this.

This command will stop the system without running any shutdown(8) scripts. Amongst other things, this means that swapping will not be disabled so that raid(4) can shutdown cleanly. You should normally use shutdown(8) unless you are running in single user mode.

BUGS
The single user shell will ignore the SIGTERM signal. To avoid waiting for the timeout when rebooting or halting from the single user shell, you have to **exec reboot** or **exec halt**.

NAME

renice — alter priority of running processes

SYNOPSIS

renice *priority* [[**-p**] *pid* . . .][**-g** *pgrp* . . .][**-u** *user* . . .]
renice **-n** *increment* [[**-p**] *pid* . . .][**-g** *pgrp* . . .][**-u** *user* . . .]

DESCRIPTION

renice alters the scheduling priority of one or more running processes. The following *who* parameters are interpreted as process ID's, process group ID's, or user names. **renice**'ing a process group causes all processes in the process group to have their scheduling priority altered. **renice**'ing a user causes all processes owned by the user to have their scheduling priority altered. By default, the processes to be affected are specified by their process ID's.

Options supported by **renice**:

-g   Force *who* parameters to be interpreted as process group ID's.

-n   Instead of changing the specified processes to the given priority, interpret the following argument as an increment to be applied to the current priority of each process.

-u   Force the *who* parameters to be interpreted as user names.

-p   Resets the *who* interpretation to be (the default) process ID's.

For example,

```
renice +1 987 -u daemon root -p 32
```

would change the priority of process ID's 987 and 32, and all processes owned by users daemon and root.

Users other than the super-user may only alter the priority of processes they own, and can only monotonically increase their "nice value" within the range 0 to PRIO_MAX (20). (This prevents overriding administrative fiats.) The super-user may alter the priority of any process and set the priority to any value in the range PRIO_MIN (−20) to PRIO_MAX.

Useful priorities are: 0, the "base" scheduling priority; 20, the affected processes will run only when nothing at the base priority wants to; anything negative, the processes will receive a scheduling preference.

FILES

/etc/passwd to map user names to user ID's

SEE ALSO

nice(1), getpriority(2), setpriority(2)

HISTORY

The **renice** command appeared in 4.0BSD.

BUGS

Non super-users can not increase scheduling priorities of their own processes, even if they were the ones that decreased the priorities in the first place.

NAME
   repquota — summarize quotas for a file system

SYNOPSIS
   repquota [**-g**] [**-u**] [**-v**] *filesystem* ...
   repquota [**-g**] [**-u**] [**-v**] **-a**

DESCRIPTION
   repquota prints a summary of the disk usage and quotas for the specified file systems.

   Available options:

   -a   Print the quotas of all the filesystems listed in /etc/fstab.

   -g   Print only group quotas (the default is to print both group and user quotas if they exist).

   -u   Print only user quotas (the default is to print both group and user quotas if they exist).

   -v   Print a header line before printing each filesystem quotas.

   For each user or group, the current number files and amount of space (in kilobytes) is printed, along with any quotas created with edquota(8).

   Only members of the operator group or the super-user may use this command.

FILES
   quota.user   at the filesystem root with user quotas
   quota.group   at the filesystem root with group quotas
   /etc/fstab   for file system names and locations

DIAGNOSTICS
   Various messages about inaccessible files; self-explanatory.

SEE ALSO
   quota(1), quotactl(2), fstab(5), edquota(8), quotacheck(8), quotaon(8)

HISTORY
   The **repquota** command appeared in 4.2BSD.

NAME

rescue — rescue utilities in `/rescue`

DESCRIPTION

The `/rescue` directory contains a collection of common utilities intended for use in recovering a badly damaged system. With the transition to a dynamically-linked root beginning with NetBSD 2.0, there is a real possibility that the standard tools in `/bin` and `/sbin` may become non-functional due to a failed upgrade or a disk error. The tools in `/rescue` are statically linked and should therefore be more resistant to damage. However, being statically linked, the tools in `/rescue` are also less functional than the standard utilities. In particular, they do not have full use of the locale, pam(3), and nsswitch libraries.

If your system fails to boot, and it shows an error message similar to:

        init: not found

try booting the system with the boot flag "**-a**" and supplying `/rescue/init`, which is the **rescue** init(8), as the init path.

If your system fails to boot, and it shows a prompt similar to:

        Enter full pathname of shell or RETURN for /bin/sh:

the first thing to try running is the standard shell, `/bin/sh`. If that fails, try running `/rescue/sh`, which is the **rescue** shell. To repair the system, the root partition must first be remounted read-write. This can be done with the following mount(8) command:

        /rescue/mount -uw /

The next step is to double-check the contents of `/bin`, `/lib`, `/libexec`, and `/sbin`, possibly mounting a NetBSD installation CD-ROM and copying files from there. Once it is possible to successfully run `/bin/sh`, `/bin/ls`, and other standard utilities, try rebooting back into the standard system.

The `/rescue` tools are compiled using crunchgen(1), which makes them considerably more compact than the standard utilities.

FILES

`/rescue` Root of the **rescue** hierarchy.

SEE ALSO

crunchgen(1)

HISTORY

The **rescue** utilities first appeared in NetBSD 2.0.

AUTHORS

The **rescue** system was written by Luke Mewburn ⟨lukem@NetBSD.org⟩. This manual page was written by Simon L. Nielsen ⟨simon@FreeBSD.org⟩, based on text by Tim Kientzle ⟨kientzle@FreeBSD.org⟩.

BUGS

Most of the **rescue** tools work even in a fairly crippled system. The most egregious exception is the **rescue** version of vi(1), which currently requires that `/usr` be mounted so that it can access the termcap(5) files. Hopefully, a failsafe termcap(3) entry will eventually be added into the curses(3) library, so that `/rescue/vi` can be used even in a system where `/usr` cannot immediately be mounted. In the meantime, the **rescue** version of the ed(1) editor can be used from `/rescue/ed` if you need to edit files, but cannot mount `/usr`.

NAME
resize_lfs — resize a mounted log-structured filesystem

SYNOPSIS
resize_lfs [**-v**] [**-s** *new-size*] *mounted-file-system*

DESCRIPTION
resize_lfs grows or shrinks a mounted log-structured filesystem to the specified size. *mounted-file-system* is the name of the filesystem to be resized, and *new-size* is the desired new filesystem size, in sectors. If *new-size* is not specified, **resize_lfs** will default to the current size of the partition containing the filesystem in question.

When growing, the partition must be large enough to contain a filesystem of the specified size; when shrinking, **resize_lfs** must first "clean" the segments that will be invalid when the filesystem is shrunk. If this cleaning process results in these segments becoming redirtied, this indicates that the given new size is not large enough to contain the existing filesystem data, and **resize_lfs** will return an error.

EXAMPLES
To resize the file system mounted at /home to 32576 sectors:
```
resize_lfs -s 32576 /home
```

SEE ALSO
fsck_lfs(8), lfs_cleanerd(8), newfs_lfs(8)

HISTORY
The **resize_lfs** command first appeared in NetBSD 3.0.

AUTHORS
Konrad Schroder ⟨perseant@NetBSD.org⟩

BUGS
resize_lfs should be able to resize an unmounted filesystem as well.

NAME

resolvconf — a framework for managing multiple DNS configurations

SYNOPSIS

resolvconf −I
resolvconf [−m *metric*] [−p] −a *interface* <file
resolvconf [−f] −d *interface*
resolvconf −il *pattern*
resolvconf −u

DESCRIPTION

resolvconf manages resolv.conf(5) files from multiple sources, such as DHCP and VPN clients. Traditionally, the host runs just one client and that updates /etc/resolv.conf. More modern systems frequently have wired and wireless interfaces and there is no guarantee both are on the same network. With the advent of VPN and other types of networking daemons, many things now contend for the contents of /etc/resolv.conf.

resolvconf solves this by letting the daemon send their resolv.conf(5) file to **resolvconf** via stdin(3) with the argument −a *interface* instead of the filesystem. **resolvconf** then updates /etc/resolv.conf as it thinks best. When a local resolver other than libc is installed, such as dnsmasq(8) or named(8), then **resolvconf** will supply files that the resolver should be configured to include.

resolvconf can mark an interfaces resolv.conf as private. This means that the name servers listed in that resolv.conf are only used for queries against the domain/search listed in the same file. This only works when a local resolver other than libc is installed. See resolvconf.conf(5) for how to configure **resolvconf** to use a local name server.

When an interface goes down, it should then call **resolvconf** with −d *interface* arguments to delete the resolv.conf file for the *interface*.

Here are some more options that **resolvconf** has:-

−I   Initialise the state directory /var/run/resolvconf. This only needs to be called if the initial system boot sequence does not automatically clean it out; for example the state directory is moved somewhere other than /var/run. If used, it should only be called once as early in the system boot sequence as possible and before **resolvconf** is used to add interfaces.

−f   Ignore non existant interfaces. Only really useful for deleting interfaces.

−i *pattern*
       List the interfaces, optionally matching *pattern*, we have resolv.conf files for.

−l *pattern*
       List the resolv.conf files we have. If *pattern* is specified then we list the files for the interfaces that match it.

−m *metric*
       Set the metric of the interface when adding it, default of 0. Lower metrics take precedence. This affects the default order of interfaces when listed.

−p   Marks the interface resolv.conf as private.

−u   Force **resolvconf** to update all it's subscribers. **resolvconf** does not update the subscribers when adding a resolv.conf that matches what it already has for that interface.

resolvconf also has some options designed to be used by it's subscribers:-

-v   Echo variables DOMAINS, SEARCH and NAMESERVERS so that the subscriber can configure
             the resolver easily.

INTERFACE ORDERING

For **resolvconf** to work effectively, it has to process the resolv.confs for the interfaces in the correct
order. **resolvconf** first processes interfaces from the **interface_order** list, then interfaces without a metic
and that match the **dynamic_order** list, then interfaces with a metric in order and finally the rest in the operating systems lexical order. See `resolvconf.conf`(5) for details on these lists.

IMPLEMENTATION NOTES

If a subscriber has the executable bit then it is executed otherwise it is assumed to be a shell script and
sourced into the current environment in a subshell. This is done so that subscribers can remain fast, but are
also not limited to the shell language.

Portable subscribers should not use anything outside of `/bin` and `/sbin` because `/usr` and others may not
be available when booting. Also, it would be unwise to assume any shell specific features.

ENVIRONMENT

IF_METRIC
If the **-m** option is not present then we use *IF_METRIC* for the metric.

IF_PRIVATE
Marks the interface `resolv.conf` as private.

FILES

`/etc/resolvconf.conf`
Configuration file for **resolvconf**.

`/libexec/resolvconf`
Directory of subscribers which are run every time **resolvconf** adds, deletes or updates.

`/libexec/resolvconf/libc.d`
Directory of subscribers which are run after the libc subscriber is run.

`/var/run/resolvconf`
State directory for **resolvconf**.

HISTORY

This implementation of **resolvconf** is called openresolv and is fully command line compatible with
Debian's resolvconf, as written by Thomas Hood.

BUGS

resolvconf does not validate any of the files given to it.

When running a local resolver other than libc, you will need to configure it to include files that
resolvconf will generate. You should consult `resolvconf.conf`(5) for instructions on how to configure your resolver.

SEE ALSO

`resolv.conf`(5), `resolvconf.conf`(5), `resolver`(3), `stdin`(3)

AUTHORS
    Roy Marples ⟨roy@marples.name⟩

BUGS
    Please report them to http://roy.marples.name/projects/openresolv

NAME
     restore, **rrestore** — restore files or file systems from backups made with dump

SYNOPSIS
     restore −i [**−cdhmuvyN**] [**−b** *bsize*] [**−D** *algorithm*] [**−f** *file*] [**−M** *mfile*]
           [**−s** *fileno*]
     restore −R [**−cduvyN**] [**−b** *bsize*] [**−D** *algorithm*] [**−f** *file*] [**−M** *mfile*]
           [**−s** *fileno*]
     restore −r [**−cduvyN**] [**−b** *bsize*] [**−D** *algorithm*] [**−f** *file*] [**−M** *mfile*]
           [**−s** *fileno*]
     restore −t [**−cdhuvy**] [**−b** *bsize*] [**−f** *file*] [**−s** *fileno*] [*file* . . .]
     restore −x [**−cdhmuvyN**] [**−b** *bsize*] [**−D** *algorithm*] [**−f** *file*] [**−M** *mfile*]
           [**−s** *fileno*] [*file* . . .]

     (The 4.3BSD option syntax is implemented for backward compatibility, but is not documented here.)

DESCRIPTION
     The **restore** command performs the inverse function of dump(8). A full backup of a file system may be restored and subsequent incremental backups layered on top of it. Single files and directory subtrees may be restored from full or partial backups. **restore** works across a network; to do this see the **−f** flag described below. Other arguments to the command are file or directory names specifying the files that are to be restored. Unless the **−h** flag is specified (see below), the appearance of a directory name refers to the files and (recursively) subdirectories of that directory.

     If any file arguments are given with the **−x** flag, or specified in the command shell with the **−i** flag, the permissions of the root directory *will not* be applied to the current directory, unless one of those file arguments explicitly represents the root inode (e.g.: a literal '.'). This is a change from the traditional behaviour, which used to be to always prompt the user.

     Exactly one of the following flags is required:

     −i   This mode allows interactive restoration of files from a dump. After reading in the directory information from the dump, **restore** provides a shell like interface that allows the user to move around the directory tree selecting files to be extracted. The available commands are given below; for those commands that require an argument, the default is the current directory.

           add [*arg*]
               The current directory or specified argument is added to the list of files to be extracted. If a directory is specified, then it and all its descendants are added to the extraction list (unless the **−h** flag is specified on the command line). Files that are on the extraction list are prepended with a "*" when they are listed by **ls**.

           cd *arg*   Change the current working directory to the specified argument.

           delete [*arg*]
               The current directory or specified argument is deleted from the list of files to be extracted. If a directory is specified, then it and all its descendants are deleted from the extraction list (unless the **−h** flag is specified on the command line). The most expedient way to extract most of the files from a directory is to add the directory to the extraction list and then delete those files that are not needed.

           extract   All the files that are on the extraction list are extracted from the dump. **restore** will ask which volume the user wishes to mount. The fastest way to extract a few files is to start with the last volume, and work towards the first volume.

help, **?**   List a summary of the available commands.

ls [*arg*]   List the current or specified directory. Entries that are directories are appended with a "/". Entries that have been marked for extraction are prepended with a "*". If the verbose flag is set the inode number of each entry is also listed.

pwd   Print the full pathname of the current working directory.

quit, **xit**
          Restore immediately exits, even if the extraction list is not empty.

setmodes   All the directories that have been added to the extraction list have their owner, modes, and times set; nothing is extracted from the dump. This is useful for cleaning up after a restore has been prematurely aborted.

verbose   The sense of the **−v** flag is toggled. When set, the verbose flag causes the **ls** command to list the inode numbers of all entries. It also causes **restore** to print out information about each file as it is extracted.

what   List dump header information.

Debug   Enable debugging.

−R   **restore** requests a particular tape of a multi volume set on which to restart a full restore (see the **−r** flag below). This is useful if the restore has been interrupted.

−r   Restore (rebuild a file system). The target file system should be made pristine with newfs(8), mounted and the user cd(1)'d into the pristine file system before starting the restoration of the initial level 0 backup. If the level 0 restores successfully, the **−r** flag may be used to restore any necessary incremental backups on top of the level 0. The **−r** flag precludes an interactive file extraction and can be detrimental to one's health if not used carefully (not to mention the disk). An example:

```
newfs /dev/rsd0g
mount /dev/sd0g /mnt
cd /mnt

restore rf /dev/rst0
```

Note that **restore** leaves a file restoresymtable in the root directory to pass information between incremental restore passes. This file should be removed when the last incremental has been restored.

restore, in conjunction with newfs(8) and dump(8), may be used to modify file system parameters such as size or block size.

−t   The names of the specified files are listed if they occur on the backup. If no file argument is given, then the root directory is listed, which results in the entire content of the backup being listed, unless the **−h** flag has been specified. Note that the **−t** flag replaces the function of the old **dumpdir** program.

−x   The named files are read from the given media. If a named file matches a directory whose contents are on the backup and the **−h** flag is not specified, the directory is recursively extracted. The owner, modification time, and mode are restored (if possible). If no file argument is given, then the root directory is extracted, which results in the entire content of the backup being extracted, unless the **−h** flag has been specified.

The following additional options may be specified:

-b *bsize*
        The number of kilobytes per dump record. If the **-b** option is not specified, **restore** tries to determine the block size dynamically.

-c   Normally, **restore** will try to determine dynamically whether the dump was made from an old (pre-4.4) or new format file system. The **-c** flag disables this check, and only allows reading a dump in the old format.

-D *algorithm*
        Computes the digest of each regular files using the *algorithm* and output to standard output. The *algorithm* is one of *md5*, *rmd160*, or *sha1*. This option doesn't imply **-N**.

-d   Enable debugging.

-f *file*
        Read the backup from *file*; *file* may be a special device file like /dev/rst0 (a tape drive), /dev/rsd1c (a disk drive), an ordinary file, or '−' (the standard input). If the name of the file is of the form "host:file", or "user@host:file", **restore** reads from the named file on the remote host using rmt(8). If the name of the file is '−', **restore** reads from standard input. Thus, dump(8) and **restore** can be used in a pipeline to dump and restore a file system with the command

            dump 0f − /usr | (cd /mnt; restore xf −)

-h   Extract the actual directory, rather than the files that it references. This prevents hierarchical restoration of complete subtrees from the dump.

-M *mfile*
        Do not set the file flags on restore. Instead, append an mtree(8) specification to *mfile*, which can be used to restore file flags with a command such as

            sort mfile | mtree −e −i −u

-m   Extract by inode numbers rather than by file name. This is useful if only a few files are being extracted, and one wants to avoid regenerating the complete pathname to the file.

-N   Do not perform actual writing to disk.

-s *fileno*
        Read from the specified *fileno* on a multi-file tape. File numbering starts at 1.

-u   The **-u** (unlink) flag removes files before extracting them. This is useful when an executable file is in use. Ignored if **-t** or **-N** flag is given.

-v   Normally **restore** does its work silently. The **-v** (verbose) flag causes it to type the name of each file it treats preceded by its file type.

-y   Do not ask the user whether to abort the restore in the event of an error. Always try to skip over the bad block(s) and continue.

ENVIRONMENT
       If the following environment variable exists it will be used by **restore**:
       TMPDIR
              The directory given in TMPDIR will be used instead of /tmp to store temporary files. Refer to environ(7) for more information.

FILES

`/dev/nrst0`	default tape unit to use. Taken from `_PATH_DEFTAPE` in `/usr/include/paths.h`.
`/dev/rst*`	raw SCSI tape interface
`/tmp/rstdir*`	file containing directories on the tape.
`/tmp/rstmode*`	owner, mode, and time stamps for directories.
`./restoresymtable`	information passed between incremental restores.

DIAGNOSTICS

Complains if it gets a read error. If **-y** has been specified, or the user responds 'y', **restore** will attempt to continue the restore.

If a backup was made using more than one tape volume, **restore** will notify the user when it is time to mount the next volume. If the **-x** or **-i** flag has been specified, **restore** will also ask which volume the user wishes to mount. The fastest way to extract a few files is to start with the last volume, and work towards the first volume.

There are numerous consistency checks that can be listed by **restore**. Most checks are self-explanatory or can "never happen". Common errors are given below.

Converting to new file system format.
  A dump tape created from the old file system has been loaded. It is automatically converted to the new file system format.

<filename>: not found on tape
  The specified file name was listed in the tape directory, but was not found on the tape. This is caused by tape read errors while looking for the file, and from using a dump tape created on an active file system.

expected next file <inumber>, got <inumber>
  A file that was not listed in the directory showed up. This can occur when using a dump created on an active file system.

Incremental dump too low
  When doing incremental restore, a dump that was written before the previous incremental dump, or that has too low an incremental level has been loaded.

Incremental dump too high
  When doing incremental restore, a dump that does not begin its coverage where the previous incremental dump left off, or that has too high an incremental level has been loaded.

Tape read error while restoring <filename>
Tape read error while skipping over inode <inumber>
Tape read error while trying to resynchronize
  A tape (or other media) read error has occurred. If a file name is specified, then its contents are probably partially wrong. If an inode is being skipped or the tape is trying to resynchronize, then no extracted files have been corrupted, though files may not be found on the tape.

resync restore, skipped <num> blocks
  After a dump read error, **restore** may have to resynchronize itself. This message lists the number of blocks that were skipped over.

SEE ALSO

`rcmd`(1), `rcmd`(3), `environ`(7), `dump`(8), `mount`(8), `newfs`(8), `rmt`(8)

HISTORY

The **restore** command appeared in 4.2 BSD.

BUGS

restore can get confused when doing incremental restores from dumps that were made on active file systems.

A level zero dump must be done after a full restore. Because **restore** runs in user code, it has no control over inode allocation; thus a full dump must be done to get a new set of directories reflecting the new inode numbering, even though the content of the files is unchanged.

The temporary files /tmp/rstdir* and /tmp/rstmode* are generated with a unique name based on the date of the dump and the process ID (see mktemp(3)), except for when −r or −R is used. Because −R allows you to restart a −r operation that may have been interrupted, the temporary files should be the same across different processes. In all other cases, the files are unique because it is possible to have two different dumps started at the same time, and separate operations shouldn't conflict with each other.

NAME

revnetgroup — generate reverse netgroup data

SYNOPSIS

revnetgroup [**-uh**] [**-f** *netgroup_file*]

DESCRIPTION

revnetgroup processes the contents of a file in netgroup(5) format into what is called reverse netgroup form. That is, where the original file shows netgroup memberships in terms of which members reside in a particular group, the reverse netgroup format specifies what groups are associated with a particular member. This information is used to generate the netgroup.byuser and netgroup.byhosts NIS maps. These reverse netgroup maps are used to help speed up netgroup lookups, particularly for the **innetgr**() library function.

For example, the standard /etc/netgroup file may list a netgroup and a list of its members. Here, the netgroup is considered the key and the member names are the data. By contrast, the reverse netgroup.byusers database lists each unique member as the key and the netgroups to which the members belong become the data. Separate databases are created to hold information pertaining to users and hosts; this allows netgroup username lookups and netgroup hostname lookups to be performed using independent keyspaces.

By constructing these reverse netgroup databases (and the corresponding NIS maps) in advance, the getnetgrent(3) library functions are spared from having to work out the dependencies themselves on the fly. This is important on networks with large numbers of users and hosts, since it can take a considerable amount of time to process very large netgroup databases.

The **revnetgroup** command prints its results on the standard output. It is usually called only by /var/yp/<domain>/Makefile when rebuilding the NIS netgroup maps.

OPTIONS

The **revnetgroup** command supports the following options:

-u   Generate netgroup.byuser output; only username information in the original netgroup file is processed.

-h   Generate netgroup.byhost output; only hostname information in the original netgroup file is processed. (Note at least one of the **-u** or **-h** flags must be specified.)

[**-f** *netgroup_file*]
          The **revnetgroup** command uses /etc/netgroup as its default input file. The **-f** flag allows the user to specify an alternate input file. Specifying "-" as the input file causes **revnetgroup** to read from the standard input.

FILES

/var/yp/<domain>/Makefile   The Makefile that calls **makedbm** and **revnetgroup** to build the NIS databases.

/etc/netgroup   The default netgroup database file. This file is most often found only on the NIS master server.

SEE ALSO

getnetgrent(3), netgroup(5), makedbm(8), nis(8)

AUTHORS
Bill Paul ⟨wpaul@ctr.columbia.edu⟩

NAME
revoke — call revoke(2)

SYNOPSIS
revoke *file*

DESCRIPTION
The **revoke** utility performs the system call **revoke**(*file*).

file must be the pathname of an existing file.

EXIT STATUS
The **revoke** utility returns EXIT_SUCCESS on success and EXIT_FAILURE if an error occurs.

SEE ALSO
revoke(2)

NAME

rexecd — remote execution server

SYNOPSIS

rexecd

DESCRIPTION

rexecd is the server for the `rexec`(3) routine. The server provides remote execution facilities with authentication based on user names and passwords.

rexecd listens for service requests at the port indicated in the "exec" service specification; see `services`(5). When a service request is received the following protocol is initiated:

1. The server reads characters from the socket up to a NUL (`'\0'`) byte. The resultant string is interpreted as an ASCII number, base 10.

2. If the number received in step 1 is non-zero, it is interpreted as the port number of a secondary stream to be used for the *stderr*. A second connection is then created to the specified port on the client's machine.

3. A NUL terminated user name of at most 16 characters is retrieved on the initial socket.

4. A NUL terminated, unencrypted password of at most 16 characters is retrieved on the initial socket.

5. A NUL terminated command to be passed to a shell is retrieved on the initial socket. The length of the command is limited by the upper bound on the size of the system's argument list.

6. **rexecd** then validates the user as is done at login time and, if the authentication was successful, changes to the user's home directory, and establishes the user and group protections of the user. If any of these steps fail the connection is aborted with a diagnostic message returned.

7. A NUL byte is returned on the initial socket and the command line is passed to the normal login shell of the user. The shell inherits the network connections established by **rexecd**.

DIAGNOSTICS

Except for the last one listed below, all diagnostic messages are returned on the initial socket, after which any network connections are closed. An error is indicated by a leading byte with a value of 1 (0 is returned in step 7 above upon successful completion of all the steps prior to the command execution).

username too long
> The name is longer than 16 characters.

password too long
> The password is longer than 16 characters.

command too long
> The command line passed exceeds the size of the argument list (as configured into the system).

Login incorrect.
> No password file entry for the user name existed.

Password incorrect.
> The wrong password was supplied.

No remote directory.
> The `chdir`(2) to the home directory failed.

Try again.
> A `fork`(2) by the server failed.

<shellname>: ...

> The user's login shell could not be started. This message is returned on the connection associated with the *stderr*, and is not preceded by a flag byte.

SEE ALSO
rexec(3)

HISTORY
The **rexecd** command appeared in 4.2BSD.

BUGS
Indicating "Login incorrect" as opposed to "Password incorrect" is a security breach which allows people to probe a system for users with null passwords.

A facility to allow all data and password exchanges to be encrypted should be present.

SECURITY CONSIDERATIONS
As the passwords exchanged by the client and **rexecd** are not encrypted, it is *strongly* recommended that this service is not enabled.

NAME
rip6query — RIPng debugging tool

SYNOPSIS
rip6query [**-I** *interface*] [**-w** *time*] *destination*

DESCRIPTION
rip6query requests remote RIPng daemon on *destination* to dump RIPng routing information. **-I** lets you specify outgoing *interface* for the query packet, and is useful when link-local address is specified for *destination*. **-w** specifies the time in seconds to wait for the initial response from a gateway. The default value is 5 seconds.

SEE ALSO
route6d(8)

HISTORY
The **rip6query** command first appeared in WIDE Hydrangea IPv6 protocol stack kit.

NAME

rlogind — remote login server

SYNOPSIS

rlogind [**-alnL**]

DESCRIPTION

rlogind is the server for the rlogin(1) program. The server provides a remote login facility with authentication based on privileged port numbers from trusted hosts.

Options supported by **rlogind**:

-a   Ask hostname for verification.

-l   Prevent any authentication based on the user's ".rhosts" file, unless the user is logging in as the superuser.

-n   Disable keep-alive messages.

-L   Log all successful accesses to syslogd(8) as auth.info messages.

rlogind listens for service requests at the port indicated in the "login" service specification; see services(5). When a service request is received the following protocol is initiated:

1.   The server checks the client's source port. If the port is not in the range 512-1023, the server aborts the connection.

2.   The server checks the client's source address and requests the corresponding host name (see getnameinfo(3), hosts(5) and named(8)). If the hostname cannot be determined, the dot-notation representation of the host address is used. If the hostname is in the same domain as the server (according to the last two components of the domain name), or if the **-a** option is given, the addresses for the hostname are requested, verifying that the name and address correspond. Normal authentication is bypassed if the address verification fails.

Once the source port and address have been checked, **rlogind** proceeds with the authentication process described in rshd(8). It then allocates a pseudo terminal (see pty(4)), and manipulates file descriptors so that the slave half of the pseudo terminal becomes the *stdin*, *stdout*, and *stderr* for a login process. The login process is an instance of the login(1) program, invoked with the **-f** option if authentication has succeeded. If automatic authentication fails, the user is prompted to log in as if on a standard terminal line.

The parent of the login process manipulates the master side of the pseudo terminal, operating as an intermediary between the login process and the client instance of the rlogin(1) program. In normal operation, the packet protocol described in pty(4) is invoked to provide ^S/^Q type facilities and propagate interrupt signals to the remote programs. The login process propagates the client terminal's baud rate and terminal type, as found in the environment variable, TERM; see environ(7). The screen or window size of the terminal is requested from the client, and window size changes from the client are propagated to the pseudo terminal.

Transport-level keepalive messages are enabled unless the **-n** option is present. The use of keepalive messages allows sessions to be timed out if the client crashes or becomes unreachable.

At the end of a login session, **rlogind** invokes the ttyaction(3) facility with an action of "rlogind" and user "root" to execute site-specific commands.

DIAGNOSTICS

All initial diagnostic messages are indicated by a leading byte with a value of 1, after which any network connections are closed. If there are no errors before login(1) is invoked, a null byte is returned as in indication of success.

Try again.
A fork(2) by the server failed.

SEE ALSO
login(1), ruserok(3), ttyaction(3), rshd(8)

HISTORY
The **rlogind** command appeared in 4.2 BSD.

BUGS
The authentication procedure used here assumes the integrity of each client machine and the connecting medium. This is insecure, but is useful in an "open" environment.

A facility to allow all data exchanges to be encrypted should be present.

A more extensible protocol should be used.

rlogind intentionally rejects accesses from IPv4 mapped address on top of AF_INET6 socket, since IPv4 mapped address complicates host-address based authentication. If you would like to accept connections from IPv4 peers, you will need to run **rlogind** on top of AF_INET socket, not AF_INET6 socket.

NAME

rmt — remote magtape protocol module

SYNOPSIS

rmt

DESCRIPTION

rmt is a program used by the remote dump and restore programs in manipulating a magnetic tape drive through an interprocess communication connection. **rmt** is normally started up with an rexec(3) or rcmd(3) call.

The **rmt** program accepts requests specific to the manipulation of magnetic tapes, performs the commands, then responds with a status indication. All responses are in ASCII and in one of two forms. Successful commands have responses of:

  A*number*\n

Number is an ASCII representation of a decimal number. Unsuccessful commands are responded to with:

  E*error-number*\n*error-message*\n

Error-number is one of the possible error numbers described in intro(2) and *error-message* is the corresponding error string as printed from a call to perror(3). The protocol comprises the following commands, which are sent as indicated - no spaces are supplied between the command and its arguments, or between its arguments, and '\n' indicates that a newline should be supplied:

O*device*\n*mode*\n
  Open the specified *device* using the indicated *mode*. *Device* is a full pathname and *mode* is an ASCII representation of a decimal number suitable for passing to open(2). If a device had already been opened, it is closed before a new open is performed.

C*device*\n
  Close the currently open device. The *device* specified is ignored.

L*offset*\n*whence*\n
  Perform an lseek(2) operation using the specified parameters. The response value is that returned from the lseek(2) call.

W*count*\n
  Write data onto the open device. **rmt** reads *count* bytes from the connection, aborting if a premature end-of-file is encountered. The response value is that returned from the write(2) call.

R*count*\n
  Read *count* bytes of data from the open device. If *count* exceeds the size of the data buffer (10 kilobytes), it is truncated to the data buffer size. **rmt** then performs the requested read(2) and responds with **A***count-read*\n if the read was successful; otherwise an error in the standard format is returned. If the read was successful, the data read is then sent.

I*operation*\n*count*\n
  Perform a MTIOCOP ioctl(2) command using the specified parameters. The parameters are interpreted as the ASCII representations of the decimal values to place in the *mt_op* and *mt_count* fields of the structure used in the ioctl(2) call. The return value is the *count* parameter when the operation is successful.

S   Return the status of the open device, as obtained with a MTIOCGET ioctl(2) call. If the operation was successful, an "ack" is sent with the size of the status buffer, then the status buffer is sent (in binary).

Any other command causes **rmt** to exit.

DIAGNOSTICS

All responses are of the form described above.

SEE ALSO

rcmd(3), rexec(3), mtio(4), rdump(8), rrestore(8)

HISTORY

The **rmt** command appeared in 4.2 BSD.

BUGS

People should be discouraged from using this for a remote file access protocol.

NAME
rndc – name server control utility

SYNOPSIS
rndc [–**b** *source–address*] [–**c** *config–file*] [–**k** *key–file*] [–**s** *server*] [–**p** *port*] [–**V**] [–**y** *key_id*]
{command}

DESCRIPTION
rndc controls the operation of a name server. It supersedes the **ndc** utility that was provided in old BIND releases. If **rndc** is invoked with no command line options or arguments, it prints a short summary of the supported commands and the available options and their arguments.

rndc communicates with the name server over a TCP connection, sending commands authenticated with digital signatures. In the current versions of **rndc** and **named**, the only supported authentication algorithm is HMAC–MD5, which uses a shared secret on each end of the connection. This provides TSIG–style authentication for the command request and the name server's response. All commands sent over the channel must be signed by a key_id known to the server.

rndc reads a configuration file to determine how to contact the name server and decide what algorithm and key it should use.

OPTIONS
–b *source–address*

    Use *source–address* as the source address for the connection to the server. Multiple instances are permitted to allow setting of both the IPv4 and IPv6 source addresses.

–c *config–file*

    Use *config–file* as the configuration file instead of the default, */etc/rndc.conf*.

–k *key–file*

    Use *key–file* as the key file instead of the default, */etc/rndc.key*. The key in */etc/rndc.key* will be used to authenticate commands sent to the server if the *config–file* does not exist.

–s *server*

    server is the name or address of the server which matches a server statement in the configuration file for **rndc**. If no server is supplied on the command line, the host named by the default–server clause in the options statement of the **rndc** configuration file will be used.

–p *port*

    Send commands to TCP port *port* instead of BIND 9's default control channel port, 953.

–V

    Enable verbose logging.

–y *key_id*

    Use the key *key_id* from the configuration file. *key_id* must be known by named with the same algorithm and secret string in order for control message validation to succeed. If no *key_id* is specified, **rndc** will first look for a key clause in the server statement of the server being used, or if no server statement is present for that host, then the default–key clause of the options statement. Note that the configuration file contains shared secrets which are used to send authenticated control commands to name servers. It should therefore not have general read or write access.

For the complete set of commands supported by **rndc**, see the BIND 9 Administrator Reference Manual or run **rndc** without arguments to see its help message.

LIMITATIONS
rndc does not yet support all the commands of the BIND 8 **ndc** utility.

There is currently no way to provide the shared secret for a **key_id** without using the configuration file.

Several error messages could be clearer.

SEE ALSO

    rndc.conf(5), **rndc−confgen**(8), **named**(8), **named.conf**(5), **ndc**(8), BIND 9 Administrator Reference Manual.

AUTHOR

    Internet Systems Consortium

COPYRIGHT

    Copyright © 2004, 2005, 2007 Internet Systems Consortium, Inc. ("ISC")

    Copyright © 2000, 2001 Internet Software Consortium.

NAME

rndctl — in-kernel random number generator management tool

SYNOPSIS

rndctl −CcEe [**−d** *devname* | **−t** *devtype*]
rndctl −ls [**−d** *devname* | **−t** *devtype*]

DESCRIPTION

The **rndctl** program displays statistics on the current state of the rnd(4) pseudo-driver, and allows the administrator to control which sources are allowed to contribute to the randomness pool maintained by rnd(4), as well as whether a given source counts as strongly random.

The following options are available:

−C   Disable collection of timing information for the given device name or device type.

−c   Enable collection of timing information for the given device name of device type.

−d   Only the device named *devname* is altered or displayed. This is mutually exclusive with **−t**.

−E   Disable entropy estimation from the collected timing information for the given device name or device type. If collection is still enabled, timing information is still collected and mixed into the internal entropy pool, but no entropy is assumed to be present.

−e   Enable entropy estimation using the collected timing information for the given device name or device type.

−l   List all sources, or, if the **−t** or **−d** flags are specified, only those specified by the *devtype* or *devname* specified.

−s   Display statistics on the current state of the random collection pool.

−t   All devices of type *devtype* are altered or displayed. This is mutually exclusive with **−d**.

        The available types are:

        disk   Physical hard drives.

        net   Network interfaces.

        tape   Tape devices.

        tty   Terminal, mouse, or other user input devices.

        rng   Random number generators.

FILES

/dev/random   Returns "good" values only.
/dev/urandom   Always returns data, degenerates to a pseudo-random generator.

SEE ALSO

rnd(4), rnd(9)

HISTORY

The **rndctl** program was first made available in NetBSD 1.3.

AUTHORS

The **rndctl** program was written by Michael Graff ⟨explorer@flame.org⟩.

BUGS

Turning on entropy estimation from unsafe or predictable sources will weaken system security, while turning on entropy collection from such sources may weaken system security.

Care should be taken when using this command.

NAME

route — manually manipulate the routing tables

SYNOPSIS

route [**-fnqSsv**] *command* [[*modifiers*] *args*]

DESCRIPTION

route is a utility used to manually manipulate the network routing tables. Except for setting up the default route, it is normally not needed, as a system routing table management daemon such as routed(8), should tend to this task.

route can be used to modify nearly any aspect of the routing policy, except packet forwarding, which can be manipulated through the sysctl(8) command.

The **route** utility supports a limited number of general options, but a rich command language, enabling the user to specify any arbitrary request that could be delivered via the programmatic interface discussed in route(4).

-f   Remove all routes (as per **flush**). If used in conjunction with the **add**, **change**, **delete** or **get** commands, **route** removes the routes before performing the command.

-n   Bypasses attempts to print host and network names symbolically when reporting actions. (The process of translating between symbolic names and numerical equivalents can be quite time consuming, and may require correct operation of the network; thus it may be expedient to forgo this, especially when attempting to repair networking operations).

-q   Suppress all output from commands that manipulate the routing table.

-S   Print a space when a flag is missing so that flags are vertically aligned instead of printing the flags that are set as a contiguous string.

-s   (short) Suppresses all output from a **get** command except for the actual gateway that will be used. How the gateway is printed depends on the type of route being looked up.

-v   (verbose) Print additional details.

The **route** utility provides several commands:

add	Add a route.
flush	Remove all routes.
flushall	Remove all routes including the default gateway.
delete	Delete a specific route.
change	Change aspects of a route (such as its gateway).
get	Lookup and display the route for a destination.
show	Print out the route table similar to "netstat -r" (see netstat(1)).
monitor	Continuously report any changes to the routing information base, routing lookup misses, or suspected network partitionings.

The monitor command has the syntax

       route [**-n**] **monitor**

The flush command has the syntax

       route [**-n**] **flush** [*family*]

If the **flush** command is specified, **route** will "flush" the routing tables of all gateway entries. When the address family is specified by any of the **-osi**, **-xns**, **-atalk**, **-inet**, or **-inet6** modifiers, only routes having destinations with addresses in the delineated family will be manipulated.

The other commands have the following syntax:

route [**-n**] *command* [**-net** | **-host**] *destination gateway*

where *destination* is the destination host or network, and *gateway* is the next-hop intermediary via
which packets should be routed. Routes to a particular host may be distinguished from those to a network by
interpreting the Internet address specified as the *destination* argument. The optional modifiers **-net**
and **-host** force the destination to be interpreted as a network or a host, respectively. Otherwise, if the
destination has a "local address part" of INADDR_ANY, or if the *destination* is the symbolic
name of a network, then the route is assumed to be to a network; otherwise, it is presumed to be a route to a
host. Optionally, the *destination* can also be specified in the *net/bits* format.

For example, 128.32 is interpreted as **-host** 128.0.0.32; 128.32.130 is interpreted as **-host**
128.32.0.130; **-net** 128.32 is interpreted as 128.32.0.0; and **-net** 128.32.130 is interpreted as 128.32.130.0.

The keyword **default** can be used as the *destination* to set up a default route to a smart *gateway*. If
no other routes match, this default route will be used as a last resort.

If the destination is directly reachable via an interface requiring no intermediary system to act as a gateway,
the **-interface** modifier should be specified; the gateway given is the address of this host on the common
network, indicating the interface to be used for transmission.

The optional modifiers **-xns**, **-osi**, **-atalk**, and **-link** specify that all subsequent addresses are in the
XNS, OSI, or AppleTalk address families, or are specified as link-level addresses, and the names must be
numeric specifications rather than symbolic names.

The optional **-netmask** qualifier is intended to achieve the effect of an OSI ESIS redirect with the netmask
option, or to manually add subnet routes with netmasks different from that of the implied network interface
(as would otherwise be communicated using the OSPF or ISIS routing protocols). One specifies an additional ensuing address parameter (to be interpreted as a network mask). The implicit network mask generated in the AF_INET case can be overridden by making sure this option follows the destination parameter.
-prefixlen is also available for similar purpose, in IPv4 and IPv6 case.

Routes have associated flags which influence operation of the protocols when sending to destinations
matched by the routes. These flags may be set (or sometimes cleared) by indicating the following corresponding modifiers:

```
-cloning       RTF_CLONING    - generates a new route on use
-nocloning     ~RTF_CLONING   - stop generating new routes on use
-cloned        RTF_CLONED     - cloned route generated by RTF_CLONING
-nocloned      ~RTF_CLONED    - prevent removal with RTF_CLONING parent
-xresolve      RTF_XRESOLVE   - emit mesg on use (for external lookup)
-iface         ~RTF_GATEWAY   - destination is directly reachable
-static        RTF_STATIC     - manually added route
-nostatic      ~RTF_STATIC    - pretend route added by kernel or daemon
-reject        RTF_REJECT     - emit an ICMP unreachable when matched
-noreject      ~RTF_REJECT    - clear reject flag
-blackhole     RTF_BLACKHOLE  - silently discard pkts (during updates)
-noblackhole   ~RTF_BLACKHOLE - clear blackhole flag
-proto1        RTF_PROTO1     - set protocol specific routing flag #1
-proto2        RTF_PROTO2     - set protocol specific routing flag #2
-llinfo        RTF_LLINFO     - validly translates proto addr to link addr
```

The optional modifiers **-rtt**, **-rttvar**, **-sendpipe**, **-recvpipe**, **-mtu**, **-hopcount**, **-expire**,
and **-ssthresh** provide initial values to quantities maintained in the routing entry by transport level protocols, such as TCP or TP4. These may be individually locked by preceding each such modifier to be locked

by the **-lock** meta-modifier, or one can specify that all ensuing metrics may be locked by the **-lockrest** meta-modifier.

In a **change** or **add** command where the destination and gateway are not sufficient to specify the route (as in the ISO case where several interfaces may have the same address), the **-ifp** or **-ifa** modifiers may be used to determine the interface or interface address.

All symbolic names specified for a *destination* or *gateway* are looked up first as a host name using gethostbyname(3). If this lookup fails, getnetbyname(3) is then used to interpret the name as that of a network.

route uses a routing socket and the new message types RTM_ADD, RTM_DELETE, RTM_GET, and RTM_CHANGE. As such, only the super-user may modify the routing tables.

EXIT STATUS

The **route** utility exits 0 on success, and >0 if an error occurs. This includes the use of the **get** command to look up a route that is incomplete.

EXAMPLES

This sets the default route to 192.168.0.1:

```
route add default 192.168.0.1
```

This shows all routes, without DNS resolution (this is useful if the DNS is not available):

```
route -n show
```

To install a static route through 10.200.0.1 to reach the network 192.168.1.0/28, use this:

```
route add -net 192.168.1.0 -netmask 255.255.255.240 10.200.0.1
```

DIAGNOSTICS

add [host | network] %s: gateway %s flags %x

The specified route is being added to the tables. The values printed are from the routing table entry supplied in the ioctl(2) call. If the gateway address used was not the primary address of the gateway (the first one returned by gethostbyname(3)), the gateway address is printed numerically as well as symbolically.

delete [host | network] %s: gateway %s flags %x

As above, but when deleting an entry.

%s %s done

When the **flush** command is specified, each routing table entry deleted is indicated with a message of this form.

Network is unreachable

An attempt to add a route failed because the gateway listed was not on a directly-connected network. The next-hop gateway must be given.

not in table

A delete operation was attempted for an entry which wasn't present in the tables.

routing table overflow

An add operation was attempted, but the system was low on resources and was unable to allocate memory to create the new entry.

Permission denied

The attempted operation is privileged. Only root may modify the routing tables. These privileges are enforced by the kernel.

SEE ALSO

esis(4), netintro(4), route(4), routed(8), sysctl(8)

HISTORY

The **route** command appeared in 4.2 BSD. IPv6 support was added by WIDE/KAME project.

BUGS

The first paragraph may have slightly exaggerated routed(8)'s abilities.

Some uses of the **-ifa** or **-ifp** modifiers with the add command will incorrectly fail with a "Network is unreachable" message if there is no default route. See case RTM_ADD in sys/net/rtsock.c:route_output for details.

NAME

route6d — RIP6 routing daemon

SYNOPSIS

route6d [-adDhlnqsS] [-R *routelog*] [-A *prefix/preflen,if1[,if2...]*]
       [-L *prefix/preflen,if1[,if2...]*] [-N *if1[,if2...]*]
       [-O *prefix/preflen,if1[,if2...]*] [-T *if1[,if2...]*] [-t *tag*]

DESCRIPTION

The **route6d** is a routing daemon which supports RIP over IPv6.

Options are:

-a   Enables aging of the statically defined routes. With this option, any statically defined routes will be removed unless corresponding updates arrive as if the routes are received at the startup of **route6d**.

-R *routelog*
       This option makes **route6d** log route changes (add/delete) to the file *routelog*.

-A *prefix/preflen,if1[,if2...]*
       This option is used for aggregating routes. *prefix/preflen* specifies the prefix and the prefix length of the aggregated route. When advertising routes, **route6d** filters specific routes covered by the aggregate and advertises the aggregated route *prefix/preflen* to the interfaces specified in the comma-separated interface list *if1[,if2...]*. **route6d** creates a static route to *prefix/preflen*, with the RTF_REJECT flag set, into the kernel routing table.

-d   Enables output of debugging messages. This option also instructs **route6d** to run in foreground mode (i.e., it does not become a daemon process).

-D   Enables extensive output of debugging messages. This option also instructs **route6d** to run in foreground mode (i.e., it does not become a daemon process).

-h   Disables split horizon processing.

-l   By default, **route6d** will not exchange site local routes for safety reasons. This is because the semantics of site local address space are rather vague, as the specification is still being worked on, and there is no good way to define the site local boundary. With **-l**, **route6d** will exchange site local routes as well. It must not be used on site boundary routers, since **-l** assumes that all interfaces are in the same site.

-L *prefix/preflen,if1[,if2...]*
       Filter incoming routes from interfaces *if1, [if2...]*. **route6d** will accept incoming routes that are in *prefix/preflen*. If multiple **-L** options are specified, all routes that match any of the options are accepted. ::/0 is treated specially as default route, not "any route that has longer prefix length than, or equal to 0". If you would like to accept any route, specify no **-L** option. For example, with " **-L** 3ffe::/16,if1 **-L** ::/0,if1" **route6d** will accept the default route and routes in the 6bone test address range, but no others.

-n   Do not update the kernel routing table.

-N *if1[,if2...]*
       Do not listen to, or advertise, route from/to interfaces specified by *if1, [if2...]*.

-O *prefix/preflen,if1[,if2...]*
       Restrict route advertisement toward interfaces specified by *if1, [if2...]*. With this option **route6d** will only advertise routes that match *prefix/preflen*.

-q   Makes **route6d** use listen-only mode. No advertisement is sent.

-s   Makes **route6d** advertise the statically defined routes which exist in the kernel routing table
           when **route6d** is invoked. Announcements obey the regular split horizon rule.

-S   This option is the same as -s, except that the split horizon rule does apply.

-T *if1[,if2...]*
           Advertise only the default route toward *if1, [if2...]*.

-t *tag*
           Attach the route tag *tag* to originated route entries. *tag* can be decimal, octal prefixed by 0, or
           hexadecimal prefixed by 0x.

Upon receipt of signal SIGINT or SIGUSR1, **route6d** will dump the current internal state into
/var/run/rcute6d_dump.

FILES
       /var/run/rcute6d_dump contains the internal state dumps created if **route6d** receives a SIGINT or
                              SIGUSR1 signal

SEE ALSO
       G. Malkin and R. Minnear, *RIPng for IPv6*, RFC 2080, January 1997.

NOTES
       route6d uses the advanced IPv6 API, defined in RFC 3542, for communicating with peers using link-local
       addresses.

       Internally **route6d** embeds interface identifiers into bits 32 to 63 of link-local addresses (fe80::xx and
       ff02::xx) so they will be visible in the internal state dump file (/var/run/route6d_dump).

       Routing table manipulation differs from IPv6 implementation to implementation. Currently **route6d** obeys
       the WIDE Hydrangea/KAME IPv6 kernel, and will not be able to run on other platforms.

       Currently, **route6d** does not reduce the rate of the triggered updates when consecutive updates arrive.

ROUTED (8)   NetBSD   ROUTED (8)

NAME

routed, rdisc — network RIP and router discovery routing daemon

SYNOPSIS

routed [-sqdghmAtv] [-T *tracefile*] [-F *net*[/mask[,metric]]] [-P *parms*]

DESCRIPTION

routed is a daemon invoked at boot time to manage the network routing tables. It uses Routing Information Protocol, RIPv1 (RFC 1058), RIPv2 (RFC 1723), and Internet Router Discovery Protocol (RFC 1256) to
maintain the kernel routing table. The RIPv1 protocol is based on the reference 4.3 BSD daemon.

It listens on the udp(4) socket for the route(8) service (see services(5)) for Routing Information Protocol packets. It also sends and receives multicast Router Discovery ICMP messages. If the host is a router,
routed periodically supplies copies of its routing tables to any directly connected hosts and networks. It
also advertises or solicits default routes using Router Discovery ICMP messages.

When started (or when a network interface is later turned on), routed uses an AF_ROUTE address family
facility to find those directly connected interfaces configured into the system and marked "up". It adds necessary routes for the interfaces to the kernel routing table. Soon after being first started, and provided there is
at least one interface on which RIP has not been disabled, routed deletes all pre-existing non-static routes
in kernel table. Static routes in the kernel table are preserved and included in RIP responses if they have a
valid RIP metric (see route(8)).

If more than one interface is present (not counting the loopback interface), it is assumed that the host should
forward packets among the connected networks. After transmitting a RIP *request* and Router Discovery
Advertisements or Solicitations on a new interface, the daemon enters a loop, listening for RIP request and
response and Router Discovery packets from other hosts.

When a *request* packet is received, routed formulates a reply based on the information maintained in its
internal tables. The *response* packet generated contains a list of known routes, each marked with a "hop
count" metric (a count of 16 or greater is considered "infinite"). The advertised metric for a route reflects the
metrics associated with interfaces (see ifconfig(8)) through which it is received and sent, so setting the
metric on an interface is an effective way to steer traffic. See also **adj_inmetric** and **adj_outmetric**
parameters below.

Responses do not include routes with a first hop on the requesting network to implement in part
split-horizon. Requests from query programs such as rtquery(8) are answered with the complete table.

The routing table maintained by the daemon includes space for several gateways for each destination to
speed recovery from a failing router. RIP *response* packets received are used to update the routing tables
provided they are from one of the several currently recognized gateways or advertise a better metric than at
least one of the existing gateways.

When an update is applied, routed records the change in its own tables and updates the kernel routing table
if the best route to the destination changes. The change in the kernel routing table is reflected in the next
batch of *response* packets sent. If the next response is not scheduled for a while, a *flash update* response
containing only recently changed routes is sent.

In addition to processing incoming packets, routed also periodically checks the routing table entries. If an
entry has not been updated for 3 minutes, the entry's metric is set to infinity and marked for deletion. Deletions are delayed until the route has been advertised with an infinite metric to ensure the invalidation is propagated throughout the local internet. This is a form of *poison reverse*.

Routes in the kernel table that are added or changed as a result of ICMP Redirect messages are deleted after
a while to minimize *black-holes*. When a TCP connection suffers a timeout, the kernel tells routed, which
deletes all redirected routes through the gateway involved, advances the age of all RIP routes through the

gateway to allow an alternate to be chosen, and advances of the age of any relevant Router Discovery Protocol default routes.

Hosts acting as internetwork routers gratuitously supply their routing tables every 30 seconds to all directly connected hosts and networks. These RIP responses are sent to the broadcast address on nets that support broadcasting, to the destination address on point-to-point links, and to the router's own address on other networks. If RIPv2 is enabled, multicast packets are sent on interfaces that support multicasting.

If no response is received on a remote interface, if there are errors while sending responses, or if there are more errors than input or output (see netstat(1)), then the cable or some other part of the interface is assumed to be disconnected or broken, and routes are adjusted appropriately.

The *Internet Router Discovery Protocol* is handled similarly. When the daemon is supplying RIP routes, it also listens for Router Discovery Solicitations and sends Advertisements. When it is quiet and listening to other RIP routers, it sends Solicitations and listens for Advertisements. If it receives a good Advertisement and it is not multi-homed, it stops listening for broadcast or multicast RIP responses. It tracks several advertising routers to speed recovery when the currently chosen router dies. If all discovered routers disappear, the daemon resumes listening to RIP responses. It continues listening to RIP while using Router Discovery if multi-homed to ensure all interfaces are used.

The Router Discovery standard requires that advertisements have a default "lifetime" of 30 minutes. That means should something happen, a client can be without a good route for 30 minutes. It is a good idea to reduce the default to 45 seconds using **-P rdisc_interval=45** on the command line or **rdisc_interval=45** in the /etc/gateways file.

While using Router Discovery (which happens by default when the system has a single network interface and a Router Discover Advertisement is received), there is a single default route and a variable number of redirected host routes in the kernel table. On a host with more than one network interface, this default route will be via only one of the interfaces. Thus, multi-homed hosts running with **-q** might need **no_rdisc** described below.

See the **pm_rdisc** facility described below to support "legacy" systems that can handle neither RIPv2 nor Router Discovery.

By default, neither Router Discovery advertisements nor solicitations are sent over point to point links (e.g. PPP). The netmask associated with point-to-point links (such as SLIP or PPP, with the IFF_POINTOPOINT flag) is used by **routed** to infer the netmask used by the remote system when RIPv1 is used.

The following options are available:

-s   force **routed** to supply routing information. This is the default if multiple network interfaces are present on which RIP or Router Discovery have not been disabled, and if the sysctl net.inet.ip.forwarding=1.

-q   is the opposite of the **-s** option. This is the default when only one interface is present. With this explicit option, the daemon is always in "quiet-mode" for RIP and does not supply routing information to other computers.

-d   do not run in the background. This option is meant for interactive use.

-g   used on internetwork routers to offer a route to the "default" destination. It is equivalent to **-F 0/0,1** and is present mostly for historical reasons. A better choice is **-P pm_rdisc** on the command line or **pm_rdisc** in the /etc/gateways file. since a larger metric will be used, reducing the spread of the potentially dangerous default route. This is typically used on a gateway to the Internet, or on a gateway that uses another routing protocol whose routes are not reported to other local routers. Notice that because a metric of 1 is used, this feature is dangerous. It is more commonly accidentally used to create chaos with a routing loop than to solve problems.

-h   cause host or point-to-point routes to not be advertised, provided there is a network route going the
            same direction. That is a limited kind of aggregation. This option is useful on gateways to Ether-
            nets that have other gateway machines connected with point-to-point links such as SLIP.

-m   cause the machine to advertise a host or point-to-point route to its primary interface. It is useful on
            multi-homed machines such as NFS servers. This option should not be used except when the cost
            of the host routes it generates is justified by the popularity of the server. It is effective only when
            the machine is supplying routing information, because there is more than one interface. The **-m**
            option overrides the **-q** option to the limited extent of advertising the host route.

-A   do not ignore RIPv2 authentication if we do not care about RIPv2 authentication. This option is
            required for conformance with RFC 1723. However, it makes no sense and breaks using RIP as a
            discovery protocol to ignore all RIPv2 packets that carry authentication when this machine does
            not care about authentication.

-t   increase the debugging level, which causes more information to be logged on the tracefile specified
            with **-T** or standard out. The debugging level can be increased or decreased with the *SIGUSR1* or
            SIGUSR2 signals or with the rtquery(8) command.

-T *tracefile*
            increases the debugging level to at least 1 and causes debugging information to be appended to the
            trace file. Note that because of security concerns, it is wisest to not run **routed** routinely with
            tracing directed to a file.

-v   displays and logs the version of daemon.

-F *net[/mask][,metric]*
            minimize routes in transmissions via interfaces with addresses that match *net/mask*, and synthe-
            sizes a default route to this machine with the *metric*. The intent is to reduce RIP traffic on slow,
            point-to-point links such as PPP links by replacing many large UDP packets of RIP information
            with a single, small packet containing a "fake" default route. If *metric* is absent, a value of 14 is
            assumed to limit the spread of the "fake" default route. This is a dangerous feature that when used
            carelessly can cause routing loops. Notice also that more than one interface can match the speci-
            fied network number and mask. See also **-g**.

-P *parms*
            is equivalent to adding the parameter line *parms* to the /etc/gateways file.

Any other argument supplied is interpreted as the name of a file in which the actions of **routed** should be
logged. It is better to use **-T** instead of appending the name of the trace file to the command.

routed also supports the notion of "distant" *passive* or *active* gateways. When **routed** is started, it reads
the file /etc/gateways to find such distant gateways which may not be located using only information
from a routing socket, to discover if some of the local gateways are *passive*, and to obtain other parameters.
Gateways specified in this manner should be marked passive if they are not expected to exchange routing
information, while gateways marked active should be willing to exchange RIP packets. Routes through
passive gateways are installed in the kernel's routing tables once upon startup and are not included in transmitted RIP responses.

Distant active gateways are treated like network interfaces. RIP responses are sent to the distant *active* gateway. If no responses are received, the associated route is deleted from the kernel table and RIP responses
advertised via other interfaces. If the distant gateway resumes sending RIP responses, the associated route is
restored.

Such gateways can be useful on media that do not support broadcasts or multicasts but otherwise act like
classic shared media like Ethernets such as some ATM networks. One can list all RIP routers reachable on
the HIPPI or ATM network in /etc/gateways with a series of "host" lines. Note that it is usually desir-

able to use RIPv2 in such situations to avoid generating lists of inferred host routes.

Gateways marked *external* are also passive, but are not placed in the kernel routing table nor are they included in routing updates. The function of external entries is to indicate that another routing process will install such a route if necessary, and that other routes to that destination should not be installed by **routed**. Such entries are only required when both routers may learn of routes to the same destination.

The /etc/gateways file is comprised of a series of lines, each in one of the following two formats or consist of parameters described later. Blank lines and lines starting with '#' are comments.

net *Nname[/mask]* **gateway** *Gname* **metric** *value* **<passive** |**active** |**extern>**

host *Hname* **gateway** *Gname* **metric** *value* **<passive** |**active** |**extern>**

Nname or *Hname* is the name of the destination network or host. It may be a symbolic network name or an Internet address specified in "dot" notation (see inet(3)). (If it is a name, then it must either be defined in /etc/networks or /etc/hosts, or named(8), must have been started before **routed**.)

Mask is an optional number between 1 and 32 indicating the netmask associated with *Nname*.

Gname is the name or address of the gateway to which RIP responses should be forwarded.

Value is the hop count to the destination host or network.   *Host hname* is equivalent to *net nname/32* .

One of the keywords **passive**, **active** or **external** must be present to indicate whether the gateway should be treated as **passive** or **active** (as described above), or whether the gateway is **external** to the scope of the RIP protocol.

As can be seen when debugging is turned on with −**t**, such lines create pseudo-interfaces. To set parameters for remote or external interfaces, a line starting with **if=alias(Hname)**, **if=remote(Hname)**, etc. should be used.

Parameters

Lines that start with neither "net" nor "host" must consist of one or more of the following parameter settings, separated by commas or blanks:

if=*ifname*
> indicates that the other parameters on the line apply to the interface name *ifname*.

subnet=*nname[/mask][,metric]*
> advertises a route to network *nname* with mask *mask* and the supplied metric (default 1). This is useful for filling "holes" in CIDR allocations. This parameter must appear by itself on a line. The network number must specify a full, 32-bit value, as in 192.0.2.0 instead of 192.0.2.
>
> Do not use this feature unless necessary. It is dangerous.

ripv1_mask=*nname/mask1,mask2*
> specifies that netmask of the network of which **nname/mask1** is a subnet should be **mask2**. For example **ripv1_mask**=*192.0.2.16/28,27* marks 192.0.2.16/28 as a subnet of 192.0.2.0/27 instead of 192.0.2.0/24. It is better to turn on RIPv2 instead of using this facility, for example with **ripv2_out**.

passwd=*XXX[|KeyID[start|stop]]*
> specifies a RIPv2 cleartext password that will be included on all RIPv2 responses sent, and checked on all RIPv2 responses received. Any blanks, tab characters, commas, or '#', '|', or NULL characters in the password must be escaped with a backslash (\). The common escape sequences \n, \r, \t, \b, and \xxx have their usual meanings. The **KeyID** must be unique but is ignored for cleartext passwords. If present, **start** and **stop** are timestamps in the form year/month/day@hour:minute.

They specify when the password is valid. The valid password with the most future is used on output packets, unless all passwords have expired, in which case the password that expired most recently is used, or unless no passwords are valid yet, in which case no password is output. Incoming packets can carry any password that is valid, will be valid within the next 24 hours, or that was valid within the preceding 24 hours. To protect the secrets, the passwd settings are valid only in the */etc/gateways* file and only when that file is readable only by UID 0.

md5_passwd=*XXX|KeyID[start|stop]*
> specifies a RIPv2 MD5 password. Except that a **KeyID** is required, this keyword is similar to **passwd**.

no_ag turns off aggregation of subnets in RIPv1 and RIPv2 responses.

no_super_ag
> turns off aggregation of networks into supernets in RIPv2 responses.

passive
> marks the interface to not be advertised in updates sent via other interfaces, and turns off all RIP and router discovery through the interface.

no_rip
> disables all RIP processing on the specified interface. If no interfaces are allowed to process RIP packets, **routed** acts purely as a router discovery daemon.

> Note that turning off RIP without explicitly turning on router discovery advertisements with **rdisc_adv** or **−s** causes **routed** to act as a client router discovery daemon, not advertising.

no_rip_mcast
> causes RIPv2 packets to be broadcast instead of multicast.

no_ripv1_in
> causes RIPv1 received responses to be ignored.

no_ripv2_in
> causes RIPv2 received responses to be ignored.

ripv2_out
> turns on RIPv2 output and causes RIPv2 advertisements to be multicast when possible.

ripv2 is equivalent to **no_ripv1_in** and **no_ripv1_out**. This enables RIPv2.

no_rdisc
> disables the Internet Router Discovery Protocol.

no_solicit
> disables the transmission of Router Discovery Solicitations.

send_solicit
> specifies that Router Discovery solicitations should be sent, even on point-to-point links, which by default only listen to Router Discovery messages.

no_rdisc_adv
> disables the transmission of Router Discovery Advertisements.

rdisc_adv
> specifies that Router Discovery Advertisements should be sent, even on point-to-point links, which by default only listen to Router Discovery messages.

bcast_rdisc
> specifies that Router Discovery packets should be broadcast instead of multicast.

rdisc_pref=*N*
> sets the preference in Router Discovery Advertisements to the optionally signed integer *N*. The default preference is 0. Default routes with larger preferences are preferred by clients.

rdisc_interval=*N*
> sets the nominal interval with which Router Discovery Advertisements are transmitted to N seconds and their lifetime to 3*N.

fake_default=*metric*
> has an identical effect to **−F** *net [/mask] [=metric]* with the network and mask coming from the specified interface.

pm_rdisc
> is similar to **fake_default**. When RIPv2 routes are multicast, so that RIPv1 listeners cannot receive them, this feature causes a RIPv1 default route to be broadcast to RIPv1 listeners. Unless modified with **fake_default**, the default route is broadcast with a metric of 14. That serves as a "poor man's router discovery" protocol.

adj_inmetric=*delta*
> adjusts the hop count or metric of received RIP routes by *delta*. The metric of every received RIP route is increased by the sum of two values associated with the interface. One is the adj_inmetric value and the other is the interface metric set with *ifconfig*(8).

adj_outmetric=*delta*
> adjusts the hop count or metric of advertised RIP routes by *delta*. The metric of every received RIP route is increased by the metric associated with the interface by which it was received, or by 1 if the interface does not have a non-zero metric. The metric of the received route is then increased by the adj_outmetric associated with the interface. Every advertised route is increased by a total of four values, the metric set for the interface by which it was received with *ifconfig*(8), the **adj_inmetric** *delta* of the receiving interface, the metric set for the interface by which it is transmitted with *ifconfig*(8), and the **adj_outmetric** *delta* of the transmitting interface.

trust_gateway=*rname[|net1/mask1|net2/mask2|...]*
> causes RIP packets from router *rname* and other routers named in other **trust_gateway** keywords to be accepted, and packets from other routers to be ignored. If networks are specified, then routes to other networks will be ignored from that router.

redirect_ok
> allows the kernel to listen ICMP Redirect messages when the system is acting as a router and forwarding packets. Otherwise, ICMP Redirect messages are overridden and deleted when the system is acting as a router.

FILES
> /etc/gateways for distant gateways

SEE ALSO
> icmp(4), udp(4), rtquery(8)

> *Internet Transport Protocols*, XSIS 028112, Xerox System Integration Standard.

HISTORY
> The **routed** command appeared in 4.2 BSD.

BUGS

It does not always detect unidirectional failures in network interfaces, for example, when the output side fails.

NAME

bootparamd, **rpc.bootparamd** — boot parameter server

SYNOPSIS

bootparamd [**-ds**] [**-i** *interface*] [**-r** *router*] [**-f** *file*]

DESCRIPTION

bootparamd is a server process that provides information to diskless clients necessary for booting. It consults the file "/etc/bootparams". It should normally be started from "/etc/rc".

This version will allow the use of aliases on the hostname in the "/etc/bootparams" file. The hostname returned in response to the booting client's whoami request will be the name that appears in the config file, not the canonical name. In this way you can keep the answer short enough so that machines that cannot handle long hostnames won't fail during boot.

While parsing, if a line containing just "+" is found, and the YP subsystem is active, the YP map bootparams will be searched immediately.

OPTIONS

-d   Display the debugging information. The daemon does not fork in this case.

-i *interface*
             Specify the interface to become the default router. **bootparamd** picks the first IPv4 address it finds on the system by default. With **-i**, you can control which interface to be used to obtain the default router address. **-r** overrides **-i**.

-s   Log the debugging information with syslog(3).

-r   Set the default router (a hostname or IP-address). This defaults to the machine running the server.

-f   Specify the file to use as boot parameter file instead of "/etc/bootparams".

FILES

/etc/bootparams default configuration file

SEE ALSO

bootparams(5)

AUTHORS

Originally written by Klas Heggemann ⟨klas@nada.kth.se⟩.

BUGS

You may find the syslog messages too verbose.

It's not clear if the non-canonical hack mentioned above is a good idea.

NAME

rpc.lockd — NFS file locking daemon

SYNOPSIS

rpc.lockd [**-d** *debug_level*] [**-g** *grace period*]

DESCRIPTION

The **rpc.lockd** daemon provides monitored and unmonitored file and record locking services in an NFS environment. To monitor the status of hosts requesting locks, the locking daemon typically operates in conjunction with rpc.statd(8).

Options and operands available for **rpc.lockd** :

-d   The **-d** option causes debugging information to be written to syslog, recording all RPC transactions to the daemon. These messages are logged with level LOG_DEBUG and facility LOG_DAEMON. Specifying a debug_level of 1 results in the generation of one log line per protocol operation. Higher debug levels can be specified, causing display of operation arguments and internal operations of the daemon.

-g   The **-g** option allow to specify the grace period, in seconds. During the grace period **rpc.lockd** only accepts requests from hosts which are reinitialising locks which existed before the server restart. Default is 30 seconds.

Error conditions are logged to syslog, irrespective of the debug level, using log level LOG_ERR and facility LOG_DAEMON.

The **rpc.lockd** daemon must NOT be invoked by inetd(8) because the protocol assumes that the daemon will run from system start time. Instead, it should be configured in rc.conf(5) to run at system startup.

FILES

/usr/include/rpcsvc/nlm_prot.x RPC protocol specification for the network lock manager protocol.

SEE ALSO

syslog(3), rc.conf(5), rpc.statd(8)

STANDARDS

The implementation is based on the specification in X/Open CAE Specification C218, "Protocols for X/Open PC Interworking: XNFS, Issue 4", ISBN 1 872630 66 9

HISTORY

A version of **rpc.lockd** appeared in SunOS 4.

BUGS

The current implementation provides only the server side of the protocol (i.e. clients running other OS types can establish locks on a NetBSD fileserver, but there is currently no means for a NetBSD client to establish locks).

The current implementation serialises locks requests that could be shared.

NAME

pcnfsd, rpc.pcnfsd – (PC)NFS authentication and print request server

SYNOPSIS

/usr/sbin/rpc.pcnfsd

DESCRIPTION

pcnfsd is an RPC server that supports Sun ONC clients on PC (DOS, OS/2, Macintosh, and other) systems. This page describes version two of the **pcnfsd** server.

rpc.pcnfsd may be started from **/etc/rc.local** or by the **inetd**(8) superdaemon. It reads the configuration file **/etc/pcnfsd.conf** if present, and then services RPC requests directed to program number 150001. This release of the **pcnfsd** daemon supports both version 1 and version 2 of the pcnfsd protocol. Consult the **rpcgen** source file **pcnfsd.x** for details of the protocols.

The requests serviced by **pcnfsd** fall into three categories: authentication, printing, and other. Only the authentication and printing services have administrative significance.

AUTHENTICATION

When **pcnfsd** receives a **PCNFSD_AUTH** or **PCNFSD2_AUTH** request, it will "log in" the user by validating the username and password and returning the corresponding uid, gids, home directory, and umask. If **pcnfsd** was built with the **WTMP** compile-time option, it will also append a record to the **wtmp**(5) data base. If you do not wish to record PC "logins" in this way, you should add a line of the form

wtmp off

to the **/etc/pcnfsd.conf** file.

PRINTING

pcnfsd supports a printing model based on the use of NFS to transfer the actual print data from the client to the server. The client system issues a **PCNFSD_PR_INIT** or **PCNFSD2_PR_INIT** request, and the server returns the path to a spool directory which the client may use and which is exported by NFS. **pcnfsd** creates a subdirectory for each of its clients: the parent directory is normally **/export/pcnfs** and the subdirectory is the hostname of the client system. If you wish to use a different parent directory, you should add a line of the form

spooldir *path*

to the **/etc/pcnfsd.conf** file.

Once a client has mounted the spool directory using NFS and has transferred print data to a file in this directory, it will issue a **PCNFSD_PR_START** or **PCNFSD2_PR_START** request. **pcnfsd** handles this, and most other print-related requests, by constructing a command based on the printing services of the server operating system and executing the command using the identity of the PC user. Since this involves set-user-id privileges, **pcnfsd** must be run as root.

Every print request from the client includes the name of the printer which is to be used. In SunOS, this name corresponds to a printer definition in the **/etc/printcap**(5) database. If you wish to define a non-standard way of processing print data, you should define a new printer and arrange for the client to print to this printer. There are two ways of setting up a new printer. The first involves the addition of an entry to **/etc/printcap**(5) and the creation of filters to perform the required processing. This is outside the scope of this discussion. In addition, **pcnfsd** includes a mechanism by which you can define virtual printers known only to **pcnfsd** clients. Each printer is defined by a line in the **/etc/pcnfsd.conf** file of the following form

printer *name alias-for command*

name is the name of the printer you want to define. *alias-for* is the name of a "real" printer which corresponds to this printer. For example, a request to display the queue for *name* will be translated into the corresponding request for the printer *alias-for*. If you have defined a printer in such a way that there is no "real" printer to which it corresponds, use a single "-" for this field. (See the definition of the printer **test** below for an example.) *command* is a command which will be executed whenever a file is printed on *name*. This command is executed by the Bourne shell, **/bin/sh** using the **-c** option. For complex operations you should construct an executable shell program and invoke that in *command*. Within *command* the following tokens will be replaced:

Token	Substitution
$FILE	Replaced by the full path name of the print data file. When the command has been executed, the file will be unlinked.
$USER	Replaced by the username of the user logged in to the client system.
$HOST	Replaced by the host name of the client system.

Consider the following example **/etc/pcnfsd.conf** file:

```
printer rotated lw /usr/local/bin/enscript -2r $FILE
printer test - /usr/bin/cp $FILE /usr/tmp/$HOST-$USER
```

If a client system prints a job on the printer **rotated** the utility **enscript** will be invoked to pre-process the file $FILE. In this case, the **-2r** option causes the file to be printed in two-column rotated format on the default PostScript® printer. If the client requests a list of the print queue for the printer **rotated** the **pcnfsd** daemon will translate this into a request for a listing for the printer **lw.**

The printer **test** is used only for testing. Any file sent to this printer will be copied into **/usr/tmp.** Any request to list the queue, check the status, etc. of printer **test** will be rejected because the *alias-for* has been specified as "-".

FILES

/etc/pcnfsd.conf	configuration file
/export/pcnfs	default print spool directory

SEE ALSO
lpr(1), **lpc**(8)

HISTORY
The **pcnfsd** source code is distributed by Sun Microsystems, Inc. with their PC/NFS product under terms described in common.h in that source code. Those terms require that you be informed that this version of **pcnfsd** was modified to run on NetBSD and is NOT supported by Sun.

NAME

   rpc.rquotad, **rquotad** — remote quota server

SYNOPSIS

   `/usr/libexec/rpc.rquotad`

DESCRIPTION

   rpc.rquotad is a `rpc`(3) server which returns quotas for a user of a local filesystem which is NFS-mounted onto a remote machine. `quota`(1) uses the results to display user quotas for remote filesystems. **rpc.rquotad** is normally invoked by `inetd`(8).

   rpc.rquotad uses an RPC protocol defined in `/usr/include/rpcsvc/rquota.x`.

SEE ALSO

   `quota`(1)

NAME

rpc.rstatd, **rstatd** — kernel statistics server

SYNOPSIS

/usr/libexec/rpc.rstatd [*interval*]

DESCRIPTION

rpc.rstatd is a server which returns performance statistics obtained from the kernel. These statistics are read using the rup(1) command. The **rpc.rstatd** daemon is normally invoked by inetd(8).

The *interval* argument specifies the number of seconds that **rpc.rstatd** should stay active, updating its internal statistics every second. If no value is specified, 20 seconds will be used. After *interval* seconds with no new RPC requests, if **rpc.rstatd** was invoked from inetd(8), **rpc.rstatd** exits. Otherwise, **rpc.rstatd** loops, becoming dormant until it receives a new RPC request, and staying active until *interval* seconds pass with no new requests.

rpc.rstatd uses an RPC protocol defined in /usr/include/rpcsvc/rstat.x.

SEE ALSO

rup(1), inetd(8)

NAME
     rpc.rusersd, **rusersd** — logged in users server

SYNOPSIS
     `/usr/libexec/rpc.rusersd`

DESCRIPTION
     rpc.rusersd is a server which returns information about users currently logged in to the system.

     The currently logged in users are queried using the `rusers`(1) command. The **rpc.rusersd** daemon is normally invoked by `inetd`(8).

     rpc.rusersd uses an RPC protocol defined in `/usr/include/rpcsvc/rnusers.x`.

SEE ALSO
     `rusers`(1), `w`(1), `who`(1), `inetd`(8)

NAME

rpc.rwalld, **rwalld** — write messages to users currently logged in server

SYNOPSIS

/usr/libexec/rpc.rwalld

DESCRIPTION

rpc.rwalld is a server which will send a message to users currently logged in to the system. This server invokes the wall(1) command to actually write the messages to the system.

Messages are sent to this server by the rwall(1) command. The **rpc.rwalld** daemon is normally invoked by inetd(8).

rpc.rwalld uses an RPC protocol defined in /usr/include/rpcsvc/rwall.x.

SEE ALSO

rwall(1), wall(1), inetd(8)

NAME

rpc.sprayd, **sprayd** — spray server

SYNOPSIS

`/usr/libexec/rpc.sprayd`

DESCRIPTION

rpc.sprayd is a server which records packets sent by the `spray`(8) command and sends a traffic report to the originator of the packets. The **rpc.sprayd** daemon is normally invoked by `inetd`(8).

rpc.sprayd uses an RPC protocol defined in `/usr/include/rpcsvc/spray.x`.

SEE ALSO

`spray`(8)

SECURITY CONSIDERATIONS

As **rpc.sprayd** responds to packets generated by `spray`(8), remote users can cause a denial of network service against the local host by saturating requests to **rpc.sprayd**.

NAME
rpc.statd — host status monitoring daemon

SYNOPSIS
rpc.statd [−d]

DESCRIPTION
rpc.statd is a daemon which co-operates with rpc.statd daemons on other hosts to provide a status monitoring service. The daemon accepts requests from programs running on the local host (typically,
rpc.lockd(8), the NFS file locking daemon) to monitor the status of specified hosts. If a monitored host
crashes and restarts, the remote daemon will notify the local daemon, which in turn will notify the local pro-
gram(s) which requested the monitoring service. Conversely, if this host crashes and restarts, when
rpc.statd restarts, it will notify all of the hosts which were being monitored at the time of the crash.

Options and operands available for rpc.statd :

−d   The −d option causes debugging information to be written to syslog, recording all RPC transactions
        to the daemon. These messages are logged with level LOG_DEBUG and facility LOG_DAEMON.
        Error conditions are logged irrespective of this option, using level LOG_ERR.

The rpc.statd daemon must NOT be invoked by inetd(8) because the protocol assumes that the daemon will run from system start time. Instead, it should be configured in rc.conf(5) to run at system
startup.

FILES
/var/db/statd.status   non-volatile record of currently monitored hosts.
/usr/include/rpcsvc/sm_inter.x   RPC protocol specification used by local applications to regis-
                                  ter monitoring requests.

SEE ALSO
syslog(3), rc.conf(5), rpc.lockd(8)

STANDARDS
The implementation is based on the specification in X/Open CAE Specification C218, "Protocols for X/Open
PC Interworking: XNFS, Issue 4", ISBN 1 872630 66 9

HISTORY
A version of rpc.statd appeared in SunOS 4.

BUGS
There is no means for the daemon to tell when a monitored host has disappeared permanently (e.g., catastrophic hardware failure), as opposed to transient failure of the host or an intermediate router. At present, it
will retry notification attempts at frequent intervals for 10 minutes, then hourly, and finally gives up after 24
hours.

The protocol requires that symmetric monitor requests are made to both the local and remote daemon in
order to establish a monitored relationship. This is convenient for the NFS locking protocol, but probably
reduces the usefulness of the monitoring system for other applications.

The current implementation uses more than 1Kbyte per monitored host in the status file (and also in VM).
This may be inefficient for NFS servers with large numbers of clients.

NAME

rpc.yppasswdd — NIS update password file daemon

SYNOPSIS

rpc.yppasswdd [**-d** *directory*] [**-noshell**] [**-nogecos**] [**-nopw**]
        [**-m** *arg1* [*arg2* ...]]

DESCRIPTION

rpc.yppasswdd must be running on the NIS master server to allow users to change information in the password file.

The options are as follows:

-d *directory*   Change the root directory of the password file from "/" to *directory*. It is important to create the binary database files (pwd.db and spwd.db) when using this switch or the password change will fail. The databases need to be created only once with the following command:

        pwd_mkdb   -d   directory
        directory/etc/master.passwd

-noshell   Don't allow changes of the shell field in the passwd file.

-nogecos   Don't allow changes of the gecos field in the passwd file.

-nopw   Don't allow changes of the password in the passwd file.

-m *arg1* [*arg2* ...]
    Additional arguments to pass to *make* in */var/yp*.

FILES

/etc/passwd
/etc/master.passwd

SEE ALSO

chpass(1), passwd(1), hosts_access(5), nis(8), ypbind(8), ypserv(8)

AUTHORS

Mats O Jansson ⟨moj@stacken.kth.se⟩

NAME

rpcbind — universal addresses to RPC program number mapper

SYNOPSIS

rpcbind [**-dilLs**]

DESCRIPTION

rpcbind is a server that converts RPC program numbers into universal addresses. It must be running on the host to be able to make RPC calls on a server on that machine.

When an RPC service is started, it tells **rpcbind** the address at which it is listening, and the RPC program numbers it is prepared to serve. When a client wishes to make an RPC call to a given program number, it first contacts **rpcbind** on the server machine to determine the address where RPC requests should be sent.

rpcbind should be started before any other RPC service. Normally, standard RPC servers are started by port monitors, so **rpcbind** must be started before port monitors are invoked.

When **rpcbind** is started, it checks that certain name-to-address translation-calls function correctly. If they fail, the network configuration databases may be corrupt. Since RPC services cannot function correctly in this situation, **rpcbind** reports the condition and terminates.

rpcbind can only be started by the super-user.

Access control is provided by /etc/hosts.allow and /etc/hosts.deny, as described in hosts_access(5) with daemon name **rpcbind**.

OPTIONS

-d   Run in debug mode. In this mode, **rpcbind** will not fork when it starts, will print additional information during operation, and will abort on certain errors. With this option, the name-to-address translation consistency checks are shown in detail.

-i   "insecure" mode. Allows calls to SET and UNSET from any host. Normally **rpcbind** accepts these requests only from the loopback interface for security reasons. This change is necessary for programs that were compiled with earlier versions of the rpc library and do not make those requests using the loopback interface.

-l   Turns on libwrap connection logging.

-s   Causes **rpcbind** to change to the user daemon as soon as possible. This causes **rpcbind** to use non-privileged ports for outgoing connections, preventing non-privileged clients from using **rpcbind** to connect to services from a privileged port.

-L   Allow old-style local connections over the loopback interface. Without this flag, local connections are only allowed over a local socket, /var/run/rpcbind.sock

NOTES

All RPC servers must be restarted if **rpcbind** is restarted.

FILES

/var/run/rpcbind.sock
/etc/hosts.allow   explicit remote host access list.
/etc/hosts.deny   explicit remote host denial of service list.

SEE ALSO

rpcbind(3), hosts_access(5), hosts_options(5), netconfig(5), rpcinfo(8)

NAME
     rpcinfo — report RPC information

SYNOPSIS
     rpcinfo [**-m** | **-s**] [*host*]
     rpcinfo **-p** [*host*]
     rpcinfo **-T** *transport host prognum* [*versnum*]
     rpcinfo **-l** [**-T** *transport*] *host prognum* [*versnum*]
     rpcinfo [**-n** *portnum*] **-u** *host prognum* [*versnum*]
     rpcinfo [**-n** *portnum*] [**-t**] *host prognum* [*versnum*]
     rpcinfo **-a** *serv_address* **-T** *transport prognum* [*versnum*]
     rpcinfo **-b** [**-T** *transport*] *prognum versnum*
     rpcinfo **-d** [**-T** *transport*] *prognum versnum*

DESCRIPTION
     rpcinfo makes an RPC call to an RPC server and reports what it finds.

     In the first synopsis, **rpcinfo** lists all the registered RPC services with **rpcbind** on *host*. If *host* is not
     specified, the local host is the default. If **-s** is used, the information is displayed in a concise format.

     In the second synopsis, **rpcinfo** lists all the RPC services registered with **rpcbind**, version 2. Also note
     that the format of the information is different in the first and the second synopsis. This is because the second
     synopsis is an older protocol used to collect the information displayed (version 2 of the **rpcbind** protocol).

     The third synopsis makes an RPC call to procedure 0 of *prognum* and *versnum* on the specified *host* and
     reports whether a response was received. *transport* is the transport which has to be used for contacting
     the given service. The remote address of the service is obtained by making a call to the remote **rpcbind**.

     The *prognum* argument is a number that represents an RPC program number. If a *versnum* is specified,
     rpcinfo attempts to call that version of the specified *prognum*. Otherwise, **rpcinfo** attempts to find all
     the registered version numbers for the specified *prognum* by calling version 0, which is presumed not to
     exist; if it does exist, **rpcinfo** attempts to obtain this information by calling an extremely high version
     number instead, and attempts to call each registered version. Note: the version number is required for **-b**
     and **-d** options.

OPTIONS
     -T *transport*
               Specify the transport on which the service is required. If this option is not specified, **rpcinfo**
               uses the transport specified in the NETPATH environment variable, or if that is unset or null, the
               transport in the netconfig(5) database is used. This is a generic option, and can be used in con-
               junction with other options as shown in the SYNOPSIS.

     -a *serv_address*
               Use *serv_address* as the (universal) address for the service on *transport* to ping procedure
               0 of the specified *prognum* and report whether a response was received. The **-T** option is
               required with the **-a** option.

               If *versnum* is not specified, **rpcinfo** tries to ping all available version numbers for that pro-
               gram number. This option avoids calls to remote **rpcbind** to find the address of the service. The
               serv_address is specified in universal address format of the given transport.

     -b   Make an RPC broadcast to procedure 0 of the specified *prognum* and *versnum* and report all
               hosts that respond. If *transport* is specified, it broadcasts its request only on the specified
               transport. If broadcasting is not supported by any transport, an error message is printed. Use of
               broadcasting should be limited because of the potential for adverse effect on other systems.

-d   Delete registration for the RPC service of the specified *prognum* and *versnum*. If *transport* is specified, unregister the service on only that transport, otherwise unregister the service on all the transports on which it was registered. Only the owner of a service can delete a registration, except the super-user who can delete any service.

-l   Display a list of entries with a given *prognum* and *versnum* on the specified *host*. Entries are returned for all transports in the same protocol family as that used to contact the remote **rpcbind**.

-m   Display a table of statistics of **rpcbind** operations on the given *host*. The table shows statistics for each version of **rpcbind** (versions 2, 3 and 4), giving the number of times each procedure was requested and successfully serviced, the number and type of remote call requests that were made, and information about RPC address lookups that were handled. This is useful for monitoring RPC activities on *host*.

-n *portnum*
             Use *portnum* as the port number for the **-t** and **-u** options instead of the port number given by **rpcbind**. Use of this option avoids a call to the remote **rpcbind** to find out the address of the service. This option is made obsolete by the **-a** option.

-p   Probe **rpcbind** on *host* using version 2 of the **rpcbind** protocol, and display a list of all registered RPC programs. If *host* is not specified, it defaults to the local host. Note: Version 2 of the **rpcbind** protocol was previously known as the portmapper protocol.

-s   Display a concise list of all registered RPC programs on *host*. If *host* is not specified, it defaults to the local host.

-t   Make an RPC call to procedure 0 of *prognum* on the specified *host* using TCP, and report whether a response was received. This option is made obsolete by the **-T** option as shown in the third synopsis.

-u   Make an RPC call to procedure 0 of *prognum* on the specified *host* using UDP, and report whether a response was received. This option is made obsolete by the **-T** option as shown in the third synopsis.

EXAMPLES
    To show all of the RPC services registered on the local machine use:

            example% rpcinfo

    To show all of the RPC services registered with **rpcbind** on the machine named **klaxon** use:

            example% rpcinfo klaxon

    The information displayed by the above commands can be quite lengthy. Use the **-s** option to display a more concise list:

            example$ rpcinfo -s klaxon

program	version(s)	netid(s)	service	owner
100000	2,3,4	local,tcp,udp,tcp6,udp6	rpcbind	super-user
100008	1	udp,tcp,udp6,tcp6	walld	super-user
100002	2,1	udp,udp6	rusersd	super-user
100001	2,3,4	udp,udp6	rstatd	super-user
100012	1	udp,tcp	sprayd	super-user
100007	3	udp,tcp	ypbind	super-user

To show whether the RPC service with program number *prognum* and version *versnum* is registered on the machine named **klaxon** for the transport TCP use:

```
example% rpcinfo -T tcp klaxon prognum versnum
```

To show all RPC services registered with version 2 of the **rpcbind** protocol on the local machine use:

```
example% rpcinfo -p
```

To delete the registration for version 1 of the **walld** (program number 100008) service for all transports use:

```
example# rpcinfo -d 100008 1
```

or

```
example# rpcinfo -d walld 1
```

SEE ALSO
    rpc(3), netconfig(5), rpc(5), rpcbind(8)

NAME

rshd — remote shell server

SYNOPSIS

rshd [**-aLln**]

DESCRIPTION

The **rshd** server is the server for the rcmd(3) routine and, consequently, for the rsh(1) program. The server provides remote execution facilities with authentication based on privileged port numbers from trusted hosts.

The **rshd** server listens for service requests at the port indicated in the "cmd" service specification; see services(5). When a service request is received the following protocol is initiated:

1.   The server checks the client's source port. If the port is not in the range 512-1023, the server aborts the connection.

2.   The server reads characters from the socket up to a null ('\0') byte. The resultant string is interpreted as an ASCII number, base 10.

3.   If the number received in step 2 is non-zero, it is interpreted as the port number of a secondary stream to be used for the *stderr*. A second connection is then created to the specified port on the client's machine. The source port of this second connection is also in the range 512-1023.

4.   The server checks the client's source address and requests the corresponding host name (see getnameinfo(3), hosts(5), and named(8)). If the hostname cannot be determined, the dot-notation representation of the host address is used. If the hostname is in the same domain as the server (according to the last two components of the domain name), or if the **-a** option is given, the addresses for the hostname are requested, verifying that the name and address correspond. If address verification fails, the connection is aborted with the message "Host address mismatch."

5.   A null terminated user name of at most 16 characters is retrieved on the initial socket. This user name is interpreted as the user identity on the *client*'s machine.

6.   A null terminated user name of at most 16 characters is retrieved on the initial socket. This user name is interpreted as a user identity to use on the **server**'s machine.

7.   A null terminated command to be passed to a shell is retrieved on the initial socket. The length of the command is limited by the upper bound on the size of the system's argument list.

8.   **rshd** then validates the user using ruserok(3), which uses the file /etc/hosts.equiv and the .rhosts file found in the user's home directory. The **-l** option prevents ruserok(3) from doing any validation based on the user's ".rhosts" file, unless the user is the superuser.

9.   If the file /etc/nologin exists and the user is not the superuser, the connection is closed.

10. A null byte is returned on the initial socket and the command line is passed to the normal login shell of the user. The shell inherits the network connections established by **rshd**.

Transport-level keepalive messages are enabled unless the **-n** option is present. The use of keepalive messages allows sessions to be timed out if the client crashes or becomes unreachable.

The **-L** option causes all successful accesses to be logged to syslogd(8) as auth.info messages.

DIAGNOSTICS

Except for the last one listed below, all diagnostic messages are returned on the initial socket, after which any network connections are closed. An error is indicated by a leading byte with a value of 1 (0 is returned in step 10 above upon successful completion of all the steps prior to the execution of the login shell).

Locuser too long.
> The name of the user on the client's machine is longer than 16 characters.

Ruser too long.
> The name of the user on the remote machine is longer than 16 characters.

Command too long.
> The command line passed exceeds the size of the argument list (as configured into the system).

Login incorrect.
> No password file entry for the user name existed.

Remote directory.
> The chdir(2) to the home directory failed.

Permission denied.
> The authentication procedure described above failed.

Can't make pipe.
> The pipe needed for the *stderr*, wasn't created.

Can't fork; try again.
> A fork(2) by the server failed.

<shellname>: ...
> The user's login shell could not be started. This message is returned on the connection associated with the *stderr*, and is not preceded by a flag byte.

SEE ALSO

rsh(1), ssh(1), rcmd(3), ruserok(3), hosts_access(5), login.conf(5), sshd(8)

BUGS

The authentication procedure used here assumes the integrity of every machine and every network that can reach the rshd/rlogind ports on the server. This is insecure, but is useful in an "open" environment. sshd(8) or a Kerberized version of this server are much more secure.

A facility to allow all data exchanges to be encrypted should be present.

A more extensible protocol (such as Telnet) should be used.

rshd intentionally rejects accesses from IPv4 mapped address on top of AF_INET6 socket, since IPv4 mapped address complicates host-address based authentication. If you would like to accept connections from IPv4 peers, you will need to run **rshd** on top of an AF_INET socket, not an AF_INET6 socket.

NAME
rtadvd — router advertisement daemon

SYNOPSIS
rtadvd [**-DdfMRs**] [**-c** *configfile*] *interface* ...

DESCRIPTION
rtadvd sends router advertisement packets to the specified interfaces.

The program will daemonize itself on invocation. It will then send router advertisement packets periodically, as well as in response to router solicitation messages sent by end hosts.

Router advertisements can be configured on a per-interface basis, as described in rtadvd.conf(5).

If there is no configuration file entry for an interface, or if the configuration file does not exist at all, **rtadvd** sets all the parameters to their default values. In particular, **rtadvd** reads all the interface routes from the routing table and advertises them as on-link prefixes.

rtadvd also watches the routing table. If an interface direct route is added on an advertising interface and no static prefixes are specified by the configuration file, **rtadvd** adds the corresponding prefix to its advertising list.

Similarly, when an interface direct route is deleted, **rtadvd** will start advertising the prefixes with zero valid and preferred lifetimes to help the receiving hosts switch to a new prefix when renumbering. Note, however, that the zero valid lifetime cannot invalidate the autoconfigured addresses at a receiving host immediately. According to the specification, the host will retain the address for a certain period, which will typically be two hours. The zero lifetimes rather intend to make the address deprecated, indicating that a new non-deprecated address should be used as the source address of a new connection. This behavior will last for two hours. Then **rtadvd** will completely remove the prefix from the advertising list, and succeeding advertisements will not contain the prefix information.

Moreover, if the status of an advertising interface changes, **rtadvd** will start or stop sending router advertisements according to the latest status.

The **-s** option may be used to disable this behavior; **rtadvd** will not watch the routing table and the whole functionality described above will be suppressed.

Basically, hosts MUST NOT send Router Advertisement messages at any time (RFC 2461, Section 6.2.3). However, it would sometimes be useful to allow hosts to advertise some parameters such as prefix information and link MTU. Thus, **rtadvd** can be invoked if router lifetime is explicitly set to zero on every advertising interface.

The command line options are:

-c *configfile*
  Specify an alternate location, *configfile*, for the configuration file. By default, /etc/rtadvd.conf is used.

-D Even more debugging information than that offered by the **-d** option is printed.

-d Print debugging information.

-f Foreground mode (useful when debugging). Log messages will be dumped to stderr when this option is specified.

-M Specify an interface to join the all-routers site-local multicast group. By default, **rtadvd** tries to join the first advertising interface appearing on the command line. This option has meaning only with the **-R** option, which enables routing renumbering protocol support.

−R   Accept router renumbering requests. If you enable it, an ipsec(4) setup is suggested for security reasons. This option is currently disabled, and is ignored by **rtadvd** with a warning message.

−s   Do not add or delete prefixes dynamically. Only statically configured prefixes, if any, will be advertised.

Upon receipt of signal SIGUSR1, **rtadvd** will dump the current internal state into /var/run/rtadvd.dump.

Use SIGTERM to kill **rtadvd** gracefully. In this case, **rtadvd** will transmit router advertisement with router lifetime 0 to all the interfaces (in accordance with RFC 2461 6.2.5).

EXIT STATUS
The **rtadvd** utility exits 0 on success, and >0 if an error occurs.

FILES
/etc/rtadvd.conf	The default configuration file.
/var/run/rtadvd.pid	Contains the PID of the currently running **rtadvd**.
/var/run/rtadvd.dump	The file in which **rtadvd** dumps its internal state.

SEE ALSO
rtadvd.conf(5), rtsol(8)

HISTORY
The **rtadvd** command first appeared in the WIDE Hydrangea IPv6 protocol stack kit.

BUGS
There used to be some text that recommended users not to let **rtadvd** advertise Router Advertisement messages on an upstream link to avoid undesirable icmp6(4) redirect messages. However, based on later discussion in the IETF IPng working group, all routers should rather advertise the messages regardless of the network topology, in order to ensure reachability.

NAME

rtcalarm — Display or set x68k's RTC alarm timer

SYNOPSIS

rtcalarm [**-w** *day-of-the-week*] [**-d** *day-of-the-month*] [[**-m** *minites*] |
        [**-s** *seconds*]] [**-c** **-channel**] *hh:mm*
rtcalarm off
rtcalarm

DESCRIPTION

rtcalarm displays or sets x68k's RTC alarm timer.

The first form of **rtcalarm** sets the alarm timer to specified time and enables it. *Day-of-the-week* is a number from 0 to 6, which means Sunday, Monday,.. etc.

If **-c** is omitted, the alarm timer starts the x68k in computer mode.

The second form disables the alarm timer.

If no arguments are supplied (the third form), **rtcalarm** displays the current settings of the alarm timer.

Note that setting the alarm timer is allowed only for the super user.

SEE ALSO

pow(4)

AUTHORS

rtcalarm was written by MINOURA Makoto <minoura@flab.fujitsu.co.jp>.

NAME

    rtquery — query routing daemons for their routing tables

SYNOPSIS

    rtquery [**-1np**] [**-a** *secret*] [**-r** *addr*] [**-w** *timeout*] *host* ...
    rtquery [**-t** *op*] *host* ...

DESCRIPTION

    rtquery is used to query a RIP network routing daemon, routed(8) or gated(8), for its routing table by sending a *request* or *poll* command. The routing information in any routing *response* packets returned is displayed numerically and symbolically.

    rtquery by default uses the *request* command. When the **-p** option is specified, **rtquery** uses the *poll* command, an undocumented extension to the RIP protocol supported by gated(8). When querying gated(8), the *poll* command is preferred over the *request* command because the response is not subject to Split Horizon and/or Poisoned Reverse, and because some versions of gated do not answer the *request* command. routed(8) does not answer the *poll* command, but recognizes *requests* coming from **rtquery** and so answers completely.

    rtquery is also used to turn tracing on or off in routed(8).

    The following options are available:

    -n   displays only the numeric network and host numbers instead of both numeric and symbolic.

    -p   uses the *poll* command to request full routing information from gated(8). This is an undocumented extension RIP protocol supported only by gated(8).

    -1   queries using RIP version 1 instead of RIP version 2.

    -w *timeout*
        changes the delay for an answer from each host. By default, each host is given 15 seconds to respond.

    -r *addr*
        asks about the route to destination *addr*.

    -a *passwd=XXX*

    -a *md5_passwd=XXX|KeyID*
        causes the query to be sent with the indicated cleartext or MD5 password.

    -t *op*   changes tracing, where *op* is one of the following. Requests from processes not running with UID 0 or on distant networks are generally ignored by the daemon except for a message in the system log. gated(8) is likely to ignore these debugging requests.

        on=tracefile
            turns tracing on into the specified file. That file must usually have been specified when the daemon was started or be the same as a fixed name, often /etc/routed.trace.

        more   increases the debugging level.

        off   turns off tracing.

        dump   dumps the daemon's routing table to the current tracefile.

RTQUERY (8)   NetBSD   RTQUERY (8)

SEE ALSO
    gated(8), routed(8), pkgsrc/net/gated

    Routing Information Protocol, RIPv1, RFC 1058, 1988.

    Routing Information Protocol, RIPv2, RFC 1723, 1994.

NAME

rtsold — router solicitation daemon

SYNOPSIS

rtsold [**−1Ddfm**] *interface* . . .
rtsold [**−1Ddfm**] **−a**
rtsol [**−Dd**] *interface* . . .
rtsol [**−Dd**] **−a**

DESCRIPTION

rtsold is the daemon program to send ICMPv6 Router Solicitation messages on the specified interfaces. If a node (re)attaches to a link, **rtsold** sends some Router Solicitations on the link destined to the link-local scope all-routers multicast address to discover new routers and to get non link-local addresses.

rtsold should be used on IPv6 hosts (non-router nodes) only.

If you invoke the program as **rtsol**, it will transmit probes from the specified *interface*, without becoming a daemon. In other words, **rtsol** behaves as "rtsold -f1 interface …".

Specifically, **rtsold** sends at most 3 Router Solicitations on an interface after one of the following events:

- Just after invocation of the **rtsold** daemon.

- The interface is up after a temporary interface failure. **rtsold** detects such failures by periodically probing to see if the status of the interface is active or not. Note that some network cards and drivers do not allow the extraction of link state. In such cases, **rtsold** cannot detect the change of the interface status.

- Every 60 seconds if the **−m** option is specified and the **rtsold** daemon cannot get the interface status. This feature does not conform to the IPv6 neighbor discovery specification, but is provided for mobile stations. The default interval for router advertisements, which is on the order of 10 minutes, is slightly long for mobile stations. This feature is provided for such stations so that they can find new routers as soon as possible when they attach to another link.

Once **rtsold** has sent a Router Solicitation, and has received a valid Router Advertisement, it refrains from sending additional solicitations on that interface, until the next time one of the above events occurs.

When sending a Router Solicitation on an interface, **rtsold** includes a Source Link-layer address option if the interface has a link-layer address.

Upon receipt of signal SIGUSR1, **rtsold** will dump the current internal state into /var/run/rtsold.dump. Also note that **rtsold** will not be able to update the kernel routing tables unless sysctl(8) reports that net.inet6.ip6.accept_rtadv=1.

The options are as follows:

−1   Perform only one probe. Transmit Router Solicitation packets until at least one valid Router Advertisement packet has arrived on each *interface*, then exit.

−a   Autoprobe outgoing interface. **rtsold** will try to find a non-loopback, non-point-to-point, IPv6-capable interface. If **rtsold** finds multiple interfaces, **rtsold** will exit with an error.

−D   Enable more debugging (than that offered by the **−d** option) including the printing of internal timer information.

−d   Enable debugging.

-f   This option prevents **rtsold** from becoming a daemon (foreground mode). Warning messages
          are generated to standard error instead of syslog(3).

-m   Enable mobility support. If this option is specified, **rtsold** sends probing packets to default
          routers that have advertised Router Advertisements when the node (re)attaches to an interface.
          Moreover, if the option is specified, **rtsold** periodically sends Router Solicitation on an interface
          that does not support the SIOCGIFMEDIA ioctl.

EXIT STATUS

The **rtsold** utility exits 0 on success, and >0 if an error occurs.

FILES

/var/run/rtsold.pid   The PID of the currently running **rtsold**.
/var/run/rtsold.dump   Internal state dump file.

SEE ALSO

rtadvd(8), sysctl(8)

HISTORY

The **rtsold** command is based on the **rtsol** command, which first appeared in the WIDE/KAME IPv6
protocol stack kit. **rtsol** is now integrated into **rtsold**.

BUGS

In some operating systems, when a PCMCIA network card is removed and reinserted, the corresponding
interface index is changed. However, **rtsold** assumes such changes will not occur, and always uses the
index that it got at invocation. As a result, **rtsold** may not work if you reinsert a network card. In such a
case, **rtsold** should be killed and restarted.

You may see kernel error messages if you try to autoconfigure a host with multiple interfaces.

NAME
rump_cd9660 — mount the cd9660 file system using a userspace server

SYNOPSIS
file-system PUFFS
pseudo-device putter

rump_cd9660 [options] *special node*

DESCRIPTION
NOTE! This manual page has been generated from a common source shared between all rump(3) file servers. Some parts of this manual page may not apply to this particular server. After reading this manual page, you may want to verify the details from mount_cd9660(8).

The **rump_cd9660** utility can be used to mount cd9660 file systems. It uses rump(3) and p2k(3) to facilitate running the file system as a server in userspace. As opposed to mount_cd9660(8), **rump_cd9660** does not use file system code within the kernel and therefore does not require kernel support except puffs(4). Apart from a minor speed penalty (starting from 10% and depending on the workload and file system in question), there is no difference to using in-kernel code.

In case mounting a file system image from a regular file, **rump_cd9660** does not require the use of vnconfig(8) unlike kernel file systems. Instead, the image path can be directly passed as the special file path. The exception is if the image contains a disklabel. In this case vnconfig is required to resolve the start offset for the correct partition within the image.

It is recommended that untrusted file system images be mounted with **rump_cd9660** instead of mount_cd9660(8). Corrupt file system images commonly cause the file system to crash the entire kernel, but with **rump_cd9660** only the userspace server process will dump core.

To use **rump_cd9660** via mount(8), the flags **-o** *rump* and **-t** *cd9660* should be given. Similarly, **rump_cd9660** is run instead of mount_cd9660(8) if "rump" is added to the options field of fstab(5).

Please see mount_cd9660(8) for a full description of the available command line options.

SEE ALSO
p2k(3), puffs(3), rump(3), mount_cd9660(8)

HISTORY
The **rump_cd9660** utility first appeared in NetBSD 5.0. It is currently considered experimental.

NAME
   rump_efs — mount the efs file system using a userspace server

SYNOPSIS
   file-system PUFFS
   pseudo-device putter

   rump_efs [options] *special node*

DESCRIPTION
   NOTE! This manual page has been generated from a common source shared between all rump(3) file servers. Some parts of this manual page may not apply to this particular server. After reading this manual page, you may want to verify the details from mount_efs(8).

   The **rump_efs** utility can be used to mount efs file systems. It uses rump(3) and p2k(3) to facilitate running the file system as a server in userspace. As opposed to mount_efs(8), **rump_efs** does not use file system code within the kernel and therefore does not require kernel support except puffs(4). Apart from a minor speed penalty (starting from 10% and depending on the workload and file system in question), there is no difference to using in-kernel code.

   In case mounting a file system image from a regular file, **rump_efs** does not require the use of vnconfig(8) unlike kernel file systems. Instead, the image path can be directly passed as the special file path. The exception is if the image contains a disklabel. In this case vnconfig is required to resolve the start offset for the correct partition within the image.

   It is recommended that untrusted file system images be mounted with **rump_efs** instead of mount_efs(8). Corrupt file system images commonly cause the file system to crash the entire kernel, but with **rump_efs** only the userspace server process will dump core.

   To use **rump_efs** via mount(8), the flags **-o** *rump* and **-t** *efs* should be given. Similarly, **rump_efs** is run instead of mount_efs(8) if "rump" is added to the options field of fstab(5).

   Please see mount_efs(8) for a full description of the available command line options.

SEE ALSO
   p2k(3), puffs(3), rump(3), mount_efs(8)

HISTORY
   The **rump_efs** utility first appeared in NetBSD 5.0. It is currently considered experimental.

NAME

rump_ext2fs — mount the ext2fs file system using a userspace server

SYNOPSIS

file-system PUFFS
pseudo-device putter

rump_ext2fs [options] *special node*

DESCRIPTION

NOTE! This manual page has been generated from a common source shared between all rump(3) file servers. Some parts of this manual page may not apply to this particular server. After reading this manual page, you may want to verify the details from mount_ext2fs(8).

The **rump_ext2fs** utility can be used to mount ext2fs file systems. It uses rump(3) and p2k(3) to facilitate running the file system as a server in userspace. As opposed to mount_ext2fs(8), **rump_ext2fs** does not use file system code within the kernel and therefore does not require kernel support except puffs(4). Apart from a minor speed penalty (starting from 10% and depending on the workload and file system in question), there is no difference to using in-kernel code.

In case mounting a file system image from a regular file, **rump_ext2fs** does not require the use of vnconfig(8) unlike kernel file systems. Instead, the image path can be directly passed as the special file path. The exception is if the image contains a disklabel. In this case vnconfig is required to resolve the start offset for the correct partition within the image.

It is recommended that untrusted file system images be mounted with **rump_ext2fs** instead of mount_ext2fs(8). Corrupt file system images commonly cause the file system to crash the entire kernel, but with **rump_ext2fs** only the userspace server process will dump core.

To use **rump_ext2fs** via mount(8), the flags **-o** *rump* and **-t** *ext2fs* should be given. Similarly, **rump_ext2fs** is run instead of mount_ext2fs(8) if "rump" is added to the options field of fstab(5).

Please see mount_ext2fs(8) for a full description of the available command line options.

SEE ALSO

p2k(3), puffs(3), rump(3), mount_ext2fs(8)

HISTORY

The **rump_ext2fs** utility first appeared in NetBSD 5.0. It is currently considered experimental.

NAME

rump_ffs — mount the ffs file system using a userspace server

SYNOPSIS

```
file-system PUFFS
pseudo-device putter
```

rump_ffs [options] *special node*

DESCRIPTION

NOTE! This manual page has been generated from a common source shared between all rump(3) file servers. Some parts of this manual page may not apply to this particular server. After reading this manual page, you may want to verify the details from mount_ffs(8).

The **rump_ffs** utility can be used to mount ffs file systems. It uses rump(3) and p2k(3) to facilitate running the file system as a server in userspace. As opposed to mount_ffs(8), **rump_ffs** does not use file system code within the kernel and therefore does not require kernel support except puffs(4). Apart from a minor speed penalty (starting from 10% and depending on the workload and file system in question), there is no difference to using in-kernel code.

In case mounting a file system image from a regular file, **rump_ffs** does not require the use of vnconfig(8) unlike kernel file systems. Instead, the image path can be directly passed as the special file path. The exception is if the image contains a disklabel. In this case vnconfig is required to resolve the start offset for the correct partition within the image.

It is recommended that untrusted file system images be mounted with **rump_ffs** instead of mount_ffs(8). Corrupt file system images commonly cause the file system to crash the entire kernel, but with **rump_ffs** only the userspace server process will dump core.

To use **rump_ffs** via mount(8), the flags **-o** *rump* and **-t** *ffs* should be given. Similarly, **rump_ffs** is run instead of mount_ffs(8) if "rump" is added to the options field of fstab(5).

Please see mount_ffs(8) for a full description of the available command line options.

SEE ALSO

p2k(3), puffs(3), rump(3), mount_ffs(8)

HISTORY

The **rump_ffs** utility first appeared in NetBSD 5.0. It is currently considered experimental.

NAME
   rump_hfs — mount the hfs file system using a userspace server

SYNOPSIS
   file-system PUFFS
   pseudo-device putter

   rump_hfs [options] *special node*

DESCRIPTION
   NOTE! This manual page has been generated from a common source shared between all rump(3) file servers. Some parts of this manual page may not apply to this particular server. After reading this manual page, you may want to verify the details from mount_hfs(8).

   The **rump_hfs** utility can be used to mount hfs file systems. It uses rump(3) and p2k(3) to facilitate running the file system as a server in userspace. As opposed to mount_hfs(8), **rump_hfs** does not use file system code within the kernel and therefore does not require kernel support except puffs(4). Apart from a minor speed penalty (starting from 10% and depending on the workload and file system in question), there is no difference to using in-kernel code.

   In case mounting a file system image from a regular file, **rump_hfs** does not require the use of vnconfig(8) unlike kernel file systems. Instead, the image path can be directly passed as the special file path. The exception is if the image contains a disklabel. In this case vnconfig is required to resolve the start offset for the correct partition within the image.

   It is recommended that untrusted file system images be mounted with **rump_hfs** instead of mount_hfs(8). Corrupt file system images commonly cause the file system to crash the entire kernel, but with **rump_hfs** only the userspace server process will dump core.

   To use **rump_hfs** via mount(8), the flags **-o** *rump* and **-t** *hfs* should be given. Similarly, **rump_hfs** is run instead of mount_hfs(8) if "rump" is added to the options field of fstab(5).

   Please see mount_hfs(8) for a full description of the available command line options.

SEE ALSO
   p2k(3), puffs(3), rump(3), mount_hfs(8)

HISTORY
   The **rump_hfs** utility first appeared in NetBSD 5.0. It is currently considered experimental.

NAME
    rump_lfs — mount the lfs file system using a userspace server

SYNOPSIS
    file-system PUFFS
    pseudo-device putter

    rump_lfs [options] *special node*

DESCRIPTION
    NOTE! This manual page has been generated from a common source shared between all rump(3) file servers. Some parts of this manual page may not apply to this particular server. After reading this manual page, you may want to verify the details from mount_lfs(8).

    The **rump_lfs** utility can be used to mount lfs file systems. It uses rump(3) and p2k(3) to facilitate running the file system as a server in userspace. As opposed to mount_lfs(8), **rump_lfs** does not use file system code within the kernel and therefore does not require kernel support except puffs(4). Apart from a minor speed penalty (starting from 10% and depending on the workload and file system in question), there is no difference to using in-kernel code.

    In case mounting a file system image from a regular file, **rump_lfs** does not require the use of vnconfig(8) unlike kernel file systems. Instead, the image path can be directly passed as the special file path. The exception is if the image contains a disklabel. In this case vnconfig is required to resolve the start offset for the correct partition within the image.

    It is recommended that untrusted file system images be mounted with **rump_lfs** instead of mount_lfs(8). Corrupt file system images commonly cause the file system to crash the entire kernel, but with **rump_lfs** only the userspace server process will dump core.

    To use **rump_lfs** via mount(8), the flags **-o** *rump* and **-t** *lfs* should be given. Similarly, **rump_lfs** is run instead of mount_lfs(8) if "rump" is added to the options field of fstab(5).

    Please see mount_lfs(8) for a full description of the available command line options.

SEE ALSO
    p2k(3), puffs(3), rump(3), mount_lfs(8)

HISTORY
    The **rump_lfs** utility first appeared in NetBSD 5.0. It is currently considered experimental.

NAME
rump_msdos — mount the msdos file system using a userspace server

SYNOPSIS
file-system PUFFS
pseudo-device putter

rump_msdos [options] *special node*

DESCRIPTION
NOTE! This manual page has been generated from a common source shared between all rump(3) file servers. Some parts of this manual page may not apply to this particular server. After reading this manual page, you may want to verify the details from mount_msdos(8).

The **rump_msdos** utility can be used to mount msdos file systems. It uses rump(3) and p2k(3) to facilitate running the file system as a server in userspace. As opposed to mount_msdos(8), **rump_msdos** does not use file system code within the kernel and therefore does not require kernel support except puffs(4). Apart from a minor speed penalty (starting from 10% and depending on the workload and file system in question), there is no difference to using in-kernel code.

In case mounting a file system image from a regular file, **rump_msdos** does not require the use of vnconfig(8) unlike kernel file systems. Instead, the image path can be directly passed as the special file path. The exception is if the image contains a disklabel. In this case vnconfig is required to resolve the start offset for the correct partition within the image.

It is recommended that untrusted file system images be mounted with **rump_msdos** instead of mount_msdos(8). Corrupt file system images commonly cause the file system to crash the entire kernel, but with **rump_msdos** only the userspace server process will dump core.

To use **rump_msdos** via mount(8), the flags **-o** *rump* and **-t** *msdos* should be given. Similarly, **rump_msdos** is run instead of mount_msdos(8) if "rump" is added to the options field of fstab(5).

Please see mount_msdos(8) for a full description of the available command line options.

SEE ALSO
p2k(3), puffs(3), rump(3), mount_msdos(8)

HISTORY
The **rump_msdos** utility first appeared in NetBSD 5.0. It is currently considered experimental.

NAME

rump_nfs — mount the nfs file system using a userspace server

SYNOPSIS

```
file-system PUFFS
pseudo-device putter
```

rump_nfs [options] *special node*

DESCRIPTION

NOTE! This manual page has been generated from a common source shared between all rump(3) file servers. Some parts of this manual page may not apply to this particular server. After reading this manual page, you may want to verify the details from mount_nfs(8).

The **rump_nfs** utility can be used to mount nfs file systems. It uses rump(3) and p2k(3) to facilitate running the file system as a server in userspace. As opposed to mount_nfs(8), **rump_nfs** does not use file system code within the kernel and therefore does not require kernel support except puffs(4). Apart from a minor speed penalty (starting from 10% and depending on the workload and file system in question), there is no difference to using in-kernel code.

In case mounting a file system image from a regular file, **rump_nfs** does not require the use of vnconfig(8) unlike kernel file systems. Instead, the image path can be directly passed as the special file path. The exception is if the image contains a disklabel. In this case vnconfig is required to resolve the start offset for the correct partition within the image.

It is recommended that untrusted file system images be mounted with **rump_nfs** instead of mount_nfs(8). Corrupt file system images commonly cause the file system to crash the entire kernel, but with **rump_nfs** only the userspace server process will dump core.

To use **rump_nfs** via mount(8), the flags **-o** *rump* and **-t** *nfs* should be given. Similarly, **rump_nfs** is run instead of mount_nfs(8) if "rump" is added to the options field of fstab(5).

Please see mount_nfs(8) for a full description of the available command line options.

SEE ALSO

p2k(3), puffs(3), rump(3), mount_nfs(8)

HISTORY

The **rump_nfs** utility first appeared in NetBSD 5.0. It is currently considered experimental.

NAME
rump_ntfs — mount the ntfs file system using a userspace server

SYNOPSIS
file-system PUFFS
pseudo-device putter

rump_ntfs [options] *special node*

DESCRIPTION
NOTE! This manual page has been generated from a common source shared between all rump(3) file servers. Some parts of this manual page may not apply to this particular server. After reading this manual page, you may want to verify the details from mount_ntfs(8).

The **rump_ntfs** utility can be used to mount ntfs file systems. It uses rump(3) and p2k(3) to facilitate running the file system as a server in userspace. As opposed to mount_ntfs(8), **rump_ntfs** does not use file system code within the kernel and therefore does not require kernel support except puffs(4). Apart from a minor speed penalty (starting from 10% and depending on the workload and file system in question), there is no difference to using in-kernel code.

In case mounting a file system image from a regular file, **rump_ntfs** does not require the use of vnconfig(8) unlike kernel file systems. Instead, the image path can be directly passed as the special file path. The exception is if the image contains a disklabel. In this case vnconfig is required to resolve the start offset for the correct partition within the image.

It is recommended that untrusted file system images be mounted with **rump_ntfs** instead of mount_ntfs(8). Corrupt file system images commonly cause the file system to crash the entire kernel, but with **rump_ntfs** only the userspace server process will dump core.

To use **rump_ntfs** via mount(8), the flags **−o** *rump* and **−t** *ntfs* should be given. Similarly, **rump_ntfs** is run instead of mount_ntfs(8) if "rump" is added to the options field of fstab(5).

Please see mount_ntfs(8) for a full description of the available command line options.

SEE ALSO
p2k(3), puffs(3), rump(3), mount_ntfs(8)

HISTORY
The **rump_ntfs** utility first appeared in NetBSD 5.0. It is currently considered experimental.

NAME

rump_smbfs — mount the smbfs file system using a userspace server

SYNOPSIS

file-system PUFFS
pseudo-device putter

rump_smbfs [options] *special node*

DESCRIPTION

NOTE! This manual page has been generated from a common source shared between all rump(3) file servers. Some parts of this manual page may not apply to this particular server. After reading this manual page, you may want to verify the details from mount_smbfs(8).

The **rump_smbfs** utility can be used to mount smbfs file systems. It uses rump(3) and p2k(3) to facilitate running the file system as a server in userspace. As opposed to mount_smbfs(8), **rump_smbfs** does not use file system code within the kernel and therefore does not require kernel support except puffs(4). Apart from a minor speed penalty (starting from 10% and depending on the workload and file system in question), there is no difference to using in-kernel code.

In case mounting a file system image from a regular file, **rump_smbfs** does not require the use of vnconfig(8) unlike kernel file systems. Instead, the image path can be directly passed as the special file path. The exception is if the image contains a disklabel. In this case vnconfig is required to resolve the start offset for the correct partition within the image.

It is recommended that untrusted file system images be mounted with **rump_smbfs** instead of mount_smbfs(8). Corrupt file system images commonly cause the file system to crash the entire kernel, but with **rump_smbfs** only the userspace server process will dump core.

To use **rump_smbfs** via mount(8), the flags **-o** *rump* and **-t** *smbfs* should be given. Similarly, **rump_smbfs** is run instead of mount_smbfs(8) if "rump" is added to the options field of fstab(5).

Please see mount_smbfs(8) for a full description of the available command line options.

SEE ALSO

p2k(3), puffs(3), rump(3), mount_smbfs(8)

HISTORY

The **rump_smbfs** utility first appeared in NetBSD 5.0. It is currently considered experimental.

NAME
rump_syspuffs — mount a puffs file server with a userspace puffs loop

SYNOPSIS
```
file-system PUFFS
pseudo-device putter
```

rump_syspuffs *file_server arguments*

DESCRIPTION
The **rump_syspuffs** utility can be used to mount any puffs(3) file server so that the requests are passed through the kernel puffs code in userspace as well. Therefore the approximate callgraph looks a little like the following, where k and u denote code running in the kernel space and userspace, respectively: puffs vfs (k) → libpuffs (u) → p2k (u) → puffs vfs (u) → libpuffs (u) → file server (u). The response path is the same, but in reverse.

In its current state, **rump_syspuffs** is most useful as a proof of concept for file system distribution and for developing and debugging the kernel portion of puffs.

EXAMPLES
Mount a file system with sshfs:
```
rump_syspuffs mount_psshfs server.address /mnt
```

Mount an ntfs file system using ntfs-3g (from pkgsrc/filesystems/fuse-ntfs-3g), set the default uid to 1323:
```
rump_syspuffs ntfs-3g -o uid=1323 /path/to/filesystem /mnt
```

SEE ALSO
p2k(3), puffs(3), rump(3), puffs(4)

HISTORY
The **rump_syspuffs** debugging utility first appeared in NetBSD 5.0.

NAME

   rump_sysvbfs — mount the sysvbfs file system using a userspace server

SYNOPSIS

   file-system PUFFS
   pseudo-device putter

   rump_sysvbfs [options] *special node*

DESCRIPTION

   NOTE! This manual page has been generated from a common source shared between all rump(3) file servers. Some parts of this manual page may not apply to this particular server. After reading this manual page, you may want to verify the details from mount_sysvbfs(8).

   The **rump_sysvbfs** utility can be used to mount sysvbfs file systems. It uses rump(3) and p2k(3) to facilitate running the file system as a server in userspace. As opposed to mount_sysvbfs(8), **rump_sysvbfs** does not use file system code within the kernel and therefore does not require kernel support except puffs(4). Apart from a minor speed penalty (starting from 10% and depending on the workload and file system in question), there is no difference to using in-kernel code.

   In case mounting a file system image from a regular file, **rump_sysvbfs** does not require the use of vnconfig(8) unlike kernel file systems. Instead, the image path can be directly passed as the special file path. The exception is if the image contains a disklabel. In this case vnconfig is required to resolve the start offset for the correct partition within the image.

   It is recommended that untrusted file system images be mounted with **rump_sysvbfs** instead of mount_sysvbfs(8). Corrupt file system images commonly cause the file system to crash the entire kernel, but with **rump_sysvbfs** only the userspace server process will dump core.

   To use **rump_sysvbfs** via mount(8), the flags **-o** *rump* and **-t** *sysvbfs* should be given. Similarly, **rump_sysvbfs** is run instead of mount_sysvbfs(8) if "rump" is added to the options field of fstab(5).

   Please see mount_sysvbfs(8) for a full description of the available command line options.

SEE ALSO

   p2k(3), puffs(3), rump(3), mount_sysvbfs(8)

HISTORY

   The **rump_sysvbfs** utility first appeared in NetBSD 5.0. It is currently considered experimental.

NAME

   rump_tmpfs — mount the tmpfs file system using a userspace server

SYNOPSIS

   file-system PUFFS
   pseudo-device putter

   rump_tmpfs [options] *special node*

DESCRIPTION

   NOTE! This manual page has been generated from a common source shared between all rump(3) file
   servers. Some parts of this manual page may not apply to this particular server. After reading this manual
   page, you may want to verify the details from mount_tmpfs(8).

   The **rump_tmpfs** utility can be used to mount tmpfs file systems. It uses rump(3) and p2k(3) to facilitate
   running the file system as a server in userspace. As opposed to mount_tmpfs(8), **rump_tmpfs** does not
   use file system code within the kernel and therefore does not require kernel support except puffs(4). Apart
   from a minor speed penalty (starting from 10% and depending on the workload and file system in question),
   there is no difference to using in-kernel code.

   In case mounting a file system image from a regular file, **rump_tmpfs** does not require the use of
   vnconfig(8) unlike kernel file systems. Instead, the image path can be directly passed as the special file
   path. The exception is if the image contains a disklabel. In this case vnconfig is required to resolve the start
   offset for the correct partition within the image.

   It is recommended that untrusted file system images be mounted with **rump_tmpfs** instead of
   mount_tmpfs(8). Corrupt file system images commonly cause the file system to crash the entire kernel,
   but with **rump_tmpfs** only the userspace server process will dump core.

   To use **rump_tmpfs** via mount(8), the flags **-o** *rump* and **-t** *tmpfs* should be given. Similarly,
   rump_tmpfs is run instead of mount_tmpfs(8) if "rump" is added to the options field of fstab(5).

   Please see mount_tmpfs(8) for a full description of the available command line options.

SEE ALSO

   p2k(3), puffs(3), rump(3), mount_tmpfs(8)

HISTORY

   The **rump_tmpfs** utility first appeared in NetBSD 5.0. It is currently considered experimental.

NAME

rump_udf — mount the udf file system using a userspace server

SYNOPSIS

file-system PUFFS
pseudo-device putter

rump_udf [options] *special node*

DESCRIPTION

NOTE! This manual page has been generated from a common source shared between all rump(3) file servers. Some parts of this manual page may not apply to this particular server. After reading this manual page, you may want to verify the details from mount_udf(8).

The **rump_udf** utility can be used to mount udf file systems. It uses rump(3) and p2k(3) to facilitate running the file system as a server in userspace. As opposed to mount_udf(8), **rump_udf** does not use file system code within the kernel and therefore does not require kernel support except puffs(4). Apart from a minor speed penalty (starting from 10% and depending on the workload and file system in question), there is no difference to using in-kernel code.

In case mounting a file system image from a regular file, **rump_udf** does not require the use of vnconfig(8) unlike kernel file systems. Instead, the image path can be directly passed as the special file path. The exception is if the image contains a disklabel. In this case vnconfig is required to resolve the start offset for the correct partition within the image.

It is recommended that untrusted file system images be mounted with **rump_udf** instead of mount_udf(8). Corrupt file system images commonly cause the file system to crash the entire kernel, but with **rump_udf** only the userspace server process will dump core.

To use **rump_udf** via mount(8), the flags **-o** *rump* and **-t** *udf* should be given. Similarly, **rump_udf** is run instead of mount_udf(8) if "rump" is added to the options field of fstab(5).

Please see mount_udf(8) for a full description of the available command line options.

SEE ALSO

p2k(3), puffs(3), rump(3), mount_udf(8)

HISTORY

The **rump_udf** utility first appeared in NetBSD 5.0. It is currently considered experimental.

NAME

rwhod — system status server

SYNOPSIS

rwhod [**-i** *interval*] [**-u** *user*]

DESCRIPTION

rwhod is the server which maintains the database used by the rwho(1) and ruptime(1) programs. Its operation is predicated on the ability to *broadcast* messages on a network.

The following options are available:

-i *interval*

> Allows for the broadcast interval to be changed from the default 3 minutes. The *interval* argument is the number of seconds to change the interval to, or if the value is suffixed by "m" then it is interpreted as minutes. The maximum allowed value for the broadcast interval is 11 minutes because higher values will cause ruptime(1) to mark the host as being down.

-u *user*   Drop privileges and become the user *user*.

rwhod operates as both a producer and consumer of status information. As a producer of information it periodically queries the state of the system and constructs status messages which are broadcast on a network. As a consumer of information, it listens for other **rwhod** servers' status messages, validating them, then recording them in a collection of files located in the directory /var/rwho.

The server transmits and receives messages at the port indicated in the "who" service specification; see services(5). The messages sent and received, are of the form:

```
struct  outmp {
        char    out_line[8];            /* tty name */
        char    out_name[8];            /* user id */
        int32_t out_time;               /* time on */
};

struct  whod {
        char    wd_vers;
        char    wd_type;
        char    wd_fill[2];
        int32_t wd_sendtime;
        int32_t wd_recvtime;
        char    wd_hostname[32];
        int32_t wd_loadav[3];
        int32_t wd_boottime;
        struct  whoent {
                struct  outmp we_utmp;
                int32_t we_idle;
        } wd_we[1024 / sizeof (struct whoent)];
};
```

All fields are converted to network byte order prior to transmission. The load averages are as calculated by the w(1) program, and represent load averages over the 5, 10, and 15 minute intervals prior to a server's transmission; they are multiplied by 100 for representation in an integer. The host name included is that returned by the gethostname(3) function call, with any trailing domain name omitted. The array at the end of the message contains information about the users logged in to the sending machine. This information includes the contents of the utmp(5) entry for each non-idle terminal line and a value indicating the time in seconds since a character was last received on the terminal line.

Messages received by the rwho(1) server are discarded unless they originated at an rwho(1) server's port. In addition, if the host's name, as specified in the message, contains any unprintable ASCII characters, the message is discarded. Valid messages received by **rwhod** are placed in files named whod.hostname in the directory /var/rwho. These files contain only the most recent message, in the format described above.

Status messages are generated by default approximately once every 3 minutes.

SEE ALSO
ruptime(1), rwho(1)

HISTORY
The **rwhod** command appeared in 4.2 BSD.

BUGS
There should be a way to relay status information between networks. Status information should be sent only upon request rather than continuously. People often interpret the server dying or network communication failures as a machine going down.

NAME

    sa — print system accounting statistics

SYNOPSIS

    sa [**-abcdDfijkKlmnqrstu**] [**-v** *cutoff*] [*file* . . .]

DESCRIPTION

    The **sa** utility reports on, cleans up, and generally maintains system accounting files.

    sa is able to condense the information in /var/account/acct into the summary files
/var/account/savacct and /var/account/usracct, which contain system statistics according
to command name and login id, respectively. This condensation is desirable because on a large system,
/var/account/acct can grow by hundreds of blocks per day. The summary files are normally read
before the accounting file, so that reports include all available information.

    If file names are supplied, they are read instead of /var/account/acct. After each file is read, if the
summary files are being updated, an updated summary will be saved to disk. Only one report is printed, after
the last file is processed.

    The labels used in the output indicate the following, except where otherwise specified by individual options:

avio   Average number of I/O operations per execution

cp   Sum of user and system time, in minutes

cpu   Same as cp

k   CPU-time averaged core usage, in 1k units

k*sec CPU storage integral, in 1k-core seconds

re   Real time, in minutes

s   System time, in minutes

tio   Total number of I/O operations

u   User time, in minutes

    The options to **sa** are:

  -a   List all command names, including those containing unprintable characters and those used only
once. By default, **sa** places all names containing unprintable characters and those used only once
under the name "∗∗∗other".

  -b   If printing command statistics, sort output by the sum of user and system time divided by number of
calls.

  -c   In addition to the number of calls and the user, system and real times for each command, print their
percentage of the total over all commands.

  -d   If printing command statistics, sort by the average number of disk I/O operations. If printing user
statistics, print the average number of disk I/O operations per user.

  -D   If printing command statistics, sort and print by the total number of disk I/O operations.

  -f   Force no interactive threshold comparison with the **-v** option.

  -i   Do not read in the summary files.

-j   Instead of the total minutes per category, give seconds per call.

-k   If printing command statistics, sort by the CPU-time average memory usage. If printing user statistics, print the CPU-time average memory usage.

-K   If printing command statistics, print and sort by the CPU-storage integral.

-l   Separate system and user time; normally they are combined.

-m   Print per-user statistics rather than per-command statistics.

-n   Sort by number of calls.

-q   Create no output other than error messages.

-r   Reverse order of sort.

-s   Truncate the accounting files when done and merge their data into the summary files.

-t   For each command, report the ratio of real time to the sum of user and system CPU times. If the CPU time is too small to report, "*ignore*" appears in this field.

-u   Superseding all other flags, for each entry in the accounting file, print the user ID, total seconds of CPU usage, total memory usage, number of I/O operations performed, and command name.

-v *cutoff*
          For each command used *cutoff* times or fewer, print the command name and await a reply from the terminal. If the reply begins with "y", add the command to the category "**junk**". This flag is used to strip garbage from the report.

By default, per-command statistics will be printed. The number of calls, the total elapsed time in minutes, total CPU and user time in minutes, average number of I/O operations, and CPU-time averaged core usage will be printed. If the **-m** option is specified, per-user statistics will be printed, including the user name, the number of commands invoked, total CPU time used (in minutes), total number of I/O operations, and CPU storage integral for each user. If the **-u** option is specified, the uid, user and system time (in seconds), CPU storage integral, I/O usage, and command name will be printed for each entry in the accounting data file.

If the **-u** flag is specified, all flags other than **-q** are ignored. If the **-m** flag is specified, only the **-b**, **-d**, **-i**, **-k**, **-q**, and **-s** flags are honored.

The **sa** utility exits 0 on success, and >0 if an error occurs.

FILES
    /var/account/acct   raw accounting data file
    /var/account/savacct   per-command accounting summary database
    /var/account/usracct   per-user accounting summary database

SEE ALSO
    lastcomm(1), acct(5), ac(8), accton(8)

HISTORY
    sa was written for NetBSD 1.0 from the specification provided by various systems' manual pages. Its date of origin is unknown to the author.

AUTHORS
    Chris G. Demetriou ⟨cgd@postgres.berkeley.edu⟩.

BUGS

The number of options to this program is absurd, especially considering that there's not much logic behind their lettering.

The field labels should be more consistent.

NetBSD's VM system does not record the CPU storage integral.

CAVEATS

While the behavior of the options in this version of **sa** was modeled after the original version, there are some intentional differences and undoubtedly some unintentional ones as well. In particular, the −**q** option has been added, and the −**m** option now understands more options than it used to.

The formats of the summary files created by this version of **sa** are very different than the those used by the original version. This is not considered a problem, however, because the accounting record format has changed as well (since user ids are now 32 bits).

NAME

savecore — save a core dump of the operating system

SYNOPSIS

savecore [**-fvz**] [**-N** *system*] [**-Z** *level*] *directory*
savecore **-c** [**-v**] [**-N** *system*]
savecore **-n** [**-v**] [**-N** *system*]

DESCRIPTION

When the NetBSD kernel encounters a fatal error, the panic(9) routine arranges for a snapshot of the contents of physical memory to be written into a dump area, typically in the swap partition.

Upon a subsequent reboot, **savecore** is typically run out of rc(8), before swapping is enabled, to copy the kernel and the saved memory image into *directory*, and enters a reboot message and information about the core dump into the system log.

The kernel and core file can then be analyzed using various tools, including crash(8), dmesg(8), fstat(1), gdb(1), iostat(8), netstat(1), ps(1), and pstat(8), to attempt to deduce the cause of the crash.

Crashes are usually the result of hardware faults or kernel bugs. If a kernel bug is suspected, a full bug report should be filed at http://www.netbsd.org/, or using send-pr(1), containing as much information as possible about the circumstances of the crash. Since crash dumps are typically very large and may contain whatever (potentially confidential) information was in memory at the time of the crash, do *NOT* include a copy of the crash dump file in the bug report; instead, save it somewhere in the event that a NetBSD developer wants to examine it.

The options are as follows:

-c   Only clears the dump without saving it, so that future invocations of **savecore** will ignore it.

-f   Forces a dump to be taken even if the dump doesn't appear correct or there is insufficient disk space.

-n   Check whether a dump is present without taking further action. The command exits with zero status if a dump is present, or with non-zero status otherwise.

-N   Use *system* as the kernel instead of the default (returned by getbootfile(3)). Note that getbootfile(3) uses secure_path(3) to check that kernel file is "secure" and will default to /netbsd if the check fails.

-v   Prints out some additional debugging information.

-z   Compresses the core dump and kernel (see gzip(1)).

-Z *level*   Set the compression level for **-z** to *level*. Defaults to 1 (the fastest compression mode). Refer to gzip(1) for more information regarding the compression level.

savecore checks the core dump in various ways to make sure that it is current and that it corresponds to the currently running system. If it passes these checks, it saves the core image in *directory*/netbsd.#.core and the system in *directory*/netbsd.# (or in *directory*/netbsd.#.core.gz and *directory*/netbsd.#.gz, respectively, if the **-z** option is used). The "#" is the number from the first line of the file *directory*/bounds, and it is incremented and stored back into the file each time **savecore** successfully runs.

savecore also checks the available disk space before attempting to make the copies. If there is insufficient disk space in the file system containing *directory*, or if the file *directory*/minfree exists and the number of free kilobytes (for non-superusers) in the file system after the copies were made would be less than the number in the first line of this file, the copies are not attempted.

If **savecore** successfully copies the kernel and the core dump, the core dump is cleared so that future invocations of **savecore** will ignore it.

SEE ALSO

fstat(1), gdb(1), gzip(1), netstat(1), ps(1), send-pr(1), crash(8), dmesg(8), iostat(8), pstat(8), rc(8), syslogd(8), panic(9)

HISTORY

The **savecore** command appeared in 4.1 BSD.

BUGS

The minfree code does not consider the effect of compression.

NAME

scache – Postfix shared connection cache server

SYNOPSIS

scache [generic Postfix daemon options]

DESCRIPTION

The **scache**(8) server maintains a shared multi-connection cache. This information can be used by, for example, Postfix SMTP clients or other Postfix delivery agents.

The connection cache is organized into logical destination names, physical endpoint names, and connections.

As a specific example, logical SMTP destinations specify (transport, domain, port), and physical SMTP endpoints specify (transport, IP address, port). An SMTP connection may be saved after a successful mail transaction.

In the general case, one logical destination may refer to zero or more physical endpoints, one physical endpoint may be referenced by zero or more logical destinations, and one endpoint may refer to zero or more connections.

The exact syntax of a logical destination or endpoint name is application dependent; the **scache**(8) server does not care. A connection is stored as a file descriptor together with application-dependent information that is needed to re-activate a connection object. Again, the **scache**(8) server is completely unaware of the details of that information.

All information is stored with a finite time to live (ttl). The connection cache daemon terminates when no client is connected for **max_idle** time units.

This server implements the following requests:

save_endp *ttl endpoint endpoint_properties file_descriptor*
> Save the specified file descriptor and connection property data under the specified endpoint name. The endpoint properties are used by the client to re-activate a passivated connection object.

find_endp *endpoint*
> Look up cached properties and a cached file descriptor for the specified endpoint.

save_dest *ttl destination destination_properties endpoint*
> Save the binding between a logical destination and an endpoint under the destination name, together with destination specific connection properties. The destination properties are used by the client to re-activate a passivated connection object.

find_dest *destination*
> Look up cached destination properties, cached endpoint properties, and a cached file descriptor for the specified logical destination.

SECURITY

The **scache**(8) server is not security-sensitive. It does not talk to the network, and it does not talk to local users. The **scache**(8) server can run chrooted at fixed low privilege.

The **scache**(8) server is not a trusted process. It must not be used to store information that is security sensitive.

DIAGNOSTICS

Problems and transactions are logged to **syslogd**(8).

BUGS

The session cache cannot be shared among multiple machines.

When a connection expires from the cache, it is closed without the appropriate protocol specific handshake.

CONFIGURATION PARAMETERS

Changes to **main.cf** are picked up automatically as **scache**(8) processes run for only a limited amount of time. Use the command "**postfix reload**" to speed up a change.

The text below provides only a parameter summary. See **postconf**(5) for more details including examples.

RESOURCE CONTROLS

connection_cache_ttl_limit (2s)

The maximal time-to-live value that the **scache**(8) connection cache server allows.

connection_cache_status_update_time (600s)

How frequently the **scache**(8) server logs usage statistics with connection cache hit and miss rates for logical destinations and for physical endpoints.

MISCELLANEOUS CONTROLS

config_directory (see 'postconf -d' output)

The default location of the Postfix main.cf and master.cf configuration files.

daemon_timeout (18000s)

How much time a Postfix daemon process may take to handle a request before it is terminated by a built-in watchdog timer.

ipc_timeout (3600s)

The time limit for sending or receiving information over an internal communication channel.

max_idle (100s)

The maximum amount of time that an idle Postfix daemon process waits for an incoming connection before terminating voluntarily.

process_id (read-only)

The process ID of a Postfix command or daemon process.

process_name (read-only)

The process name of a Postfix command or daemon process.

syslog_facility (mail)

The syslog facility of Postfix logging.

syslog_name (see 'postconf -d' output)

The mail system name that is prepended to the process name in syslog records, so that "smtpd" becomes, for example, "postfix/smtpd".

SEE ALSO

smtp(8), SMTP client
postconf(5), configuration parameters
master(8), process manager
syslogd(8), system logging

README FILES

Use "**postconf readme_directory**" or "**postconf html_directory**" to locate this information.
CONNECTION_CACHE_README, Postfix connection cache

LICENSE

The Secure Mailer license must be distributed with this software.

HISTORY

This service was introduced with Postfix version 2.2.

AUTHOR(S)

Wietse Venema
IBM T.J. Watson Research
P.O. Box 704

Yorktown Heights, NY 10598, USA

NAME

    scan_ffs, **scan_lfs** — find FFSv1/FFSv2/LFS partitions on a disk or file

SYNOPSIS

    scan_ffs [**-blv**] [**-e** *end*] [**-F** *file*] [**-s** *start*] *device*

DESCRIPTION

    scan_ffs will take a raw disk device that covers the whole disk or a file and will find all possible FFSv[12]/LFS partitions, independent of block sizes on it. It will show the file system type (FFSv1, FFSv2, or LFS), size, and offset. Also it has an option to show the values with a disklabel-alike output.

    The options are as follows:

        -b   Report every superblock found with its sector address, rather than trying to report the partition boundaries. This option can be useful to find the other superblocks in a partition if the first superblock has become corrupted. It is most useful if *device* refers to the raw device for the partition, rather than the entire disk.

        -e *end*   Where to stop searching for file systems. The *end* argument specifies the last sector that will be searched. Default is the last sector of *device*.

        -F *file*   Path to a file containing possible partitions inside of it.

        -l   Print out a string looking much like the input to disklabel. With a little massaging, this output can usually be used by disklabel(8).

        -s *start*   Where to start searching for file systems. This makes it easier to skip swap partitions or other large non-UFS/FFS partitions. The *start* argument specifies the first sector that will be searched. Default is the first sector of *device*.

        -v   Be verbose about what **scan_ffs** is doing, and what has been found.

    The *device* argument specifies which device **scan_ffs** should scan for file systems.

    scan_lfs is just another name for the same program, both behave in exactly the same way.

SEE ALSO

    disklabel(8)

HISTORY

    The **scan_ffs** program first appeared in OpenBSD 2.3 and then in NetBSD 3.1. Support for searching in files was added in NetBSD 4.0.

AUTHORS

    scan_ffs was written for OpenBSD by Niklas Hallqvist and Tobias Weingartner. It was ported to NetBSD by Juan Romero Pardines, who added support for LFS/FFSv2, partitions with fragsize/blocksize greater than 2048/16384 for FFSv1, searching on files, etc.

BUGS

    Currently **scan_ffs** won't find partitions with fragsize/blocksize greater than 8192/65536.

SCHEDCTL (8)   NetBSD   SCHEDCTL (8)

NAME

schedctl — control scheduling of processes and threads

SYNOPSIS

schedctl [-A cpus] [-C class] [-P pri] [-t lid] -p pid | command

DESCRIPTION

The schedctl command can be used to control the scheduling of processes and threads. It also returns information about the current scheduling parameters of the process or thread. Only the super-user may change the scheduling parameters. schedctl can also be used to start a new command using the specified parameters.

Available options:

-A cpus

Set of the processors on which process or thread should run, that is, affinity. Processors are defined as numbers (starting from zero) and separated by commas. A value of −1 is used to unset the affinity.

-C class

Scheduling class (policy), one of:

SCHED_OTHER   Time-sharing (TS) scheduling policy. The default policy in NetBSD.

SCHED_FIFO   First in, first out (FIFO) scheduling policy.

SCHED_RR   Round-robin scheduling policy.

-P pri

Priority for the process or thread. Value should be in the range from SCHED_PRI_MIN (0) to SCHED_PRI_MAX (63). Setting of priority for the process or thread running at SCHED_OTHER policy is not allowed.

-p pid

The target process which will be affected. If the process has more than one thread, all of them will be affected.

If −p is not given, a command to execute must be given on the command line.

-t lid

Thread in the specified process. If specified, only this thread in the process will be affected. May only be specified if −p is also given.

EXAMPLES

Show scheduling information about the process whose ID is "123":

```
# schedctl -p 123
```

Set the affinity to CPU 0 and CPU 1, policy to SCHED_RR, and priority to 63 for thread whose ID is "1" in process whose ID is "123":

```
# schedctl -p 123 -t 1 -A 0,1 -C SCHED_RR -P 63
```

Run the top(1) command with real-time priority:

```
# schedctl -C SCHED_FIFO top
```

SEE ALSO

    nice(1), getpriority(2), setpriority(2), psrset(8), renice(8)

HISTORY

    The **schedctl** command first appeared in NetBSD 5.0.

NAME

    `screenblank` — screen saver daemon for wscons and FBIO machines

SYNOPSIS

    `screenblank` [`-k` | `-m`] [`-d` *inactivity-timeout*] [`-e` *wakeup-delay*]
              [`-f` *framebuffer*] [`-i` *input-device*]
    `screenblank` {`-b` | `-u`}

DESCRIPTION

    `screenblank` disables the framebuffer if the keyboard and mouse are idle for a period of time, and re-enables the framebuffer when keyboard or mouse activity resumes.

    When killed with a SIGINT, SIGHUP, or SIGTERM, `screenblank` will re-enable the framebuffer. The pid can be found in the file `/var/run/screenblank.pid`.

    The options are as follows:

    `-b`   Overriding the other options, simply try (once) to blank the framebuffer, then exit.

    `-d` *inactivity-timeout*
          Wait the number of seconds specified by *inactivity-timeout*, expressed in the format "xxx.xxx", before disabling the framebuffer due to inactivity. The default is 600 seconds (10 minutes).

    `-e` *wakeup-delay*
          Wait the number of seconds specified by *wakeup-delay*, expressed in the format "xxx.xxx", before re-enabling the framebuffer once activity resumes. The default is .25 seconds.

    `-f` *framebuffer*
          Use the framebuffer device *framebuffer* instead of the default `/dev/fb`.

    `-i` *input-device*
          Add *input-device* to the list of devices to monitor for activity.

    `-k`   Do not check the keyboard for activity.

    `-m`   Do not check the mouse for activity.

    `-u`   Overriding the other options, simply try (once) to unblank the framebuffer, then exit.

    Note that the `-k` and `-m` flags are mutually exclusive.

FILES

/dev/kbd	The keyboard device.
/dev/mouse	The mouse device.
/dev/console	The console device.
/dev/fb	The default framebuffer.
/dev/wskbd	The keyboard for wscons machines.
/dev/wsmouse	The mouse device for wscons machines.
/dev/ttyE0	The console device for wscons machines.
/var/run/screenblank.pid	File containing the pid of **screenblank**.

NAME

scsictl — a program to manipulate SCSI devices and busses

SYNOPSIS

scsictl *device command* [*arg* [...]]

DESCRIPTION

scsictl allows a user or system administrator to issue commands to and otherwise control SCSI devices and busses. It is used by specifying a device or bus to manipulate, the command to perform, and any arguments the command may require. **scsictl** determines if the specified device is an actual device or a SCSI bus automatically, and selects the appropriate command set.

For commands which **scsictl** issues a SCSI command to the device directly, any returned sense information will be decoded by **scsictl** and displayed to the standard output.

DEVICE COMMANDS

The following commands are supported for SCSI devices:

defects [primary] [grown] [block|byte|physical]

Read the primary and/or grown defect lists from the specified device in block, byte from index, or physical sector format. The default is to return both the primary and grown defect lists in physical sector format. This command is only supported on direct access devices.

format [blocksize [immediate]]

(Low level) format the named device. If the optional blocksize parameter is provided, the device geometry will be modified to use the specified blocksize. If this parameter is different form the Current or Default Mode Page 3 parameters, the device will update Mode Page 3 at the successful completion of the Format. Device geometry may change as a result of using a new device blocksize. When the optional blocksize parameter is specified, the Defect List on the drive will revert to the original primary defect list created at the time of manufacture if available. The drive will usually recertify itself during the Format and add any other defective blocks to the new Defect List. Some disks may not support the ability to change the blocksize and may enter a Degraded Mode when fed a Format command of this type. If this happens the standard recovery for the drive requires issuing a correct Format command, i.e. one without the blocksize parameter.

When the immediate parameter is also specified, the disk is instructed to return from the format command right away. It continues to format, and every ten seconds **scsictl** issues a TEST UNIT READY command to check the associated sense data. This associated sense data has a progress indicator which indicates how far the format is progressing. Note well that most SCSI disk drives prior to a few years ago do not support this option.

identify

Identify the specified device, displaying the device's SCSI bus, target, and lun, as well as the device's vendor, product, and revision strings.

reassign *blkno* [blkno [...]]

Issues a REASSIGN BLOCKS command to the device, adding the specified blocks to the grown defect list. This command is only supported on direct access devices.

release

Send a "RELEASE" command to the device to release a reservation on it.

reserve

Send a "RESERVE" command to the device to place a reservation on it.

reset

Reset the device. This command is only supported for devices which support the SCIOCRESET ioctl.

start

Send a "START" command to the device. This is useful typically only for disk devices.

stop

Send a "STOP" command to the device. This is useful typically only for disk devices.

tur

Send a "TEST UNIT READY" command to the device. This is useful for generating current device status.

getcache

Returns basic cache parameters for the device.

setcache *none | r | w | rw* [*save*]

Set basic cache parameters for the device. The cache may be disabled (none), the read cache enabled (r), the write cache enabled (w), or both read and write cache enabled (rw). If the drive's cache parameters are savable, specifying *save* after the cache enable state will cause the parameters to be saved in non-volatile storage.

flushcache

Explicitly flushes the write cache.

setspeed *speed*

Set the highest speed that the optical drive should use for reading data. The units are multiples of a single speed CDROM (150 KB/s). Specify 0 to use the drive's fastest speed.

BUS COMMANDS

The following commands are supported for SCSI busses:

reset

Reset the SCSI bus. This command is only supported if the host adapter supports the SCBUSIORESET ioctl.

scan *target lun*

Scan the SCSI bus for devices. This is useful if a device was not connected or powered on when the system was booted. The *target* and *lun* arguments specify which SCSI target and lun on the bus is to be scanned. Either may be wildcarded by specifying the keyword "any" or "all".

detach *target lun*

Detach the specified device from the bus. Useful if a device is powered down after use. The *target* and *lun* arguments have the same meaning as for the **scan** command, and may also be wildcarded.

NOTES

When scanning the SCSI bus, information about newly recognized devices is printed to console. No information is printed for already probed devices.

FILES
/dev/scsibus* - for commands operating on SCSI busses

SEE ALSO
ioctl(2), cd(4), ch(4), sd(4), se(4), ss(4), st(4), uk(4), atactl(8), dkctl(8)

HISTORY
The **scsictl** command first appeared in NetBSD 1.4.

AUTHORS
The **scsictl** command was written by Jason R. Thorpe of the Numerical Aerospace Simulation Facility, NASA Ames Research Center.

NAME

sdpd — Bluetooth Service Discovery Protocol daemon

SYNOPSIS

sdpd [**-dh**] [**-c** *path*] [**-G** *group*] [**-g** *group*] [**-u** *user*]

DESCRIPTION

The **sdpd** daemon keeps a database of Bluetooth Service Records registered on the host and responds to Service Discovery inquiries from remote Bluetooth devices.

In order to discover services, remote Bluetooth devices send Service Search and Service Attribute or Service Search Attribute requests over Bluetooth L2CAP connections on the SDP PSM (0x0001). The **sdpd** daemon will try to find matching Service Records in its Service Database and will return the requested record extracts for the remote device to interpret. The remote device will then make a separate connection in order to access the service.

Bluetooth applications, running on the host, are able to insert, remove and update Service Records with the **sdpd** daemon via the control socket. It is possible to query entire contents of the Service Database locally with sdpquery(1) using the **-l** option.

The command line options are as follows:

-c *path*
> Specify path to the control socket. The default path is /var/run/sdp.

-d
> Do not detach from the controlling terminal.

-G *group*
> Grant permission to members of the *group* to modify the **sdpd** Service Database.

-g *group*
> Specifies the group the **sdpd** should run as after it initializes. The value specified may be either a group name or a numeric group ID. This only works if **sdpd** was started as root. The default group name is "_sdpd".

-h
> Display usage message and exit.

-u *user*
> Specifies the user the **sdpd** should run as after it initializes. The value specified may be either a user name or a numeric user ID. This only works if **sdpd** was started as root. The default user name is "_sdpd".

FILES

/var/run/sdp

SEE ALSO

sdpquery(1), sdp(3)

The "Service Discovery Protocol" section of the Bluetooth Core specifications, available at "http://www.bluetooth.com/"

HISTORY

The original **sdpd** daemon first appeared in FreeBSD 5.3 and was imported into NetBSD 4.0 by Iain Hibbert under the sponsorship of Itronix, Inc. This version was rewritten by Iain Hibbert for NetBSD 6.0 in order to allow Bluetooth applications to fully specify service records.

AUTHORS

Maksim Yevmenkin ⟨m_evmenkin@yahoo.com⟩

Iain Hibbert

CAVEATS

The **sdpd** daemon will listen for incoming L2CAP connections on a wildcard BD_ADDR.

In case of multiple Bluetooth controllers connected to the same host it is possible to limit visibility of Service Records according to the controller the connection is made through.

Requests to insert, remove or update service records can only be made via the control socket. The **sdpd** daemon will check the peer's credentials and will only accept the request when the peer is the superuser, of if the peer is a member of the group specified with the −**G** option.

The **sdpd** daemon does not check for duplicated Service Records and only performs minimal validation of the record data sent in the Insert/Update Record requests. It is assumed that application must obtain all required resources such as RFCOMM channels etc., before registering the service.

BUGS

sdpd only ever generates 16-bit sequence headers, so if a response was to grow over UINT16_MAX, the sequence header will be wrong.

There is no way for clients to discover the maximum packet size that **sdpd** will accept on the local socket. Currently this is SDP_LOCAL_MTU as defined in <bluetooth/sdp.h>.

NAME

security — NetBSD security features

DESCRIPTION

NetBSD supports a variety of security features. Below is a brief description of them with some quick usage examples that will help you get started.

Contents:

- Veriexec (file integrity)
- Exploit mitigation
- Per-user /tmp directory
- Information filtering

VERIEXEC

Veriexec is a file integrity subsystem.

For more information about it, and a quick guide on how to use it, please see veriexec(8).

In a nutshell, once enabled, *Veriexec* can be started as follows:

```
# veriexecgen && veriexecctl load
```

EXPLOIT MITIGATION

NetBSD incorporates some exploit mitigation features. The purpose of exploit mitigation features is to interfere with the way exploits work, in order to prevent them from succeeding. Due to that, some features may have other impacts on the system, so be sure to fully understand the implications of each feature.

NetBSD provides the following exploit mitigation features:

- PaX ASLR (Address Space Layout Randomization).
- PaX MPROTECT (mprotect(2) restrictions)
- PaX SegvGuard
- gcc(1) stack-smashing protection (SSP)
- bounds checked libc functions (FORTIFY_SOURCE)

PaX ASLR

PaX ASLR implements Address Space Layout Randomization (ASLR), meant to complement non-executable mappings. Its purpose is to harden prediction of the address space layout, namely location of library and application functions that can be used by an attacker to circumvent non-executable mappings by using a technique called "return to library" to bypass the need to write new code to (potentially executable) regions of memory.

When *PaX ASLR* is used, it is more likely the attacker will fail to predict the addresses of such functions, causing the application to segfault. To detect cases where an attacker might try and brute-force the return address of respawning services, *PaX Segvguard* can be used (see below).

For non-PIE (Position Independent Executable) executables, the NetBSD *PaX ASLR* implementation introduces randomization to the following memory regions:

1. The data segment
2. The stack

For PIE executables:

1.   The program itself (exec base)
2.   All shared libraries
3.   The data segment
4.   The stack

While it can be enabled globally, NetBSD provides a tool, paxctl(8), to enable *PaX ASLR* on a per-program basis.

Example usage:

```
# paxctl +A /usr/sbin/sshd
```

Enabling *PaX ASLR* globally:

```
# sysctl -w security.pax.aslr.global=1
```

PaX MPROTECT

PaX MPROTECT implements memory protection restrictions, meant to complement non-executable mappings. The purpose is to prevent situations where malicious code attempts to mark writable memory regions as executable, often by trashing arguments to an mprotect(2) call.

While it can be enabled globally, NetBSD provides a tool, paxctl(8), to enable *PaX MPROTECT* on a per-program basis.

Example usage:

```
# paxctl +M /usr/sbin/sshd
```

Enabling *PaX MPROTECT* globally:

```
# sysctl -w security.pax.mprotect.global=1
```

PaX Segvguard

PaX Segvguard monitors the number of segmentation faults in a program on a per-user basis, in an attempt to detect on-going exploitation attempts and possibly prevent them. For instance, *PaX Segvguard* can help detect when an attacker tries to brute-force a function return address, when attempting to perform a return-to-lib attack.

PaX Segvguard consumes kernel memory, so use it wisely. While it provides rate-limiting protections, records are tracked for all users on a per-program basis, meaning that irresponsible use may result in tracking all segmentation faults in the system, possibly consuming all kernel memory.

For this reason, it is highly recommended to have *PaX Segvguard* enabled explicitly only for network services or other processes deemed as critical to system security. Enabling *PaX Segvguard* explicitly works like this:

```
# paxctl +G /usr/sbin/sshd
```

However, a global knob is still provided, for use in strict environments with no local users (for example, some network appliances, embedded devices, and firewalls)

```
# sysctl -w security.pax.segvguard.global=1
```

Explicitly disabling *PaX Segvguard* is also possible:

```
# paxctl +g /bin/ls
```

In addition, *PaX Segvguard* provides several tunable options. For example, to limit a program to 5 segmentation faults from the same user in a 60 second timeframe:

```
# sysctl -w security.pax.segvguard.max_crashes=5
# sysctl -w security.pax.segvguard.expiry_timeout=60
```

The number of seconds a user will be suspended from running the culprit program is also configurable. For example, 10 minutes seem like a sane setting:

```
# sysctl -w security.pax.segvguard.suspend_timeout=600
```

GCC Stack Smashing Protection (SSP)

As of NetBSD 4.0, gcc(1) includes *SSP*, a set of compiler extensions to raise the bar on exploitation attempts by detecting corruption of variables and buffer overruns, which may be used to affect program control flow.

Upon detection of a buffer overrun, *SSP* will immediately abort execution of the program and send a log message to syslog(3).

The system (userland and kernel) can be built with *SSP* by using the "USE_SSP" flag in /etc/mk.conf:

```
USE_SSP=yes
```

You are encouraged to use *SSP* for software you build, by providing one of the **-fstack-protector** or **-fstack-protector-all** flags to gcc(1). Keep in mind, however, that *SSP* will not work for functions that make use of alloca(3), as the latter modifies the stack size during run-time, while *SSP* relies on it being a compile-time static.

Use of *SSP* is especially encouraged on platforms without per-page execute bit granularity such as i386. As of NetBSD 6.0, *SSP* is used by default on i386 and amd64 architectures.

FORTIFY_SOURCE

The so-called *FORTIFY_SOURCE* is a relatively simple technique to detect a subset of buffer overflows before these can do damage. It is integrated to gcc(1) together with some common memory and string functions in the standard C library of NetBSD.

The underlying idea builds on the observation that there are cases where the compiler knows the size of a buffer. If a buffer overflow is suspected in a function that does little or no bounds checking, either a compile time warning can be issued or a safer substitute function can be used at runtime. Refer to ssp(3) for additional details.

The *FORTIFY_SOURCE* is enabled by default in some parts of the NetBSD source tree. It is also possible to explicitly enable it by defining the following in mk.conf(5):

```
USE_FORT=yes
```

PER-USER TEMPORARY STORAGE

It is possible to configure per-user temporary storage to avoid potential security issues (race conditions, etc.) in programs that do not make secure usage of /tmp.

To enable per-user temporary storage, add the following line to rc.conf(5):

```
per_user_tmp=YES
```

If /tmp is a mount point, you will also need to update its fstab(5) entry to use "/private/tmp" (or whatever directory you want, if you override the default using the "per_user_tmp_dir" rc.conf(5) keyword) instead of "/tmp".

Following that, run:

```
# /etc/rc.d/perusertmp start
```

The per-user temporary storage is implemented by using "magic symlinks". These are further described in `symlink(7)`.

INFORMATION FILTERING

NetBSD provides administrators the ability to restrict information passed from the kernel to userland so that users can only view information they "own".

The hooks that manage this restriction are located in various parts of the system and affect programs such as `ps(1)`, `fstat(1)`, and `netstat(1)`. Information filtering is enabled as follows:

```
# sysctl -w security.curtain=1
```

SEE ALSO

`sysctl(3)`, `options(4)`, `paxctl(8)`, `sysctl(8)`, `veriexec(8)`, `veriexecctl(8)`, `veriexecgen(8)`

AUTHORS

Elad Efrat ⟨elad@NetBSD.org⟩

NAME

sendmail – Postfix to Sendmail compatibility interface

SYNOPSIS

sendmail [*option ...*] [*recipient ...*]

mailq
sendmail -bp

newaliases
sendmail -I

DESCRIPTION

The Postfix **sendmail**(1) command implements the Postfix to Sendmail compatibility interface. For the sake of compatibility with existing applications, some Sendmail command-line options are recognized but silently ignored.

By default, Postfix **sendmail**(1) reads a message from standard input until EOF or until it reads a line with only a **.** character, and arranges for delivery. Postfix **sendmail**(1) relies on the **postdrop**(1) command to create a queue file in the **maildrop** directory.

Specific command aliases are provided for other common modes of operation:

mailq   List the mail queue. Each entry shows the queue file ID, message size, arrival time, sender, and the recipients that still need to be delivered. If mail could not be delivered upon the last attempt, the reason for failure is shown. The queue ID string is followed by an optional status character:

    *   The message is in the **active** queue, i.e. the message is selected for delivery.

    !   The message is in the **hold** queue, i.e. no further delivery attempt will be made until the mail is taken off hold.

    This mode of operation is implemented by executing the **postqueue**(1) command.

newaliases

    Initialize the alias database. If no input file is specified (with the **-oA** option, see below), the program processes the file(s) specified with the **alias_database** configuration parameter. If no alias database type is specified, the program uses the type specified with the **default_database_type** configuration parameter. This mode of operation is implemented by running the **postalias**(1) command.

    Note: it may take a minute or so before an alias database update becomes visible. Use the "**postfix reload**" command to eliminate this delay.

These and other features can be selected by specifying the appropriate combination of command-line options. Some features are controlled by parameters in the **main.cf** configuration file.

The following options are recognized:

-Am (ignored)

-Ac (ignored)

    Postfix sendmail uses the same configuration file regardless of whether or not a message is an initial submission.

-B *body_type*

    The message body MIME type: **7BIT** or **8BITMIME**.

-bd   Go into daemon mode. This mode of operation is implemented by executing the "**postfix start**" command.

-bh (ignored)

-bH (ignored)

  Postfix has no persistent host status database.

-bi Initialize alias database. See the **newaliases** command above.

-bm Read mail from standard input and arrange for delivery. This is the default mode of operation.

-bp List the mail queue. See the **mailq** command above.

-bs Stand-alone SMTP server mode. Read SMTP commands from standard input, and write responses to standard output. In stand-alone SMTP server mode, mail relaying and other access controls are disabled by default. To enable them, run the process as the **mail_owner** user.

  This mode of operation is implemented by running the **smtpd**(8) daemon.

-bv Do not collect or deliver a message. Instead, send an email report after verifying each recipient address. This is useful for testing address rewriting and routing configurations.

  This feature is available in Postfix version 2.1 and later.

-C *config_file*

-C *config_dir*

  The path name of the Postfix **main.cf** file, or of its parent directory. This information is ignored with Postfix versions before 2.3.

  With all Postfix versions, you can specify a directory pathname with the MAIL_CONFIG environment variable to override the location of configuration files.

-F *full_name*

  Set the sender full name. This overrides the NAME environment variable, and is used only with messages that have no **From:** message header.

-f *sender*

  Set the envelope sender address. This is the address where delivery problems are sent to. With Postfix versions before 2.1, the **Errors-To:** message header overrides the error return address.

-G Gateway (relay) submission, as opposed to initial user submission. Either do not rewrite addresses at all, or update incomplete addresses with the domain information specified with **remote_header_rewrite_domain**.

  This option is ignored before Postfix version 2.3.

-h *hop_count* (ignored)

  Hop count limit. Use the **hopcount_limit** configuration parameter instead.

-I Initialize alias database. See the **newaliases** command above.

-i When reading a message from standard input, don´t treat a line with only a **.** character as the end of input.

-L *label* (ignored)

  The logging label. Use the **syslog_name** configuration parameter instead.

-m (ignored)

  Backwards compatibility.

-N *dsn* (default: 'delay, failure')

  Delivery status notification control. Specify either a comma-separated list with one or more of **failure** (send notification when delivery fails), **delay** (send notification when delivery is delayed), or **success** (send notification when the message is delivered); or specify **never** (don't send any notifications at all).

2

This feature is available in Postfix 2.3 and later.

-n (ignored)
> Backwards compatibility.

-oAalias_database
> Non-default alias database. Specify *pathname* or *type*:*pathname*. See **postalias**(1) for details.

-O *option*=*value* (ignored)
> Backwards compatibility.

-o7 (ignored)

-o8 (ignored)
> To send 8-bit or binary content, use an appropriate MIME encapsulation and specify the appropriate **-B** command-line option.

-oi
> When reading a message from standard input, don´t treat a line with only a **.** character as the end of input.

-om (ignored)
> The sender is never eliminated from alias etc. expansions.

-o *x value* (ignored)
> Set option *x* to *value*. Use the equivalent configuration parameter in **main.cf** instead.

-r *sender*
> Set the envelope sender address. This is the address where delivery problems are sent to. With Postfix versions before 2.1, the **Errors-To:** message header overrides the error return address.

-R *return_limit* (ignored)
> Limit the size of bounced mail. Use the **bounce_size_limit** configuration parameter instead.

-q
> Attempt to deliver all queued mail. This is implemented by executing the **postqueue**(1) command.
>
> Warning: flushing undeliverable mail frequently will result in poor delivery performance of all other mail.

-qinterval (ignored)
> The interval between queue runs. Use the **queue_run_delay** configuration parameter instead.

-qIqueueid
> Schedule immediate delivery of mail with the specified queue ID. This option is implemented by executing the **postqueue**(1) command, and is available with Postfix version 2.4 and later.

-qRsite
> Schedule immediate delivery of all mail that is queued for the named *site*. This option accepts only *site* names that are eligible for the "fast flush" service, and is implemented by executing the **postqueue**(1) command. See **flush**(8) for more information about the "fast flush" service.

-qSsite
> This command is not implemented. Use the slower "**sendmail -q**" command instead.

-t
> Extract recipients from message headers. These are added to any recipients specified on the command line.
>
> With Postfix versions prior to 2.1, this option requires that no recipient addresses are specified on the command line.

-U (ignored)
> Initial user submission.

-V *envid*
> Specify the envelope ID for notification by servers that support DSN.
>
> This feature is available in Postfix 2.3 and later.

3

-XV (Postfix 2.2 and earlier: **-V**)

Variable Envelope Return Path. Given an envelope sender address of the form *owner-list-name@origin*, each recipient *user@domain* receives mail with a personalized envelope sender address.

By default, the personalized envelope sender address is *owner-listname+user=domain@origin*. The default + and = characters are configurable with the **default_verp_delimiters** configuration parameter.

-XV*xy* (Postfix 2.2 and earlier: **-V***xy*)

As **-XV**, but uses *x* and *y* as the VERP delimiter characters, instead of the characters specified with the **default_verp_delimiters** configuration parameter.

-v   Send an email report of the first delivery attempt (Postfix versions 2.1 and later). Mail delivery always happens in the background. When multiple **-v** options are given, enable verbose logging for debugging purposes.

-X *log_file* (ignored)

Log mailer traffic. Use the **debug_peer_list** and **debug_peer_level** configuration parameters instead.

SECURITY

By design, this program is not set-user (or group) id. However, it must handle data from untrusted, possibly remote, users. Thus, the usual precautions need to be taken against malicious inputs.

DIAGNOSTICS

Problems are logged to **syslogd**(8) and to the standard error stream.

ENVIRONMENT

MAIL_CONFIG

Directory with Postfix configuration files.

MAIL_VERBOSE (value does not matter)

Enable verbose logging for debugging purposes.

MAIL_DEBUG (value does not matter)

Enable debugging with an external command, as specified with the **debugger_command** configuration parameter.

NAME   The sender full name. This is used only with messages that have no **From:** message header. See also the **-F** option above.

CONFIGURATION PARAMETERS

The following **main.cf** parameters are especially relevant to this program. The text below provides only a parameter summary. See **postconf**(5) for more details including examples.

TROUBLE SHOOTING CONTROLS

The DEBUG_README file gives examples of how to trouble shoot a Postfix system.

debugger_command (empty)

The external command to execute when a Postfix daemon program is invoked with the -D option.

debug_peer_level (2)

The increment in verbose logging level when a remote client or server matches a pattern in the debug_peer_list parameter.

debug_peer_list (empty)

Optional list of remote client or server hostname or network address patterns that cause the verbose logging level to increase by the amount specified in $debug_peer_level.

ACCESS CONTROLS

Available in Postfix version 2.2 and later:

authorized_flush_users (static:anyone)
> List of users who are authorized to flush the queue.

authorized_mailq_users (static:anyone)
> List of users who are authorized to view the queue.

authorized_submit_users (static:anyone)
> List of users who are authorized to submit mail with the **sendmail**(1) command (and with the privileged **postdrop**(1) helper command).

RESOURCE AND RATE CONTROLS

bounce_size_limit (50000)
> The maximal amount of original message text that is sent in a non-delivery notification.

fork_attempts (5)
> The maximal number of attempts to fork() a child process.

fork_delay (1s)
> The delay between attempts to fork() a child process.

hopcount_limit (50)
> The maximal number of Received: message headers that is allowed in the primary message headers.

queue_run_delay (300s)
> The time between deferred queue scans by the queue manager; prior to Postfix 2.4 the default value was 1000s.

FAST FLUSH CONTROLS

The ETRN_README file describes configuration and operation details for the Postfix "fast flush" service.

fast_flush_domains ($relay_domains)
> Optional list of destinations that are eligible for per-destination logfiles with mail that is queued to those destinations.

VERP CONTROLS

The VERP_README file describes configuration and operation details of Postfix support for variable envelope return path addresses.

default_verp_delimiters (+=)
> The two default VERP delimiter characters.

verp_delimiter_filter (-=+)
> The characters Postfix accepts as VERP delimiter characters on the Postfix **sendmail**(1) command line and in SMTP commands.

MISCELLANEOUS CONTROLS

alias_database (see 'postconf -d' output)
> The alias databases for **local**(8) delivery that are updated with "**newaliases**" or with "**sendmail -bi**".

command_directory (see 'postconf -d' output)
> The location of all postfix administrative commands.

config_directory (see 'postconf -d' output)
> The default location of the Postfix main.cf and master.cf configuration files.

daemon_directory (see 'postconf -d' output)
> The directory with Postfix support programs and daemon programs.

default_database_type (see 'postconf -d' output)
> The default database type for use in **newaliases**(1), **postalias**(1) and **postmap**(1) commands.

delay_warning_time (0h)
> The time after which the sender receives the message headers of mail that is still queued.

enable_errors_to (no)
> Report mail delivery errors to the address specified with the non-standard Errors-To: message header, instead of the envelope sender address (this feature is removed with Postfix version 2.2, is turned off by default with Postfix version 2.1, and is always turned on with older Postfix versions).

mail_owner (postfix)
> The UNIX system account that owns the Postfix queue and most Postfix daemon processes.

queue_directory (see 'postconf -d' output)
> The location of the Postfix top-level queue directory.

remote_header_rewrite_domain (empty)
> Don't rewrite message headers from remote clients at all when this parameter is empty; otherwise, rewrite message headers and append the specified domain name to incomplete addresses.

syslog_facility (mail)
> The syslog facility of Postfix logging.

syslog_name (see 'postconf -d' output)
> The mail system name that is prepended to the process name in syslog records, so that "smtpd" becomes, for example, "postfix/smtpd".

FILES
/var/spool/postfix, mail queue
/etc/postfix, configuration files

SEE ALSO
pickup(8), mail pickup daemon
qmgr(8), queue manager
smtpd(8), SMTP server
flush(8), fast flush service
postsuper(1), queue maintenance
postalias(1), create/update/query alias database
postdrop(1), mail posting utility
postfix(1), mail system control
postqueue(1), mail queue control
syslogd(8), system logging

README_FILES
Use "**postconf readme_directory**" or "**postconf html_directory**" to locate this information.
DEBUG_README, Postfix debugging howto
ETRN_README, Postfix ETRN howto
VERP_README, Postfix VERP howto

LICENSE
The Secure Mailer license must be distributed with this software.

AUTHOR(S)
Wietse Venema
IBM T.J. Watson Research
P.O. Box 704
Yorktown Heights, NY 10598, USA

NAME

    services_mkdb — generate the services databases

SYNOPSIS

    services_mkdb [**-qv**] [**-o** *database*] [**-V** *style*] [*file*]
    services_mkdb **-u** [*file*]

DESCRIPTION

    services_mkdb creates a db(3) database for the specified file. If no file is specified, then /etc/services is used. The database is installed into /var/db/services.cdb for CDB format and into /var/db/services.db for DB format (see **-V**). The file must be in the correct format (see services(5)).

The options are as follows:

-o *database*
    Put the output databases in the named file.

-q   Don't warn about duplicate services. This is the default behavior.

-u   Print the services file to stdout, omitting duplicate entries and comments.

-V   Create a specific version of the database style. *style* can be cdb to request the CDB format (default) or db to request the DB format. The DB format is useful for compatibility with old statically linked binaries.

-v   Warn about duplicate services.

The databases are used by the C library services routines (see getservent(3)).

services_mkdb exits zero on success, non-zero on failure.

FILES

    /var/db/services.db   The current services database.
    /var/db/services.db.tmp
                              A temporary file.
    /etc/services   The current services file.

SEE ALSO

    db(3), getservent(3), services(5)

BUGS

    Because **services_mkdb** guarantees not to install a partial destination file it must build a temporary file in the same file system and if successful use rename(2) to install over the destination file.

If **services_mkdb** fails it will leave the previous version of the destination file intact.

NAME
sesd — monitor SCSI Environmental Services Devices

SYNOPSIS
sesd [**-d**] [**-t** *poll-interval*] *device* [*device* ...]

DESCRIPTION
sesd monitors SCSI Environmental Services (or SAF-TE) devices for changes in state and logs such changes changes to the system error logger (see syslogd(8)). At least one device must be specified. When no other options are supplied, **sesd** detaches and becomes a daemon, by default waking up every 30 seconds to poll each device for a change in state.

The following options may be used:

-d   Instead of detaching and becoming a daemon, stay attached to the controlling terminal and log changes there as well as via the system logger.

-p *poll-interval*
    Change the interval of polling from the default 30 seconds to the number of seconds specified.

The user may then use getencstat(8) to get more detailed information about the state of the over enclosure device or objects within the enclosure device.

FILES
/dev/sesN SCSI Environmental Services Devices

SEE ALSO
ses(4), getencstat(8), setencstat(8), setobjstat(8), syslogd(8)

BUGS
This is something of a toy, but it is better than nothing.

SETENCSTAT (8)   NetBSD   SETENCSTAT (8)

NAME
  setencstat — set SCSI Environmental Services Device enclosure status

SYNOPSIS
  setencstat *device enclosure_status*

DESCRIPTION
  setencstat sets summary status for a SCSI Environmental Services (or SAF-TE) device. The enclosure status argument may take on the values:

  0   Set the status to an **OK** state.

  1   Set the status to an **UNRECOVERABLE** state.

  2   Set the status to an **CRITICAL** state.

  4   Set the status to an **NON-CRITICAL** state.

  8   Set the status to an **INFORMATIONAL** state.

  All the non-zero options may be combined.

  Note that devices may simply and silently ignore the setting of these values.

FILES
  /dev/sesN SCSI Environmental Services Devices

SEE ALSO
  ses(4), getencstat(8), sesd(8), setobjstat(8)

NAME
setkey — manually manipulate the IPsec SA/SP database

SYNOPSIS
setkey [−knrv] *file* . . .
setkey [−knrv] −c
setkey [−krv] −f *filename*
setkey [−aklPrv] −D
setkey [−Pvp] −F
setkey [−H] −x
setkey [−?V]

DESCRIPTION
setkey adds, updates, dumps, or flushes Security Association Database (SAD) entries as well as Security Policy Database (SPD) entries in the kernel.

setkey takes a series of operations from standard input (if invoked with −c) or the file named *filename* (if invoked with −f *filename*).

(no flag)
        Dump the SAD entries or SPD entries contained in the specified *file*.

−?   Print short help.

−a   setkey usually does not display dead SAD entries with −D. If −a is also specified, the dead SAD entries will be displayed as well. A dead SAD entry is one that has expired but remains in the system because it is referenced by some SPD entries.

−D   Dump the SAD entries. If −P is also specified, the SPD entries are dumped. If −p is specified, the ports are displayed.

−F   Flush the SAD entries. If −P is also specified, the SPD entries are flushed.

−H   Add hexadecimal dump in −x mode.

−h   On NetBSD, synonym for −H. On other systems, synonym for − ?.

−k   Use semantics used in kernel. Available only in Linux. See also −r.

−l   Loop forever with short output on −D.

−n   No action. The program will check validity of the input, but no changes to the SPD will be made.

−r   Use semantics described in IPsec RFCs. This mode is default. For details see section **RFC vs Linux kernel semantics**. Available only in Linux. See also −k.

−x   Loop forever and dump all the messages transmitted to the PF_KEY socket. −xx prints the unformatted timestamps.

−V   Print version string.

−v   Be verbose. The program will dump messages exchanged on the PF_KEY socket, including messages sent from other processes to the kernel.

Configuration syntax
With −c or −f on the command line, setkey accepts the following configuration syntax. Lines starting with hash signs ('#') are treated as comment lines.

add [**-46n**] `src dst protocol spi` [`extensions`] `algorithm` ... ;
  Add an SAD entry. add can fail for multiple reasons, including when the key length does not
  match the specified algorithm.

get [**-46n**] `src dst protocol spi` ;
  Show an SAD entry.

delete [**-46n**] `src dst protocol spi` ;
  Remove an SAD entry.

deleteall [**-46n**] `src dst protocol` ;
  Remove all SAD entries that match the specification.

flush [`protocol`];
  Clear all SAD entries matched by the options. **-F** on the command line achieves the same functionality.

dump [`protocol`];
  Dumps all SAD entries matched by the options. **-D** on the command line achieves the same functionality.

spdadd [**-46n**] `src_range dst_range upperspec label policy` ;
  Add an SPD entry.

spdadd tagged `tag policy` ;
  Add an SPD entry based on a PF tag. `tag` must be a string surrounded by double quotes.

spdupdate [**-46n**] `src_range dst_range upperspec label policy` ;
  Updates an SPD entry.

spdupdate tagged `tag policy` ;
  Update an SPD entry based on a PF tag. `tag` must be a string surrounded by double quotes.

spddelete [**-46n**] `src_range dst_range upperspec` **-P** `direction` ;
  Delete an SPD entry.

spdflush ;
  Clear all SPD entries. **-FP** on the command line achieves the same functionality.

spddump ;
  Dumps all SPD entries. **-DP** on the command line achieves the same functionality.

Meta-arguments are as follows:

`src`
`dst`   Source/destination of the secure communication is specified as an IPv4/v6 address, and an optional
        port number between square brackets. **setkey** can resolve a FQDN into numeric addresses. If the
        FQDN resolves into multiple addresses, **setkey** will install multiple SAD/SPD entries into the ker-
        nel by trying all possible combinations. **-4**, **-6**, and **-n** restrict the address resolution of FQDN in
        certain ways. **-4** and **-6** restrict results into IPv4/v6 addresses only, respectively. **-n** avoids
        FQDN resolution and requires addresses to be numeric addresses.

`protocol`
        `protocol` is one of following:
        `esp`   ESP based on rfc2406
        `esp-old`   ESP based on rfc1827
        `ah`   AH based on rfc2402

> ah-old   AH based on rfc1826
> ipcomp   IPComp
> tcp   TCP-MD5 based on rfc2385

spi Security Parameter Index (SPI) for the SAD and the SPD. *spi* must be a decimal number, or a hexadecimal number with a "0x" prefix. SPI values between 0 and 255 are reserved for future use by IANA and cannot be used. TCP-MD5 associations must use 0x1000 and therefore only have per-host granularity at this time.

extensions
  take some of the following:

  −m *mode* Specify a security protocol mode for use. *mode* is one of following: transport, tunnel, or any. The default value is any.

  −r *size* Specify window size of bytes for replay prevention. *size* must be decimal number in 32-bit word. If *size* is zero or not specified, replay checks don't take place.

  −u *id* Specify the identifier of the policy entry in the SPD. See *policy*.

  −f *pad_option*
    defines the content of the ESP padding. *pad_option* is one of following:
    zero-pad All the paddings are zero.
    random-pad A series of randomized values are used.
    seq-pad A series of sequential increasing numbers started from 1 are used.

  −f nocyclic-seq
    Don't allow cyclic sequence numbers.

  −lh *time*
  −ls *time* Specify hard/soft life time duration of the SA measured in seconds.

  −bh *bytes*
  −bs *bytes*
    Specify hard/soft life time duration of the SA measured in bytes transported.

  −ctx *doi algorithm context-name*
    Specify an access control label. The access control label is interpreted by the LSM (e.g., SELinux). Ultimately, it enables MAC on network communications.
    doi The domain of interpretation, which is used by the IKE daemon to identify the domain in which negotiation takes place.
    algorithm
      Indicates the LSM for which the label is generated (e.g., SELinux).
    context-name
      The string representation of the label that is interpreted by the LSM.

algorithm
  −E *ealgo key*
    Specify an encryption algorithm *ealgo* for ESP.

  −E *ealgo key* **−A** *aalgo key*
    Specify an encryption algorithm *ealgo*, as well as a payload authentication algorithm *aalgo*, for ESP.

  −A *aalgo key*
    Specify an authentication algorithm for AH.

  −C *calgo* [**−R**]
    Specify a compression algorithm for IPComp. If **−R** is specified, the *spi* field value will be used as the IPComp CPI (compression parameter index) on wire as-is. If **−R** is not specified, the kernel will use well-known CPI on wire, and *spi* field will be used only as an index for kernel internal usage.

key must be a double-quoted character string, or a series of hexadecimal digits preceded by "0x".

Possible values for *ealgo*, *aalgo*, and *calgo* are specified in the **Algorithms** sections.

src_range
dst_range
> These select the communications that should be secured by IPsec. They can be an IPv4/v6 address or an IPv4/v6 address range, and may be accompanied by a TCP/UDP port specification. This takes the following form:
>
> *address*
> *address/prefixlen*
> *address[port]*
> *address/prefixlen[port]*
>
> *prefixlen* and *port* must be decimal numbers. The square brackets around *port* are really necessary, they are not man page meta-characters. For FQDN resolution, the rules applicable to *src* and *dst* apply here as well.

upperspec
> Upper-layer protocol to be used. You can use one of the words in /etc/protocols as *upperspec*, or icmp6, ip4, or any. any stands for "any protocol". You can also use the protocol number. You can specify a type and/or a code of ICMPv6 when the upper-layer protocol is ICMPv6. The specification can be placed after icmp6. A type is separated from a code by single comma. A code must always be specified. When a zero is specified, the kernel deals with it as a wildcard. Note that the kernel can not distinguish a wildcard from an ICPMv6 type of zero. For example, the following means that the policy doesn't require IPsec for any inbound Neighbor Solicitation.
>
> > spdadd ::/0 ::/0 icmp6 135,0 -P in none;

Note: *upperspec* does not work against forwarding case at this moment, as it requires extra reassembly at the forwarding node (not implemented at this moment). There are many protocols in /etc/protocols, but all protocols except of TCP, UDP, and ICMP may not be suitable to use with IPsec. You have to consider carefully what to use.

label label is the access control label for the policy. This label is interpreted by the LSM (e.g., SELinux). Ultimately, it enables MAC on network communications. When a policy contains an access control label, SAs negotiated with this policy will contain the label. Its format:
> **-ctx** *doi algorithm context-name*
> > *doi*   The domain of interpretation, which is used by the IKE daemon to identify the domain in which negotiation takes place.
> > *algorithm*
> > > Indicates the LSM for which the label is generated (e.g., SELinux).
> > *context-name*
> > > The string representation of the label that is interpreted by the LSM.

policy
> *policy* is in one of the following three formats:
> **-P** *direction [priority specification]* discard
> **-P** *direction [priority specification]* none
> **-P**   *direction*   *[priority   specification]*   ipsec
> *protocol/mode/src-dst/level* [...]

You must specify the direction of its policy as *direction*. Either *out*, *in*, or *fwd* can be used.

priority specification is used to control the placement of the policy within the SPD. Policy position is determined by a signed integer where higher priorities indicate the policy is placed closer to the beginning of the list and lower priorities indicate the policy is placed closer to the end of the list. Policies with equal priorities are added at the end of groups of such policies.

Priority can only be specified when setkey has been compiled against kernel headers that support policy priorities (Linux >= 2.6.6). If the kernel does not support priorities, a warning message will be printed the first time a priority specification is used. Policy priority takes one of the following formats:

{priority,prio} offset
> *offset* is an integer in the range from −2147483647 to 214783648.

{priority,prio} base {+,-} offset
> *base* is either low (−1073741824), def (0), or high (1073741824)

> *offset* is an unsigned integer. It can be up to 1073741824 for positive offsets, and up to 1073741823 for negative offsets.

discard means the packet matching indexes will be discarded. none means that IPsec operation will not take place onto the packet. ipsec means that IPsec operation will take place onto the packet.

The *protocol/mode/src-dst/level* part specifies the rule how to process the packet. Either ah, esp, or ipcomp must be used as *protocol*. *mode* is either transport or tunnel. If *mode* is tunnel, you must specify the end-point addresses of the SA as *src* and *dst* with '-' between these addresses, which is used to specify the SA to use. If *mode* is transport, both *src* and *dst* can be omitted. *level* is to be one of the following: default, use, require, or unique. If the SA is not available in every level, the kernel will ask the key exchange daemon to establish a suitable SA. default means the kernel consults the system wide default for the protocol you specified, e.g. the esp_trans_deflev sysctl variable, when the kernel processes the packet. use means that the kernel uses an SA if it's available, otherwise the kernel keeps normal operation. require means SA is required whenever the kernel sends a packet matched with the policy. unique is the same as require; in addition, it allows the policy to match the unique out-bound SA. You just specify the policy level unique, racoon(8) will configure the SA for the policy. If you configure the SA by manual keying for that policy, you can put a decimal number as the policy identifier after unique separated by a colon ':' like: unique:number in order to bind this policy to the SA. number must be between 1 and 32767. It corresponds to *extensions* −u of the manual SA configuration. When you want to use SA bundle, you can define multiple rules. For example, if an IP header was followed by an AH header followed by an ESP header followed by an upper layer protocol header, the rule would be:

        esp/transport//require ah/transport//require;
The rule order is very important.

When NAT-T is enabled in the kernel, policy matching for ESP over UDP packets may be done on endpoint addresses and port (this depends on the system. System that do not perform the port check cannot support multiple endpoints behind the same NAT). When using ESP over UDP, you can specify port numbers in the endpoint addresses to get the correct matching. Here is an example:

    spdadd 10.0.11.0/24[any] 10.0.11.33/32[any] any −P out ipsec
        esp/tunnel/192.168.0.1[4500]-192.168.1.2[30000]/require ;

These ports must be left unspecified (which defaults to 0) for anything other than ESP over UDP. They can be displayed in SPD dump using **setkey −DPp**.

Note that "discard" and "none" are not in the syntax described in ipsec_set_policy(3). There are a few differences in the syntax. See ipsec_set_policy(3) for detail.

Algorithms

The following list shows the supported algorithms. **protocol** and **algorithm** are almost orthogonal. These authentication algorithms can be used as *aalgo* in **−A** *aalgo* of the *protocol* parameter:

```
algorithm       keylen (bits)
hmac-md5        128                 ah: rfc2403
                128                 ah-old: rfc2085
hmac-sha1       160                 ah: rfc2404
                160                 ah-old: 128bit ICV (no document)
keyed-md5       128                 ah: 96bit ICV (no document)
                128                 ah-old: rfc1828
keyed-sha1      160                 ah: 96bit ICV (no document)
                160                 ah-old: 128bit ICV (no document)
null            0 to 2048           for debugging
hmac-sha256     256                 ah: 96bit ICV
                                    (draft-ietf-ipsec-ciph-sha-256-00)
                256                 ah-old: 128bit ICV (no document)
hmac-sha384     384                 ah: 96bit ICV (no document)
                384                 ah-old: 128bit ICV (no document)
hmac-sha512     512                 ah: 96bit ICV (no document)
                512                 ah-old: 128bit ICV (no document)
hmac-ripemd160  160                 ah: 96bit ICV (RFC2857)
                                    ah-old: 128bit ICV (no document)
aes-xcbc-mac    128                 ah: 96bit ICV (RFC3566)
                128                 ah-old: 128bit ICV (no document)
tcp-md5         8 to 640            tcp: rfc2385
```

These encryption algorithms can be used as *ealgo* in **−E** *ealgo* of the *protocol* parameter:

```
algorithm       keylen (bits)
des-cbc         64                  esp-old: rfc1829, esp: rfc2405
3des-cbc        192                 rfc2451
null            0 to 2048           rfc2410
blowfish-cbc    40 to 448           rfc2451
cast128-cbc     40 to 128           rfc2451
des-deriv       64                  ipsec-ciph-des-derived-01
3des-deriv      192                 no document
rijndael-cbc    128/192/256         rfc3602
twofish-cbc     0 to 256            draft-ietf-ipsec-ciph-aes-cbc-01
aes-ctr         160/224/288         draft-ietf-ipsec-ciph-aes-ctr-03
camellia-cbc    128/192/256         rfc4312
```

Note that the first 128 bits of a key for aes-ctr will be used as AES key, and the remaining 32 bits will be used as nonce.

These compression algorithms can be used as *calgo* in **−C** *calgo* of the *protocol* parameter:

```
algorithm
deflate         rfc2394
```

RFC vs Linux kernel semantics

The Linux kernel uses the *fwd* policy instead of the *in* policy for packets what are forwarded through that particular box.

In *kernel* mode, **setkey** manages and shows policies and SAs exactly as they are stored in the kernel.

In *RFC* mode, **setkey**

creates *fwd* policies for every *in* policy inserted

(not implemented yet) filters out all *fwd* policies

RETURN VALUES

The command exits with 0 on success, and non-zero on errors.

EXAMPLES

```
add 3ffe:501:4819::1 3ffe:501:481d::1 esp 123457
      -E des-cbc 0x3ffe05014819ffff ;

add -6 myhost.example.com yourhost.example.com ah 123456
      -A hmac-sha1 "AH SA configuration!" ;

add 10.0.11.41 10.0.11.33 esp 0x10001
      -E des-cbc 0x3ffe05014819ffff
      -A hmac-md5 "authentication!!" ;

get 3ffe:501:4819::1 3ffe:501:481d::1 ah 123456 ;

flush ;

dump esp ;

spdadd 10.0.11.41/32[21] 10.0.11.33/32[any] any
      -P out ipsec esp/tunnel/192.168.0.1-192.168.1.2/require ;

add 10.1.10.34 10.1.10.36 tcp 0x1000 -A tcp-md5 "TCP-MD5 BGP secret" ;

add 10.0.11.41 10.0.11.33 esp 0x10001
      -ctx 1 1 "system_u:system_r:unconfined_t:SystemLow-SystemHigh"
      -E des-cbc 0x3ffe05014819ffff;

spdadd 10.0.11.41 10.0.11.33 any
      -ctx 1 1 "system_u:system_r:unconfined_t:SystemLow-SystemHigh"
      -P out ipsec esp/transport//require ;
```

SEE ALSO

ipsec_set_policy(3), racoon(8), sysctl(8)

Changed manual key configuration for IPsec, October 1999.

HISTORY

The **setkey** command first appeared in the WIDE Hydrangea IPv6 protocol stack kit. The command was completely re-designed in June 1998.

BUGS

    setkey should report and handle syntax errors better.

    For IPsec gateway configuration, *src_range* and *dst_range* with TCP/UDP port numbers does not work, as the gateway does not reassemble packets (it cannot inspect upper-layer headers).

NAME

setnetbootinfo — configure Alpha network bootstrap program

SYNOPSIS

/usr/mdec/setnetbootinfo [**-vf**] [**-o** *outfile*] [**-a** *ether-address* | **-h**
ether-host] *infile*
/usr/mdec/setnetbootinfo [**-v**] **-u** **-o** *outfile infile*

DESCRIPTION

The **setnetbootinfo** utility configures the NetBSD/alpha network bootstrap program so that it can be used to bootstrap systems with old firmware revisions.

The NetBSD/alpha network bootstrap program needs to have the ethernet address of the interface being used to boot the system available when querying other hosts on the network for bootstrapping information. Alpha systems with old firmware revisions provide no way for network bootstrap programs to determine the ethernet address of the interface that they are booting from, and so the NetBSD/alpha network bootstrap program must find that information in another way. (Newer firmware revisions include the ethernet address in the name of the device that is being booted from.) The **setnetbootinfo** utility encodes an ethernet address (and other information) directly into the network bootstrap program.

The options recognized by **setnetbootinfo** are as follows:

-a *ether-address*
Encode the given ethernet address into the network bootstrap program. (This option and the **-h** option are mutually exclusive.)

-f   Force the address information being encoded in the bootstrap program to be used regardless of whether or not the bootstrap program can get address information from the booting system's firmware.

-h *ether-host*
Encode the ethernet address of the specified host into the network bootstrap program. The host's name is translated to an ethernet address using the ether_hostton(3) function. (This option and the **-a** option are mutually exclusive.)

-o *outfile*
Output the resulting bootstrap program into the file named by *outfile*, replacing it if it already exists. If the **-o** flag is not specified, the output file name will be the name of the input bootstrap program concatenated with a period and the digits of the ethernet address being encoded. For instance, if the input file is named /usr/mdec/netboot and is being configured to encode the ethernet address 08:00:2b:bd:5d:fd, then the default output file name would be /usr/mdec/netboot.08002bbd5dfd. It is safe to set the output file name to be the same as the input file name; the input file is read in its entirety before the output file is modified.

-u   Remove configuration information from the specified network bootstrap program. If this option is used, an output file name must be specified with the **-o** option, and neither the **-a** or the **-h** options may be specified.

-v   Verbose mode.

FILES

/usr/mdec/netboot   network bootstrap program

SEE ALSO
boot(8), bootpd(8)

HISTORY
The NetBSD/alpha **setnetbootinfo** command first appeared in NetBSD 1.3.

AUTHORS
The **setnetbootinfo** utility was written by Chris Demetriou.

NAME
    setobjstat — set SCSI Environmental Services Device object status

SYNOPSIS
    setobjstat *device objectid stat0 stat1 stat2 stat3*

DESCRIPTION
    setobjstat sets the object status for a SCSI Environmental Services (or SAF-TE) device. The *objectid* argument may be determined by running getencstat(8).

    The status fields are partially common (first byte only, which must have a value of 0x80 contained in it), but otherwise quite device specific. A complete discussion of the possible values is impractical here. Please refer to the ANSI SCSI specification (available on the FTP site ftp.t10.org).

    Note that devices may simply and silently ignore the setting of these values.

FILES
    /dev/ses*N* SCSI Environmental Services Devices

SEE ALSO
    ses(4), getencstat(8), sesd(8), setencstat(8)

NAME
sftp-server — SFTP server subsystem

SYNOPSIS
sftp-server [**-f** *log_facility*] [**-l** *log_level*]

DESCRIPTION
sftp-server is a program that speaks the server side of SFTP protocol to stdout and expects client requests from stdin. **sftp-server** is not intended to be called directly, but from sshd(8) using the **Subsystem** option.

Command-line flags to **sftp-server** should be specified in the **Subsystem** declaration. See sshd_config(5) for more information.

Valid options are:

-f *log_facility*
> Specifies the facility code that is used when logging messages from **sftp-server**. The possible values are: DAEMON, USER, AUTH, LOCAL0, LOCAL1, LOCAL2, LOCAL3, LOCAL4, LOCAL5, LOCAL6, LOCAL7. The default is AUTH.

-l *log_level*
> Specifies which messages will be logged by **sftp-server**. The possible values are: QUIET, FATAL, ERROR, INFO, VERBOSE, DEBUG, DEBUG1, DEBUG2, and DEBUG3. INFO and VERBOSE log transactions that **sftp-server** performs on behalf of the client. DEBUG and DEBUG1 are equivalent. DEBUG2 and DEBUG3 each specify higher levels of debugging output. The default is ERROR.

For logging to work, **sftp-server** must be able to access /dev/log. Use of **sftp-server** in a chroot configuration therefore requires that syslogd(8) establish a logging socket inside the chroot directory.

SEE ALSO
sftp(1), ssh(1), sshd_config(5), sshd(8)

T. Ylonen and S. Lehtinen, *SSH File Transfer Protocol*, draft-ietf-secsh-filexfer-00.txt, January 2001, work in progress material.

HISTORY
sftp-server first appeared in OpenBSD 2.8.

AUTHORS
Markus Friedl ⟨markus@openbsd.org⟩

NAME

/usr/mdec/sgivol — configure SGI Volume Header

SYNOPSIS

/usr/mdec/sgivol [-fq] *device*
/usr/mdec/sgivol [-fq] -i [-h *vhsize*] *device*
/usr/mdec/sgivol [-fq] -r *vhfilename diskfilename device*
/usr/mdec/sgivol [-fq] -w *vhfilename diskfilename device*
/usr/mdec/sgivol [-fq] -d *vhfilename device*
/usr/mdec/sgivol [-fq] -m *vhfilename vhfilename device*
/usr/mdec/sgivol [-fq] -p *partno partfirst partblocks parttype device*

DESCRIPTION

The /usr/mdec/sgivol program prepares an SGI Volume Header to be used to boot NetBSD. The SGI PROM is able to load executables within the header, which in turn are used to load the kernel from another file system.

OPTIONS

The following options are available:

-f   Force the operation. Do not ask the user before proceeding.

-h   Set the size of the newly initialized volume header in blocks. One block is 512 bytes. The default volume header size is 3135 blocks (1.53MB).

-q   Suppress output.

PARTITION TYPES

The numerical partition types for the volume header include:

0:	Volume Header
1:	Replicated Tracks
2:	Replicated Sectors
3:	Raw
4:	BSD4.2 file system
5:	SysV file system
6:	Entire Volume (all disk blocks)
7:	EFS
8:	Logical Volume
9:	Raw Logical Volume
10:	XFS
11:	XFS Log
12:	XLV Volume
13:	XVM Volume

EXAMPLES

To display the existing volume header and partition table on disk "sd0":

    sgivol sd0

To initialize a new volume header 42 512-byte blocks large on disk "sd0":

    sgivol -i -h 42 sd0

To copy a file boot from the volume header to local file /tmp/boot on disk "sd0":

    sgivol -r boot /tmp/boot sd0

To copy a local file /usr/mdec/ip2xboot to the volume header as boot on disk "sd0":

        sgivol −w boot /usr/mdec/ip2xboot sd0

To delete the existing file boot from the volume header on disk "sd0":

        sgivol −d boot sd0

To move (rename) an existing file file1 to file2 in the volume header on disk "sd0":

        sgivol −m file1 file2 sd0

To change partition 0 to type 4 (BSD4.2) beginning at block offset 3200 and continue for 28000 blocks on disk "sd0":

        sgivol −p 0 3200 28000 4 sd0

SEE ALSO

        boot(8)

NAME
   showmount — show remote NFS mounts on host

SYNOPSIS
   showmount [**-ade3**] [*host*]

DESCRIPTION
   showmount shows status information about the NFS server on *host*. By default it prints the names of all
   hosts that have NFS file systems mounted on the host. See *NFS: Network File System Protocol Specification*,
   RFC 1094, Appendix A, and *NFS: Network File System Version 3 Protocol Specification*, Appendix I, for a
   detailed description of the protocol.

   -a   List all mount points in the form:
                   host:*dirpath*

   -d   List directory paths of mount points instead of hosts

   -e   Show the *host*'s exports list

   -3   Use mount protocol Version 3, compatible with NFS Version 3.

SEE ALSO
   mount(8), mountd(8)

HISTORY
   The **showmount** utility first appeared in 4.4BSD.

BUGS
   The mount daemon running on the server only has an idea of the actual mounts, since the NFS server is state-
   less. **showmount** will only display the information as accurately as the mount daemon reports it.

NAME
showq – list the Postfix mail queue

SYNOPSIS
showq [generic Postfix daemon options]

DESCRIPTION
The **showq**(8) daemon reports the Postfix mail queue status. It is the program that emulates the sendmail 'mailq' command.

The **showq**(8) daemon can also be run in stand-alone mode by the superuser. This mode of operation is used to emulate the 'mailq' command while the Postfix mail system is down.

SECURITY
The **showq**(8) daemon can run in a chroot jail at fixed low privilege, and takes no input from the client. Its service port is accessible to local untrusted users, so the service can be susceptible to denial of service attacks.

STANDARDS
None. The **showq**(8) daemon does not interact with the outside world.

DIAGNOSTICS
Problems and transactions are logged to **syslogd**(8).

CONFIGURATION PARAMETERS
Changes to **main.cf** are picked up automatically as **showq**(8) processes run for only a limited amount of time. Use the command "**postfix reload**" to speed up a change.

The text below provides only a parameter summary. See **postconf**(5) for more details including examples.

config_directory (see 'postconf -d' output)
The default location of the Postfix main.cf and master.cf configuration files.

daemon_timeout (18000s)
How much time a Postfix daemon process may take to handle a request before it is terminated by a built-in watchdog timer.

duplicate_filter_limit (1000)
The maximal number of addresses remembered by the address duplicate filter for **aliases**(5) or **virtual**(5) alias expansion, or for **showq**(8) queue displays.

empty_address_recipient (MAILER-DAEMON)
The recipient of mail addressed to the null address.

ipc_timeout (3600s)
The time limit for sending or receiving information over an internal communication channel.

max_idle (100s)
The maximum amount of time that an idle Postfix daemon process waits for an incoming connection before terminating voluntarily.

max_use (100)
The maximal number of incoming connections that a Postfix daemon process will service before terminating voluntarily.

process_id (read-only)
The process ID of a Postfix command or daemon process.

process_name (read-only)
The process name of a Postfix command or daemon process.

queue_directory (see 'postconf -d' output)
The location of the Postfix top-level queue directory.

syslog_facility (mail)
> The syslog facility of Postfix logging.

syslog_name (see 'postconf -d' output)
> The mail system name that is prepended to the process name in syslog records, so that "smtpd" becomes, for example, "postfix/smtpd".

FILES
/var/spool/postfix, queue directories

SEE ALSO
pickup(8), local mail pickup service
cleanup(8), canonicalize and enqueue mail
qmgr(8), queue manager
postconf(5), configuration parameters
master(8), process manager
syslogd(8), system logging

LICENSE
The Secure Mailer license must be distributed with this software.

AUTHOR(S)
Wietse Venema
IBM T.J. Watson Research
P.O. Box 704
Yorktown Heights, NY 10598, USA

NAME

shutdown — close down the system at a given time

SYNOPSIS

shutdown [**-b** *bootstr*] [**-Ddfhknpr**] *time* [*message* . . . | -]

DESCRIPTION

shutdown provides an automated shutdown procedure for super-users to nicely notify users when the system is shutting down, saving them from system administrators, hackers, and gurus, who would otherwise not bother with such niceties.

Available friendlinesses:

-b *bootstr*
> The given *bootstr* is passed to reboot(8) for the benefit of those systems that can pass boot arguments to the firmware. Currently, this only affects sun3 and sparc machines.

-d
> **shutdown** will pass the **-d** flag to reboot(8) or halt(8) to request a kernel core dump. If neither the **-h** or **-r** flags are specified, then **-d** also implies **-r**.

-f
> **shutdown** arranges, in the manner of fastboot(8), for the file systems *not to be* checked on reboot.

-h
> The system is halted at the specified *time*, using halt(8).

-k
> Kick everybody off. The **-k** option does not actually halt the system, but leaves the system multi-user with logins disabled (for all but super-user).

-n
> Prevent the normal sync(2) before stopping.

-p
> The system is powered down at the specified *time*, using halt(8). If the powerdown fails, or the system does not support software powerdown, the system will simply halt instead.

-r
> The system is rebooted at the specified *time*, using reboot(8).

-D
> Prevents **shutdown** from detaching from the tty with fork(2)/ exit(3).

time
> *Time* is the time at which **shutdown** will bring the system down and may be the word *now* or a future time in one of two formats: *+number*, or *[[[[[cc]yy]mm]dd]hh]mn*, where the century, year, month, day, and hour may be defaulted to the current system values. The first form brings the system down *number* minutes from the current time; the second brings the system down at the absolute time specified. If the century is not specified, it defaults to 1900 for years between 69 and 99, or 2000 for years between 0 and 68. A leading zero in the "yy" value is *not* optional.

message . . .
> Any other arguments comprise the warning message that is broadcast to users currently logged into the system.

-
> If - is supplied as the only argument after the time, the warning message is read from the standard input.

BEHAVIOR

At intervals, becoming more frequent as apocalypse approaches and starting at ten hours before shutdown, warning messages are displayed on the terminals of all users logged in. Five minutes before shutdown, or immediately if shutdown is in less than 5 minutes, logins are disabled by creating /etc/nologin and copying the warning message there. If this file exists when a user attempts to log in, login(1) prints its contents and exits. The file is removed just before **shutdown** exits.

SHUTDOWN (8)   NetBSD   SHUTDOWN (8)

At shutdown time, a message is written in the system log containing the time of shutdown, who initiated the shutdown, and the reason. Next a message is printed announcing the start of the system shutdown hooks. Then the shutdown hooks in `/etc/rc.shutdown` are run, and a message is printed indicating that they have completed. After a short delay, **shutdown** runs `halt`(8) or `reboot`(8), or sends a terminate signal to `init`(8) to bring the system down to single-user mode, depending on the choice of options.

The time of the shutdown and the warning message are placed in `/etc/nologin` and should be used to tell the users why the system is going down, when it will be back up, and to share any other pertinent information.

FILES
    `/etc/nologin`   tells `login`(1) not to let anyone log in
    `/fastboot`   tells `rc`(8) not to run `fsck`(8) when rebooting
    `/etc/rc.shutdown` System shutdown commands

SEE ALSO
    `login`(1), `wall`(1), `fastboot`(8), `halt`(8), `init`(8), `poweroff`(8), `reboot`(8), `rescue`(8)

BACKWARD COMPATIBILITY
    The hours and minutes in the second time format may be separated by a colon (":") for backward compatibility.

HISTORY
    The **shutdown** command appeared in 4.0BSD.

NAME

    slattach — attach serial lines as network interfaces

SYNOPSIS

    slattach [**-Hhlmn**] [**-s** *baudrate*] [**-t** *ldisc*] *ttyname*

DESCRIPTION

    slattach is used to assign a tty line to a network interface which uses asynchronous serial lines.

    Currently the **slattach** command is used to attach sl(4) or strip(4) interfaces. These interfaces have to be created using the ifconfig(8) **create** subcommand before the **slattach** command. The network source and destination addresses and other interface parameters are configured via ifconfig(8).

    The following operands are supported by **slattach**:

    -H   Turn on DTR/CTS flow control. By default, no flow control is done.

    -h   Turn on RTS/CTS flow control. By default, no flow control is done.

    -l   Turn on the CLOCAL flag, making it possible to run SLIP on a cable without modem control signals (e.g. DTR, DSR, DCD).

    -m   Maintain modem control signals after closing the line. Specifically, this disables HUPCL.

    -n   Don't detach from invoking tty.

    -s *baudrate*

          Specifies the speed of the connection. If not specified, the default of 9600 is used.

    -t *ldisc*   Specifies the line discipline to use for the tty. Supported line disciplines are "slip" (creates a sl(4) instance) and "strip" (creates a strip(4) instance). If this option is not specified, the default is "slip".

    ttyname   Specifies the name of the tty device. *ttyname* should be a string of the form ttyXX, or /dev/ttyXX.

    Only the super-user may attach a network interface.

    To detach the interface, use "ifconfig interface-name down" after killing off the **slattach** process. *Interface-name* is the name that is shown by netstat(1).

EXAMPLES

        slattach ttyh8
        slattach -s 4800 /dev/tty01

DIAGNOSTICS

    Messages indicating that the specified interface is not configured or created, the requested address is unknown, or that the user is not privileged but tried to alter an interface's configuration.

SEE ALSO

    netstat(1), daemon(3), netintro(4), sl(4), strip(4), ifconfig(8), rc(8), sliplogin(8), slstats(8)

HISTORY

    The **slattach** command appeared in 4.3 BSD.

BUGS

There is no way to specify the interface name (sl%d etc.) to be attached by the **slattach** command. There is no way to see which interface is assigned to the specified tty by the **slattach** command, either.

It would be better if the network interfaces were created by the **slattach** command rather than by using the ifconfig(8) **create** subcommand before the **slattach** command.

NAME

sliplogin — attach a serial line network interface

SYNOPSIS

sliplogin [*loginname*]

DESCRIPTION

sliplogin is used to turn the terminal line on standard input into a Serial Line IP (SLIP) link to a remote host. To do this, the program searches the file /etc/sliphome/slip.hosts for an entry matching *loginname* (which defaults to the current login name if omitted). If a matching entry is found, the line is configured appropriately for slip (8-bit transparent i/o) and converted to SLIP line discipline. Then a shell script is invoked to initialize the slip interface with the appropriate local and remote IP address, netmask, etc.

The usual initialization script is /etc/sliphome/slip.login but, if particular hosts need special initialization, the file /etc/sliphome/slip.login.*loginname* will be executed instead if it exists. The script is invoked with the parameters

slipunit   The unit number of the slip interface assigned to this line. E.g., **0** for **sl0**.

speed   The speed of the line.

args   The arguments from the /etc/sliphome/slip.hosts entry, in order starting with *loginname*.

Only the super-user may attach a network interface. The interface is automatically detached when the other end hangs up or the **sliplogin** process dies. If the kernel slip module has been configured for it, all routes through that interface will also disappear at the same time. If there is other processing a site would like done on hangup, the file /etc/sliphome/slip.logcut or /etc/sliphome/slip.logout.*loginname* is executed if it exists. It is given the same arguments as the login script.

Format of /etc/sliphome/slip.hosts

Comments (lines starting with a '#') and blank lines are ignored. Other lines must start with a *loginname* but the remaining arguments can be whatever is appropriate for the slip.login file that will be executed for that name. Arguments are separated by white space and follow normal sh(1) quoting conventions (however, *loginname* cannot be quoted). Usually, lines have the form

        loginname local-address remote-address netmask opt-args

where *local-address* and *remote-address* are the IP host names or addresses of the local and remote ends of the slip line and *netmask* is the appropriate IP netmask. These arguments are passed directly to ifconfig(8). *opt-args* are optional arguments used to configure the line.

EXAMPLES

The normal use of **sliplogin** is to create a /etc/passwd entry for each legal, remote slip site with **sliplogin** as the shell for that entry. E.g.,

Sfoo:ikhuy6:2010:1:slip line to foo:/tmp:/usr/sbin/sliplogin

(Our convention is to name the account used by remote host *hostname* as *Shostname*.) Then an entry is added to slip.hosts that looks like:

        Sfoo   'hostname'   foo   netmask

where *'hostname'* will be evaluated by sh(1) to the local host name and *netmask* is the local host IP netmask.

Note that **sliplogin** must be setuid to root and, while not a security hole, moral defectives can use it to place terminal lines in an unusable state and/or deny access to legitimate users of a remote slip line. To prevent this, a site can create a group, say *slip*, that only the slip login accounts are put in then make sure that /usr/sbin/sliplogin is in group *slip* and mode 4550 (setuid root, only group *slip* can execute binary).

DIAGNOSTICS

sliplogin logs various information to the system log daemon, syslogd(8), with a facility code of *daemon*. The messages are listed here, grouped by severity level.

Error Severity
ioctl (TCGETS): *reason*
> A TCGETS **ioctl**() to get the line parameters failed.

ioctl (TCSETS): *reason*
> A TCSETS **ioctl**() to set the line parameters failed.

/etc/sliphome/slip.hosts: *reason*
> The /etc/sliphome/slip.hosts file could not be opened.

access denied for *user*
> No entry for *user* was found in /etc/sliphome/slip.hosts.

Notice Severity
attaching slip unit *unit* **for** loginname
> SLIP unit *unit* was successfully attached.

SEE ALSO
sl(4), slattach(8), syslogd(8)

HISTORY
The **sliplogin** command is currently in beta test.

NAME

smtp – Postfix SMTP+LMTP client

SYNOPSIS

smtp [generic Postfix daemon options]

DESCRIPTION

The Postfix SMTP+LMTP client implements the SMTP and LMTP mail delivery protocols. It processes message delivery requests from the queue manager. Each request specifies a queue file, a sender address, a domain or host to deliver to, and recipient information. This program expects to be run from the **master**(8) process manager.

The SMTP+LMTP client updates the queue file and marks recipients as finished, or it informs the queue manager that delivery should be tried again at a later time. Delivery status reports are sent to the **bounce**(8), **defer**(8) or **trace**(8) daemon as appropriate.

The SMTP+LMTP client looks up a list of mail exchanger addresses for the destination host, sorts the list by preference, and connects to each listed address until it finds a server that responds.

When a server is not reachable, or when mail delivery fails due to a recoverable error condition, the SMTP+LMTP client will try to deliver the mail to an alternate host.

After a successful mail transaction, a connection may be saved to the **scache**(8) connection cache server, so that it may be used by any SMTP+LMTP client for a subsequent transaction.

By default, connection caching is enabled temporarily for destinations that have a high volume of mail in the active queue. Connection caching can be enabled permanently for specific destinations.

SMTP DESTINATION SYNTAX

SMTP destinations have the following form:

domainname

domainname:port

> Look up the mail exchangers for the specified domain, and connect to the specified port (default: **smtp**).

[*hostname*]

[*hostname*]:*port*

> Look up the address(es) of the specified host, and connect to the specified port (default: **smtp**).

[*address*]

[*address*]:*port*

> Connect to the host at the specified address, and connect to the specified port (default: **smtp**). An IPv6 address must be formatted as [**ipv6**:*address*].

LMTP DESTINATION SYNTAX

LMTP destinations have the following form:

unix:*pathname*

> Connect to the local UNIX-domain server that is bound to the specified *pathname*. If the process runs chrooted, an absolute pathname is interpreted relative to the Postfix queue directory.

inet:*hostname*

inet:*hostname*:*port*

inet:[*address*]

> **inet**:[*address*]:*port*
> Connect to the specified TCP port on the specified local or remote host. If no port is specified, connect to the port defined as **lmtp** in **services**(4). If no such service is found, the **lmtp_tcp_port** configuration parameter (default value of 24) will be used. An IPv6 address must be formatted as [**ipv6**:*address*].

SECURITY

The SMTP+LMTP client is moderately security-sensitive. It talks to SMTP or LMTP servers and to DNS servers on the network. The SMTP+LMTP client can be run chrooted at fixed low privilege.

STANDARDS

RFC 821 (SMTP protocol)
RFC 822 (ARPA Internet Text Messages)
RFC 1651 (SMTP service extensions)
RFC 1652 (8bit-MIME transport)
RFC 1870 (Message Size Declaration)
RFC 2033 (LMTP protocol)
RFC 2034 (SMTP Enhanced Error Codes)
RFC 2045 (MIME: Format of Internet Message Bodies)
RFC 2046 (MIME: Media Types)
RFC 2554 (AUTH command)
RFC 2821 (SMTP protocol)
RFC 2920 (SMTP Pipelining)
RFC 3207 (STARTTLS command)
RFC 3461 (SMTP DSN Extension)
RFC 3463 (Enhanced Status Codes)
RFC 4954 (AUTH command)

DIAGNOSTICS

Problems and transactions are logged to **syslogd**(8). Corrupted message files are marked so that the queue manager can move them to the **corrupt** queue for further inspection.

Depending on the setting of the **notify_classes** parameter, the postmaster is notified of bounces, protocol problems, and of other trouble.

BUGS

SMTP and LMTP connection caching does not work with TLS. The necessary support for TLS object passivation and re-activation does not exist without closing the session, which defeats the purpose.

SMTP and LMTP connection caching assumes that SASL credentials are valid for all destinations that map onto the same IP address and TCP port.

CONFIGURATION PARAMETERS

Before Postfix version 2.3, the LMTP client is a separate program that implements only a subset of the functionality available with SMTP: there is no support for TLS, and connections are cached in-process, making it ineffective when the client is used for multiple domains.

Most smtp_*xxx* configuration parameters have an lmtp_*xxx* "mirror" parameter for the equivalent LMTP feature. This document describes only those LMTP-related parameters that aren't simply "mirror" parameters.

Changes to **main.cf** are picked up automatically, as **smtp**(8) processes run for only a limited amount of time. Use the command "**postfix reload**" to speed up a change.

The text below provides only a parameter summary. See **postconf**(5) for more details including examples.

COMPATIBILITY CONTROLS

ignore_mx_lookup_error (no)

> Ignore DNS MX lookups that produce no response.

smtp_always_send_ehlo (yes)

> Always send EHLO at the start of an SMTP session.

smtp_never_send_ehlo (no)

> Never send EHLO at the start of an SMTP session.

smtp_defer_if_no_mx_address_found (no)

> Defer mail delivery when no MX record resolves to an IP address.

smtp_line_length_limit (990)

> The maximal length of message header and body lines that Postfix will send via SMTP.

smtp_pix_workaround_delay_time (10s)

> How long the Postfix SMTP client pauses before sending ".<CR><LF>" in order to work around the PIX firewall "<CR><LF>.<CR><LF>" bug.

smtp_pix_workaround_threshold_time (500s)

> How long a message must be queued before the Postfix SMTP client turns on the PIX firewall "<CR><LF>.<CR><LF>" bug workaround for delivery through firewalls with "smtp fixup" mode turned on.

smtp_pix_workarounds (disable_esmtp, delay_dotcrlf)

> A list that specifies zero or more workarounds for CISCO PIX firewall bugs.

smtp_pix_workaround_maps (empty)

> Lookup tables, indexed by the remote SMTP server address, with per-destination workarounds for CISCO PIX firewall bugs.

smtp_quote_rfc821_envelope (yes)

> Quote addresses in SMTP MAIL FROM and RCPT TO commands as required by RFC 2821.

smtp_skip_5xx_greeting (yes)

> Skip SMTP servers that greet with a 5XX status code (go away, do not try again later).

smtp_skip_quit_response (yes)

> Do not wait for the response to the SMTP QUIT command.

Available in Postfix version 2.0 and earlier:

smtp_skip_4xx_greeting (yes)

> Skip SMTP servers that greet with a 4XX status code (go away, try again later).

Available in Postfix version 2.2 and later:

smtp_discard_ehlo_keyword_address_maps (empty)

> Lookup tables, indexed by the remote SMTP server address, with case insensitive lists of EHLO keywords (pipelining, starttls, auth, etc.) that the Postfix SMTP client will ignore in the EHLO response from a remote SMTP server.

smtp_discard_ehlo_keywords (empty)

> A case insensitive list of EHLO keywords (pipelining, starttls, auth, etc.) that the Postfix SMTP client will ignore in the EHLO response from a remote SMTP server.

smtp_generic_maps (empty)

> Optional lookup tables that perform address rewriting in the SMTP client, typically to transform a locally valid address into a globally valid address when sending mail across the Internet.

Available in Postfix version 2.2.9 and later:

smtp_cname_overrides_servername (version dependent)

> Allow DNS CNAME records to override the servername that the Postfix SMTP client uses for logging, SASL password lookup, TLS policy decisions, or TLS certificate verification.

Available in Postfix version 2.3 and later:

lmtp_discard_lhlo_keyword_address_maps (empty)
> Lookup tables, indexed by the remote LMTP server address, with case insensitive lists of LHLO keywords (pipelining, starttls, auth, etc.) that the LMTP client will ignore in the LHLO response from a remote LMTP server.

lmtp_discard_lhlo_keywords (empty)
> A case insensitive list of LHLO keywords (pipelining, starttls, auth, etc.) that the LMTP client will ignore in the LHLO response from a remote LMTP server.

Available in Postfix version 2.4.4 and later:

send_cyrus_sasl_authzid (no)
> When authenticating to a remote SMTP or LMTP server with the default setting "no", send no SASL authoriZation ID (authzid); send only the SASL authentiCation ID (authcid) plus the authcid's password.

Available in Postfix version 2.5 and later:

smtp_header_checks (empty)
> Restricted **header_checks**(5) tables for the Postfix SMTP client.

smtp_mime_header_checks (empty)
> Restricted **mime_header_checks**(5) tables for the Postfix SMTP client.

smtp_nested_header_checks (empty)
> Restricted **nested_header_checks**(5) tables for the Postfix SMTP client.

smtp_body_checks (empty)
> Restricted **body_checks**(5) tables for the Postfix SMTP client.

Available in Postfix version 2.6 and later:

tcp_windowsize (0)
> An optional workaround for routers that break TCP window scaling.

MIME PROCESSING CONTROLS
Available in Postfix version 2.0 and later:

disable_mime_output_conversion (no)
> Disable the conversion of 8BITMIME format to 7BIT format.

mime_boundary_length_limit (2048)
> The maximal length of MIME multipart boundary strings.

mime_nesting_limit (100)
> The maximal recursion level that the MIME processor will handle.

EXTERNAL CONTENT INSPECTION CONTROLS
Available in Postfix version 2.1 and later:

smtp_send_xforward_command (no)
> Send the non-standard XFORWARD command when the Postfix SMTP server EHLO response announces XFORWARD support.

SASL AUTHENTICATION CONTROLS
smtp_sasl_auth_enable (no)
> Enable SASL authentication in the Postfix SMTP client.

smtp_sasl_password_maps (empty)
> Optional SMTP client lookup tables with one username:password entry per remote hostname or domain, or sender address when sender-dependent authentication is enabled.

smtp_sasl_security_options (noplaintext, noanonymous)

> Postfix SMTP client SASL security options; as of Postfix 2.3 the list of available features depends on the SASL client implementation that is selected with **smtp_sasl_type**.

Available in Postfix version 2.2 and later:

smtp_sasl_mechanism_filter (empty)

> If non-empty, a Postfix SMTP client filter for the remote SMTP server's list of offered SASL mechanisms.

Available in Postfix version 2.3 and later:

smtp_sender_dependent_authentication (no)

> Enable sender-dependent authentication in the Postfix SMTP client; this is available only with SASL authentication, and disables SMTP connection caching to ensure that mail from different senders will use the appropriate credentials.

smtp_sasl_path (empty)

> Implementation-specific information that the Postfix SMTP client passes through to the SASL plug-in implementation that is selected with **smtp_sasl_type**.

smtp_sasl_type (cyrus)

> The SASL plug-in type that the Postfix SMTP client should use for authentication.

Available in Postfix version 2.5 and later:

smtp_sasl_auth_cache_name (empty)

> An optional table to prevent repeated SASL authentication failures with the same remote SMTP server hostname, username and password.

smtp_sasl_auth_cache_time (90d)

> The maximal age of an smtp_sasl_auth_cache_name entry before it is removed.

smtp_sasl_auth_soft_bounce (yes)

> When a remote SMTP server rejects a SASL authentication request with a 535 reply code, defer mail delivery instead of returning mail as undeliverable.

STARTTLS SUPPORT CONTROLS

Detailed information about STARTTLS configuration may be found in the TLS_README document.

smtp_tls_security_level (empty)

> The default SMTP TLS security level for the Postfix SMTP client; when a non-empty value is specified, this overrides the obsolete parameters smtp_use_tls, smtp_enforce_tls, and smtp_tls_enforce_peername.

smtp_sasl_tls_security_options ($smtp_sasl_security_options)

> The SASL authentication security options that the Postfix SMTP client uses for TLS encrypted SMTP sessions.

smtp_starttls_timeout (300s)

> Time limit for Postfix SMTP client write and read operations during TLS startup and shutdown handshake procedures.

smtp_tls_CAfile (empty)

> A file containing CA certificates of root CAs trusted to sign either remote SMTP server certificates or intermediate CA certificates.

smtp_tls_CApath (empty)

> Directory with PEM format certificate authority certificates that the Postfix SMTP client uses to verify a remote SMTP server certificate.

smtp_tls_cert_file (empty)

> File with the Postfix SMTP client RSA certificate in PEM format.

5

smtp_tls_mandatory_ciphers (medium)
> The minimum TLS cipher grade that the Postfix SMTP client will use with mandatory TLS encryption.

smtp_tls_exclude_ciphers (empty)
> List of ciphers or cipher types to exclude from the Postfix SMTP client cipher list at all TLS security levels.

smtp_tls_mandatory_exclude_ciphers (empty)
> Additional list of ciphers or cipher types to exclude from the SMTP client cipher list at mandatory TLS security levels.

smtp_tls_dcert_file (empty)
> File with the Postfix SMTP client DSA certificate in PEM format.

smtp_tls_dkey_file ($smtp_tls_dcert_file)
> File with the Postfix SMTP client DSA private key in PEM format.

smtp_tls_key_file ($smtp_tls_cert_file)
> File with the Postfix SMTP client RSA private key in PEM format.

smtp_tls_loglevel (0)
> Enable additional Postfix SMTP client logging of TLS activity.

smtp_tls_note_starttls_offer (no)
> Log the hostname of a remote SMTP server that offers STARTTLS, when TLS is not already enabled for that server.

smtp_tls_policy_maps (empty)
> Optional lookup tables with the Postfix SMTP client TLS security policy by next-hop destination; when a non-empty value is specified, this overrides the obsolete smtp_tls_per_site parameter.

smtp_tls_mandatory_protocols (SSLv3, TLSv1)
> List of SSL/TLS protocols that the Postfix SMTP client will use with mandatory TLS encryption.

smtp_tls_scert_verifydepth (9)
> The verification depth for remote SMTP server certificates.

smtp_tls_secure_cert_match (nexthop, dot-nexthop)
> The server certificate peername verification method for the "secure" TLS security level.

smtp_tls_session_cache_database (empty)
> Name of the file containing the optional Postfix SMTP client TLS session cache.

smtp_tls_session_cache_timeout (3600s)
> The expiration time of Postfix SMTP client TLS session cache information.

smtp_tls_verify_cert_match (hostname)
> The server certificate peername verification method for the "verify" TLS security level.

tls_daemon_random_bytes (32)
> The number of pseudo-random bytes that an **smtp**(8) or **smtpd**(8) process requests from the **tlsmgr**(8) server in order to seed its internal pseudo random number generator (PRNG).

tls_high_cipherlist (ALL:!EXPORT:!LOW:!MEDIUM:+RC4:@STRENGTH)
> The OpenSSL cipherlist for "HIGH" grade ciphers.

tls_medium_cipherlist (ALL:!EXPORT:!LOW:+RC4:@STRENGTH)
> The OpenSSL cipherlist for "MEDIUM" or higher grade ciphers.

tls_low_cipherlist (ALL:!EXPORT:+RC4:@STRENGTH)
> The OpenSSL cipherlist for "LOW" or higher grade ciphers.

tls_export_cipherlist (ALL:+RC4:@STRENGTH)
> The OpenSSL cipherlist for "EXPORT" or higher grade ciphers.

tls_null_cipherlist (eNULL:!aNULL)
> The OpenSSL cipherlist for "NULL" grade ciphers that provide authentication without encryption.

Available in Postfix version 2.4 and later:

smtp_sasl_tls_verified_security_options ($smtp_sasl_tls_security_options)
> The SASL authentication security options that the Postfix SMTP client uses for TLS encrypted SMTP sessions with a verified server certificate.

Available in Postfix version 2.5 and later:

smtp_tls_fingerprint_cert_match (empty)
> List of acceptable remote SMTP server certificate fingerprints for the "fingerprint" TLS security level (**smtp_tls_security_level** = fingerprint).

smtp_tls_fingerprint_digest (md5)
> The message digest algorithm used to construct remote SMTP server certificate fingerprints.

Available in Postfix version 2.6 and later:

smtp_tls_protocols (!SSLv2)
> List of TLS protocols that the Postfix SMTP client will exclude or include with opportunistic TLS encryption.

smtp_tls_ciphers (export)
> The minimum TLS cipher grade that the Postfix SMTP client will use with opportunistic TLS encryption.

smtp_tls_eccert_file (empty)
> File with the Postfix SMTP client ECDSA certificate in PEM format.

smtp_tls_eckey_file ($smtp_tls_eccert_file)
> File with the Postfix SMTP client ECDSA private key in PEM format.

OBSOLETE STARTTLS CONTROLS

The following configuration parameters exist for compatibility with Postfix versions before 2.3. Support for these will be removed in a future release.

smtp_use_tls (no)
> Opportunistic mode: use TLS when a remote SMTP server announces STARTTLS support, otherwise send the mail in the clear.

smtp_enforce_tls (no)
> Enforcement mode: require that remote SMTP servers use TLS encryption, and never send mail in the clear.

smtp_tls_enforce_peername (yes)
> With mandatory TLS encryption, require that the remote SMTP server hostname matches the information in the remote SMTP server certificate.

smtp_tls_per_site (empty)
> Optional lookup tables with the Postfix SMTP client TLS usage policy by next-hop destination and by remote SMTP server hostname.

smtp_tls_cipherlist (empty)
> Obsolete Postfix < 2.3 control for the Postfix SMTP client TLS cipher list.

RESOURCE AND RATE CONTROLS

smtp_destination_concurrency_limit ($default_destination_concurrency_limit)
> The maximal number of parallel deliveries to the same destination via the smtp message delivery transport.

smtp_destination_recipient_limit ($default_destination_recipient_limit)
> The maximal number of recipients per message for the smtp message delivery transport.

smtp_connect_timeout (30s)
> The SMTP client time limit for completing a TCP connection, or zero (use the operating system built-in time limit).

smtp_helo_timeout (300s)
> The SMTP client time limit for sending the HELO or EHLO command, and for receiving the initial server response.

lmtp_lhlo_timeout (300s)
> The LMTP client time limit for sending the LHLO command, and for receiving the initial server response.

smtp_xforward_timeout (300s)
> The SMTP client time limit for sending the XFORWARD command, and for receiving the server response.

smtp_mail_timeout (300s)
> The SMTP client time limit for sending the MAIL FROM command, and for receiving the server response.

smtp_rcpt_timeout (300s)
> The SMTP client time limit for sending the SMTP RCPT TO command, and for receiving the server response.

smtp_data_init_timeout (120s)
> The SMTP client time limit for sending the SMTP DATA command, and for receiving the server response.

smtp_data_xfer_timeout (180s)
> The SMTP client time limit for sending the SMTP message content.

smtp_data_done_timeout (600s)
> The SMTP client time limit for sending the SMTP ".", and for receiving the server response.

smtp_quit_timeout (300s)
> The SMTP client time limit for sending the QUIT command, and for receiving the server response.

Available in Postfix version 2.1 and later:

smtp_mx_address_limit (5)
> The maximal number of MX (mail exchanger) IP addresses that can result from mail exchanger lookups, or zero (no limit).

smtp_mx_session_limit (2)
> The maximal number of SMTP sessions per delivery request before giving up or delivering to a fall-back relay host, or zero (no limit).

smtp_rset_timeout (20s)
> The SMTP client time limit for sending the RSET command, and for receiving the server response.

Available in Postfix version 2.2 and earlier:

lmtp_cache_connection (yes)
> Keep Postfix LMTP client connections open for up to $max_idle seconds.

Available in Postfix version 2.2 and later:

smtp_connection_cache_destinations (empty)
> Permanently enable SMTP connection caching for the specified destinations.

smtp_connection_cache_on_demand (yes)
> Temporarily enable SMTP connection caching while a destination has a high volume of mail in the active queue.

smtp_connection_reuse_time_limit (300s)
> The amount of time during which Postfix will use an SMTP connection repeatedly.

smtp_connection_cache_time_limit (2s)
> When SMTP connection caching is enabled, the amount of time that an unused SMTP client socket is kept open before it is closed.

Available in Postfix version 2.3 and later:

connection_cache_protocol_timeout (5s)
> Time limit for connection cache connect, send or receive operations.

TROUBLE SHOOTING CONTROLS

debug_peer_level (2)
> The increment in verbose logging level when a remote client or server matches a pattern in the debug_peer_list parameter.

debug_peer_list (empty)
> Optional list of remote client or server hostname or network address patterns that cause the verbose logging level to increase by the amount specified in $debug_peer_level.

error_notice_recipient (postmaster)
> The recipient of postmaster notifications about mail delivery problems that are caused by policy, resource, software or protocol errors.

internal_mail_filter_classes (empty)
> What categories of Postfix-generated mail are subject to before-queue content inspection by non_smtpd_milters, header_checks and body_checks.

notify_classes (resource, software)
> The list of error classes that are reported to the postmaster.

MISCELLANEOUS CONTROLS

best_mx_transport (empty)
> Where the Postfix SMTP client should deliver mail when it detects a "mail loops back to myself" error condition.

config_directory (see 'postconf -d' output)
> The default location of the Postfix main.cf and master.cf configuration files.

daemon_timeout (18000s)
> How much time a Postfix daemon process may take to handle a request before it is terminated by a built-in watchdog timer.

delay_logging_resolution_limit (2)
> The maximal number of digits after the decimal point when logging sub-second delay values.

disable_dns_lookups (no)
> Disable DNS lookups in the Postfix SMTP and LMTP clients.

inet_interfaces (all)
> The network interface addresses that this mail system receives mail on.

inet_protocols (ipv4)
> The Internet protocols Postfix will attempt to use when making or accepting connections.

ipc_timeout (3600s)
> The time limit for sending or receiving information over an internal communication channel.

lmtp_assume_final (no)
> When an LMTP server announces no DSN support, assume that the server performs final delivery, and send "delivered" delivery status notifications instead of "relayed".

lmtp_tcp_port (24)
> The default TCP port that the Postfix LMTP client connects to.

max_idle (100s)
> The maximum amount of time that an idle Postfix daemon process waits for an incoming connection before terminating voluntarily.

max_use (100)
> The maximal number of incoming connections that a Postfix daemon process will service before terminating voluntarily.

process_id (read-only)
> The process ID of a Postfix command or daemon process.

process_name (read-only)
> The process name of a Postfix command or daemon process.

proxy_interfaces (empty)
> The network interface addresses that this mail system receives mail on by way of a proxy or network address translation unit.

smtp_bind_address (empty)
> An optional numerical network address that the Postfix SMTP client should bind to when making an IPv4 connection.

smtp_bind_address6 (empty)
> An optional numerical network address that the Postfix SMTP client should bind to when making an IPv6 connection.

smtp_helo_name ($myhostname)
> The hostname to send in the SMTP EHLO or HELO command.

lmtp_lhlo_name ($myhostname)
> The hostname to send in the LMTP LHLO command.

smtp_host_lookup (dns)
> What mechanisms when the Postfix SMTP client uses to look up a host's IP address.

smtp_randomize_addresses (yes)
> Randomize the order of equal-preference MX host addresses.

syslog_facility (mail)
> The syslog facility of Postfix logging.

syslog_name (see 'postconf -d' output)
> The mail system name that is prepended to the process name in syslog records, so that "smtpd" becomes, for example, "postfix/smtpd".

Available with Postfix 2.2 and earlier:

fallback_relay (empty)
> Optional list of relay hosts for SMTP destinations that can't be found or that are unreachable.

Available with Postfix 2.3 and later:

smtp_fallback_relay ($fallback_relay)
> Optional list of relay hosts for SMTP destinations that can't be found or that are unreachable.

SEE ALSO

generic(5), output address rewriting
header_checks(5), message header content inspection
body_checks(5), body parts content inspection
qmgr(8), queue manager
bounce(8), delivery status reports
scache(8), connection cache server

> postconf(5), configuration parameters
> master(5), generic daemon options
> master(8), process manager
> tlsmgr(8), TLS session and PRNG management
> syslogd(8), system logging

README FILES

> Use "**postconf readme_directory**" or "**postconf html_directory**" to locate this information.
> SASL_README, Postfix SASL howto
> TLS_README, Postfix STARTTLS howto

LICENSE

> The Secure Mailer license must be distributed with this software.

AUTHOR(S)

> Wietse Venema
> IBM T.J. Watson Research
> P.O. Box 704
> Yorktown Heights, NY 10598, USA
>
> Command pipelining in cooperation with:
> Jon Ribbens
> Oaktree Internet Solutions Ltd.,
> Internet House,
> Canal Basin,
> Coventry,
> CV1 4LY, United Kingdom.
>
> SASL support originally by:
> Till Franke
> SuSE Rhein/Main AG
> 65760 Eschborn, Germany
>
> TLS support originally by:
> Lutz Jaenicke
> BTU Cottbus
> Allgemeine Elektrotechnik
> Universitaetsplatz 3-4
> D-03044 Cottbus, Germany
>
> Revised TLS and SMTP connection cache support by:
> Victor Duchovni
> Morgan Stanley

NAME

smtpd – Postfix SMTP server

SYNOPSIS

smtpd [generic Postfix daemon options]

sendmail -bs

DESCRIPTION

The SMTP server accepts network connection requests and performs zero or more SMTP transactions per connection. Each received message is piped through the **cleanup**(8) daemon, and is placed into the **incoming** queue as one single queue file. For this mode of operation, the program expects to be run from the **master**(8) process manager.

Alternatively, the SMTP server be can run in stand-alone mode; this is traditionally obtained with "**sendmail -bs**". When the SMTP server runs stand-alone with non $**mail_owner** privileges, it receives mail even while the mail system is not running, deposits messages directly into the **maildrop** queue, and disables the SMTP server's access policies. As of Postfix version 2.3, the SMTP server refuses to receive mail from the network when it runs with non $**mail_owner** privileges.

The SMTP server implements a variety of policies for connection requests, and for parameters given to **HELO, ETRN, MAIL FROM, VRFY** and **RCPT TO** commands. They are detailed below and in the **main.cf** configuration file.

SECURITY

The SMTP server is moderately security-sensitive. It talks to SMTP clients and to DNS servers on the network. The SMTP server can be run chrooted at fixed low privilege.

STANDARDS

RFC 821 (SMTP protocol)
RFC 1123 (Host requirements)
RFC 1652 (8bit-MIME transport)
RFC 1869 (SMTP service extensions)
RFC 1870 (Message Size Declaration)
RFC 1985 (ETRN command)
RFC 2034 (SMTP Enhanced Error Codes)
RFC 2554 (AUTH command)
RFC 2821 (SMTP protocol)
RFC 2920 (SMTP Pipelining)
RFC 3207 (STARTTLS command)
RFC 3461 (SMTP DSN Extension)
RFC 3463 (Enhanced Status Codes)
RFC 3848 (ESMTP Transmission Types)
RFC 4954 (AUTH command)

DIAGNOSTICS

Problems and transactions are logged to **syslogd**(8).

Depending on the setting of the **notify_classes** parameter, the postmaster is notified of bounces, protocol problems, policy violations, and of other trouble.

CONFIGURATION PARAMETERS

Changes to **main.cf** are picked up automatically, as **smtpd**(8) processes run for only a limited amount of time. Use the command "**postfix reload**" to speed up a change.

The text below provides only a parameter summary. See **postconf**(5) for more details including examples.

COMPATIBILITY CONTROLS

The following parameters work around implementation errors in other software, and/or allow you to override standards in order to prevent undesirable use.

broken_sasl_auth_clients (no)
> Enable inter-operability with SMTP clients that implement an obsolete version of the AUTH command (RFC 4954).

disable_vrfy_command (no)
> Disable the SMTP VRFY command.

smtpd_noop_commands (empty)
> List of commands that the Postfix SMTP server replies to with "250 Ok", without doing any syntax checks and without changing state.

strict_rfc821_envelopes (no)
> Require that addresses received in SMTP MAIL FROM and RCPT TO commands are enclosed with <>, and that those addresses do not contain RFC 822 style comments or phrases.

Available in Postfix version 2.1 and later:

resolve_null_domain (no)
> Resolve an address that ends in the "@" null domain as if the local hostname were specified, instead of rejecting the address as invalid.

smtpd_reject_unlisted_sender (no)
> Request that the Postfix SMTP server rejects mail from unknown sender addresses, even when no explicit reject_unlisted_sender access restriction is specified.

smtpd_sasl_exceptions_networks (empty)
> What remote SMTP clients the Postfix SMTP server will not offer AUTH support to.

Available in Postfix version 2.2 and later:

smtpd_discard_ehlo_keyword_address_maps (empty)
> Lookup tables, indexed by the remote SMTP client address, with case insensitive lists of EHLO keywords (pipelining, starttls, auth, etc.) that the SMTP server will not send in the EHLO response to a remote SMTP client.

smtpd_discard_ehlo_keywords (empty)
> A case insensitive list of EHLO keywords (pipelining, starttls, auth, etc.) that the SMTP server will not send in the EHLO response to a remote SMTP client.

smtpd_delay_open_until_valid_rcpt (yes)
> Postpone the start of an SMTP mail transaction until a valid RCPT TO command is received.

Available in Postfix version 2.3 and later:

smtpd_tls_always_issue_session_ids (yes)
> Force the Postfix SMTP server to issue a TLS session id, even when TLS session caching is turned off (smtpd_tls_session_cache_database is empty).

Available in Postfix version 2.6 and later:

tcp_windowsize (0)
> An optional workaround for routers that break TCP window scaling.

ADDRESS REWRITING CONTROLS

See the ADDRESS_REWRITING_README document for a detailed discussion of Postfix address rewriting.

receive_override_options (empty)
> Enable or disable recipient validation, built-in content filtering, or address mapping.

Available in Postfix version 2.2 and later:

local_header_rewrite_clients (permit_inet_interfaces)

Rewrite message header addresses in mail from these clients and update incomplete addresses with the domain name in $myorigin or $mydomain; either don't rewrite message headers from other clients at all, or rewrite message headers and update incomplete addresses with the domain specified in the remote_header_rewrite_domain parameter.

AFTER QUEUE EXTERNAL CONTENT INSPECTION CONTROLS

As of version 1.0, Postfix can be configured to send new mail to an external content filter AFTER the mail is queued. This content filter is expected to inject mail back into a (Postfix or other) MTA for further delivery. See the FILTER_README document for details.

content_filter (empty)

The name of a mail delivery transport that filters mail after it is queued.

BEFORE QUEUE EXTERNAL CONTENT INSPECTION CONTROLS

As of version 2.1, the Postfix SMTP server can be configured to send incoming mail to a real-time SMTP-based content filter BEFORE mail is queued. This content filter is expected to inject mail back into Postfix. See the SMTPD_PROXY_README document for details on how to configure and operate this feature.

smtpd_proxy_filter (empty)

The hostname and TCP port of the mail filtering proxy server.

smtpd_proxy_ehlo ($myhostname)

How the Postfix SMTP server announces itself to the proxy filter.

smtpd_proxy_timeout (100s)

The time limit for connecting to a proxy filter and for sending or receiving information.

BEFORE QUEUE MILTER CONTROLS

As of version 2.3, Postfix supports the Sendmail version 8 Milter (mail filter) protocol. These content filters run outside Postfix. They can inspect the SMTP command stream and the message content, and can request modifications before mail is queued. For details see the MILTER_README document.

smtpd_milters (empty)

A list of Milter (mail filter) applications for new mail that arrives via the Postfix **smtpd**(8) server.

milter_protocol (6)

The mail filter protocol version and optional protocol extensions for communication with a Milter application; prior to Postfix 2.6 the default protocol is 2.

milter_default_action (tempfail)

The default action when a Milter (mail filter) application is unavailable or mis-configured.

milter_macro_daemon_name ($myhostname)

The {daemon_name} macro value for Milter (mail filter) applications.

milter_macro_v ($mail_name $mail_version)

The {v} macro value for Milter (mail filter) applications.

milter_connect_timeout (30s)

The time limit for connecting to a Milter (mail filter) application, and for negotiating protocol options.

milter_command_timeout (30s)

The time limit for sending an SMTP command to a Milter (mail filter) application, and for receiving the response.

milter_content_timeout (300s)

The time limit for sending message content to a Milter (mail filter) application, and for receiving the response.

milter_connect_macros (see 'postconf -d' output)

The macros that are sent to Milter (mail filter) applications after completion of an SMTP connection.

milter_helo_macros (see 'postconf -d' output)
> The macros that are sent to Milter (mail filter) applications after the SMTP HELO or EHLO command.

milter_mail_macros (see 'postconf -d' output)
> The macros that are sent to Milter (mail filter) applications after the SMTP MAIL FROM command.

milter_rcpt_macros (see 'postconf -d' output)
> The macros that are sent to Milter (mail filter) applications after the SMTP RCPT TO command.

milter_data_macros (see 'postconf -d' output)
> The macros that are sent to version 4 or higher Milter (mail filter) applications after the SMTP DATA command.

milter_unknown_command_macros (see 'postconf -d' output)
> The macros that are sent to version 3 or higher Milter (mail filter) applications after an unknown SMTP command.

milter_end_of_header_macros (see 'postconf -d' output)
> The macros that are sent to Milter (mail filter) applications after the end of the message header.

milter_end_of_data_macros (see 'postconf -d' output)
> The macros that are sent to Milter (mail filter) applications after the message end-of-data.

GENERAL CONTENT INSPECTION CONTROLS
The following parameters are applicable for both built-in and external content filters.

Available in Postfix version 2.1 and later:

receive_override_options (empty)
> Enable or disable recipient validation, built-in content filtering, or address mapping.

EXTERNAL CONTENT INSPECTION CONTROLS
The following parameters are applicable for both before-queue and after-queue content filtering.

Available in Postfix version 2.1 and later:

smtpd_authorized_xforward_hosts (empty)
> What SMTP clients are allowed to use the XFORWARD feature.

SASL AUTHENTICATION CONTROLS
Postfix SASL support (RFC 4954) can be used to authenticate remote SMTP clients to the Postfix SMTP server, and to authenticate the Postfix SMTP client to a remote SMTP server. See the SASL_README document for details.

broken_sasl_auth_clients (no)
> Enable inter-operability with SMTP clients that implement an obsolete version of the AUTH command (RFC 4954).

smtpd_sasl_auth_enable (no)
> Enable SASL authentication in the Postfix SMTP server.

smtpd_sasl_local_domain (empty)
> The name of the Postfix SMTP server's local SASL authentication realm.

smtpd_sasl_security_options (noanonymous)
> Postfix SMTP server SASL security options; as of Postfix 2.3 the list of available features depends on the SASL server implementation that is selected with **smtpd_sasl_type**.

smtpd_sender_login_maps (empty)
> Optional lookup table with the SASL login names that own sender (MAIL FROM) addresses.

Available in Postfix version 2.1 and later:

smtpd_sasl_exceptions_networks (empty)
> What remote SMTP clients the Postfix SMTP server will not offer AUTH support to.

Available in Postfix version 2.1 and 2.2:

smtpd_sasl_application_name (smtpd)
> The application name that the Postfix SMTP server uses for SASL server initialization.

Available in Postfix version 2.3 and later:

smtpd_sasl_authenticated_header (no)
> Report the SASL authenticated user name in the **smtpd**(8) Received message header.

smtpd_sasl_path (smtpd)
> Implementation-specific information that the Postfix SMTP server passes through to the SASL plug-in implementation that is selected with **smtpd_sasl_type**.

smtpd_sasl_type (cyrus)
> The SASL plug-in type that the Postfix SMTP server should use for authentication.

Available in Postfix version 2.5 and later:

cyrus_sasl_config_path (empty)
> Search path for Cyrus SASL application configuration files, currently used only to locate the $smtpd_sasl_path.conf file.

STARTTLS SUPPORT CONTROLS
Detailed information about STARTTLS configuration may be found in the TLS_README document.

smtpd_tls_security_level (empty)
> The SMTP TLS security level for the Postfix SMTP server; when a non-empty value is specified, this overrides the obsolete parameters smtpd_use_tls and smtpd_enforce_tls.

smtpd_sasl_tls_security_options ($smtpd_sasl_security_options)
> The SASL authentication security options that the Postfix SMTP server uses for TLS encrypted SMTP sessions.

smtpd_starttls_timeout (300s)
> The time limit for Postfix SMTP server write and read operations during TLS startup and shutdown handshake procedures.

smtpd_tls_CAfile (empty)
> A file containing (PEM format) CA certificates of root CAs trusted to sign either remote SMTP client certificates or intermediate CA certificates.

smtpd_tls_CApath (empty)
> A directory containing (PEM format) CA certificates of root CAs trusted to sign either remote SMTP client certificates or intermediate CA certificates.

smtpd_tls_always_issue_session_ids (yes)
> Force the Postfix SMTP server to issue a TLS session id, even when TLS session caching is turned off (smtpd_tls_session_cache_database is empty).

smtpd_tls_ask_ccert (no)
> Ask a remote SMTP client for a client certificate.

smtpd_tls_auth_only (no)
> When TLS encryption is optional in the Postfix SMTP server, do not announce or accept SASL authentication over unencrypted connections.

smtpd_tls_ccert_verifydepth (9)
> The verification depth for remote SMTP client certificates.

smtpd_tls_cert_file (empty)
> File with the Postfix SMTP server RSA certificate in PEM format.

smtpd_tls_exclude_ciphers (empty)
    List of ciphers or cipher types to exclude from the SMTP server cipher list at all TLS security levels.

smtpd_tls_dcert_file (empty)
    File with the Postfix SMTP server DSA certificate in PEM format.

smtpd_tls_dh1024_param_file (empty)
    File with DH parameters that the Postfix SMTP server should use with EDH ciphers.

smtpd_tls_dh512_param_file (empty)
    File with DH parameters that the Postfix SMTP server should use with EDH ciphers.

smtpd_tls_dkey_file ($smtpd_tls_dcert_file)
    File with the Postfix SMTP server DSA private key in PEM format.

smtpd_tls_key_file ($smtpd_tls_cert_file)
    File with the Postfix SMTP server RSA private key in PEM format.

smtpd_tls_loglevel (0)
    Enable additional Postfix SMTP server logging of TLS activity.

smtpd_tls_mandatory_ciphers (medium)
    The minimum TLS cipher grade that the Postfix SMTP server will use with mandatory TLS encryption.

smtpd_tls_mandatory_exclude_ciphers (empty)
    Additional list of ciphers or cipher types to exclude from the SMTP server cipher list at mandatory TLS security levels.

smtpd_tls_mandatory_protocols (SSLv3, TLSv1)
    The SSL/TLS protocols accepted by the Postfix SMTP server with mandatory TLS encryption.

smtpd_tls_received_header (no)
    Request that the Postfix SMTP server produces Received: message headers that include information about the protocol and cipher used, as well as the client CommonName and client certificate issuer CommonName.

smtpd_tls_req_ccert (no)
    With mandatory TLS encryption, require a trusted remote SMTP client certificate in order to allow TLS connections to proceed.

smtpd_tls_session_cache_database (empty)
    Name of the file containing the optional Postfix SMTP server TLS session cache.

smtpd_tls_session_cache_timeout (3600s)
    The expiration time of Postfix SMTP server TLS session cache information.

smtpd_tls_wrappermode (no)
    Run the Postfix SMTP server in the non-standard "wrapper" mode, instead of using the STARTTLS command.

tls_daemon_random_bytes (32)
    The number of pseudo-random bytes that an **smtp**(8) or **smtpd**(8) process requests from the **tlsmgr**(8) server in order to seed its internal pseudo random number generator (PRNG).

tls_high_cipherlist (ALL:!EXPORT:!LOW:!MEDIUM:+RC4:@STRENGTH)
    The OpenSSL cipherlist for "HIGH" grade ciphers.

tls_medium_cipherlist (ALL:!EXPORT:!LOW:+RC4:@STRENGTH)
    The OpenSSL cipherlist for "MEDIUM" or higher grade ciphers.

tls_low_cipherlist (ALL:!EXPORT:+RC4:@STRENGTH)
    The OpenSSL cipherlist for "LOW" or higher grade ciphers.

tls_export_cipherlist (ALL:+RC4:@STRENGTH)
>   The OpenSSL cipherlist for "EXPORT" or higher grade ciphers.

tls_null_cipherlist (eNULL:!aNULL)
>   The OpenSSL cipherlist for "NULL" grade ciphers that provide authentication without encryption.

Available in Postfix version 2.5 and later:

smtpd_tls_fingerprint_digest (md5)
>   The message digest algorithm used to construct client-certificate fingerprints for
>   **check_ccert_access** and **permit_tls_clientcerts**.

Available in Postfix version 2.6 and later:

smtpd_tls_protocols (empty)
>   List of TLS protocols that the Postfix SMTP server will exclude or include with opportunistic TLS
>   encryption.

smtpd_tls_ciphers (export)
>   The minimum TLS cipher grade that the Postfix SMTP server will use with opportunistic TLS
>   encryption.

smtpd_tls_eccert_file (empty)
>   File with the Postfix SMTP server ECDSA certificate in PEM format.

smtpd_tls_eckey_file ($smtpd_tls_eccert_file)
>   File with the Postfix SMTP server ECDSA private key in PEM format.

smtpd_tls_eecdh_grade (see 'postconf -d' output)
>   The Postfix SMTP server security grade for ephemeral elliptic-curve Diffie-Hellman (EECDH)
>   key exchange.

tls_eecdh_strong_curve (prime256v1)
>   The elliptic curve used by the SMTP server for sensibly strong ephemeral ECDH key exchange.

tls_eecdh_ultra_curve (secp384r1)
>   The elliptic curve used by the SMTP server for maximally strong ephemeral ECDH key exchange.

OBSOLETE STARTTLS CONTROLS

The following configuration parameters exist for compatibility with Postfix versions before 2.3. Support for
these will be removed in a future release.

smtpd_use_tls (no)
>   Opportunistic TLS: announce STARTTLS support to SMTP clients, but do not require that clients
>   use TLS encryption.

smtpd_enforce_tls (no)
>   Mandatory TLS: announce STARTTLS support to SMTP clients, and require that clients use TLS
>   encryption.

smtpd_tls_cipherlist (empty)
>   Obsolete Postfix < 2.3 control for the Postfix SMTP server TLS cipher list.

VERP SUPPORT CONTROLS

With VERP style delivery, each recipient of a message receives a customized copy of the message with
his/her own recipient address encoded in the envelope sender address. The VERP_README file describes
configuration and operation details of Postfix support for variable envelope return path addresses. VERP
style delivery is requested with the SMTP XVERP command or with the "sendmail -V" command-line
option and is available in Postfix version 1.1 and later.

default_verp_delimiters (+=)
>   The two default VERP delimiter characters.

verp_delimiter_filter (-=+)
> The characters Postfix accepts as VERP delimiter characters on the Postfix **sendmail**(1) command line and in SMTP commands.

Available in Postfix version 1.1 and 2.0:

authorized_verp_clients ($mynetworks)
> What SMTP clients are allowed to specify the XVERP command.

Available in Postfix version 2.1 and later:

smtpd_authorized_verp_clients ($authorized_verp_clients)
> What SMTP clients are allowed to specify the XVERP command.

TROUBLE SHOOTING CONTROLS

The DEBUG_README document describes how to debug parts of the Postfix mail system. The methods vary from making the software log a lot of detail, to running some daemon processes under control of a call tracer or debugger.

debug_peer_level (2)
> The increment in verbose logging level when a remote client or server matches a pattern in the debug_peer_list parameter.

debug_peer_list (empty)
> Optional list of remote client or server hostname or network address patterns that cause the verbose logging level to increase by the amount specified in $debug_peer_level.

error_notice_recipient (postmaster)
> The recipient of postmaster notifications about mail delivery problems that are caused by policy, resource, software or protocol errors.

internal_mail_filter_classes (empty)
> What categories of Postfix-generated mail are subject to before-queue content inspection by non_smtpd_milters, header_checks and body_checks.

notify_classes (resource, software)
> The list of error classes that are reported to the postmaster.

soft_bounce (no)
> Safety net to keep mail queued that would otherwise be returned to the sender.

Available in Postfix version 2.1 and later:

smtpd_authorized_xclient_hosts (empty)
> What SMTP clients are allowed to use the XCLIENT feature.

KNOWN VERSUS UNKNOWN RECIPIENT CONTROLS

As of Postfix version 2.0, the SMTP server rejects mail for unknown recipients. This prevents the mail queue from clogging up with undeliverable MAILER-DAEMON messages. Additional information on this topic is in the LOCAL_RECIPIENT_README and ADDRESS_CLASS_README documents.

show_user_unknown_table_name (yes)
> Display the name of the recipient table in the "User unknown" responses.

canonical_maps (empty)
> Optional address mapping lookup tables for message headers and envelopes.

recipient_canonical_maps (empty)
> Optional address mapping lookup tables for envelope and header recipient addresses.

Parameters concerning known/unknown local recipients:

mydestination ($myhostname, localhost.$mydomain, localhost)
> The list of domains that are delivered via the $local_transport mail delivery transport.

inet_interfaces (all)
> The network interface addresses that this mail system receives mail on.

proxy_interfaces (empty)
> The network interface addresses that this mail system receives mail on by way of a proxy or network address translation unit.

inet_protocols (ipv4)
> The Internet protocols Postfix will attempt to use when making or accepting connections.

local_recipient_maps (proxy:unix:passwd.byname $alias_maps)
> Lookup tables with all names or addresses of local recipients: a recipient address is local when its domain matches $mydestination, $inet_interfaces or $proxy_interfaces.

unknown_local_recipient_reject_code (550)
> The numerical Postfix SMTP server response code when a recipient address is local, and $local_recipient_maps specifies a list of lookup tables that does not match the recipient.

Parameters concerning known/unknown recipients of relay destinations:

relay_domains ($mydestination)
> What destination domains (and subdomains thereof) this system will relay mail to.

relay_recipient_maps (empty)
> Optional lookup tables with all valid addresses in the domains that match $relay_domains.

unknown_relay_recipient_reject_code (550)
> The numerical Postfix SMTP server reply code when a recipient address matches $relay_domains, and relay_recipient_maps specifies a list of lookup tables that does not match the recipient address.

Parameters concerning known/unknown recipients in virtual alias domains:

virtual_alias_domains ($virtual_alias_maps)
> Postfix is final destination for the specified list of virtual alias domains, that is, domains for which all addresses are aliased to addresses in other local or remote domains.

virtual_alias_maps ($virtual_maps)
> Optional lookup tables that alias specific mail addresses or domains to other local or remote address.

unknown_virtual_alias_reject_code (550)
> The SMTP server reply code when a recipient address matches $virtual_alias_domains, and $virtual_alias_maps specifies a list of lookup tables that does not match the recipient address.

Parameters concerning known/unknown recipients in virtual mailbox domains:

virtual_mailbox_domains ($virtual_mailbox_maps)
> Postfix is final destination for the specified list of domains; mail is delivered via the $virtual_transport mail delivery transport.

virtual_mailbox_maps (empty)
> Optional lookup tables with all valid addresses in the domains that match $virtual_mailbox_domains.

unknown_virtual_mailbox_reject_code (550)
> The SMTP server reply code when a recipient address matches $virtual_mailbox_domains, and $virtual_mailbox_maps specifies a list of lookup tables that does not match the recipient address.

RESOURCE AND RATE CONTROLS
The following parameters limit resource usage by the SMTP server and/or control client request rates.

line_length_limit (2048)
> Upon input, long lines are chopped up into pieces of at most this length; upon delivery, long lines are reconstructed.

queue_minfree (0)
> The minimal amount of free space in bytes in the queue file system that is needed to receive mail.

message_size_limit (10240000)
> The maximal size in bytes of a message, including envelope information.

smtpd_recipient_limit (1000)
> The maximal number of recipients that the Postfix SMTP server accepts per message delivery request.

smtpd_timeout (normal: 300s, stress: 10s)
> The time limit for sending a Postfix SMTP server response and for receiving a remote SMTP client request.

smtpd_history_flush_threshold (100)
> The maximal number of lines in the Postfix SMTP server command history before it is flushed upon receipt of EHLO, RSET, or end of DATA.

Available in Postfix version 2.3 and later:

smtpd_peername_lookup (yes)
> Attempt to look up the remote SMTP client hostname, and verify that the name matches the client IP address.

The per SMTP client connection count and request rate limits are implemented in co-operation with the **anvil**(8) service, and are available in Postfix version 2.2 and later.

smtpd_client_connection_count_limit (50)
> How many simultaneous connections any client is allowed to make to this service.

smtpd_client_connection_rate_limit (0)
> The maximal number of connection attempts any client is allowed to make to this service per time unit.

smtpd_client_message_rate_limit (0)
> The maximal number of message delivery requests that any client is allowed to make to this service per time unit, regardless of whether or not Postfix actually accepts those messages.

smtpd_client_recipient_rate_limit (0)
> The maximal number of recipient addresses that any client is allowed to send to this service per time unit, regardless of whether or not Postfix actually accepts those recipients.

smtpd_client_event_limit_exceptions ($mynetworks)
> Clients that are excluded from connection count, connection rate, or SMTP request rate restrictions.

Available in Postfix version 2.3 and later:

smtpd_client_new_tls_session_rate_limit (0)
> The maximal number of new (i.e., uncached) TLS sessions that a remote SMTP client is allowed to negotiate with this service per time unit.

TARPIT CONTROLS

When a remote SMTP client makes errors, the Postfix SMTP server can insert delays before responding. This can help to slow down run-away software. The behavior is controlled by an error counter that counts the number of errors within an SMTP session that a client makes without delivering mail.

smtpd_error_sleep_time (1s)
> With Postfix version 2.1 and later: the SMTP server response delay after a client has made more than $smtpd_soft_error_limit errors, and fewer than $smtpd_hard_error_limit errors, without delivering mail.

smtpd_soft_error_limit (10)
> The number of errors a remote SMTP client is allowed to make without delivering mail before the Postfix SMTP server slows down all its responses.

smtpd_hard_error_limit (normal: 20, stress: 1)
> The maximal number of errors a remote SMTP client is allowed to make without delivering mail.

smtpd_junk_command_limit (normal: 100, stress: 1)
> The number of junk commands (NOOP, VRFY, ETRN or RSET) that a remote SMTP client can send before the Postfix SMTP server starts to increment the error counter with each junk command.

Available in Postfix version 2.1 and later:

smtpd_recipient_overshoot_limit (1000)
> The number of recipients that a remote SMTP client can send in excess of the limit specified with $smtpd_recipient_limit, before the Postfix SMTP server increments the per-session error count for each excess recipient.

ACCESS POLICY DELEGATION CONTROLS

As of version 2.1, Postfix can be configured to delegate access policy decisions to an external server that runs outside Postfix. See the file SMTPD_POLICY_README for more information.

smtpd_policy_service_max_idle (300s)
> The time after which an idle SMTPD policy service connection is closed.

smtpd_policy_service_max_ttl (1000s)
> The time after which an active SMTPD policy service connection is closed.

smtpd_policy_service_timeout (100s)
> The time limit for connecting to, writing to or receiving from a delegated SMTPD policy server.

ACCESS CONTROLS

The SMTPD_ACCESS_README document gives an introduction to all the SMTP server access control features.

smtpd_delay_reject (yes)
> Wait until the RCPT TO command before evaluating $smtpd_client_restrictions, $smtpd_helo_restrictions and $smtpd_sender_restrictions, or wait until the ETRN command before evaluating $smtpd_client_restrictions and $smtpd_helo_restrictions.

parent_domain_matches_subdomains (see 'postconf -d' output)
> What Postfix features match subdomains of "domain.tld" automatically, instead of requiring an explicit ".domain.tld" pattern.

smtpd_client_restrictions (empty)
> Optional SMTP server access restrictions in the context of a client SMTP connection request.

smtpd_helo_required (no)
> Require that a remote SMTP client introduces itself at the beginning of an SMTP session with the HELO or EHLO command.

smtpd_helo_restrictions (empty)
> Optional restrictions that the Postfix SMTP server applies in the context of the SMTP HELO command.

smtpd_sender_restrictions (empty)
> Optional restrictions that the Postfix SMTP server applies in the context of the MAIL FROM command.

smtpd_recipient_restrictions (permit_mynetworks, reject_unauth_destination)
> The access restrictions that the Postfix SMTP server applies in the context of the RCPT TO command.

smtpd_etrn_restrictions (empty)
> Optional SMTP server access restrictions in the context of a client ETRN request.

allow_untrusted_routing (no)
> Forward mail with sender-specified routing (user[@%!]remote[@%!]site) from untrusted clients to destinations matching $relay_domains.

smtpd_restriction_classes (empty)
> User-defined aliases for groups of access restrictions.

smtpd_null_access_lookup_key (<>)
> The lookup key to be used in SMTP **access**(5) tables instead of the null sender address.

permit_mx_backup_networks (empty)
> Restrict the use of the permit_mx_backup SMTP access feature to only domains whose primary MX hosts match the listed networks.

Available in Postfix version 2.0 and later:

smtpd_data_restrictions (empty)
> Optional access restrictions that the Postfix SMTP server applies in the context of the SMTP DATA command.

smtpd_expansion_filter (see 'postconf -d' output)
> What characters are allowed in $name expansions of RBL reply templates.

Available in Postfix version 2.1 and later:

smtpd_reject_unlisted_sender (no)
> Request that the Postfix SMTP server rejects mail from unknown sender addresses, even when no explicit reject_unlisted_sender access restriction is specified.

smtpd_reject_unlisted_recipient (yes)
> Request that the Postfix SMTP server rejects mail for unknown recipient addresses, even when no explicit reject_unlisted_recipient access restriction is specified.

Available in Postfix version 2.2 and later:

smtpd_end_of_data_restrictions (empty)
> Optional access restrictions that the Postfix SMTP server applies in the context of the SMTP END-OF-DATA command.

SENDER AND RECIPIENT ADDRESS VERIFICATION CONTROLS

Postfix version 2.1 introduces sender and recipient address verification. This feature is implemented by sending probe email messages that are not actually delivered. This feature is requested via the reject_unverified_sender and reject_unverified_recipient access restrictions. The status of verification probes is maintained by the **verify**(8) server. See the file ADDRESS_VERIFICATION_README for information about how to configure and operate the Postfix sender/recipient address verification service.

address_verify_poll_count (3)
> How many times to query the **verify**(8) service for the completion of an address verification request in progress.

address_verify_poll_delay (3s)
> The delay between queries for the completion of an address verification request in progress.

address_verify_sender ($double_bounce_sender)
> The sender address to use in address verification probes; prior to Postfix 2.5 the default was "postmaster".

unverified_sender_reject_code (450)
> The numerical Postfix SMTP server response code when a recipient address is rejected by the reject_unverified_sender restriction.

unverified_recipient_reject_code (450)
> The numerical Postfix SMTP server response when a recipient address is rejected by the reject_unverified_recipient restriction.

Available in Postfix version 2.6 and later:

unverified_sender_defer_code (450)
> The numerical Postfix SMTP server response code when a sender address probe fails due to a temporary error condition.

unverified_recipient_defer_code (450)
> The numerical Postfix SMTP server response when a recipient address probe fails due to a temporary error condition.

unverified_sender_reject_reason (empty)
> The Postfix SMTP server's reply when rejecting mail with reject_unverified_sender.

unverified_recipient_reject_reason (empty)
> The Postfix SMTP server's reply when rejecting mail with reject_unverified_recipient.

unverified_sender_tempfail_action ($reject_tempfail_action)
> The Postfix SMTP server's action when reject_unverified_sender fails due to a temporary error condition.

unverified_recipient_tempfail_action ($reject_tempfail_action)
> The Postfix SMTP server's action when reject_unverified_recipient fails due to a temporary error condition.

ACCESS CONTROL RESPONSES
The following parameters control numerical SMTP reply codes and/or text responses.

access_map_reject_code (554)
> The numerical Postfix SMTP server response code for an **access**(5) map "reject" action.

defer_code (450)
> The numerical Postfix SMTP server response code when a remote SMTP client request is rejected by the "defer" restriction.

invalid_hostname_reject_code (501)
> The numerical Postfix SMTP server response code when the client HELO or EHLO command parameter is rejected by the reject_invalid_helo_hostname restriction.

maps_rbl_reject_code (554)
> The numerical Postfix SMTP server response code when a remote SMTP client request is blocked by the reject_rbl_client, reject_rhsbl_client, reject_rhsbl_sender or reject_rhsbl_recipient restriction.

non_fqdn_reject_code (504)
> The numerical Postfix SMTP server reply code when a client request is rejected by the reject_non_fqdn_helo_hostname, reject_non_fqdn_sender or reject_non_fqdn_recipient restriction.

plaintext_reject_code (450)
> The numerical Postfix SMTP server response code when a request is rejected by the **reject_plaintext_session** restriction.

reject_code (554)
> The numerical Postfix SMTP server response code when a remote SMTP client request is rejected by the "reject" restriction.

relay_domains_reject_code (554)
> The numerical Postfix SMTP server response code when a client request is rejected by the reject_unauth_destination recipient restriction.

unknown_address_reject_code (450)
> The numerical Postfix SMTP server response code when a sender or recipient address is rejected by the reject_unknown_sender_domain or reject_unknown_recipient_domain restriction.

unknown_client_reject_code (450)
> The numerical Postfix SMTP server response code when a client without valid address <=> name mapping is rejected by the reject_unknown_client_hostname restriction.

unknown_hostname_reject_code (450)
> The numerical Postfix SMTP server response code when the hostname specified with the HELO or EHLO command is rejected by the reject_unknown_helo_hostname restriction.

Available in Postfix version 2.0 and later:

default_rbl_reply (see 'postconf -d' output)
> The default SMTP server response template for a request that is rejected by an RBL-based restriction.

multi_recipient_bounce_reject_code (550)
> The numerical Postfix SMTP server response code when a remote SMTP client request is blocked by the reject_multi_recipient_bounce restriction.

rbl_reply_maps (empty)
> Optional lookup tables with RBL response templates.

Available in Postfix version 2.6 and later:

access_map_defer_code (450)
> The numerical Postfix SMTP server response code for an **access**(5) map "defer" action, including "defer_if_permit" or "defer_if_reject".

reject_tempfail_action (defer_if_permit)
> The Postfix SMTP server's action when a reject-type restriction fails due to a temporary error condition.

unknown_helo_hostname_tempfail_action ($reject_tempfail_action)
> The Postfix SMTP server's action when reject_unknown_helo_hostname fails due to an temporary error condition.

unknown_address_tempfail_action ($reject_tempfail_action)
> The Postfix SMTP server's action when reject_unknown_sender_domain or reject_unknown_recipient_domain fail due to a temporary error condition.

MISCELLANEOUS CONTROLS
config_directory (see 'postconf -d' output)
> The default location of the Postfix main.cf and master.cf configuration files.

daemon_timeout (18000s)
> How much time a Postfix daemon process may take to handle a request before it is terminated by a built-in watchdog timer.

command_directory (see 'postconf -d' output)
> The location of all postfix administrative commands.

double_bounce_sender (double-bounce)
> The sender address of postmaster notifications that are generated by the mail system.

ipc_timeout (3600s)
> The time limit for sending or receiving information over an internal communication channel.

mail_name (Postfix)
> The mail system name that is displayed in Received: headers, in the SMTP greeting banner, and in bounced mail.

mail_owner (postfix)
> The UNIX system account that owns the Postfix queue and most Postfix daemon processes.

max_idle (100s)
> The maximum amount of time that an idle Postfix daemon process waits for an incoming connection before terminating voluntarily.

max_use (100)
> The maximal number of incoming connections that a Postfix daemon process will service before terminating voluntarily.

myhostname (see 'postconf -d' output)
> The internet hostname of this mail system.

mynetworks (see 'postconf -d' output)
> The list of "trusted" SMTP clients that have more privileges than "strangers".

myorigin ($myhostname)
> The domain name that locally-posted mail appears to come from, and that locally posted mail is delivered to.

process_id (read-only)
> The process ID of a Postfix command or daemon process.

process_name (read-only)
> The process name of a Postfix command or daemon process.

queue_directory (see 'postconf -d' output)
> The location of the Postfix top-level queue directory.

recipient_delimiter (empty)
> The separator between user names and address extensions (user+foo).

smtpd_banner ($myhostname ESMTP $mail_name)
> The text that follows the 220 status code in the SMTP greeting banner.

syslog_facility (mail)
> The syslog facility of Postfix logging.

syslog_name (see 'postconf -d' output)
> The mail system name that is prepended to the process name in syslog records, so that "smtpd" becomes, for example, "postfix/smtpd".

Available in Postfix version 2.2 and later:

smtpd_forbidden_commands (CONNECT, GET, POST)
> List of commands that causes the Postfix SMTP server to immediately terminate the session with a 221 code.

Available in Postfix version 2.5 and later:

smtpd_client_port_logging (no)
> Enable logging of the remote SMTP client port in addition to the hostname and IP address.

SEE ALSO
> anvil(8), connection/rate limiting
> cleanup(8), message canonicalization
> tlsmgr(8), TLS session and PRNG management
> trivial-rewrite(8), address resolver
> verify(8), address verification service
> postconf(5), configuration parameters
> master(5), generic daemon options
> master(8), process manager
> syslogd(8), system logging

README FILES
> Use "**postconf readme_directory**" or "**postconf html_directory**" to locate this information.
> ADDRESS_CLASS_README, blocking unknown hosted or relay recipients

ADDRESS_REWRITING_README Postfix address manipulation
FILTER_README, external after-queue content filter
LOCAL_RECIPIENT_README, blocking unknown local recipients
MILTER_README, before-queue mail filter applications
SMTPD_ACCESS_README, built-in access policies
SMTPD_POLICY_README, external policy server
SMTPD_PROXY_README, external before-queue content filter
SASL_README, Postfix SASL howto
TLS_README, Postfix STARTTLS howto
VERP_README, Postfix XVERP extension
XCLIENT_README, Postfix XCLIENT extension
XFORWARD_README, Postfix XFORWARD extension

LICENSE

The Secure Mailer license must be distributed with this software.

AUTHOR(S)

Wietse Venema
IBM T.J. Watson Research
P.O. Box 704
Yorktown Heights, NY 10598, USA

SASL support originally by:
Till Franke
SuSE Rhein/Main AG
65760 Eschborn, Germany

TLS support originally by:
Lutz Jaenicke
BTU Cottbus
Allgemeine Elektrotechnik
Universitaetsplatz 3-4
D-03044 Cottbus, Germany

Revised TLS support by:
Victor Duchovni
Morgan Stanley

NAME

    sntp – standard SNTP program

SYNOPSIS

    sntp [*–flag* [*value*]]... [*––opt-name* [[=|]*value*]]...

    All arguments must be options.

DESCRIPTION

    This manual page documents, briefly, the **sntp** command. *sntp* can be used as a SNTP client to query a
    NTP or SNTP server and either display the time or set the local system's time (given suitable privilege). It
    can be run as an interactive command or in a *cron* job. NTP is the Network Time Protocol (RFC 1305) and
    SNTP is the Simple Network Time Protocol (RFC 2030, which supersedes RFC 1769).

  Options

    sntp recognizes the following options:

    –v   indicates that diagnostic messages for non-fatal errors and a limited amount of tracing should be
            written to standard error. Fatal ones always produce a diagnostic. This option should be set when
            there is a suspected problem with the server, network or the source.

    –V   requests more and less comprehensible output, mainly for investigating problems with apparently
            inconsistent timestamps. This option should be set when the program fails with a message indicat-
            ing that is the trouble.

    –W   requests very verbose debugging output, and will interfere with the timing when writing to the ter-
            minal (because of line buffered output from C). Note that the times produced by this are the cor-
            rections needed, and not the error in the local clock. This option should be set only when debug-
            ging the source.

    –q   indicates that it should query a daemon save file being maintained by it. This needs no privilege
            and will change neither the save file nor the clock.

    The default is that it should behave as a client, and the following options are then relevant:

    –r   indicates that the system clock should be reset by *settimeofday*. Naturally, this will work only if
            the user has enough privilege.

    –a   indicates that the system clock should be reset by *adjtime*. Naturally, this will work only if the
            user has enough privilege.

    The default is to write the estimated correct local date and time (i.e. not UTC) to the standard output in a
    format like **'1996 Oct 15 20:17:25.123 + 4.567 +/- 0.089 secs'**, where the **'+ 4.567 +/- 0.089 secs'** indi-
    cates the estimated error in the time on the local system.

  –l *lockfile*

            sets the name of the lock file to ensure that there is only one copy of *sntp* running at once. The
            default is installation-dependent, but will usually be */etc/sntp.pid*.

  –e *minerr*

            sets the maximum ignorable variation between the clocks to *minerr*. Acceptable values are from
            0.001 to 1, and the default is 0.1 if a NTP host is is specified and 0.5 otherwise.

  –E *maxerr*

            sets the maximum value of various delays that are deemed acceptable to *maxerr*. Acceptable val-
            ues are from 1 to 60, and the default is 5. It should sometimes be increased if there are problems
            with the network, NTP server or system clock, but take care.

  –P *prompt*

            sets the maximum clock change that will be made automatically to *maxerr*. Acceptable values are
            from 1 to 3600 or *no*, and the default is 30. If the program is being run interactively in ordinary
            client mode, and the system clock is to be changed, larger corrections will prompt the user for con-
            firmation. Specifying *no* will disable this and the correction will be made regardless.

−c *count*

        sets the maximum number of NTP packets required to *count*. Acceptable values are from 1 to 25 if a NTP host is specified and from 5 to 25 otherwise, and the default is 5. If the maximum isn't enough, the system needs a better consistency algorithm than this program uses.

−d *delay*

        sets a rough limit on the total running time to *delay* seconds. Acceptable values are from 1 to 3600, and the default is 15 if a NTP host is specified and 300 otherwise.

−4   force IPv4 DNS resolution.

−6   force IPv6 DNS resolution.

address(es) are the DNS names or IP numbers of hosts to use for the challenge and response protocol; if no names are given, the program waits for broadcasts. Polling a server is vastly more reliable than listening to broadcasts. Note that a single component numeric address is not allowed, to avoid ambiguities. If more than one name is give, they will be used in a round-robin fashion.

Constraints:

        minerr must be less than **maxerr** which must be less than **delay** (or, if a NTP host is not specified **delay/count**), and **count** must be less than half of **delay**.

        In update mode, **maxerr** must be less than **prompt.**

Note that none of the above values are closely linked to the limits described in the NTP protocol (RFC 1305).

USAGE

The simplest use of this program is as an unprivileged command to check the current time and error in the local clock. For example:

        sntp ntpserver.somewhere

With suitable privilege, it can be run as a command or in a *cron* job to reset the local clock from a reliable server, like the *ntpdate* and *rdate* commands. For example:

        sntp −a ntpserver.somewhere

More information on how to use this utility is given in the *README* file in the distribution. In particular, this *man* page does not describe how to set it up as a server, which needs special care to avoid propagating misinformation.

RETURN VALUE

When used as a client in non-daemon mode, the program returns a zero exit status for success, and a non-zero one otherwise. When used as a daemon (either client or server), it does not return except after a serious error.

BUGS

The program implements the SNTP protocol, and does not provide all NTP facilities. In particular, it contains no checks against any form of spoofing. If this is a serious concern, some network security mechanism (like a firewall or even just *tcpwrappers*) should be installed.

There are some errors, ambiguities and inconsistencies in the RFCs, and this code may not interwork with all other NTP implementations. Any unreasonable restrictions should be reported as bugs to whoever is responsible. It may be difficult to find out who that is.

The program will stop as soon as it feels that things have got out of control. In client daemon mode, it will usually fail during an extended period of network or server inaccessibility or excessively slow performance, or when the local clock is reset by another process. It will then need restarting manually. Experienced system administrators can write a shell script, a *cron* job or put it in *inittab*, to do this automatically.

The error cannot be estimated reliably with broadcast packets or for the drift in daemon mode (even with client-server packets), and the guess made by the program may be wrong (possibly even very wrong). If this is a problem, then setting the −c option to a larger value may help. Or it may not.

AUTHOR

sntp was developed by N.M. Maclaren of the University of Cambridge Computing Service.

OPTIONS

−4, −−ipv4

> Force IPv4 DNS name resolution. This option is a member of the ipv4 class of options.
>
> Force DNS resolution of following host names on the command line to the IPv4 namespace.

−6, −−ipv6

> Force IPv6 DNS name resolution. This option is a member of the ipv4 class of options.
>
> Force DNS resolution of following host names on the command line to the IPv6 namespace.

−u, −−unprivport

> Use an unprivileged port.
>
> Use an unprivilegded UDP port for our queries.

−v, −−normalverbose

> Slightly verbose. This option must not appear in combination with any of the following options: extraverbose, megaverbose.
>
> Diagnostic messages for non-fatal errors and a limited amount of tracing should be written to standard error. Fatal ones always produce a diagnostic. This option should be set when there is a suspected problem with the server, network or the source.

−V, −−extraverbose

> Extra verbose. This option must not appear in combination with any of the following options: normalverbose, megaverbose.
>
> Produce more and less comprehensible output, mainly for investigating problems with apparently inconsistent timestamps. This option should be set when the program fails with a message indicating that is the trouble.

−W, −−megaverbose

> Mega verbose. This option must not appear in combination with any of the following options: normalverbose, extraverbose.
>
> Very verbose debugging output that will interfere with the timing when writing to the terminal (because of line buffered output from C). Note that the times produced by this are the corrections needed, and not the error in the local clock. This option should be set only when debugging the source.

−r, −−settimeofday

> Set (step) the time with settimeofday(). This option must not appear in combination with any of the following options: adjtime.

−a, −−adjtime

> Set (slew) the time with adjtime(). This option must not appear in combination with any of the following options: settimeofday.

−?, −−help

> Display usage information and exit.

–!, −−**more-help**
    Extended usage information passed thru pager.

–> [*rcfile*], −−**save-opts**[=*rcfile*]
    Save the option state to *rcfile*. The default is the *last* configuration file listed in the **OPTION PRESETS** section, below.

–< *rcfile*, −−**load-opts**=*rcfile*, −−**no-load-opts**
    Load options from *rcfile*. The *no-load-opts* form will disable the loading of earlier RC/INI files. *--no-load-opts* is handled early, out of order.

–**v** [{*v|c|n*}], −−**version**[=*{v|c|n}*]
    Output version of program and exit. The default mode is 'v', a simple version. The 'c' mode will print copyright information and 'n' will print the full copyright notice.

OPTION PRESETS

Any option that is not marked as *not presettable* may be preset by loading values from configuration ("RC" or ".INI") file(s) and values from environment variables named:
    SNTP_<option-name> or **SNTP**
The environmental presets take precedence (are processed later than) the configuration files. The *homerc* files are "*$HOME*", and ".". If any of these are directories, then the file *.ntprc* is searched for within those directories.

AUTHOR

ntp.org
Please send bug reports to: http://bugs.ntp.org, bugs@ntp.org

    General Public Licence for the software known as MSNTP
    −−

      (c) Copyright, N.M. Maclaren, 1996, 1997, 2000
      (c) Copyright, University of Cambridge, 1996, 1997, 2000

Free use of MSNTP in source and binary forms is permitted, provided that this entire licence is duplicated in all copies, and that any documentation, announcements, and other materials related to use acknowledge that the software was developed by N.M. Maclaren (hereafter refered to as the Author) at the University of Cambridge. Neither the name of the Author nor the University of Cambridge may be used to endorse or promote products derived from this material without specific prior written permission.

The Author and the University of Cambridge retain the copyright and all other legal rights to the software and make it available non-exclusively. All users must ensure that the software in all its derivations carries a copyright notice in the form:
      (c) Copyright N.M. Maclaren,
      (c) Copyright University of Cambridge.

      NO WARRANTY

Because the MSNTP software is licensed free of charge, the Author and the University of Cambridge provide absolutely no warranty, either expressed or implied, including, but not limited to, the implied warranties of

merchantability and fitness for a particular purpose. The entire risk as to
the quality and performance of the MSNTP software is with you. Should MSNTP
prove defective, you assume the cost of all necessary servicing or repair.

In no event, unless required by law, will the Author or the University of
Cambridge, or any other party who may modify and redistribute this software as
permitted in accordance with the provisions below, be liable for damages for
any losses whatsoever, including but not limited to lost profits, lost monies,
lost or corrupted data, or other special, incidental or consequential losses
that may arise out of the use or inability to use the MSNTP software.

COPYING POLICY

Permission is hereby granted for copying and distribution of copies of the
MSNTP source and binary files, and of any part thereof, subject to the
following licence conditions:

1. You may distribute MSNTP or components of MSNTP, with or without additions
developed by you or by others. No charge, other than an "at-cost" distribution
fee, may be charged for copies, derivations, or distributions of this material
without the express written consent of the copyright holders.

2. You may also distribute MSNTP along with any other product for sale,
provided that the cost of the bundled package is the same regardless of whether
MSNTP is included or not, and provided that those interested only in MSNTP must
be notified that it is a product freely available from the University of
Cambridge.

3. If you distribute MSNTP software or parts of MSNTP, with or without
additions developed by you or others, then you must either make available the
source to all portions of the MSNTP system (exclusive of any additions made by
you or by others) upon request, or instead you may notify anyone requesting
source that it is freely available from the University of Cambridge.

4. You may not omit any of the copyright notices on either the source files,
the executable files, or the documentation.

5. You may not omit transmission of this License agreement with whatever
portions of MSNTP that are distributed.

6. Any users of this software must be notified that it is without warranty or
guarantee of any nature, express or implied, nor is there any fitness for use
represented.

October 1996
April 1997
October 2000

This manual page was *AutoGen*-erated from the **sntp** option definitions.

NAME
spawn – Postfix external command spawner

SYNOPSIS
spawn [generic Postfix daemon options] command_attributes...

DESCRIPTION
The **spawn**(8) daemon provides the Postfix equivalent of **inetd**. It listens on a port as specified in the Postfix **master.cf** file and spawns an external command whenever a connection is established. The connection can be made over local IPC (such as UNIX-domain sockets) or over non-local IPC (such as TCP sockets). The command's standard input, output and error streams are connected directly to the communication endpoint.

This daemon expects to be run from the **master**(8) process manager.

COMMAND ATTRIBUTE SYNTAX
The external command attributes are given in the **master.cf** file at the end of a service definition. The syntax is as follows:

user=*username* (required)

user=*username*:*groupname*

The external command is executed with the rights of the specified *username*. The software refuses to execute commands with root privileges, or with the privileges of the mail system owner. If *groupname* is specified, the corresponding group ID is used instead of the group ID of *username*.

argv=*command*... (required)

The command to be executed. This must be specified as the last command attribute. The command is executed directly, i.e. without interpretation of shell meta characters by a shell command interpreter.

BUGS
In order to enforce standard Postfix process resource controls, the **spawn**(8) daemon runs only one external command at a time. As such, it presents a noticeable overhead by wasting precious process resources. The **spawn**(8) daemon is expected to be replaced by a more structural solution.

DIAGNOSTICS
The **spawn**(8) daemon reports abnormal child exits. Problems are logged to **syslogd**(8).

SECURITY
This program needs root privilege in order to execute external commands as the specified user. It is therefore security sensitive. However the **spawn**(8) daemon does not talk to the external command and thus is not vulnerable to data-driven attacks.

CONFIGURATION PARAMETERS
Changes to **main.cf** are picked up automatically as **spawn**(8) processes run for only a limited amount of time. Use the command "**postfix reload**" to speed up a change.

The text below provides only a parameter summary. See **postconf**(5) for more details including examples.

In the text below, *transport* is the first field of the entry in the **master.cf** file.

RESOURCE AND RATE CONTROL
*transport*_**time_limit** (**$command_time_limit**)

The amount of time the command is allowed to run before it is terminated.

Postfix 2.4 and later support a suffix that specifies the time unit: s (seconds), m (minutes), h (hours), d (days), w (weeks). The default time unit is seconds.

MISCELLANEOUS

config_directory (see 'postconf -d' output)
> The default location of the Postfix main.cf and master.cf configuration files.

daemon_timeout (18000s)
> How much time a Postfix daemon process may take to handle a request before it is terminated by a built-in watchdog timer.

export_environment (see 'postconf -d' output)
> The list of environment variables that a Postfix process will export to non-Postfix processes.

ipc_timeout (3600s)
> The time limit for sending or receiving information over an internal communication channel.

mail_owner (postfix)
> The UNIX system account that owns the Postfix queue and most Postfix daemon processes.

max_idle (100s)
> The maximum amount of time that an idle Postfix daemon process waits for an incoming connection before terminating voluntarily.

max_use (100)
> The maximal number of incoming connections that a Postfix daemon process will service before terminating voluntarily.

process_id (read-only)
> The process ID of a Postfix command or daemon process.

process_name (read-only)
> The process name of a Postfix command or daemon process.

queue_directory (see 'postconf -d' output)
> The location of the Postfix top-level queue directory.

syslog_facility (mail)
> The syslog facility of Postfix logging.

syslog_name (see 'postconf -d' output)
> The mail system name that is prepended to the process name in syslog records, so that "smtpd" becomes, for example, "postfix/smtpd".

SEE ALSO

postconf(5), configuration parameters
master(8), process manager
syslogd(8), system logging

LICENSE

The Secure Mailer license must be distributed with this software.

AUTHOR(S)

Wietse Venema
IBM T.J. Watson Research
P.O. Box 704
Yorktown Heights, NY 10598, USA

NAME

spray — send many packets to host

SYNOPSIS

spray [**-c** *count*] [**-d** *delay*] [**-l** *length*] *host* . . .

DESCRIPTION

spray sends multiple RPC packets to *host* and records how many of them were correctly received and how long it took.

The options are as follows:

-c *count*
> Send *count* packets.

-d *delay*
> Pause *delay* microseconds between sending each packet.

-l *length*
> Set the length of the packet that holds the RPC call message to *length* bytes. Not all values of *length* are possible because RPC data is encoded using XDR. **spray** rounds up to the nearest possible value.

spray is intended for use in network testing, measurement, and management. This command *can be very hard on a network and should be used with caution.*

SEE ALSO

netstat(1), ifconfig(8), ping(8), rpc.sprayd(8)

NAME

srtconfig — configure srt interfaces

SYNOPSIS

srtconfig *srtX*
srtconfig *srtX N*
srtconfig *srtX* del *N*
srtconfig *srtX* add *srcaddr mask dstif dstaddr*
srtconfig *srtX* set *N srcaddr mask dstif dstaddr*

DESCRIPTION

srtconfig configures, or queries the configuration of, srt(4) interfaces. An srt(4) interface parcels packets out to other interfaces based on their source addresses (the normal routing mechanisms handle routing decisions based on destination addresses). An interface may have any number of routing choices; they are examined in order until one matching the packet is found. The packet is sent to the corresponding interface. (Any interface, even another **srt** interface, may be specified; if the configurations collaborate to cause a packet to loop forever, the system will lock up or crash.)

When run with only one argument, **srtconfig** prints the settings for the specified interface.

When run with two arguments, **srtconfig** prints the settings for the routing choice whose number is given as the second argument.

The form with 'del' deletes a routing choice, identified by its number. Other choices with higher numbers, if any, will be renumbered accordingly.

The 'add' form adds a choice; the other arguments describe it, and are documented below. The new choice is added at the end of the list.

The 'set' form replaces an existing choice, given its number. The other arguments describe the new choice which is to replace whatever currently exists at the given number *N*.

A choice is described by four pieces of information: a source address and mask, which are used to determine which choice an outgoing packet uses, a destination interface, and a destination address for the new interface. The source address and mask are specified like any Internet addresses (for convenience, the mask may instead be specified as a '/' followed by a small integer, CIDR-style; note that in this case the mask must still be a separate argument; it cannot be appended to the end of the source address argument).

Each srt interface also has ordinary source and destination addresses which are set with ifconfig(8) like any other interface; these should not be confused with any of the above.

AUTHORS

der Mouse ⟨mouse@rodents.montreal.qc.ca⟩

NAME

ssh-keysign — ssh helper program for host-based authentication

SYNOPSIS

ssh-keysign

DESCRIPTION

ssh-keysign is used by ssh(1) to access the local host keys and generate the digital signature required during host-based authentication with SSH protocol version 2.

ssh-keysign is disabled by default and can only be enabled in the global client configuration file /etc/ssh/ssh_config by setting **EnableSSHKeysign** to "yes".

ssh-keysign is not intended to be invoked by the user, but from ssh(1). See ssh(1) and sshd(8) for more information about host-based authentication.

FILES

/etc/ssh/ssh_config
> Controls whether **ssh-keysign** is enabled.

/etc/ssh/ssh_host_dsa_key, /etc/ssh/ssh_host_rsa_key
> These files contain the private parts of the host keys used to generate the digital signature. They should be owned by root, readable only by root, and not accessible to others. Since they are readable only by root, **ssh-keysign** must be set-uid root if host-based authentication is used.

SEE ALSO

ssh(1), ssh-keygen(1), ssh_config(5), sshd(8)

HISTORY

ssh-keysign first appeared in OpenBSD 3.2.

AUTHORS

Markus Friedl ⟨markus@openbsd.org⟩

NAME

   sshd — OpenSSH SSH daemon

SYNOPSIS

   sshd [**-46DdeiqTt**] [**-b** *bits*] [**-C** *connection_spec*] [**-f** *config_file*]
        [**-g** *login_grace_time*] [**-h** *host_key_file*] [**-k** *key_gen_time*] [**-o** *option*]
        [**-p** *port*] [**-u** *len*]

DESCRIPTION

   sshd (OpenSSH Daemon) is the daemon program for ssh(1). Together these programs replace rlogin(1) and rsh(1), and provide secure encrypted communications between two untrusted hosts over an insecure network.

   sshd listens for connections from clients. It is normally started at boot from /etc/rc.d/sshd. It forks a new daemon for each incoming connection. The forked daemons handle key exchange, encryption, authentication, command execution, and data exchange.

   sshd can be configured using command-line options or a configuration file (by default sshd_config(5)); command-line options override values specified in the configuration file. **sshd** rereads its configuration file when it receives a hangup signal, SIGHUP, by executing itself with the name and options it was started with, e.g. /usr/sbin/sshd.

   The options are as follows:

   -4   Forces **sshd** to use IPv4 addresses only.

   -6   Forces **sshd** to use IPv6 addresses only.

   -b *bits*
             Specifies the number of bits in the ephemeral protocol version 1 server key (default 1024).

   -C *connection_spec*
             Specify the connection parameters to use for the **-T** extended test mode. If provided, any **Match** directives in the configuration file that would apply to the specified user, host, and address will be set before the configuration is written to standard output. The connection parameters are supplied as keyword=value pairs. The keywords are "user", "host", and "addr". All are required and may be supplied in any order, either with multiple **-C** options or as a comma-separated list.

   -D   When this option is specified, **sshd** will not detach and does not become a daemon. This allows easy monitoring of **sshd**.

   -d   Debug mode. The server sends verbose debug output to the system log, and does not put itself in the background. The server also will not fork and will only process one connection. This option is only intended for debugging for the server. Multiple **-d** options increase the debugging level. Maximum is 3.

   -e   When this option is specified, **sshd** will send the output to the standard error instead of the system log.

   -f *config_file*
             Specifies the name of the configuration file. The default is /etc/ssh/sshd_config. **sshd** refuses to start if there is no configuration file.

   -g *login_grace_time*
             Gives the grace time for clients to authenticate themselves (default 120 seconds). If the client fails to authenticate the user within this many seconds, the server disconnects and exits. A value of zero indicates no limit.

-h *host_key_file*
> Specifies a file from which a host key is read. This option must be given if **sshd** is not run as root (as the normal host key files are normally not readable by anyone but root). The default is /etc/ssh/ssh_host_key for protocol version 1, and /etc/ssh/ssh_host_rsa_key and /etc/ssh/ssh_host_dsa_key for protocol version 2. It is possible to have multiple host key files for the different protocol versions and host key algorithms.

-i
> Specifies that **sshd** is being run from inetd(8). **sshd** is normally not run from inetd because it needs to generate the server key before it can respond to the client, and this may take tens of seconds. Clients would have to wait too long if the key was regenerated every time. However, with small key sizes (e.g. 512) using **sshd** from inetd may be feasible.

-k *key_gen_time*
> Specifies how often the ephemeral protocol version 1 server key is regenerated (default 3600 seconds, or one hour). The motivation for regenerating the key fairly often is that the key is not stored anywhere, and after about an hour it becomes impossible to recover the key for decrypting intercepted communications even if the machine is cracked into or physically seized. A value of zero indicates that the key will never be regenerated.

-o *option*
> Can be used to give options in the format used in the configuration file. This is useful for specifying options for which there is no separate command-line flag. For full details of the options, and their values, see sshd_config(5).

-p *port*
> Specifies the port on which the server listens for connections (default 22). Multiple port options are permitted. Ports specified in the configuration file with the **Port** option are ignored when a command-line port is specified. Ports specified using the **ListenAddress** option override command-line ports.

-q
> Quiet mode. Nothing is sent to the system log. Normally the beginning, authentication, and termination of each connection is logged.

-T
> Extended test mode. Check the validity of the configuration file, output the effective configuration to stdout and then exit. Optionally, **Match** rules may be applied by specifying the connection parameters using one or more **-C** options.

-t
> Test mode. Only check the validity of the configuration file and sanity of the keys. This is useful for updating **sshd** reliably as configuration options may change.

-u *len*
> This option is used to specify the size of the field in the utmp structure that holds the remote host name. If the resolved host name is longer than *len*, the dotted decimal value will be used instead. This allows hosts with very long host names that overflow this field to still be uniquely identified. Specifying **-u0** indicates that only dotted decimal addresses should be put into the utmp file. **-u0** may also be used to prevent **sshd** from making DNS requests unless the authentication mechanism or configuration requires it. Authentication mechanisms that may require DNS include **RhostsRSAAuthentication**, **HostbasedAuthentication**, and using a **from="pattern-list"** option in a key file. Configuration options that require DNS include using a USER@HOST pattern in **AllowUsers** or **DenyUsers**.

AUTHENTICATION

The OpenSSH SSH daemon supports SSH protocols 1 and 2. Both protocols are supported by default, though this can be changed via the **Protocol** option in sshd_config(5). Protocol 2 supports both RSA and DSA keys; protocol 1 only supports RSA keys. For both protocols, each host has a host-specific key, normally 2048 bits, used to identify the host.

Forward security for protocol 1 is provided through an additional server key, normally 768 bits, generated when the server starts. This key is normally regenerated every hour if it has been used, and is never stored on disk. Whenever a client connects, the daemon responds with its public host and server keys. The client compares the RSA host key against its own database to verify that it has not changed. The client then generates a 256-bit random number. It encrypts this random number using both the host key and the server key, and sends the encrypted number to the server. Both sides then use this random number as a session key which is used to encrypt all further communications in the session. The rest of the session is encrypted using a conventional cipher, currently Blowfish or 3DES, with 3DES being used by default. The client selects the encryption algorithm to use from those offered by the server.

For protocol 2, forward security is provided through a Diffie-Hellman key agreement. This key agreement results in a shared session key. The rest of the session is encrypted using a symmetric cipher, currently 128-bit AES, Blowfish, 3DES, CAST128, Arcfour, 192-bit AES, or 256-bit AES. The client selects the encryption algorithm to use from those offered by the server. Additionally, session integrity is provided through a cryptographic message authentication code (hmac-md5, hmac-sha1, umac-64 or hmac-ripemd160).

Finally, the server and the client enter an authentication dialog. The client tries to authenticate itself using host-based authentication, public key authentication, challenge-response authentication, or password authentication.

If the client successfully authenticates itself, a dialog for preparing the session is entered. At this time the client may request things like allocating a pseudo-tty, forwarding X11 connections, forwarding TCP connections, or forwarding the authentication agent connection over the secure channel.

After this, the client either requests a shell or execution of a command. The sides then enter session mode. In this mode, either side may send data at any time, and such data is forwarded to/from the shell or command on the server side, and the user terminal in the client side.

When the user program terminates and all forwarded X11 and other connections have been closed, the server sends command exit status to the client, and both sides exit.

LOGIN PROCESS

When a user successfully logs in, **sshd** does the following:

1. If the login is on a tty, and no command has been specified, prints last login time and `/etc/motd` (unless prevented in the configuration file or by `~/.hushlogin`; see the **FILES** section).

2. If the login is on a tty, records login time.

3. Checks `/etc/nologin`; if it exists, prints contents and quits (unless root).

4. Changes to run with normal user privileges.

5. Sets up basic environment.

6. Reads the file `~/.ssh/environment`, if it exists, and users are allowed to change their environment. See the **PermitUserEnvironment** option in sshd_config(5).

7. Changes to user's home directory.

8. If `~/.ssh/rc` exists, runs it; else if `/etc/ssh/sshrc` exists, runs it; otherwise runs xauth. The "rc" files are given the X11 authentication protocol and cookie in standard input. See **SSHRC**, below.

9. Runs user's shell or command.

SSHRC

If the file ˜/.ssh/rc exists, sh(1) runs it after reading the environment files but before starting the user's shell or command. It must not produce any output on stdout; stderr must be used instead. If X11 forwarding is in use, it will receive the "proto cookie" pair in its standard input (and DISPLAY in its environment). The script must call xauth(1) because **sshd** will not run xauth automatically to add X11 cookies.

The primary purpose of this file is to run any initialization routines which may be needed before the user's home directory becomes accessible; AFS is a particular example of such an environment.

This file will probably contain some initialization code followed by something similar to:

```
if read proto cookie && [ -n "$DISPLAY" ]; then
        if [ 'echo $DISPLAY | cut -c1-10' = 'localhost:' ]; then
                # X11UseLocalhost=yes
                echo add unix:'echo $DISPLAY |
                    cut -c11-' $proto $cookie
        else
                # X11UseLocalhost=no
                echo add $DISPLAY $proto $cookie
        fi | xauth -q -
fi
```

If this file does not exist, /etc/ssh/sshrc is run, and if that does not exist either, xauth is used to add the cookie.

AUTHORIZED_KEYS FILE FORMAT

AuthorizedKeysFile specifies the file containing public keys for public key authentication; if none is specified, the default is ˜/.ssh/authorized_keys. Each line of the file contains one key (empty lines and lines starting with a '#' are ignored as comments). Protocol 1 public keys consist of the following space-separated fields: options, bits, exponent, modulus, comment. Protocol 2 public key consist of: options, keytype, base64-encoded key, comment. The options field is optional; its presence is determined by whether the line starts with a number or not (the options field never starts with a number). The bits, exponent, modulus, and comment fields give the RSA key for protocol version 1; the comment field is not used for anything (but may be convenient for the user to identify the key). For protocol version 2 the keytype is "ssh-dss" or "ssh-rsa".

Note that lines in this file are usually several hundred bytes long (because of the size of the public key encoding) up to a limit of 8 kilobytes, which permits DSA keys up to 8 kilobits and RSA keys up to 16 kilobits. You don't want to type them in; instead, copy the identity.pub, id_dsa.pub, or the id_rsa.pub file and edit it.

sshd enforces a minimum RSA key modulus size for protocol 1 and protocol 2 keys of 768 bits.

The options (if present) consist of comma-separated option specifications. No spaces are permitted, except within double quotes. The following option specifications are supported (note that option keywords are case-insensitive):

command="command"

Specifies that the command is executed whenever this key is used for authentication. The command supplied by the user (if any) is ignored. The command is run on a pty if the client requests a pty; otherwise it is run without a tty. If an 8-bit clean channel is required, one must not request a pty or should specify **no-pty**. A quote may be included in the command by quoting it with a backslash. This option might be useful to restrict certain public keys to perform just a specific operation. An example might be a key that permits remote backups but nothing else. Note that the client may specify TCP and/or X11 forwarding unless they are explicitly prohibited. The command originally supplied by the client is available in the SSH_ORIGINAL_COMMAND environment variable. Note that this option applies to shell, command or subsystem execution.

environment="NAME=value"
Specifies that the string is to be added to the environment when logging in using this key. Environment variables set this way override other default environment values. Multiple options of this type are permitted. Environment processing is disabled by default and is controlled via the **PermitUserEnvironment** option. This option is automatically disabled if **UseLogin** is enabled.

from="pattern-list"
Specifies that in addition to public key authentication, either the canonical name of the remote host or its IP address must be present in the comma-separated list of patterns. See **PATTERNS** in ssh_config(5) for more information on patterns.

In addition to the wildcard matching that may be applied to hostnames or addresses, a **from** stanza may match IP addresses using CIDR address/masklen notation.

The purpose of this option is to optionally increase security: public key authentication by itself does not trust the network or name servers or anything (but the key); however, if somebody somehow steals the key, the key permits an intruder to log in from anywhere in the world. This additional option makes using a stolen key more difficult (name servers and/or routers would have to be compromised in addition to just the key).

no-agent-forwarding
Forbids authentication agent forwarding when this key is used for authentication.

no-port-forwarding
Forbids TCP forwarding when this key is used for authentication. Any port forward requests by the client will return an error. This might be used, e.g. in connection with the **command** option.

no-pty
Prevents tty allocation (a request to allocate a pty will fail).

no-user-rc
Disables execution of ~/.ssh/rc.

no-X11-forwarding
Forbids X11 forwarding when this key is used for authentication. Any X11 forward requests by the client will return an error.

permitopen="host:port"
Limit local ''ssh -L'' port forwarding such that it may only connect to the specified host and port. IPv6 addresses can be specified with an alternative syntax: *host/port*. Multiple **permitopen** options may be applied separated by commas. No pattern matching is performed on the specified hostnames, they must be literal domains or addresses.

tunnel="n"
Force a tun(4) device on the server. Without this option, the next available device will be used if the client requests a tunnel.

An example authorized_keys file:

```
# Comments allowed at start of line
ssh-rsa AAAAB3Nza...LiPk== user@example.net
from="*.sales.example.net,!pc.sales.example.net" ssh-rsa
AAAAB2...19Q== john@example.net
command="dump /home",no-pty,no-port-forwarding ssh-dss
AAAAC3...51R== example.net
```

SSHD(8)   NetBSD   SSHD(8)

```
permitopen="192.0.2.1:80",permitopen="192.0.2.2:25" ssh-dss
AAAAB5...21S==
tunnel="0",command="sh /etc/netstart tun0" ssh-rsa AAAA...==
jane@example.net
```

SSH_KNOWN_HOSTS FILE FORMAT

The `/etc/ssh/ssh_known_hosts` and `~/.ssh/known_hosts` files contain host public keys for all
known hosts. The global file should be prepared by the administrator (optional), and the per-user file is
maintained automatically: whenever the user connects from an unknown host, its key is added to the per-user
file.

Each line in these files contains the following fields: hostnames, bits, exponent, modulus, comment. The
fields are separated by spaces.

Hostnames is a comma-separated list of patterns ('*' and '?' act as wildcards); each pattern in turn is
matched against the canonical host name (when authenticating a client) or against the user-supplied name
(when authenticating a server). A pattern may also be preceded by '!' to indicate negation: if the host name
matches a negated pattern, it is not accepted (by that line) even if it matched another pattern on the line. A
hostname or address may optionally be enclosed within '[' and ']' brackets then followed by ':' and a non-
standard port number.

Alternately, hostnames may be stored in a hashed form which hides host names and addresses should the
file's contents be disclosed. Hashed hostnames start with a '|' character. Only one hashed hostname may
appear on a single line and none of the above negation or wildcard operators may be applied.

Bits, exponent, and modulus are taken directly from the RSA host key; they can be obtained, for example,
from `/etc/ssh/ssh_host_key.pub`. The optional comment field continues to the end of the line, and
is not used.

Lines starting with '#' and empty lines are ignored as comments.

When performing host authentication, authentication is accepted if any matching line has the proper key. It
is thus permissible (but not recommended) to have several lines or different host keys for the same names.
This will inevitably happen when short forms of host names from different domains are put in the file. It is
possible that the files contain conflicting information; authentication is accepted if valid information can be
found from either file.

Note that the lines in these files are typically hundreds of characters long, and you definitely don't want to
type in the host keys by hand. Rather, generate them by a script or by taking
`/etc/ssh/ssh_host_key.pub` and adding the host names at the front.

An example ssh_known_hosts file:

```
# Comments allowed at start of line
closenet,...,192.0.2.53 1024 37 159...93 closenet.example.net
cvs.example.net,192.0.2.10 ssh-rsa AAAA1234.....=
# A hashed hostname
|1|JfKTdBh7rNbXkVAQCRp4OQoPfmI=|USECr3SWf1JUPsms5AqfD5QfxkM= ssh-rsa
AAAA1234.....=
```

FILES

~/.hushlogin

This file is used to suppress printing the last login time and `/etc/motd`, if **PrintLastLog** and
PrintMotd, respectively, are enabled. It does not suppress printing of the banner specified by
Banner.

˜/.rhosts

    This file is used for host-based authentication (see ssh(1) for more information). On some machines this file may need to be world-readable if the user's home directory is on an NFS partition, because **sshd** reads it as root. Additionally, this file must be owned by the user, and must not have write permissions for anyone else. The recommended permission for most machines is read/write for the user, and not accessible by others.

˜/.shosts

    This file is used in exactly the same way as .rhosts, but allows host-based authentication without permitting login with rlogin/rsh.

˜/.ssh/   This directory is the default location for all user-specific configuration and authentication information. There is no general requirement to keep the entire contents of this directory secret, but the recommended permissions are read/write/execute for the user, and not accessible by others.

˜/.ssh/authorized_keys

    Lists the public keys (RSA/DSA) that can be used for logging in as this user. The format of this file is described above. The content of the file is not highly sensitive, but the recommended permissions are read/write for the user, and not accessible by others.

    If this file, the ˜/.ssh directory, or the user's home directory are writable by other users, then the file could be modified or replaced by unauthorized users. In this case, **sshd** will not allow it to be used unless the **StrictModes** option has been set to "no".

˜/.ssh/environment

    This file is read into the environment at login (if it exists). It can only contain empty lines, comment lines (that start with '#'), and assignment lines of the form name=value. The file should be writable only by the user; it need not be readable by anyone else. Environment processing is disabled by default and is controlled via the **PermitUserEnvironment** option.

˜/.ssh/known_hosts

    Contains a list of host keys for all hosts the user has logged into that are not already in the systemwide list of known host keys. The format of this file is described above. This file should be writable only by root/the owner and can, but need not be, world-readable.

˜/.ssh/rc

    Contains initialization routines to be run before the user's home directory becomes accessible. This file should be writable only by the user, and need not be readable by anyone else.

/etc/hosts.allow
/etc/hosts.deny

    Access controls that should be enforced by tcp-wrappers are defined here. Further details are described in hosts_access(5).

/etc/hosts.equiv

    This file is for host-based authentication (see ssh(1)). It should only be writable by root.

/etc/moduli

    Contains Diffie-Hellman groups used for the "Diffie-Hellman Group Exchange". The file format is described in moduli(5).

/etc/motd

    See motd(5).

/etc/nologin

    If this file exists, **sshd** refuses to let anyone except root log in. The contents of the file are displayed to anyone trying to log in, and non-root connections are refused. The file should be world-readable.

/etc/shosts.equiv

    This file is used in exactly the same way as `hosts.equiv`, but allows host-based authentication without permitting login with rlogin/rsh.

/etc/ssh/ssh_host_key
/etc/ssh/ssh_host_dsa_key
/etc/ssh/ssh_host_rsa_key

    These three files contain the private parts of the host keys. These files should only be owned by root, readable only by root, and not accessible to others. Note that **sshd** does not start if these files are group/world-accessible.

/etc/ssh/ssh_host_key.pub
/etc/ssh/ssh_host_dsa_key.pub
/etc/ssh/ssh_host_rsa_key.pub

    These three files contain the public parts of the host keys. These files should be world-readable but writable only by root. Their contents should match the respective private parts. These files are not really used for anything; they are provided for the convenience of the user so their contents can be copied to known hosts files. These files are created using `ssh-keygen`(1).

/etc/ssh/ssh_known_hosts

    Systemwide list of known host keys. This file should be prepared by the system administrator to contain the public host keys of all machines in the organization. The format of this file is described above. This file should be writable only by root/the owner and should be world-readable.

/etc/ssh/sshd_config

    Contains configuration data for **sshd**. The file format and configuration options are described in `sshd_config`(5).

/etc/ssh/sshrc

    Similar to `~/.ssh/rc`, it can be used to specify machine-specific login-time initializations globally. This file should be writable only by root, and should be world-readable.

/var/empty

    `chroot`(2) directory used by **sshd** during privilege separation in the pre-authentication phase. The directory should not contain any files and must be owned by root and not group or world-writable.

/var/run/sshd.pid

    Contains the process ID of the **sshd** listening for connections (if there are several daemons running concurrently for different ports, this contains the process ID of the one started last). The content of this file is not sensitive; it can be world-readable.

SEE ALSO

    `scp`(1), `sftp`(1), `ssh`(1), `ssh-add`(1), `ssh-agent`(1), `ssh-keygen`(1), `ssh-keyscan`(1), `chroot`(2), `hosts_access`(5), `login.conf`(5), `moduli`(5), `sshd_config`(5), `inetd`(8), `sftp-server`(8)

AUTHORS

    OpenSSH is a derivative of the original and free ssh 1.2.12 release by Tatu Ylonen. Aaron Campbell, Bob Beck, Markus Friedl, Niels Provos, Theo de Raadt and Dug Song removed many bugs, re-added newer features and created OpenSSH. Markus Friedl contributed the support for SSH protocol versions 1.5 and 2.0. Niels Provos and Markus Friedl contributed support for privilege separation.

CAVEATS

System security is not improved unless **rshd**, **rlogind**, and **rexecd** are disabled (thus completely disabling `rlogin` and `rsh` into the machine).

NAME

stdethers — a NIS filter program

SYNOPSIS

stdethers [*file*]

DESCRIPTION

stdethers parses the ethers(5) style input stream (stdin, or *file* if given), and outputs lines containing only the MAC address and host name.

stdethers is used by other NIS programs when creating some of the NIS maps.

SEE ALSO

nis(8), ypserv(8)

AUTHORS

Mats O Jansson ⟨moj@stacken.kth.se⟩

NAME

   stdhosts — a NIS filter program

SYNOPSIS

   stdhosts [**-n**] [*file*]

DESCRIPTION

   stdhosts parses the hosts(5) style input stream (stdin, or *file* if given), and outputs lines containing only the IPv4 address and host name.

   stdhosts is used by other NIS programs when creating some of the NIS maps.

   -n allows other address types in the output, including IPv6 addresses.

SEE ALSO

   nis(8), ypserv(8)

AUTHORS

   Mats O Jansson ⟨moj@stacken.kth.se⟩

STI (8)   NetBSD   STI (8)

NAME
     sti — Simulate Terminal Input: send characters to a tty device

SYNOPSIS
     sti *tty* [*string ...*]

DESCRIPTION
     sti will send the provided *string* to the *tty* specified in the command line using ioctl(2) TIOCSTI,
     or send the standard input if no *string* is supplied. This ioctl(2) is limited to the superuser.

     The *string* is interpreted using unvis(3).

SEE ALSO
     ioctl(2), unvis(3)

HISTORY
     The **sti** first appeared at NetBSD 4.0.

AUTHORS
     The **sti** command was written by Christos Zoulas ⟨christos@NetBSD.org⟩.

NAME
strfile, **unstr** — create a random access file for storing strings

SYNOPSIS
strfile [**-iorsx**] [**-c** *char*] *source_file* [*output_file*]
unstr *source_file*

DESCRIPTION
strfile reads a file containing groups of lines separated by a line containing a single percent '%' sign and creates a data file which contains a header structure and a table of file offsets for each group of lines. This allows random access of the strings.

The output file, if not specified on the command line, is named *source_file*.**dat**.

The options are as follows:

-c *char*
  Change the delimiting character from the percent sign to *char*.

-i
  Ignore case when ordering the strings.

-o
  Order the strings in alphabetical order. The offset table will be sorted in the alphabetical order of the groups of lines referenced. Any initial non-alphanumeric characters are ignored. This option causes the STR_ORDERED bit in the header *str_flags* field to be set.

-r
  Randomize access to the strings. Entries in the offset table will be randomly ordered. This option causes the STR_RANDOM bit in the header *str_flags* field to be set.

-s
  Run silently; don't give a summary message when finished.

-x
  Note that each alphabetic character in the groups of lines is rotated 13 positions in a simple caesar cipher. This option causes the STR_ROTATED bit in the header *str_flags* field to be set.

The format of the header is:

```
#define VERSION 1
unsigned long   str_version;    /* version number */
unsigned long   str_numstr;     /* # of strings in the file */
unsigned long   str_longlen;    /* length of longest string */
unsigned long   str_shortlen;   /* length of shortest string */
#define STR_RANDOM      0x1     /* randomized pointers */
#define STR_ORDERED     0x2     /* ordered pointers */
#define STR_ROTATED     0x4     /* rot-13'd text */
unsigned long   str_flags;      /* bit field for flags */
char str_delim;                         /* delimiting character */
```

All fields are written in big-endian byte order.

The purpose of **unstr** is to undo the work of **strfile**. It prints out the strings contained in the file *source_file* in the order that they are listed in the header file *source_file*.**dat** to standard output. It is possible to create sorted versions of input files by using **-o** when **strfile** is run and then using **unstr** to dump them out in the table order.

FILES
strfile.dat default output file.

SEE ALSO
     byteorder(3), fortune(6)

HISTORY
     The **strfile** utility first appeared in 4.4 BSD.

NAME

string2key — map a password into a key

SYNOPSIS

string2key [**-5** | **--version5**][**-4** | **--version4**][**-a** | **--afs**][**-c** *cell* |
                --cell=*cell*][**-w** *password* | **--password**=*password*][**-p** *principal* |
                --principal=*principal*][**-k** *string* | **--keytype**=*string*] *password*

DESCRIPTION

string2key performs the string-to-key function. This is useful when you want to handle the raw key instead of the password. Supported options:

-5, **--version5**
    Output Kerberos v5 string-to-key

-4, **--version4**
    Output Kerberos v4 string-to-key

-a, **--afs**
    Output AFS string-to-key

-c *cell*, **--cell**=*cell*
    AFS cell to use

-w *password*, **--password**=*password*
    Password to use

-p *principal*, **--principal**=*principal*
    Kerberos v5 principal to use

-k *string*, **--keytype**=*string*
    Keytype

--version
    print version

--help

NAME

   sunlabel — read or modify a SunOS disk label

SYNOPSIS

   sunlabel [**-mnqs**] *device*

DESCRIPTION

   sunlabel reads or modifies a SunOS disk label on *device*, which is used by the PROM on NetBSD/sparc hardware to find partitions to boot from. **sunlabel** only reads/writes the first 512 bytes of *device*.

   The supported options are:

   -m   Ignore an incorrect magic number in the disk label.

   -n   Synthesize a new label rather than reading what is there.

   -q   Quiet mode - don't print unnecessary babble (currently this suppresses the "sunlabel>" prompt).

   -s   Ignore checksum errors when reading the label.

   Note that **-m** is dangerous, especially when combined with **-s**, since it will then happily believe whatever garbage it may find in the label. When using these flags, all values should be checked carefully, both those printed by **L** and the partition table printed by **P**.

   sunlabel prints a prompt "sunlabel>" and expects commands. The following commands are understood:

   ?   Show a short help message.

   [abcdefghijklmnop] *<cylno> <size>*
                        Change partition (see below).

   L   Print label, except for the partition table.

   P   Print the partition table.

   Q   Quit program (error if no write since last change).

   Q!   Quit program (unconditionally) [EOF also quits].

   S   Set label in the kernel (orthogonal to **W**).

   V *<name> <value>*
                        Change a non-partition label value.

   W   Write (possibly modified) label out.

   The **a** through **p** commands will accept, for the *<size>* parameter, the *nnn/nnn/nnn* syntax used by SunOS 4.x **format**. (For those not familiar with this syntax, *a/b/c* means *a* cylinders + *b* tracks + *c* sectors. For example, if the disk has 16 tracks of 32 sectors, *3/4/5* means (3*16*32)+(4*32)+5=1669. This calculation always uses the *nsect* and *ntrack* values as printed by the **L** command; in particular, if they are zero (which they will initially be if **-n** is used), this syntax is not very useful. Some additional strings are accepted. For the *<cylno>* parameter, "end-X" (where *X* is a partition letter) indicates that the partition should start with the first free cylinder after partition *X*; "start-X" indicates that the partition should start at the same place as partition *X*. For the *<size>* parameter, "end-X" indicates that the partition should end at the same place as partition *X* (even if partition *X* ends partway through a cylinder); "start-X" indicates that the partition should end with the last cylinder before partition *X*; and "size-X" means that the partition's size should exactly match partition *X*'s size.

Note that **sunlabel** supports 16 partitions. SunOS supports only 8. Labels written by **sunlabel**, when partitions *i* through *p* are all set *offset=0 size=0*, are identical to Sun labels. If any of the "extended" partitions are nontrivial, information about them is tucked into some otherwise unused space in the Sun label format.

The **V** command changes fields printed by the **L** command. For example, if the **L** command prints

```
ascii: ST15230N cyl 5657 alt 2 hd 19 sec 78
rpm: 0          pcyl: 0         apc: 0          obs1: 0
obs2: 0         intrlv: 1       ncyl: 5657      acyl: 0
nhead: 19       nsect: 78       obs3: 0         obs4: 0
```

then **V** *ncyl 6204* would set the *ncyl* value to 6204, or **V** *ascii Seagate ST15230N cyl 5657 hd 19 sec varying* would set the ascii-label string to that string. **sunlabel** performs very few consistency checks on the values you supply, and the ones it does perform never generate errors, only warnings.

AUTHORS

der Mouse ⟨mouse@rodents.montreal.qc.ca⟩

BUGS

It may be that the space in the label where the information for the extended partitions is saved is used by SunOS.

Not very many consistency checks are done on the **V** arguments, and those only produce warnings.

NetBSD doesn't support 16 partitions in a Sun disk label yet.

NAME

sup – software upgrade protocol

SYNOPSIS

sup [*flags*] [*supfile*] [*collection* ...]

DESCRIPTION

Sup is a program used for upgrading collections of files from other machines to your machine. You execute *sup*, the *client* program, which talks over the network using IP/TCP to a *file server* process. The file server process cooperates with *sup* to determine which files of the collection need to be upgraded on your machine.

Sup collections can have multiple releases. One use for such releases is to provide different versions of the same files. At CMU, for example, system binaries have alpha, beta and default release corresponding to different staging levels of the software. We also use release names default and minimal to provide complete releases or subset releases. In both of these cases, it only makes sense to sup one release of the collections. Releases have also been used in private or external sups to provide subsets of collections where it makes sense to pick up several of the releases. For example the Mach 3.0 kernel sources has a default release of machine independent sources and separate releases of machine dependent sources for each supported platform.

In performing an upgrade, the file server constructs a list of files included in the specified release of the collection. The list is sent to your machine, which determines which files are needed. Those files are then sent from the file server. It will be most useful to run *sup* as a daemon each night so you will continually have the latest version of the files in the needed collections.

The only required argument to *sup* is the name of a supfile. It must either be given explicitly on the command line, or the **-s** flag must be specified. If the **-s** flag is given, the system supfile will be used and a supfile command argument should not be specified. The list of collections is optional and if specified will be the only collections upgraded. The following flags affect all collections specified:

-s   As described above.

-t   When this flag is given, *sup* will print the time that each collection was last upgraded, rather than performing actual upgrades.

-u   When this flag is given, *sup* will not try to restore the user access and modified times of files in the collections from the server.

-S   Operate silently printing messages only on errors.

-N   *Sup* will trace network messages sent and received that implement the *sup* network protocol.

-P   Sup will use a set of non-privileged network ports reserved for debugging purposes.

The remaining flags affect all collections unless an explicit list of collections are given with the flags. Multiple flags may be specified together that affect the same collections. For the sake of convenience, any flags that always affect all collections can be specified with flags that affect only some collections. For example, **sup -sde=coll1,coll2** would perform a system upgrade, and the first two collections would allow both file deletions and command executions. Note that this is not the same command as **sup -sde=coll1 coll2**, which would perform a system upgrade of just the coll2 collection and would ignore the flags given for the coll1 collection.

-a   All files in the collection will be copied from the repository, regardless of their status on the current machine. Because of this, it is a very expensive operation and should only be done for small collections if data corruption is suspected and been confirmed. In most cases, the **-o** flag should be sufficient.

-b   If the **-b** flag if given, or the **backup** supfile option is specified, the contents of regular files on the local system will be saved before they are overwritten with new data. The file collection maintainer can designate specific files to be worthy of backing up whenever they are upgraded. However, such backup will only take place if you specify this flag or the **backup** option to allow backups for a file collection on your machine. The backup mechanism will create a copy of the current version of a file immediately before a new copy is received from the file server; the copy is given the same name as the original file but is put into a directory called **BACKUP** within the directory containing the original file. For example, **/usr/sas/src/foo.c** would have a backup copy called **/usr/sas/src/BACKUP/foo.c**. There is no provision for automatically maintaining multiple old versions of files; you would have to do this yourself.

-B   The -B flag overrides and disables the -b flag and the **backup** supfile option.

-d   Files that are no longer in the collection on the repository will be deleted if present on the local machine and were put there by a previous sup. This may also be specified in a supfile with the **delete** option.

-D   The -D flag overrides and disables the -d flag and the **delete** supfile option.

-e   Sup will execute commands sent from the repository that should be run when a file is upgraded. If the -e flag is omitted, Sup will print a message that specifies the command to execute. This may also be specified in a supfile with the **execute** option.

-E   The -E flag overrides and disables the -e flag and the **execute** supfile option.

-f   A *list-only* upgrade will be performed. Messages will be printed that indicate what would happen if an actual upgrade were done.

-k   *Sup* will check the modification times of files on the local disk before updating them. Only files which are newer on the repository than on the local disk will be updated; files that are newer on the local disk will be kept as they are. This may also be specified in a supfile with the **keep** option.

-K   The -K flag overrides and disables the -k flag and the **keep** supfile option.

-l   Normally, *sup* will not upgrade a collection if the repository is on the same machine. This allows users to run upgrades on all machines without having to make special checks for the repository machine. If the -l flag is specified, collections will be upgraded even if the repository is local.

-m   Normally, *sup* used standard output for messages. If the -m flag if given, *sup* will send mail to the user running *sup*, or a user specified with the **notify** supfile option, that contains messages printed by *sup*.

-M <user>
       like -m but send mail to the specified user.

-o   *Sup* will normally only upgrade files that have changed on the repository since the last time an upgrade was performed. That is, if the file in the repository is newer than the date stored in the *when* file on the client. The -o flag, or the **old** supfile option, will cause *sup* to check all files in the collection for changes instead of just the new ones.

-O   The -O flag overrides and disables the -o flag and the **old** supfile option.

-z   Normally sup transfers files directly without any other processing, but with the -z flag, or the **compress** supfile option, sup will compress the file before sending it across the network and uncompress it and restore all the correct file attributes at the receiving end.

-Z   The -Z flag overrides and disables the -z flag and the **compress** supfile option.

-v   Normally, *sup* will only print messages if there are problems. This flag causes *sup* to also print messages during normal progress showing what *sup* is doing.

SETTING UP UPGRADES

Each file collection to be upgraded must have a *base directory* which contains a subdirectory called **sup** that will be used by the *sup* program; it will be created automatically if you do not create it. *Sup* will put subdirectories and files into this directory as needed.

Sup will look for a subdirectory with the same name as the collection within the **sup** subdirectory of the *base directory*. If it exists it may contain any of the following files:

when.<rel-suffix>

This file is automatically updated by *sup* when a collection is successfully upgraded and contains the time that the file server, or possibly *supscan*, created the list of files in the upgrade list. *Sup* will send this time to the file server for generating the list of files that have been changed on the repository machine.

refuse   This file contains a list of files and directories, one per line, that the client is not interested in that should not be upgraded.

lock   This file is used by *sup* to lock a collection while it is being upgraded. *Sup* will get exclusive access to the lock file using *flock*(2), preventing more than one *sup* from upgrading the same collection at the same time.

last.<rel-suffix>

This file contains a list of files and directories, one per line, that have been upgraded by *sup* in the past. This information is used when the **delete** option, or the **-d** flag is used to locate files previously upgraded that are no longer in the collection that should be deleted.

Each file collection must also be described in one or more supfiles. When *sup* is executed, it reads the specified supfile to determine what file collections and releases to upgrade. Each collection-release set is described by a single line of text in the supfile; this line must contain the name of the collection, and possibly one or more options separated by spaces. The options are:

release=*releasename*

If a collection contains multiple releases, you need to specify which release you want. You can only specify one release per line, so if you want multiple releases from the same collections, you will need to specify the collection more than once. In this case, you should use the *use-rel-suffix* option in the supfile to keep the last and when files for the two releases separate.

base=*directory*

The usual default name of the base directory for a collection is described below (see FILES); if you want to specify another directory name, use this option specifying the desired directory.

prefix=*directory*

Each collection may also have an associated *prefix directory* which is used instead of the base directory to specify in what directory files within the collection will be placed.

host=*hostname*
hostbase=*directory*

System collections are supported by the system maintainers, and *sup* will automatically find out the name of the host machine and base directory on that machine. However, you can also upgrade *private* collections; you simply specify with these options the *hostname* of the machine containing the files and the *directory* used as a base directory for the file server on that machine. Details of setting up a file collection are given in the section below.

login=*accountid*
password=*password*
crypt=*key*

Files on the file server may be protected, and network transmissions may be encrypted. This prevents unauthorized access to files via *sup*. When files are not accessible to the default account (e.g. the **anon** anonymous account), you can specify an alternative *accountid* and *password* for the file server to use on the repository host. Network transmission of the password will be always be encrypted. You can also have the actual file data encrypted by specifying a *key*; the file collection on the repository must specify the same key or else *sup* will not be able to upgrade files from that collection. In this case, the default account used by the file server on the repository machine will be the owner of the encryption key file (see FILES) rather than the **anon** anonymous account.

notify=*address*

  If you use the **-m** option to receive log messages by mail, you can have the mail sent to different user, possibly on another host, than the user running the sup program. Messages will be sent to the specified *address*, which can be any legal netmail address. In particular, a project maintainer can be designated to receive mail for that project's file collection from all users running *sup* to upgrade that collection.

backup

  As described above under the **-b** flag.

delete As described above under the **-d** flag.

execute

  As described above under the **-e** flag.

keep As described above under the **-k** flag.

old As described above under the **-o** flag.

use-rel-suffix

  Causes the release name to be used as a suffix to the *last* and *when* files. This is necessary whenever you are supping more than one release in the same collection.

PREPARING A FILE COLLECTION REPOSITORY

A set of files residing on a repository must be prepared before *sup* client processes can upgrade those files. The collection must be given a *name* and a *base directory*. If it is a private collection, client users must be told the name of the collection, repository host, and base directory; these will be specified in the supfile via the **host** and **hostbase** options. For a system-maintained file collection, entries must be placed into the host list file and directory list file as described in *supservers*(8).

Within the base directory, a subdirectory must be created called **sup** . Within this directory there must be a subdirectory for each collection using that base directory, whose name is the name of the collection; within each of these directories will be a list file and possibly a prefix file, a host file, an encryption key file, a log file and a scan file. The filenames are listed under FILES below.

prefix Normally, all files in the collection are relative to the base directory. This file contains a single line which is the name of a directory to be used in place of the base directory for file references.

host Normally, all remote host machines are allowed access to a file collection. If you wish to restrict access to specific remote hosts for this collection, put each allowed hostname on a separate line of text in this file. If a host has more than one name, only one of its names needs to be listed. The name **LOCAL** can be used to grant access to all hosts on the local network. The host name may be a numeric network address or a network name. If a crypt appears on the same line as the host name, that crypt will be used for that host. Otherwise, the crypt appearing in the *crypt* file, if any will be used.

crypt If you wish to use the *sup* data encryption mechanism, create an encryption file containing, on a single line of text, the desired encryption key. Client processes must then specify the same key with the **crypt** option in the supfile or they will be denied access to the files. In addition, actual network transmission of file contents and filenames will be encrypted.

list This file describes the actual list of files to be included in this file collection, in a format described below.

releases

  This file describes any releases that the collection may have. Each line starts with the release name and then may specify any of the following files: *prefix=<dirname>* to use a different parent directory for the files in this release. *list=<listname>* to specify the list of files in the release. *scan=<scanfile>* must be used in multi-release collections that are scanned to keep the scan files for the different releases separate. *host=<hostfile>* to allow different host restrictions for this release. *next=<release>* used to chain releases together. This has the effect of making one release be a combination of several other releases. If the same file appears in more than one chained release, the first one found will be used. If these files are not specified for a release the default names: prefix,list,scan and host will be used.

scan   This file, created by *supscan*, is the list of filenames that correspond to the instructions in the list file. The scan file is only used for frequently updated file collections; it makes the file server run much faster. See *supservers*(8) for more information.

lock   As previously mentioned, this file is used to indicate that the collection should be locked while upgrades are in progress. All file servers will try to get shared access to the lock file with *flock*(2).

logfile If a log file exists in the collection directory, the file server will append the last time an upgrade was successfully completed, the time the last upgrade started and finished, and the name of the host requesting the upgrade.

It should be noted that *sup* allows several different named collections to use the same base directory. Separate encryption, remote host access, and file lists are used for each collection, since these files reside in subdirectories *<basedir>/sup/<coll.name>*.

The list file is a text file with one command on each line. Each command contains a keyword and a number of operands separated by spaces. All filenames in the list file are evaluated on the repository machine relative to the host's base directory, or prefix directory if one is specified, and on your machine with respect to the base, or prefix, directory for the client. The *filenames* below (except *exec-command*) may all include wild-cards and meta-characters as used by *csh*(1) including *, ?, [...], and {...}. The commands are:

upgrade *filename* ...
    The specified file(s) (or directories) will be included in the list of files to be upgraded. If a directory name is given, it recursively includes all subdirectories and files within that directory.

always *filename* ...
    The always command is identical to upgrade, except that omit and omitany commands do not affect filenames specified with the always command.

omit *filename* ...
    The specified file(s) (or directories) will be excluded from the list of files to be upgraded. For example, by specifying **upgrade /usr/vision** and **omit /usr/vision/exp,** the generated list of files would include all subdirectories and files of /usr/vision except /usr/vision/exp (and its subdirectories and files).

omitany *pattern* ...
    The specified patterns are compared against the files in the upgrade list. If a pattern matches, the file is omitted. The omitany command currently supports all wild-card patterns except {...}. Also, the pattern must match the entire filename, so a leading */, or a trailing /*, may be necessary in the pattern.

backup *filename* ...
    The specified file(s) are marked for backup; if they are upgraded and the client has specified the **backup** option in the corresponding line of the supfile, then backup copies will be created as described above. Directories may not be specified, and no recursive filename construction is performed; you must specify the names of the specific files to be backed up before upgrading.

noaccount *filename* ...
    The accounting information of the specified file(s) will not be preserved by *sup*. Accounting information consists of the owner, group, mode and modified time of a file.

symlink *filename* ...
    The specified file(s) are to be treated as symbolic links and will be transferred as such and not followed. By default, *sup* will follow symbolic links.

rsymlink *dirname* ...
    All symbolic links in the specified directory and its subdirectories are to be treated as symbolic links. That is the links will be transferred and not the files to which they point.

execute *exec-command* (*filename* ...)

> The *exec-command* you specified will be executed on the client process whenever any of the files listed in parentheses are upgraded. A special token, **%s,** may be specified in the *exec-command* and will be replaced by the name of the file that was upgraded. For example, if you say **execute ranlib %s (libc.a)**, then whenever libc.a is upgraded, the client machine will execute **ranlib libc.a.** As described above, the client must invoke *sup* with the **-e** flag to allow the automatic execution of command files.

include *listfile* ...

> The specified *listfiles* will be read at this point. This is useful when one collection subsumes other collections; the larger collection can simply specify the listfiles for the smaller collections contained within it.

The order in which the command lines appear in the list file does not matter. Blank lines may appear freely in the list file.

FILES

Files on the client machine for *sup*:

/etc/supfiles/coll.list
> supfile used for -s flag

/etc/supfiles/coll.what
> supfile used for -s flag when -t flag is also specified

/etc/supfiles/coll.host
> host name list for system collections

<base-directory>/**sup**/*<collection>*/**last**<*.release*>
> recorded list of files in collection as of last upgrade

<base-directory>/**sup**/*<collection>*/**lock**
> file used to lock collection

<base-directory>/**sup**/*<collection>*/**refuse**
> list of files to refuse in collection

<base-directory>/**sup**/*<collection>*/**when**<*.release*>
> recorded time of last upgrade

/usr/sup/<*collection*>
> default base directory for file collection

Files needed on each repository machine for the file server:

/etc/supfiles/coll.dir
> base directory list for system collections

<base-directory>/**sup**/*<collection>*/**crypt**
> data encryption key for a collection. the owner of this file is the default account used when data encryption is specified

<base-directory>/**sup**/*<collection>*/**host**
> list of remote hosts allowed to upgrade a collection

<base-directory>/**sup**/*<collection>*/**list**
> list file for a collection

<base-directory>/**sup**/*<collection>*/**lock**
> lock file for a collection

<base-directory>/**sup**/*<collection>*/**logfile**
> log file for a collection

    <base-directory>/**sup**/*<collection>*/**prefix**
        file containing the name of the prefix directory for a collection

    <base-directory>/**sup**/*<collection>*/**scan**
        scan file for a collection

    /usr/*<collection>*
        default base directory for a file collection

SEE ALSO

    supservers(8)
    The SUP Software Upgrade Protocol, S. A. Shafer, CMU Computer Science Department, 1985.

EXAMPLE

    <example>

BUGS

    The encryption mechanism should be strengthened, although it's not trivial.

    sup can delete files it should not with the delete option. This is because in the delete pass, it tries to delete all files in the old list that don't exist in the new list. This is a problem when a directory becomes a symlink to a hierarchy that contains the same names. Then sup will cross the symlink and start deleting files and directories from the destination. This is not easily fixed. Don't use sup with symlink/rsymlink and the delete option at the same time or *be careful*!

NAME

supfilesrv, supscan – sup server processes

SYNOPSIS

supfilesrv [*-4*] [*-6*] [*-d*] [*-l*] [*-q*] [*-N*] [*-P*] [*-C MaxChildren*]

supscan [*-v*] [*-s*] [*collection*] [*basedir*]

DESCRIPTION

Supfilesrv is the server processes used to interact with *sup* client processes via the IP/TCP network proto-col. This server normally is expected to be running on server machines at all times. Each machine with files of interest to users on other machines is expected to be a file server and should run *supfilesrv*.

A file server machine will service requests for both "private" and "system" file collections. No special action is necessary to support private collections, as the client user is expected to supply all necessary infor-mation. For system collections, if the base directory is not the default (see FILES below), an entry must be put into the directory list file; this entry is a single text line containing the name of the collection, one or more spaces, and the name of the base directory for that collection.

Each collection should have an entry in the host list file; this entry is a single text line containing the name of the collection, one or more spaces, and the name of the host machine acting as file server for that collec-tion.

Details of setting up a file collection for the file server are described in the manual entry for *sup(1)*.

Supfilesrv generally runs as a network server process that listens for connections, and for each connection (double-)forks a process to handle the interaction with the client. However, with the -d flag, no forking will take place: the server will listen for a network connection, handle it, and exit. This is useful for debugging the servers in "live" mode rather than as daemons.

For debugging purposes, the -P "debugging ports" flag can be used. It will cause the selection of an alter-nate, non-privileged set of TCP ports instead of the usual ports, which are reserved for the active server pro-cesses. The -N "network debugging" flag can be used to produce voluminous messages describing the net-work communication progress and status. The more -N switches that you use the more output you get. Use 3 (separated by spaces: -N -N -N) to get a complete record of all network messages. Log messages are printed by *syslog* on *daemon.log* . To suppress log messages, the -q "quiet" flag can be used.

supfilesrv uses libwrap style access control (the /etc/hosts.allow and /etc/hosts.deny files) with service name "supfilesrv". The -l "log" flag turn on loggin of accepted connections (denied connections are always logged).

Normally the *supfilesrv* will only respond to 3 requests simultaneously, forking a child process for each client. If it gets additional requests it will respond with the error FSSETUPBUSY. The -C MaxChildren switch can be used to increase (or decrease) this number.

supfilesrv listens to IPv4 listening socket by default. With the -6 flag, it will listen to IPv6 listening socket. For dual stack support you will want to run two instances of *supfilesrv*.

SUPSCAN

It is possible to pre-compile a list of the files in a collection to make *supfilesrv* service that collection much faster. This can be done by running *supscan* on the desired collection on the repository machine. This pro-duces a list of all the files in the collection at the time of the *supscan;* subsequent upgrades will be based on this list of files rather than actually scanning the disk at the time of the upgrade. Of course, the upgrade will consequently bring the client machine up to the status of the repository machine as of the time of the *supscan* rather than as of the time of the upgrade; hence, if *supscan* is used, it should be run periodically on the collection. This facility is useful for extremely large file collections that are upgraded many times per day, such as the CMU UNIX system software. The "verbose" flag *-v* will cause *supscan* to produce output messages as it scans the files in the collection. The "system" flag *-s* will cause *supscan* to scan all system collections residing on the current host. The *basedir* parameter must be specified if the collection is a private collection whose base directory is not the default.

FILES

/usr   default base directory for a collection

/etc/supfiles/coll.dir
            base directory list for system collections

/etc/supfiles/coll.host
            host name list for system collections

<base-directory>/sup/<collection>/*
            files used by file server (see *sup(1)*)

<base-directory>/sup/<collection>/list
            list file used by *supscan* to create file list

<base-directory>/sup/<collection>/scan
            file list created by *supscan* from list file

SEE ALSO

sup(1) hosts_access(5) hosts_options(5)
The SUP Software Upgrade Protocol, S. A. Shafer, CMU Computer Science Dept., 1985.

DIAGNOSTICS

The file server places log messages on the standard and diagnostic output files. The process name and process id number generally accompany each message for diagnostic purposes.

HISTORY

31-July-92 Mary Thompson (mrt) at Carnegie Mellon University
            Removed references to supnameserver which has not existed for a long time. Update a few file names. Added -C switch.

21-May-87 Glenn Marcy (gm0w) at Carnegie-Mellon University
            Updated documentation for 4.3; changed /usr/cmu to /usr/cs.

15-Jan-86 Glenn Marcy (gm0w) at Carnegie-Mellon University
            Updated documentation; -s switch to supscan.

23-May-85 Steven Shafer (sas) at Carnegie-Mellon University
            Supscan created and documented; also -N flag.

04-Apr-85 Steven Shafer (sas) at Carnegie-Mellon University
            Created.

SVHLABEL (8)   NetBSD   SVHLABEL (8)

NAME

  svhlabel — update disk label from SGI Volume Header

SYNOPSIS

  svhlabel [**-fqrw**] *device*

DESCRIPTION

  svhlabel is used to update a NetBSD disk label from the Silicon Graphics Volume Header on disks that were previously used on IRIX systems.

  svhlabel scans the Volume Header contained in the first blocks of the disk and generates additional partition entries for the disk from the entries found.

  Each Volume Header entry which does not have an equivalent partition in the disk label (equivalent in having the same size and offset) is added to the first free partition slot in the disk label. A free partition slot is defined as one with an fstype of 'unused' and a size of zero ('0'). If there are not enough free slots in the disk label, a warning will be issued.

  The raw partition (typically partition *c*, but *d* on i386 and some other platforms) is left alone during this process.

  By default, the proposed changed disk label will be displayed and no disk label update will occur.

  Available options:

  -f

    Force an update, even if there has been no change.

  -q

    Performs operations in a quiet fashion.

  -r

    In conjunction with **-w**, also update the on-disk label. You probably do not want to do this.

  -w

    Update the in-core label if it has been changed.

SEE ALSO

  disklabel(8), dkctl(8), mount_efs(8), sgivol(8)

HISTORY

  The **svhlabel** command appeared in NetBSD 5.0.

NAME
swapctl, swapon — system swap management tool

SYNOPSIS
swapctl −A [−f | −o] [−n] [−p *priority*] [−t *blk|noblk|auto*]
swapctl −D *dumpdev|none*
swapctl −U [−n] [−t *blk|noblk|auto*]
swapctl −a [−p *priority*] *path*
swapctl −c −p *priority path*
swapctl −d *path*
swapctl −l | −s [−k | −m | −g | −h]
swapctl −q
swapctl −z
swapon −a [−t *blk|noblk*]
swapon *path*

DESCRIPTION
The **swapctl** program adds, removes, lists and prioritizes swap devices and files for the system. The **swapon** program acts the same as the **swapctl** program, as if called with the −a option, except if **swapon** itself is called with −a in which case, **swapon** acts as **swapctl** with the −A option.

The following options are available:

−A   This option causes **swapctl** to read the /etc/fstab file for devices and files with a "sw" or "dp" type, and adds all "sw" type entries as swap devices and sets the last "dp" type entry as the dump device. If no swap devices are configured, **swapctl** will exit with an error code. If used together with −t *auto* this option will not read /etc/fstab but query the kernel for all swap partitions on local hard disks.

−a   The −a option requires that a *path* also be in the argument list. The *path* is added to the kernel's list of swap devices using the swapctl(2) system call. When using the **swapon** form of this command, the −a option is treated the same as the −A option, for backwards compatibility.

−c   The −c option changes the priority of the listed swap device or file.

−D   The −D option requires that a *dumpdev* also be in the argument list. The kernel dump device is set to *dumpdev*. The word "none" can be used instead of a *dumpdev* to disable the currently set dump device. This change is made via the swapctl(2) system call. The dump device is used when the system crashes to write a current snapshot of real memory, to be saved later with savecore(8) at system reboot, and analyzed to determine the problem.

−d   The −d option removes the listed *path* from the kernel's list of swap devices or files.

−f   Used in combination with the −A command and −t *auto* flag this option makes **swapctl** use the first discovered swap device to also become the dump device. The −f option is mutually exclusive with the −o option.

−g   The −g option uses (1024 ∗ 1024 ∗ 1024) byte blocks instead of the default 512 byte.

−h   The −h option uses humanize_number(3) to display the sizes.

−k   The −k option uses 1024 byte blocks instead of the default 512 byte.

−l   The −l option lists the current swap devices and files, and their usage statistics.

−m   The −m option uses (1024 ∗ 1024) byte blocks instead of the default 512 byte.

-n   Used with the **-A** or **-U** command, the **-n** option makes **swapctl** print the action it would take, but not actually change any swap or dump devices.

-o   Similar to the **-f** flag, this "Dump Only" option makes **swapctl** find the first swap device and configure it as dump device. No swap device is changed. This option needs to be used in combination with **-A** **-t** *auto* and is mutually exclusive with **-f**.

-p   The **-p** option sets the priority of swap devices or files to the *priority* argument. This works with the **-a**, **-c**, and **-l** options.

-q   Query /etc/fstab, checking for any defined swap or dump devices. If any are found, **swapctl** returns with an exit status of 0, if none are found the exit status will be 1.

-s   The **-s** option displays a single line summary of current swap statistics.

-t   This flag modifies the function of the **-A** and **-U** options. The **-t** option allows the type of device to add to be specified. An argument of *blk* causes all block devices in /etc/fstab to be added. An argument of *noblk* causes all non-block devices in /etc/fstab to be added. An argument of *auto* causes all swap partitions on local hard disks to be used. This option is useful in early system startup, where swapping may be needed before all file systems are available, such as during disk checks of large file systems.

-U   This option causes **swapctl** to read the /etc/fstab file for devices and files with a "sw" type, and remove all these entries as swap devices. If no swap devices are unconfigured, **swapctl** will exit with an error code. If used together with **-t** *auto* this option will not read /etc/fstab but unconfigure all local swap partitions.

-z   The **-z** option displays the current dump device.

SWAP PRIORITY
The NetBSD swap system allows different swap devices and files to be assigned different priorities, to allow the faster resources to be used first. Swap devices at the same priority are used in a round-robin fashion until there is no more space available at this priority, when the next priority level will be used. The default priority is 0, the highest. This value can be any valid integer, with higher values receiving less priority.

SWAP OPTIONS
When parsing the /etc/fstab file for swap devices, the following options are recognized:

priority=N   This option sets the priority of the specified swap device to N.
nfsmntpt=/path   This option is useful for swapping to NFS files. It specifies the local mount point to mount an NFS filesystem. The mount point must exist as a directory. Typically, once this mount has succeeded, the file to be used for swapping on will be available under this point mount. For example:

```
server:/export/swap/client none swap sw,nfsmntpt=/swap
```

EXIT STATUS
If the requested operation was successful, the **swapctl** utility exits with status 0. If an error occurred, the exit status is 1.

The **-A** and **-U** operations (add or remove swap devices listed in fstab(5)) return an exit status of 2 to report that no suitable swap devices were found.

The **-z** operation (query dump device) and **-l** (list swap partitions) return an exit status of 1 if no dump device or swap partition has been configured. If any swap partition is available or a dump device is set, the respective query returns 0.

SEE ALSO
swapctl(2), fstab(5), mount_nfs(8)

HISTORY
The **swapctl** program was first made available in NetBSD 1.3. The original **swapon** program, provided for backwards compatibility, appeared in 4.0BSD.

AUTHORS
The **swapctl** program was written by Matthew R. Green ⟨mrg@eterna.com.au⟩.

CAVEATS
Using the automatic swap partition detection done by the **−A −t** auto option may be dangereous. Depending on the on-disk partitioning scheme used, the type of a partition may not be accurately recognizable as a swap partition. The autodetection might recognize and use partitions on removable media like USB sticks. An easy way to test the autoconfiguration is to use **swapctl** with the **−n** option.

BUGS
If no swap information is specified in /etc/fstab, the system startup scripts (see rc(8)) will configure no swap space and your machine will behave very badly if (more likely when) it runs out of real memory.

Local and remote swap files cannot be configured until after the file systems they reside on are mounted read/write. The system startup scripts need to fsck(8) all local file systems before this can happen. This process requires substantial amounts of memory on some systems. If you configure no local block swap devices on a machine that has local file systems to check and rely only on swap files, the machine will have no swap space at all during system fsck(8) and may run out of real memory, causing fsck to abnormally exit and startup scripts to fail.

NAME

sync — force completion of pending disk writes (flush cache)

SYNOPSIS

sync

DESCRIPTION

The **sync** program can be called to ensure that all disk writes have been completed before the processor is halted in a way not suitably done by reboot(8) or halt(8). Generally, it is preferable to use reboot(8) or halt(8) to shut down the system, as they may perform additional actions such as resynchronizing the hardware clock and flushing internal caches before performing a final **sync**.

The **sync** program simply invokes the sync(2) system call.

SEE ALSO

fsync(2), sync(2), halt(8), reboot(8)

HISTORY

A **sync** command appeared in Version 6 AT&T UNIX.

NAME

sysctl — get or set kernel state

SYNOPSIS

sysctl [**-AdeMn**] [**-r** | **-x**] [*name* . . .]
sysctl [**-nq**] [**-r** | **-x**] **-w** *name* [?]=*value* . . .
sysctl [**-en**] [**-r** | **-x**] **-a**
sysctl [**-nq**] [**-r** | **-x**] **-f** *file*

DESCRIPTION

The **sysctl** utility retrieves kernel state and allows processes with appropriate privilege to set kernel state. The state to be retrieved or set is described using a "Management Information Base" ("MIB") style name, described as a dotted set of components. The '/' character may also be used as a separator and a leading separator character is accepted. If *name* specifies a non-leaf node in the MIB, all the nodes underneath *name* will be printed.

The following options are available:

-A   List all the known MIB names including tables, unless any MIB arguments or **-f** *file* are given. Those with string or integer values will be printed as with the **-a** flag; for table or structure values that **sysctl** is not able to print, the name of the utility to retrieve them is given. Errors in retrieving or setting values will be directed to stdout instead of stderr.

-a   List all the currently available string or integer values. The use of a solitary separator character (either '.' or '/') by itself has the same effect. Any given *name* arguments are ignored if this option is specified.

-d   Descriptions of each of the nodes selected will be printed instead of their values.

-e   Separate the name and the value of the variable(s) with '='. This is useful for producing output which can be fed back to the **sysctl** utility. This option is ignored if **-n** is specified or a variable is being set.

-f   Specifies the name of a file to read and process. Blank lines and comments (beginning with '#') are ignored. Line continuations with '\' are permitted. Remaining lines are processed similarly to command line arguments of the form *name* or *name=value*. The **-w** flag is implied by **-f**. Any *name* arguments are ignored.

-M   Makes **sysctl** print the MIB instead of any of the actual values contained in the MIB. This causes the entire MIB to be printed unless specific MIB arguments or **-f** *file* are also given.

-n   Specifies that the printing of the field name should be suppressed and that only its value should be output. This flag is useful for setting shell variables. For example, to save the pagesize in variable psize, use:

```
set psize='sysctl -n hw.pagesize'
```

-q   Used to indicate that nothing should be printed for writes unless an error is detected.

-r   Raw output form. Values printed are in their raw binary forms as retrieved directly from the kernel. Some additional nodes that **sysctl** cannot print directly can be retrieved with this flag. This option conflicts with the **-x** option.

-w   Sets the MIB style name given to the value given. The MIB style name and value must be separated by '=' with no whitespace. To prevent an error if the MIB style name does not exist (as would be the case with optional kernel components), one can separate the MIB style name and the value with '?='. Only integral and string values can be set via this method.

-x   Makes **sysctl** print the requested value in a hexadecimal representation instead of its regular form. If specified more than once, the output for each value resembles that of hexdump(1) when given the −C flag. This option conflicts with the −r option.

The proc top-level MIB has a special semantic: it represent per-process values and as such may differ from one process to another. The second-level name is the pid of the process (in decimal form), or the special word curproc. For variables below proc.⟨pid⟩.rlimit, the integer value may be replaced with the string unlimited if it matches the magic value used to disable a limit.

The information available from **sysctl** consists of integers, strings, and tables. The tabular information can only be retrieved by special purpose programs such as **ps**, **systat**, and **netstat**. See sysctl(7) for description of available MIBs.

CREATION AND DELETION

New nodes are allowed to be created by the superuser when the kernel is running at security level 0. These new nodes may refer to existing kernel data or to new data that is only instrumented by sysctl(3) itself.

The syntax for creating new nodes is "//create=new.node.path" followed by one or more of the following attributes separated by commas. The use of a double separator (both '/' and '.' can be used as separators) as the prefix tells sysctl that the first series of tokens is not a MIB name, but a command. It is recommended that the double separator preceding the command not be the same as the separator used in naming the MIB entry so as to avoid possible parse conflicts. The "value" assigned, if one is given, must be last.

- type=⟨T⟩ where T must be one of "node", "int", "string", "quad", or "struct". If the type is omitted, the "node" type is assumed.
- size=⟨S⟩ here, S asserts the size of the new node. Nodes of type "node" should not have a size set. The size may be omitted for nodes of types "int" or "quad". If the size is omitted for a node of type "string", the size will be determined by the length of the given value, or by the kernel for kernel strings. Nodes of type "struct" must have their size explicitly set.
- addr=⟨A⟩ or symbol=⟨A⟩ The kernel address of the data being instrumented. If "symbol" is used, the symbol must be globally visible to the in-kernel ksyms(4) driver.
- n=⟨N⟩ The MIB number to be assigned to the new node. If no number is specified, the kernel will assign a value.
- flags=⟨F⟩ A concatenated string of single letters that govern the behavior of the node. Flags currently available are:

a   Allow anyone to write to the node, if it is writable.

h   "Hidden". **sysctl** must be invoked with −A or the hidden node must be specifically requested in order to see it

i   "Immediate". Makes the node store data in itself, rather than allocating new space for it. This is the default for nodes of type "int" and "quad". This is the opposite of owning data.

o   "Own". When the node is created, separate space will be allocated to store the data to be instrumented. This is the default for nodes of type "string" and "struct" where it is not possible to guarantee sufficient space to store the data in the node itself.

p   "Private". Nodes that are marked private, and children of nodes so marked, are only viewable by the superuser. Be aware that the immediate data that some nodes may store is not necessarily protected by this.

x   "Hexadecimal". Make **sysctl** default to hexadecimal display of the retrieved value

r   "Read-only". The data instrumented by the given node is read-only. Note that other mechanisms may still exist for changing the data. This is the default for nodes that instrument data.

    w   "Writable". The data instrumented by the given node is writable at any time. This is the default for nodes that can have children.

- *value=*⟨*V*⟩ An initial starting value for a new node that does not reference existing kernel data. Initial values can only be assigned for nodes of the "int", "quad", and "string" types.

New nodes must fit the following set of criteria:

- If the new node is to address an existing kernel object, only one of the "symbol" or "addr" arguments may be given.
- The size for a "struct" type node must be specified; no initial value is expected or permitted.
- Either the size or the initial value for a "string" node must be given.
- The node which will be the parent of the new node must be writable.

If any of the given parameters describes an invalid configuration, **sysctl** will emit a diagnostic message to the standard error and exit.

Descriptions can be added by the super-user to any node that does not have one, provided that the node is not marked with the "PERMANENT" flag. The syntax is similar to the syntax for creating new nodes with the exception of the keyword that follows the double separator at the start of the command: "//describe=new.node.path=new node description". Once a description has been added, it cannot be changed or removed.

When destroying nodes, only the path to the node is necessary, i.e., "//destroy=old.node.path". No other parameters are expected or permitted. Nodes being destroyed must have no children, and their parent must be writable. Nodes that are marked with the "PERMANENT" flag (as assigned by the kernel) may not be deleted.

In all cases, the initial '=' that follows the command (eg, "create", "destroy", or "describe") may be replaced with another instance of the separator character, provided that the same separator character is used for the length of the name specification.

FILES
    /etc/sysctl.conf **sysctl** variables set at boot time

EXAMPLES
    For example, to retrieve the maximum number of processes allowed in the system, one would use the following request:

        `sysctl kern.maxproc`

To set the maximum number of processes allowed in the system to 1000, one would use the following request:

        `sysctl -w kern.maxproc=1000`

Information about the system clock rate may be obtained with:

        `sysctl kern.clockrate`

Information about the load average history may be obtained with:

        `sysctl vm.loadavg`

To view the values of the per-process variables of the current shell, the request:

        `sysctl proc.$$`

can be used if the shell interpreter replaces $$ with its pid (this is true for most shells).

To redirect core dumps to the /var/tmp/⟨username⟩ directory,

        `sysctl -w proc.$$.corename=/var/tmp/%u/%n.core`

should be used.

```
sysctl -w proc.curproc.corename=/var/tmp/%u/%n.core
```
changes the value for the sysctl process itself, and will not have the desired effect.

To create the root of a new sub-tree called "local" add some children to the new node, and some descriptions:
```
sysctl -w //create=local
sysctl -w //describe=local=my local sysctl tree
sysctl -w //create=local.esm_debug,type=int,symbol=esm_debug,flags=w
sysctl -w //describe=local.esm_debug=esm driver debug knob
sysctl -w //create=local.audiodebug,type=int,symbol=audiodebug,flags=w
sysctl -w //describe=local.audiodebug=generic audio debug knob
```
Note that the children are made writable so that the two debug settings in question can be tuned arbitrarily.

To destroy that same subtree:
```
sysctl -w //destroy=local.esm_debug
sysctl -w //destroy=local.audiodebug
sysctl -w //destroy=local
```

SEE ALSO
sysctl(3), ksyms(4), sysctl(7)

HISTORY
sysctl first appeared in 4.4 BSD.

NAME

sysinst — install or upgrade a NetBSD system

SYNOPSIS

sysinst

DESCRIPTION

sysinst is a menu-based program that may be used to install or upgrade a NetBSD system. It is usually invoked automatically when the system is booted from appropriate installation media.

sysinst is usually not present on a NetBSD system that has been fully installed.

SEE ALSO

release(7), afterboot(8), boot(8), diskless(8), *<machine>*/INSTALL.* files on CD-ROM installation media, .../NetBSD-*<rel>*/*<machine>*/INSTALL.* files in NetBSD releases or snapshots.

HISTORY

A **sysinst** command appeared in NetBSD 1.3.

NAME

syslogd — log systems messages

SYNOPSIS

syslogd [**-dnrSsTUv**] [**-b** *bind_address*] [**-f** *config_file*] [**-g** *group*]
[**-m** *mark_interval*] [**-o** *output_format*] [**-P** *file_list*] [**-p** *log_socket*
[**-p** *log_socket2* . . .]] [**-t** *chroot_dir*] [**-u** *user*]

DESCRIPTION

syslogd reads and logs messages to the system console, log files, other machines and/or users as specified by its configuration file. The options are as follows:

-b *bind_address*

Specify one specific IP address or hostname to bind to. If a hostname is specified, the IPv4 or IPv6 address which corresponds to it is used.

-d

Enable debugging to the standard output, and do not disassociate from the controlling terminal.

-f *config_file*

Specify the pathname of an alternative configuration file; the default is /etc/syslog.conf.

-g *group*   Set GID to *group* after the sockets and log files have been opened.

-m *mark_interval*

Select the number of minutes between "mark" messages; the default is 20 minutes.

-n   Do not perform hostname lookups; report only numeric addresses.

-o *output_format*

Select output message format.

rfc3164 traditional BSD Syslog format (default)

syslog   new syslog-protocol format

-P   Specify the pathname of a file containing a list of sockets to be created. The format of the file is simply one socket per line.

-p *log_socket*

Specify the pathname of a log socket. Multiple **-p** options create multiple log sockets. If no **-p** arguments are created, the default socket of /var/run/log is used.

-r   Disable the compression of repeated instances of the same line into a single line of the form "last message repeated N times".

-S   Sync kernel messages to disk immediately.

-s   Select "secure" mode, in which **syslogd** does not listen on a UDP socket but only communicates over a UNIX domain socket. This is valuable when the machine on which **syslogd** runs is subject to attack over the network and it is desired that the machine be protected from attempts to remotely fill logs and similar attacks.

-t *chroot_dir*

chroot(2) to *chroot_dir* after the sockets and log files have been opened.

-T   Always use the local time and date for messages received from the network, instead of the timestamp field supplied in the message by the remote host. This is useful if some of the originating hosts can't keep time properly or are unable to generate a correct timestamp.

−u *user*   Set UID to *user* after the sockets and log files have been opened.

−U   Unique priority logging. Only log messages at the priority specified by the selector in the configuration file. Without this option, messages at the specified priority or higher are logged. This option changes the default priority comparison from '>=' to '='.

−v   Verbose logging. If specified once, the numeric facility and priority are logged with each locally-written message. If specified more than once, the names of the facility and priority are logged with each locally-written message.

syslogd reads its configuration file when it starts up and whenever it receives a hangup signal. For information on the format of the configuration file, see `syslog.conf`(5).

syslogd reads messages from the UNIX domain socket `/var/run/log`, from an Internet domain socket specified in `/etc/services`, and from the special device `/dev/klog` (to read kernel messages).

syslogd creates the file `/var/run/syslogd.pid`, and stores its process id there. This can be used to kill or reconfigure **syslogd**.

By using multiple **−p** options, one can set up many chroot environments by passing the pathname to the log socket (`/var/run/log`) in each chroot area to **syslogd**. For example:

```
syslogd -p /var/run/log -p /web/var/run/log -p /ftp/var/run/log
```

Note: the normal log socket must now also be passed to **syslogd**.

The logged message includes the date, time, and hostname (or pathname of the log socket). Commonly, the program name and the process id is included.

The date and time are taken from the received message. If the format of the timestamp field is incorrect, time obtained from the local host is used instead. This can be overridden by the **−T** flag.

Accesses from UDP socket can be filtered by libwrap configuration files, like `/etc/hosts.deny`. Specify "syslogd" in *daemon_list* portion of the configuration files. Refer to `hosts_access`(5) for details.

SYSLOG PROTOCOL NOTES

syslogd accepts messages in traditional BSD Syslog or in newer Syslog Protocol format. See RFC 3164 (BSD Syslog) and RFC 5424 (Syslog Protocol) for detailed description of the message format. Messages from the local kernel that are not tagged with a priority code receive the default facility `LOG_KERN` and priority `LOG_NOTICE`. All other untagged messages receive the default facility `LOG_USER` and priority `LOG_NOTICE`.

FILES

`/etc/syslog.conf`	The configuration file.
`/var/run/syslogd.pid`	The process id of current **syslogd**.
`/var/run/log`	Name of the UNIX domain datagram log socket.
`/dev/klog`	The kernel log device.

SEE ALSO

`logger`(1), `syslog`(3), `services`(5), `syslog.conf`(5), `newsyslog`(8)

The BSD syslog Protocol, RFC, 3164, August 2001.

The Syslog Protocol, RFC, 5424, March 2009.

HISTORY

The **syslogd** command appeared in 4.3 BSD. Support for multiple log sockets appeared in NetBSD 1.4. libwrap support appeared in NetBSD 1.6.

NAME
   tadpolectl — get or set tadpole microcontroller state

SYNOPSIS
   tadpolectl [**-n**] *name* . . .
   tadpolectl [**-n**] **-w** *name=value* . . .
   tadpolectl [**-n**] **-a**

DESCRIPTION
   The **tadpolectl** utility retrieves values from the ts102 microcontroller and allows processes with appropriate privilege to set some values. The state to be retrieved or set is described using a "Management Information Base" ("MIB") style name, described as a dotted set of components. The **-a** flag can be used to list all the currently available string or integer values.

   The **-n** flag specifies that the printing of the field name should be suppressed and that only its value should be output. This flag is useful for setting shell variables. For example, to save the mains power status in variable mains, use:
       set mains='tadpolectl -n hw.power.mains'

   If just a MIB style name is given, the corresponding value is retrieved. If a value is to be set, the **-w** flag must be specified and the MIB name followed by an equal sign and the new value to be used.

   The information available from **tadpolectl** consists of only integers. Some registers can be modified, but have no way of reading what the current value is. Those registers will always display "0".

   The changeable column indicates whether a process with appropriate privilege can change the value, and if a displayed value is valid.

Name	Changeable	Valid
hw.microcontroller.version	no	yes
hw.version	no	yes
hw.poweroncycles	no	yes
hw.poweronseconds	no	yes
hw.power.mains	no	yes
hw.power.battery.int	no	yes
hw.power.battery.ext	no	yes
hw.power.battery.chargedisabled	yes	yes
hw.power.battery.int.chargerate	yes	yes
hw.power.battery.ext.chargerate	yes	yes
hw.power.battery.int.chargelevel	no	yes
hw.power.battery.ext.chargelevel	no	yes
hw.video.external	no	yes
hw.video.lid	no	yes
hw.video.syncinva	yes	yes
hw.video.syncinvb	yes	yes
hw.video.compsync	yes	yes
hw.video.tft.brightness	yes	yes
hw.speaker.freq	yes	no
hw.speaker.volume	yes	yes
hw.kbd.repeat.delay	yes	yes
hw.kbd.repeat.speed	yes	yes
hw.kbd.click	yes	yes

hw.mouse.recalibrate	yes	no
hw.mouse.disable	yes	yes
hw.mouse.intclick	yes	yes
hw.mouse.extclick	yes	yes
hw.mouse.sensitivity	yes	yes
hw.serial.power	yes	yes

EXAMPLES

For example, to retrieve the current internal battery charge level, one would use the following request:

```
tadpolectl hw.power.battery.int.chargelevel
```

To set the speaker beep frequency of the system to 1000, one would use the following request:

```
tadpolectl -w hw.speaker.freq=1000
```

SEE ALSO

sysctl(8)

HISTORY

tadpolectl first appeared in NetBSD 1.5.

NAME

    tbrconfig — configure a token bucket regulator for an output queue

SYNOPSIS

    tbrconfig *interface* [*tokenrate* [*bucketsize*]]
    tbrconfig -d *interface*
    tbrconfig -a

DESCRIPTION

    tbrconfig configures a token bucket regulator for the output network interface queue. A token bucket regulator limits both the average amount and instantaneous amount of packets that the underlying driver can dequeue from the network interface within the kernel.

    Conceptually, tokens accumulate in a bucket at the average *tokenrate*, up to the *bucketsize*. The driver can dequeue packets as long as there are positive amount of tokens, and the length of the dequeued packet is subtracted from the remaining tokens. Tokens can be negative as a deficit, and packets are not dequeued from the interface queue until the tokens become positive again. The *tokenrate* limits the average rate, and the *bucketsize* limits the maximum burst size.

    Limiting the burst size is essential to packet scheduling, since the scheduler schedules packets backlogged at the network interface. Limiting the burst size is also needed for drivers which dequeues more packets than they can send and end up with discarding excess packets.

    When the *tokenrate* is set to higher than the actual transmission rate, the transmission complete interrupt will trigger the next dequeue. On the other hand, when the *tokenrate* is set to lower than the actual transmission rate, the transmission complete interrupt would occur before the tokens become positive. In this case, the next dequeue will be triggered by a timer event. Because the kernel timer has a limited granularity, a larger *bucketsize* is required for a higher *tokenrate*.

    The *interface* parameter is a string of the form "name unit", for example, "en0".

    The *tokenrate* parameter specifies the average rate in bits per second, and "K" or "M" can be appended to *tokenrate* as a short hand of "Kilo-bps" or "Mega-bps", respectively. When *tokenrate* is omitted, **tbrconfig** displays the current parameter values.

    The *bucketsize* parameter specifies the bucket size in bytes, and "K" can be appended to *bucketsize* as a short hand of "Kilo-bytes". When *bucketsize* is omitted, **tbrconfig** assumes the regulator is driven by transmission complete interrupts and, using heuristics, assigns a small bucket size according to the *tokenrate*. When the keyword "auto" is given as *bucketsize*, **tbrconfig** assumes the regulator is driven by the kernel timer, and computes the bucket size from *tokenrate* and the kernel clock frequency.

    If the **-d** flag is passed before an interface name, **tbrconfig** will remove the token bucket regulator for the specified interface.

    Optionally, the **-a** flag may be used instead of an interface name. This flag instructs **tbrconfig** to display information about all interfaces in the system.

EXAMPLES

    To configure a token bucket regulator for the interface en0 with 10Mbps token rate and 8KB bucket size,

```
# tbrconfig en0 10M 8K
```

    To rate-limit the interface en0 up to 3Mbps,

```
# tbrconfig en0 3M auto
```

SEE ALSO
     altq.conf(5), altqd(8)

HISTORY
     The **tbrconfig** command first appeared in WIDE/KAME IPv6 protocol stack kit as part of ALTQ tools.

NAME
tcpdchk – tcp wrapper configuration checker

SYNOPSIS
tcpdchk [-a] [-d] [-i inet_conf] [-v]

DESCRIPTION
tcpdchk examines your tcp wrapper configuration and reports all potential and real problems it can find. The program examines the *tcpd* access control files (by default, these are */etc/hosts.allow* and */etc/hosts.deny*), and compares the entries in these files against entries in the *inetd* or *tlid* network configuration files.

tcpdchk reports problems such as non-existent pathnames; services that appear in *tcpd* access control rules, but are not controlled by *tcpd*; services that should not be wrapped; non-existent host names or non-internet address forms; occurrences of host aliases instead of official host names; hosts with a name/address conflict; inappropriate use of wildcard patterns; inappropriate use of NIS netgroups or references to non-existent NIS netgroups; references to non-existent options; invalid arguments to options; and so on.

Where possible, *tcpdchk* provides a helpful suggestion to fix the problem.

OPTIONS
-a   Report access control rules that permit access without an explicit ALLOW keyword. This applies only when the extended access control language is enabled (build with -DPROCESS_OPTIONS).

-d   Examine *hosts.allow* and *hosts.deny* files in the current directory instead of the default ones.

-i inet_conf
          Specify this option when *tcpdchk* is unable to find your *inetd.conf* or *tlid.conf* network configuration file, or when you suspect that the program uses the wrong one.

-v   Display the contents of each access control rule. Daemon lists, client lists, shell commands and options are shown in a pretty-printed format; this makes it easier for you to spot any discrepancies between what you want and what the program understands.

FILES
The default locations of the *tcpd* access control tables are:

/etc/hosts.allow
/etc/hosts.deny

SEE ALSO
tcpdmatch(8), explain what tcpd would do in specific cases.
hosts_access(5), format of the tcpd access control tables.
hosts_options(5), format of the language extensions.
inetd.conf(5), format of the inetd control file.

AUTHORS
Wietse Venema (wietse@wzv.win.tue.nl),
Department of Mathematics and Computing Science,
Eindhoven University of Technology
Den Dolech 2, P.O. Box 513,
5600 MB Eindhoven, The Netherlands

NAME
tcpdmatch – tcp wrapper oracle

SYNOPSIS
tcpdmatch [-d] [-i inet_conf] daemon client

tcpdmatch [-d] [-i inet_conf] daemon[@server] [user@]client

DESCRIPTION
tcpdmatch predicts how the tcp wrapper would handle a specific request for service. Examples are given below.

The program examines the *tcpd* access control tables (default */etc/hosts.allow* and */etc/hosts.deny*) and prints its conclusion. For maximal accuracy, it extracts additional information from your *inetd* or *tlid* network configuration file.

When *tcpdmatch* finds a match in the access control tables, it identifies the matched rule. In addition, it displays the optional shell commands or options in a pretty-printed format; this makes it easier for you to spot any discrepancies between what you want and what the program understands.

ARGUMENTS
The following two arguments are always required:

daemon

A daemon process name. Typically, the last component of a daemon executable pathname.

client   A host name or network address, or one of the 'unknown' or 'paranoid' wildcard patterns.

When a client host name is specified, *tcpdmatch* gives a prediction for each address listed for that client.

When a client address is specified, *tcpdmatch* predicts what *tcpd* would do when client name lookup fails.

Optional information specified with the *daemon@server* form:

server   A host name or network address, or one of the 'unknown' or 'paranoid' wildcard patterns. The default server name is 'unknown'.

Optional information specified with the *user@client* form:

user   A client user identifier. Typically, a login name or a numeric userid. The default user name is 'unknown'.

OPTIONS
-d   Examine *hosts.allow* and *hosts.deny* files in the current directory instead of the default ones.

-i inet_conf
Specify this option when *tcpdmatch* is unable to find your *inetd.conf* or *tlid.conf* network configuration file, or when you suspect that the program uses the wrong one.

EXAMPLES
To predict how *tcpd* would handle a telnet request from the local system:

tcpdmatch in.telnetd localhost

The same request, pretending that hostname lookup failed:

tcpdmatch in.telnetd 127.0.0.1

To predict what tcpd would do when the client name does not match the client address:

tcpdmatch in.telnetd paranoid

On some systems, daemon names have no 'in.' prefix, or *tcpdmatch* may need some help to locate the inetd

1

configuration file.

FILES

The default locations of the *tcpd* access control tables are:

/etc/hosts.allow
/etc/hosts.deny

SEE ALSO

tcpdchk(8), tcpd configuration checker
hosts_access(5), format of the tcpd access control tables.
hosts_options(5), format of the language extensions.
inetd.conf(5), format of the inetd control file.

AUTHORS

Wietse Venema (wietse@wzv.win.tue.nl),
Department of Mathematics and Computing Science,
Eindhoven University of Technology
Den Dolech 2, P.O. Box 513,
5600 MB Eindhoven, The Netherlands

BUGS

If you specify FQDN hostname as client, they will be recognized only as IPv4 or IPv6 address, which
should be recognized as both.

NAME
tcpdrop — drop a TCP connection

SYNOPSIS
tcpdrop *laddr lport faddr fport*

DESCRIPTION
The **tcpdrop** command drops the TCP connection specified by the local address *laddr*, port *lport* and the foreign address *faddr*, port *fport*. Addresses and ports can be specified by name or numeric value.

EXAMPLES
If a connection to httpd(8) is causing congestion on a network link, one can drop the TCP session in charge:

```
$ fstat | grep 'httpd.*internet.*<--'
www       httpd       21307    3* internet stream tcp \
          0xd1007ca8 192.168.5.41:80 <-- 192.168.5.1:26747
```

The following command will drop the connection:

```
# tcpdrop 192.168.5.41 80 192.168.5.1 26747
```

SEE ALSO
fstat(1), netstat(1)

NAME

tcpdump – dump traffic on a network

SYNOPSIS

tcpdump [**−AdDefILnNOpqRStuUvxX**] [**−c** *count*]
             [**−C** *file_size*] [**−F** *file*]
             [**−i** *interface*] [**−m** *module*] [**−M** *secret*]
             [**−r** *file*] [**−s** *snaplen*] [**−T** *type*] [**−w** *file*]
             [**−W** *filecount*]
             [**−E** *spi@ipaddr algo:secret,...*]
             [**−y** *datalinktype*] [**−Z** *user*]
             [*expression*]

DESCRIPTION

Tcpdump prints out a description of the contents of packets on a network interface that match the boolean *expression*. It can also be run with the **−w** flag, which causes it to save the packet data to a file for later analysis, and/or with the **−r** flag, which causes it to read from a saved packet file rather than to read packets from a network interface. In all cases, only packets that match *expression* will be processed by *tcpdump*.

Tcpdump will, if not run with the **−c** flag, continue capturing packets until it is interrupted by a SIGINT signal (generated, for example, by typing your interrupt character, typically control-C) or a SIGTERM signal (typically generated with the **kill**(1) command); if run with the **−c** flag, it will capture packets until it is interrupted by a SIGINT or SIGTERM signal or the specified number of packets have been processed.

When *tcpdump* finishes capturing packets, it will report counts of:

> packets "captured" (this is the number of packets that *tcpdump* has received and processed);

> packets "received by filter" (the meaning of this depends on the OS on which you're running *tcpdump*, and possibly on the way the OS was configured - if a filter was specified on the command line, on some OSes it counts packets regardless of whether they were matched by the filter expression and, even if they were matched by the filter expression, regardless of whether *tcpdump* has read and processed them yet, on other OSes it counts only packets that were matched by the filter expression regardless of whether *tcpdump* has read and processed them yet, and on other OSes it counts only packets that were matched by the filter expression and were processed by *tcpdump*);

> packets "dropped by kernel" (this is the number of packets that were dropped, due to a lack of buffer space, by the packet capture mechanism in the OS on which *tcpdump* is running, if the OS reports that information to applications; if not, it will be reported as 0).

On platforms that support the SIGINFO signal, such as most BSDs (including Mac OS X) and Digital/Tru64 UNIX, it will report those counts when it receives a SIGINFO signal (generated, for example, by typing your "status" character, typically control-T) and will continue capturing packets.

Reading packets from a network interface may require that you have special privileges: You must have read access to */dev/bpf*.

Reading a saved packet file doesn't require special privileges.

OPTIONS

−A   Print each packet (minus its link level header) in ASCII. Handy for capturing web pages.

−a   Attempt to convert network and broadcast addresses to names.

−c   Exit after receiving *count* packets.

−C   Before writing a raw packet to a savefile, check whether the file is currently larger than *file_size* and, if so, close the current savefile and open a new one. Savefiles after the first savefile will have the name specified with the **−w** flag, with a number after it, starting at 1 and continuing upward. The units of *file_size* are millions of bytes (1,000,000 bytes, not 1,048,576 bytes).

−d   Dump the compiled packet-matching code in a human readable form to standard output and stop.

−dd   Dump packet-matching code as a **C** program fragment.

−ddd   Dump packet-matching code as decimal numbers (preceded with a count).

−D   Print the list of the network interfaces available on the system and on which *tcpdump* can capture packets. For each network interface, a number and an interface name, possibly followed by a text description of the interface, is printed. The interface name or the number can be supplied to the **−i** flag to specify an interface on which to capture.

This can be useful on systems that don't have a command to list them (e.g., Windows systems, or UNIX systems lacking **ifconfig −a**); the number can be useful on Windows 2000 and later systems, where the interface name is a somewhat complex string.

The **−D** flag will not be supported if *tcpdump* was built with an older version of *libpcap* that lacks the **pcap_findalldevs()** function.

−e   Print the link-level header on each dump line.

−E   Use *spi@ipaddr algo:secret* for decrypting IPsec ESP packets that are addressed to *addr* and contain Security Parameter Index value *spi*. This combination may be repeated with comma or newline seperation.

Note that setting the secret for IPv4 ESP packets is supported at this time.

Algorithms may be **des-cbc**, **3des-cbc**, **blowfish-cbc**, **rc3-cbc**, **cast128-cbc**, or **none**. The default is **des-cbc**. The ability to decrypt packets is only present if *tcpdump* was compiled with cryptography enabled.

secret is the ASCII text for ESP secret key. If preceded by 0x, then a hex value will be read.

The option assumes RFC2406 ESP, not RFC1827 ESP. The option is only for debugging purposes, and the use of this option with a true 'secret' key is discouraged. By presenting IPsec secret key onto command line you make it visible to others, via *ps*(1) and other occasions.

In addition to the above syntax, the syntax *file name* may be used to have tcpdump read the provided file in. The file is opened upon receiving the first ESP packet, so any special permissions that tcpdump may have been given should already have been given up.

−f   Print 'foreign' IPv4 addresses numerically rather than symbolically (this option is intended to get around serious brain damage in Sun's NIS server — usually it hangs forever translating non-local internet numbers).

The test for 'foreign' IPv4 addresses is done using the IPv4 address and netmask of the interface on which capture is being done. If that address or netmask are not available, available, either because the interface on which capture is being done has no address or netmask or because the capture is being done on the Linux "any" interface, which can capture on more than one interface, this option will not work correctly.

−F   Use *file* as input for the filter expression. An additional expression given on the command line is ignored.

−i   Listen on *interface*. If unspecified, *tcpdump* searches the system interface list for the lowest numbered, configured up interface (excluding loopback). Ties are broken by choosing the earliest match.

If the **−D** flag is supported, an interface number as printed by that flag can be used as the *interface* argument.

−l   Make stdout line buffered. Useful if you want to see the data while capturing it. E.g., "tcpdump −l | tee dat" or "tcpdump −l > dat & tail −f dat".

−L   List the known data link types for the interface and exit.

−m   Load SMI MIB module definitions from file *module*. This option can be used several times to load several MIB modules into *tcpdump*.

−M   Use *secret* as a shared secret for validating the digests found in TCP segments with the TCP-MD5 option (RFC 2385), if present.

−n   Don't convert addresses (i.e., host addresses, port numbers, etc.) to names.

−N   Don't print domain name qualification of host names. E.g., if you give this flag then *tcpdump* will print "nic" instead of "nic.ddn.mil".

−O   Do not run the packet-matching code optimizer. This is useful only if you suspect a bug in the optimizer.

−p   *Don't* put the interface into promiscuous mode. Note that the interface might be in promiscuous mode for some other reason; hence, '-p' cannot be used as an abbreviation for 'ether host {local-hw-addr} or ether broadcast'.

−q   Quick (quiet?) output. Print less protocol information so output lines are shorter.

−R   Assume ESP/AH packets to be based on old specification (RFC1825 to RFC1829). If specified, *tcpdump* will not print replay prevention field. Since there is no protocol version field in ESP/AH specification, *tcpdump* cannot deduce the version of ESP/AH protocol.

−r   Read packets from *file* (which was created with the **−w** option). Standard input is used if *file* is "-".

−S   Print absolute, rather than relative, TCP sequence numbers.

−s   Snarf *snaplen* bytes of data from each packet rather than the default of 68 (with SunOS's NIT, the minimum is actually 96). 68 bytes is adequate for IP, ICMP, TCP and UDP but may truncate protocol information from name server and NFS packets (see below). Packets truncated because of a limited snapshot are indicated in the output with "[|*proto*]", where *proto* is the name of the protocol level at which the truncation has occurred. Note that taking larger snapshots both increases the amount of time it takes to process packets and, effectively, decreases the amount of packet buffering. This may cause packets to be lost. You should limit *snaplen* to the smallest number that will capture the protocol information you're interested in. Setting *snaplen* to 0 means use the required length to catch whole packets.

−T   Force packets selected by "*expression*" to be interpreted the specified *type*. Currently known types are **aodv** (Ad-hoc On-demand Distance Vector protocol), **cnfp** (Cisco NetFlow protocol), **rpc** (Remote Procedure Call), **rtp** (Real-Time Applications protocol), **rtcp** (Real-Time Applications control protocol), **snmp** (Simple Network Management Protocol), **tftp** (Trivial File Transfer Protocol), **vat** (Visual Audio Tool), and **wb** (distributed White Board).

−t   *Don't* print a timestamp on each dump line.

−tt   Print an unformatted timestamp on each dump line.

−ttt   Print a delta (in micro-seconds) between current and previous line on each dump line.

−tttt   Print a timestamp in default format proceeded by date on each dump line.

−u   Print undecoded NFS handles.

−U   Make output saved via the **−w** option "packet-buffered"; i.e., as each packet is saved, it will be written to the output file, rather than being written only when the output buffer fills.

           The **−U** flag will not be supported if *tcpdump* was built with an older version of *libpcap* that lacks the **pcap_dump_flush()** function.

−v   When parsing and printing, produce (slightly more) verbose output. For example, the time to live, identification, total length and options in an IP packet are printed. Also enables additional packet integrity checks such as verifying the IP and ICMP header checksum.

           When writing to a file with the **−w** option, report, every 10 seconds, the number of packets captured.

−vv   Even more verbose output. For example, additional fields are printed from NFS reply packets, and SMB packets are fully decoded.

−vvv   Even more verbose output. For example, telnet **SB** ... **SE** options are printed in full. With **−X** Telnet options are printed in hex as well.

−w   Write the raw packets to *file* rather than parsing and printing them out. They can later be printed with the −r option. Standard output is used if *file* is "-".

−W   Used in conjunction with the −C option, this will limit the number of files created to the specified number, and begin overwriting files from the beginning, thus creating a 'rotating' buffer. In addition, it will name the files with enough leading 0s to support the maximum number of files, allowing them to sort correctly.

−x   When parsing and printing, in addition to printing the headers of each packet, print the data of each packet (minus its link level header) in hex. The smaller of the entire packet or *snaplen* bytes will be printed. Note that this is the entire link-layer packet, so for link layers that pad (e.g. Ethernet), the padding bytes will also be printed when the higher layer packet is shorter than the required padding.

−xx   When parsing and printing, in addition to printing the headers of each packet, print the data of each packet, *including* its link level header, in hex.

−X   When parsing and printing, in addition to printing the headers of each packet, print the data of each packet (minus its link level header) in hex and ASCII. This is very handy for analysing new protocols.

−XX   When parsing and printing, in addition to printing the headers of each packet, print the data of each packet, *including* its link level header, in hex and ASCII.

−y   Set the data link type to use while capturing packets to *datalinktype*. The available data link types may be found using the −L option.

−Z   Drops privileges (if root) and changes user ID to *user* and the group ID to the primary group of *user*.

          This behavior can also be enabled by default at compile time.

expression

          selects which packets will be dumped. If no *expression* is given, all packets on the net will be dumped. Otherwise, only packets for which *expression* is 'true' will be dumped.

          The *expression* consists of one or more *primitives*. Primitives usually consist of an *id* (name or number) preceded by one or more qualifiers. There are three different kinds of qualifier:

type   qualifiers say what kind of thing the id name or number refers to. Possible types are **host**, **net , port** and **portrange**. E.g., 'host foo', 'net 128.3', 'port 20', 'portrange 6000-6008'. If there is no type qualifier, **host** is assumed.

dir   qualifiers specify a particular transfer direction to and/or from *id*. Possible directions are **src**, **dst**, **src or dst** and **src and dst**. E.g., 'src foo', 'dst net 128.3', 'src or dst port ftp-data'. If there is no dir qualifier, **src or dst** is assumed. For some link layers, such as SLIP and the "cooked" Linux capture mode used for the "any" device and for some other device types, the **inbound** and **outbound** qualifiers can be used to specify a desired direction.

proto   qualifiers restrict the match to a particular protocol. Possible protos are: **ether**, **fddi**, **tr**, **wlan**, **ip**, **ip6**, **arp**, **rarp**, **decnet**, **tcp** and **udp**. E.g., 'ether src foo', 'arp net 128.3', 'tcp port 21', 'udp portrange 7000-7009'. If there is no proto qualifier, all protocols consistent with the type are assumed. E.g., 'src foo' means '(ip or arp or rarp) src foo' (except the latter is not legal syntax), 'net bar' means '(ip or arp or rarp) net bar' and 'port 53' means '(tcp or udp) port 53'.

          ['fddi' is actually an alias for 'ether'; the parser treats them identically as meaning "the data link level used on the specified network interface." FDDI headers contain Ethernet-like source and destination addresses, and often contain Ethernet-like packet types, so you can filter on these FDDI fields just as with the analogous Ethernet fields. FDDI headers also contain other fields, but you cannot name them explicitly in a filter expression.

Similarly, 'tr' and 'wlan' are aliases for 'ether'; the previous paragraph's statements about FDDI headers also apply to Token Ring and 802.11 wireless LAN headers. For 802.11 headers, the destination address is the DA field and the source address is the SA field; the BSSID, RA, and TA fields aren't tested.]

In addition to the above, there are some special 'primitive' keywords that don't follow the pattern: **gateway**, **broadcast**, **less**, **greater** and arithmetic expressions. All of these are described below.

More complex filter expressions are built up by using the words **and**, **or** and **not** to combine primitives. E.g., 'host foo and not port ftp and not port ftp-data'. To save typing, identical qualifier lists can be omitted. E.g., 'tcp dst port ftp or ftp-data or domain' is exactly the same as 'tcp dst port ftp or tcp dst port ftp-data or tcp dst port domain'.

Allowable primitives are:

dst host *host*
> True if the IPv4/v6 destination field of the packet is *host*, which may be either an address or a name.

src host *host*
> True if the IPv4/v6 source field of the packet is *host*.

host *host*
> True if either the IPv4/v6 source or destination of the packet is *host*.
>
> Any of the above host expressions can be prepended with the keywords, **ip**, **arp**, **rarp**, or **ip6** as in:
>> **ip host** *host*
> which is equivalent to:
>> **ether proto** *ip* **and host** *host*
> If *host* is a name with multiple IP addresses, each address will be checked for a match.

ether dst *ehost*
> True if the Ethernet destination address is *ehost*. *Ehost* may be either a name from /etc/ethers or a number (see *ethers*(3N) for numeric format).

ether src *ehost*
> True if the Ethernet source address is *ehost*.

ether host *ehost*
> True if either the Ethernet source or destination address is *ehost*.

gateway *host*
> True if the packet used *host* as a gateway. I.e., the Ethernet source or destination address was *host* but neither the IP source nor the IP destination was *host*. *Host* must be a name and must be found both by the machine's host-name-to-IP-address resolution mechanisms (host name file, DNS, NIS, etc.) and by the machine's host-name-to-Ethernet-address resolution mechanism (/etc/ethers, etc.). (An equivalent expression is
>> **ether host** *ehost* **and not host** *host*
> which can be used with either names or numbers for *host / ehost*.) This syntax does not work in IPv6-enabled configuration at this moment.

dst net *net*
> True if the IPv4/v6 destination address of the packet has a network number of *net*. *Net* may be either a name from the networks database (/etc/networks, etc.) or a network number. An IPv4 network number can be written as a dotted quad (e.g., 192.168.1.0), dotted triple (e.g., 192.168.1), dotted pair (e.g, 172.16), or single number (e.g., 10); the netmask

is 255.255.255.255 for a dotted quad (which means that it's really a host match), 255.255.255.0 for a dotted triple, 255.255.0.0 for a dotted pair, or 255.0.0.0 for a single number. An IPv6 network number must be written out fully; the netmask is ff:ff:ff:ff:ff:ff:ff:ff, so IPv6 "network" matches are really always host matches, and a network match requires a netmask length.

src net *net*
> True if the IPv4/v6 source address of the packet has a network number of *net*.

net *net*   True if either the IPv4/v6 source or destination address of the packet has a network number of *net*.

net *net* **mask** *netmask*
> True if the IPv4 address matches *net* with the specific *netmask*. May be qualified with **src** or **dst**. Note that this syntax is not valid for IPv6 *net*.

net *net/len*
> True if the IPv4/v6 address matches *net* with a netmask *len* bits wide. May be qualified with **src** or **dst**.

dst port *port*
> True if the packet is ip/tcp, ip/udp, ip6/tcp or ip6/udp and has a destination port value of *port*. The *port* can be a number or a name used in /etc/services (see *tcp*(4P) and *udp*(4P)). If a name is used, both the port number and protocol are checked. If a number or ambiguous name is used, only the port number is checked (e.g., **dst port 513** will print both tcp/login traffic and udp/who traffic, and **port domain** will print both tcp/domain and udp/domain traffic).

src port *port*
> True if the packet has a source port value of *port*.

port *port*
> True if either the source or destination port of the packet is *port*.

dst portrange *port1-port2*
> True if the packet is ip/tcp, ip/udp, ip6/tcp or ip6/udp and has a destination port value between *port1* and *port2*. *port1* and *port2* are interpreted in the same fashion as the *port* parameter for **port**.

src portrange *port1-port2*
> True if the packet has a source port value between *port1* and *port2*.

portrange *port1-port2*
> True if either the source or destination port of the packet is between *port1* and *port2*.

> Any of the above port or port range expressions can be prepended with the keywords, **tcp** or **udp**, as in:
>> **tcp src port** *port*
> which matches only tcp packets whose source port is *port*.

less *length*
> True if the packet has a length less than or equal to *length*. This is equivalent to:
>> **len <=** *length.*

greater *length*
> True if the packet has a length greater than or equal to *length*. This is equivalent to:
>> **len >=** *length.*

ip proto *protocol*
> True if the packet is an IPv4 packet (see *ip*(4P)) of protocol type *protocol*. *Protocol* can be a number or one of the names **icmp**, **icmp6**, **igmp**, **igrp**, **pim**, **ah**, **esp**, **vrrp**, **udp**, or **tcp**. Note that the identifiers **tcp**, **udp**, and **icmp** are also keywords and must be escaped via backslash (\), which is \\ in the C-shell. Note that this primitive does not chase the

protocol header chain.

ip6 proto *protocol*

True if the packet is an IPv6 packet of protocol type *protocol*. Note that this primitive does not chase the protocol header chain.

ip6 protochain *protocol*

True if the packet is IPv6 packet, and contains protocol header with type *protocol* in its protocol header chain. For example,

ip6 protochain 6

matches any IPv6 packet with TCP protocol header in the protocol header chain. The packet may contain, for example, authentication header, routing header, or hop-by-hop option header, between IPv6 header and TCP header. The BPF code emitted by this primitive is complex and cannot be optimized by BPF optimizer code in *tcpdump*, so this can be somewhat slow.

ip protochain *protocol*

Equivalent to **ip6 protochain** *protocol*, but this is for IPv4.

ether broadcast

True if the packet is an Ethernet broadcast packet. The *ether* keyword is optional.

ip broadcast

True if the packet is an IPv4 broadcast packet. It checks for both the all-zeroes and all-ones broadcast conventions, and looks up the subnet mask on the interface on which the capture is being done.

If the subnet mask of the interface on which the capture is being done is not available, either because the interface on which capture is being done has no netmask or because the capture is being done on the Linux "any" interface, which can capture on more than one interface, this check will not work correctly.

ether multicast

True if the packet is an Ethernet multicast packet. The **ether** keyword is optional. This is shorthand for '**ether[0] & 1 != 0**'.

ip multicast

True if the packet is an IPv4 multicast packet.

ip6 multicast

True if the packet is an IPv6 multicast packet.

ether proto *protocol*

True if the packet is of ether type *protocol*. *Protocol* can be a number or one of the names **ip**, **ip6**, **arp**, **rarp**, **atalk**, **aarp**, **decnet**, **sca**, **lat**, **mopdl**, **moprc**, **iso**, **stp**, **ipx**, or **netbeui**. Note these identifiers are also keywords and must be escaped via backslash (\).

[In the case of FDDI (e.g., '**fddi protocol arp**'), Token Ring (e.g., '**tr protocol arp**'), and IEEE 802.11 wireless LANS (e.g., '**wlan protocol arp**'), for most of those protocols, the protocol identification comes from the 802.2 Logical Link Control (LLC) header, which is usually layered on top of the FDDI, Token Ring, or 802.11 header.

When filtering for most protocol identifiers on FDDI, Token Ring, or 802.11, *tcpdump* checks only the protocol ID field of an LLC header in so-called SNAP format with an Organizational Unit Identifier (OUI) of 0x000000, for encapsulated Ethernet; it doesn't check whether the packet is in SNAP format with an OUI of 0x000000. The exceptions are:

iso   *tcpdump* checks the DSAP (Destination Service Access Point) and SSAP (Source Service Access Point) fields of the LLC header;

stp and **netbeui**
> *tcpdump* checks the DSAP of the LLC header;

atalk   *tcpdump* checks for a SNAP-format packet with an OUI of 0x080007 and the AppleTalk etype.

In the case of Ethernet, *tcpdump* checks the Ethernet type field for most of those protocols. The exceptions are:

iso, **stp**, and **netbeui**
> *tcpdump* checks for an 802.3 frame and then checks the LLC header as it does for FDDI, Token Ring, and 802.11;

atalk   *tcpdump* checks both for the AppleTalk etype in an Ethernet frame and for a SNAP-format packet as it does for FDDI, Token Ring, and 802.11;

aarp   *tcpdump* checks for the AppleTalk ARP etype in either an Ethernet frame or an 802.2 SNAP frame with an OUI of 0x000000;

ipx   *tcpdump* checks for the IPX etype in an Ethernet frame, the IPX DSAP in the LLC header, the 802.3-with-no-LLC-header encapsulation of IPX, and the IPX etype in a SNAP frame.

decnet src *host*
> True if the DECNET source address is *host*, which may be an address of the form "10.123", or a DECNET host name. [DECNET host name support is only available on ULTRIX systems that are configured to run DECNET.]

decnet dst *host*
> True if the DECNET destination address is *host*.

decnet host *host*
> True if either the DECNET source or destination address is *host*.

ifname *interface*
> True if the packet was logged as coming from the specified interface (applies only to packets logged by OpenBSD's **pf**(4)).

on *interface*
> Synonymous with the **ifname** modifier.

rnr *num*
> True if the packet was logged as matching the specified PF rule number (applies only to packets logged by OpenBSD's **pf**(4)).

rulenum *num*
> Synonomous with the **rnr** modifier.

reason *code*
> True if the packet was logged with the specified PF reason code. The known codes are: **match**, **bad-offset**, **fragment**, **short**, **normalize**, and **memory** (applies only to packets logged by OpenBSD's **pf**(4)).

rset *name*
> True if the packet was logged as matching the specified PF ruleset name of an anchored ruleset (applies only to packets logged by **pf**(4)).

ruleset *name*
> Synonomous with the **rset** modifier.

srnr *num*
> True if the packet was logged as matching the specified PF rule number of an anchored ruleset (applies only to packets logged by **pf**(4)).

subrulenum *num*
> Synonomous with the **srnr** modifier.

action *act*
> True if PF took the specified action when the packet was logged. Known actions are: **pass** and **block** (applies only to packets logged by OpenBSD's **pf**(4)).

ip, **ip6**, **arp**, **rarp**, **atalk**, **aarp**, **decnet**, **iso**, **stp**, **ipx**, *netbeui*
> Abbreviations for:
>> **ether proto** *p*
> where *p* is one of the above protocols.

lat, **moprc**, **mopdl**
> Abbreviations for:
>> **ether proto** *p*
> where *p* is one of the above protocols. Note that *tcpdump* does not currently know how to parse these protocols.

vlan *[vlan_id]*
> True if the packet is an IEEE 802.1Q VLAN packet. If *[vlan_id]* is specified, only true if the packet has the specified *vlan_id*. Note that the first **vlan** keyword encountered in *expression* changes the decoding offsets for the remainder of *expression* on the assumption that the packet is a VLAN packet. The **vlan** *[vlan_id]* expression may be used more than once, to filter on VLAN hierarchies. Each use of that expression increments the filter offsets by 4.
>
> For example:
>> **vlan 100 && vlan 200**
> filters on VLAN 200 encapsulated within VLAN 100, and
>> **vlan && vlan 300 && ip**
> filters IPv4 protocols encapsulated in VLAN 300 encapsulated within any higher order VLAN.

mpls *[label_num]*
> True if the packet is an MPLS packet. If *[label_num]* is specified, only true is the packet has the specified *label_num*. Note that the first **mpls** keyword encountered in *expression* changes the decoding offsets for the remainder of *expression* on the assumption that the packet is a MPLS-encapsulated IP packet. The **mpls** *[label_num]* expression may be used more than once, to filter on MPLS hierarchies. Each use of that expression increments the filter offsets by 4.
>
> For example:
>> **mpls 100000 && mpls 1024**
> filters packets with an outer label of 100000 and an inner label of 1024, and
>> **mpls && mpls 1024 && host 192.9.200.1**
> filters packets to or from 192.9.200.1 with an inner label of 1024 and any outer label.

pppoed
> True if the packet is a PPP-over-Ethernet Discovery packet (Ethernet type 0x8863).

pppoes True if the packet is a PPP-over-Ethernet Session packet (Ethernet type 0x8864). Note that the first **pppoes** keyword encountered in *expression* changes the decoding offsets for the remainder of *expression* on the assumption that the packet is a PPPoE session packet.
> For example:
>> **pppoes && ip**
> filters IPv4 protocols encapsulated in PPPoE.

tcp, **udp**, **icmp**
> Abbreviations for:
>> **ip proto** *p* **or ip6 proto** *p*

where p is one of the above protocols.

iso proto *protocol*
> True if the packet is an OSI packet of protocol type *protocol*. *Protocol* can be a number or one of the names **clnp**, **esis**, or **isis**.

clnp, **esis**, **isis**
> Abbreviations for:
> > **iso proto** *p*
> where p is one of the above protocols.

l1, **l2**, **iih**, **lsp**, **snp**, **csnp**, **psnp**
> Abbreviations for IS-IS PDU types.

vpi *n*   True if the packet is an ATM packet, for SunATM on Solaris, with a virtual path identifier of n.

vci *n*   True if the packet is an ATM packet, for SunATM on Solaris, with a virtual channel identifier of n.

lane   True if the packet is an ATM packet, for SunATM on Solaris, and is an ATM LANE packet. Note that the first **lane** keyword encountered in *expression* changes the tests done in the remainder of *expression* on the assumption that the packet is either a LANE emulated Ethernet packet or a LANE LE Control packet. If **lane** isn't specified, the tests are done under the assumption that the packet is an LLC-encapsulated packet.

llc   True if the packet is an ATM packet, for SunATM on Solaris, and is an LLC-encapsulated packet.

oamf4s True if the packet is an ATM packet, for SunATM on Solaris, and is a segment OAM F4 flow cell (VPI=0 & VCI=3).

oamf4e
> True if the packet is an ATM packet, for SunATM on Solaris, and is an end-to-end OAM F4 flow cell (VPI=0 & VCI=4).

oamf4   True if the packet is an ATM packet, for SunATM on Solaris, and is a segment or end-to-end OAM F4 flow cell (VPI=0 & (VCI=3 | VCI=4)).

oam   True if the packet is an ATM packet, for SunATM on Solaris, and is a segment or end-to-end OAM F4 flow cell (VPI=0 & (VCI=3 | VCI=4)).

metac   True if the packet is an ATM packet, for SunATM on Solaris, and is on a meta signaling circuit (VPI=0 & VCI=1).

bcc   True if the packet is an ATM packet, for SunATM on Solaris, and is on a broadcast signaling circuit (VPI=0 & VCI=2).

sc   True if the packet is an ATM packet, for SunATM on Solaris, and is on a signaling circuit (VPI=0 & VCI=5).

ilmic   True if the packet is an ATM packet, for SunATM on Solaris, and is on an ILMI circuit (VPI=0 & VCI=16).

connectmsg
> True if the packet is an ATM packet, for SunATM on Solaris, and is on a signaling circuit and is a Q.2931 Setup, Call Proceeding, Connect, Connect Ack, Release, or Release Done message.

metaconnect
> True if the packet is an ATM packet, for SunATM on Solaris, and is on a meta signaling circuit and is a Q.2931 Setup, Call Proceeding, Connect, Release, or Release Done message.

expr relop expr

True if the relation holds, where *relop* is one of >, <, >=, <=, =, !=, and *expr* is an arithmetic expression composed of integer constants (expressed in standard C syntax), the normal binary operators [+, -, *, /, &, |, <<, >>], a length operator, and special packet data accessors. Note that all comparisons are unsigned, so that, for example, 0x80000000 and 0xffffffff are > 0. To access data inside the packet, use the following syntax:

   proto [*expr* : *size*]

Proto is one of **ether, fddi, tr, wlan, ppp, slip, link, ip, arp, rarp, tcp, udp, icmp, ip6** or **radio**, and indicates the protocol layer for the index operation. (**ether, fddi, wlan, tr, ppp, slip** and **link** all refer to the link layer. **radio** refers to the "radio header" added to some 802.11 captures.) Note that *tcp, udp* and other upper-layer protocol types only apply to IPv4, not IPv6 (this will be fixed in the future). The byte offset, relative to the indicated protocol layer, is given by *expr*. *Size* is optional and indicates the number of bytes in the field of interest; it can be either one, two, or four, and defaults to one. The length operator, indicated by the keyword **len**, gives the length of the packet.

For example, '**ether[0] & 1 != 0**' catches all multicast traffic. The expression '**ip[0] & 0xf != 5**' catches all IPv4 packets with options. The expression '**ip[6:2] & 0x1fff = 0**' catches only unfragmented IPv4 datagrams and frag zero of fragmented IPv4 datagrams. This check is implicitly applied to the **tcp** and **udp** index operations. For instance, **tcp[0]** always means the first byte of the TCP *header*, and never means the first byte of an intervening fragment.

Some offsets and field values may be expressed as names rather than as numeric values. The following protocol header field offsets are available: **icmptype** (ICMP type field), **icmpcode** (ICMP code field), and **tcpflags** (TCP flags field).

The following ICMP type field values are available: **icmp-echoreply, icmp-unreach, icmp-sourcequench, icmp-redirect, icmp-echo, icmp-routeradvert, icmp-routersolicit, icmp-timxceed, icmp-paramprob, icmp-tstamp, icmp-tstampreply, icmp-ireq, icmp-ireqreply, icmp-maskreq, icmp-maskreply.**

The following TCP flags field values are available: **tcp-fin, tcp-syn, tcp-rst, tcp-push, tcp-ack, tcp-urg.**

Primitives may be combined using:

A parenthesized group of primitives and operators (parentheses are special to the Shell and must be escaped).

Negation ('**!**' or '**not**').

Concatenation ('**&&**' or '**and**').

Alternation ('**||**' or '**or**').

Negation has highest precedence. Alternation and concatenation have equal precedence and associate left to right. Note that explicit **and** tokens, not juxtaposition, are now required for concatenation.

If an identifier is given without a keyword, the most recent keyword is assumed. For example,

   not host vs and ace

is short for

   not host vs and host ace

which should not be confused with

   not (host vs or ace)

Expression arguments can be passed to *tcpdump* as either a single argument or as multiple arguments, whichever is more convenient. Generally, if the expression contains Shell metacharacters, it is easier to pass it as a single, quoted argument. Multiple arguments are concatenated with spaces before being parsed.

EXAMPLES

To print all packets arriving at or departing from *sundown*:

tcpdump host sundown

To print traffic between *helios* and either *hot* or *ace*:

tcpdump host helios and \(hot or ace \)

To print all IP packets between *ace* and any host except *helios*:

tcpdump ip host ace and not helios

To print all traffic between local hosts and hosts at Berkeley:

tcpdump net ucb-ether

To print all ftp traffic through internet gateway *snup*: (note that the expression is quoted to prevent the shell from (mis-)interpreting the parentheses):

tcpdump 'gateway snup and (port ftp or ftp-data)'

To print traffic neither sourced from nor destined for local hosts (if you gateway to one other net, this stuff should never make it onto your local net).

tcpdump ip and not net *localnet*

To print the start and end packets (the SYN and FIN packets) of each TCP conversation that involves a non-local host.

tcpdump 'tcp[tcpflags] & (tcp-syn|tcp-fin) != 0 and not src and dst net *localnet***'**

To print all IPv4 HTTP packets to and from port 80, i.e. print only packets that contain data, not, for example, SYN and FIN packets and ACK-only packets. (IPv6 is left as an exercise for the reader.)

tcpdump 'tcp port 80 and (((ip[2:2] - ((ip[0]&0xf)<<2)) - ((tcp[12]&0xf0)>>2)) != 0)'

To print IP packets longer than 576 bytes sent through gateway *snup*:

tcpdump 'gateway snup and ip[2:2] > 576'

To print IP broadcast or multicast packets that were *not* sent via Ethernet broadcast or multicast:

tcpdump 'ether[0] & 1 = 0 and ip[16] >= 224'

To print all ICMP packets that are not echo requests/replies (i.e., not ping packets):

tcpdump 'icmp[icmptype] != icmp-echo and icmp[icmptype] != icmp-echoreply'

OUTPUT FORMAT

The output of *tcpdump* is protocol dependent. The following gives a brief description and examples of most of the formats.

Link Level Headers

If the '-e' option is given, the link level header is printed out. On Ethernets, the source and destination addresses, protocol, and packet length are printed.

On FDDI networks, the '-e' option causes *tcpdump* to print the 'frame control' field, the source and destination addresses, and the packet length. (The 'frame control' field governs the interpretation of the rest of the packet. Normal packets (such as those containing IP datagrams) are 'async' packets, with a priority value between 0 and 7; for example, '**async4**'. Such packets are assumed to contain an 802.2 Logical Link Control (LLC) packet; the LLC header is printed if it is *not* an ISO datagram or a so-called SNAP packet.

On Token Ring networks, the '-e' option causes *tcpdump* to print the 'access control' and 'frame control' fields, the source and destination addresses, and the packet length. As on FDDI networks, packets are assumed to contain an LLC packet. Regardless of whether the '-e' option is specified or not, the source routing information is printed for source-routed packets.

On 802.11 networks, the '-e' option causes *tcpdump* to print the 'frame control' fields, all of the addresses in the 802.11 header, and the packet length. As on FDDI networks, packets are assumed to contain an LLC packet.

(N.B.: The following description assumes familiarity with the SLIP compression algorithm described in RFC-1144.)

On SLIP links, a direction indicator ("I" for inbound, "O" for outbound), packet type, and compression information are printed out. The packet type is printed first. The three types are *ip*, *utcp*, and *ctcp*. No further link information is printed for *ip* packets. For TCP packets, the connection identifier is printed following the type. If the packet is compressed, its encoded header is printed out. The special cases are printed out as ***S+***n* and ***SA+***n*, where *n* is the amount by which the sequence number (or sequence number and ack) has changed. If it is not a special case, zero or more changes are printed. A change is indicated by U (urgent pointer), W (window), A (ack), S (sequence number), and I (packet ID), followed by a delta (+n or -n), or a new value (=n). Finally, the amount of data in the packet and compressed header length are printed.

For example, the following line shows an outbound compressed TCP packet, with an implicit connection identifier; the ack has changed by 6, the sequence number by 49, and the packet ID by 6; there are 3 bytes of data and 6 bytes of compressed header:

O ctcp * A+6 S+49 I+6 3 (6)

ARP/RARP Packets

Arp/rarp output shows the type of request and its arguments. The format is intended to be self explanatory. Here is a short sample taken from the start of an 'rlogin' from host *rtsg* to host *csam*:

```
arp who-has csam tell rtsg
arp reply csam is-at CSAM
```

The first line says that rtsg sent an arp packet asking for the Ethernet address of internet host csam. Csam replies with its Ethernet address (in this example, Ethernet addresses are in caps and internet addresses in lower case).

This would look less redundant if we had done *tcpdump* −*n*:

```
arp who-has 128.3.254.6 tell 128.3.254.68
arp reply 128.3.254.6 is-at 02:07:01:00:01:c4
```

If we had done *tcpdump* −*e*, the fact that the first packet is broadcast and the second is point-to-point would be visible:

```
RTSG Broadcast 0806  64: arp who-has csam tell rtsg
CSAM RTSG 0806  64: arp reply csam is-at CSAM
```

For the first packet this says the Ethernet source address is RTSG, the destination is the Ethernet broadcast address, the type field contained hex 0806 (type ETHER_ARP) and the total length was 64 bytes.

TCP Packets

(N.B.:The following description assumes familiarity with the TCP protocol described in RFC-793. If you are not familiar with the protocol, neither this description nor tcpdump will be of much use to you.)

The general format of a tcp protocol line is:

src > dst: flags data-seqno ack window urgent options

Src and *dst* are the source and destination IP addresses and ports. *Flags* are some combination of S (SYN), F (FIN), P (PUSH), R (RST), W (ECN CWR) or E (ECN-Echo), or a single '.' (no flags). *Data-seqno* describes the portion of sequence space covered by the data in this packet (see example below). *Ack* is sequence number of the next data expected the other direction on this connection. *Window* is the number of bytes of receive buffer space available the other direction on this connection. *Urg* indicates there is 'urgent' data in the packet. *Options* are tcp options enclosed in angle brackets (e.g., <mss 1024>).

Src, dst and *flags* are always present. The other fields depend on the contents of the packet's tcp protocol header and are output only if appropriate.

Here is the opening portion of an rlogin from host *rtsg* to host *csam*.

```
rtsg.1023 > csam.login: S 768512:768512(0) win 4096 <mss 1024>
csam.login > rtsg.1023: S 947648:947648(0) ack 768513 win 4096 <mss 1024>
rtsg.1023 > csam.login: . ack 1 win 4096
rtsg.1023 > csam.login: P 1:2(1) ack 1 win 4096
csam.login > rtsg.1023: . ack 2 win 4096
rtsg.1023 > csam.login: P 2:21(19) ack 1 win 4096
csam.login > rtsg.1023: P 1:2(1) ack 21 win 4077
csam.login > rtsg.1023: P 2:3(1) ack 21 win 4077 urg 1
csam.login > rtsg.1023: P 3:4(1) ack 21 win 4077 urg 1
```

The first line says that tcp port 1023 on rtsg sent a packet to port *login* on csam. The **S** indicates that the *SYN* flag was set. The packet sequence number was 768512 and it contained no data. (The notation is 'first:last(nbytes)' which means 'sequence numbers *first* up to but not including *last* which is *nbytes* bytes of user data'.) There was no piggy-backed ack, the available receive window was 4096 bytes and there was a max-segment-size option requesting an mss of 1024 bytes.

Csam replies with a similar packet except it includes a piggy-backed ack for rtsg's SYN. Rtsg then acks csam's SYN. The '.' means no flags were set. The packet contained no data so there is no data sequence number. Note that the ack sequence number is a small integer (1). The first time *tcpdump* sees a tcp 'conversation', it prints the sequence number from the packet. On subsequent packets of the conversation, the difference between the current packet's sequence number and this initial sequence number is printed. This means that sequence numbers after the first can be interpreted as relative byte positions in the conversation's data stream (with the first data byte each direction being '1'). '-S' will override this feature, causing the original sequence numbers to be output.

On the 6th line, rtsg sends csam 19 bytes of data (bytes 2 through 20 in the rtsg → csam side of the conversation). The PUSH flag is set in the packet. On the 7th line, csam says it's received data sent by rtsg up to but not including byte 21. Most of this data is apparently sitting in the socket buffer since csam's receive window has gotten 19 bytes smaller. Csam also sends one byte of data to rtsg in this packet. On the 8th and 9th lines, csam sends two bytes of urgent, pushed data to rtsg.

If the snapshot was small enough that *tcpdump* didn't capture the full TCP header, it interprets as much of the header as it can and then reports "[|*tcp*]" to indicate the remainder could not be interpreted. If the header contains a bogus option (one with a length that's either too small or beyond the end of the header), *tcpdump* reports it as "[*bad opt*]" and does not interpret any further options (since it's impossible to tell where they start). If the header length indicates options are present but the IP datagram length is not long enough for the options to actually be there, *tcpdump* reports it as "[*bad hdr length*]".

Capturing TCP packets with particular flag combinations (SYN-ACK, URG-ACK, etc.)

There are 8 bits in the control bits section of the TCP header:

CWR | ECE | URG | ACK | PSH | RST | SYN | FIN

Let's assume that we want to watch packets used in establishing a TCP connection. Recall that TCP uses a 3-way handshake protocol when it initializes a new connection; the connection sequence with regard to the TCP control bits is

    1) Caller sends SYN
    2) Recipient responds with SYN, ACK
    3) Caller sends ACK

Now we're interested in capturing packets that have only the SYN bit set (Step 1). Note that we don't want packets from step 2 (SYN-ACK), just a plain initial SYN. What we need is a correct filter expression for *tcpdump*.

Recall the structure of a TCP header without options:

0   15   31

```
-----------------------------------------------------------------
|       source port       |     destination port     |
-----------------------------------------------------------------
|                  sequence number               |
-----------------------------------------------------------------
|                acknowledgment number             |
-----------------------------------------------------------------
| HL  | rsvd |C|E|U|A|P|R|S|F|      window size       |
-----------------------------------------------------------------
|      TCP checksum      |     urgent pointer      |
-----------------------------------------------------------------
```

A TCP header usually holds 20 octets of data, unless options are present. The first line of the graph contains octets 0 - 3, the second line shows octets 4 - 7 etc.

Starting to count with 0, the relevant TCP control bits are contained in octet 13:

```
0        7|        15|        23|        31
----------------|----------------|----------------|----------------
| HL  | rsvd |C|E|U|A|P|R|S|F|      window size       |
----------------|----------------|----------------|----------------
|        | 13th octet |        |        |
```

Let's have a closer look at octet no. 13:

```
        |          |
        |---------------|
        |C|E|U|A|P|R|S|F|
        |---------------|
        |7   5   3    0|
```

These are the TCP control bits we are interested in. We have numbered the bits in this octet from 0 to 7, right to left, so the PSH bit is bit number 3, while the URG bit is number 5.

Recall that we want to capture packets with only SYN set. Let's see what happens to octet 13 if a TCP datagram arrives with the SYN bit set in its header:

```
        |C|E|U|A|P|R|S|F|
        |---------------|
        |0 0 0 0 0 0 1 0|
        |---------------|
        |7 6 5 4 3 2 1 0|
```

Looking at the control bits section we see that only bit number 1 (SYN) is set.

Assuming that octet number 13 is an 8-bit unsigned integer in network byte order, the binary value of this octet is

    00000010

and its decimal representation is

```
  7   6   5   4   3   2   1   0
0*2 + 0*2 + 0*2 + 0*2 + 0*2 + 0*2 + 1*2 + 0*2  =  2
```

We're almost done, because now we know that if only SYN is set, the value of the 13th octet in the TCP header, when interpreted as a 8-bit unsigned integer in network byte order, must be exactly 2.

This relationship can be expressed as
    tcp[13] == 2

We can use this expression as the filter for *tcpdump* in order to watch packets which have only SYN set:
    tcpdump -i xl0 tcp[13] == 2

The expression says "let the 13th octet of a TCP datagram have the decimal value 2", which is exactly what we want.

Now, let's assume that we need to capture SYN packets, but we don't care if ACK or any other TCP control bit is set at the same time. Let's see what happens to octet 13 when a TCP datagram with SYN-ACK set arrives:

```
|C|E|U|A|P|R|S|F|
|---------------|
|0 0 0 1 0 0 1 0|
|---------------|
|7 6 5 4 3 2 1 0|
```

Now bits 1 and 4 are set in the 13th octet. The binary value of octet 13 is

          00010010

which translates to decimal

   7   6   5   4   3   2   1   0
$0*2 + 0*2 + 0*2 + 1*2 + 0*2 + 0*2 + 1*2 + 0*2 = 18$

Now we can't just use 'tcp[13] == 18' in the *tcpdump* filter expression, because that would select only those packets that have SYN-ACK set, but not those with only SYN set. Remember that we don't care if ACK or any other control bit is set as long as SYN is set.

In order to achieve our goal, we need to logically AND the binary value of octet 13 with some other value to preserve the SYN bit. We know that we want SYN to be set in any case, so we'll logically AND the value in the 13th octet with the binary value of a SYN:

```
    00010010 SYN-ACK          00000010 SYN
AND 00000010 (we want SYN)  AND 00000010 (we want SYN)
    --------                    --------
  = 00000010               =  00000010
```

We see that this AND operation delivers the same result regardless whether ACK or another TCP control bit is set. The decimal representation of the AND value as well as the result of this operation is 2 (binary 00000010), so we know that for packets with SYN set the following relation must hold true:

          ((value of octet 13) AND (2)) == (2)

This points us to the *tcpdump* filter expression
          tcpdump -i xl0 'tcp[13] & 2 == 2'

Note that you should use single quotes or a backslash in the expression to hide the AND ('&') special character from the shell.

UDP Packets

UDP format is illustrated by this rwho packet:

```
        actinide.who > broadcast.who: udp 84
```

This says that port *who* on host *actinide* sent a udp datagram to port *who* on host *broadcast*, the Internet broadcast address. The packet contained 84 bytes of user data.

Some UDP services are recognized (from the source or destination port number) and the higher level protocol information printed. In particular, Domain Name service requests (RFC-1034/1035) and Sun RPC calls (RFC-1050) to NFS.

UDP Name Server Requests

(N.B.:The following description assumes familiarity with the Domain Service protocol described in RFC-1035. If you are not familiar with the protocol, the following description will appear to be written in

greek.)

Name server requests are formatted as

> *src > dst: id op? flags qtype qclass name (len)*

```
h2opolo.1538 > helios.domain: 3+ A? ucbvax.berkeley.edu. (37)
```

Host *h2opolo* asked the domain server on *helios* for an address record (qtype=A) associated with the name *ucbvax.berkeley.edu.* The query id was '3'. The '+' indicates the *recursion desired* flag was set. The query length was 37 bytes, not including the UDP and IP protocol headers. The query operation was the normal one, *Query*, so the op field was omitted. If the op had been anything else, it would have been printed between the '3' and the '+'. Similarly, the qclass was the normal one, *C_IN*, and omitted. Any other qclass would have been printed immediately after the 'A'.

A few anomalies are checked and may result in extra fields enclosed in square brackets: If a query contains an answer, authority records or additional records section, *ancount*, *nscount*, or *arcount* are printed as '[*n*a]', '[*n*n]' or '[*n*au]' where *n* is the appropriate count. If any of the response bits are set (AA, RA or rcode) or any of the 'must be zero' bits are set in bytes two and three, '[b2&3=*x*]' is printed, where *x* is the hex value of header bytes two and three.

UDP Name Server Responses

Name server responses are formatted as

> *src > dst: id op rcode flags a/n/au type class data (len)*

```
helios.domain > h2opolo.1538: 3 3/3/7 A 128.32.137.3 (273)
helios.domain > h2opolo.1537: 2 NXDomain* 0/1/0 (97)
```

In the first example, *helios* responds to query id 3 from *h2opolo* with 3 answer records, 3 name server records and 7 additional records. The first answer record is type A (address) and its data is internet address 128.32.137.3. The total size of the response was 273 bytes, excluding UDP and IP headers. The op (Query) and response code (NoError) were omitted, as was the class (C_IN) of the A record.

In the second example, *helios* responds to query 2 with a response code of non-existent domain (NXDomain) with no answers, one name server and no authority records. The '*' indicates that the *authoritative answer* bit was set. Since there were no answers, no type, class or data were printed.

Other flag characters that might appear are '–' (recursion available, RA, *not* set) and 'l' (truncated message, TC, set). If the 'question' section doesn't contain exactly one entry, '[nq]' is printed.

Note that name server requests and responses tend to be large and the default *snaplen* of 68 bytes may not capture enough of the packet to print. Use the **–s** flag to increase the snaplen if you need to seriously investigate name server traffic. '**–s 128**' has worked well for me.

SMB/CIFS decoding

tcpdump now includes fairly extensive SMB/CIFS/NBT decoding for data on UDP/137, UDP/138 and TCP/139. Some primitive decoding of IPX and NetBEUI SMB data is also done.

By default a fairly minimal decode is done, with a much more detailed decode done if -v is used. Be warned that with -v a single SMB packet may take up a page or more, so only use -v if you really want all the gory details.

For information on SMB packet formats and what all te fields mean see www.cifs.org or the pub/samba/specs/ directory on your favorite samba.org mirror site. The SMB patches were written by Andrew Tridgell (tridge@samba.org).

NFS Requests and Replies

Sun NFS (Network File System) requests and replies are printed as:

> *src.xid > dst.nfs: len op args*
> *src.nfs > dst.xid: reply stat len op results*

```
sushi.6709 > wrl.nfs: 112 readlink fh 21,24/10.73165
wrl.nfs > sushi.6709: reply ok 40 readlink "../var"
sushi.201b > wrl.nfs:
      144 lookup fh 9,74/4096.6878 "xcolors"
wrl.nfs > sushi.201b:
      reply ok 128 lookup fh 9,74/4134.3150
```

In the first line, host *sushi* sends a transaction with id *6709* to *wrl* (note that the number following the src host is a transaction id, *not* the source port). The request was 112 bytes, excluding the UDP and IP headers. The operation was a *readlink* (read symbolic link) on file handle (*fh*) 21,24/10.731657119. (If one is lucky, as in this case, the file handle can be interpreted as a major,minor device number pair, followed by the inode number and generation number.) *Wrl* replies 'ok' with the contents of the link.

In the third line, *sushi* asks *wrl* to lookup the name '*xcolors*' in directory file 9,74/4096.6878. Note that the data printed depends on the operation type. The format is intended to be self explanatory if read in conjunction with an NFS protocol spec.

If the −v (verbose) flag is given, additional information is printed. For example:

```
sushi.1372a > wrl.nfs:
      148 read fh 21,11/12.195 8192 bytes @ 24576
wrl.nfs > sushi.1372a:
      reply ok 1472 read REG 100664 ids 417/0 sz 29388
```

(−v also prints the IP header TTL, ID, length, and fragmentation fields, which have been omitted from this example.) In the first line, *sushi* asks *wrl* to read 8192 bytes from file 21,11/12.195, at byte offset 24576. *Wrl* replies 'ok'; the packet shown on the second line is the first fragment of the reply, and hence is only 1472 bytes long (the other bytes will follow in subsequent fragments, but these fragments do not have NFS or even UDP headers and so might not be printed, depending on the filter expression used). Because the −v flag is given, some of the file attributes (which are returned in addition to the file data) are printed: the file type ("REG", for regular file), the file mode (in octal), the uid and gid, and the file size.

If the −v flag is given more than once, even more details are printed.

Note that NFS requests are very large and much of the detail won't be printed unless *snaplen* is increased. Try using '**−s 192**' to watch NFS traffic.

NFS reply packets do not explicitly identify the RPC operation. Instead, *tcpdump* keeps track of "recent" requests, and matches them to the replies using the transaction ID. If a reply does not closely follow the corresponding request, it might not be parsable.

AFS Requests and Replies

Transarc AFS (Andrew File System) requests and replies are printed as:

> *src.sport > dst.dport: rx packet-type*
> *src.sport > dst.dport: rx packet-type service call call-name args*
> *src.sport > dst.dport: rx packet-type service reply call-name args*

```
elvis.7001 > pike.afsfs:
      rx data fs call rename old fid 536876964/1/1 ".newsrc.new"
      new fid 536876964/1/1 ".newsrc"
pike.afsfs > elvis.7001: rx data fs reply rename
```

In the first line, host elvis sends a RX packet to pike. This was a RX data packet to the fs (fileserver) service, and is the start of an RPC call. The RPC call was a rename, with the old directory file id of 536876964/1/1 and an old filename of '.newsrc.new', and a new directory file id of 536876964/1/1 and a new filename of '.newsrc'. The host pike responds with a RPC reply to the rename call (which was successful, because it was a data packet and not an abort packet).

In general, all AFS RPCs are decoded at least by RPC call name. Most AFS RPCs have at least some of the arguments decoded (generally only the 'interesting' arguments, for some definition of interesting).

The format is intended to be self-describing, but it will probably not be useful to people who are not familiar with the workings of AFS and RX.

If the -v (verbose) flag is given twice, acknowledgement packets and additional header information is printed, such as the the RX call ID, call number, sequence number, serial number, and the RX packet flags.

If the -v flag is given twice, additional information is printed, such as the the RX call ID, serial number, and the RX packet flags. The MTU negotiation information is also printed from RX ack packets.

If the -v flag is given three times, the security index and service id are printed.

Error codes are printed for abort packets, with the exception of Ubik beacon packets (because abort packets are used to signify a yes vote for the Ubik protocol).

Note that AFS requests are very large and many of the arguments won't be printed unless *snaplen* is increased. Try using '-s 256' to watch AFS traffic.

AFS reply packets do not explicitly identify the RPC operation. Instead, *tcpdump* keeps track of "recent" requests, and matches them to the replies using the call number and service ID. If a reply does not closely follow the corresponding request, it might not be parsable.

KIP AppleTalk (DDP in UDP)

AppleTalk DDP packets encapsulated in UDP datagrams are de-encapsulated and dumped as DDP packets (i.e., all the UDP header information is discarded). The file */etc/atalk.names* is used to translate AppleTalk net and node numbers to names. Lines in this file have the form

        number name

```
1.254        ether
16.1         icsd-net
1.254.110    ace
```

The first two lines give the names of AppleTalk networks. The third line gives the name of a particular host (a host is distinguished from a net by the 3rd octet in the number – a net number *must* have two octets and a host number *must* have three octets.) The number and name should be separated by whitespace (blanks or tabs). The */etc/atalk.names* file may contain blank lines or comment lines (lines starting with a '#').

AppleTalk addresses are printed in the form

        net.host.port

```
144.1.209.2 > icsd-net.112.220
office.2 > icsd-net.112.220
jssmag.149.235 > icsd-net.2
```

(If the */etc/atalk.names* doesn't exist or doesn't contain an entry for some AppleTalk host/net number, addresses are printed in numeric form.) In the first example, NBP (DDP port 2) on net 144.1 node 209 is sending to whatever is listening on port 220 of net icsd node 112. The second line is the same except the full name of the source node is known ('office'). The third line is a send from port 235 on net jssmag node 149 to broadcast on the icsd-net NBP port (note that the broadcast address (255) is indicated by a net name with no host number – for this reason it's a good idea to keep node names and net names distinct in

/etc/atalk.names).

NBP (name binding protocol) and ATP (AppleTalk transaction protocol) packets have their contents inter-preted. Other protocols just dump the protocol name (or number if no name is registered for the protocol) and packet size.

NBP packets are formatted like the following examples:

```
icsd-net.112.220 > jssmag.2: nbp-lkup 190: "=:LaserWriter@*"
jssmag.209.2 > icsd-net.112.220: nbp-reply 190: "RM1140:LaserWriter@*" 250
techpit.2 > icsd-net.112.220: nbp-reply 190: "techpit:LaserWriter@*" 186
```

The first line is a name lookup request for laserwriters sent by net icsd host 112 and broadcast on net jss-mag. The nbp id for the lookup is 190. The second line shows a reply for this request (note that it has the same id) from host jssmag.209 saying that it has a laserwriter resource named "RM1140" registered on port 250. The third line is another reply to the same request saying host techpit has laserwriter "techpit" regis-tered on port 186.

ATP packet formatting is demonstrated by the following example:

```
jssmag.209.165 > helios.132: atp-req  12266<0-7> 0xae030001
helios.132 > jssmag.209.165: atp-resp 12266:0 (512) 0xae040000
helios.132 > jssmag.209.165: atp-resp 12266:1 (512) 0xae040000
helios.132 > jssmag.209.165: atp-resp 12266:2 (512) 0xae040000
helios.132 > jssmag.209.165: atp-resp 12266:3 (512) 0xae040000
helios.132 > jssmag.209.165: atp-resp 12266:4 (512) 0xae040000
helios.132 > jssmag.209.165: atp-resp 12266:5 (512) 0xae040000
helios.132 > jssmag.209.165: atp-resp 12266:6 (512) 0xae040000
helios.132 > jssmag.209.165: atp-resp*12266:7 (512) 0xae040000
jssmag.209.165 > helios.132: atp-req  12266<3,5> 0xae030001
helios.132 > jssmag.209.165: atp-resp 12266:3 (512) 0xae040000
helios.132 > jssmag.209.165: atp-resp 12266:5 (512) 0xae040000
jssmag.209.165 > helios.132: atp-rel  12266<0-7> 0xae030001
jssmag.209.133 > helios.132: atp-req* 12267<0-7> 0xae030002
```

Jssmag.209 initiates transaction id 12266 with host helios by requesting up to 8 packets (the '<0-7>'). The hex number at the end of the line is the value of the 'userdata' field in the request.

Helios responds with 8 512-byte packets. The ':digit' following the transaction id gives the packet sequence number in the transaction and the number in parens is the amount of data in the packet, excluding the atp header. The '*' on packet 7 indicates that the EOM bit was set.

Jssmag.209 then requests that packets 3 & 5 be retransmitted. Helios resends them then jssmag.209 releases the transaction. Finally, jssmag.209 initiates the next request. The '*' on the request indicates that XO ('exactly once') was *not* set.

IP Fragmentation

Fragmented Internet datagrams are printed as

> (**frag** *id*:*size*@*offset*+)
> (**frag** *id*:*size*@*offset*)

(The first form indicates there are more fragments. The second indicates this is the last fragment.)

Id is the fragment id. *Size* is the fragment size (in bytes) excluding the IP header. *Offset* is this fragment's offset (in bytes) in the original datagram.

The fragment information is output for each fragment. The first fragment contains the higher level protocol header and the frag info is printed after the protocol info. Fragments after the first contain no higher level protocol header and the frag info is printed after the source and destination addresses. For example, here is part of an ftp from arizona.edu to lbl-rtsg.arpa over a CSNET connection that doesn't appear to handle 576 byte datagrams:

```
arizona.ftp-data > rtsg.1170: . 1024:1332(308) ack 1 win 4096 (frag 595a:328@0+)
arizona > rtsg: (frag 595a:204@328)
rtsg.1170 > arizona.ftp-data: . ack 1536 win 2560
```

There are a couple of things to note here: First, addresses in the 2nd line don't include port numbers. This is because the TCP protocol information is all in the first fragment and we have no idea what the port or sequence numbers are when we print the later fragments. Second, the tcp sequence information in the first line is printed as if there were 308 bytes of user data when, in fact, there are 512 bytes (308 in the first frag and 204 in the second). If you are looking for holes in the sequence space or trying to match up acks with packets, this can fool you.

A packet with the IP *don't fragment* flag is marked with a trailing **(DF)**.

Timestamps

By default, all output lines are preceded by a timestamp. The timestamp is the current clock time in the form

    hh:mm:ss.frac

and is as accurate as the kernel's clock. The timestamp reflects the time the kernel first saw the packet. No attempt is made to account for the time lag between when the Ethernet interface removed the packet from the wire and when the kernel serviced the 'new packet' interrupt.

SEE ALSO

bpf(4), pcap(3)

AUTHORS

The original authors are:

Van Jacobson, Craig Leres and Steven McCanne, all of the Lawrence Berkeley National Laboratory, University of California, Berkeley, CA.

It is currently being maintained by tcpdump.org.

The current version is available via http:

    http://www.tcpdump.org/

The original distribution is available via anonymous ftp:

    ftp://ftp.ee.lbl.gov/tcpdump.tar.Z

IPv6/IPsec support is added by WIDE/KAME project. This program uses Eric Young's SSLeay library, under specific configuration.

BUGS

Please send problems, bugs, questions, desirable enhancements, etc. to:

    tcpdump-workers@tcpdump.org

Please send source code contributions, etc. to:

    patches@tcpdump.org

Some attempt should be made to reassemble IP fragments or, at least to compute the right length for the higher level protocol.

Name server inverse queries are not dumped correctly: the (empty) question section is printed rather than real query in the answer section. Some believe that inverse queries are themselves a bug and prefer to fix the program generating them rather than *tcpdump*.

A packet trace that crosses a daylight savings time change will give skewed time stamps (the time change is ignored).

Filter expressions on fields other than those in Token Ring headers will not correctly handle source-routed Token Ring packets.

Filter expressions on fields other than those in 802.11 headers will not correctly handle 802.11 data packets with both To DS and From DS set.

ip6 proto should chase header chain, but at this moment it does not. **ip6 protochain** is supplied for this behavior.

Arithmetic expression against transport layer headers, like **tcp[0]**, does not work against IPv6 packets. It only looks at IPv4 packets.

NAME

  telnetd — DARPA TELNET protocol server

SYNOPSIS

  /usr/libexec/telnetd [**-Uhlkns46**] [**-D** *debugmode*] [**-S** *tos*] [**-X** *authtype*]
      [**-a** *authmode*] [**-edebug**] [**-g** *gettyent*] [**-u** *len*]
      [**-debug** [*port*]]

DESCRIPTION

  The **telnetd** command is a server which supports the DARPA standard TELNET virtual terminal protocol. **telnetd** is normally invoked by the internet server (see inetd(8)) for requests to connect to the TELNET port as indicated by the /etc/services file (see services(5)). The **-debug** option may be used to start up **telnetd** manually, instead of through inetd(8). If started up this way, *port* may be specified to run **telnetd** on an alternate TCP port number.

  The **telnetd** command accepts the following options:

-a *authmode*

    This option may be used for specifying what mode should be used for authentication. Note that this option is only useful if **telnetd** has been compiled with support for the AUTHENTICATION option. There are several valid values for *authmode*:

    debug Turns on authentication debugging code.

    user Only allow connections when the remote user can provide valid authentication information to identify the remote user, and is allowed access to the specified account without providing a password.

    valid Only allow connections when the remote user can provide valid authentication information to identify the remote user. The login(1) command will provide any additional user verification needed if the remote user is not allowed automatic access to the specified account.

    other Only allow connections that supply some authentication information. This option is currently not supported by any of the existing authentication mechanisms, and is thus the same as specifying **-a valid**.

    none This is the default state. Authentication information is not required. If no or insufficient authentication information is provided, then the login(1) program will provide the necessary user verification.

    off This disables the authentication code. All user verification will happen through the login(1) program.

-D *debugmode*

    This option may be used for debugging purposes. This allows **telnetd** to print out debugging information to the connection, allowing the user to see what **telnetd** is doing. There are several possible values for *debugmode*:

    options Prints information about the negotiation of TELNET options.

    report Prints the **options** information, plus some additional information about what processing is going on.

    netdata Displays the data stream received by **telnetd**.

ptydata   Displays data written to the pty.

exercise Has not been implemented yet.

−debug   Enables debugging on each socket created by **telnetd** (see SO_DEBUG in socket(2)).

−edebug   If **telnetd** has been compiled with support for data encryption, then the **−edebug** option may be used to enable encryption debugging code.

−g *gettyent*

Specifies which entry from /etc/gettytab should be used to get banner strings, login program and other information. The default entry is default.

−h   Disables the printing of host-specific information before login has been completed.

−k   This option is only useful if **telnetd** has been compiled with both linemode and kludge linemode support. If the **−k** option is specified, then if the remote client does not support the LINEMODE option, then **telnetd** will operate in character at a time mode. It will still support kludge linemode, but will only go into kludge linemode if the remote client requests it. (This is done by by the client sending DONT SUPPRESS-GO-AHEAD and DONT ECHO.) The **−k** option is most useful when there are remote clients that do not support kludge linemode, but pass the heuristic (if they respond with WILL TIMING-MARK in response to a DO TIMING-MARK) for kludge linemode support.

−l   Specifies line mode. Tries to force clients to use line-at-a-time mode. If the LINEMODE option is not supported, it will go into kludge linemode.

−n   Disable TCP keep-alives. Normally **telnetd** enables the TCP keep-alive mechanism to probe connections that have been idle for some period of time to determine if the client is still there, so that idle connections from machines that have crashed or can no longer be reached may be cleaned up.

−s   This option is only enabled if **telnetd** is compiled with support for secure logins. It causes the **−s** option to be passed on to login(1), and thus is only useful if login(1) supports the **−s** flag to indicate that only Kerberos or S/Key validated logins are allowed, and is usually useful for controlling remote logins from outside of a firewall.

−S *tos*   This option sets the IP Type-of Service (TOS) option on the connection to the value tos, which may be a numeric TOS value or a symbolic TOS name found in the /etc/iptos file. This option has no effect on NetBSD.

−u *len*   This option is used to specify the size of the field in the utmp structure that holds the remote host name. If the resolved host name is longer than *len*, the dotted decimal value will be used instead. This allows hosts with very long host names that overflow this field to still be uniquely identified. Specifying **−u0** indicates that only dotted decimal addresses should be put into the utmp file.

−U   This option causes **telnetd** to refuse connections from addresses that cannot be mapped back into a symbolic name via the getnameinfo(3) routine.

−X *authtype*

This option is only valid if **telnetd** has been built with support for the authentication option. It disables the use of *authtype* authentication, and can be used to temporarily disable a specific authentication type without having to recompile **telnetd**.

−4

-6   Specifies address family to be used on **-debug** mode. During normal operation (called from inetd(8)) **telnetd** will use the file descriptor passed from inetd(8).

telnetd operates by allocating a pseudo-terminal device (see pty(4)) for a client, then creating a login process which has the slave side of the pseudo-terminal as stdin, stdout and stderr. **telnetd** manipulates the master side of the pseudo-terminal, implementing the TELNET protocol and passing characters between the remote client and the login process.

When a TELNET session is started up, **telnetd** sends TELNET options to the client side indicating a willingness to do the following TELNET options, which are described in more detail below:

```
DO AUTHENTICATION
WILL ENCRYPT
DO TERMINAL TYPE
DO TSPEED
DO XDISPLOC
DO NEW-ENVIRON
DO ENVIRON
WILL SUPPRESS GO AHEAD
DO ECHO
DO LINEMODE
DO NAWS
WILL STATUS
DO LFLOW
DO TIMING-MARK
```

The pseudo-terminal allocated to the client is configured to operate in cooked mode, and with XTABS and CRMOD enabled (see tty(4)).

telnetd has support for enabling locally the following TELNET options:

WILL ECHO   When the LINEMODE option is enabled, a WILL ECHO or WONT ECHO will be sent to the client to indicate the current state of terminal echoing. When terminal echo is not desired, a WILL ECHO is sent to indicate that telnetd will take care of echoing any data that needs to be echoed to the terminal, and then nothing is echoed. When terminal echo is desired, a WONT ECHO is sent to indicate that telnetd will not be doing any terminal echoing, so the client should do any terminal echoing that is needed.

WILL BINARY   Indicates that the client is willing to send a 8 bits of data, rather than the normal 7 bits of the Network Virtual Terminal.

WILL SGA   Indicates that it will not be sending IAC GA, go ahead, commands.

WILL STATUS   Indicates a willingness to send the client, upon request, of the current status of all TELNET options.

WILL TIMING-MARK Whenever a DO TIMING-MARK command is received, it is always responded to with a WILL TIMING-MARK

WILL LOGOUT   When a DO LOGOUT is received, a WILL LOGOUT is sent in response, and the TELNET session is shut down.

WILL ENCRYPT   Only sent if **telnetd** is compiled with support for data encryption, and indicates a willingness to decrypt the data stream.

telnetd has support for enabling remotely the following TELNET options:

DO BINARY	Sent to indicate that telnetd is willing to receive an 8 bit data stream.
DO LFLOW	Requests that the client handle flow control characters remotely.
DO ECHO	This is not really supported, but is sent to identify a 4.2BSD telnet(1) client, which will improperly respond with WILL ECHO. If a WILL ECHO is received, a DONT ECHO will be sent in response.
DO TERMINAL-TYPE	Indicates a desire to be able to request the name of the type of terminal that is attached to the client side of the connection.
DO SGA	Indicates that it does not need to receive IAC GA, the go ahead command.
DO NAWS	Requests that the client inform the server when the window (display) size changes.
DO TERMINAL-SPEED	
	Indicates a desire to be able to request information about the speed of the serial line to which the client is attached.
DO XDISPLOC	Indicates a desire to be able to request the name of the X windows display that is associated with the telnet client.
DO NEW-ENVIRON	Indicates a desire to be able to request environment variable information, as described in RFC 1572.
DO ENVIRON	Indicates a desire to be able to request environment variable information, as described in RFC 1408.
DO LINEMODE	Only sent if **telnetd** is compiled with support for linemode, and requests that the client do line by line processing.
DO TIMING-MARK	Only sent if **telnetd** is compiled with support for both linemode and kludge linemode, and the client responded with WONT LINEMODE. If the client responds with WILL TM, the it is assumed that the client supports kludge linemode. Note that the [**−k**] option can be used to disable this.
DO AUTHENTICATION	
	Only sent if **telnetd** is compiled with support for authentication, and indicates a willingness to receive authentication information for automatic login.
DO ENCRYPT	Only sent if **telnetd** is compiled with support for data encryption, and indicates a willingness to decrypt the data stream.

At the end of a login session, **telnetd** invokes the ttyaction(3) facility with an action of "telnetd" and user "root" to execute site-specific commands.

FILES
```
/etc/services
/etc/iptos (if supported)
```

SEE ALSO
login(1), skey(1), telnet(1), ttyaction(3)

STANDARDS
RFC 854	TELNET PROTOCOL SPECIFICATION
RFC 855	TELNET OPTION SPECIFICATIONS

RFC 856	TELNET BINARY TRANSMISSION
RFC 857	TELNET ECHO OPTION
RFC 858	TELNET SUPPRESS GO AHEAD OPTION
RFC 859	TELNET STATUS OPTION
RFC 860	TELNET TIMING MARK OPTION
RFC 861	TELNET EXTENDED OPTIONS - LIST OPTION
RFC 885	TELNET END OF RECORD OPTION
RFC 1073	Telnet Window Size Option
RFC 1079	Telnet Terminal Speed Option
RFC 1091	Telnet Terminal-Type Option
RFC 1096	Telnet X Display Location Option
RFC 1123	Requirements for Internet Hosts -- Application and Support
RFC 1184	Telnet Linemode Option
RFC 1372	Telnet Remote Flow Control Option
RFC 1416	Telnet Authentication Option
RFC 1411	Telnet Authentication: Kerberos Version 4
RFC 1412	Telnet Authentication: SPX
RFC 1571	Telnet Environment Option Interoperability Issues
RFC 1572	Telnet Environment Option

BUGS

Some TELNET commands are only partially implemented.

Because of bugs in the original 4.2BSD telnet(1), **telnetd** performs some dubious protocol exchanges to try to discover if the remote client is, in fact, a 4.2BSD telnet(1).

Binary mode has no common interpretation except between similar operating systems (UNIX in this case).

The terminal type name received from the remote client is converted to lower case.

telnetd never sends TELNET IAC GA (go ahead) commands.

NAME

tftp-proxy — Internet Trivial File Transfer Protocol proxy

SYNOPSIS

tftp-proxy [**-v**] [**-w** *transwait*]

DESCRIPTION

tftp-proxy is a proxy for the Internet Trivial File Transfer Protocol invoked by the inetd(8) internet server. TFTP connections should be redirected to the proxy using the pf(4) *rdr* command, after which the proxy connects to the server on behalf of the client.

The proxy establishes a pf(4) *rdr* rule using the *anchor* facility to rewrite packets between the client and the server. Once the rule is established, **tftp-proxy** forwards the initial request from the client to the server to begin the transfer. After *transwait* seconds, the pf(4) NAT state is assumed to have been established and the *rdr* rule is deleted and the program exits. Once the transfer between the client and the server is completed, the NAT state will naturally expire.

Assuming the TFTP command request is from $client to $server, the proxy connected to the server using the $proxy source address, and $port is negotiated, **tftp-proxy** adds the following rule to the anchor:

```
rdr proto udp from $server to $proxy port $port -> $client
```

The options are as follows:

-v   Log the connection and request information to syslogd(8).

-w *transwait*

     Number of seconds to wait for the data transmission to begin before removing the pf(4) *rdr* rule. The default is 2 seconds.

CONFIGURATION

To make use of the proxy, pf.conf(5) needs the following rules. The anchors are mandatory. Adjust the rules as needed for your configuration.

In the NAT section:

```
nat on $ext_if from $int_if -> ($ext_if:0)

no nat on $ext_if to port tftp

rdr-anchor "tftp-proxy/*"
rdr on $int_if proto udp from $lan to any port tftp -> \
    127.0.0.1 port 6969
```

In the filter section, an anchor must be added to hold the pass rules:

```
anchor "tftp-proxy/*"
```

inetd(8) must be configured to spawn the proxy on the port that packets are being forwarded to by pf(4). An example inetd.conf(5) entry follows:

```
127.0.0.1:6969 dgram   udp     wait    root \
        /usr/libexec/tftp-proxy         tftp-proxy
```

SEE ALSO

tftp(1), pf(4), pf.conf(5), ftp-proxy(8), inetd(8), syslogd(8), tftpd(8)

CAVEATS

    tftp-proxy chroots to `/var/chroot/tftp-proxy` and changes to user "_proxy" to drop privileges.

NAME

tftpd — DARPA Internet Trivial File Transfer Protocol server

SYNOPSIS

tftpd [**-cdln**] [**-g** *group*] [**-p** *pathsep*] [**-s** *directory*] [**-u** *user*]
      [*directory* ...]

DESCRIPTION

tftpd is a server which supports the DARPA Trivial File Transfer Protocol. The TFTP server operates at the port indicated in the `tftp` service description; see `services`(5). The server is normally started by `inetd`(8).

The use of `tftp`(1) does not require an account or password on the remote system. Due to the lack of authentication information, **tftpd** will allow only publicly readable files to be accessed. Filenames beginning in "`../`" or containing "`/../`" are not allowed. Unless **-c** is used, files may be written to only if they already exist and are publicly writable.

Note that this extends the concept of "public" to include all users on all hosts that can be reached through the network; this may not be appropriate on all systems, and its implications should be considered before enabling tftp service. The server should have the user ID with the lowest possible privilege.

Access to files may be restricted by invoking **tftpd** with a list of directories by including up to 20 pathnames as server program arguments in `/etc/inetd.conf`. In this case access is restricted to files whose names are prefixed by the one of the given directories. The given directories are also treated as a search path for relative filename requests.

The options are:

-c
    Allow unrestricted creation of new files. Without this flag, only existing publicly writable files can be overwritten.

-d
    Enable verbose debugging messages to `syslogd`(8).

-g *group*
    Change gid to that of *group* on startup. If this isn't specified, the gid is set to that of the *user* specified with **-u**.

-l
    Logs all requests using `syslog`(3).

-n
    Suppresses negative acknowledgement of requests for nonexistent relative filenames.

-p *pathsep*
    All occurances of the single character *pathsep* (path separator) in the requested filename are replaced with '/'.

-s *directory*
    tftpd will `chroot`(2) to *directory* on startup. This is recommended for security reasons (so that files other than those in the `/tftpboot` directory aren't accessible). If the remote host passes the directory name as part of the file name to transfer, you may have to create a symbolic link from 'tftpboot' to '.' under `/tftpboot`.

-u *user*
    Change uid to that of *user* on startup. If **-u** isn't given, *user* defaults to "nobody". If **-g** isn't also given, change the gid to that of *user* as well.

SEE ALSO

`tftp`(1), `inetd`(8)

The TFTP Protocol (Revision 2), RFC, 1350, July 1992.

TFTP Option Extension, RFC, 2347, May 1998.

TFTP Blocksize Option, RFC, 2348, May 1998.

TFTP Timeout Interval and Transfer Size Options, RFC, 2349, May 1998.

HISTORY

The **tftpd** command appeared in 4.2 BSD.

The **−s** flag appeared in NetBSD 1.0.

The **−g** and **−u** flags appeared in NetBSD 1.4.

IPv6 support was implemented by WIDE/KAME project in 1999.

TFTP options were implemented by Wasabi Systems, Inc., in 2003, and first appeared in NetBSD 2.0.

BUGS

Files larger than 33,553,919 octets (65535 blocks, last one less than 512 octets) cannot be correctly transferred without client and server supporting blocksize negotiation (RFCs 2347 and 2348). As a kludge, **tftpd** accepts a sequence of block numbers which wrap to zero after 65535.

Many tftp clients will not transfer files over 16,776,703 octets (32767 blocks), as they incorrectly count the block number using a signed rather than unsigned 16-bit integer.

SECURITY CONSIDERATIONS

You are *strongly* advised to set up **tftpd** using the **−s** flag in conjunction with the name of the directory that contains the files that **tftpd** will serve to remote hosts (e.g., /tftpboot). This ensures that only the files that should be served to remote hosts can be accessed by them.

Because there is no user-login or validation within the TFTP protocol, the remote site will probably have some sort of file-access restrictions in place. The exact methods are specific to each site and therefore difficult to document here.

If unrestricted file upload is enabled via the **−c** option, care should be taken that this can be used to fill up disk space in an uncontrolled manner if this is used in an insecure environment.

NAME

timed — time server daemon

SYNOPSIS

timed [-dMt] [-F *host* ...] [-G *netgroup*] [-i *network* | -n *network*]

DESCRIPTION

The **timed** utility is a time server daemon which is normally invoked at boot time from the rc(8) file. It synchronizes the host's time with the time of other machines, which are also running **timed**, in a local area network. These time servers will slow down the clocks of some machines and speed up the clocks of others to bring them to the average network time. The average network time is computed from measurements of clock differences using the ICMP timestamp request message.

The following options are available:

-d   Enable debugging mode; do not detach from the terminal.

-F *host* ...
            Create a list of trusted hosts. The **timed** utility will only accept trusted hosts as masters. If it finds an untrusted host claiming to be master, **timed** will suppress incoming messages from that host and call for a new election. This option implies the -M option. If this option is not specified, all hosts on the connected networks are treated as trustworthy.

-G *netgroup*
            Specify a netgroup of trustworthy hosts, in addition to any masters specified with the -M flag. This option may only be specified once.

-i *network*
            Add *network* to the list of networks to ignore. All other networks to which the machine is directly connected are used by **timed**. This option may be specified multiple times to add more than one network to the list.

-M   Allow this host to become a **timed** master if necessary.

-n *network*
            Add *network* to the list of allowed networks. All other networks to which the machine is directly connected are ignored by **timed**. This option may be specified multiple times to add more than one network to the list.

-t   Enable tracing of received messages and log to the file /var/log/timed.log. Tracing can be turned on or off while **timed** is running with the timedc(8) utility.

The -n and -i flags are mutually exclusive and require as arguments real networks to which the host is connected (see networks(5)). If neither flag is specified, **timed** will listen on all connected networks.

A **timed** running without the -M nor -F flags will always remain a slave. If the -F flag is not used, **timed** will treat all machines as trustworthy.

The **timed** utility is based on a master-slave scheme. When **timed** is started on a machine, it asks the master for the network time and sets the host's clock to that time. After that, it accepts synchronization messages periodically sent by the master and calls adjtime(2) to perform the needed corrections on the host's clock.

It also communicates with date(1) in order to set the date globally, and with timedc(8), a **timed** control utility. If the machine running the master becomes unreachable, the slaves will elect a new master from among those slaves which are running with at least one of the -M and -F flags.

At startup **timed** normally checks for a master time server on each network to which it is connected, except as modified by the **−n** and **−i** options described above. It will request synchronization service from the first master server located. If permitted by the **−M** or **−F** flags, it will provide synchronization service on any attached networks on which no trusted master server was detected. Such a server propagates the time computed by the top-level master. The **timed** utility will periodically check for the presence of a master on those networks for which it is operating as a slave. If it finds that there are no trusted masters on a network, it will begin the election process on that network.

One way to synchronize a group of machines is to use ntpd(8) to synchronize the clock of one machine to a distant standard or a radio receiver and **−F** *hostname* to tell its **timed** to trust only itself.

Messages printed by the kernel on the system console occur with interrupts disabled. This means that the clock stops while they are printing. A machine with many disk or network hardware problems and consequent messages cannot keep good time by itself. Each message typically causes the clock to lose a dozen milliseconds. A time daemon can correct the result.

Messages in the system log about machines that failed to respond usually indicate machines that crashed or were turned off. Complaints about machines that failed to respond to initial time settings are often associated with "multi-homed" machines that looked for time masters on more than one network and eventually chose to become a slave on the other network.

WARNINGS

Temporal chaos will result if two or more time daemons attempt to adjust the same clock. If both **timed** and another time daemon are run on the same machine, ensure that the **−F** flag is used, so that **timed** never attempts to adjust the local clock.

The protocol is based on UDP/IP broadcasts. All machines within the range of a broadcast that are using the TSP protocol must cooperate. There cannot be more than a single administrative domain using the **−F** flag among all machines reached by a broadcast packet. Failure to follow this rule is usually indicated by complaints concerning "untrusted" machines in the system log.

FILES

```
/var/log/timed.log          tracing file for timed
/var/log/timed.masterlog    log file for master timed
```

SEE ALSO

date(1), adjtime(2), gettimeofday(2), icmp(4), netgroup(5), networks(5), ntpd(8), timedc(8)

R. Gusella and S. Zatti, *TSP: The Time Synchronization Protocol for UNIX 4.3BSD*.

HISTORY

The **timed** utility appeared in 4.3 BSD.

NAME
   timedc — timed control program

SYNOPSIS
   timedc [*command* [*argument* . . .]]

DESCRIPTION
   timedc is used to control the operation of the timed(8) program. It may be used to:

   • Measure the differences between machines' clocks,

   • Find the location where the master time server is running,

   • Enable or disable tracing of messages received by timed(8), and

   • Perform various debugging actions.

   Without any arguments, **timedc** will prompt for commands from the standard input. If arguments are supplied, **timedc** interprets the first argument as a command and the remaining arguments as parameters to the
   command. The standard input may be redirected causing **timedc** to read commands from a file. Commands may be abbreviated; recognized commands are:

   ? [*command* . . .]

   help [*command* . . .]
         Print a short description of each command specified in the argument list, or, if no arguments are
         given, a list of the recognized commands.

   clockdiff *host* . . .
         Compute the differences between the clock of the host machine and the clocks of the machines
         given as arguments.

   msite [*host* . . .]
         Show the master time server for specified host(s).

   trace { *on* | *off* }
         Enable or disable the tracing of incoming messages to timed(8) in the file
         /var/log/timed.log.

   election *host*
         Asks the daemon on the target host to reset its "election" timers and to ensure that a time master has
         been elected.

   quit   Exit from timedc.

   Other commands may be included for use in testing and debugging timed(8); the help command and the
   program source may be consulted for details.

FILES
   /var/log/timed.log   tracing file for timed
   /var/log/timed.masterlog log file for master timed

DIAGNOSTICS
   ?Ambiguous command
         abbreviation matches more than one command
   ?Invalid command
         no match found

SEE ALSO

    date(1), adjtime(2), icmp(4), timed(8)

R. Gusella and S. Zatti, *TSP: The Time Synchronization Protocol for UNIX 4.3BSD*.

HISTORY

The **timedc** command appeared in 4.3 BSD.

NAME
tlsmgr – Postfix TLS session cache and PRNG manager

SYNOPSIS
tlsmgr [generic Postfix daemon options]

DESCRIPTION
The **tlsmgr**(8) manages the Postfix TLS session caches. It stores and retrieves cache entries on request by **smtpd**(8) and **smtp**(8) processes, and periodically removes entries that have expired.

The **tlsmgr**(8) also manages the PRNG (pseudo random number generator) pool. It answers queries by the **smtpd**(8) and **smtp**(8) processes to seed their internal PRNG pools.

The **tlsmgr**(8)'s PRNG pool is initially seeded from an external source (EGD, /dev/urandom, or regular file). It is updated at configurable pseudo-random intervals with data from the external source. It is updated periodically with data from TLS session cache entries and with the time of day, and is updated with the time of day whenever a process requests **tlsmgr**(8) service.

The **tlsmgr**(8) saves the PRNG state to an exchange file periodically and when the process terminates, and reads the exchange file when initializing its PRNG.

SECURITY
The **tlsmgr**(8) is not security-sensitive. The code that maintains the external and internal PRNG pools does not "trust" the data that it manipulates, and the code that maintains the TLS session cache does not touch the contents of the cached entries, except for seeding its internal PRNG pool.

The **tlsmgr**(8) can be run chrooted and with reduced privileges. At process startup it connects to the entropy source and exchange file, and creates or truncates the optional TLS session cache files.

With Postfix version 2.5 and later, the **tlsmgr**(8) no longer uses root privileges when opening cache files. These files should now be stored under the Postfix-owned **data_directory**. As a migration aid, an attempt to open a cache file under a non-Postfix directory is redirected to the Postfix-owned **data_directory**, and a warning is logged.

DIAGNOSTICS
Problems and transactions are logged to the syslog daemon.

BUGS
There is no automatic means to limit the number of entries in the TLS session caches and/or the size of the TLS cache files.

CONFIGURATION PARAMETERS
Changes to **main.cf** are not picked up automatically, because **tlsmgr**(8) is a persistent processes. Use the command "**postfix reload**" after a configuration change.

The text below provides only a parameter summary. See **postconf**(5) for more details including examples.

TLS SESSION CACHE
lmtp_tls_loglevel (0)
> The LMTP-specific version of the smtp_tls_loglevel configuration parameter.

lmtp_tls_session_cache_database (empty)
> The LMTP-specific version of the smtp_tls_session_cache_database configuration parameter.

lmtp_tls_session_cache_timeout (3600s)
> The LMTP-specific version of the smtp_tls_session_cache_timeout configuration parameter.

smtp_tls_loglevel (0)
> Enable additional Postfix SMTP client logging of TLS activity.

smtp_tls_session_cache_database (empty)
> Name of the file containing the optional Postfix SMTP client TLS session cache.

smtp_tls_session_cache_timeout (3600s)
> The expiration time of Postfix SMTP client TLS session cache information.

smtpd_tls_loglevel (0)
> Enable additional Postfix SMTP server logging of TLS activity.

smtpd_tls_session_cache_database (empty)
> Name of the file containing the optional Postfix SMTP server TLS session cache.

smtpd_tls_session_cache_timeout (3600s)
> The expiration time of Postfix SMTP server TLS session cache information.

PSEUDO RANDOM NUMBER GENERATOR

tls_random_source (see 'postconf -d' output)
> The external entropy source for the in-memory **tlsmgr**(8) pseudo random number generator (PRNG) pool.

tls_random_bytes (32)
> The number of bytes that **tlsmgr**(8) reads from $tls_random_source when (re)seeding the in-memory pseudo random number generator (PRNG) pool.

tls_random_exchange_name (see 'postconf -d' output)
> Name of the pseudo random number generator (PRNG) state file that is maintained by **tlsmgr**(8).

tls_random_prng_update_period (3600s)
> The time between attempts by **tlsmgr**(8) to save the state of the pseudo random number generator (PRNG) to the file specified with $tls_random_exchange_name.

tls_random_reseed_period (3600s)
> The maximal time between attempts by **tlsmgr**(8) to re-seed the in-memory pseudo random number generator (PRNG) pool from external sources.

MISCELLANEOUS CONTROLS

config_directory (see 'postconf -d' output)
> The default location of the Postfix main.cf and master.cf configuration files.

data_directory (see 'postconf -d' output)
> The directory with Postfix-writable data files (for example: caches, pseudo-random numbers).

daemon_timeout (18000s)
> How much time a Postfix daemon process may take to handle a request before it is terminated by a built-in watchdog timer.

process_id (read-only)
> The process ID of a Postfix command or daemon process.

process_name (read-only)
> The process name of a Postfix command or daemon process.

syslog_facility (mail)
> The syslog facility of Postfix logging.

syslog_name (see 'postconf -d' output)
> The mail system name that is prepended to the process name in syslog records, so that "smtpd" becomes, for example, "postfix/smtpd".

SEE ALSO

> smtp(8), Postfix SMTP client
> smtpd(8), Postfix SMTP server
> postconf(5), configuration parameters
> master(5), generic daemon options
> master(8), process manager

syslogd(8), system logging

README FILES
Use "**postconf readme_directory**" or "**postconf html_directory**" to locate this information.
TLS_README, Postfix TLS configuration and operation

LICENSE
The Secure Mailer license must be distributed with this software.

AUTHOR(S)
Lutz Jaenicke
BTU Cottbus
Allgemeine Elektrotechnik
Universitaetsplatz 3-4
D-03044 Cottbus, Germany

Adapted by:
Wietse Venema
IBM T.J. Watson Research
P.O. Box 704
Yorktown Heights, NY 10598, USA

NAME
tpctl — touch panel calibration utility

SYNOPSIS
tpctl [**-D** *dispdevname*] [**-d** *devname*] [**-f** *filename*] [**-hnuv**]

DESCRIPTION
tpctl is a touch panel calibration utility. **tpctl** calibrates a touch panel and saves and restores the calibration parameters into/from a parameter database file.

Available command-line flags are:

-D *dispdevname*	Specify display device name.
-d *devname*	Specify touch panel device name.
-f *filename*	Specify alternate parameter database file name.
-h	Print brief description.
-n	Do not change the parameter database file.
-u	Force calibration. Without this flag, **tpctl** won't do calibration if the database file already contains parameters for the touch panel.
-v	Verbose mode.

You calibrate the touch panel the first time you run **tpctl**. If you see a cross cursor on the screen, you should tap the center of the cursor to calibrate the touch panel, or you can abort the calibration with the 'ESC' key. Five cursors will appear on the screen in turn. Once calibration is done, **tpctl** saves the calibration parameters into the database file and uses the saved parameters to calibrate the touch panel.

You can run **tpctl** automatically with /etc/rc.d/tpctl.

FILES
/etc/tpctl.dat	The default calibration parameter database file. The **-f** flag may be used to specify an alternate database file name. **tpctl** will create an empty database file if it doesn't exist.
/dev/ttyE0	The default display device, which is used to display the cursor during calibration. The **-D** flag may be used to specify an alternate display device name. The display device must provide the 'hpcfb' interface as defined in /usr/include/dev/hpc/hpcfbio.h.
/dev/wsmux0	The default touch panel device. The **-d** flag may be used to specify an alternate touch panel device name.

SEE ALSO
rc.conf(5)

BUGS
tpctl isn't available on all ports because it requires a display device which provides the 'hpcfb' interface.

NAME
traceroute – print the route packets take to network host

SYNOPSIS
traceroute [**–aDFPIdlMnrvx**] [**–f** *first_ttl*]
            [**–g** *gateway*] [**–i** *iface*] [**–m** max_ttl]
            [**–p** *port*] [**–q** *nqueries*] [**–s** *src_addr*]
            [**–t** *tos*] [**–w** *waittime*] [**–A** *as_server*]
            host [*packetlen*]

DESCRIPTION
The Internet is a large and complex aggregation of network hardware, connected together by gateways. Tracking the route one's packets follow (or finding the miscreant gateway that's discarding your packets) can be difficult. *Traceroute* uses the IP protocol 'time to live' field and attempts to elicit an ICMP TIME_EXCEEDED response from each gateway along the path to some host.

The only mandatory parameter is the destination host name or IP number. The default probe datagram length is 40 bytes, but this may be increased by specifying a packet length (in bytes) after the destination host name.

Other options are:

–a   Turn on AS# lookups for each hop encountered.

–A   Turn on AS# lookups and use the given server instead of the default.

–d   Turn on socket-level debugging.

–D   Dump the packet data to standard error before transmitting it.

–f   Set the initial time-to-live used in the first outgoing probe packet.

–F   Set the "don't fragment" bit.

–g   Specify a loose source route gateway (8 maximum).

–i   Specify a network interface to obtain the source IP address for outgoing probe packets. This is normally only useful on a multi-homed host. (See the **–s** flag for another way to do this.)

–I   Use ICMP ECHO instead of UDP datagrams.

–l   Display the ttl value of the returned packet. This is useful for checking for asymmetric routing.

–m   Set the max time-to-live (max number of hops) used in outgoing probe packets. The default value is taken from the *net.inet.ip.ttl* sysctl(3) variable.

–M   If found, show the MPLS Label and the Experimental (EXP) bit for the hop.

–n   Print hop addresses numerically rather than symbolically and numerically (saves a nameserver address-to-name lookup for each gateway found on the path).

–p   Set the base UDP port number used in probes (default is 33434). Traceroute hopes that nothing is listening on UDP ports *base* to *base* + *nhops* – *1* at the destination host (so an ICMP PORT_UNREACHABLE message will be returned to terminate the route tracing). If something is listening on a port in the default range, this option can be used to pick an unused port range.

–P   Set the "don't fragment" bit, and use the next hop mtu each time we get the "need fragmentation" error, thus probing the path MTU.

–q   Set the number of probe packets sent for each hop. By default, traceroute sends three probe packets.

–r   Bypass the normal routing tables and send directly to a host on an attached network. If the host is not on a directly-attached network, an error is returned. This option can be used to ping a local host through an interface that has no route through it (e.g., after the interface was dropped by *routed*(8)).

−s   Use the following IP address (which usually is given as an IP number, not a hostname) as the source address in outgoing probe packets. On multi-homed hosts (those with more than one IP address), this option can be used to force the source address to be something other than the IP address of the interface the probe packet is sent on. If the IP address is not one of this machine's interface addresses, an error is returned and nothing is sent. (See the **−i** flag for another way to do this.)

−t   Set the *type-of-service* in probe packets to the following value (default zero). The value must be a decimal integer in the range 0 to 255. This option can be used to see if different types-of-service result in different paths. (If you are not running 4.4BSD, this may be academic since the normal network services like telnet and ftp don't let you control the TOS). Not all values of TOS are legal or meaningful – see the IP spec for definitions. Useful values are probably '**-t** *16*' (low delay) and '**-t** *8*' (high throughput).

−v   Verbose output. Received ICMP packets other than TIME_EXCEEDED and UNREACHABLEs are listed.

−w   Set the time (in seconds) to wait for a response to a probe (default 5 sec.).

−x   Toggle checksums. Normally, this prevents traceroute from calculating checksums. In some cases, the operating system can overwrite parts of the outgoing packet but not recalculate the checksum (so in some cases the default is to not calculate checksums and using **−x** causes them to be calculated). Note that checksums are usually required for the last hop when using ICMP ECHO probes (**−I**).

This program attempts to trace the route an IP packet would follow to some internet host by launching UDP probe packets with a small ttl (time to live) then listening for an ICMP "time exceeded" reply from a gateway. We start our probes with a ttl of one and increase by one until we get an ICMP "port unreachable" (which means we got to "host") or hit a max (which defaults to 30 hops & can be changed with the **−m** flag). Three probes (change with **−q** flag) are sent at each ttl setting and a line is printed showing the ttl, address of the gateway and round trip time of each probe. If the probe answers come from different gateways, the address of each responding system will be printed. If there is no response within a 5 sec. timeout interval (changed with the **−w** flag), a "*" is printed for that probe.

We don't want the destination host to process the UDP probe packets so the destination port is set to an unlikely value (if some clod on the destination is using that value, it can be changed with the **−p** flag).

A sample use and output might be:

```
        [yak 71]% traceroute nis.nsf.net.
        traceroute to nis.nsf.net (35.1.1.48), 30 hops max, 38 byte packet
         1  helios.ee.lbl.gov (128.3.112.1)  19 ms  19 ms  0 ms
         2  lilac-dmc.Berkeley.EDU (128.32.216.1)  39 ms  39 ms  19 ms
         3  lilac-dmc.Berkeley.EDU (128.32.216.1)  39 ms  39 ms  19 ms
         4  ccngw-ner-cc.Berkeley.EDU (128.32.136.23)  39 ms  40 ms  39 ms
         5  ccn-nerif22.Berkeley.EDU (128.32.168.22)  39 ms  39 ms  39 ms
         6  128.32.197.4 (128.32.197.4)  40 ms  59 ms  59 ms
         7  131.119.2.5 (131.119.2.5)  59 ms  59 ms  59 ms
         8  129.140.70.13 (129.140.70.13)  99 ms  99 ms  80 ms
         9  129.140.71.6 (129.140.71.6)  139 ms  239 ms  319 ms
        10  129.140.81.7 (129.140.81.7)  220 ms  199 ms  199 ms
        11  nic.merit.edu (35.1.1.48)  239 ms  239 ms  239 ms
```

Note that lines 2 & 3 are the same. This is due to a buggy kernel on the 2nd hop system – lilac-dmc.Berkeley.EDU – that forwards packets with a zero ttl (a bug in the distributed version of 4.3BSD). Note that you have to guess what path the packets are taking cross-country since the NSFNET (129.140) doesn't supply address-to-name translations for its NSSes.

A more interesting example is:

```
[yak 72]% traceroute allspice.lcs.mit.edu.
traceroute to allspice.lcs.mit.edu (18.26.0.115), 30 hops max
 1  helios.ee.lbl.gov (128.3.112.1)  0 ms  0 ms  0 ms
 2  lilac-dmc.Berkeley.EDU (128.32.216.1)  19 ms  19 ms  19 ms
 3  lilac-dmc.Berkeley.EDU (128.32.216.1)  39 ms  19 ms  19 ms
 4  ccngw-ner-cc.Berkeley.EDU (128.32.136.23)  19 ms  39 ms  39 ms
 5  ccn-nerif22.Berkeley.EDU (128.32.168.22)  20 ms  39 ms  39 ms
 6  128.32.197.4 (128.32.197.4)  59 ms  119 ms  39 ms
 7  131.119.2.5 (131.119.2.5)  59 ms  59 ms  39 ms
 8  129.140.70.13 (129.140.70.13)  80 ms  79 ms  99 ms
 9  129.140.71.6 (129.140.71.6)  139 ms  139 ms  159 ms
10  129.140.81.7 (129.140.81.7)  199 ms  180 ms  300 ms
11  129.140.72.17 (129.140.72.17)  300 ms  239 ms  239 ms
12  * * *
13  128.121.54.72 (128.121.54.72)  259 ms  499 ms  279 ms
14  * * *
15  * * *
16  * * *
17  * * *
18  ALLSPICE.LCS.MIT.EDU (18.26.0.115)  339 ms  279 ms  279 ms
```

Note that the gateways 12, 14, 15, 16 & 17 hops away either don't send ICMP "time exceeded" messages or send them with a ttl too small to reach us. 14 − 17 are running the MIT C Gateway code that doesn't send "time exceeded"s. God only knows what's going on with 12.

The silent gateway 12 in the above may be the result of a bug in the 4.[23]BSD network code (and its derivatives): 4.x (x ≤ 3) sends an unreachable message using whatever ttl remains in the original datagram. Since, for gateways, the remaining ttl is zero, the ICMP "time exceeded" is guaranteed to not make it back to us. The behavior of this bug is slightly more interesting when it appears on the destination system:

```
 1  helios.ee.lbl.gov (128.3.112.1)  0 ms  0 ms  0 ms
 2  lilac-dmc.Berkeley.EDU (128.32.216.1)  39 ms  19 ms  39 ms
 3  lilac-dmc.Berkeley.EDU (128.32.216.1)  19 ms  39 ms  19 ms
 4  ccngw-ner-cc.Berkeley.EDU (128.32.136.23)  39 ms  40 ms  19 ms
 5  ccn-nerif35.Berkeley.EDU (128.32.168.35)  39 ms  39 ms  39 ms
 6  csgw.Berkeley.EDU (128.32.133.254)  39 ms  59 ms  39 ms
 7  * * *
 8  * * *
 9  * * *
10  * * *
11  * * *
12  * * *
13  rip.Berkeley.EDU (128.32.131.22)  59 ms !  39 ms !  39 ms !
```

Notice that there are 12 "gateways" (13 is the final destination) and exactly the last half of them are "missing". What's really happening is that rip (a Sun-3 running Sun OS3.5) is using the ttl from our arriving datagram as the ttl in its ICMP reply. So, the reply will time out on the return path (with no notice sent to anyone since ICMP's aren't sent for ICMP's) until we probe with a ttl that's at least twice the path length. I.e., rip is really only 7 hops away. A reply that returns with a ttl of 1 is a clue this problem exists. Traceroute prints a "!" after the time if the ttl is ≤ 1. Since vendors ship a lot of obsolete (DEC's ULTRIX, Sun 3.x) or non-standard (HP-UX) software, expect to see this problem frequently and/or take care picking the target host of your probes.

Other possible annotations after the time are !H, !N, or !P (got a host, network or protocol unreachable, respectively), !S or !F (source route failed or fragmentation needed − neither of these should ever occur and the associated gateway is busted if you see one), **!X** (communication administratively prohibited), or **!<N>** (ICMP unreachable code N). If almost all the probes result in some kind of unreachable, traceroute will give up and exit.

      traceroute −g 10.3.0.5 128.182.0.0

will show the path from the Cambridge Mailbridge to PSC, while

      traceroute −g 192.5.146.4 −g 10.3.0.5 35.0.0.0

will show the path from the Cambridge Mailbridge to Merit, using PSC to reach the Mailbridge.

This program is intended for use in network testing, measurement and management. It should be used primarily for manual fault isolation. Because of the load it could impose on the network, it is unwise to use *traceroute* during normal operations or from automated scripts.

SEE ALSO

      netstat(1), ping(8)

AUTHOR

      Implemented by Van Jacobson from a suggestion by Steve Deering. Debugged by a cast of thousands with particularly cogent suggestions or fixes from C. Philip Wood, Tim Seaver and Ken Adelman.

      The current version is available via anonymous ftp:

            ftp://ftp.ee.lbl.gov/traceroute.tar.Z

BUGS

      Please send bug reports to traceroute@ee.lbl.gov.

      The AS number capability reports information that may sometimes be inaccurate due to discrepancies between the contents of the routing database server and the current state of the Internet.

NAME
traceroute6 — print the route IPv6 packets will take to the destination

SYNOPSIS
traceroute6 [**-dIlnrv**] [**-f** *firsthop*] [**-g** *gateway*] [**-m** *hoplimit*] [**-p** *port*]
         [**-q** *probes*] [**-s** *src*] [**-w** *waittime*] *target* [*datalen*]

DESCRIPTION
-d   Debug mode.

-f *firsthop*
        Specify how many hops to skip in trace.

-g *gateway*
        Specify intermediate gateway (**traceroute6** uses routing header).

-I   Use ICMP6 ECHO instead of UDP datagrams.

-l   Print both host hostnames and numeric addresses. Normally **traceroute6** prints only hostnames
        if **-n** is not specified, and only numeric addresses if **-n** is specified.

-m *hoplimit*
        Specify maximum hoplimit.

-n   Do not resolve numeric address to hostname.

-p *port*
        Set UDP port number to *port*.

-q *probes*
        Set the number of probe per hop count to *probes*.

-r   Bypass the normal routing tables and send directly to a host on an attached network. If the host is
        not on a directly-attached network, an error is returned. This option can be used to send probes to a
        local host through an interface that has no route through it (e.g., after the interface was dropped by
        route6d(8)).

-s *src*
        Src specifies the source IPv6 address to be used.

-v   Be verbose.

-w *waittime*
        Specify the delay time between probes.

EXIT STATUS
The **traceroute6** command exits 0 on success, and >0 on errors.

# SEE ALSO
ping(8), ping6(8), traceroute(8)

HISTORY
The **traceroute6** command first appeared in WIDE hydrangea IPv6 protocol stack kit.

NAME

trivial-rewrite – Postfix address rewriting and resolving daemon

SYNOPSIS

trivial-rewrite [generic Postfix daemon options]

DESCRIPTION

The **trivial-rewrite**(8) daemon processes three types of client service requests:

rewrite *context address*

> Rewrite an address to standard form, according to the address rewriting context:

> **local**   Append the domain names specified with **$myorigin** or **$mydomain** to incomplete addresses; do **swap_bangpath** and **allow_percent_hack** processing as described below, and strip source routed addresses (*@site, @site:user@domain*) to *user@domain* form.

> **remote** Append the domain name specified with **$remote_header_rewrite_domain** to incomplete addresses. Otherwise the result is identical to that of the **local** address rewriting context. This prevents Postfix from appending the local domain to spam from poorly written remote clients.

resolve *sender address*

> Resolve the address to a (*transport*, *nexthop*, *recipient*, *flags*) quadruple. The meaning of the results is as follows:

> *transport*
> > The delivery agent to use. This is the first field of an entry in the **master.cf** file.

> *nexthop*
> > The host to send to and optional delivery method information.

> *recipient*
> > The envelope recipient address that is passed on to *nexthop*.

> *flags*   The address class, whether the address requires relaying, whether the address has problems, and whether the request failed.

verify *sender address*

> Resolve the address for address verification purposes.

SERVER PROCESS MANAGEMENT

The **trivial-rewrite**(8) servers run under control by the Postfix master server. Each server can handle multiple simultaneous connections. When all servers are busy while a client connects, the master creates a new server process, provided that the trivial-rewrite server process limit is not exceeded. Each trivial-rewrite server terminates after serving at least **$max_use** clients of after **$max_idle** seconds of idle time.

STANDARDS

None. The command does not interact with the outside world.

SECURITY

The **trivial-rewrite**(8) daemon is not security sensitive. By default, this daemon does not talk to remote or local users. It can run at a fixed low privilege in a chrooted environment.

DIAGNOSTICS

Problems and transactions are logged to **syslogd**(8).

CONFIGURATION PARAMETERS

On busy mail systems a long time may pass before a **main.cf** change affecting **trivial-rewrite**(8) is picked up. Use the command "**postfix reload**" to speed up a change.

The text below provides only a parameter summary. See **postconf**(5) for more details including examples.

COMPATIBILITY CONTROLS

resolve_dequoted_address (yes)
> Resolve a recipient address safely instead of correctly, by looking inside quotes.

resolve_null_domain (no)
> Resolve an address that ends in the "@" null domain as if the local hostname were specified, instead of rejecting the address as invalid.

resolve_numeric_domain (no)
> Resolve "user@ipaddress" as "user@[ipaddress]", instead of rejecting the address as invalid.

Available with Postfix version 2.5 and later:

allow_min_user (no)
> Allow a sender or recipient address to have '-' as the first character.

ADDRESS REWRITING CONTROLS
myorigin ($myhostname)
> The domain name that locally-posted mail appears to come from, and that locally posted mail is delivered to.

allow_percent_hack (yes)
> Enable the rewriting of the form "user%domain" to "user@domain".

append_at_myorigin (yes)
> With locally submitted mail, append the string "@$myorigin" to mail addresses without domain information.

append_dot_mydomain (yes)
> With locally submitted mail, append the string ".$mydomain" to addresses that have no ".domain" information.

recipient_delimiter (empty)
> The separator between user names and address extensions (user+foo).

swap_bangpath (yes)
> Enable the rewriting of "site!user" into "user@site".

Available in Postfix 2.2 and later:

remote_header_rewrite_domain (empty)
> Don't rewrite message headers from remote clients at all when this parameter is empty; otherwise, rewrite message headers and append the specified domain name to incomplete addresses.

ROUTING CONTROLS
The following is applicable to Postfix version 2.0 and later. Earlier versions do not have support for: virtual_transport, relay_transport, virtual_alias_domains, virtual_mailbox_domains or proxy_interfaces.

local_transport (local:$myhostname)
> The default mail delivery transport and next-hop destination for final delivery to domains listed with mydestination, and for [ipaddress] destinations that match $inet_interfaces or $proxy_interfaces.

virtual_transport (virtual)
> The default mail delivery transport and next-hop destination for final delivery to domains listed with $virtual_mailbox_domains.

relay_transport (relay)
> The default mail delivery transport and next-hop destination for remote delivery to domains listed with $relay_domains.

default_transport (smtp)
> The default mail delivery transport and next-hop destination for destinations that do not match $mydestination, $inet_interfaces, $proxy_interfaces, $virtual_alias_domains, $virtual_mailbox_domains, or $relay_domains.

parent_domain_matches_subdomains (see 'postconf -d' output)
 What Postfix features match subdomains of "domain.tld" automatically, instead of requiring an explicit ".domain.tld" pattern.

relayhost (empty)
 The next-hop destination of non-local mail; overrides non-local domains in recipient addresses.

transport_maps (empty)
 Optional lookup tables with mappings from recipient address to (message delivery transport, next-hop destination).

Available in Postfix version 2.3 and later:

sender_dependent_relayhost_maps (empty)
 A sender-dependent override for the global relayhost parameter setting.

Available in Postfix version 2.5 and later:

empty_address_relayhost_maps_lookup_key (<>)
 The sender_dependent_relayhost_maps search string that will be used instead of the null sender address.

ADDRESS VERIFICATION CONTROLS

Postfix version 2.1 introduces sender and recipient address verification. This feature is implemented by sending probe email messages that are not actually delivered. By default, address verification probes use the same route as regular mail. To override specific aspects of message routing for address verification probes, specify one or more of the following:

address_verify_local_transport ($local_transport)
 Overrides the local_transport parameter setting for address verification probes.

address_verify_virtual_transport ($virtual_transport)
 Overrides the virtual_transport parameter setting for address verification probes.

address_verify_relay_transport ($relay_transport)
 Overrides the relay_transport parameter setting for address verification probes.

address_verify_default_transport ($default_transport)
 Overrides the default_transport parameter setting for address verification probes.

address_verify_relayhost ($relayhost)
 Overrides the relayhost parameter setting for address verification probes.

address_verify_transport_maps ($transport_maps)
 Overrides the transport_maps parameter setting for address verification probes.

Available in Postfix version 2.3 and later:

address_verify_sender_dependent_relayhost_maps ($sender_dependent_relayhost_maps)
 Overrides the sender_dependent_relayhost_maps parameter setting for address verification probes.

MISCELLANEOUS CONTROLS

config_directory (see 'postconf -d' output)
 The default location of the Postfix main.cf and master.cf configuration files.

daemon_timeout (18000s)
 How much time a Postfix daemon process may take to handle a request before it is terminated by a built-in watchdog timer.

empty_address_recipient (MAILER-DAEMON)
 The recipient of mail addressed to the null address.

ipc_timeout (3600s)
 The time limit for sending or receiving information over an internal communication channel.

max_idle (100s)
> The maximum amount of time that an idle Postfix daemon process waits for an incoming connection before terminating voluntarily.

max_use (100)
> The maximal number of incoming connections that a Postfix daemon process will service before terminating voluntarily.

relocated_maps (empty)
> Optional lookup tables with new contact information for users or domains that no longer exist.

process_id (read-only)
> The process ID of a Postfix command or daemon process.

process_name (read-only)
> The process name of a Postfix command or daemon process.

queue_directory (see 'postconf -d' output)
> The location of the Postfix top-level queue directory.

show_user_unknown_table_name (yes)
> Display the name of the recipient table in the "User unknown" responses.

syslog_facility (mail)
> The syslog facility of Postfix logging.

syslog_name (see 'postconf -d' output)
> The mail system name that is prepended to the process name in syslog records, so that "smtpd" becomes, for example, "postfix/smtpd".

Available in Postfix version 2.0 and later:

helpful_warnings (yes)
> Log warnings about problematic configuration settings, and provide helpful suggestions.

SEE ALSO
postconf(5), configuration parameters
transport(5), transport table format
relocated(5), format of the "user has moved" table
master(8), process manager
syslogd(8), system logging

README FILES
Use "**postconf readme_directory**" or "**postconf html_directory**" to locate this information.
ADDRESS_CLASS_README, Postfix address classes howto
ADDRESS_VERIFICATION_README, Postfix address verification

LICENSE
The Secure Mailer license must be distributed with this software.

AUTHOR(S)
Wietse Venema
IBM T.J. Watson Research
P.O. Box 704
Yorktown Heights, NY 10598, USA

NAME

trpt — transliterate protocol trace

SYNOPSIS

trpt [**-a**] [**-f**] [**-j**] [**-p** *hex-address*] [**-s**] [**-t**] [**-N** *system*] [**-M** *core*]

DESCRIPTION

trpt interrogates the buffer of TCP trace records created when a socket is marked for "debugging" (see setsockopt(2)), and prints a readable description of these records. When no options are supplied, **trpt** prints all the trace records found in the system grouped according to TCP connection protocol control block (PCB). The following options may be used to alter this behavior.

-a   In addition to the normal output, print the values of the source and destination addresses for each packet recorded.

-f   Follow the trace as it occurs, waiting a short time for additional records each time the end of the log is reached.

-j   Just give a list of the protocol control block addresses for which there are trace records.

-p   Show only trace records associated with the protocol control block at the given address *hex-address*.

-s   In addition to the normal output, print a detailed description of the packet sequencing information.

-t   in addition to the normal output, print the values for all timers at each point in the trace.

-M *core*
        Extract values associated with the name list from core.

-N *system*
        Extract the name list from system.

The recommended use of **trpt** is as follows. Isolate the problem and enable debugging on the socket(s) involved in the connection. Find the address of the protocol control blocks associated with the sockets using the **-A** option to netstat(1). Then run **trpt** with the **-p** option, supplying the associated protocol control block addresses. The **-f** option can be used to follow the trace log once the trace is located. If there are many sockets using the debugging option, the **-j** option may be useful in checking to see if any trace records are present for the socket in question.

SYSCTLS

The following sysctls are used by **trpt**. The TCP_DEBUG kernel option must be enabled.

net.inet.tcp.debug   Structure containing TCP sockets information used by **trpt**.

net.inet.tcp.debx   Number of TCP debug messages.

DIAGNOSTICS

no namelist
        When the image doesn't contain the proper symbols to find the trace buffer; others which should be self explanatory.

SEE ALSO

netstat(1), setsockopt(2)

HISTORY

The **trpt** command appeared in 4.2 BSD.

BUGS

Should also print the data for each input or output, but this is not saved in the trace record.

The output format is inscrutable and should be described here.

NAME

ttyflags — set device-specific flags for terminals

SYNOPSIS

ttyflags [**-v**] [**-a** | *tty* ...]

DESCRIPTION

ttyflags sets the device-specific flags for terminals using TIOCSFLAGS, based on the flags found on the terminal's line in /etc/ttys.

The options are as follows:

-a   Set the flags for all terminals in /etc/ttys.

-v   Be verbose about what the terminals' flags will be set to.

The *tty* arguments are optional, but must not be specified if the **-a** flag is used. If specified, the *tty* arguments should be the base names of the ttys, as found in /etc/ttys.

FILES

/etc/ttys

SEE ALSO

getttyent(3), tty(4), ttys(5)

HISTORY

The **ttyflags** utility appeared in NetBSD 1.0.

BUGS

The conditions on which to report an error are ill-defined. **ttyflags** tries to report all significant errors, perhaps going over-board at times.

NAME
tunefs — tune up an existing file system

SYNOPSIS
tunefs [**-AFN**] [**-e** *maxbpg*] [**-g** *avgfilesize*] [**-h** *avgfpdir*] [**-l** *logsize*]
[**-m** *minfree*] [**-o** *optimize_preference*] *special* | *filesys*

DESCRIPTION
tunefs is designed to change the dynamic parameters of a file system which affect the layout policies.

The following options are supported by **tunefs**:

-A   Cause the values to be updated in all the alternate superblocks instead of just the standard superblock. If this option is not used, then use of a backup superblock by fsck(8) will lose anything changed by **tunefs**. **-A** is ignored when **-N** is specified.

-F   Indicates that *special* is a file system image, rather than a device name or file system mount point. *special* will be accessed 'as-is'.

-N   Display all the settable options (after any changes from the tuning options) but do not cause any of them to be changed.

-e *maxbpg*
This indicates the maximum number of blocks any single file can allocate out of a cylinder group before it is forced to begin allocating blocks from another cylinder group. Typically this value is set to about one quarter of the total blocks in a cylinder group. The intent is to prevent any single file from using up all the blocks in a single cylinder group, thus degrading access times for all files subsequently allocated in that cylinder group. The effect of this limit is to cause big files to do long seeks more frequently than if they were allowed to allocate all the blocks in a cylinder group before seeking elsewhere. For file systems with exclusively large files, this parameter should be set higher.

-g *avgfilesize*
This specifies the expected average file size.

-h *avgfpdir*
This specifies the expected number of files per directory.

-l *logsize*
This value specifies the size of the in-filesystem journaling log file. The default journaling log file size is described in wapbl(4). Specifying a size of zero will cause the in-filesystem journaling log file to be removed the next time the filesystem is mounted. The size of an existing in-filesystem journaling log file can not be changed.

-m *minfree*
This value specifies the percentage of space held back from normal users; the minimum free space threshold. The default value is set during creation of the filesystem, see newfs(8). This value can be set to zero, however up to a factor of three in throughput will be lost over the performance obtained at a 5% threshold. Note that if the value is raised above the current usage level, users will be unable to allocate files until enough files have been deleted to get under the higher threshold.

-o *optimize_preference*
The file system can either try to minimize the time spent allocating blocks, or it can attempt to minimize the space fragmentation on the disk. If the value of minfree (see above) is less than 5%, then the file system should optimize for space to avoid running out of full sized blocks. For values of minfree greater than or equal to 5%, fragmentation is unlikely to be problematical, and the file system can be optimized for time.

optimize_preference can be specified as either space or time.

SEE ALSO

wapbl(4), fs(5), dumpfs(8), fsck_ffs(8), newfs(8)

M. McKusick, W. Joy, S. Leffler, and R. Fabry, "A Fast File System for UNIX", *ACM Transactions on Computer Systems 2*, 3, pp 181-197, August 1984, (reprinted in the BSD System Manager's Manual, SMM:5).

HISTORY

The **tunefs** command appeared in 4.2 BSD.

BUGS

This program should work on mounted and active file systems. Because the super-block is not kept in the buffer cache, the changes will only take effect if the program is run on unmounted file systems. To change the root file system, the system must be rebooted after the file system is tuned.

You can tune a file system, but you can't tune a fish.

NAME
umount — unmount filesystems

SYNOPSIS
umount [**−fvFR**] [**−t** *fstypelist*] *special* | *node*
umount **−a** [**−fvF**] [**−h** *host*] [**−t** *fstypelist*]

DESCRIPTION
The **umount** command calls the unmount(2) system call to remove a *special device* or the remote node (rhost:path) from the filesystem tree at the point *node*. If either *special* or *node* are not provided, the appropriate information is taken from the fstab(5) file.

The options are as follows:

−a   All the currently mounted filesystems except the root are unmounted.

−f   The filesystem is forcibly unmounted. Active special devices continue to work, but all other files return errors if further accesses are attempted. The root filesystem cannot be forcibly unmounted.

−F   Fake the unmount; perform all other processing but do not actually attempt the unmount. (This is most useful in conjunction with **−v**, to see what **umount** would attempt to do).

−R   Take the *special* | *node* argument as a path to be passed directly to unmount(2), bypassing all attempts to be smart about mechanically determining the correct path from the argument. This option is incompatible with any option that potentially unmounts more than one filesystem, such as **−a**, but it can be used with **−f** and/or **−v**. This is the only way to unmount something that does not appear as a directory (such as a nullfs mount of a plain file); there are probably other cases where it is necessary.

−h *host*
         Only filesystems mounted from the specified host will be unmounted. This option is implies the **−a** option and, unless otherwise specified with the **−t** option, will only unmount NFS filesystems.

−t *fstypelist*
         Is used to indicate the actions should only be taken on filesystems of the specified type. More than one type may be specified in a comma separated list. The list of filesystem types can be prefixed with "no" to specify the filesystem types for which action should *not* be taken. For example, the **umount** command:

             umount −a −t nfs,mfs

         unmounts all filesystems of the type NFS and MFS, whereas the **umount** command:

             umount −a −t nonfs,mfs

         unmounts all file systems except those of type NFS and MFS.

−v   Verbose, additional information is printed out as each filesystem is unmounted.

FILES
/etc/fstab filesystem table

SEE ALSO
unmount(2), fstab(5), mount(8)

HISTORY

A **umount** command appeared in Version 6 AT&T UNIX.

NAME

      unlink — call the unlink function

SYNOPSIS

      unlink *file*

DESCRIPTION

      The **unlink** utility performs the function call **unlink**(*file*).

      file must be the pathname of an existing file.

EXIT STATUS

      The **unlink** utility exits 0 on success, and >0 if an error occurs.

SEE ALSO

      rm(1), rmdir(1), unlink(2), link(8)

STANDARDS

      The **unlink** utility conforms to X/Open Commands and Utilities Issue 5 ("XCU5").

NAME

usbdevs — show USB devices connected to the system

SYNOPSIS

usbdevs [-a *addr*] [-d] [-f *dev*] [-v]

DESCRIPTION

usbdevs prints a listing of all USB devices connected to the system with some information about each device. The indentation of each line indicates its distance from the root.

The options are as follows:

-a *addr*   only print information about the device at the given address.

-d   Show the device drivers associated with each device.

-f *dev*   only print information for the given USB controller.

-v   Be verbose.

FILES

/dev/usb[0-9]   Default USB controllers.

SEE ALSO

usb(4)

HISTORY

The usbdevs command appeared in NetBSD 1.4.

USER (8)   NetBSD   USER (8)

NAME

    user — manage user login information on the system

SYNOPSIS

    user add −**D** [options]
    user add [options] *user*
    user del −**D** [options]
    user del [options] *user*
    user info [options] *user*
    user mod [options] *user*

DESCRIPTION

    The **user** utility acts as a frontend to the useradd(8), usermod(8), userinfo(8), and userdel(8) commands. The utilities by default are built with EXTENSIONS. This allows for further functionality.

    For a full explanation of the options available, please see the relevant manual page.

EXIT STATUS

    The **user** utility exits 0 on success, and >0 if an error occurs.

FILES

    /etc/skel/.[A−z]*   Skeleton files for new user
    /etc/usermgmt.conf   Configuration file for **user**, group(8) and the backend commands mentioned above.

SEE ALSO

    chpass(1), group(5), passwd(5), usermgmt.conf(5), useradd(8), userdel(8), userinfo(8), usermod(8)

HISTORY

    The **user** utility first appeared in NetBSD 1.5. It is based on the *addnerd* package by the same author.

AUTHORS

    The **user** utility was written by Alistair G. Crooks ⟨agc@NetBSD.org⟩.

NAME

　　useradd — add a user to the system

SYNOPSIS

　　useradd −D [**−F**] [**−b** *base-dir*] [**−e** *expiry-time*] [**−f** *inactive-time*]
　　　　　　[**−g** *gid* | *name* | =uid] [**−k** *skel-dir*] [**−L** *login-class*] [**−M** *home-perm*]
　　　　　　[**−r** *lowuid..highuid*] [**−s** *shell*]
　　useradd [**−moSv**] [**−b** *base-dir*] [**−c** *comment*] [**−d** *home-dir*] [**−e** *expiry-time*]
　　　　　　[**−f** *inactive-time*] [**−G** *secondary-group*] [**−g** *gid* | *name* | =uid]
　　　　　　[**−k** *skel-dir*] [**−L** *login-class*] [**−M** *home-perm*] [**−p** *password*]
　　　　　　[**−r** *lowuid..highuid*] [**−s** *shell*] [**−u** *uid*] *user*

DESCRIPTION

　　The **useradd** utility adds a user to the system, creating and populating a home directory if necessary. Any
　　skeleton files will be provided for the new user if they exist in the *skel-dir* directory (see the **−k** option).
　　Default values for the base directory, the time of password expiry, the time of account expiry, primary group,
　　the skeleton directory, the range from which the uid will be allocated, and default login shell can be provided
　　in the /etc/usermgmt.conf file, which, if running as root, is created using the built-in defaults if it does
　　not exist.

　　The first form of the command shown above (using the **−D** option) sets and displays the defaults for the
　　useradd utility.

　　See user(8) for more information about EXTENSIONS.

　　−b *base-dir*
　　　　　　Set the default base directory. This is the directory to which the user directory is added, which will
　　　　　　be created if the **−m** option is specified and no **−d** option is specified.

　　−D　　without any further options, **−D** will show the current defaults which will be used by the **useradd**
　　　　　　utility. Together with one of the options shown for the first version of the command, **−D** will set the
　　　　　　default to be the new value. See usermgmt.conf(5) for more information.

　　−e *expiry-time*
　　　　　　Set the time at which the new user accounts will expire. It should be entered in the form "month
　　　　　　day year", where month is the month name (the first three characters are sufficient), day is the day of
　　　　　　the month, and year is the year. Time in seconds since the epoch (UTC) is also valid. A value of 0
　　　　　　can be used to disable this feature.

　　−F　　Force the user to change their password upon next login.

　　−f *inactive-time*
　　　　　　Set the time at which passwords for the new user accounts will expire. Also see the **−e** option
　　　　　　above.

　　−g *gid* | *groupname* | =uid
　　　　　　Set the default group for new users.

　　−k *skel-dir*
　　　　　　Set the skeleton directory in which to find files with which to populate new users' home directories.

　　−L *login-class*
　　　　　　Set the default login class for new users. See login.conf(5) for more information on user login
　　　　　　classes. This option is included if built with EXTENSIONS.

−M *home-perm*
: sets the default permissions of the newly created home directory if **−m** is given. The permission is specified as an octal number, with or without a leading zero.

−r *lowuid..highuid*
: Set the low and high bounds of uid ranges for new users. A new user can only be created if there are uids which can be assigned from one of the free ranges. This option is included if built with EXTENSIONS.

−s *shell*
: Set the default login shell for new users.

In the second form of the command, after setting any defaults, and then reading values from /etc/usermgmt.conf, the following command line options are processed:

−b *base-directory*
: Set the base directory name, in which the user's new home directory will be created, should the **−m** option be specified.

−c *comment*
: Set the comment field (also, for historical reasons known as the GECOS field) which will be added for the user, and typically will include the user's full name, and, perhaps, contact information for the user.

−d *home-directory*
: Set the home directory which will be created and populated for the user, should the **−m** option be specified.

−e *expiry-time*
: Set the time at which the current password will expire for new users. It should be entered in the form "month day year", where month is the month name (the first three characters are sufficient), day is the day of the month, and year is the year. Time in seconds since the epoch (UTC) is also valid. A value of 0 can be used to disable this feature. See passwd(5) for more details.

−f *inactive-time*
: Set the time at which new user accounts will expire. Also see the **−e** option above.

−G *secondary-group*
: Add the user to the secondary group *secondary-group* in the /etc/group file. The *secondary-group* may be a comma-delimited list for multiple groups. Or the option may be repeated for multiple groups. (16 groups maximum.)

−g *gid | name | =uid*
: Give the group name or identifier to be used for the new user's primary group. If this is =uid, then a uid and gid will be picked which are both unique and the same, and a line added to /etc/group to describe the new group.

−k *skeleton directory*
: Give the skeleton directory in which to find files with which to populate the new user's home directory.

−L *login-class*
: Set the login class for the user being created. See login.conf(5) for more information on user login classes. This option is included if built with EXTENSIONS.

−M *home-perm*
: sets the permissions of the newly created home directory if **−m** is given. The permission is specified as an octal number, with or without a leading zero.

-m   Create a new home directory for the new user.

-o   Allow the new user to have a uid which is already in use for another user.

-p *password*
          Specify an already-encrypted password for the new user. Encrypted passwords can be generated
          with pwhash(1). The password can be changed later by using chpass(1) or passwd(1). This
          option is included if built with EXTENSIONS.

-S   Allow samba user names with a trailing dollar sign to be added to the system. This option is
          included if built with EXTENSIONS.

-s *shell*
          Specify the login shell for the new user.

-u *uid*
          Specify a uid for the new user. Boundaries for this value can be preset for all users by using the
          range field in the /etc/usermgmt.conf file.

-v   Enable verbose mode - explain the commands as they are executed. This option is included if built
          with EXTENSIONS.

Once the information has been verified, **useradd** uses pwd_mkdb(8) to update the user database. This is
run in the background, and, at very large sites could take several minutes. Until this update is completed, the
password file is unavailable for other updates and the new information is not available to programs.

EXIT STATUS
        The **useradd** utility exits 0 on success, and >0 if an error occurs.

FILES
        /etc/usermgmt.conf
        /etc/skel/*
        /etc/login.conf

SEE ALSO
        chpass(1), passwd(1), pwhash(1), group(5), login.conf(5), passwd(5), usermgmt.conf(5),
        pwd_mkdb(8), user(8), userdel(8), usermod(8)

HISTORY
        The **useradd** utility first appeared in NetBSD 1.5. It is based on the *addnerd* package by the same author.

AUTHORS
        The **useradd** utility was written by Alistair G. Crooks ⟨agc@NetBSD.org⟩.

        Support for setting permissions of home directories was added by Hubert Feyrer.

NAME
userdel — remove a user from the system

SYNOPSIS
userdel **-D** [**-p** *preserve-value*]
userdel [**-rSv**] [**-p** *preserve-value*] *user*

DESCRIPTION
The **userdel** utility removes a user from the system, optionally removing that user's home directory and any subdirectories.

Default values are taken from the information provided in the /etc/usermgmt.conf file, which, if running as root, is created using the built-in defaults if it does not exist.

The first form of the command shown above (using the **-D** option) sets and displays the defaults for the **userdel** utility.

See user(8) for more information about EXTENSIONS.

-D   Without any further options, **-D** will show the current defaults which will be used by the **userdel** utility. Together with one of the options shown for the first version of the command, **-D** will set the default to be the new value. This option is included if built with EXTENSIONS.

-p *preserve-value*
     Set the preservation value. If this value is one of true, yes, or a non-zero number, then the user login information will be preserved. This option is included if built with EXTENSIONS.

In the second form of the command, after setting any defaults, and then reading values from /etc/usermgmt.conf, the following command line options are processed:

-p *preserve-value*
     Preserve the user information in the password file, but do not allow the user to login, by switching the password to an "impossible" one, and by setting the user's shell to the nologin(8) program. This option can be helpful in preserving a user's files for later use by members of that person's group after the user has moved on. This value can also be set in the /etc/usermgmt.conf file, using the preserve field. If the field has any of the values true, yes, or a non-zero number, then user information preservation will take place. This option is included if built with EXTENSIONS.

-r   Remove the user's home directory, any subdirectories, and any files and other entries in them.

-S   Allow a samba user name (with a trailing dollar sign) to be deleted. This option is included if built with EXTENSIONS.

-v   Perform any actions in a verbose manner. This option is included if built with EXTENSIONS.

Once the information has been verified, **userdel** uses pwd_mkdb(8) to update the user database. This is run in the background, and, at very large sites could take several minutes. Until this update is completed, the password file is unavailable for other updates and the new information is not available to programs.

EXIT STATUS
The **userdel** utility exits 0 on success, and >0 if an error occurs.

FILES
/etc/usermgmt.conf

USERDEL (8)   NetBSD   USERDEL (8)

SEE ALSO
passwd(5), usermgmt.conf(5), group(8), nologin(8), pwd_mkdb(8), user(8), useradd(8)

HISTORY
The **userdel** utility first appeared in NetBSD 1.5. It is based on the *addnerd* package by the same author.

AUTHORS
The **userdel** utility was written by Alistair G. Crooks ⟨agc@NetBSD.org⟩.

NAME

    userinfo — displays user information

SYNOPSIS

    userinfo [**-e**] *user*

DESCRIPTION

    The **userinfo** utility retrieves the user information from the system. The **userinfo** utility is only available if built with EXTENSIONS. See user(8) for more information.

    The following command line option is recognised:

    -e   Return 0 if the user exists, and non-zero if the user does not exist, on the system. No information is displayed. This form of the command is useful for scripts which need to check whether a particular user name or uid is already in use on the system.

    The *user* argument may either be a user's name, or a uid.

EXIT STATUS

    The **userinfo** utility exits 0 on success, and >0 if an error occurs.

SEE ALSO

    passwd(5), group(8), user(8), useradd(8), userdel(8)

HISTORY

    The **userinfo** utility first appeared in NetBSD 1.5. It is based on the *addnerd* package by the same author.

AUTHORS

    The **userinfo** utility was written by Alistair G. Crooks ⟨agc@NetBSD.org⟩.

NAME
   usermod — modify user login information

SYNOPSIS
   usermod [**-FmoSv**] [**-C** *yes/no*] [**-c** *comment*] [**-d** *home-dir*] [**-e** *expiry-time*]
             [**-f** *inactive-time*] [**-G** *secondary-group*] [**-g** *gid* | *name* | =uid]
             [**-L** *login-class*] [**-l** *new-login*] [**-p** *password*] [**-s** *shell*] [**-u** *uid*]
             user

DESCRIPTION
   The **usermod** utility modifies user login information on the system.

   Default values are taken from the information provided in the /etc/usermgmt.conf file, which, if running as root, is created using the built-in defaults if it does not exist.

   See user(8) for more information about EXTENSIONS.

   After setting any defaults, and then reading values from /etc/usermgmt.conf, the following command line options are processed:

   -C *yes/no*
       Enable user accounts to be temporary locked/closed. The *yes/no* operand can be given as "*yes*" to lock the account or "*no*" to unlock the account.

   -c *comment*
       Set the comment field (also, for historical reasons known as the GECOS field) for the user. The comment field will typically include the user's full name and, perhaps, contact information for the user.

   -d *home-directory*
       Set the home directory without populating it; if the **-m** option is specified, tries to move the old home directory to *home-directory*.

   -e *expiry-time*
       Set the time at which the account expires. This can be used to implement password aging. It should be entered in the form "month day year", where month is the month name (the first three characters are sufficient), day is the day of the month, and year is the year. Time in seconds since the epoch (UTC) is also valid. A value of 0 can be used to disable this feature. This value can be preset for all users using the *expire* field in the /etc/usermgmt.conf file. See usermgmt.conf(5) for more details.

   -F Force the user to change their password upon next login.

   -f *inactive-time*
       Set the time at which the password expires. See the **-e** option.

   -G *secondary-group*
       Specify a secondary group to which the user will be added in the /etc/group file. The *secondary-group* may be a comma-delimited list for multiple groups. Or the option may be repeated for multiple groups. (16 groups maximum.)

   -g *gid* | *name* | =uid
       Give the group name or identifier to be used for the user's primary group. If this is =uid, then a uid and gid will be picked which are both unique and the same, and a line will be added to /etc/group to describe the new group. This value can be preset for all users by using the *group* field in the /etc/usermgmt.conf file. See usermgmt.conf(5) for more details.

−L *login-class*
>   Set the login class for the user. See login.conf(5) for more information on user login classes. This value can be preset for all users by using the *class* field in the /etc/usermgmt.conf file. See usermgmt.conf(5) for more details. This option is included if built with EXTENSIONS.

−l *new-user*
>   Give the new user name. It can consist of alphanumeric characters and the characters '.', '−', and '_'.

−m
>   Move the home directory from its old position to the new one. If **−d** is not specified, the *new-user* argument of the **−l** option is used; one of **−d** and **−l** is needed.

−o
>   Allow duplicate uids to be given.

−p *password*
>   Specify an already-encrypted password for the user. This password can then be changed by using the chpass(1) utility. This value can be preset for all users by using the *password* field in the /etc/usermgmt.conf file. See usermgmt.conf(5) for more details. This option is included if built with EXTENSIONS.

−S
>   Allow samba user names with a trailing dollar sign to be modified. This option is included if built with EXTENSIONS.

−s *shell*
>   Specify the login shell for the user. This value can be preset for all users by using the *shell* field in the /etc/usermgmt.conf file. See usermgmt.conf(5) for more details.

−u *uid*
>   Specify a new uid for the user. Boundaries for this value can be preset for all users by using the *range* field in the /etc/usermgmt.conf file. See usermgmt.conf(5) for more details.

−v
>   Enable verbose mode - explain the commands as they are executed. This option is included if built with EXTENSIONS.

Once the information has been verified, **usermod** uses pwd_mkdb(8) to update the user database. This is run in the background. At very large sites this can take several minutes. Until this update is completed, the password file is unavailable for other updates and the new information is not available to programs.

EXIT STATUS
The **usermod** utility exits 0 on success, and >0 if an error occurs.

FILES
/etc/usermgmt.conf

SEE ALSO
chpass(1), group(5), passwd(5), usermgmt.conf(5), pwd_mkdb(8), user(8), useradd(8), userdel(8)

HISTORY
The **usermod** utility first appeared in NetBSD 1.5. It is based on the *addnerd* package by the same author.

AUTHORS
The **usermod** utility was written by Alistair G. Crooks ⟨agc@NetBSD.org⟩.

NAME

    utmp_update — update utmpx database

SYNOPSIS

    utmp_update *utmpx_entry*

DESCRIPTION

    utmp_update is a helper program to allow a user to update his own utmpx(5) entry. **utmp_update** does some consistency checks on the strvis(3)-encoded *utmpx_entry* and then updates the utmpx(5) database of currently logged in users.

    utmp_update should not be called directly, but will normally only be called by pututxline(3) if the privileges of the calling user are not sufficient.

EXIT STATUS

    utmp_update returns 0 on success, and 1 if an error occurred.

SEE ALSO

    pututxline(3), utmpx(5)

NAME

veriexec — file integrity subsystem

DESCRIPTION

Veriexec is an in-kernel, real-time, file-system independent, file integrity subsystem. It can be used for a variety of purposes, including defense against trojaned binaries, indirect attacks via third-party remote file-systems, and malicious configuration file corruption.

CONFIGURATION

Signatures Database

Veriexec requires a signatures database -- a list of monitored files, along with their digital fingerprint and (optionally) access modes. The format of this file is described by veriexec(5).

NetBSD provides a tool, veriexecgen(8), for generating the signatures database. Example usage:

```
# veriexecgen
```

Although it should be loaded on system boot (see "RC Configuration" below), this list can be loaded manually using veriexecctl(8):

```
# veriexecctl load
```

Kernel Configuration

Veriexec requires a pseudo-device to run:

```
pseudo-device veriexec 1
```

Additionally, one or more options for digital fingerprint algorithm support:

```
options VERIFIED_EXEC_FP_SHA256
options VERIFIED_EXEC_FP_SHA512
```

Some kernels already enable *Veriexec* by default. See your kernel's config file for more information.

RC Configuration

Veriexec also allows loading signatures and setting the strict level (see below) during the boot process using the following variables set in rc.conf(5):

```
veriexec=YES
veriexec_strict=1 # IDS mode
```

STRICT LEVELS

Veriexec can operate in four modes, also referred to as strict levels:

Learning mode (strict level 0)

The only level at which the fingerprint tables can be modified, this level is used to help fine-tune the signature database. No enforcement is made, and verbose information is provided (fingerprint matches and mismatches, file removals, incorrect access, etc.).

IDS mode (strict level 1)

IDS (intrusion detection system) mode provides an adequate level of integrity for the files it monitors. Implications:

− Monitored files cannot be removed
− If raw disk access is granted to a disk with monitored files on it, all monitored files' fingerprints will be invalidated

- Access to files with mismatched fingerprints is denied
- Write access to monitored files is allowed
- Access type is not enforced

IPS mode (strict level 2)

IPS (intrusion prevention system) mode provides a high level of integrity for the files it monitors. Implications:

- All implications of IDS mode
- Write access to monitored files is denied
- Access type is enforced
- Raw disk access to disk devices with monitored files on them is denied
- Execution of non-monitored files is denied
- Write access to kernel memory via /dev/mem and /dev/kmem is denied

Lockdown mode (strict level 3)

Lockdown mode provides high assurance integrity for the entire system. Implications:

- All implications of IPS mode
- Access to non-monitored files is denied
- Write access to files is allowed only if the file was opened before the strict level was raised to this mode
- Creation of new files is denied
- Raw access to system disks is denied

RUNTIME INFORMATION

Veriexec exports runtime information that may be useful for various purposes.

It reports the currently supported fingerprinting algorithms, for example:

```
# /sbin/sysctl kern.veriexec.algorithms
kern.veriexec.algorithms = RMD160 SHA256 SHA384 SHA512 SHA1 MD5
```

It reports the current verbosity and strict levels, for example:

```
# /sbin/sysctl kern.veriexec.{verbose,strict}
kern.veriexec.verbose = 0
kern.veriexec.strict = 1
```

It reports a summary of currently loaded files and the mount-points they're on, for example:

```
# /sbin/sysctl kern.veriexec.count
kern.veriexec.count.table0.mntpt = /
kern.veriexec.count.table0.fstype = ffs
kern.veriexec.count.table0.nentries = 33
```

Other information may be retrieved using veriexecctl(8).

SEE ALSO

options(4), veriexec(5), sysctl(7), sysctl(8), veriexecctl(8), veriexecgen(8)

AUTHORS

Elad Efrat ⟨elad@NetBSD.org⟩

NAME
veriexecctl — manage the *Veriexec* subsystem

SYNOPSIS
veriexecctl [-ekv] load [file]
veriexecctl delete *file | mount_point*
veriexecctl dump
veriexecctl flush
veriexecctl query *file*

DESCRIPTION
The **veriexecctl** command is used to manipulate *Veriexec*, the NetBSD file integrity subsystem.

Commands
load [file]
> Load the fingerprint entries contained in *file*, if specified, or the default signatures file otherwise.

> This operation is only allowed in learning mode (strict level zero).

> The following flags are allowed with this command:

> -e   Evaluate fingerprint on load, as opposed to when the file is accessed.

> -k   Keep the filenames in the entry for more accurate logging.

> -v   Enable verbose output.

delete *file | mount_point*
> Delete either a single entry *file* or all entries on *mount_point* from being monitored by *Veriexec*.

dump   Dump the *Veriexec* database from the kernel. Only entries that have the filename will be presented.

> This can be used to recover a lost database:

>   # veriexecctl dump > /etc/signatures

flush
> Delete all entries in the *Veriexec* database.

query *file*
> Query *Veriexec* for information associated with *file*: Filename, mount, fingerprint, fingerprint algorithm, evaluation status, and entry type.

FILES
/dev/veriexec   *Veriexec* pseudo-device
/etc/signatures   default signatures file

SEE ALSO
veriexec(4), veriexec(5), security(8), veriexec(8), veriexecgen(8)

HISTORY
veriexecctl first appeared in NetBSD 2.0.

AUTHORS
Brett Lymn ⟨blymn@NetBSD.org⟩
Elad Efrat ⟨elad@NetBSD.org⟩

NOTES
The kernel is expected to have the "veriexec" pseudo-device.

NAME
veriexecgen — generate fingerprints for Veriexec

SYNOPSIS
veriexecgen [**-AaDrSTvW**] [**-d** dir] [**-o** fingerprintdb] [**-p** prefix]
              [**-t** algorithm]
veriexecgen [**-h**]

DESCRIPTION
veriexecgen can be used to create a fingerprint database for use with *Veriexec*.

If no command line arguments were specified, **veriexecgen** will resort to default operation, implying **-D**
-o /etc/signatures **-t** sha256.

If the output file already exists, **veriexecgen** will save a backup copy in the same file only with a ".old"
suffix.

The following options are available:

-A   Append to the output file, don't overwrite it.

-a   Add fingerprints for non-executable files as well.

-D   Search system directories, /bin, /sbin, /usr/bin, /usr/sbin, /lib, /usr/lib,
                    /libexec, and /usr/libexec.

-d dir   Scan for files in dir. Multiple uses of this flag can specify more than one directory.

-h   Display the help screen.

-o fingerprintdb
                    Save the generated fingerprint database to fingerprintdb.

-p prefix   When storing files in the fingerprint database, store the full pathnames of files with the lead-
                    ing "prefix" of the filenames removed.

-r   Scan recursively.

-S   Set the immutable flag on the created signatures file when done writing it.

-T   Put a timestamp on the generated file.

-t algorithm
                    Use algorithm for the fingerprints. Must be one of "md5", "sha1", "sha256", "sha384",
                    "sha512", or "rmd160".

-v   Verbose mode. Print messages describing what operations are being done.

-W   By default, **veriexecgen** will exit when an error condition is encountered. This option
                 will treat errors such as not being able to follow a symbolic link, not being able to find the
                 real path for a directory entry, or not being able to calculate a hash of an entry as a warning,
                 rather than an error. If errors are treated as warnings, **veriexecgen** will continue process-
                 ing. The default behaviour is to treat errors as fatal.

FILES
/etc/signatures

EXAMPLES

Fingerprint files in the common system directories using the default hashing algorithm "sha256" and save to the default fingerprint database in `/etc/signatures`:

```
# veriexecgen
```

Fingerprint files in `/etc`, appending to the default fingerprint database:

```
# veriexecgen -A -d /etc
```

Fingerprint files in `/path/to/somewhere` using "rmd160" as the hashing algorithm, saving to `/etc/somewhere.fp`:

```
# veriexecgen -d /path/to/somewhere -t rmd160 -o /etc/somewhere.fp
```

SEE ALSO

veriexec(4), veriexec(5), security(8), veriexec(8), veriexecctl(8)

NAME

verify – Postfix address verification server

SYNOPSIS

verify [generic Postfix daemon options]

DESCRIPTION

The **verify**(8) address verification server maintains a record of what recipient addresses are known to be deliverable or undeliverable.

Addresses are verified by injecting probe messages into the Postfix queue. Probe messages are run through all the routing and rewriting machinery except for final delivery, and are discarded rather than being deferred or bounced.

Address verification relies on the answer from the nearest MTA for the specified address, and will therefore not detect all undeliverable addresses.

The **verify**(8) server is designed to run under control by the Postfix master server. It maintains an optional persistent database. To avoid being interrupted by "postfix stop" in the middle of a database update, the process runs in a separate process group.

The **verify**(8) server implements the following requests:

update *address status text*

Update the status and text of the specified address.

query *address*

Look up the *status* and *text* for the specified address. If the status is unknown, a probe is sent and an "in progress" status is returned.

SECURITY

The address verification server is not security-sensitive. It does not talk to the network, and it does not talk to local users. The verify server can run chrooted at fixed low privilege.

The address verification server can be coerced to store unlimited amounts of garbage. Limiting the cache size trades one problem (disk space exhaustion) for another one (poor response time to client requests).

With Postfix version 2.5 and later, the **verify**(8) server no longer uses root privileges when opening the **address_verify_map** cache file. The file should now be stored under the Postfix-owned **data_directory**. As a migration aid, an attempt to open a cache file under a non-Postfix directory is redirected to the Postfix-owned **data_directory**, and a warning is logged.

DIAGNOSTICS

Problems and transactions are logged to **syslogd**(8).

BUGS

The address verification service is suitable only for sites that handle a low mail volume. Verification probes add additional traffic to the mail queue and perform poorly under high load. Servers may blacklist sites that probe excessively, or that probe excessively for non-existent recipient addresses.

If the persistent database ever gets corrupted then the world comes to an end and human intervention is needed. This violates a basic Postfix principle.

CONFIGURATION PARAMETERS

Changes to **main.cf** are not picked up automatically, as **verify**(8) processes are persistent. Use the command "**postfix reload**" after a configuration change.

The text below provides only a parameter summary. See **postconf**(5) for more details including examples.

CACHE CONTROLS

address_verify_map (empty)
> Optional lookup table for persistent address verification status storage.

address_verify_sender ($double_bounce_sender)
> The sender address to use in address verification probes; prior to Postfix 2.5 the default was "post-master".

address_verify_positive_expire_time (31d)
> The time after which a successful probe expires from the address verification cache.

address_verify_positive_refresh_time (7d)
> The time after which a successful address verification probe needs to be refreshed.

address_verify_negative_cache (yes)
> Enable caching of failed address verification probe results.

address_verify_negative_expire_time (3d)
> The time after which a failed probe expires from the address verification cache.

address_verify_negative_refresh_time (3h)
> The time after which a failed address verification probe needs to be refreshed.

PROBE MESSAGE ROUTING CONTROLS

By default, probe messages are delivered via the same route as regular messages. The following parameters can be used to override specific message routing mechanisms.

address_verify_relayhost ($relayhost)
> Overrides the relayhost parameter setting for address verification probes.

address_verify_transport_maps ($transport_maps)
> Overrides the transport_maps parameter setting for address verification probes.

address_verify_local_transport ($local_transport)
> Overrides the local_transport parameter setting for address verification probes.

address_verify_virtual_transport ($virtual_transport)
> Overrides the virtual_transport parameter setting for address verification probes.

address_verify_relay_transport ($relay_transport)
> Overrides the relay_transport parameter setting for address verification probes.

address_verify_default_transport ($default_transport)
> Overrides the default_transport parameter setting for address verification probes.

MISCELLANEOUS CONTROLS

config_directory (see 'postconf -d' output)
> The default location of the Postfix main.cf and master.cf configuration files.

daemon_timeout (18000s)
> How much time a Postfix daemon process may take to handle a request before it is terminated by a built-in watchdog timer.

ipc_timeout (3600s)
> The time limit for sending or receiving information over an internal communication channel.

process_id (read-only)
> The process ID of a Postfix command or daemon process.

process_name (read-only)
> The process name of a Postfix command or daemon process.

queue_directory (see 'postconf -d' output)
> The location of the Postfix top-level queue directory.

syslog_facility (mail)
> The syslog facility of Postfix logging.

syslog_name (see 'postconf -d' output)
> The mail system name that is prepended to the process name in syslog records, so that "smtpd" becomes, for example, "postfix/smtpd".

SEE ALSO

smtpd(8), Postfix SMTP server
cleanup(8), enqueue Postfix message
postconf(5), configuration parameters
syslogd(5), system logging

README FILES

Use "**postconf readme_directory**" or "**postconf html_directory**" to locate this information.
ADDRESS_VERIFICATION_README, address verification howto

LICENSE

The Secure Mailer license must be distributed with this software.

HISTORY

This service was introduced with Postfix version 2.1.

AUTHOR(S)

Wietse Venema
IBM T.J. Watson Research
P.O. Box 704
Yorktown Heights, NY 10598, USA

NAME

verify_krb5_conf — checks krb5.conf for obvious errors

SYNOPSIS

verify_krb5_conf *[config-file]*

DESCRIPTION

verify_krb5_conf reads the configuration file krb5.conf, or the file given on the command line, and parses it, thereby verifying that the syntax is not correctly wrong.

If the file is syntactically correct, **verify_krb5_conf** tries to verify that the contents of the file is of relevant nature.

ENVIRONMENT

KRB5_CONFIG points to the configuration file to read.

FILES

/etc/krb5.conf Kerberos 5 configuration file

DIAGNOSTICS

Possible output from **verify_krb5_conf** include:

<path>: failed to parse <something> as size/time/number/boolean
> Usually means that <something> is misspelled, or that it contains weird characters. The parsing done by **verify_krb5_conf** is more strict than the one performed by libkrb5, so strings that work in real life might be reported as bad.

<path>: host not found (<hostname>)
> Means that <path> is supposed to point to a host, but it can't be recognised as one.

<path>: unknown or wrong type
> Means that <path> is either a string when it should be a list, vice versa, or just that **verify_krb5_conf** is confused.

<path>: unknown entry
> Means that <string> is not known by **verify_krb5_conf**.

SEE ALSO

krb5.conf(5)

BUGS

Since each application can put almost anything in the config file, it's hard to come up with a watertight verification process. Most of the default settings are sanity checked, but this does not mean that every problem is discovered, or that everything that is reported as a possible problem actually is one. This tool should thus be used with some care.

It should warn about obsolete data, or bad practice, but currently doesn't.

NAME

vgcfgbackup – backup volume group descriptor area

SYNOPSIS

vgcfgbackup [**–d**|**––debug**] [**–f**|**––file** filename] [**–h**|**––help**] [**––ignorelockingfailure**] [**–P**|**––partial**] [**–v**|**––verbose**] [*VolumeGroupName*...]

DESCRIPTION

vgcfgbackup allows you to backup the metadata of your volume groups. If you don't name any volume groups on the command line, all of them will be backed up.

In a default installation, each volume group gets backed up into a separate file bearing the name of the volume group in the directory /etc/lvm/backup. You can write the backup to an alternative file using -f. In this case if you are backing up more than one volume group the filename is treated as a template, and %s gets replaced by the volume group name.

NB. This DOESN'T backup user/system data in logical volume(s)! Backup /etc/lvm regularly too.

OPTIONS

See **lvm** for common options.

SEE ALSO

lvm(8), **vgcfgrestore**(8)

NAME

vgcfgrestore – restore volume group descriptor area

SYNOPSIS

vgcfgrestore [−d|−−**debug**] [−f|−−**file** filename] [−l[l]|−−**list**] [−h|−−**help**] [−M|−−**Metadatatype**1|2]
[−t|−−**test**] [−v|−−**verbose**] *VolumeGroupName*

DESCRIPTION

vgcfgrestore allows you to restore the metadata of *VolumeGroupName* from a text backup file produced by
vgcfgbackup. You can specify a backup file with **--file**. If no backup file is specified, the most recent one
is used. Use **--list** for a list of the available backup and archive files of *VolumeGroupName*.

OPTIONS

-l | --list — List files pertaining to *VolumeGroupName*

List metadata backup and archive files pertaining to *VolumeGroupName*. May be used with the **-f**
option. Does not restore *VolumeGroupName*.

-f | --file filename — Name of LVM metadata backup file

Specifies a metadata backup or archive file to be used for restoring VolumeGroupName. Often
this file has been created with **vgcfgbackup**.

See **lvm** for common options.

REPLACING PHYSICAL VOLUMES

vgdisplay --partial --verbose will show you the UUIDs and sizes of any PVs that are no longer present. If
a PV in the VG is lost and you wish to substitute another of the same size, use **pvcreate --restorefile filename --uuid uuid** (plus additional arguments as appropriate) to initialise it with the same UUID as the
missing PV. Repeat for all other missing PVs in the VG. Then use **vgcfgrestore --file filename** to restore
the volume group's metadata.

SEE ALSO

lvm(8), **vgcreate**(8)

NAME
    vgchange – change attributes of a volume group

SYNOPSIS
    vgchange [**--addtag** *Tag*] [**--alloc** *AllocationPolicy*] [**-A**|**--autobackup** {y|n}] [**-a**|**--available** [e|l]
    {y|n}] [**--monitor** {y|n}] [**-c**|**--clustered** {y|n}] [**-u**|**--uuid**] [**-d**|**--debug**] [**--deltag** *Tag*] [**-h**|**--help**]
    [**--ignorelockingfailure**] [**--ignoremonitoring**] [**-l**|**--logicalvolume** *MaxLogicalVolumes*] [**-p**|**--max-**
    physicalvolumes *MaxPhysicalVolumes*] [**-P**|**--partial**] [**-s**|**--physicalextentsize** *PhysicalExtent-*
    Size[**kKmMgGtT**]] [**-t**|**--test**] [**-v**|**--verbose**] [**--version**] [**-x**|**--resizeable** {y|n}] [*VolumeGroup-*
    Name...]

DESCRIPTION
    vgchange allows you to change the attributes of one or more volume groups. Its main purpose is to activate
    and deactivate *VolumeGroupName*, or all volume groups if none is specified. Only active volume groups
    are subject to changes and allow access to their logical volumes. [Not yet implemented: During volume
    group activation, if **vgchange** recognizes snapshot logical volumes which were dropped because they ran
    out of space, it displays a message informing the administrator that such snapshots should be removed (see
    lvremove(8)).]

OPTIONS
    See **lvm** for common options.

    -A, --autobackup {y|n}
        Controls automatic backup of metadata after the change. See **vgcfgbackup (8)**. Default is yes.

    -a, --available [e|l]{y|n}
        Controls the availability of the logical volumes in the volume group for input/output. In other
        words, makes the logical volumes known/unknown to the kernel.

        If clustered locking is enabled, add 'e' to activate/deactivate exclusively on one node or 'l' to acti-
        vate/deactivate only on the local node. Logical volumes with single-host snapshots are always
        activated exclusively because they can only be used on one node at once.

    -c, --clustered {y|n}
        If clustered locking is enabled, this indicates whether this Volume Group is shared with other
        nodes in the cluster or whether it contains only local disks that are not visible on the other nodes.
        If the cluster infrastructure is unavailable on a particular node at a particular time, you may still be
        able to use Volume Groups that are not marked as clustered.

    -u, --uuid
        Generate new random UUID for specified Volume Groups.

    --monitor {y|n}
        Controls whether or not a mirrored logical volume is monitored by dmeventd, if it is installed. If a
        device used by a monitored mirror reports an I/O error, the failure is handled according to **mir-**
        ror_image_fault_policy and **mirror_log_fault_policy** set in **lvm.conf**(5).

    --ignoremonitoring
        Make no attempt to interact with dmeventd unless **--monitor** is specified. Do not use this if
        dmeventd is already monitoring a device.

    -l, --logicalvolume *MaxLogicalVolumes*
        Changes the maximum logical volume number of an existing inactive volume group.

    -p, --maxphysicalvolumes *MaxPhysicalVolumes*
        Changes the maximum number of physical volumes that can belong to this volume group. For
        volume groups with metadata in lvm1 format, the limit is 255. If the metadata uses lvm2 format,
        the value 0 removes this restriction: there is then no limit. If you have a large number of physical
        volumes in a volume group with metadata in lvm2 format, for tool performance reasons, you
        should consider some use of **--metadatacopies 0** as described in **pvcreate**(8).

−s, −−physicalextentsize *PhysicalExtentSize*[**kKmMgGtT**]

> Changes the physical extent size on physical volumes of this volume group. A size suffix (k for kilobytes up to t for terabytes) is optional, megabytes is the default if no suffix is present. The default is 4 MB and it must be at least 1 KB and a power of 2.

> Before increasing the physical extent size, you might need to use lvresize, pvresize and/or pvmove so that everything fits. For example, every contiguous range of extents used in a logical volume must start and end on an extent boundary.

> If the volume group metadata uses lvm1 format, extents can vary in size from 8KB to 16GB and there is a limit of 65534 extents in each logical volume. The default of 4 MB leads to a maximum logical volume size of around 256GB.

> If the volume group metadata uses lvm2 format those restrictions do not apply, but having a large number of extents will slow down the tools but have no impact on I/O performance to the logical volume. The smallest PE is 1KB.

> The 2.4 kernel has a limitation of 2TB per block device.

−x, −−resizeable {y|n}

> Enables or disables the extension/reduction of this volume group with/by physical volumes.

EXAMPLES

> To activate all known volume groups in the system:

> > vgchange -a y

> To change the maximum number of logical volumes of inactive volume group **vg00** to 128.

> > vgchange -l 128 /dev/vg00

SEE ALSO

> **lvchange**(8), **lvm**(8), **vgcreate**(8)

NAME
       vgck – check volume group metadata

SYNOPSIS
       vgck [–d|––debug] [–h|–?|––help] [–v|––verbose] [VolumeGroupName...]

DESCRIPTION
       vgck checks LVM metadata for each named volume group for consistency.

OPTIONS
       See **lvm** for common options.

SEE ALSO
       lvm(8), **vgcreate**(8), **vgchange**(8), **vgscan**(8)

NAME
vgconvert – convert volume group metadata format

SYNOPSIS
vgconvert [**–d**|**––debug**] [**–h**|**––help**] [**–t**|**––test**] [**–v**|**––verbose**] [**––labelsector**] [**–M**|**––metadatatype**-type] [**––metadatacopies**#copies] [**––metadatasize**size] [**––version**] *VolumeGroupName* [*VolumeGroup-Name...*]

DESCRIPTION
vgconvert converts *VolumeGroupName* metadata from one format to another provided that the metadata fits into the same space.

OPTIONS
See **lvm**(8) and **pvcreate**(8) for options.

EXAMPLE
Convert volume group vg1 from LVM1 metadata format to the new LVM2 metadata format.

vgconvert -M2 vg1

RECOVERY
Use **pvscan**(8) to see which PVs lost their metadata. Run **pvcreate**(8) with the --uuid and --restorefile options on each such PV to reformat it as it was, using the archive file that **vgconvert**(8) created at the start of the procedure. Finally run **vgcfgrestore**(8) with that archive file to restore the original metadata.

SEE ALSO
lvm(8), **pvcreate**(8), **vgcfgrestore**(8)

NAME
vgcreate – create a volume group

SYNOPSIS
vgcreate [−−**addtag** *Tag*] [−−**alloc** *AllocationPolicy*] [−**A**|−−**autobackup** {y|n}] [−**c**|−−**clustered** {y|n}] [−**d**|−−**debug**] [−**h**|−−**help**] [−**l**|−−**maxlogicalvolumes** *MaxLogicalVolumes*] [-**M**|−−**metadatatype**type] [-**p**|−−**maxphysicalvolumes** *MaxPhysicalVolumes*] [−**s**|−−**physicalextentsize** *PhysicalExtentSize*[kKm-MgGtT]] [−**t**|−−**test**] [−**v**|−−**verbose**] [−−**version**] *VolumeGroupName PhysicalVolumePath* [*PhysicalVolumePath*...]

DESCRIPTION
vgcreate creates a new volume group called *VolumeGroupName* using the block special device *PhysicalVolumePath* previously configured for LVM with **pvcreate**(8).

OPTIONS
See **lvm** for common options.

−**c**, −−**clustered** {y|n}
> If clustered locking is enabled, this defaults to **y** indicating that this Volume Group is shared with other nodes in the cluster.
>
> If the new Volume Group contains only local disks that are not visible on the other nodes, you must specify −−**clustered n**. If the cluster infrastructure is unavailable on a particular node at a particular time, you may still be able to use such Volume Groups.

−**l**, −−**maxlogicalvolumes** *MaxLogicalVolumes*
> Sets the maximum number of logical volumes allowed in this volume group. The setting can be changed with **vgchange**. For volume groups with metadata in lvm1 format, the limit and default value is 255. If the metadata uses lvm2 format, the default value is 0 which removes this restriction: there is then no limit.

−**p**, −−**maxphysicalvolumes** *MaxPhysicalVolumes*
> Sets the maximum number of physical volumes that can belong to this volume group. The setting can be changed with **vgchange**. For volume groups with metadata in lvm1 format, the limit and default value is 255. If the metadata uses lvm2 format, the default value is 0 which removes this restriction: there is then no limit. If you have a large number of physical volumes in a volume group with metadata in lvm2 format, for tool performance reasons, you should consider some use of --**metadatacopies 0** as described in **pvcreate**(8).

−**s**, −−**physicalextentsize** *PhysicalExtentSize*[kKmMgGtT]
> Sets the physical extent size on physical volumes of this volume group. A size suffix (k for kilobytes up to t for terabytes) is optional, megabytes is the default if no suffix is present. The default is 4 MB and it must be at least 1 KB and a power of 2.
>
> Once this value has been set, it is difficult to change it without recreating the volume group which would involve backing up and restoring data on any logical volumes. However, if no extents need moving for the new value to apply, it can be altered using vgchange −s.
>
> If the volume group metadata uses lvm1 format, extents can vary in size from 8KB to 16GB and there is a limit of 65534 extents in each logical volume. The default of 4 MB leads to a maximum logical volume size of around 256GB.
>
> If the volume group metadata uses lvm2 format those restrictions do not apply, but having a large number of extents will slow down the tools but have no impact on I/O performance to the logical volume. The smallest PE is 1KB.
>
> The 2.4 kernel has a limitation of 2TB per block device.

EXAMPLES

To create a volume group named **test_vg** using physical volumes **/dev/hdk1**, and **/dev/hdl1** with default physical extent size of 4MB:

vgcreate test_vg /dev/sdk1 /dev/sdl1

SEE ALSO

lvm(8), **pvdisplay**(8), **pvcreate**(8), **vgdisplay**(8), **vgextend**(8), **vgreduce**(8), **lvcreate**(8), **lvdisplay**(8), **lvextend**(8), **lvreduce**(8)

NAME
vgdisplay – display attributes of volume groups

SYNOPSIS
vgdisplay [−A|−−activevolumegroups] [−c|−−colon] [−d|−−debug] [−h|−−help] [−−ignorelockingfailure] [−P|−−partial] [−s|−−short] [−v[v]|−−verbose [−−verbose]] [−−version] [*VolumeGroupName*...]

DESCRIPTION
vgdisplay allows you to see the attributes of *VolumeGroupName* (or all volume groups if none is given) with it's physical and logical volumes and their sizes etc.

vgs (8) is an alternative that provides the same information in the style of **ps** (1).

OPTIONS
See **lvm** for common options.

−A, −−activevolumegroups
> Only select the active volume groups.

−c, −−colon
> Generate colon separated output for easier parsing in scripts or programs. N.B. **vgs** (8) provides considerably more control over the output.

> The values are:

> 1 volume group name
> 2 volume group access
> 3 volume group status
> 4 internal volume group number
> 5 maximum number of logical volumes
> 6 current number of logical volumes
> 7 open count of all logical volumes in this volume group
> 8 maximum logical volume size
> 9 maximum number of physical volumes
> 10 current number of physical volumes
> 11 actual number of physical volumes
> 12 size of volume group in kilobytes
> 13 physical extent size
> 14 total number of physical extents for this volume group
> 15 allocated number of physical extents for this volume group
> 16 free number of physical extents for this volume group
> 17 uuid of volume group

−s, −−short
> Give a short listing showing the existence of volume groups.

−v, −−verbose
> Display verbose information containing long listings of physical and logical volumes. If given twice, also display verbose runtime information of vgdisplay's activities.

−−version
> Display version and exit successfully.

SEE ALSO
lvm(8), **vgs**(8), **pvcreate**(8), **vgcreate**(8), **lvcreate**(8)

NAME
vgexport – make volume groups unknown to the system

SYNOPSIS
vgexport [–a|––all] [–d|––debug] [–h|–?|––help] [–v|––verbose] VolumeGroupName [VolumeGroup-Name...]

DESCRIPTION
vgexport allows you to make the inactive *VolumeGroupName*(s) unknown to the system. You can then move all the Physical Volumes in that Volume Group to a different system for later **vgimport**(8). Most LVM2 tools ignore exported Volume Groups.

OPTIONS
See **lvm** for common options.

–a, ––all
        Export all inactive Volume Groups.

SEE ALSO
lvm(8), **pvscan**(8), **vgimport**(8), **vgscan**(8)

NAME
vgextend – add physical volumes to a volume group

SYNOPSIS
vgextend [−A|−−autobackup y|n] [−d|−−debug] [−h|−?|−−help] [−t|−−test] [−v|−−verbose] VolumeGroup-
Name PhysicalDevicePath [PhysicalDevicePath...]

DESCRIPTION
vgextend allows you to add one or more initialized physical volumes (see **pvcreate(8)**) to an existing volume group to extend it in size.

OPTIONS
See **lvm** for common options.

Examples
"vgextend vg00 /dev/sda4 /dev/sdn1" tries to extend the existing volume group "vg00" by the new physical
volumes (see **pvcreate(8)**) "/dev/sdn1" and /dev/sda4".

SEE ALSO
lvm(8), **vgcreate**(8), **vgreduce**(8), **pvcreate**(8)

NAME

vgimport – make exported volume groups known to the system

SYNOPSIS

vgimport [–a|––all] [–d|––debug] [–h|–?|––help] [–v|––verbose] VolumeGroupName [VolumeGroup-Name...]

DESCRIPTION

vgimport allows you to make a Volume Group that was previously exported using **vgexport**(8) known to the system again, perhaps after moving its Physical Volumes from a different machine.

OPTIONS

See **lvm** for common options.

–a, ––all

Import all exported Volume Groups.

SEE ALSO

lvm(8), **pvscan**(8), **vgexport**(8), **vgscan**(8)

NAME

vgmerge – merge two volume groups

SYNOPSIS

vgmerge [−A|−−autobackup y|n] [−d|−−debug] [−h|−?|−−help] [−l|−−list] [−t|−−test] [−v|−−verbose] Destination VolumeGroupName Source VolumeGroupName

DESCRIPTION

vgmerge merges two existing volume groups. The inactive Source VolumeGroupName will be merged into the Destination VolumeGroupName if physical extent sizes are equal and physical and logical volume summaries of both volume groups fit into Destination VolumeGroupName's limits.

OPTIONS

See **lvm** for common options. −l, −−list Display merged Destination VolumeGroupName like "vgdisplay -v".

−t, −−test

Do a test run WITHOUT making any real changes.

Examples

"vgmerge -v databases my_vg" merges the inactive volume group named "my_vg" into the active or inactive volume group named "databases" giving verbose runtime information.

SEE ALSO

lvm(8), **vgcreate**(8), **vgextend**(8), **vgreduce**(8)

NAME

vgmknodes – recreate volume group directory and logical volume special files

SYNOPSIS

vgmknodes [–d|––debug] [–h|–?|––help] [–v|––verbose] [[VolumeGroupName | LogicalVolumePath]...]

DESCRIPTION

Checks the LVM2 special files in /dev that are needed for active logical volumes and creates any missing ones and removes unused ones.

OPTIONS

See **lvm** for common options.

SEE ALSO

lvm(8), **vgscan**(8), **dmsetup**(8)

NAME
vgreduce – reduce a volume group

SYNOPSIS
vgreduce [−a|−−all] [−A|−−autobackup y|n] [−d|−−debug] [−h|−?|−−help] [−−removemissing] [−t|−−test]
[−v|−−verbose] VolumeGroupName [PhysicalVolumePath...]

DESCRIPTION
vgreduce allows you to remove one or more unused physical volumes from a volume group.

OPTIONS
See **lvm** for common options.

−a, −−all

Removes all empty physical volumes if none are given on command line.

−−removemissing

Removes all missing physical volumes from the volume group, if there are no logical volumes
allocated on those. This resumes normal operation of the volume group (new logical volumes may
again be created, changed and so on).

If this is not possible (there are logical volumes referencing the missing physical volumes) and you
cannot or do not want to remove them manually, you can run this option with --force to have vgreduce remove any partial LVs.

Any logical volumes and dependent snapshots that were partly on the missing disks get removed
completely. This includes those parts that lie on disks that are still present.

If your logical volumes spanned several disks including the ones that are lost, you might want to
try to salvage data first by activating your logical volumes with --partial as described in **lvm (8)**.

SEE ALSO
lvm(8), **vgextend**(8)

NAME
vgremove – remove a volume group

SYNOPSIS
vgremove [–d|––debug] [–f|––force] [–h|–?|––help] [–t|––test] [–v|––verbose] VolumeGroupName [VolumeGroupName...]

DESCRIPTION
vgremove allows you to remove one or more volume groups. If one or more physical volumes in the volume group are lost, consider **vgreduce --removemissing** to make the volume group metadata consistent again.

If there are logical volumes that exist in the volume group, a prompt will be given to confirm removal. You can override the prompt with **-f**.

OPTIONS
See **lvm** for common options.

–f, ––force
  Force the removal of any logical volumes on the volume group without confirmation.

SEE ALSO
lvm(8), **lvremove**(8), **vgcreate**(8), **vgreduce**(8)

NAME

vgrename – rename a volume group

SYNOPSIS

vgrename [–A|––autobackup y|n] [–d|––debug] [–h|–?|––help] [–t|––test] [–v|––verbose] *OldVolumeGroup{Path|Name|UUID} NewVolumeGroup{Path|Name}*

DESCRIPTION

vgrename renames an existing (see **vgcreate(8)**) volume group from *OldVolumeGroup{Name|Path|UUID}* to *NewVolumeGroup{Name|Path}*.

OPTIONS

See **lvm** for common options.

Examples

"vgrename /dev/vg02 /dev/my_volume_group" renames existing volume group "vg02" to "my_volume_group".

"vgrename vg02 my_volume_group" does the same.

"vgrename Zvlifi-Ep3t-e0Ng-U42h-o0ye-KHu1-nl7Ns4 VolGroup00_tmp" changes the name of the Volume Group with UUID Zvlifi-Ep3t-e0Ng-U42h-o0ye-KHu1-nl7Ns4 to "VolGroup00_tmp".

All the Volume Groups visible to a system need to have different names. Otherwise many LVM2 commands will refuse to run or give warning messages.

This situation could arise when disks are moved between machines. If a disk is connected and it contains a Volume Group with the same name as the Volume Group containing your root filesystem the machine might not even boot correctly. However, the two Volume Groups should have different UUIDs (unless the disk was cloned) so you can rename one of the conflicting Volume Groups with **vgrename**.

SEE ALSO

lvm(8), **vgchange**(8), **vgcreate**(8), **lvrename**(8)

NAME

vgs – report information about volume groups

SYNOPSIS

vgs [--aligned] [-d|--debug] [-h|-?|--help] [--ignorelockingfailure] [--nameprefixes] [--noheadings] [--nosuffix] [-o|--options [+]Field[,Field]] [-O|--sort [+|-]Key1[,[+|-]Key2[,...]]] [-P|--partial] [--rows] [--separator Separator] [--unbuffered] [--units hsbkmgtHKMGT] [--unquoted] [-v|--verbose] [--version] [VolumeGroupName [VolumeGroupName...]]

DESCRIPTION

vgs produces formatted output about volume groups.

OPTIONS

See **lvm** for common options.

--aligned

    Use with --separator to align the output columns.

--nameprefixes

    Add an "LVM2_" prefix plus the field name to the output. Useful with --noheadings to produce a list of field=value pairs that can be used to set environment variables (for example, in **udev (7)** rules).

--noheadings

    Suppress the headings line that is normally the first line of output. Useful if grepping the output.

--nosuffix

    Suppress the suffix on output sizes. Use with --units (except h and H) if processing the output.

-o, --options

    Comma-separated ordered list of columns. Precede the list with '+' to append to the default selection of columns. Column names are: vg_fmt, vg_uuid, vg_name, vg_attr, vg_size, vg_free, vg_sysid, vg_extent_size, vg_extent_count, vg_free_count, max_lv, max_pv, pv_count, lv_count, snap_count, vg_seqno, vg_tags, vg_mda_count, vg_mda_free, and vg_mda_size. Any "vg_" prefixes are optional. Columns mentioned in either **pvs (8)** or **lvs (8)** can also be chosen, but columns cannot be taken from both at the same time. Use -o help to view the full list of fields available.

    The vg_attr bits are:

    1   Permissions: (w)riteable, (r)ead-only

    2   Resi(z)eable

    3   E(x)ported

    4   (p)artial

    5   Allocation policy: (c)ontiguous, c(l)ing, (n)ormal, (a)nywhere, (i)nherited

    6   (c)lustered

-O, --sort

    Comma-separated ordered list of columns to sort by. Replaces the default selection. Precede any column with - for a reverse sort on that column.

--rows

    Output columns as rows.

--separator Separator

    String to use to separate each column. Useful if grepping the output.

--unbuffered

    Produce output immediately without sorting or aligning the columns properly.

      −−units hsbkmgtHKMGT
          All sizes are output in these units: (h)uman-readable, (s)ectors, (b)ytes, (k)ilobytes, (m)egabytes, (g)igabytes, (t)erabytes. Capitalise to use multiples of 1000 (S.I.) instead of 1024. Can also specify custom (u)nits e.g. −−units 3M

      −−unquoted
          When used with --nameprefixes, output values in the field=value pairs are not quoted.

SEE ALSO
      lvm(8), **vgdisplay**(8), **pvs**(8), **lvs**(8)

NAME
vgscan – scan all disks for volume groups and rebuild caches

SYNOPSIS
vgscan [–d|––debug] [–h|–?|––help] [––ignorelockingfailure] [––mknodes] [–P|––partial] [–v|––verbose]

DESCRIPTION
vgscan scans all SCSI, (E)IDE disks, multiple devices and a bunch of other disk devices in the system looking for LVM physical volumes and volume groups. Define a filter in **lvm.conf**(5) to restrict the scan to
avoid a CD ROM, for example.

In LVM2, vgscans take place automatically; but you might still need to run one explicitly after changing
hardware.

OPTIONS
See **lvm** for common options.

––mknodes

> Also checks the LVM special files in /dev that are needed for active logical volumes and creates
> any missing ones and removes unused ones.

SEE ALSO
lvm(8), **vgcreate**(8), **vgchange**(8)

NAME
vgsplit – split a volume group into two

SYNOPSIS
vgsplit [**--alloc** *AllocationPolicy*] [**-A**|**--autobackup** {**y**|**n**}] [**-c**|**--clustered** {**y**|**n**}] [**-d**|**--debug**] [**-h**|**--help**] [**-l**|**--maxlogicalvolumes** *MaxLogicalVolumes*] [**-M**|**--metadatatype** *type*] [**-p**|**--maxphysicalvolumes** *MaxPhysicalVolumes*] [**-n**|**--name** *LogicalVolumeName*] [**-t**|**--test**] [**-v**|**--verbose**] SourceVolumeGroupName DestinationVolumeGroupName [PhysicalVolumePath ...]

DESCRIPTION
vgsplit moves one or more physical volumes from *SourceVolumeGroupName* into *DestinationVolumeGroupName*. The physical volumes moved can be specified either explicitly via *PhysicalVolumePath*, or implicitly by **-n** *LogicalVolumeName*, in which case only physical volumes underlying the specified logical volume will be moved.

If *DestinationVolumeGroupName* does not exist, a new volume group will be created. The default attributes for the new volume group can be specified with **--alloc**, **--clustered**, **--maxlogicalvolumes**, **--metadatatype**, and **--maxphysicalvolumes** (see **vgcreate(8)** for a description of these options). If any of these options are not given, default attribute(s) are taken from *SourceVolumeGroupName*.

If *DestinationVolumeGroupName* does exist, it will be checked for compatibility with *SourceVolumeGroupName* before the physical volumes are moved. Specifying any of the above default volume group attributes with an existing destination volume group is an error, and no split will occur.

Logical volumes cannot be split between volume groups. **Vgsplit(8)** only moves complete physical volumes: To move part of a physical volume, use **pvmove(8)**. Each existing logical volume must be entirely on the physical volumes forming either the source or the destination volume group. For this reason, **vgsplit(8)** may fail with an error if a split would result in a logical volume being split across volume groups.

OPTIONS
See **lvm** for common options.

SEE ALSO
lvm(8), **vgcreate**(8), **vgextend**(8), **vgreduce**(8), **vgmerge**(8)

NAME
vipw — edit the password file

SYNOPSIS
vipw [**-d** *directory*]

DESCRIPTION
vipw edits the password file after setting the appropriate locks, and does any necessary processing after the password file is unlocked. If the password file is already locked for editing by another user, **vipw** will ask you to try again later. The default editor for **vipw** is vi(1).

vipw performs a number of consistency checks on the password entries, and will not allow a password file with a "mangled" entry to be installed. If **vipw** rejects the new password file, the user is prompted to re-enter the edit session.

Once the information has been verified, **vipw** uses pwd_mkdb(8) to update the user database. This is run in the background, and, at very large sites could take several minutes. Until this update is completed, the password file is unavailable for other updates and the new information is not available to programs.

The options are as follows:

-d *directory*
    Change the root directory of the password file from "/" to *directory*.

If a **vipw** session is killed it may leave "/etc/ptmp", which will cause future **vipw** executions to fail with "vipw: the passwd file is busy", until it is removed.

ENVIRONMENT
If the following environment variable exists it will be used by **vipw**:

EDITOR The editor specified by the string EDITOR will be invoked instead of the default editor vi(1).

FILES
/etc/master.passwd	The current password file.
/etc/ptmp	Temporary copy of the password file used while editing.

SEE ALSO
chpass(1), passwd(1), pwhash(1), passwd(5), passwd.conf(5), pwd_mkdb(8), user(8)

HISTORY
The **vipw** command appeared in 4.0BSD.

NAME

virecover — report recovered vi edit sessions

SYNOPSIS

/usr/libexec/virecover

DESCRIPTION

The **virecover** utility sends emails to users who have $vi(1)$ recovery files.

This email gives the name of the file that was saved for recovery and instructions for recovering most, if not all, of the changes to the file. This is done by using the **-r** option with $vi(1)$. See the **-r** option in $vi(1)$ for details.

If the backup files have the execute bit set or are zero length, then they have not been modified, so **virecover** deletes them to clean up. **virecover** also removes recovery files that are corrupted, zero length, or do not have a corresponding backup file.

virecover is normally run automatically at boot time using /etc/rc.d/virecover.

FILES

/var/tmp/vi.recover/recover.* $vi(1)$ recovery files
/var/tmp/vi.recover/vi.* $vi(1)$ editor backup files

SEE ALSO

$vi(1)$, rc.conf(5)

HISTORY

This script, previously known as **recover.script**, is from nvi and was added to NetBSD in 1996. It was renamed in 2001.

AUTHORS

This man page was written by Jeremy C. Reed ⟨reed@reedmedia.net⟩.

NAME

virtual – Postfix virtual domain mail delivery agent

SYNOPSIS

virtual [generic Postfix daemon options]

DESCRIPTION

The **virtual**(8) delivery agent is designed for virtual mail hosting services. Originally based on the Postfix **local**(8) delivery agent, this agent looks up recipients with map lookups of their full recipient address, instead of using hard-coded unix password file lookups of the address local part only.

This delivery agent only delivers mail. Other features such as mail forwarding, out-of-office notifications, etc., must be configured via virtual_alias maps or via similar lookup mechanisms.

MAILBOX LOCATION

The mailbox location is controlled by the **virtual_mailbox_base** and **virtual_mailbox_maps** configuration parameters (see below). The **virtual_mailbox_maps** table is indexed by the recipient address as described under TABLE SEARCH ORDER below.

The mailbox pathname is constructed as follows:

$virtual_mailbox_base/$virtual_mailbox_maps(*recipient*)

where *recipient* is the full recipient address.

UNIX MAILBOX FORMAT

When the mailbox location does not end in /, the message is delivered in UNIX mailbox format. This format stores multiple messages in one textfile.

The **virtual**(8) delivery agent prepends a "**From** *sender time_stamp*" envelope header to each message, prepends a **Delivered-To:** message header with the envelope recipient address, prepends an **X-Original-To:** header with the recipient address as given to Postfix, prepends a **Return-Path:** message header with the envelope sender address, prepends a **>** character to lines beginning with "**From** ", and appends an empty line.

The mailbox is locked for exclusive access while delivery is in progress. In case of problems, an attempt is made to truncate the mailbox to its original length.

QMAIL MAILDIR FORMAT

When the mailbox location ends in /, the message is delivered in qmail **maildir** format. This format stores one message per file.

The **virtual**(8) delivery agent prepends a **Delivered-To:** message header with the final envelope recipient address, prepends an **X-Original-To:** header with the recipient address as given to Postfix, and prepends a **Return-Path:** message header with the envelope sender address.

By definition, **maildir** format does not require application-level file locking during mail delivery or retrieval.

MAILBOX OWNERSHIP

Mailbox ownership is controlled by the **virtual_uid_maps** and **virtual_gid_maps** lookup tables, which are indexed with the full recipient address. Each table provides a string with the numerical user and group ID, respectively.

The **virtual_minimum_uid** parameter imposes a lower bound on numerical user ID values that may be specified in any **virtual_uid_maps**.

CASE FOLDING

All delivery decisions are made using the full recipient address, folded to lower case. See also the next section for a few exceptions with optional address extensions.

TABLE SEARCH ORDER

Normally, a lookup table is specified as a text file that serves as input to the **postmap**(1) command. The result, an indexed file in **dbm** or **db** format, is used for fast searching by the mail system.

The search order is as follows. The search stops upon the first successful lookup.

- When the recipient has an optional address extension the *user+extension@domain.tld* address is looked up first.

  With Postfix versions before 2.1, the optional address extension is always ignored.

- The *user@domain.tld* address, without address extension, is looked up next.

- Finally, the recipient *@domain* is looked up.

When the table is provided via other means such as NIS, LDAP or SQL, the same lookups are done as for ordinary indexed files.

Alternatively, a table can be provided as a regular-expression map where patterns are given as regular expressions. In that case, only the full recipient address is given to the regular-expression map.

SECURITY

The **virtual**(8) delivery agent is not security sensitive, provided that the lookup tables with recipient user/group ID information are adequately protected. This program is not designed to run chrooted.

The **virtual**(8) delivery agent disallows regular expression substitution of $1 etc. in regular expression lookup tables, because that would open a security hole.

The **virtual**(8) delivery agent will silently ignore requests to use the **proxymap**(8) server. Instead it will open the table directly. Before Postfix version 2.2, the virtual delivery agent will terminate with a fatal error.

STANDARDS

RFC 822 (ARPA Internet Text Messages)

DIAGNOSTICS

Mail bounces when the recipient has no mailbox or when the recipient is over disk quota. In all other cases, mail for an existing recipient is deferred and a warning is logged.

Problems and transactions are logged to **syslogd**(8). Corrupted message files are marked so that the queue manager can move them to the **corrupt** queue afterwards.

Depending on the setting of the **notify_classes** parameter, the postmaster is notified of bounces and of other trouble.

BUGS

This delivery agent supports address extensions in email addresses and in lookup table keys, but does not propagate address extension information to the result of table lookup.

Postfix should have lookup tables that can return multiple result attributes. In order to avoid the inconvenience of maintaining three tables, use an LDAP or MYSQL database.

CONFIGURATION PARAMETERS

Changes to **main.cf** are picked up automatically, as **virtual**(8) processes run for only a limited amount of time. Use the command "**postfix reload**" to speed up a change.

The text below provides only a parameter summary. See **postconf**(5) for more details including examples.

MAILBOX DELIVERY CONTROLS

virtual_mailbox_base (empty)

A prefix that the **virtual**(8) delivery agent prepends to all pathname results from $virtual_mailbox_maps table lookups.

virtual_mailbox_maps (empty)

Optional lookup tables with all valid addresses in the domains that match $virtual_mailbox_domains.

virtual_minimum_uid (100)

The minimum user ID value that the **virtual**(8) delivery agent accepts as a result from $virtual_uid_maps table lookup.

virtual_uid_maps (empty)

Lookup tables with the per-recipient user ID that the **virtual**(8) delivery agent uses while writing to the recipient's mailbox.

virtual_gid_maps (empty)

Lookup tables with the per-recipient group ID for **virtual**(8) mailbox delivery.

Available in Postfix version 2.0 and later:

virtual_mailbox_domains ($virtual_mailbox_maps)

Postfix is final destination for the specified list of domains; mail is delivered via the $virtual_transport mail delivery transport.

virtual_transport (virtual)

The default mail delivery transport and next-hop destination for final delivery to domains listed with $virtual_mailbox_domains.

Available in Postfix version 2.5.3 and later:

strict_mailbox_ownership (yes)

Defer delivery when a mailbox file is not owned by its recipient.

LOCKING CONTROLS

virtual_mailbox_lock (see 'postconf -d' output)

How to lock a UNIX-style **virtual**(8) mailbox before attempting delivery.

deliver_lock_attempts (20)

The maximal number of attempts to acquire an exclusive lock on a mailbox file or **bounce**(8) logfile.

deliver_lock_delay (1s)

The time between attempts to acquire an exclusive lock on a mailbox file or **bounce**(8) logfile.

stale_lock_time (500s)

The time after which a stale exclusive mailbox lockfile is removed.

RESOURCE AND RATE CONTROLS

virtual_destination_concurrency_limit ($default_destination_concurrency_limit)

The maximal number of parallel deliveries to the same destination via the virtual message delivery transport.

virtual_destination_recipient_limit ($default_destination_recipient_limit)

The maximal number of recipients per message for the virtual message delivery transport.

virtual_mailbox_limit (51200000)

The maximal size in bytes of an individual mailbox or maildir file, or zero (no limit).

MISCELLANEOUS CONTROLS

config_directory (see 'postconf -d' output)
> The default location of the Postfix main.cf and master.cf configuration files.

daemon_timeout (18000s)
> How much time a Postfix daemon process may take to handle a request before it is terminated by a built-in watchdog timer.

delay_logging_resolution_limit (2)
> The maximal number of digits after the decimal point when logging sub-second delay values.

ipc_timeout (3600s)
> The time limit for sending or receiving information over an internal communication channel.

max_idle (100s)
> The maximum amount of time that an idle Postfix daemon process waits for an incoming connection before terminating voluntarily.

max_use (100)
> The maximal number of incoming connections that a Postfix daemon process will service before terminating voluntarily.

process_id (read-only)
> The process ID of a Postfix command or daemon process.

process_name (read-only)
> The process name of a Postfix command or daemon process.

queue_directory (see 'postconf -d' output)
> The location of the Postfix top-level queue directory.

syslog_facility (mail)
> The syslog facility of Postfix logging.

syslog_name (see 'postconf -d' output)
> The mail system name that is prepended to the process name in syslog records, so that "smtpd" becomes, for example, "postfix/smtpd".

SEE ALSO
qmgr(8), queue manager
bounce(8), delivery status reports
postconf(5), configuration parameters
syslogd(8), system logging

README_FILES
Use "**postconf readme_directory**" or
"**postconf html_directory**" to locate this information.
VIRTUAL_README, domain hosting howto

LICENSE
The Secure Mailer license must be distributed with this software.

HISTORY
This delivery agent was originally based on the Postfix local delivery agent. Modifications mainly consisted of removing code that either was not applicable or that was not safe in this context: aliases, ~user/.forward files, delivery to "|command" or to /file/name.

The **Delivered-To:** message header appears in the **qmail** system by Daniel Bernstein.

The **maildir** structure appears in the **qmail** system by Daniel Bernstein.

AUTHOR(S)
Wietse Venema
IBM T.J. Watson Research

P.O. Box 704
Yorktown Heights, NY 10598, USA

Andrew McNamara
andrewm@connect.com.au
connect.com.au Pty. Ltd.
Level 3, 213 Miller St
North Sydney 2060, NSW, Australia

NAME
vnconfig — configure vnode disks

SYNOPSIS
vnconfig [**-crvz**] [**-f** *disktab*] [**-t** *typename*] *vnode_disk regular_file*
     [*geomspec*]
vnconfig **-u** [**-Fv**] *vnode_disk*
vnconfig **-l** [*vnode_disk*]

DESCRIPTION
The **vnconfig** command configures vnode pseudo disk devices. It will associate the vnode disk *vnode_disk* with the regular file *regular_file* allowing the latter to be accessed as though it were a disk. Hence a regular file within the filesystem can be used for swapping or can contain a filesystem that is mounted in the name space. The *vnode_disk* is a special file of raw partition or name of vnode disk like vnd0.

Options indicate an action to be performed:

-c   Configures the device. If successful, references to *vnode_disk* will access the contents of *regular_file*.

          If *geomspec* is specified, the vnode device will emulate the specified disk geometry. The format of the *geomspec* argument is:

            secsize/nsectors/ntracks/ncylinders

          If geometry is not specified, the kernel will choose a default based on 1MB cylinders. *secsize* is the number of bytes per sector. It must be an even multiple of 512. *nsectors* is the number of sectors per track. *ntracks* is the number of tracks per cylinder. *ncylinders* is the number of cylinders in the device.

-F   Force unconfiguration if the device is in use. Does not imply **-u**.

-f *disktab*
          Specifies that the **-t** option should look up in *disktab* instead of in /etc/disktab.

-l   List the vnd devices and indicate which ones are in use. If a specific *vnode_disk* is given, then only that will be described.

-t *typename*
          If configuring the device, look up *typename* in /etc/disktab and use the geometry specified in the entry. This option and the *geomspec* argument are mutually exclusive.

-r   Configure the device as read-only.

-u   Unconfigures the device.

-v   Print messages to stdout describing actions taken.

-z   Assume that *regular_file* is a compressed disk image in cloop2 format, and configure it read-only. See the vndcompress(1) manpage on how to create such an image.

If no action option is given, **-c** is assumed.

FILES
/dev/rvnd??

```
/dev/vnd??
/etc/disktab
```

EXAMPLES

```
      vnconfig vnd0 /tmp/diskimage
```
or
```
      vnconfig /dev/rvnd0c /tmp/diskimage
```

Configures the vnode disk vnd0. Please note that use of the second form of the command is discouraged because it requires knowledge of the raw partition which varies between architectures.

```
      vnconfig vnd0 /tmp/floppy.img 512/18/2/80
```

Configures the vnode disk vnd0 emulating the geometry of 512 bytes per sector, 18 sectors per track, 2 tracks per cylinder, and 80 cylinders total.

```
      vnconfig -t floppy vnd0 /tmp/floppy.img
```

Configures the vnode disk vnd0 using the geometry specified in the floppy entry in /etc/disktab.

```
      vnconfig -u vnd0
```

Unconfigures the vnd0 device.

SEE ALSO

opendisk(3), vnd(4), mount(8), swapctl(8), umount(8)

HISTORY

The **vnconfig** command appeared in NetBSD 1.0.

BUGS

This command should really be named **vndconfig**.

NAME

wake — send Wake on LAN frames to hosts on a local Ethernet network

SYNOPSIS

wake [*interface*] *lladdr* [*lladdr* ...]

DESCRIPTION

The **wake** program is used to send Wake on LAN (WoL) frames over a local Ethernet network to one or more hosts using their link layer (hardware) addresses. WoL functionality is generally enabled in a machine's BIOS and can be used to power on machines from a remote system without having physical access to them.

interface is an Ethernet interface of the local machine and is used to send the Wake on LAN frames over it. If there is only one Ethernet device available that is up and running, then the *interface* argument can be omitted. *lladdr* is the link layer address of the remote machine. This can be specified as the actual hardware address (six hexadecimal numbers separated by colons) or as a hostname entry in /etc/ethers. **wake** accepts multiple *lladdr* addresses. Link layer addresses can be determined and set using ifconfig(8).

FILES

/etc/ethers   Ethernet host name data base.

SEE ALSO

ethers(5), ifconfig(8)

AUTHORS

wake was written by Marc Balmer ⟨marc@msys.ch⟩.

NAME

   wdogctl — Watchdog timer control utility

SYNOPSIS

   wdogctl
   wdogctl -d
   wdogctl -e [**-A**] [**-p** *seconds*] *timer*
   wdogctl -k [**-A**] [**-p** *seconds*] *timer*
   wdogctl -t
   wdogctl -u [**-A**] [**-p** *seconds*] *timer*
   wdogctl -x [**-A**] [**-p** *seconds*] *timer*

DESCRIPTION

   wdogctl is used to manipulate watchdog timers. Watchdog timers provide a means of ensuring that a system continues to make progress. This is accomplished by use of a timer, provided by either hardware or software; when the timer expires, the watchdog resets the system. In this case of a hardware watchdog timer, this is accomplished by asserting the system's hardware reset signal. In the case of a software watchdog timer, this is accomplished by calling the kernel's normal reboot path. In order to prevent the system from rebooting, something must refresh the timer to prevent it from expiring.

   The NetBSD kernel provides three basic modes in which watchdog timers may operate: kernel tickle mode, user tickle mode, and external tickle mode. In kernel tickle mode, a timer in the kernel refreshes the watchdog timer. In user tickle mode, **wdogctl** runs in the background and refreshes the watchdog timer. In kernel tickle mode, progress of the kernel is ensured. In user tickle mode, the ability for user programs to run within a known period of time is ensured. Note that user tickle mode must be used with caution: on a heavily loaded system, the timer may expire accidentally, even though user programs may be making (very slow) progress. A user-mode timer is disarmed (if possible) when the device is closed, unless the timer is activated with the **-x** option.

   External-mode watchdogs are similar to user-mode watchdogs, except that the tickle must be done explicitly by a separate invocation of the program with the **-t** option.

   In the first two modes, an attempt is made to refresh the watchdog timer in one half the timer's configured period. That is, if the watchdog timer has a period of 30 seconds, a refresh attempt is made every 15 seconds.

   If called without arguments, **wdogctl** will list the timers available on the system. When arming a watchdog timer, the *timer* argument is the name of the timer to arm.

   Only one timer may be armed at a time; if an attempt is made to arm a timer when one is already armed, an error message will be displayed and no action will be taken.

   The options are as follows:

   -A   When arming a timer, this flag indicates that an audible alarm is to sound when the watchdog timer expires and resets the system. If the selected timer does not support an audible alarm, this option will be silently ignored.

   -d   This flag disarms the currently active timer. Note that not all watchdog timers can be disabled once armed. If the selected timer can not be disabled, an error message will be displayed and the timer will remain armed.

   -e   Arm *timer* in external tickle mode.

   -k   Arm *timer* in kernel tickle mode.

-p *period*	When arming a timer, this flag configures the timer period to *period* seconds. If the specified period is outside the timer's range, an error message will be displayed and no action will be taken.
-t	This flag tickles an external mode timer.
-u	Arm *timer* in user tickle mode.
-x	Arm *timer* in a modified user tickle mode: closing the device will not disarm the timer.

FILES

/dev/watchdog -- the system monitor watchdog timer device

SEE ALSO

evbarm/iopwdog(4), i386/elansc(4), i386/gcscpcib(4), i386/geodewdog(4), ichlpcib(4), ipmi(4), itesio(4), pcweasel(4), swwdog(4)

HISTORY

The **wdogctl** command first appeared in NetBSD 1.5.1.

AUTHORS

The **wdogctl** command and the NetBSD watchdog timer framework were written by Jason R. Thorpe ⟨thorpej@zembu.com⟩, and contributed by Zembu Labs, Inc.

NAME

wiconfig — configure WaveLAN/IEEE devices

SYNOPSIS

wiconfig *interface* [**-Dho**] [**-A** *1/2*] [**-a** *access_point_density*]
            [**-d** *max_data_length*] [**-M** *0/1*] [**-R** *1/3*] [**-s** *station_name*]

DESCRIPTION

The **wiconfig** command controls the operation of WaveLAN/IEEE wireless networking devices via the
wi(4) and awi(4) drivers. The **wiconfig** command can also be used to view the current settings of these
parameters and to dump out the values of the card's statistics counters.

Most of the parameters that can be changed relate to the IEEE 802.11 protocol which the WaveLAN implements. This includes the station name, whether the station is operating in ad-hoc (point to point) or BSS
(service set) mode, and the network name of a service set to join (IBSS) if BSS mode is enabled.

The *interface* argument given to **wiconfig** should be the logical interface name associated with the
WaveLAN/IEEE device (e.g., wi0, wi1, etc.).

OPTIONS

With no extra options, **wiconfig** will display the current settings of the specified WaveLAN/IEEE interface.

The options are as follows:

-A *1/2*   Set the authentication type for a specified interface. Permitted values are *1* (Open System
             Authentication) or *2* (Shared Key Authentication). The default is 1.

-a *access_point_density*
             Specify the *access point density* for a given interface. Legal values are 1 (low), 2
             (medium), and 3 (high). This setting influences some of the radio modem threshold settings.

-D   This forces the driver to initiate one round of access point scanning. All of the access points
             found are displayed.

-d *max_data_length*
             Set the maximum receive and transmit frame size for a specified interface. The *max data
             length* can be any number from 256 to 2346. The default is 2304.

-h   Display a short help.

-M *0/1*   Enable or disable "microwave oven robustness" on a given interface. This should only be used
             if needed.

             In cases of slow performance where there is a good quality signal but also high levels of noise
             (i.e., the signal to noise ratio is bad but the signal strength is good), or a microwave oven is
             operating near the antenna of the WLAN peer or access point, this option may be of use.

             In bad signal-to-noise conditions, the link layer will switch to lower transmit rates. However at
             lower transmit rates, individual frames take longer to transmit, making them more vulnerable to
             bursty noise. The option works by enabling data fragmentation in the link layer as the transmit
             speed lowers in an attempt to shorten the transmit time of each frame so that individual frames
             are more likely to be transmitted without error.

             Note that this does not impact the visible MTU of the link.

-o   Print out the statistics counters instead of the card settings. Note that, however, the statistics
             will only be updated every minute or so.

−R *1 | 3* Enable or disable roaming function on a given interface. The legal values are *1* (Roaming handled by firmware) and *3* (Roaming Disabled). The default is 1.

−r *RTS_threshold*

−f *fragmentation_threshold*

−m *MAC_address*

 These options are deprecated since NetBSD 6.0. Use ifconfig(8) to set the link-layer address, the fragmentation threshold, and the RTS threshold.

−s *station_name*

 Sets the *station_name* for the specified interface. The *station_name* is used for diagnostic purposes. The Lucent WaveMANAGER software can poll the names of remote hosts.

SEE ALSO
awi(4), wi(4), ifconfig(8)

HISTORY
The **wiconfig** command first appeared in FreeBSD 3.0, as **wicontrol**. It was added to NetBSD 1.5 under its present name.

AUTHORS
The **wiconfig** command was written by Bill Paul ⟨wpaul@ctr.columbia.edu⟩.

NAME

wire-test – test your network interfaces and local IP address

SYNOPSIS

wire-test [*host*]

DESCRIPTION

wire-test is used to find out what amd thinks are the first two network interfaces and network names/numbers used, as well as the IP address used for amd to NFS-mount itself.

If *host* is specified, then **wire-test** will test for the working combinations of NFS protocol and version from the current client to the NFS server *host*. If not specified, *host* defaults to "localhost".

SEE ALSO

amd(8).

"am-utils" **info**(1) entry.

Linux NFS and Automounter Administration by Erez Zadok, ISBN 0-7821-2739-8, (Sybex, 2001).

http://www.am-utils.org

Amd – The 4.4 BSD Automounter

AUTHORS

Erez Zadok <ezk@cs.sunysb.edu>, Computer Science Department, Stony Brook University, Stony Brook, New York, USA.

Other authors and contributors to am-utils are listed in the **AUTHORS** file distributed with am-utils.

NAME
wizd — automatically correct typographical errors in man pages

SYNOPSIS
wizd

DESCRIPTION
wizd automatically checks and corrects spelling errors, usage problems with mdoc(7) macros, and other typographical errors in man pages.

wizd is invoked by any cvs(1) commit to a man page. A standalone mode is also available by sending mail to ⟨wiz@NetBSD.org⟩.

SEE ALSO
cvs(1), intro(1), man(1), mdoc(7)

HISTORY
wizd appeared in NetBSD 1.5.

CAVEATS
wizd is not only copyrighted, but also registered.

BUGS
Sleeps sometimes.

NAME

      wlanctl — examine IEEE 802.11 wireless LAN client/peer table

SYNOPSIS

      wlanctl [**-p**] *interface* [...]
      wlanctl [**-p**] **-a**

DESCRIPTION

      Use the **wlanctl** utility to print node tables from IEEE 802.11 interfaces. Use the **-a** flag to print the nodes for all interfaces, or list one or more 802.11 interfaces to select their tables for examination. The **-p** flag causes only nodes that do not have encryption enabled to be printed. For example, to examine the node tables for atw0, use:

```
wlanctl atw0
```

wlanctl may print this node table, for example:

```
atw0: mac 00:02:6f:20:f6:2e bss 02:02:6f:20:f6:2e
        node flags 0001<bss>
        ess <netbsd>
        chan 11 freq 2462MHz flags 00a0<cck,2.4GHz>
        capabilities 0022<ibss,short preamble>
        beacon-interval 100 TU tsft 18425852102545544165 us
        rates [1.0] 2.0 5.5 11.0
        assoc-id 0 assoc-failed 0 inactivity 0s
        rssi 161 txseq 10 rxseq 1420
atw0: mac 00:02:2d:2e:3c:f4 bss 02:02:6f:20:f6:2e
        node flags 0000
        ess <netbsd>
        chan 11 freq 2462MHz flags 00a0<cck,2.4GHz>
        capabilities 0002<ibss>
        beacon-interval 100 TU tsft 18425852105450086784 us
        rates [1.0] 2.0 5.5 11.0
        assoc-id 0 assoc-failed 0 inactivity 0s
        rssi 159 txseq 2 rxseq 551
atw0: mac 00:02:6f:20:f6:2e bss 02:02:6f:20:f6:2e
        node flags 0000
        ess <netbsd>
        chan 11 freq 2462MHz flags 00a0<cck,2.4GHz>
        capabilities 0022<ibss,short preamble>
        beacon-interval 100 TU tsft 18425852102558548069 us
        rates [1.0] 2.0 5.5 6.0 9.0 11.0 12.0 18.0 24.0 36.0 48.0 54.0
        assoc-id 0 assoc-failed 0 inactivity 145s
        rssi 163 txseq 9 rxseq 2563
```

      This example is taken from a network consisting of three stations running in ad hoc mode. The key for interpreting the node print-outs follows:

mac   In the example node table, the first network node has MAC number 00:02:6f:20:f6:2e.

bss   The first node belongs to the 802.11 network identified by Basic Service Set Identifier (BSSID) 02:02:6f:20:f6:2e.

node flags   Only three node flags, "bss", "sta", and "scan", are presently defined. The first node is distinguished from the rest by its node flags: flag "bss" indicates that the node represents the 802.11 network that the interface has joined or created. The MAC number for the node is the same as the MAC number for the interface.

ess   the name of the (Extended) Service Set we have joined. This is the same as the network name set by `ifconfig`(8) with the "ssid" option.

chan   **wlanctl** prints the channel number, the center frequency in megahertz, and the channel flags. The channel flags indicate the frequency band ("2.4GHz" or "5GHz"), modulation ("cck", "gfsk", "ofdm", "turbo", and "dynamic cck-ofdm"), and operation constraints ("passive scan"). Common combinations of band and modulation are these:

Band	Modulation	Description
2.4GHz	cck	11Mb/s DSSS 802.11b
2.4GHz	gfsk	1-2Mb/s FHSS 802.11
2.4GHz	ofdm	54Mb/s 802.11g
2.4GHz	dynamic cck-ofdm	mixed 802.11b/g network
5GHz	ofdm	54Mb/s 802.11a
5GHz	turbo	108Mb/s 802.11a

capabilities ad hoc-mode and AP-mode 802.11 stations advertise their capabilities in 802.11 Beacons and Probe Responses. **wlanctl** understands these capability flags:

Flag	Description
ess	infrastructure (access point) network
ibss	ad hoc network (no access point)
cf pollable	TBD
request cf poll	TBD
privacy	WEP encryption
short preamble	reduce 802.11b overhead
pbcc	22Mbps "802.11b+"
channel agility	change channel for licensed services
short slot-time	TBD
rsn	TBD Real Soon Now
dsss-ofdm	TBD

beacon-interval

           In the example, beacons are sent once every 100 Time Units. A Time Unit (TU) is 1024 microseconds (a "kilo-microsecond" or "kus"). Thus 100 TU is about one tenth of a second.

tsft   802.11 stations keep a Time Synchronization Function Timer (TSFT) which counts up in microseconds. Ad hoc-mode stations synchronize time with their peers. Infrastructure-mode stations synchronize time with their access point. Power-saving stations wake and sleep at intervals measured by the TSF Timer. The TSF Timer has a role in the coalescence of 802.11 ad hoc networks ("IBSS merges").

rates   802.11 stations indicate the bit-rates they support, in units of 100kb/s in 802.11 Beacons, Probe Responses, and Association Requests. **wlanctl** prints a station's supported bit-rates in 1Mb/s units. A station's basic rates are flagged by an asterisk ("*"). The last bit-rate at which a packet was sent to the station is enclosed by square brackets.

assoc-id   In an infrastructure network, the access point assigns each client an Association Identifier which is used to indicate traffic for power-saving stations.

assoc-failed The number of times the station tried and failed to associate with its access point. Only

inactivity Seconds elapsed since a packet was last received from the station. When this value reaches net.link.ieee80211.maxinact, the station is eligible to be purged from the node table. See `sysctl`(8).

rssi   Unitless Received Signal Strength Indication (RSSI). Higher numbers indicate stronger signals. Zero is the lowest possible RSSI. On a hostap- or adhoc-mode interface, the node with *node flag* "bss" set uses *rssi* to indicate the signal strength for the last packet received from a station that does not belong to the network. On an infrastructure-mode station, the node with *node flag* "bss" set indicates the strength of packets from the access point.

txseq   The next 802.11 packet sent to this station will carry this transmit sequence number. The 802.11 MAC uses the transmit sequence number to detect duplicate packets.

rxseq   The last packet received from this station carried this transmit sequence number.

SEE ALSO

sysctl(8)

HISTORY

wlanctl first appeared in NetBSD 3.0.

AUTHORS

David Young ⟨dyoung@NetBSD.org⟩

NAME
   wpa_cli — text-based frontend program for interacting with wpa_supplicant

SYNOPSIS
   wpa_cli [*commands*]

DESCRIPTION
   The **wpa_cli** utility is a text-based frontend program for interacting with wpa_supplicant(8). It is used to query current status, change configuration, trigger events, and request interactive user input.

   The **wpa_cli** utility can show the current authentication status, selected security mode, dot11 and dot1x MIBs, etc. In addition, **wpa_cli** can configure EAPOL state machine parameters and trigger events such as reassociation and IEEE 802.1X logoff/logon.

   The **wpa_cli** utility provides an interface to supply authentication information such as username and password when it is not provided in the wpa_supplicant.conf(5) configuration file. This can be used, for example, to implement one-time passwords or generic token card authentication where the authentication is based on a challenge-response that uses an external device for generating the response.

   The **wpa_cli** utility supports two modes: interactive and command line. Both modes share the same command set and the main difference is that in interactive mode, **wpa_cli** provides access to unsolicited messages (event messages, username/password requests).

   Interactive mode is started when **wpa_cli** is executed without any parameters on the command line. Commands are then entered from the controlling terminal in response to the **wpa_cli** prompt. In command line mode, the same commands are entered as command line arguments.

   The control interface of wpa_supplicant(8) can be configured to allow non-root user access by using the *ctrl_interface_group* parameter in the wpa_supplicant.conf(5) configuration file. This makes it possible to run **wpa_cli** with a normal user account.

AUTHENTICATION PARAMETERS
   When wpa_supplicant(8) needs authentication parameters, such as username and password, that are not present in the configuration file, it sends a request message to all attached frontend programs, e.g., **wpa_cli** in interactive mode. The **wpa_cli** utility shows these requests with a "CTRL-REQ-⟨*type*⟩-⟨*id*⟩:⟨*text*⟩" prefix, where ⟨*type*⟩ is IDENTITY, PASSWORD, or OTP (one-time password), ⟨*id*⟩ is a unique identifier for the current network, and ⟨*text*⟩ is description of the request. In the case of a OTP (One Time Password) request, it includes the challenge from the authentication server.

   A user must supply wpa_supplicant(8) the needed parameters in response to these requests.

   For example,

```
CTRL-REQ-PASSWORD-1:Password needed for SSID foobar
> password 1 mysecretpassword

Example request for generic token card challenge-response:

CTRL-REQ-OTP-2:Challenge 1235663 needed for SSID foobar
> otp 2 9876
```

COMMANDS
   The following commands may be supplied on the command line or at a prompt when operating interactively.

status Report the current WPA/EAPOL/EAP status for the current interface.

mib Report MIB variables (dot1x, dot11) for the current interface.

help Show usage help.

interface [*ifname*]
> Show available interfaces and/or set the current interface when multiple are available.

level *debug_level*
> Change the debugging level in wpa_supplicant(8). Larger numbers generate more messages.

license
> Display the full license for **wpa_cli**.

logoff Send the IEEE 802.1X EAPOL state machine into the "logoff" state.

logon Send the IEEE 802.1X EAPOL state machine into the "logon" state.

set [*settings*]
> Set variables. When no arguments are supplied, the known variables and their settings are displayed.

pmksa Show the contents of the PMKSA cache.

reassociate
> Force a reassociation to the current access point.

reconfigure
> Force wpa_supplicant(8) to re-read its configuration file.

preauthenticate *BSSID*
> Force preauthentication of the specified *BSSID*.

identity *network_id identity*
> Configure an identity for an SSID.

password *network_id password*
> Configure a password for an SSID.

otp *network_id password*
> Configure a one-time password for an SSID.

terminate
> Force wpa_supplicant(8) to terminate.

quit Exit **wpa_cli**.

SEE ALSO
> wpa_supplicant.conf(5), wpa_supplicant(8)

HISTORY
> The **wpa_cli** utility first appeared in NetBSD 4.0.

AUTHORS
> The **wpa_cli** utility was written by Jouni Malinen ⟨jkmaline@cc.hut.fi⟩. This manual page is derived from the README file included in the **wpa_supplicant** distribution.

NAME

wpa_passphrase — Set WPA passphrase for a SSID

SYNOPSIS

wpa_passphrase *ssid passphrase*

DESCRIPTION

The **wpa_passphrase** utility pre-computes PSK entries for network configuration blocks of a wpa_supplicant.conf(5) file. It prints a single network configuration block to standard output.

The following arguments must be specified on the command line:

ssid   The SSID whose passphrase should be derived.

passphrase The passphrase to use. If not included on the command line, passphrase will be read from standard input. The passphrase must be 8 to 63 characters in length.

SEE ALSO

wpa_supplicant.conf(5), ifconfig(8), wpa_cli(8), wpa_supplicant(8)

HISTORY

The **wpa_passphrase** utility first appeared in NetBSD 4.0.

AUTHORS

The **wpa_passphrase** utility was written by Jouni Malinen ⟨jkmaline@cc.hut.fi⟩. This manual page is derived from the wpa_passphrase.sgml file included in the wpa_supplicant(8) distribution.

NAME

wpa_supplicant — WPA/802.11i Supplicant for wireless network devices

SYNOPSIS

wpa_supplicant [**-BdehLqvw**] [**-f** *debug-file*] **-i** *ifname* **-c** *config-file*
           [**-N** **-i** *ifname* **-c** *config-file* ...]

DESCRIPTION

The **wpa_supplicant** utility is an implementation of the WPA Supplicant component, i.e., the part that runs in the client stations. It implements WPA key negotiation with a WPA Authenticator and EAP authentication with an Authentication Server. In addition, **wpa_supplicant** controls the roaming and IEEE 802.11 authentication/association support and can be used to configure static WEP keys based on identified networks.

The **wpa_supplicant** utility is designed to be a "daemon" program that runs in the background and acts as the backend component controlling the wireless connection. It supports separate frontend programs such as the text-based wpa_cli(8) program.

The following arguments must be specified on the command line:

-i *ifname*
> Use the specified wireless interface.

-c *config-file*
> Use the settings in the specified configuration file when managing the wireless interface. See wpa_supplicant.conf(5) for a description of the configuration file syntax and contents.
>
> Changes to the configuration file can be reloaded by sending a SIGHUP signal to the **wpa_supplicant** process or with the wpa_cli(8) utility, using "wpa_cli reconfigure".

OPTIONS

The following options are available:

-B
> Detach from the controlling terminal and run as a daemon process in the background.

-d
> Enable debugging messages. If this option is supplied twice, more verbose messages are displayed. Messages are sent to stdout by default, even when daemonised. This can be changed with the **-f** flag.

-e
> Use an external IEEE 802.1X Supplicant program and disable the internal Supplicant. This option is not normally used.

-f
> Specifies a file to send debug messages to when enabled with the **-d** flag.

-h
> Show help text.

-K
> Include key information in debugging output.

-L
> Display the license for this program on the terminal and exit.

-N **-i** *ifname* **-c** *config-file* ...
> Specify an additional interface and configuration file. If multiple interfaces are specified then **wpa_supplicant** will manage them all with a single process.

-q
> Decrease debugging verbosity (i.e., counteract the use of the **-d** flag).

      -v   Display version information on the terminal and exit.

      -w   If the specified interface is not present, wait for it to be added; e.g. a cardbus device to be inserted.

SEE ALSO

    ath(4), ipw(4), iwi(4), ral(4), wi(4), wpa_supplicant.conf(5), ifconfig(8), wpa_cli(8)

HISTORY

    The **wpa_supplicant** utility first appeared in NetBSD 4.0.

AUTHORS

    The **wpa_supplicant** utility was written by Jouni Malinen ⟨jkmaline@cc.hut.fi⟩. This manual page is derived from the README file included in the **wpa_supplicant** distribution.

NAME

wsconscfg — configure and switch between virtual terminals on a wscons display

SYNOPSIS

wsconscfg [**-e** *emul*] [**-f** *ctldev*] [**-t** *type*] *index*
wsconscfg **-d** [**-F**] [**-f** *ctldev*] *index*
wsconscfg **-g** [**-f** *ctldev*]
wsconscfg **-k** | **-m** [**-d**] [**-f** *ctldev*] [*index*]
wsconscfg **-s** [**-f** *ctldev*] *index*

DESCRIPTION

The **wsconscfg** tool allows to create, delete and switch between virtual terminals on display devices controlled by the wscons terminal framework if the underlying display hardware driver supports multiple screens. Further it controls the assignment of keyboards to displays. The *index* argument specifies which virtual terminal is to be configured; the allowed numbers are from 0 to an implementation-specified value (currently 7, allowing for 8 virtual terminals on a display). In keyboard configuration mode, it specifies the wskbd(4) device to attach or detach. Without further option arguments, a virtual terminal is created with implementation specific properties and a default terminal emulation variant selected at kernel compile time.

The options are:

-d   Delete the specified terminal. A terminal opened by a program will not be deleted unless the **-F** option is applied. Terminals used by the operating system console or a graphics program (X server) cannot be deleted. With the **-k** flag, the keyboard specified by *index* will be detached from the wscons display. With the **-m** flag, the multiplexor specified by *index* will be detached from the wscons display.

-e *emul*   Specify the terminal emulation to use for the virtual terminal. The set of available terminal emulations is determined at kernel compile time. See wscons(4) for details.

-F   Force deleting of a terminal even if it is in use by a user space program.

-f *ctldev*
             Specify the control device of the wscons display to operate on. Default is /dev/ttyEcfg.

-g   Print the index of the current virtual terminal.

-k   Do keyboard related operations instead of virtual screen configuration. Without other flags, a keyboard will be attached to the display device. The *index* argument can be omitted, in this case the first free keyboard will be used.

-m   Do multiplexor related operations instead of virtual screen configuration. Without other flags, a multiplexor will be attached to the display device.

-s   Switch to the specified virtual terminal.

-t *type*   Specify a screen type to use. Screen types refer to display format, colour depth and other low-level display properties. Valid *type* arguments are defined by the underlying display device driver.

Typically, the **wsconscfg** utility will be invoked in system startup by the /etc/rc.d/wscons script, controlled by the /etc/wscons.conf configuration file.

FILES

/etc/wscons.conf

EXAMPLES

        wsconscfg -t 80x50 -e vt100 1

Configure screen 1 (i.e., the second), it will get the type 80x50 and use the VT100 terminal emulation. (Note: 80x50 is a screen type offered by the vga(4) display driver. In this particular case, an 8×8-font must be loaded before to make the screen useful. See wsfontload(8).)

        wsconscfg -k

Connect the first unconnected keyboard to the display.

        wsconscfg 3

Create screen 3.

        wsconscfg -d 3

Delete screen 3.

        wsconscfg -s 2

Switch to screen 2.

SEE ALSO
wscons(4), wskbd(4), wsconsctl(8), wsfontload(8)

BUGS
There should be an easy way to get a list of the screen types available on a display, and of the emulations supported by the kernel.

WSCONSCTL (8)   NetBSD   WSCONSCTL (8)

NAME

wsconsctl — get or set wscons state

SYNOPSIS

wsconsctl [**-dkmn**] [**-f** *file*] **-a**
wsconsctl [**-dkmn**] [**-f** *file*] *name* . . .
wsconsctl [**-dkmn**] [**-f** *file*] **-w** *name=value* . . .
wsconsctl [**-dkmn**] [**-f** *file*] **-w** *name+=value* . . .

DESCRIPTION

The **wsconsctl** command displays or sets various wscons system driver variables. If a list of variables is present on the command line, then **wsconsctl** prints the current value of those variables for the specified device.

-a   Specify all variables for the device.

-d   Select the display portion of the device.

-f *file*
         Specify an alternative control device.

-k   Select the keyboard portion of the device (this is the default).

-m   Select the mouse portion of the device.

-n   Suppress the printing of the variable name in the output - only the value will appear.

-w   Set or modify the specified variables to the given values. The value can be specified as either an absolute value, by using the '=' symbol or as a relative value, by using the '+=' symbol. See the **EXAMPLES** section for more details.

The **wsconsctl** utility can be used to view and modify aspects of the keyboard, display, and mouse, using the standard, machine-independent workstation console device driver wscons(4).

The keyboard type can be modified, the keyboard bell's pitch, period, and duration can be modified, the *typematic* value can be changed, and the keyboard encoding can be modified to switch keys, should the user find a keyboard's default layout difficult to use. The keyboard types and other relevant definitions can all be found in the /usr/include/dev/wscons/wsksymdef.h file.

The mouse types are defined in the /usr/include/dev/wscons/wsconsio.h file.

The display types, height, width, depth (bits per pixel), color map size, and color map are defined in the /usr/include/dev/wscons/wsconsio.h file. There are also definitions relating to video control and cursor control, which are not applicable to all display types, and to text emulation and graphics (mapped) modes.

In addition to British, US, and US-Dvorak keyboard encodings, support currently exists for the following languages: Belgian, Danish, Finnish, French, German, Greek, Hungarian, Italian, Japanese, Norwegian, Polish, Portugese, Russian, Spanish, Swedish, Swiss, and Ukrainian. Additionally, a user-defined encoding is supported.

FILES

/dev/wskbd   keyboard control device

/dev/wsmouse   mouse control device

/dev/ttyE0   display control device

EXAMPLES

The following are just a few examples of **wsconsctl** and its functionality.

```
wsconsctl -w encoding=uk
```

Set a UK keyboard encoding.

```
wsconsctl -w map+="keysym Caps_Lock = Control_L"
```

Modify the current keyboard encoding so that when the *Caps Lock* key is pressed, the same encoding sequence as *Left Control* is sent. For a full list of keysyms and keycodes, please refer to the `/usr/include/dev/wscons/wksymdef.h` file.

```
wsconsctl -w encoding=us.swapctrlcaps
```

Set a US keyboard encoding, with the *Caps Lock* and *Left Control* keys swapped. The *.swapctrlcaps* encoding does not work for all national keyboard encodings. For most purposes, the ability to set the value returned by the *Caps Lock* key is enough - see the previous example for details.

```
wsconsctl -w bell.pitch=1200
```

Set the bell pitch to be 1200.

```
wsconsctl -w bell.pitch+=200
```

Add 200 to the current pitch of the bell.

```
wsconsctl  -d  -w  msg.kernel.attrs=color,hilit  msg.kernel.bg=red
msg.kernel.fg=brown
```

Set the color of kernel messages to brown on red with the highlighting flag set (becoming yellow on red).

```
wsconsctl -w repeat.del1=200 repeat.deln=50
```

Set the initial delay for keyboard auto repeat to 200ms, and subsequent delays to 50ms.

```
wsconsctl -w repeat.del1=0
```

Turn off auto repeat.

```
wsconsctl -d -w scroll.fastlines=50
```

If scroll support is enabled in the kernel, set the number of lines used in the fast scroll function to 50.

```
wsconsctl -d -w scroll.slowlines=2
```

If scroll support is enabled in the kernel, set the number of lines used in the slow scroll function to 2. In order to use this function, you have to have `Cmd_ScrollSlowDown` and `Cmd_ScrollSlowUp` defined in your keyboard map.

SEE ALSO

pckbd(4), wscons(4), wscons.conf(5), wsconscfg(8), wsfontload(8)

HISTORY

The **wsconsctl** command first appeared in NetBSD 1.4.

WSFONTLOAD (8)   NetBSD   WSFONTLOAD (8)

NAME
wsfontload — load a font bitmap into the wsfont pool or a wscons display device

SYNOPSIS
wsfontload [**-f** *wsdev*] [**-w** *width*] [**-h** *height*] [**-e** *encoding*] [**-N** *name*] [**-b**] [**-B**]
        [**-v**] [*fontfile*]

DESCRIPTION
The **wsfontload** utility loads a font bitmap into the wsfont font pool (or a wscons device if the device driver supports this). The font gets assigned a name in this process which it can be referred to by later for use on a display screen. The font is loaded from the specified *fontfile*, or from standard input if *fontfile* is not provided.

The options are:

-f *wsdev*   Specify the device to operate on. Default is /dev/wsfont.

-w *width*   Sets the width of a font character in pixels. Default is 8.

-h *height*   Sets the height of a font character in pixels. Default is 16.

-e *encoding*

            Sets the encoding of the font. This can be either a symbolic abbreviation or a numeric value. Currently recognized abbreviations are iso for ISO-8859-1 encoding, ibm for IBM encoded fonts and pcvt for the custom encoding of the supplemental fonts which came with the BSD "pcvt" console driver. Per default, iso is assumed.

-N *name*   Specifies a name which can be used later to refer to the font. If none is given, the *fontfile* name is used to create one.

-b   Specifies that the font data is ordered right-to-left bit wise. The default is left-to-right.

-B   Specifies that the font data is ordered right-to-left byte wise. The default is left-to-right.

-v   Prints the font's properties before loading it.

Typically, the **wsfontload** utility will be executed in system startup by the /etc/rc.d/wscons script, controlled by the /etc/wscons.conf configuration file.

FILES
/etc/wscons.conf /usr/share/wscons/fonts

EXAMPLES
       wsfontload -N myname -h 8 -e ibm /usr/share/wscons/fonts/vt2201.808

Load the IBM-encoded 8×8-font from the wscons(4) distribution. This (or another 8×8-font) is necessary to use the 50-line screen type on vga(4) displays.

       wsfontload -N orator -e ibm /usr/share/wscons/fonts/orator.816
       wsconsctl -dw font=orator

Load the "orator" IBM-encoded 8×16 font and switch the first console screen (ttyE0, wsconsctl's default) to this alternate font.

SEE ALSO
wscons(4), wsconscfg(8), wsconsctl(8)

WSFONTLOAD (8)   NetBSD   WSFONTLOAD (8)

BUGS

    Many features are missing.

    There is no way to remove a loaded font.

NAME

wsmoused — multipurpose mouse daemon

SYNOPSIS

wsmoused [**-d** *device*] [**-f** *conf_file*] [**-m** *modes*] [**-n**]

DESCRIPTION

The **wsmoused** daemon provides mouse support in console, allowing copying and pasting text. The left mouse button is used to select text when held and you use the right button to paste it in the active console.

Supported options are as follows:

-d *device*	specifies the device file to be used as the wsmouse(4) device. Defaults to /dev/wsmouse.
-f *conf_file*	specifies the configuration file to be used. Defaults to /etc/wsmoused.conf.
-m *modes*	specifies which modes should be activated. Mode names are given in the argument as a whitespace separated list. Overrides the 'modes' directive in the configuration file.
-n	do not fork in the background (for debugging purposes). Overrides the 'nodaemon' directive in the configuration file.

Many other details can be tuned. See wsmoused.conf(5) for more information.

wsmoused is designed to be a multipurpose mouse daemon. Functionality is provided through independent *modes*, enabled either through the **-m** flag or through the 'modes' property in the configuration file (the former takes precedence).

The action mode

The 'action' mode executes commands upon receiving mouse button events. Commands can be associated on a button basis, and can differentiate between push or release events.

The selection mode

The 'selection' mode provides visual copy and paste support in text consoles when using the wscons(4) device. A selection is created by clicking with the primary mouse button at any point on the screen and dragging it while clicked. When the button is released, the selected text is copied to an internal buffer for further pasting with the secondary button.

FILES

/dev/ttyE[0-n]	tty devices
/dev/ttyEstat	wsdisplay status notification device
/dev/wsmouse[0-n]	mouse control device
/etc/wsmoused.conf	default configuration file

SECURITY CONSIDERATIONS

When using the 'action' mode, commands specified in the configuration file are executed as the user who started the daemon. By default, this user is 'root' when using the rc.subr(8) framework. You should set 'wsmoused_user="<some_user>"' in rc.conf(5) to a safer user (and adjust file permissions accordingly) if the commands you want to execute do not require superuser privileges. An alternative is to use su(1) as part of the command string in the configuration file.

NOTES

The following notes apply to all work modes:

- When switching from the X screen to a text terminal, there is a small delay (five seconds) until the mouse works again. This time is used by X to close the mouse device properly.

The following notes apply to the 'selection' mode only:

- The mouse cursor is only visible for a short period of time. It will disappear when you stop moving it to avoid console corruption (which happens if it is visible and there is text output).

- You need to change the getty program which is run in the first virtual terminal to use `/dev/ttyE0` instead of `/dev/console`. To do this, edit `/etc/ttys` and `/etc/wscons.conf`.

SEE ALSO

`su(1)`, `wscons(4)`, `wsdisplay(4)`, `wsmouse(4)`, `rc.conf(5)`, `ttys(5)`, `wscons.conf(5)`, `wsmoused.conf(5)`, `moused(8)`, `rc.subr(8)`

HISTORY

The **wsmoused** command first appeared in NetBSD 2.0.

AUTHORS

The **wsmoused** command was developed by Julio M. Merino Vidal ⟨jmmv@NetBSD.org⟩.

WSMUXCTL (8)   NetBSD   WSMUXCTL (8)

NAME

   wsmuxctl — configure wsmuxes

SYNOPSIS

   wsmuxctl [**−a** *dev*] **−f** *ctldev* [**−l**] [**−L**] [**−r** *dev*]

DESCRIPTION

   The **wsmuxctl** allows to adding and removing devices connected to a wsmux(4).

   Added and removed devices are specified by a name, not a path name. Simply use *wsmouseN*, *wskbdN*, or
   wsmuxN where N is the number of the device.

   The options are:

   −a *dev*   Add the specified device to the mux.

   −f *ctldev*
                 Specify the control device of the wsmux to operate on. A number may be given, which is then
                 taken to be the number of the mux.

   −l   List all devices connected to a mux.

   −L   List all devices connected to a mux and recursively list mux subdevices.

   −r *dev*   Remove the specified device from the mux.

SEE ALSO

   wsmux(4)

NAME
   ypbind — create and maintain a binding to a NIS server

SYNOPSIS
   ypbind [**-broadcast**] [**-insecure**] [**-ypset**] [**-ypsetme**]

DESCRIPTION
   ypbind finds the server for a particular NIS domain and stores information about it in a "binding file". This binding information includes the IP address of the server associated with that particular domain and which port the server is using. This information is stored in the directory /var/yp/binding in a file named with the convention <domain>.version, where ⟨domain⟩ is the relevant domain. The NIS system only supplies information on version 2.

   If **ypbind** is started without the **-broadcast** option, **ypbind** steps through the list of NIS servers specified in /var/yp/binding/<domain>.ypservers and contacts each in turn attempting to bind to that server. It is strongly recommended that these hosts are in the local hosts file, and that hosts are looked up in local files before the NIS hosts map.

   If **ypbind** is started with the **-broadcast** option, or if /var/yp/binding/<domain>.ypservers does not exist, **ypbind** broadcasts to find a process willing to serve maps for the client's domain.

   Once a binding is established, **ypbind** maintains this binding by periodically communicating with the server to which it is bound. If the binding is somehow lost, e.g by server reboot, **ypbind** marks the domain as unbound and attempts to re-establish the binding. When the binding is once again successful, **ypbind** marks the domain as bound and resumes its periodic check.

   The options are as follows:

   -broadcast
               sends a broadcast requesting a NIS server to which to bind.

   -insecure   do not require that the server is running on a reserved port. This may be necessary when connecting to SunOS 3.x or ULTRIX NIS servers.

   -ypset   ypset(8) may be used to change the server to which a domain is bound.

   -ypsetme   ypset(8) may be used only from this machine to change the server to which a domain is bound.

   The **-broadcast -ypset**, and **-ypsetme**, options are inherently insecure and should be avoided.

FILES
   /var/yp/binding/<domain>.version   -   binding   file   for   <domain>.
   /var/yp/binding/<domain>.ypservers - explicit list of servers to bind to for <domain>.

DIAGNOSTICS
   Messages are sent to syslogd(8) using the LOG_DAEMON facility.

SEE ALSO
   domainname(1), ypcat(1), ypmatch(1), ypwhich(1), nis(8), yppoll(8), ypset(8)

AUTHORS
   This version of **ypbind** was originally implemented by Theo de Raadt. The ypservers support was implemented by Luke Mewburn.

NAME
ypinit — initialize NIS subsystem

SYNOPSIS
ypinit **−c** [*domainname*] [**−l** *server1,...,serverN*]
ypinit **−m** [*domainname*] [**−l** *server1,...,serverN*]
ypinit **−s** *master_server* [*domainname*] [**−l** *server1,...,serverN*]

DESCRIPTION
ypinit initializes the files and directories that are required for a NIS client or server.

If *domainname* isn't specified, the default domain (as returned by domainname(1)) is used.

The following options are available:

−c   Create a NIS client. Initializes /var/yp/binding/<domain>.ypservers to contain a list
            of ypservers for ypbind(8) to connect to.

−l *server1,...,serverN*
            Set the list of client servers from the command line rather than prompting for them interactively.
            The format is a comma separated list of server names with no spaces.

−m   Create a master NIS server. Generates map data from local files (/etc/master.passwd,
            /etc/group, etc.).

−s *master_server*
            Create a slave server. Downloads the maps from *master_server*, which should be the active
            master NIS server.

To rebuild or refresh the maps for the NIS domain <domain>, change to the /var/yp/<domain> directory
and run **make**.

FILES
/var/yp   master NIS directory; contains the template makefiles.
/var/yp/<domain>   directory to store NIS maps for <domain>.
/var/yp/binding/<domain>.ypservers
                              list of NIS servers to bind to.

SEE ALSO
domainname(1), make(1), makedbm(8), mknetid(8), nis(8), stdethers(8), stdhosts(8),
ypbind(8), yppush(8), ypserv(8)

AUTHORS
Originally written by Mats O Jansson ⟨moj@stacken.kth.se⟩. Modified by Jason R. Thorpe
⟨thorpej@NetBSD.org⟩.

NAME

yppoll — ask version of NIS map from NIS server

SYNOPSIS

yppoll [**-T**] [**-h** *host*] [**-d** *domain*] *mapname*

DESCRIPTION

yppoll asks a NIS server process for the order number and which host is the master server for *mapname*.

The options are as follows:

-T   Use TCP protocol instead of UDP for request if *−h* option is present.

-h *host*

Ask the NIS server process running on *host* for information about *mapname*. If *host* is not specified, the server polled is the default server returned by ypwhich(1).

-d *domain*

Use the NIS domain *domain* instead of the default domain as returned by domainname(1).

SEE ALSO

domainname(1), ypcat(1), ypmatch(1), ypwhich(1), nis(8), ypbind(8), ypset(8)

AUTHORS

Theo de Raadt and John Brezak

NAME

yppush — force distribution of NIS map

SYNOPSIS

yppush [**−v**] [**−d** *domainname*] [**−h** *hostname*] *mapname*

DESCRIPTION

yppush is used to distribute a NIS map from a master server to any slave server in the domain. The list of servers of `domainname` are fetched from the NIS map `ypservers`.

The options are as follows:

−d *domainname*
                     NIS domain to use instead of the default domain.

−h *hostname*   Distribute map only to one host and not to the hosts in the ypserver map.

−v   Verbose. Announce what the program is doing.

SEE ALSO

`domainname`(1), `nis`(8), `ypserv`(8)

AUTHORS

Charles D. Cranor

NAME

ypserv — NIS server daemon

SYNOPSIS

ypserv [**-dfl**] [**-p** *port*]

DESCRIPTION

ypserv is a fundamental part of the network information system called NIS. This server provides information from NIS maps to the NIS clients on the network.

A NIS map is stored on the server as a db(3) database. A number of NIS maps is grouped together in a domain. **ypserv** determines the domains it serves by looking for a directory with the domain name in */var/yp*.

In an effort to improve the security of NIS (which has, historically, not been very good), this **ypserv** has support for libwrap-based access control. See hosts_access(5) for more information. The *daemon* used for access control is the name which **ypserv** was invoked as (typically "ypserv"). If a host is not allowed to query this NIS server, **ypserv** will return the NIS result code YP_NODOM. To avoid problems with DNS lookups causing **ypserv** to hang, **ypserv** disables DNS lookups for its client hosts_access(5) lists. The result is that **ypserv** can only use address based patterns. This also means that wildcard patterns such as LOCAL or KNOWN will not work.

The process pid of the **ypserv** process can be found in the file /var/run/ypserv.pid.

The options are as follows:

-d   Use internet Domain Name System. If a query to map hosts.byname or hosts.byaddr fails, make a DNS query and return the result if successful.

-f   Run in the foreground.

-l   Enable logging of all requests.

-p *port*
           Bind to the specified *port* instead of dynamically allocating one.

All messages are sent to the system log with the facility LOG_DAEMON. Error messages have the priority LOG_ERR. Refused requests are logged with the priority LOG_WARNING. All other messages are logged with the priority LOG_INFO.

FILES

/var/run/ypserv.pid

SEE ALSO

syslog(3), hosts_access(5), nis(8), syslogd(8), ypbind(8), ypinit(8)

AUTHORS

This implementation of **ypserv** was originally written by Mats O Jansson ⟨moj@stacken.kth.se⟩. The access control code was later re-written from scratch by
Jason R. Thorpe ⟨thorpej@NetBSD.org⟩.

NAME

ypset — tell ypbind(8) which NIS server process to use

SYNOPSIS

ypset [**-h** *host*] [**-d** *domain*] *server*

DESCRIPTION

ypset tells the ypbind(8) process on the current machine which NIS server process to communicate with. If *server* is down or is not running a NIS server process, it is not discovered until a NIS client process attempts to access a NIS map, at which time ypbind(8) tests the binding and takes appropriate action.

ypset is most useful for binding a NIS client that is not on the same broadcast network as the closest NIS server, but can also be used for debugging a local network's NIS configuration, testing specific NIS client programs, or binding to a specific server when there are many servers on the local network supplying NIS maps.

The options are as follows:

-h *host*

Set the NIS binding on *host* instead of the local machine.

-d *domain*

Use the NIS domain *domain* instead of the default domain as returned by domainname(1).

SEE ALSO

domainname(1), ypcat(1), ypmatch(1), ypwhich(1), nis(8), ypbind(8), yppoll(8)

AUTHORS

Theo de Raadt

NAME
yptest — calls different NIS routines

SYNOPSIS
yptest

DESCRIPTION
yptest is a utility written to check if the NIS server works as expected.

SEE ALSO
nis(8), ypserv(8)

AUTHORS
Mats O Jansson ⟨moj@stacken.kth.se⟩

NAME

ypxfr — get a NIS map from NIS server

SYNOPSIS

ypxfr [**-bcf**] [**-C** *tid prog ipadd port*] [**-d** *domain*] [**-h** *host*] [**-s** *domain*]
     mapname

DESCRIPTION

ypxfr is the utility in NIS that transfers maps to the local host.

The options are as follows:

-b   Preserve the entry in the database informing a NIS server to use DNS to get information about unknown hosts. This option will only have effect on the maps `hosts.byname` and `hosts.byaddr`.

-c   Don't send a "Clear current map" to local **ypserv** process. Useful if **ypserv** isn't running locally to avoid timeout message.

-C *tid prog ipadd port*
     This option is only used by **ypserv**. This is to open communication with **yppush** on another host.

-d *domain*
     Don't use default domain, use the specified domain.

-f   Force map transfer, even if the master's version is older than the local copy.

-h *host*
     Get map from host instead of the maps master host.

-s *domain*
     Specify a source domain other than the target domain.

SEE ALSO

nis(8), yppush(8), ypserv(8)

AUTHORS

Mats O Jansson ⟨moj@stacken.kth.se⟩

NAME
zdb – ZFS debugger

SYNOPSIS
zdb *pool*

DESCRIPTION
The **zdb** command is used by support engineers to diagnose failures and gather statistics. Since the **ZFS** file system is always consistent on disk and is self-repairing, **zdb** should only be run under the direction by a support engineer.

If no arguments are specified, **zdb**, performs basic consistency checks on the pool and associated datasets, and report any problems detected.

Any options supported by this command are internal to Sun and subject to change at any time.

EXIT STATUS
The following exit values are returned:

0   The pool is consistent.

1   An error was detected.

2   Invalid command line options were specified.

ATTRIBUTES
See **attributes**(5) for descriptions of the following attributes:

ATTRIBUTE TYPE	ATTRIBUTE VALUE
Availability	SUNWzfsu
Interface Stability	Unstable

SEE ALSO
zfs(1M), **zpool**(1M), **attributes**(5)

NAME

zdump — time zone dumper

SYNOPSIS

zdump [**--version**] [**-v**] [**-c** *[loyear,]highyear*] [*zonename* . . .]

DESCRIPTION

zdump prints the current time in each *zonename* named on the command line.

These options are available:

--version

Output version information and exit.

-v   For each *zonename* on the command line, print the time at the lowest possible time value, the time one day after the lowest possible time value, the times both one second before and exactly at each detected time discontinuity, the time at one day less than the highest possible time value, and the time at the highest possible time value, Each line ends with

isdst=1

if the given time is Daylight Saving Time or

isdst=0

otherwise.

-c *[loyear,]highyear*

Cut off the verbose output near the start of the given year(s). By default, the program cuts off verbose output near the starts of the years -500 and 2500.

LIMITATIONS

The **-v** option may not be used on systems with floating-point time_t values that are neither float nor double.

Time discontinuities are found by sampling the results returned by localtime at twelve-hour intervals. This works in all real-world cases; one can construct artificial time zones for which this fails.

SEE ALSO

ctime(3), tzfile(5), zic(8)

NAME

zfs – configures ZFS file systems

SYNOPSIS

zfs [**-?**]

zfs create [[**-o** property=*value*]]... *filesystem*

zfs create [**-s**] [**-b** *blocksize*] [[**-o** property=*value*]]... **-V** *size volume*

zfs destroy [**-rRf**] *filesystem\volume\snapshot*

zfs clone *snapshot filesystem\volume*

zfs promote *filesystem*

zfs rename *filesystem\volume\snapshot*
   [*filesystem\volume\snapshot*]

zfs snapshot [**-r**] *filesystem@name\volume@name*

zfs rollback [**-rRf**] *snapshot*

zfs list [**-rH**] [**-o** *prop*[,*prop*]]... [**-t** *type*[,*type*]...]
   [**-s** *prop* [**-s** *prop*]... [**-S** *prop* [**-S** *prop*]...
   [*filesystem\volume\snapshot\/pathname\./pathname ...*

zfs set *property=value filesystem\volume ...*

zfs get [**-rHp**] [**-o** *field*[,*field*]...]
   [**-s** *source*[,*source*]...] all | *property*[,*property*]...
   filesystem\volume\snapshot ...

zfs inherit [**-r**] *property filesystem\volume... ...*

zfs mount

zfs mount [**-o** *options*] [**-O**] **-a**

zfs mount [**-o** *options*] [**-O**] *filesystem*

zfs unmount [**-f**] **-a**

zfs unmount [**-f**] *filesystem\mountpoint*

zfs share -a

        zfs share *filesystem*

        zfs unshare [**-f**] **-a**

        zfs unshare [**-f**] *filesystem\mountpoint*

        zfs send [**-i** *snapshot1*] *snapshot2*

        zfs receive [**-vnF**] *filesystem\volume\snapshot*

        zfs receive [**-vnF**] **-d** *filesystem*

        zfs jail jailid *filesystem*

        zfs unjail jailid *filesystem*

DESCRIPTION

The **zfs** command configures **ZFS** datasets within a **ZFS** storage pool, as described in **zpool**(1M). A dataset is identified by a unique path within the **ZFS** namespace. For example:

        pool/{filesystem,volume,snapshot}

where the maximum length of a dataset name is **MAXNAMELEN** (256 bytes).

A dataset can be one of the following:

file system   A standard **POSIX** file system. **ZFS** file systems can be mounted within the standard file system namespace and behave like any other file system.

volume   A logical volume exported as a raw or block device. This type of dataset should only be used under special circumstances. File systems are typically used in most environments. Volumes cannot be used in a non-global zone.

snapshot   A read-only version of a file system or volume at a given point in time. It is specified as *filesystem@name* or *volume@name*.

ZFS File System Hierarchy

A **ZFS** storage pool is a logical collection of devices that provide space for datasets. A storage pool is also the root of the **ZFS** file system hierarchy.

The root of the pool can be accessed as a file system, such as mounting and unmounting, taking snapshots, and setting properties. The physical storage characteristics, however, are managed by the **zpool**(1M) command.

See **zpool**(1M) for more information on creating and administering pools.

Snapshots

A snapshot is a read-only copy of a file system or volume. Snapshots can be created extremely quickly, and initially consume no additional space within the pool. As data within the active dataset changes, the snapshot consumes more data than would otherwise be shared with the active dataset.

Snapshots can have arbitrary names. Snapshots of volumes can be cloned or rolled back, but cannot be accessed independently.

File system snapshots can be accessed under the ".zfs/snapshot" directory in the root of the file system. Snapshots are automatically mounted on demand and may be unmounted at regular intervals. The visibility of the ".zfs" directory can be controlled by the "snapdir" property.

Clones

A clone is a writable volume or file system whose initial contents are the same as another dataset. As with snapshots, creating a clone is nearly instantaneous, and initially consumes no additional space.

Clones can only be created from a snapshot. When a snapshot is cloned, it creates an implicit dependency between the parent and child. Even though the clone is created somewhere else in the dataset hierarchy, the original snapshot cannot be destroyed as long as a clone exists. The "origin" property exposes this dependency, and the **destroy** command lists any such dependencies, if they exist.

The clone parent-child dependency relationship can be reversed by using the "**promote**" subcommand. This causes the "origin" file system to become a clone of the specified file system, which makes it possible to destroy the file system that the clone was created from.

Mount Points

Creating a **ZFS** file system is a simple operation, so the number of file systems per system will likely be numerous. To cope with this, **ZFS** automatically manages mounting and unmounting file systems without the need to edit the **/etc/vfstab** file. All automatically managed file systems are mounted by **ZFS** at boot time.

By default, file systems are mounted under */path*, where *path* is the name of the file system in the **ZFS** namespace. Directories are created and destroyed as needed.

A file system can also have a mount point set in the "mountpoint" property. This directory is created as needed, and **ZFS** automatically mounts the file system when the "**zfs mount -a**" command is invoked (without editing **/etc/vfstab**). The mountpoint property can be inherited, so if **pool/home** has a mount point of **/export/stuff**, then **pool/home/user** automatically inherits a mount point of **/export/stuff/user**.

A file system mountpoint property of "none" prevents the file system from being mounted.

If needed, **ZFS** file systems can also be managed with traditional tools (**mount, umount, /etc/vfstab**). If a file system's mount point is set to "legacy", **ZFS** makes no attempt to manage the file system, and the administrator is responsible for mounting and unmounting the file system.

Zones

A **ZFS** file system can be added to a non-global zone by using zonecfg's "**add fs**" subcommand. A **ZFS** file system that is added to a non-global zone must have its mountpoint property set to legacy.

The physical properties of an added file system are controlled by the global administrator. However, the zone administrator can create, modify, or destroy files within the added file system, depending on how the file system is mounted.

A dataset can also be delegated to a non-global zone by using zonecfg's "**add dataset**" subcommand. You cannot delegate a dataset to one zone and the children of the same dataset to another zone. The zone administrator can change properties of the dataset or any of its children. However, the "quota" property is controlled by the global administrator.

A **ZFS** volume can be added as a device to a non-global zone by using zonecfg's "**add device**" subcommand. However, its physical properties can only be modified by the global administrator.

For more information about **zonecfg** syntax, see **zonecfg**(1M).

After a dataset is delegated to a non-global zone, the "zoned" property is automatically set. A zoned file system cannot be mounted in the global zone, since the zone administrator might have to set the mount point to an unacceptable value.

The global administrator can forcibly clear the "zoned" property, though this should be done with extreme care. The global administrator should verify that all the mount points are acceptable before clearing the property.

Native Properties

Properties are divided into two types, native properties and user defined properties. Native properties either export internal statistics or control **ZFS** behavior. In addition, native properties are either editable or read-only. User properties have no effect on **ZFS** behavior, but you can use them to annotate datasets in a way that is meaningful in your environment. For more information about user properties, see the "User Properties" section.

Every dataset has a set of properties that export statistics about the dataset as well as control various behavior. Properties are inherited from the parent unless overridden by the child. Snapshot properties can not be edited; they always inherit their inheritable properties. Properties that are not applicable to snapshots are not displayed.

The values of numeric properties can be specified using the following human-readable suffixes (for example, "k", "KB", "M", "Gb", etc, up to Z for zettabyte). The following are all valid (and equal) specifications:

    "1536M", "1.5g", "1.50GB".

The values of non-numeric properties are case sensitive and must be lowercase, except for "mountpoint" and "sharenfs".

The first set of properties consist of read-only statistics about the dataset. These properties cannot be set, nor are they inherited. Native properties apply to all dataset types unless otherwise noted.

type   The type of dataset: "filesystem", "volume", "snapshot", or "clone".

creation   The time this dataset was created.

used   The amount of space consumed by this dataset and all its descendants. This is the value that is checked against this dataset's quota and reservation. The space used does not include this dataset's reservation, but does take into account the reservations of any descendant datasets. The amount of space that a dataset consumes from its parent, as well as the amount of space that will be freed if this dataset is recursively destroyed, is the greater of its space used and its reservation.

When snapshots (see the "Snapshots" section) are created, their space is initially shared between the snapshot and the file system, and possibly with previous snapshots. As the file system changes, space that was previously shared becomes unique to the snapshot, and counted in the snapshot's space used. Additionally, deleting snapshots can increase the amount of space unique to (and used by) other snapshots.

The amount of space used, available, or referenced does not take into account pending changes. Pending changes are generally accounted for within a few seconds. Committing a change to a disk using **fsync**(3c) or **O_SYNC** does not necessarily guarantee that the space usage information is updated immediately.

available   The amount of space available to the dataset and all its children, assuming that there is no other activity in the pool. Because space is shared within a pool, availability can be limited by any number of factors, including physical pool size, quotas, reservations, or other datasets within the pool.

This property can also be referred to by its shortened column name, "avail".

referenced   The amount of data that is accessible by this dataset, which may or may not be shared with other datasets in the pool. When a snapshot or clone is created, it initially references the same amount of space as the file system or snapshot it was created from, since its contents are identical.

This property can also be referred to by its shortened column name, "refer".

compressratio   The compression ratio achieved for this dataset, expressed as a multiplier. Compression can be turned on by running "zfs set compression=on *dataset*". The default value is "off".

mounted   For file systems, indicates whether the file system is currently mounted. This property can be either "yes" or "no".

origin   For cloned file systems or volumes, the snapshot from which the clone was created. The origin cannot be destroyed (even with the **-r** or **-f** options) so long as a clone exists.

The following two properties can be set to control the way space is allocated between datasets. These properties are not inherited, but do affect their descendants.

quota=_size | none_

Limits the amount of space a dataset and its descendants can consume. This property enforces a hard limit on the amount of space used. This includes all space consumed by descendants, including file systems and snapshots. Setting a quota on a descendant of a dataset that already has a quota does not override the ancestor's quota, but rather imposes an additional limit.

Quotas cannot be set on volumes, as the "volsize" property acts as an implicit quota.

reservation=_size | none_

The minimum amount of space guaranteed to a dataset and its descendants. When the amount of space used is below this value, the dataset is treated as if it were taking up the amount of space specified by its reservation. Reservations are accounted for in the parent datasets' space used, and count against the parent datasets' quotas and reservations.

This property can also be referred to by its shortened column name, "reserv".

volsize=_size_

For volumes, specifies the logical size of the volume. By default, creating a volume establishes a reservation of equal size. Any changes to **volsize** are reflected in an equivalent change to the reservation. The **volsize** can only be set to a multiple of **volblocksize**, and cannot be zero.

The reservation is kept equal to the volume's logical size to prevent unexpected behavior for consumers. Without the reservation, the volume could run out of space, resulting in undefined behavior or data corruption, depending on how the volume is used. These effects can also occur when the volume size is changed while it is in use (particularly when shrinking the size). Extreme care should be used when adjusting the volume size.

Though not recommended, a "sparse volume" (also known as "thin provisioning") can be created by specifying the **-s** option to the "**zfs create -V**" command, or by changing the reservation after the volume has been created. A "sparse volume" is a volume where the reservation is less then the volume size. Consequently, writes to a sparse volume can fail with **ENOSPC** when the pool is low on space. For a sparse volume, changes to **volsize** are not reflected in the reservation.

volblocksize=_blocksize_

For volumes, specifies the block size of the volume. The **blocksize** cannot be changed once the volume has been written, so it should be set at volume creation time. The default **blocksize** for volumes is 8 Kbytes. Any power of 2 from 512 bytes to 128 Kbytes is valid.

This property can also be referred to by its shortened column name, "volblock".

recordsize=_size_

Specifies a suggested block size for files in the file system. This property is designed solely for use with database workloads that access files in fixed-size records. **ZFS** automatically tunes block sizes according to internal algorithms optimized for typical access patterns.

For databases that create very large files but access them in small random chunks, these algorithms may be suboptimal. Specifying a "recordsize" greater than or equal to the record size of the database can result in significant performance gains. Use of this property for general purpose file systems is strongly discouraged, and may adversely affect performance.

The size specified must be a power of two greater than or equal to 512 and less than or equal to 128 Kbytes.

Changing the file system's **recordsize** only affects files created afterward; existing files are unaffected.

This property can also be referred to by its shortened column name, "recsize".

mountpoint=_path_ | _none_ | _legacy_

Controls the mount point used for this file system. See the "Mount Points" section for more information on how this property is used.

When the mountpoint property is changed for a file system, the file system and any children that inherit the mount point are unmounted. If the new value is "legacy", then they remain unmounted. Otherwise, they are automatically remounted in the new location if the property was previously "legacy" or "none", or if they were mounted before the property was changed. In addition, any shared file systems are unshared and shared in the new location.

sharenfs=_on_ | _off_ | _opts_

Controls whether the file system is shared via **NFS**, and what options are used. A file system with a sharenfs property of "off" is managed through traditional tools such as **share**(1M), **unshare**(1M), and **dfstab**(4). Otherwise, the file system is automatically shared and unshared with the "**zfs share**" and "**zfs unshare**" commands. If the property is set to "on", the **share**(1M) command is invoked with no options. Otherwise, the **share**(1M) command is invoked with options equivalent to the contents of this property.

When the "sharenfs" property is changed for a dataset, the dataset and any children inheriting the property are re-shared with the new options, only if the property was previously "off", or if they were shared before the property was changed. If the new property is "off", the file systems are unshared.

shareiscsi=_on | off_

Like the "sharenfs" property, "shareiscsi" indicates whether a **ZFS** volume is exported as an **iSCSI** target. The acceptable values for this property are "on", "off", and "type=disk". The default value is "off". In the future, other target types might be supported. For example, "tape".

You might want to set "shareiscsi=on" for a file system so that all **ZFS** volumes within the file system are shared by default. Setting this property on a file system has no direct effect, however.

checksum=_on | off | fletcher2, | fletcher4 | sha256_

Controls the checksum used to verify data integrity. The default value is "on", which automatically selects an appropriate algorithm (currently, _fletcher2_, but this may change in future releases). The value "off" disables integrity checking on user data. Disabling checksums is NOT a recommended practice.

compression=_on | off | lzjb | gzip | gzip-N_

Controls the compression algorithm used for this dataset. The "lzjb" compression algorithm is optimized for performance while providing decent data compression. Setting compression to "on" uses the "lzjb" compression algorithm. The "gzip" compression algorithm uses the same compression as the **gzip**(1) command. You can specify the "gzip" level by using the value "gzip-_N_", where _N_ is an integer from 1 (fastest) to 9 (best compression ratio). Currently, "gzip" is equivalent to "gzip-6" (which is also the default for **gzip**(1)).

This property can also be referred to by its shortened column name "compress".

atime=_on | off_

Controls whether the access time for files is updated when they are read. Turning this property off avoids producing write traffic when reading files and can result in significant performance gains, though it might confuse mailers and other similar utilities. The default value is "on".

devices=_on | off_

Controls whether device nodes can be opened on this file system. The default value is "on".

exec=_on | off_

Controls whether processes can be executed from within this file system. The default value is "on".

setuid=_on | off_

Controls whether the set-**UID** bit is respected for the file system. The default value is "on".

readonly=*on* | *off*

>   Controls whether this dataset can be modified. The default value is "off".

>   This property can also be referred to by its shortened column name, "rdonly".

zoned=*on* | *off*

>   Controls whether the dataset is managed from a non-global zone. See the "Zones" section for more information. The default value is "off".

snapdir=*hidden* | *visible*

>   Controls whether the ".zfs" directory is hidden or visible in the root of the file system as discussed in the "Snapshots" section. The default value is "hidden".

aclmode=discard | groupmask | passthrough

>   Controls how an **ACL** is modified during **chmod**(2). A file system with an "aclmode" property of "**discard**" deletes all **ACL** entries that do not represent the mode of the file. An "aclmode" property of "**groupmask**" (the default) reduces user or group permissions. The permissions are reduced, such that they are no greater than the group permission bits, unless it is a user entry that has the same **UID** as the owner of the file or directory. In this case, the **ACL** permissions are reduced so that they are no greater than owner permission bits. A file system with an "aclmode" property of "**passthrough**" indicates that no changes will be made to the **ACL** other than generating the necessary **ACL** entries to represent the new mode of the file or directory.

aclinherit=discard | noallow | secure | passthrough

>   Controls how **ACL** entries are inherited when files and directories are created. A file system with an "aclinherit" property of "**discard**" does not inherit any **ACL** entries. A file system with an "aclinherit" property value of "**noallow**" only inherits inheritable **ACL** entries that specify "deny" permissions. The property value "**secure**" (the default) removes the "**write_acl**" and "**write_owner**" permissions when the **ACL** entry is inherited. A file system with an "aclinherit" property value of "**passthrough**" inherits all inheritable **ACL** entries without any modifications made to the **ACL** entries when they are inherited.

canmount=on | off

>   If this property is set to "**off**", the file system cannot be mounted, and is ignored by "**zfs mount -a**". This is similar to setting the "mountpoint" property to "**none**", except that the dataset still has a normal "mountpoint" property which can be inherited. This allows datasets to be used solely as a mechanism to inherit properties. One use case is to have two logically separate datasets have the same mountpoint, so that the children of both datasets appear in the same directory, but may have different inherited characteristics. The default value is "**on**".

>   This property is not inherited.

xattr=on | off

>   Controls whether extended attributes are enabled for this file system. The default value is "**on**".

copies=1 | 2 | 3

> Controls the number of copies of data stored for this dataset. These copies are in addition to any redundancy provided by the pool, for example, mirroring or raid-z. The copies are stored on different disks, if possible. The space used by multiple copies is charged to the associated file and dataset, changing the "used" property and counting against quotas and reservations.
>
> Changing this property only affects newly-written data. Therefore, set this property at file system creation time by using the "**-o** copies=" option.

jailed=_on | off_

> Controls whether the dataset is managed from within a jail. The default value is "off".

iscsioptions

This read-only property, which is hidden, is used by the **iSCSI** target daemon to store persistent information, such as the **IQN**. It cannot be viewed or modified using the **zfs** command. The contents are not intended for external consumers.

Temporary Mount Point Properties

When a file system is mounted, either through **mount**(1M) for legacy mounts or the "**zfs mount**" command for normal file systems, its mount options are set according to its properties. The correlation between properties and mount options is as follows:

PROPERTY	MOUNT OPTION
devices	devices/nodevices
exec	exec/noexec
readonly	ro/rw
setuid	setuid/nosetuid
xattr	xattr/noxattr

In addition, these options can be set on a per-mount basis using the **-o** option, without affecting the property that is stored on disk. The values specified on the command line override the values stored in the dataset. The **-nosuid** option is an alias for "nodevices,nosetuid". These properties are reported as "temporary" by the "**zfs get**" command. If the properties are changed while the dataset is mounted, the new setting overrides any temporary settings.

User Properties

In addition to the standard native properties, **ZFS** supports arbitrary user properties. User properties have no effect on **ZFS** behavior, but applications or administrators can use them to annotate datasets.

User property names must contain a colon (":") character, to distinguish them from native properties. They might contain lowercase letters, numbers, and the following punctuation characters: colon (":"), dash ("-"), period ("."), and underscore ("_"). The expected convention is that the property name is divided into two portions such as "_module:property_", but this namespace is not enforced by **ZFS**. User property names can be at most 256 characters, and cannot begin with a dash ("-").

When making programmatic use of user properties, it is strongly suggested to use a reversed **DNS** domain name for the _module_ component of property names to reduce the chance that two independently-developed packages use the same property name for different purposes. Property names beginning with "com.sun." are reserved for use by Sun Microsystems.

The values of user properties are arbitrary strings, are always inherited, and are never validated. All of the commands that operate on properties ("zfs list", "zfs get", "zfs set", etc.) can be used to manipulate both native properties and user properties. Use the "**zfs inherit**" command to clear a user property . If the property is not defined in any parent dataset, it is removed entirely. Property values are limited to 1024 characters.

Volumes as Swap or Dump Devices

To set up a swap area, create a **ZFS** volume of a specific size and then enable swap on that device. For more information, see the EXAMPLES section.

Do not swap to a file on a **ZFS** file system. A **ZFS** swap file configuration is not supported.

Using a **ZFS** volume as a dump device is not supported.

SUBCOMMANDS

All subcommands that modify state are logged persistently to the pool in their original form.

zfs ?

> Displays a help message.

zfs create [[-o property=value]...] *filesystem*

> Creates a new **ZFS** file system. The file system is automatically mounted according to the "mount-point" property inherited from the parent.

> **-o** property=value   Sets the specified property as if "**zfs set property=value**" was invoked at the same time the dataset was created. Any editable **ZFS** property can also be set at creation time. Multiple **-o** options can be specified. An error results if the same property is specified in multiple **-o** options.

zfs create [-s] [-b *blocksize*] [[-o property=value]...] **-V** *size volume*

> Creates a volume of the given size. The volume is exported as a block device in **/dev/zvol/{dsk,rdsk}/***path*, where *path* is the name of the volume in the **ZFS** namespace. The size represents the logical size as exported by the device. By default, a reservation of equal size is created.

> *size* is automatically rounded up to the nearest 128 Kbytes to ensure that the volume has an integral number of blocks regardless of *blocksize*.

> **-s**   Creates a sparse volume with no reservation. See "volsize" in the Native Properties section for more information about sparse volumes.

> **-o** property=value   Sets the specified property as if "**zfs set property=value**" was invoked at the same time the dataset was created. Any editable **ZFS** property can also be set at creation time. Multiple **-o** options can be specified. An error results if the same property is specified in multiple **-o** options.

> **-b** *blocksize*   Equivalent to "**-o volblocksize=***blocksize*". If this option is specified in conjunction with "**-o volblocksize**", the resulting behavior is undefined.

zfs destroy [-rRf] *filesystem|volume|snapshot*

> Destroys the given dataset. By default, the command unshares any file systems that are currently

shared, unmounts any file systems that are currently mounted, and refuses to destroy a dataset that has active dependents (children, snapshots, clones).

-r   Recursively destroy all children. If a snapshot is specified, destroy all snapshots with this name in descendant file systems.

-R   Recursively destroy all dependents, including cloned file systems outside the target hierarchy. If a snapshot is specified, destroy all snapshots with this name in descendant file systems.

-f   Force an unmount of any file systems using the "**unmount -f**" command. This option has no effect on non-file systems or unmounted file systems.

Extreme care should be taken when applying either the **-r** or the **-f** options, as they can destroy large portions of a pool and cause unexpected behavior for mounted file systems in use.

zfs clone *snapshot filesystem\volume*

Creates a clone of the given snapshot. See the "Clones" section for details. The target dataset can be located anywhere in the **ZFS** hierarchy, and is created as the same type as the original.

zfs promote *filesystem*

Promotes a clone file system to no longer be dependent on its "origin" snapshot. This makes it possible to destroy the file system that the clone was created from. The clone parent-child dependency relationship is reversed, so that the "origin" file system becomes a clone of the specified file system.

The snaphot that was cloned, and any snapshots previous to this snapshot, are now owned by the promoted clone. The space they use moves from the "origin" file system to the promoted clone, so enough space must be available to accommodate these snapshots. No new space is consumed by this operation, but the space accounting is adjusted. The promoted clone must not have any conflicting snapshot names of its own. The "**rename**" subcommand can be used to rename any conflicting snapshots.

zfs rename *filesystem\volume\snapshot filesystem\volume\snapshot*

Renames the given dataset. The new target can be located anywhere in the **ZFS** hierarchy, with the exception of snapshots. Snapshots can only be renamed within the parent file system or volume. When renaming a snapshot, the parent file system of the snapshot does not need to be specified as part of the second argument. Renamed file systems can inherit new mount points, in which case they are unmounted and remounted at the new mount point.

zfs snapshot [**-r**] *filesystem@name\volume@name*

Creates a snapshot with the given name. See the "Snapshots" section for details.

-r   Recursively create snapshots of all descendant datasets. Snapshots are taken atomically, so that all recursive snapshots correspond to the same moment in time.

zfs rollback [-rRf] *snapshot*

Roll back the given dataset to a previous snapshot. When a dataset is rolled back, all data that has changed since the snapshot is discarded, and the dataset reverts to the state at the time of the snapshot. By default, the command refuses to roll back to a snapshot other than the most recent one. In order to do so, all intermediate snapshots must be destroyed by specifying the **-r** option. The file system is unmounted and remounted, if necessary.

-r   Recursively destroy any snapshots more recent than the one specified.

-R   Recursively destroy any more recent snapshots, as well as any clones of those snapshots.

-f   Force an unmount of any file systems using the "**unmount -f**" command.

zfs list [-rH] [-o *prop*[,*prop*]]... [**-t** *type*[,*type*]...] [**-s** *prop* [**-s** *prop*]... [**-S** *prop* [**-S** *prop*]... [*filesystem\vol-ume\snapshot\/pathname\./pathname* ...

Lists the property information for the given datasets in tabular form. If specified, you can list property information by the absolute pathname or the relative pathname. By default, all datasets are displayed and contain the following fields:

    name,used,available,referenced,mountpoint

-H   Used for scripting mode. Do not print headers and separate fields by a single tab instead of arbitrary whitespace.

-r   Recursively display any children of the dataset on the command line.

-o *prop*   A comma-separated list of properties to display. The property must be one of the proper-ties described in the "Native Properties" section, or the special value "name" to display the dataset name.

-s *prop*   A property to use for sorting the output by column in ascending order based on the value of the property. The property must be one of the properties described in the "Properties" section, or the special value "name" to sort by the dataset name. Multiple properties can be specified at one time using multiple **-s** property options. Multiple **-s** options are evalu-ated from left to right in decreasing order of importance.

             The following is a list of sorting criteria:
             •   Numeric types sort in numeric order.
             •   String types sort in alphabetical order.
             •   Types inappropriate for a row sort that row to the literal bottom, regardless of the specified ordering.
             •   If no sorting options are specified the existing behavior of "**zfs list**" is pre-served.

-S *prop*   Same as the **-s** option, but sorts by property in descending order.

-t *type*   A comma-separated list of types to display, where "type" is one of "filesystem", "snapshot" or "volume". For example, specifying "**-t snapshot**" displays only snapshots.

zfs set *property=value filesystem\volume ...*

Sets the property to the given value for each dataset. Only some properties can be edited. See the "Properties" section for more information on what properties can be set and acceptable values. Numeric values can be specified as exact values, or in a human-readable form with a suffix of "B", "K", "M", "G", "T", "P", "E", "Z" (for bytes, Kbytes, Mbytes, gigabytes, terabytes, petabytes, exabytes, or zettabytes, respectively). Properties cannot be set on snapshots.

zfs get [**-rHp**] [**-o** *field*[,*field*]...] [**-s** *source*[,*source*]...] *all* | *property*[,*property*]... *filesystem\volume\snapshot*
...

Displays properties for the given datasets. If no datasets are specified, then the command displays properties for all datasets on the system. For each property, the following columns are displayed:

  name Dataset name
  property Property name
  value Property value
  source Property source. Can either be local, default,
       temporary, inherited, or none (-).

All columns are displayed by default, though this can be controlled by using the **-o** option. This command takes a comma-separated list of properties as described in the "Native Properties" and "User Properties" sections.

The special value "all" can be used to display all properties for the given dataset.

-r   Recursively display properties for any children.

-H   Display output in a form more easily parsed by scripts. Any headers are omitted, and fields are explicitly separated by a single tab instead of an arbitrary amount of space.

-o *field*   A comma-separated list of columns to display. "name,property,value,source" is the default value.

-s *source*   A comma-separated list of sources to display. Those properties coming from a source other than those in this list are ignored. Each source must be one of the following: "local,default,inherited,temporary,none". The default value is all sources.

-p   Display numbers in parsable (exact) values.

zfs inherit [**-r**] *property filesystem|volume* ...

Clears the specified property, causing it to be inherited from an ancestor. If no ancestor has the property set, then the default value is used. See the "Properties" section for a listing of default values, and details on which properties can be inherited.

-r   Recursively inherit the given property for all children.

zfs mount

Displays all **ZFS** file systems currently mounted.

zfs mount[**-o** *opts*] [**-O**] **-a**

Mounts all available **ZFS** file systems. Invoked automatically as part of the boot process.

-o *opts*   An optional comma-separated list of mount options to use temporarily for the duration of the mount. See the "Temporary Mount Point Properties" section for details.

-O   Perform an overlay mount. See **mount**(1M) for more information.

zfs mount [**-o** *opts*] [**-O**] *filesystem*

Mounts a specific **ZFS** file system. This is typically not necessary, as file systems are automatically mounted when they are created or the mountpoint property has changed. See the "Mount Points" section for details.

-o *opts*   An optional comma-separated list of mount options to use temporarily for the duration of the mount. See the "Temporary Mount Point Properties" section for details.

-O   Perform an overlay mount. See **mount**(1M) for more information.

zfs unmount -a

Unmounts all currently mounted **ZFS** file systems. Invoked automatically as part of the shutdown process.

zfs unmount [**-f**] *filesystem|mountpoint*

Unmounts the given file system. The command can also be given a path to a **ZFS** file system mount point on the system.

-f   Forcefully unmount the file system, even if it is currently in use.

zfs share -a

Shares all available **ZFS** file systems. This is invoked automatically as part of the boot process.

zfs share *filesystem*

Shares a specific **ZFS** file system according to the "sharenfs" property. File systems are shared when the "sharenfs" property is set.

zfs unshare -a

Unshares all currently shared **ZFS** file systems. This is invoked automatically as part of the shutdown process.

zfs unshare [**-F**] *filesystem\mountpoint*

Unshares the given file system. The command can also be given a path to a **ZFS** file system shared on the system.

-F   Forcefully unshare the file system, even if it is currently in use.

zfs send [**-i** *snapshot1*] *snapshot2*

Creates a stream representation of snapshot2, which is written to standard output. The output can be redirected to a file or to a different system (for example, using **ssh**(1). By default, a full stream is generated.

-i *snapshot1*   Generate an incremental stream from *snapshot1* to *snapshot2*. The incremental source *snapshot1* can be specified as the last component of the snapshot name (for example, the part after the "@"), and it is assumed to be from the same file system as *snapshot2*.

The format of the stream is evolving. No backwards compatibility is guaranteed. You may not be able to receive your streams on future versions of **ZFS**.

zfs receive [**-vnF**] *filesystem\volume\snapshot*
zfs receive [**-vnF**] **-d** *filesystem*

Creates a snapshot whose contents are as specified in the stream provided on standard input. If a full stream is received, then a new file system is created as well. Streams are created using the "**zfs send**" subcommand, which by default creates a full stream. "**zfs recv**" can be used as an alias for "**zfs receive**".

If an incremental stream is received, then the destination file system must already exist, and its most recent snapshot must match the incremental stream's source. The destination file system and all of its child file systems are unmounted and cannot be accessed during the receive operation.

The name of the snapshot (and file system, if a full stream is received) that this subcommand creates depends on the argument type and the **-d** option.

If the argument is a snapshot name, the specified *snapshot* is created. If the argument is a file system or volume name, a snapshot with the same name as the sent snapshot is created within the specified *filesystem* or *volume*. If the **-d** option is specified, the snapshot name is determined by appending the sent snapshot's name to the specified *filesystem*. If the **-d** option is specified, any required file systems within the specified one are created.

-d   Use the name of the sent snapshot to determine the name of the new snapshot as described in the paragraph above.

-v   Print verbose information about the stream and the time required to perform the receive operation.

-n   Do not actually receive the stream. This can be useful in conjunction with the **-v** option to determine what name the receive operation would use.

-F   Force a rollback of the *filesystem* to the most recent snapshot before performing the receive operation.

zfs jail *jailid filesystem*

Attaches the given file system to the given jail. From now on this file system tree can be managed from within a jail if the "**jailed**" property has been set. To use this functionality, sysctl **security.jail.enforce_statfs** should be set to 0 and sysctl **security.jail.mount_allowed** should be set to 1.

zfs unjail *jailid filesystem*

Detaches the given file system from the given jail.

EXAMPLES

Example 1 Creating a ZFS File System Hierarchy

The following commands create a file system named "**pool/home**" and a file system named "**pool/home/bob**". The mount point "**/export/home**" is set for the parent file system, and automatically inherited by the child file system.

```
# zfs create pool/home
# zfs set mountpoint=/export/home pool/home
# zfs create pool/home/bob
```

Example 2 Creating a ZFS Snapshot

The following command creates a snapshot named "yesterday". This snapshot is mounted on demand in the ".zfs/snapshot" directory at the root of the "**pool/home/bob**" file system.

```
# zfs snapshot pool/home/bob@yesterday
```

Example 3 Taking and destroying multiple snapshots

The following command creates snapshots named "**yesterday**" of "**pool/home**" and all of its descendant file systems. Each snapshot is mounted on demand in the ".zfs/snapshot" directory at the root of its file system. The second command destroys the newly created snapshots.

```
# zfs snapshot -r pool/home@yesterday
# zfs destroy -r pool/home@yesterday
```

Example 4 Turning Off Compression

The following commands turn compression off for all file systems under "**pool/home**", but explicitly turns it on for "**pool/home/anne**".

```
# zfs set compression=off pool/home
# zfs set compression=on pool/home/anne
```

Example 5 Listing ZFS Datasets

The following command lists all active file systems and volumes in the system.

```
# zfs list
```

```
NAME                    USED  AVAIL  REFER  MOUNTPOINT
pool               100G  60G     -   /pool
pool/home                 100G  60G     -   /export/home
pool/home/bob              40G  60G   40G   /export/home/bob
pool/home/bob@yesterday    3M    -    40G   -
pool/home/anne             60G  60G   40G   /export/home/anne
```

Example 6 Setting a Quota on a ZFS File System

The following command sets a quota of 50 gbytes for "**pool/home/bob**".

```
# zfs set quota=50G pool/home/bob
```

Example 7 Listing ZFS Properties

The following command lists all properties for "**pool/home/bob**".

```
# zfs get all pool/home/bob
```

```
NAME          PROPERTY   VALUE              SOURCE
pool/home/bob  type       filesystem         -
pool/home/bob  creation    Fri Feb 23 14:20 2007  -
```

```
pool/home/bob used          24.5K        -
pool/home/bob available      50.0G        -
pool/home/bob referenced     24.5K        -
pool/home/bob compressratio  1.00x        -
pool/home/bob mounted        yes          -
pool/home/bob quota          50G          local
pool/home/bob reservation    none         default
pool/home/bob recordsize     128K         default
pool/home/bob mountpoint     /pool/home/bob   default
pool/home/bob sharenfs       off          default
pool/home/bob shareiscsi     off          default
pool/home/bob checksum       on           default
pool/home/bob compression    off          default
pool/home/bob atime          on           default
pool/home/bob devices        on           default
pool/home/bob exec           on           default
pool/home/bob setuid         on           default
pool/home/bob readonly       off          default
pool/home/bob zoned          off          default
pool/home/bob snapdir        hidden       default
pool/home/bob aclmode        groupmask    default
pool/home/bob aclinherit     secure       default
pool/home/bob canmount       on           default
pool/home/bob xattr          on           default
```

The following command gets a single property value.

 # zfs get -H -o value compression pool/home/bob
on

The following command lists all properties with local settings for "**pool/home/bob**".

 # zfs get -r -s local -o name,property,value all pool/home/bob

```
NAME          PROPERTY      VALUE
pool          compression   on
pool/home     checksum      off
```

Example 8 Rolling Back a ZFS File System

The following command reverts the contents of "**pool/home/anne**" to the snapshot named "**yesterday**", deleting all intermediate snapshots.

 # zfs rollback -r pool/home/anne@yesterday

Example 9 Creating a ZFS Clone

The following command creates a writable file system whose initial contents are the same as "**pool/home/bob@yesterday**".

> # **zfs clone pool/home/bob@yesterday pool/clone**

Example 10 Promoting a ZFS Clone

The following commands illustrate how to test out changes to a file system, and then replace the original file system with the changed one, using clones, clone promotion, and renaming:

> # **zfs create pool/project/production**
> populate /pool/project/production with data
> # **zfs snapshot pool/project/production@today**
> # **zfs clone pool/project/production@today pool/project/beta**
> make changes to /pool/project/beta and test them
> # **zfs promote pool/project/beta**
> # **zfs rename pool/project/production pool/project/legacy**
> # **zfs rename pool/project/beta pool/project/production**
> once the legacy version is no longer needed, it can be
> destroyed
> # **zfs destroy pool/project/legacy**

Example 11 Inheriting ZFS Properties

The following command causes "**pool/home/bob**" and "**pool/home/anne**" to inherit the "checksum" property from their parent.

> # **zfs inherit checksum pool/home/bob pool/home/anne**

Example 12 Remotely Replicating ZFS Data

The following commands send a full stream and then an incremental stream to a remote machine, restoring them into "**poolB/received/fs@a**" and "**poolB/received/fs@b**", respectively. "**poolB**" must contain the file system "**poolB/received**", and must not initially contain "**poolB/received/fs**".

> # zfs send pool/fs@a | \
>   ssh host zfs receive poolB/received/fs@a
> # zfs send -i a pool/fs@b | ssh host \
>   zfs receive poolB/received/fs

Example 13 Using the zfs receive -d Option

The following command sends a full stream of "**poolA/fsA/fsB@snap**" to a remote machine, receiving it into "**poolB/received/fsA/fsB@snap**". The "**fsA/fsB@snap**" portion of the received snapshot's name is determined from the name of the sent snapshot. "**poolB**" must contain the file system "**poolB/received**". If "**poolB/received/fsA**" does not exist, it will be created as an empty file system.

```
# zfs send poolA/fsA/fsB@snap | \
  ssh host zfs receive -d poolB/received
```

Example 14 Creating a ZFS volume as a Swap Device

The following example shows how to create a 5-Gbyte ZFS volume and then add the volume as a swap device.

```
# zfs create  -V 5gb tank/vol
# swap -a /dev/zvol/dsk/tank/vol
```

Example 15 Setting User Properties

The following example sets the user defined "com.example:department" property for a dataset.

```
# zfs set com.example:department=12345 tank/accounting
```

Example 16 Creating a ZFS Volume as a iSCSI Target Device

The following example shows how to create a **ZFS** volume as an **iSCSI** target.

```
# zfs create -V 2g pool/volumes/vol1
# zfs set shareiscsi=on pool/volumes/vol1
# iscsitadm list target
Target: pool/volumes/vol1
iSCSI Name:
iqn.1986-03.com.sun:02:7b4b02a6-3277-eb1b-e686-a24762c52a8c
Connections: 0
```

After the **iSCSI** target is created, set up the **iSCSI** initiator. For more information about the Solaris **iSCSI** initiator, see the Solaris Administration Guide: Devices and File Systems.

EXIT STATUS

The following exit values are returned:

0   Successful completion.

1   An error occurred.

2   Invalid command line options were specified.

ATTRIBUTES

See **attributes**(5) for descriptions of the following attributes:

ATTRIBUTE TYPE	ATTRIBUTE VALUE
Availability	SUNWzfsu
Interface Stability	Evolving

SEE ALSO

    gzip(1), **ssh**(1), **mount**(1M), **share**(1M), **unshare**(1M), **zonecfg**(1M), **zpool**(1M), **chmod**(2), **stat**(2), **fsync**(3c), **dfstab**(4), **attributes**(5)

NAME

zic — time zone compiler

SYNOPSIS

zic [**--version**] [**-d** *directory*] [**-L** *leapsecondfilename*] [**-l** *localtime*]
    [**-p** *posixrules*] [**-s**] [**-v**] [**-y** *command*] [*Filename* . . .]

DESCRIPTION

zic reads text from the file(s) named on the command line and creates the time conversion information files specified in this input. If a *filename* is -, the standard input is read.

These options are available:

--version Output version information and exit.

-d *directory*
        Create time conversion information files in the named directory rather than in the standard directory named below.

-L *leapsecondfilename*
        Read leap second information from the file with the given name. If this option is not used, no leap second information appears in output files.

-l *timezone*
        Use the given time zone as local time. **zic** will act as if the input contained a link line of the form

              Link   timezone   localtime

-p *timezone*
        Use the given time zone's rules when handling POSIX-format time zone environment variables. **zic** will act as if the input contained a link line of the form

              Link   timezone   posixrules

-s   Limit time values stored in output files to values that are the same whether they're taken to be signed or unsigned. You can use this option to generate SVVS-compatible files.

-v   Complain if a year that appears in a data file is outside the range of years representable by time(3) values. Also complain if a time of 24:00 (which cannot be handled by pre-1998 versions of **zic**) appears in the input.

-y *command*
        Use the given *command* rather than *yearistype* when checking year types (see below).

        Input lines are made up of fields. Fields are separated from one another by any number of white space characters. Leading and trailing white space on input lines is ignored. An unquoted sharp character (#) in the input introduces a comment which extends to the end of the line the sharp character appears on. White space characters and sharp characters may be enclosed in double quotes (") if they're to be used as part of a field. Any line that is blank (after comment stripping) is ignored. Non-blank lines are expected to be of one of three types: rule lines, zone lines, and link lines.

        A rule line has the form

            Rule   NAME   FROM   TO   TYPE   IN   ON   AT   SAVE   LETTER/S

For example:

            Rule   US   1967   1973   -   Apr   lastSun   2:00   1:00   D

The fields that make up a rule line are:

NAME   Gives the (arbitrary) name of the set of rules this rule is part of.

FROM   Gives the first year in which the rule applies. Any integer year can be supplied; the Gregorian calendar is assumed. The word *minimum* (or an abbreviation) means the minimum year representable as an integer. The word *maximum* (or an abbreviation) means the maximum year representable as an integer. Rules can describe times that are not representable as time values, with the unrepresentable times ignored; this allows rules to be portable among hosts with differing time value types.

TO   Gives the final year in which the rule applies. In addition to *minimum* and *maximum* (as above), the word *only* (or an abbreviation) may be used to repeat the value of the *FROM* field.

TYPE   Gives the type of year in which the rule applies. If *TYPE* is - then the rule applies in all years between *FROM* and *TO* inclusive. If *TYPE* is something else, then **zic** executes the command

          yearistype *year type*

          to check the type of a year: an exit status of zero is taken to mean that the year is of the given type; an exit status of one is taken to mean that the year is not of the given type.

IN   Names the month in which the rule takes effect. Month names may be abbreviated.

ON   Gives the day on which the rule takes effect. Recognized forms include:
          | 5 | the fifth of the month |
          | lastSun | the last Sunday in the month |
          | lastMon | the last Monday in the month |
          | Sun≥8 | first Sunday on or after the eighth |
          | Sun≤25 | last Sunday on or before the 25th |

          Names of days of the week may be abbreviated or spelled out in full. Note that there must be no spaces within the *ON* field.

AT   Gives the time of day at which the rule takes effect. Recognized forms include:
          | 2 | time in hours |
          | 2:00 | time in hours and minutes |
          | 15:00 | 24-hour format time (for times after noon) |
          | 1:28:14 | time in hours, minutes, and seconds |
          | – | equivalent to 0 |

          where hour 0 is midnight at the start of the day, and hour 24 is midnight at the end of the day. Any of these forms may be followed by the letter *w* if the given time is local "wall clock" time, *s* if the given time is local "standard" time, or *u* (or *g* or *z*) if the given time is universal time; in the absence of an indicator, wall clock time is assumed.

SAVE   Gives the amount of time to be added to local standard time when the rule is in effect. This field has the same format as the *AT* field (although, of course, the *w* and *s* suffixes are not used).

LETTER/S Gives the "variable part" (for example, the "S" or "D" in "EST" or "EDT") of time zone abbreviations to be used when this rule is in effect. If this field is -, the variable part is null.

A zone line has the form

```
     Zone  NAME             GMTOFF      RULES/SAVE  FORMAT      [
     [MONTH [DAY [TIME]]]]
```
For example:
```
     Zone  Australia/Adelaide     9:30  Aus   CST   1971  Oct
     31 2:00
```
The fields that make up a zone line are:

NAME   The name of the time zone. This is the name used in creating the time con-
                version information file for the zone.

GMTOFF   The amount of time to add to UTC to get standard time in this zone. This
                field has the same format as the *AT* and *SAVE* fields of rule lines; begin the
                field with a minus sign if time must be subtracted from UTC.

RULES/SAVE   The name of the rule(s) that apply in the time zone or, alternatively, an
                amount of time to add to local standard time. If this field is - then standard
                time always applies in the time zone.

FORMAT   The format for time zone abbreviations in this time zone. The pair of char-
                acters %s is used to show where the "variable part" of the time zone abbrevi-
                ation goes. Alternatively, a slash (/) separates standard and daylight abbre-
                viations.

UNTILYEAR [MONTH [DAY [TIME]]]
                The time at which the UTC offset or the rule(s) change for a location. It is
                specified as a year, a month, a day, and a time of day. If this is specified, the
                time zone information is generated from the given UTC offset and rule
                change until the time specified. The month, day, and time of day have the
                same format as the IN, ON, and AT fields of a rule; trailing fields can be
                omitted, and default to the earliest possible value for the missing fields.

The next line must be a "continuation" line; this has the same form as a zone line except that
the string "Zone" and the name are omitted, as the continuation line will place information
starting at the time specified as the *until* information in the previous line in the file used by
the previous line. Continuation lines may contain *until* information, just as zone lines do,
indicating that the next line is a further continuation.

A link line has the form
        Link   LINK-FROM   LINK-TO
For example:
        Link   Europe/Istanbul   Asia/Istanbul
The *LINK-FROM* field should appear as the *NAME* field in some zone line; the *LINK-TO*
field is used as an alternative name for that zone.

Except for continuation lines, lines may appear in any order in the input.

Lines in the file that describes leap seconds have the following form:
        Leap   YEAR   MONTH DAY   HH:MM:SS   CORR   R/S
For example:
        Leap   1974   Dec   31   23:59:60   +   S
The *YEAR*, *MONTH*, *DAY*, and *HH:MM:SS* fields tell when the leap second happened. The
CORR field should be "+" if a second was added or "-" if a second was skipped. The *R/S*
field should be (an abbreviation of) "Stationary" if the leap second time given by the other
fields should be interpreted as UTC or (an abbreviation of) "Rolling" if the leap second time
given by the other fields should be interpreted as local wall clock time.

EXTENDED EXAMPLE

Here is an extended example of **zic** input, intended to illustrate many of its features.

# Rule NAME	FROM	TO TYPE	IN	ON	AT	SAVELETTER/S
Rule Swiss 1940	only -	Nov	2	0:00	1:00	S
Rule Swiss 1940	only -	Dec31	0:00	0	-	
Rule Swiss 1941	1942 -	May	Sun>=1	2:00	1:00S	
Rule Swiss 1941	1942 -	Oct Sun>=10:00	0			

```
Rule  EU  1977  1980 -    Apr Sun>=11 1:00u 1:00  S
Rule  EU  1977  only -    Sep lastSun  1:00u 0     -
Rule  EU  1978  only -    Oct  1       1:00u 0     -
Rule  EU  1979  1995 -    Sep lastSun  1:00u 0     -
Rule  EU  1981  max  -    Mar lastSun  1:00u 1:00  S
Rule  EU  1996  max  -    Oct lastSun  1:00u 0     -

# Zone NAME        GMTOFF      RULES   FORMAT UNTIL
Zone  Europe/Zurich 0:34:08 -  LMT     1848 Sep 12
                    0:29:44 -  BMT     1894 Jun
                    1:00  Swiss CE%sT  1981
                    1:00  EU   CE%sT
Link  Europe/Zurich Switzerland
```

In this example, the zone is named Europe/Zurich but it has an alias as Switzerland. Zurich was 34 minutes and 8 seconds west of GMT until 1848-09-12 at 00:00, when the offset changed to 29 minutes and 44 seconds. After 1894-06-01 at 00:00 Swiss daylight saving rules (defined with lines beginning with "Rule Swiss") apply, and the GMT offset became one hour. From 1981 to the present, EU daylight saving rules have applied, and the UTC offset has remained at one hour.

In 1940, daylight saving time applied from November 2 at 00:00 to December 31 at 00:00. In 1941 and 1942, daylight saving time applied from the first Sunday in May at 02:00 to the first Sunday in October at 00:00. The pre-1981 EU daylight-saving rules have no effect here, but are included for completeness. Since 1981, daylight saving has begun on the last Sunday in March at 01:00 UTC. Until 1995 it ended the last Sunday in September at 01:00 UTC, but this changed to the last Sunday in October starting in 1996.

For purposes of display, "LMT" and "BMT" were initially used, respectively. Since Swiss rules and later EU rules were applied, the display name for the timezone has been CET for standard time and CEST for daylight saving time.

NOTES

For areas with more than two types of local time, you may need to use local standard time in the *AT* field of the earliest transition time's rule to ensure that the earliest transition time recorded in the compiled file is correct.

If, for a particular zone, a clock advance caused by the start of daylight saving coincides with and is equal to a clock retreat caused by a change in UTC offset, **zic** produces a single transition to daylight saving at the new UTC offset (without any change in wall clock time). To get separate transitions use multiple zone continuation lines specifying transition instants using universal time.

FILES

/usr/share/zoneinfo - standard directory used for created files

SEE ALSO

ctime(3), tzfile(5), zdump(8)

NAME
zpool – configures ZFS storage pools

SYNOPSIS
zpool [**-?**]

zpool create [**-fn**] [**-R** *root*] [**-m** *mountpoint*] *pool vdev* ...

zpool destroy [**-f**] *pool*

zpool add [**-fn**] *pool vdev*

zpool remove *pool vdev*

zpool list [**-H**] [**-o** *field*[*,field*]*] [*pool*] ...

zpool iostat [**-v**] [*pool*] ... [*interval* [*count*]]

zpool status [**-xv**] [*pool*] ...

zpool offline [**-t**] *pool device* ...

zpool online *pool device* ...

zpool clear *pool* [*device*] ...

zpool attach [**-f**] *pool device new_device*

zpool detach *pool device*

zpool replace [**-f**] *pool device* [*new_device*]

zpool scrub [**-s**] *pool* ...

zpool export [**-f**] *pool*

zpool import [**-d** *dir*] [**-D**]

zpool import [**-d** *dir*] [**-D**] [**-f**] [**-o** *opts*] [**-R** *root*] *pool* | *id*
    [*newpool*]

zpool import [**-d** *dir*] [**-D**] [**-f**] [**-a**]

zpool upgrade

zpool upgrade -v

zpool upgrade [**-a** | *pool*]

zpool history [*pool*] ...

DESCRIPTION

The **zpool** command configures **ZFS** storage pools. A storage pool is a collection of devices that provides physical storage and data replication for **ZFS** datasets.

All datasets within a storage pool share the same space. See **zfs**(1M) for information on managing datasets.

Virtual Devices (vdevs)

A "virtual device" describes a single device or a collection of devices organized according to certain performance and fault characteristics. The following virtual devices are supported:

disk   A block device, typically located under "/dev/dsk". **ZFS** can use individual slices or partitions, though the recommended mode of operation is to use whole disks. A disk can be specified by a full path, or it can be a shorthand name (the relative portion of the path under "/dev/dsk"). A whole disk can be specified by omitting the slice or partition designation. For example, "c0t0d0" is equivalent to "/dev/dsk/c0t0d0s2". When given a whole disk, **ZFS** automatically labels the disk, if necessary.

file   A regular file. The use of files as a backing store is strongly discouraged. It is designed primarily for experimental purposes, as the fault tolerance of a file is only as good as the file system of which it is a part. A file must be specified by a full path.

mirror A mirror of two or more devices. Data is replicated in an identical fashion across all components of a mirror. A mirror with N disks of size X can hold X bytes and can withstand $(N-1)$ devices failing before data integrity is compromised.

raidz   A variation on **RAID-5** that allows for better distribution of parity and eliminates the "**RAID-5**
raidz1 write hole" (in which data and parity become inconsistent after a power loss). Data and parity
raidz2 is striped across all disks within a **raidz** group.

A **raidz** group can have either single- or double-parity, meaning that the **raidz** group can sustain one or two failures respectively without losing any data. The **raidz1 vdev** type specifies a single-parity **raidz** group and the **raidz2 vdev** type specifies a double-parity **raidz** group. The **raidz vdev** type is an alias for **raidz1**.

A **raidz** group with N disks of size X with P parity disks can hold approximately $(N-P)*X$ bytes and can withstand one device failing before data integrity is compromised. The minimum number of devices in a **raidz** group is one more than the number of parity disks. The recommended number is between 3 and 9.

spare   A special pseudo-**vdev** which keeps track of available hot spares for a pool. For more information, see the "Hot Spares" section.

Virtual devices cannot be nested, so a mirror or **raidz** virtual device can only contain files or disks. Mirrors of mirrors (or other combinations) are not allowed.

A pool can have any number of virtual devices at the top of the configuration (known as "root vdevs"). Data is dynamically distributed across all top-level devices to balance data among devices. As new virtual devices are added, **ZFS** automatically places data on the newly available devices.

Virtual devices are specified one at a time on the command line, separated by whitespace. The keywords "mirror" and "raidz" are used to distinguish where a group ends and another begins. For example, the following creates two root vdevs, each a mirror of two disks:

> # **zpool create mypool mirror c0t0d0 c0t1d0 mirror c1t0d0 c1t1d0**

Device Failure and Recovery

ZFS supports a rich set of mechanisms for handling device failure and data corruption. All metadata and data is checksummed, and **ZFS** automatically repairs bad data from a good copy when corruption is detected.

In order to take advantage of these features, a pool must make use of some form of redundancy, using either mirrored or **raidz** groups. While **ZFS** supports running in a non-redundant configuration, where each root vdev is simply a disk or file, this is strongly discouraged. A single case of bit corruption can render some or all of your data unavailable.

A pool's health status is described by one of three states: online, degraded, or faulted. An online pool has all devices operating normally. A degraded pool is one in which one or more devices have failed, but the data is still available due to a redundant configuration. A faulted pool has one or more failed devices, and there is insufficient redundancy to replicate the missing data.

Hot Spares

ZFS allows devices to be associated with pools as "hot spares". These devices are not actively used in the pool, but when an active device fails, it is automatically replaced by a hot spare. To create a pool with hot spares, specify a "spare" **vdev** with any number of devices. For example,

> # zpool create pool mirror c0d0 c1d0 spare c2d0 c3d0

Spares can be shared across multiple pools, and can be added with the "zpool add" command and removed with the "zpool remove" command. Once a spare replacement is initiated, a new "spare" **vdev** is created within the configuration that will remain there until the original device is replaced. At this point, the hot spare becomes available again if another device fails.

An in-progress spare replacement can be cancelled by detaching the hot spare. If the original faulted device is detached, then the hot spare assumes its place in the configuration, and is removed from the spare list of all active pools.

Alternate Root Pools

The "zpool create -R" and "zpool import -R" commands allow users to create and import a pool with a different root path. By default, whenever a pool is created or imported on a system, it is permanently added so that it is available whenever the system boots. For removable media, or when in recovery situations, this may not always be desirable. An alternate root pool does not persist on the system. Instead, it exists only until exported or the system is rebooted, at which point it will have to be imported again.

In addition, all mount points in the pool are prefixed with the given root, so a pool can be constrained to a particular area of the file system. This is most useful when importing unknown pools from removable media, as the mount points of any file systems cannot be trusted.

When creating an alternate root pool, the default mount point is "/", rather than the normal default "/*pool*".

Subcommands

All subcommands that modify state are logged persistently to the pool in their original form.

The **zpool** command provides subcommands to create and destroy storage pools, add capacity to storage pools, and provide information about the storage pools. The following subcommands are supported:

zpool -?

> Displays a help message.

zpool create [**-fn**] [**-R** *root*] [**-m** *mountpoint*] *pool vdev* ...

> Creates a new storage pool containing the virtual devices specified on the command line. The pool name must begin with a letter, and can only contain alphanumeric characters as well as underscore ("_"), dash ("-"), and period ("."). The pool names "mirror", "raidz", and "spare" are reserved, as are names beginning with the pattern "c[0-9]". The **vdev** specification is described in the "Virtual Devices" section.

> The command verifies that each device specified is accessible and not currently in use by another sub-system. There are some uses, such as being currently mounted, or specified as the dedicated dump device, that prevents a device from ever being used by **ZFS**. Other uses, such as having a preexisting **UFS** file system, can be overridden with the **-f** option.

> The command also checks that the replication strategy for the pool is consistent. An attempt to combine redundant and non-redundant storage in a single pool, or to mix disks and files, results in an error unless **-f** is specified. The use of differently sized devices within a single **raidz** or mirror group is also flagged as an error unless **-f** is specified.

> Unless the **-R** option is specified, the default mount point is "/*pool*". The mount point must not exist or must be empty, or else the root dataset cannot be mounted. This can be overridden with the **-m** option.

> | | |
> |---|---|
> | **-f** | Forces use of **vdev**s, even if they appear in use or specify a conflicting replication level. Not all devices can be overridden in this manner. |
> | **-n** | Displays the configuration that would be used without actually creating the pool. The actual pool creation can still fail due to insufficient privileges or device sharing. |
> | **-R** *root* | Creates the pool with an alternate *root*. See the "Alternate Root Pools" section. The root dataset has its mount point set to "/" as part of this operation. |
> | **-m** *mountpoint* | Sets the mount point for the root dataset. The default mount point is "/*pool*". The mount point must be an absolute path, "**legacy**", or "**none**". For more information on dataset mount points, see **zfs**(1M). |

zpool destroy [**-f**] *pool*

> Destroys the given pool, freeing up any devices for other use. This command tries to unmount any active datasets before destroying the pool.

> | | |
> |---|---|
> | **-f** | Forces any active datasets contained within the pool to be unmounted. |

zpool add [**-fn**] *pool vdev* ...

Adds the specified virtual devices to the given pool. The *vdev* specification is described in the "Virtual Devices" section. The behavior of the **-f** option, and the device checks performed are described in the "zpool create" subcommand.

-f   Forces use of **vdev**s, even if they appear in use or specify a conflicting replication level. Not all devices can be overridden in this manner.

-n   Displays the configuration that would be used without actually adding the **vdev**s. The actual pool creation can still fail due to insufficient privileges or device sharing.

Do not add a disk that is currently configured as a quorum device to a zpool. Once a disk is in a zpool, that disk can then be configured as a quorum device.

zpool remove *pool vdev*

Removes the given **vdev** from the pool. This command currently only supports removing hot spares. Devices which are part of a mirror can be removed using the "zpool detach" command. **Raidz** and top-level **vdevs** cannot be removed from a pool.

zpool list [**-H**] [**-o** *field*[,*field**]] [*pool*] ...

Lists the given pools along with a health status and space usage. When given no arguments, all pools in the system are listed.

-**H**   Scripted mode. Do not display headers, and separate fields by a single tab instead of arbitrary space.

-**o** *field*   Comma-separated list of fields to display. Each field must be one of:

name	Pool name
size	Total size
used	Amount of space used
available	Amount of space available
capacity	Percentage of pool space used
health	Health status

The default is all fields.

This command reports actual physical space available to the storage pool. The physical space can be different from the total amount of space that any contained datasets can actually use. The amount of space used in a **raidz** configuration depends on the characteristics of the data being written. In addition, **ZFS** reserves some space for internal accounting that the **zfs**(1M) command takes into account, but the **zpool** command does not. For non-full pools of a reasonable size, these effects should be invisible. For small pools, or pools that are close to being completely full, these discrepancies may become more noticeable.

zpool iostat [**-v**] [*pool*] ... [*interval* [*count*]]

> Displays **I/O** statistics for the given pools. When given an interval, the statistics are printed every *interval* seconds until **Ctrl-C** is pressed. If no *pools* are specified, statistics for every pool in the system is shown. If *count* is specified, the command exits after *count* reports are printed.
>
> **-v**   Verbose statistics. Reports usage statistics for individual *vdevs* within the pool, in addition to the pool-wide statistics.

zpool status [**-xv**] [*pool*] ...

> Displays the detailed health status for the given pools. If no *pool* is specified, then the status of each pool in the system is displayed.
>
> If a scrub or resilver is in progress, this command reports the percentage done and the estimated time to completion. Both of these are only approximate, because the amount of data in the pool and the other workloads on the system can change.
>
> **-x**   Only display status for pools that are exhibiting errors or are otherwise unavailable.
>
> **-v**   Displays verbose data error information, printing out a complete list of all data errors since the last complete pool scrub.

zpool offline [**-t**] *pool device* ...

> Takes the specified physical device offline. While the *device* is offline, no attempt is made to read or write to the device.
>
> This command is not applicable to spares.
>
> **-t**   Temporary. Upon reboot, the specified physical device reverts to its previous state.

zpool online *pool device* ...

> Brings the specified physical device online.
>
> This command is not applicable to spares.

zpool clear *pool* [*device*] ...

> Clears device errors in a pool. If no arguments are specified, all device errors within the pool are cleared. If one or more devices is specified, only those errors associated with the specified device or devices are cleared.

zpool attach [**-f**] *pool device new_device*

> Attaches *new_device* to an existing **zpool** device. The existing device cannot be part of a **raidz** configuration. If *device* is not currently part of a mirrored configuration, *device* automatically transforms into

a two-way mirror of *device* and *new_device*. If *device* is part of a two-way mirror, attaching *new_device* creates a three-way mirror, and so on. In either case, *new_device* begins to resilver immediately.

-f   Forces use of *new_device*, even if its appears to be in use. Not all devices can be overridden in this manner.

zpool detach *pool device*

Detaches *device* from a mirror. The operation is refused if there are no other valid replicas of the data.

zpool replace [-f] *pool old_device* [*new_device*]

Replaces *old_device* with *new_device*. This is equivalent to attaching *new_device*, waiting for it to resilver, and then detaching *old_device*.

The size of *new_device* must be greater than or equal to the minimum size of all the devices in a mirror or **raidz** configuration.

If *new_device* is not specified, it defaults to *old_device*. This form of replacement is useful after an existing disk has failed and has been physically replaced. In this case, the new disk may have the same **/dev/dsk** path as the old device, even though it is actually a different disk. **ZFS** recognizes this.

-f   Forces use of *new_device*, even if its appears to be in use. Not all devices can be overridden in this manner.

zpool scrub [-s] *pool* ...

Begins a scrub. The scrub examines all data in the specified pools to verify that it checksums correctly. For replicated (mirror or **raidz**) devices, **ZFS** automatically repairs any damage discovered during the scrub. The "**zpool status**" command reports the progress of the scrub and summarizes the results of the scrub upon completion.

Scrubbing and resilvering are very similar operations. The difference is that resilvering only examines data that **ZFS** knows to be out of date (for example, when attaching a new device to a mirror or replacing an existing device), whereas scrubbing examines all data to discover silent errors due to hardware faults or disk failure.

Because scrubbing and resilvering are **I/O**-intensive operations, **ZFS** only allows one at a time. If a scrub is already in progress, the "**zpool scrub**" command terminates it and starts a new scrub. If a resilver is in progress, **ZFS** does not allow a scrub to be started until the resilver completes.

-s   Stop scrubbing.

zpool export [-f] *pool* ...

Exports the given pools from the system. All devices are marked as exported, but are still considered in use by other subsystems. The devices can be moved between systems (even those of different endianness) and imported as long as a sufficient number of devices are present.

Before exporting the pool, all datasets within the pool are unmounted.

For pools to be portable, you must give the **zpool** command whole disks, not just slices, so that **ZFS** can label the disks with portable **EFI** labels. Otherwise, disk drivers on platforms of different endianness will not recognize the disks.

-**f**   Forcefully unmount all datasets, using the "**unmount -f**" command.

zpool import [-**d** *dir*] [-**D**]

Lists pools available to import. If the -**d** option is not specified, this command searches for devices in "/dev/dsk". The -**d** option can be specified multiple times, and all directories are searched. If the device appears to be part of an exported pool, this command displays a summary of the pool with the name of the pool, a numeric identifier, as well as the *vdev* layout and current health of the device for each device or file. Destroyed pools, pools that were previously destroyed with the "-**zpool destroy**" command, are not listed unless the -**D** option is specified.

The numeric identifier is unique, and can be used instead of the pool name when multiple exported pools of the same name are available.

-**d** *dir*   Searches for devices or files in *dir*. The -**d** option can be specified multiple times.

-**D**   Lists destroyed pools only.

zpool import [-**d** *dir*] [-**D**] [-**f**] [-**o** *opts*] [-**R** *root*] *pool* | *id* [*newpool*]

Imports a specific pool. A pool can be identified by its name or the numeric identifier. If *newpool* is specified, the pool is imported using the name *newpool*. Otherwise, it is imported with the same name as its exported name.

If a device is removed from a system without running "**zpool export**" first, the device appears as potentially active. It cannot be determined if this was a failed export, or whether the device is really in use from another host. To import a pool in this state, the -**f** option is required.

-**d** *dir*   Searches for devices or files in *dir*. The -**d** option can be specified multiple times.

-**D**   Imports destroyed pool. The -**f** option is also required.

-**f**   Forces import, even if the pool appears to be potentially active.

-**o** *opts*   Comma-separated list of mount options to use when mounting datasets within the pool. See **zfs**(1M) for a description of dataset properties and mount options.

-**R** *root*   Imports pool(s) with an alternate *root*. See the "Alternate Root Pools" section.

zpool import [-d *dir*] [-**D**] [-**f**] [-**a**]

Imports all pools found in the search directories. Identical to the previous command, except that all pools with a sufficient number of devices available are imported. Destroyed pools, pools that were previously destroyed with the "-**zpool destroy**" command, will not be imported unless the -**D** option is specified.

-**d** *dir*   Searches for devices or files in *dir*. The -**d** option can be specified multiple times.

-**D**   Imports destroyed pools only. The -**f** option is also required.

-**f**   Forces import, even if the pool appears to be potentially active.

zpool upgrade

Displays all pools formatted using a different **ZFS** on-disk version. Older versions can continue to be used, but some features may not be available. These pools can be upgraded using "**zpool upgrade -a**". Pools that are formatted with a more recent version are also displayed, although these pools will be inaccessible on the system.

zpool upgrade -v

Displays **ZFS** versions supported by the current software. The current **ZFS** versions and all previous supportedversions are displayed, along with an explanation of the features provided with each version.

zpool upgrade [-**a** | *pool*]

Upgrades the given pool to the latest on-disk version. Once this is done, the pool will no longer be accessible on systems running older versions of the software.

-**a**   Upgrades all pools.

zpool history [*pool*] ...

Displays the command history of the specified pools (or all pools if no pool is specified).

EXAMPLES

Example 1 Creating a RAID-Z Storage Pool

The following command creates a pool with a single **raidz** root *vdev* that consists of six disks.

 # zpool create tank raidz c0t0d0 c0t1d0 c0t2d0 c0t3d0 c0t4d0 c0t5d0

Example 2 Creating a Mirrored Storage Pool

The following command creates a pool with two mirrors, where each mirror contains two disks.

zpool create tank mirror c0t0d0 c0t1d0 mirror c0t2d0 c0t3d0

Example 3 Creating a ZFS Storage Pool by Using Slices

The following command creates an unmirrored pool using two disk slices.

zpool create tank /dev/dsk/c0t0d0s1 c0t1d0s4

Example 4 Creating a ZFS Storage Pool by Using Files

The following command creates an unmirrored pool using files. While not recommended, a pool based on files can be useful for experimental purposes.

zpool create tank /path/to/file/a /path/to/file/b

Example 5 Adding a Mirror to a ZFS Storage Pool

The following command adds two mirrored disks to the pool "*tank*", assuming the pool is already made up of two-way mirrors. The additional space is immediately available to any datasets within the pool.

zpool add tank mirror c1t0d0 c1t1d0

Example 6 Listing Available ZFS Storage Pools

The following command lists all available pools on the system. In this case, the pool *zion* is faulted due to a missing device.

The results from this command are similar to the following:

```
# zpool list
  NAME        SIZE   USED  AVAIL  CAP HEALTH    ALTROOT
  pool        67.5G  2.92M 67.5G   0% ONLINE    -
  tank        67.5G  2.92M 67.5G   0% ONLINE    -
  zion         -      -     -      0% FAULTED   -
```

Example 7 Destroying a ZFS Storage Pool

The following command destroys the pool "*tank*" and any datasets contained within.

zpool destroy -f tank

Example 8 Exporting a ZFS Storage Pool

The following command exports the devices in pool *tank* so that they can be relocated or later imported.

      # **zpool export tank**

Example 9 Importing a ZFS Storage Pool

The following command displays available pools, and then imports the pool "tank" for use on the system.

The results from this command are similar to the following:

      # **zpool import**
      pool: tank
       id: 15451357997522795478
      state: ONLINE
      action: The pool can be imported using its name or numeric identifier.
      config:

          tank   ONLINE
           mirror   ONLINE
            c1t2d0 ONLINE
            c1t3d0 ONLINE

      # **zpool import tank**

Example 10 Upgrading All ZFS Storage Pools to the Current Version

The following command upgrades all ZFS Storage pools to the current version of the software.

      # **zpool upgrade -a**
      This system is currently running ZFS version 2.

Example 11 Managing Hot Spares

The following command creates a new pool with an available hot spare:

      # **zpool create tank mirror c0t0d0 c0t1d0 spare c0t2d0**

If one of the disks were to fail, the pool would be reduced to the degraded state. The failed device can be replaced using the following command:

      # **zpool replace tank c0t0d0 c0t3d0**

Once the data has been resilvered, the spare is automatically removed and is made available should another device fails. The hot spare can be permanently removed from the pool using the following command:

      # **zpool remove tank c0t2d0**

EXIT STATUS

The following exit values are returned:

0   Successful completion.

1   An error occurred.

2   Invalid command line options were specified.

ATTRIBUTES

See **attributes**(5) for descriptions of the following attributes:

ATTRIBUTE TYPE	ATTRIBUTE VALUE
Availability	SUNWzfsu
Interface Stability	Evolving

SEE ALSO

zfs(1M), **attributes**(5)

Copyrights and Licenses

The following is a list of the known copyrights and licenses for the documentation used in the two volumes of the NetBSD System Manager's Manual. This represents over 110 licenses and many more copyrights. You'll notice that many of the licenses are near verbatim, but all have slight differences. (If you notice any duplicates here, please let the publisher know.)

---

intro.8

Copyright (c) 1983, 1991, 1993 The Regents of the University of California. All rights reserved.

arp.8

Copyright (c) 1985, 1991, 1993 The Regents of the University of California. All rights reserved.

bad144.8

Copyright (c) 1980, 1988, 1991, 1993 The Regents of the University of California. All rights reserved.

badsect.8

Copyright (c) 1985, 1991, 1993 The Regents of the University of California. All rights reserved.

boot.8

Copyright (c) 1991, 1993 The Regents of the University of California. All rights reserved.

amiga/boot.8

Copyright (c) 1990, 1991 The Regents of the University of California. All rights reserved.

atari/boot.8

Copyright (c) 1990, 1991 The Regents of the University of California. All rights reserved.

cobalt/boot.8

Copyright (c) 1991, 1993 The Regents of the University of California. All rights reserved.

hp300/boot.8

Copyright (c) 1990, 1991, 1993 The Regents of the University of California. All rights reserved.

i386/boot.8

Copyright (c) 1991, 1993 The Regents of the University of California. All rights reserved.

mac68k/boot.8

Copyright (c) 1990, 1991 The Regents of the University of California. All rights reserved.

mvme68k/boot.8

Copyright (c) 1992, 1993 The Regents of the University of California. All rights reserved.

next68k/boot.8

Copyright (c) 1990, 1991, 1993 The Regents of the University of California. All rights reserved.

pmax/boot.8

Copyright (c) 1990, 1991 The Regents of the University of California. All rights reserved.

sparc/boot.8

Copyright (c) 1992, 1993 The Regents of the University of California. All rights reserved.

sparc64/boot.8

Copyright (c) 1992, 1993 The Regents of the University of California. All rights reserved.

sun2/boot.8

Copyright (c) 1992, 1993 The Regents of the University of California. All rights reserved.

sun3/boot.8

Copyright (c) 1992, 1993 The Regents of the University of California. All rights reserved.

vax/boot.8

Copyright (c) 1980, 1991, 1993 The Regents of the University of California. All rights reserved.

x68k/boot.8

Copyright (c) 1980, 1991, 1993 The Regents of the University of California. All rights reserved.

chown.8

Copyright (c) 1990, 1991, 1993, 1994, 2003 The Regents of the University of California. All rights reserved.

chroot.8

Copyright (c) 1988, 1991, 1993 The Regents of the University of California. All rights reserved.

clri.8

Copyright (c) 1980, 1993 The Regents of the University of California. All rights reserved.

comsat.8

Copyright (c) 1983, 1991, 1993 The Regents of the University of California. All rights reserved.

hp300/crash.8

Copyright (c) 1990, 1991, 1993 The Regents of the University of California. All rights reserved.

vax/crash.8

Copyright (c) 1980, 1991, 1993 The Regents of the University of California. All rights reserved.

dev_mkdb.8

Copyright (c) 1990, 1993 The Regents of the University of California. All rights reserved.

disklabel.8

Copyright (c) 1987, 1988, 1991, 1993 The Regents of the University of California. All rights reserved.

diskpart.8

Copyright (c) 1983, 1991, 1993 The Regents of the University of California. All rights reserved.

dm.8

Copyright (c) 1987, 1991, 1993 The Regents of the University of California. All rights reserved.

dmesg.8

Copyright (c) 1980, 1991, 1993 The Regents of the University of California. All rights reserved.

vax/drtest.8

Copyright (c) 1983, 1991, 1993 The Regents of the University of California. All rights reserved.

dump.8

Copyright (c) 1980, 1991, 1993 Regents of the University of California. All rights reserved.

dump_lfs.8

Copyright (c) 1980, 1991, 1993 Regents of the University of California. All rights reserved.

dumpfs.8

Copyright (c) 1983, 1991, 1993 The Regents of the University of California. All rights reserved.

dumplfs.8

Copyright (c) 1993 The Regents of the University of California. All rights reserved.

edquota.8

mount_fdesc.8

mount_ffs.8

mount_kernfs.8

mount_lfs.8

mount_mfs.8

mount_nfs.8

mount_null.8

mount_overlay.8

mount_portal.8

mount_procfs.8

mount_sysvbfs.8

mount_umap.8

mount_union.8

mountd.8

newfs.8

newfs_ext2fs.8

newfs_lfs.8

newfs_sysvbfs.8

nfsd.8

nologin.8

ntalkd.8

pac.8

by Christopher G. Demetriou. 4. Neither the name of the University nor the names of its contributors may be used to endorse or promote products derived from this software without specific prior written permission.

accton.8

alpha/mkbootimage.8

modload.8

modstat.8

modunload.8

mount_ados.8

mount_msdos.8

mount_nilfs.8

mount_udf.8

sa.8

alpha/setnetbootinfo.8

ttyflags.8

acpidump.8

Copyright (c) 1999 Doug Rabson <dfr@FreeBSD.org>

Copyright (c) 2000 Mitsuru IWASAKI <iwasaki@FreeBSD.org>

Copyright (c) 2000 Yasuo YOKOYAMA <yokoyama@jp.FreeBSD.org>

Copyright (c) 2000 Hiroki Sato <hrs@FreeBSD.org> All rights reserved.

amldb.8

Copyright (c) 2000 Takanori Watanabe <takawata@FreeBSD.org>

Copyright (c) 2000 Mitsuru IWASAKI <iwasaki@FreeBSD.org>

Copyright (c) 2000 Yasuo YOKOYAMA <yokoyama@jp.FreeBSD.org>

Copyright (c) 2000 Norihiro KUMAGAI <kumagai@home.com>

afterboot.8

Copyright (c) 2002-2008 The NetBSD Foundation, Inc. All rights reserved.

Copyright (c) 1997 Marshall M. Midden All rights reserved.

compat_netbsd32.8

Copyright (c) 2001 Matthew R. Green All rights reserved.

compat_svr4.8

Copyright (c) 1996 Christos Zoulas All rights reserved.

fsck.8

Copyright (c) 1996 Christos Zoulas. All rights reserved.

getNAME.8

Copyright (c) 1997 Matthew R. Green All rights reserved.

httpd.8

Copyright (c) 1997-2010 Matthew R. Green All rights reserved.

mopchk.1

Copyright (c) 1996 Mats O Jansson. All rights reserved.

mopcopy.1

Copyright (c) 1996 Mats O Jansson. All rights reserved.

mopd.8

Copyright (c) 1993-96 Mats O Jansson. All rights reserved.

mopprobe.1

Copyright (c) 1996 Mats O Jansson. All rights reserved.

moptrace.1

Copyright (c) 1993-95 Mats O Jansson. All rights reserved.

netgroup_mkdb.8

Copyright (c) 1994 Christos Zoulas All rights reserved.

rdate.8

Copyright (c) 1994 Christos Zoulas All rights reserved.

rpc.rquotad.8

Copyright (c) 1994 Theo de Raadt All rights reserved.

rpc.sprayd.8

Copyright (c) 1994 Christos Zoulas All rights reserved.

scan_ffs.8

Copyright (c) 2005 Juan Romero Pardines

Copyright (c) 1997 Niklas Hallqvist, Tobias Weingartner All rights reserved.

sftp-server.8

Copyright (c) 2000 Markus Friedl. All rights reserved.

ssh-keysign.8

Copyright (c) 2002 Markus Friedl. All rights reserved.

swapctl.8

Copyright (c) 1997 Matthew R. Green All rights reserved.

anvil.8

bounce.8

cleanup.8

discard.8

error.8

flush.8

local.8

master.8

oqmgr.8

pickup.8

pipe.8

postalias.1

postcat.1

postconf.1

postdrop.1

postfix.1

postkick.1

postlock.1

postlog.1

postmap.1

postmulti.1

Copyright (c) 1997,1998,1999, International Business Machines Corporation and others. All Rights Reserved.

postqueue.1

Copyright (c) 1997,1998,1999, International Business Machines Corporation and others. All Rights Reserved.

postsuper.1

Copyright (c) 1997,1998,1999, International Business Machines Corporation and others. All Rights Reserved.

proxymap.8

Copyright (c) 1997,1998,1999, International Business Machines Corporation and others. All Rights Reserved.

qmgr.8

Copyright (c) 1997,1998,1999, International Business Machines Corporation and others. All Rights Reserved.

scache.8

Copyright (c) 1997,1998,1999, International Business Machines Corporation and others. All Rights Reserved.

sendmail.1

Copyright (c) 1997,1998,1999, International Business Machines Corporation and others. All Rights Reserved.

showq.8

Copyright (c) 1997,1998,1999, International Business Machines Corporation and others. All Rights Reserved.

smtp.8

Copyright (c) 1997,1998,1999, International Business Machines Corporation and others. All Rights Reserved.

smtpd.8

Copyright (c) 1997,1998,1999, International Business Machines Corporation and others. All Rights Reserved.

spawn.8

Copyright (c) 1997,1998,1999, International Business Machines Corporation and others. All Rights Reserved.

tlsmgr.8

Copyright (c) 1997,1998,1999, International Business Machines Corporation and others. All Rights Reserved.

trivial-rewrite.8

Copyright (c) 1997,1998,1999, International Business Machines Corporation and others. All Rights Reserved.

verify.8

Copyright (c) 1997,1998,1999, International Business Machines Corporation and others. All Rights Reserved.

virtual.8

Copyright (c) 1997,1998,1999, International Business Machines Corporation and others. All Rights Reserved.

IBM PUBLIC LICENSE VERSION 1.0 - SECURE MAILER

THE ACCOMPANYING PROGRAM IS PROVIDED UNDER THE TERMS OF THIS IBM PUBLIC LICENSE ("AGREE-MENT"). ANY USE, REPRODUCTION OR DISTRIBUTION OF THE PROGRAM CONSTITUTES RECIPIENT'S ACCEPTANCE OF THIS AGREEMENT.

1. DEFINITIONS

"Contribution" means: a) in the case of International Business Machines Corporation ("IBM"), the Original Program, and b) in the case of each Contributor, i) changes to the Program, and ii) additions to the Program; where such changes and/or additions to the Program originate from and are distributed by that particular Contributor. A Contribution 'originates' from a Contributor if it was added to the Program by such Contributor itself or anyone acting on such Contributor's behalf. Contributions do not include additions to the Program which: (i) are separate modules of software distributed in conjunction with the Program under their own license agreement, and (ii) are not derivative works of the Program.

"Contributor" means IBM and any other entity that distributes the Program.

"Licensed Patents " mean patent claims licensable by a Contributor which are necessarily infringed by the use or sale of its Contribution alone or when combined with the Program.

"Original Program" means the original version of the software accompanying this Agreement as released by IBM, including source code, object code and documentation, if any.

"Program" means the Original Program and Contributions.

"Recipient" means anyone who receives the Program under this Agreement, including all Contributors.

2. GRANT OF RIGHTS

a) Subject to the terms of this Agreement, each Contributor hereby grants Recipient a non-exclusive, worldwide, royalty-free copyright license to reproduce, prepare derivative works of, publicly display, publicly perform, distribute and sublicense the Contribution of such Contributor, if any, and such derivative works, in source code and object code form.

b) Subject to the terms of this Agreement, each Contributor hereby grants Recipient a non-exclusive, worldwide, royalty-free patent license under Licensed Patents to make, use, sell, offer to sell, import and otherwise transfer the Contribution of such Contributor, if any, in source code and object code form. This patent license shall apply to the combination of the Contribution and the Program if, at the time the Contribution is added by the Contributor, such addition of the Contribution causes such combination to be covered by the Licensed Patents. The patent license shall not apply to any other combinations which include the Contribution. No hardware per se is licensed hereunder.

c) Recipient understands that although each Contributor grants the licenses to its Contributions set forth herein, no assurances are provided by any Contributor that the Program does not infringe the patent or other intellectual property rights of any other entity. Each Contributor disclaims any liability to Recipient for claims brought by any other entity based on infringement of intellectual property rights or otherwise. As a condition to exercising the rights and licenses granted hereunder, each Recipient hereby assumes sole responsibility to secure any other intellectual property rights needed, if any. For example, if a third party patent license is required to allow Recipient to distribute the Program, it is Recipient's responsibility to acquire that license before distributing the Program.

d) Each Contributor represents that to its knowledge it has sufficient copyright rights in its Contribution, if any, to grant the copyright license set forth in this Agreement.

3. REQUIREMENTS

A Contributor may choose to distribute the Program in object code form under its own license agreement, provided that: a) it complies with the terms and conditions of this Agreement; and b) its license agreement: i) effectively disclaims on behalf of all Contributors all warranties and conditions, express and implied, including warranties or conditions of title and non-infringement, and implied warranties or conditions of merchantability and fitness for a particular purpose; ii) effectively excludes on behalf of all Contributors all liability for damages, including direct, indirect, special, incidental and consequential damages, such as lost profits; iii) states that any provisions which differ from this Agreement are offered by that Contributor alone and not by any other party; and iv) states that source code for the Program is available from such Contributor, and informs licensees how to obtain it in a reasonable manner on or through a medium customarily used for software exchange.

When the Program is made available in source code form: a) it must be made available under this Agreement; and b) a copy of this Agreement must be included with each copy of the Program.

Each Contributor must include the following in a conspicuous location in the Program:

In addition, each Contributor must identify itself as the originator of its Contribution, if any, in a manner that reasonably allows subsequent Recipients to identify the originator of the Contribution.

4. COMMERCIAL DISTRIBUTION

Commercial distributors of software may accept certain responsibilities with respect to end users, business partners and the like. While this license is intended to facilitate the commercial use of the Program, the Contributor who includes the Program in a commercial product offering should do so in a manner which does not create potential liability for other Contributors. Therefore, if a Contributor includes the Program in a commercial product offering, such Contributor ("Commercial Contributor") hereby agrees to defend and indemnify every other Contributor ("Indemnified Contributor") against any losses, damages and costs (collectively "Losses") arising from claims, lawsuits and other legal actions brought by a third party against the Indemnified Contributor to the extent caused by the acts or omissions of such Commercial Contributor in connection with its distribution of the Program in a commercial product offering. The obligations in this section do not apply to any claims or Losses relating to any actual or alleged intellectual property infringement. In order to qualify, an Indemnified Contributor must: a) promptly notify the Commercial Contributor in writing of such claim, and b) allow the Commercial Contributor to control, and cooperate with the Commercial Contributor in, the defense and any related settlement negotiations. The Indemnified Contributor may participate in any such claim at its own expense.

For example, a Contributor might include the Program in a commercial product offering, Product X. That Contributor is then a Commercial Contributor. If that Commercial Contributor then makes performance claims, or offers warranties related to Product X, those performance claims and warranties are such Commercial Contributor's responsibility alone. Under this section, the Commercial Contributor would have to defend claims against the other Contributors related to those performance claims and warranties, and if a court requires any other Contributor to pay any damages as a result, the Commercial Contributor must pay those damages.

5. NO WARRANTY

EXCEPT AS EXPRESSLY SET FORTH IN THIS AGREEMENT, THE PROGRAM IS PROVIDED ON AN "AS IS" BASIS, WITHOUT WARRANTIES OR CONDITIONS OF ANY KIND, EITHER EXPRESS OR IMPLIED INCLUDING, WITHOUT LIMITATION, ANY WARRANTIES OR CONDITIONS OF TITLE, NON-INFRINGEMENT, MERCHANTABILITY OR FITNESS FOR A PARTICULAR PURPOSE. Each Recipient is solely responsible for determining the appropriateness of using and distributing the Program and assumes all risks associated with its exercise of rights under this Agreement, including but not limited to the risks and costs of program errors, compliance with applicable laws, damage to or loss of data, programs or equipment, and unavailability or interruption of operations.

6. DISCLAIMER OF LIABILITY

---

compat_30.8

compat_osf1.8

cpuctl.8

crash.8

daicctl.1

dkscan_bsdlabel.8

eeprom.8

envstat.8

eshconfig.8

etcupdate.8

fsdb.8

fsirand.8

fssconfig.8

amiga/grfconfig.8

gspa.8

hdaudioctl.8

iasl.8

ifwatchd.8

installboot.8

amiga/installboot.8

atari/installboot.8

iopctl.8

resize_lfs.8

Copyright (c) 2005 The NetBSD Foundation, Inc. All rights reserved.

revoke.8

Copyright (c) 2006 The NetBSD Foundation, Inc. All rights reserved.

schedctl.8

Copyright (c) 2008 The NetBSD Foundation, Inc. All rights reserved.

screenblank.1

Copyright (c) 1996-2002 The NetBSD Foundation, Inc. All rights reserved.

scsictl.8

Copyright (c) 1998, 2002 The NetBSD Foundation, Inc. All rights reserved.

services_mkdb.8

Copyright (c) 1999 The NetBSD Foundation, Inc. All rights reserved.

sti.8

Copyright (c) 2005 The NetBSD Foundation, Inc. All rights reserved.

sunlabel.8

Copyright (c) 2002 The NetBSD Foundation, Inc. All rights reserved.

sysinst.8

Copyright (c) 2007 The NetBSD Foundation, Inc. All rights reserved.

sparc/tadpolectl.8

Copyright (c) 1999 The NetBSD Foundation, Inc. All rights reserved.

tpctl.8

Copyright (c) 2002 The NetBSD Foundation, Inc. All rights reserved.

unlink.8

Copyright (c) 1999 The NetBSD Foundation, Inc. All rights reserved.

usbdevs.8

Copyright (c) 1999 The NetBSD Foundation, Inc. All rights reserved.

utmp_update.8

Copyright (c) 2002 The NetBSD Foundation, Inc. All rights reserved.

veriexecgen.8

Copyright (c) 2006 The NetBSD Foundation, Inc. All rights reserved.

virecover.8

Copyright (c) 2006 The NetBSD Foundation, Inc. All rights reserved.

wizd.8

Copyright (c) 2003 The NetBSD Foundation, Inc. All rights reserved.

wsmuxctl.8

Copyright (c) 2001 The NetBSD Foundation, Inc. All rights reserved.

ypbind.8

Copyright (c) 1996 The NetBSD Foundation, Inc. All rights reserved.

ypinit.8

Copyright (c) 1997 The NetBSD Foundation, Inc. All rights reserved.

yppoll.8

Copyright (c) 1996 The NetBSD Foundation, Inc. All rights reserved.

ypset.8

---

apmlabel.8

mbrlabel.8

quot.8

svhlabel.8

---

atf-cleanup.1

atf-format.1

---

atrun.8

hpcmips/boot.8

cron.8

dbsym.8

dmsetup.8

fdisk.8

mvme68k/installboot.8

ipfstat.8

ipnat.8

x68k/loadbsd.8

i386/mbr.8

mscdlabel.8

hpcmips/pbsdboot.8

pdisk.8

pppdump.8

pppstats.8

pvcsif.8

rpc.bootparamd.8

rpc.pcnfsd.8

rpcbind.8

Copyright 1989 AT&T

Copyright 1991 Sun Microsystems, Inc.

rpcinfo.8

Copyright 1989 AT&T

Copyright 1991 Sun Microsystems, Inc.

rtquery.8

wpa_passphrase.8

Missing license. See the website for details.

---

authpf.8

Copyright (c) 1998-2007 Bob Beck (beck@openbsd.org>. All rights reserved.

ftp-proxy.8

Copyright (c) 2004, 2005 Camiel Dobbelaar, <cd@sentia.nl>

gpioctl.8

Copyright (c) 2009 Marc Balmer <marc@msys.ch>

Copyright (c) 2004 Alexander Yurchenko <grange@openbsd.org>

wake.8

Copyright (c) 2009, 2010 Marc Balmer <marc@msys.ch>

amiga/binpatch.8

atari/binpatch.8

iteconfig.8

bioctl.8

alpha/boot.8

hp700/boot.8

hpcarm/boot.8

hpcsh/boot.8

hpcboot.8

sgimips/boot.8

sgimips/sgivol.8

i386/boot_console.8

dhcpcd.8

dhcpcd-run-hooks.8

i386/dosboot.8

drvctl.8

dtmfdecode.1

extattrctl.8

hostapd.8

hostapd_cli.8

isdnd.8

isdnmonitor.8

isdntel.8

isdntelctl.8

isdntrace.8

mount_9p.8

acorn26/boot26.8

---

bootptest.8

---

brconfig.8

dkctl.8

makefs.8

pcictl.8

powerd.8

---

btattach.8

compat_sunos.8

Copyright (c) 1984 Theo de Raadt All rights reserved.

fwctl.8

Copyright (c) 2005 KIYOHARA Takashi All rights reserved.

Copyright (c) 2002 Hidetoshi Shimokawa All rights reserved.

makedbm.8

Copyright (c) 1994 Mats O Jansson <moj@stacken.kth.se> All rights reserved.

mkalias.8

Copyright (c) 1997 Mats O Jansson <moj@stacken.kth.se> All rights reserved.

mknetid.8

Copyright (c) 1996 Mats O Jansson <moj@stacken.kth.se> All rights reserved.

rescue.8

Copyright (c) 2003 Tim Kientzle <kientzle@acm.org>

Copyright (c) 2003 Simon L. Nielsen <simon@FreeBSD.org> All rights reserved.

rpc.yppasswdd.8

Copyright (c) 1994 Mats O Jansson <moj@stacken.kth.se> All rights reserved.

stdethers.8

Copyright (c) 1995 Mats O Jansson <moj@stacken.kth.se> All rights reserved.

stdhosts.8

Copyright (c) 1994 Mats O Jansson <moj@stacken.kth.se> All rights reserved.

yppush.8

Copyright (c) 1995 Mats O Jansson <moj@stacken.kth.se> All rights reserved.

ypserv.8

Copyright (c) 1994 Mats O Jansson <moj@stacken.kth.se> All rights reserved.

yptest.8

Copyright (c) 1994 Mats O Jansson <moj@stacken.kth.se> All rights reserved.

ypxfr.8

Copyright (c) 1994 Mats O Jansson <moj@stacken.kth.se> All rights reserved.

---

btconfig.8

Copyright (c) 2006 Itronix Inc. All rights reserved.

---

btdevctl.8

bthcid.8

---

catman.8

chat.8

The chat program is in public domain. This is not the GNU public license. If it breaks then you get to keep both pieces.

cnwctl.8

compat_darwin.8

compat_freebsd.8

compat_linux.8

A PARTICULAR PURPOSE ARE DISCLAIMED. IN NO EVENT SHALL THE AUTHOR BE LIABLE FOR ANY DI-RECT, INDIRECT, INCIDENTAL, SPECIAL, EXEMPLARY, OR CONSEQUENTIAL DAMAGES (INCLUDING, BUT NOT LIMITED TO, PROCUREMENT OF SUBSTITUTE GOODS OR SERVICES; LOSS OF USE, DATA, OR PROF-ITS; OR BUSINESS INTERRUPTION) HOWEVER CAUSED AND ON ANY THEORY OF LIABILITY, WHETHER IN CONTRACT, STRICT LIABILITY, OR TORT (INCLUDING NEGLIGENCE OR OTHERWISE) ARISING IN ANY WAY OUT OF THE USE OF THIS SOFTWARE, EVEN IF ADVISED OF THE POSSIBILITY OF SUCH DAMAGE.

rndc.8

---

faithd.8

ifmcstat.8

mld6query.8

ndp.8

ping6.8

racoon.8

racoonctl.8

rip6query.8

rtadvd.8

rtsold.8

setkey.8

traceroute6.8

hprop.8

Copyright (c) 2000 - 2004 Kungliga Tekniska Högskolan (Royal Institute of Technology, Stockholm, Sweden). All rights reserved.

hpropd.8

Copyright (c) 1997, 2000 - 2003 Kungliga Tekniska Högskolan (Royal Institute of Technology, Stockholm, Sweden). All rights reserved.

iprop.8

Copyright (c) 2005 Kungliga Tekniska Högskolan (Royal Institute of Technology, Stockholm, Sweden). All rights reserved.

iprop-log.8

Copyright (c) 2005 - 2007 Kungliga Tekniska Högskolan (Royal Institute of Technology, Stockholm, Sweden). All rights reserved.

kadmin.8

Copyright (c) 2000 - 2007 Kungliga Tekniska Högskolan (Royal Institute of Technology, Stockholm, Sweden). All rights reserved.

kadmind.8

Copyright (c) 2002 - 2004 Kungliga Tekniska Högskolan (Royal Institute of Technology, Stockholm, Sweden). All rights reserved.

kcm.8

Copyright (c) 2005 Kungliga Tekniska Högskolan (Royal Institute of Technology, Stockholm, Sweden). All rights reserved.

kdc.8

Copyright (c) 2003 - 2004 Kungliga Tekniska Högskolan (Royal Institute of Technology, Stockholm, Sweden). All rights reserved.

kerberos.8

Copyright (c) 2000 Kungliga Tekniska Högskolan (Royal Institute of Technology, Stockholm, Sweden). All rights reserved.

kimpersonate.1

Copyright (c) 2002 - 2007 Kungliga Tekniska Högskolan (Royal Institute of Technology, Stockholm, Sweden). All rights reserved.

kpasswdd.8

Copyright (c) 1997, 2000 - 2005 Kungliga Tekniska Högskolan (Royal Institute of Technology, Stockholm, Sweden). All rights reserved.

kstash.8

Copyright (c) 1997 - 2004 Kungliga Tekniska Högskolan (Royal Institute of Technology, Stockholm, Sweden). All rights reserved.

ktutil.8

Copyright (c) 1997-2004 Kungliga Tekniska Högskolan (Royal Institute of Technology, Stockholm, Sweden). All rights reserved.

string2key.8

CONTRIBUTORS BE LIABLE FOR ANY DIRECT, INDIRECT, INCIDENTAL, SPECIAL, EXEMPLARY, OR CONSEQUENTIAL DAMAGES (INCLUDING, BUT NOT LIMITED TO, PROCUREMENT OF SUBSTITUTE GOODS OR SERVICES; LOSS OF USE, DATA, OR PROFITS; OR BUSINESS INTERRUPTION) HOWEVER CAUSED AND ON ANY THEORY OF LIABILITY, WHETHER IN CONTRACT, STRICT LIABILITY, OR TORT (INCLUDING NEGLIGENCE OR OTHERWISE) ARISING IN ANY WAY OUT OF THE USE OF THIS SOFTWARE, EVEN IF ADVISED OF THE POSSIBILITY OF SUCH DAMAGE.

I hate legalese, don't you ?

---

ipwctl.8

iwictl.8

Redistribution and use in source and binary forms, with or without modification, are permitted provided that the following conditions are met: 1. Redistributions of source code must retain the above copyright notice unmodified, this list of conditions, and the following disclaimer. 2. Redistributions in binary form must reproduce the above copyright notice, this list of conditions and the following disclaimer in the documentation and/or other materials provided with the distribution.

THIS SOFTWARE IS PROVIDED BY THE AUTHOR AND CONTRIBUTORS "AS IS" AND ANY EXPRESS OR IMPLIED WARRANTIES, INCLUDING, BUT NOT LIMITED TO, THE IMPLIED WARRANTIES OF MERCHANTABILITY AND FITNESS FOR A PARTICULAR PURPOSE ARE DISCLAIMED. IN NO EVENT SHALL THE AUTHOR OR CONTRIBUTORS BE LIABLE FOR ANY DIRECT, INDIRECT, INCIDENTAL, SPECIAL, EXEMPLARY, OR CONSEQUENTIAL DAMAGES (INCLUDING, BUT NOT LIMITED TO, PROCUREMENT OF SUBSTITUTE GOODS OR SERVICES; LOSS OF USE, DATA, OR PROFITS; OR BUSINESS INTERRUPTION) HOWEVER CAUSED AND ON ANY THEORY OF LIABILITY, WHETHER IN CONTRACT, STRICT LIABILITY, OR TORT (INCLUDING NEGLIGENCE OR OTHERWISE) ARISING IN ANY WAY OUT OF THE USE OF THIS SOFTWARE, EVEN IF ADVISED OF THE POSSIBILITY OF SUCH DAMAGE.

---

kdigest.8

Redistribution and use in source and binary forms, with or without modification, are permitted provided that the following conditions are met:

1. Redistributions of source code must retain the above copyright notice, this list of conditions and the following disclaimer.

2. Redistributions in binary form must reproduce the above copyright notice, this list of conditions and the following disclaimer in the documentation and/or other materials provided with the distribution.

3. Neither the name of the Institute nor the names of its contributors may be used to endorse or promote products derived from this software without specific prior written permission.

THIS SOFTWARE IS PROVIDED BY THE INSTITUTE AND CONTRIBUTORS "AS IS" AND ANY EXPRESS OR IMPLIED WARRANTIES, INCLUDING, BUT NOT LIMITED TO, THE IMPLIED WARRANTIES OF MERCHANTABILITY AND FITNESS FOR A PARTICULAR PURPOSE ARE DISCLAIMED. IN NO EVENT SHALL THE INSTITUTE OR CONTRIBUTORS BE LIABLE FOR ANY DIRECT, INDIRECT, INCIDENTAL, SPECIAL, EXEMPLARY, OR CONSEQUENTIAL DAMAGES (INCLUDING, BUT NOT LIMITED TO, PROCUREMENT OF SUBSTITUTE GOODS OR SERVICES; LOSS OF USE, DATA, OR PROFITS; OR BUSINESS INTERRUPTION) HOWEVER CAUSED AND ON ANY THEORY OF LIABILITY, WHETHER IN CONTRACT, STRICT LIABILITY, OR TORT (INCLUDING NEGLIGENCE OR OTHERWISE) ARISING IN ANY WAY OUT OF THE USE OF THIS SOFTWARE, EVEN IF ADVISED OF THE POSSIBILITY OF SUCH DAMAGE.

Id

---

lastlogin.8

Redistribution and use in source and binary forms, with or without modification, are permitted provided that the following conditions are met: 1. Redistributions of source code must retain the above copyright notice, this list of conditions and the following disclaimer. 2. Redistributions in binary form must reproduce the above copyright notice, this list of conditions and the following disclaimer in the documentation and/or other materials provided with the distribution. 3. All advertising materials mentioning features or use of this software must display the following acknowledgement: This product includes software developed for the NetBSD Project by John M. Vinopal. 4. The name of the author may not be used to endorse or promote products derived from this software without specific prior written permission.

lmcconfig.8

BSD License:

GNU General Public License:

lvchange.8

lvconvert.8

lvcreate.8

lvdisplay.8

lvextend.8

lvm.8

lvmchange.8

lvmdiskscan.8

lvmdump.8

lvreduce.8

lvremove.8

lvrename.8

lvresize.8

lvs.8

lvscan.8

pvchange.8

pvck.8

pvcreate.8

pvdisplay.8

pvmove.8

pvremove.8

pvresize.8

pvs.8

pvscan.8

vgcfgbackup.8

vgcfgrestore.8

vgchange.8

vgck.8

vgconvert.8

vgcreate.8

vgdisplay.8

vgexport.8

vgextend.8

vgimport.8

vgmerge.8

vgmknodes.8

vgreduce.8

vgremove.8

vgrename.8

vgs.8

vgscan.8

vgsplit.8

GNU GENERAL PUBLIC LICENSE Version 2, June 1991

Preamble

The licenses for most software are designed to take away your freedom to share and change it. By contrast, the GNU General Public License is intended to guarantee your freedom to share and change free software–to make sure the software is free for all its users. This General Public License applies to most of the Free Software Foundation's software and to any other program whose authors commit to using it. (Some other Free Software Foundation software is covered by the GNU Library General Public License instead.) You can apply it to your programs, too.

When we speak of free software, we are referring to freedom, not price. Our General Public Licenses are designed to make sure that you have the freedom to distribute copies of free software (and charge for this service if you wish), that you receive source code or can get it if you want it, that you can change the software or use pieces of it in new free programs; and that you know you can do these things.

To protect your rights, we need to make restrictions that forbid anyone to deny you these rights or to ask you to surrender the rights. These restrictions translate to certain responsibilities for you if you distribute copies of the software, or if you modify it.

For example, if you distribute copies of such a program, whether gratis or for a fee, you must give the recipients all the rights that you have. You must make sure that they, too, receive or can get the source code. And you must show them these terms so they know their rights.

We protect your rights with two steps: (1) copyright the software, and (2) offer you this license which gives you legal permission to copy, distribute and/or modify the software.

Also, for each author's protection and ours, we want to make certain that everyone understands that there is no warranty for this free software. If the software is modified by someone else and passed on, we want its recipients to know that what they have is not the original, so that any problems introduced by others will not reflect on the original authors' reputations.

Finally, any free program is threatened constantly by software patents. We wish to avoid the danger that redistributors of a free program will individually obtain patent licenses, in effect making the program proprietary. To prevent this, we have made it clear that any patent must be licensed for everyone's free use or not licensed at all.

The precise terms and conditions for copying, distribution and modification follow.

GNU GENERAL PUBLIC LICENSE TERMS AND CONDITIONS FOR COPYING, DISTRIBUTION AND MODIFICATION

0. This License applies to any program or other work which contains a notice placed by the copyright holder saying it may be distributed under the terms of this General Public License. The "Program", below, refers to any such program or work, and a "work based on the Program" means either the Program or any derivative work under copyright law: that is to say, a work containing the Program or a portion of it, either verbatim or with modifications and/or translated into another language. (Hereinafter, translation is included without limitation in the term "modification".) Each licensee is addressed as "you".

Activities other than copying, distribution and modification are not covered by this License; they are outside its scope. The act of running the Program is not restricted, and the output from the Program is covered only if its contents constitute a work based on the Program (independent of having been made by running the Program). Whether that is true depends on what the Program does.

1. You may copy and distribute verbatim copies of the Program's source code as you receive it, in any medium, provided that you conspicuously and appropriately publish on each copy an appropriate copyright notice and disclaimer of warranty; keep intact all the notices that refer to this License and to the absence of any warranty; and give any other recipients of the Program a copy of this License along with the Program.

You may charge a fee for the physical act of transferring a copy, and you may at your option offer warranty protection in exchange for a fee.

2. You may modify your copy or copies of the Program or any portion of it, thus forming a work based on the Program, and copy and distribute such modifications or work under the terms of Section 1 above, provided that you also meet all of these conditions:

a) You must cause the modified files to carry prominent notices stating that you changed the files and the date of any change.

b) You must cause any work that you distribute or publish, that in whole or in part contains or is derived from the Program or any part thereof, to be licensed as a whole at no charge to all third parties under the terms of this License.

c) If the modified program normally reads commands interactively when run, you must cause it, when started running for such interactive use in the most ordinary way, to print or display an announcement including an appropriate copyright notice and a notice that there is no warranty (or else, saying that you provide a warranty) and that users may redistribute the program under these conditions, and telling the user how to view a copy of this License. (Exception: if the Program itself is interactive but does not normally print such an announcement, your work based on the Program is not required to print an announcement.)

These requirements apply to the modified work as a whole. If identifiable sections of that work are not derived from the Program, and can be reasonably considered independent and separate works in themselves, then this License, and its terms, do not apply to those sections when you distribute them as separate works. But when you distribute the same sections as part of a whole which is a work based on the Program, the distribution of the whole must be on the terms of this License, whose permissions for other licensees extend to the entire whole, and thus to each and every part regardless of who wrote it.

Thus, it is not the intent of this section to claim rights or contest your rights to work written entirely by you; rather, the intent is to exercise the right to control the distribution of derivative or collective works based on the Program.

In addition, mere aggregation of another work not based on the Program with the Program (or with a work based on the Program) on a volume of a storage or distribution medium does not bring the other work under the scope of this License.

3. You may copy and distribute the Program (or a work based on it, under Section 2) in object code or executable form under the terms of Sections 1 and 2 above provided that you also do one of the following:

a) Accompany it with the complete corresponding machine-readable source code, which must be distributed under the terms of Sections 1 and 2 above on a medium customarily used for software interchange; or,

b) Accompany it with a written offer, valid for at least three years, to give any third party, for a charge no more than your cost of physically performing source distribution, a complete machine-readable copy of the corresponding source code, to be distributed under the terms of Sections 1 and 2 above on a medium customarily used for software interchange; or,

c) Accompany it with the information you received as to the offer to distribute corresponding source code. (This alternative is allowed only for noncommercial distribution and only if you received the program in object code or executable form with such an offer, in accord with Subsection b above.)

The source code for a work means the preferred form of the work for making modifications to it. For an executable work, complete source code means all the source code for all modules it contains, plus any associated interface definition files, plus the scripts used to control compilation and installation of the executable. However, as a special exception, the source code distributed need not include anything that is normally distributed (in either source or binary form) with the major components (compiler, kernel, and so on) of the operating system on which the executable runs, unless that component itself accompanies the executable.

If distribution of executable or object code is made by offering access to copy from a designated place, then offering equivalent access to copy the source code from the same place counts as distribution of the source code, even though third parties are not compelled to copy the source along with the object code.

4. You may not copy, modify, sublicense, or distribute the Program except as expressly provided under this License. Any attempt otherwise to copy, modify, sublicense or distribute the Program is void, and will automatically terminate your rights under this License. However, parties who have received copies, or rights, from you under this License will not have their licenses terminated so long as such parties remain in full compliance.

5. You are not required to accept this License, since you have not signed it. However, nothing else grants you permission to modify or distribute the Program or its derivative works. These actions are prohibited by law if you do not accept this License. Therefore, by modifying or distributing the Program (or any work based on the Program), you indicate your acceptance of this License to do so, and all its terms and conditions for copying, distributing or modifying the Program or works based on it.

6. Each time you redistribute the Program (or any work based on the Program), the recipient automatically receives a license from the original licensor to copy, distribute or modify the Program subject to these terms and conditions. You may not impose any further restrictions on the recipients' exercise of the rights granted herein. You are not responsible for enforcing compliance by third parties to this License.

7. If, as a consequence of a court judgment or allegation of patent infringement or for any other reason (not limited to patent issues), conditions are imposed on you (whether by court order, agreement or otherwise) that contradict the conditions of this License, they do not excuse you from the conditions of this License. If you cannot distribute so as to satisfy simultaneously your obligations under this License and any other pertinent obligations, then as a consequence you may not distribute the Program at all. For example, if a patent license would not permit royalty-free redistribution of the Program by all those who receive copies directly or indirectly through you, then the only way you could satisfy both it and this License would be to refrain entirely from distribution of the Program.

If any portion of this section is held invalid or unenforceable under any particular circumstance, the balance of the section is intended to apply and the section as a whole is intended to apply in other circumstances.

It is not the purpose of this section to induce you to infringe any patents or other property right claims or to contest validity of any such claims; this section has the sole purpose of protecting the integrity of the free software distribution system, which is implemented by public license practices. Many people have made generous contributions to the wide range of software distributed through that system in reliance on consistent application of that system; it is up to the author/donor to decide if he or she is willing to distribute software through any other system and a licensee cannot impose that choice.

This section is intended to make thoroughly clear what is believed to be a consequence of the rest of this License.

8. If the distribution and/or use of the Program is restricted in certain countries either by patents or by copyrighted interfaces, the original copyright holder who places the Program under this License may add an explicit geographical distribution limitation excluding those countries, so that distribution is permitted only in or among countries not thus excluded. In such case, this License incorporates the limitation as if written in the body of this License.

9. The Free Software Foundation may publish revised and/or new versions of the General Public License from time to time. Such new versions will be similar in spirit to the present version, but may differ in detail to address new problems or concerns.

Each version is given a distinguishing version number. If the Program specifies a version number of this License which applies to it and "any later version", you have the option of following the terms and conditions either of that version or of any later version published by the Free Software Foundation. If the Program does not specify a version number of this License, you may choose any version ever published by the Free Software Foundation.

10. If you wish to incorporate parts of the Program into other free programs whose distribution conditions are different, write to the author to ask for permission. For software which is copyrighted by the Free Software Foundation, write to the Free Software Foundation; we sometimes make exceptions for this. Our decision will be guided by the two goals of preserving the free status of all derivatives of our free software and of promoting the sharing and reuse of software generally.

NO WARRANTY

11. BECAUSE THE PROGRAM IS LICENSED FREE OF CHARGE, THERE IS NO WARRANTY FOR THE PRO-GRAM, TO THE EXTENT PERMITTED BY APPLICABLE LAW. EXCEPT WHEN OTHERWISE STATED IN WRIT-ING THE COPYRIGHT HOLDERS AND/OR OTHER PARTIES PROVIDE THE PROGRAM "AS IS" WITHOUT WAR-RANTY OF ANY KIND, EITHER EXPRESSED OR IMPLIED, INCLUDING, BUT NOT LIMITED TO, THE IMPLIED WARRANTIES OF MERCHANTABILITY AND FITNESS FOR A PARTICULAR PURPOSE. THE ENTIRE RISK AS TO THE QUALITY AND PERFORMANCE OF THE PROGRAM IS WITH YOU. SHOULD THE PROGRAM PROVE DEFECTIVE, YOU ASSUME THE COST OF ALL NECESSARY SERVICING, REPAIR OR CORRECTION.

12. IN NO EVENT UNLESS REQUIRED BY APPLICABLE LAW OR AGREED TO IN WRITING WILL ANY COPY-RIGHT HOLDER, OR ANY OTHER PARTY WHO MAY MODIFY AND/OR REDISTRIBUTE THE PROGRAM AS PERMITTED ABOVE, BE LIABLE TO YOU FOR DAMAGES, INCLUDING ANY GENERAL, SPECIAL, INCIDEN-TAL OR CONSEQUENTIAL DAMAGES ARISING OUT OF THE USE OR INABILITY TO USE THE PROGRAM (INCLUDING BUT NOT LIMITED TO LOSS OF DATA OR DATA BEING RENDERED INACCURATE OR LOSSES SUSTAINED BY YOU OR THIRD PARTIES OR A FAILURE OF THE PROGRAM TO OPERATE WITH ANY OTHER PROGRAMS), EVEN IF SUCH HOLDER OR OTHER PARTY HAS BEEN ADVISED OF THE POSSIBILITY OF SUCH DAMAGES.

END OF TERMS AND CONDITIONS

How to Apply These Terms to Your New Programs

If you develop a new program, and you want it to be of the greatest possible use to the public, the best way to achieve this is to make it free software which everyone can redistribute and change under these terms.

To do so, attach the following notices to the program. It is safest to attach them to the start of each source file to most effectively convey the exclusion of warranty; and each file should have at least the "copyright" line and a pointer to where the full notice is found.

<one line to give the program's name and a brief idea of what it does.> Copyright (C) <year> <name of author>

This program is free software; you can redistribute it and/or modify it under the terms of the GNU General Public License as published by the Free Software Foundation; either version 2 of the License, or (at your option) any later version.

This program is distributed in the hope that it will be useful, but WITHOUT ANY WARRANTY; without even the implied warranty of MERCHANTABILITY or FITNESS FOR A PARTICULAR PURPOSE. See the GNU General Public License for more details.

You should have received a copy of the GNU General Public License along with this program; if not, write to the Free Software Foundation, Inc., 59 Temple Place, Suite 330, Boston, MA 02111-1307 USA

Also add information on how to contact you by electronic and paper mail.

If the program is interactive, make it output a short notice like this when it starts in an interactive mode:

Gnomovision version 69, Copyright (C) year name of author Gnomovision comes with ABSOLUTELY NO WARRANTY; for details type 'show w'. This is free software, and you are welcome to redistribute it under certain conditions; type 'show c' for details.

The hypothetical commands 'show w' and 'show c' should show the appropriate parts of the General Public License. Of course, the commands you use may be called something other than 'show w' and 'show c'; they could even be mouse-clicks or menu items—whatever suits your program.

You should also get your employer (if you work as a programmer) or your school, if any, to sign a "copyright disclaimer" for the program, if necessary. Here is a sample; alter the names:

Yoyodyne, Inc., hereby disclaims all copyright interest in the program 'Gnomovision' (which makes passes at compilers) written by James Hacker.

<signature of Ty Coon>, 1 April 1989 Ty Coon, President of Vice

This General Public License does not permit incorporating your program into proprietary programs. If your program is a subroutine library, you may consider it more useful to permit linking proprietary applications with the library. If this is what you want to do, use the GNU Library General Public License instead of this License.

mailwrapper.8

The following requests are required for all man pages.

map-mbone.8

mdnsd.8

Apache License Version 2.0, January 2004 http://www.apache.org/licenses/

TERMS AND CONDITIONS FOR USE, REPRODUCTION, AND DISTRIBUTION

1. Definitions.

"License" shall mean the terms and conditions for use, reproduction, and distribution as defined by Sections 1 through 9 of this document.

"Licensor" shall mean the copyright owner or entity authorized by the copyright owner that is granting the License.

"Legal Entity" shall mean the union of the acting entity and all other entities that control, are controlled by, or are under common control with that entity. For the purposes of this definition, "control" means (i) the power, direct or indirect, to cause the direction or management of such entity, whether by contract or otherwise, or (ii) ownership of fifty percent (50%) or more of the outstanding shares, or (iii) beneficial ownership of such entity.

"You" (or "Your") shall mean an individual or Legal Entity exercising permissions granted by this License.

"Source" form shall mean the preferred form for making modifications, including but not limited to software source code, documentation source, and configuration files.

"Object" form shall mean any form resulting from mechanical transformation or translation of a Source form, including but not limited to compiled object code, generated documentation, and conversions to other media types.

"Work" shall mean the work of authorship, whether in Source or Object form, made available under the License, as indicated by a copyright notice that is included in or attached to the work (an example is provided in the Appendix below).

"Derivative Works" shall mean any work, whether in Source or Object form, that is based on (or derived from) the Work and for which the editorial revisions, annotations, elaborations, or other modifications represent, as a whole, an original work of authorship. For the purposes of this License, Derivative Works shall not include works that remain separable from, or merely link (or bind by name) to the interfaces of, the Work and Derivative Works thereof.

"Contribution" shall mean any work of authorship, including the original version of the Work and any modifications or additions to that Work or Derivative Works thereof, that is intentionally submitted to Licensor for inclusion in the Work by the copyright owner or by an individual or Legal Entity authorized to submit on behalf of the copyright owner. For the purposes of this definition, "submitted" means any form of electronic, verbal, or written communication sent to the Licensor or its representatives, including but not limited to communication on electronic mailing lists, source code control systems, and issue tracking systems that are managed by, or on behalf of, the Licensor for the purpose of discussing and improving the Work, but excluding communication that is conspicuously marked or otherwise designated in writing by the copyright owner as "Not a Contribution."

"Contributor" shall mean Licensor and any individual or Legal Entity on behalf of whom a Contribution has been received by Licensor and subsequently incorporated within the Work.

2. Grant of Copyright License. Subject to the terms and conditions of this License, each Contributor hereby grants to You a perpetual, worldwide, non-exclusive, no-charge, royalty-free, irrevocable copyright license to reproduce, prepare Derivative Works of, publicly display, publicly perform, sublicense, and distribute the Work and such Derivative Works in Source or Object form.

3. Grant of Patent License. Subject to the terms and conditions of this License, each Contributor hereby grants to You a perpetual, worldwide, non-exclusive, no-charge, royalty-free, irrevocable (except as stated in this section) patent license to make, have made, use, offer to sell, sell, import, and otherwise transfer the Work, where such license applies only to those patent claims licensable by such Contributor that are necessarily infringed by their Contribution(s) alone or by combination of their Contribution(s) with the Work to which such Contribution(s) was submitted. If You institute patent litigation against any entity (including a cross-claim or counterclaim in a lawsuit) alleging that the Work or a Contribution incorporated within the Work constitutes direct or contributory patent infringement, then any patent licenses granted to You under this License for that Work shall terminate as of the date such litigation is filed.

4. Redistribution. You may reproduce and distribute copies of the Work or Derivative Works thereof in any medium, with or without modifications, and in Source or Object form, provided that You meet the following conditions:

(a) You must give any other recipients of the Work or Derivative Works a copy of this License; and

(b) You must cause any modified files to carry prominent notices stating that You changed the files; and

(c) You must retain, in the Source form of any Derivative Works that You distribute, all copyright, patent, trademark, and attribution notices from the Source form of the Work, excluding those notices that do not pertain to any part of the Derivative Works; and

(d) If the Work includes a "NOTICE" text file as part of its distribution, then any Derivative Works that You distribute must include a readable copy of the attribution notices contained within such NOTICE file, excluding those notices that do not pertain to any part of the Derivative Works, in at least one of the following places: within a NOTICE text file distributed as part of the Derivative Works; within the Source form or documentation, if provided along with the Derivative Works; or, within a display generated by the Derivative Works, if and wherever such third-party notices normally appear. The contents of the NOTICE file are for informational purposes only and do not modify the License. You may add Your own attribution notices within Derivative Works that You distribute, alongside or as an addendum to the NOTICE text from the Work, provided that such additional attribution notices cannot be construed as modifying the License.

You may add Your own copyright statement to Your modifications and may provide additional or different license terms and conditions for use, reproduction, or distribution of Your modifications, or for any such Derivative Works as a whole, provided Your use, reproduction, and distribution of the Work otherwise complies with the conditions stated in this License.

5. Submission of Contributions. Unless You explicitly state otherwise, any Contribution intentionally submitted for inclusion in the Work by You to the Licensor shall be under the terms and conditions of this License, without any additional terms or conditions. Notwithstanding the above, nothing herein shall supersede or modify the terms of any separate license agreement you may have executed with Licensor regarding such Contributions.

6. Trademarks. This License does not grant permission to use the trade names, trademarks, service marks, or product names of the Licensor, except as required for reasonable and customary use in describing the origin of the Work and reproducing the content of the NOTICE file.

7. Disclaimer of Warranty. Unless required by applicable law or agreed to in writing, Licensor provides the Work (and each Contributor provides its Contributions) on an "AS IS" BASIS, WITHOUT WARRANTIES OR CONDITIONS OF ANY KIND, either express or implied, including, without limitation, any warranties or conditions of TITLE, NON-INFRINGEMENT, MERCHANTABILITY, or FITNESS FOR A PARTICULAR PURPOSE. You are solely responsible

for determining the appropriateness of using or redistributing the Work and assume any risks associated with Your exercise of permissions under this License.

8. Limitation of Liability. In no event and under no legal theory, whether in tort (including negligence), contract, or otherwise, unless required by applicable law (such as deliberate and grossly negligent acts) or agreed to in writing, shall any Contributor be liable to You for damages, including any direct, indirect, special, incidental, or consequential damages of any character arising as a result of this License or out of the use or inability to use the Work (including but not limited to damages for loss of goodwill, work stoppage, computer failure or malfunction, or any and all other commercial damages or losses), even if such Contributor has been advised of the possibility of such damages.

9. Accepting Warranty or Additional Liability. While redistributing the Work or Derivative Works thereof, You may choose to offer, and charge a fee for, acceptance of support, warranty, indemnity, or other liability obligations and/or rights consistent with this License. However, in accepting such obligations, You may act only on Your own behalf and on Your sole responsibility, not on behalf of any other Contributor, and only if You agree to indemnify, defend, and hold each Contributor harmless for any liability incurred by, or claims asserted against, such Contributor by reason of your accepting any such warranty or additional liability.

END OF TERMS AND CONDITIONS

---

mmcformat.8

newfs_msdos.8

newfs_udf.8

pppoectl.8

mount_filecore.8

mount_ntfs.8

moused.8

mrinfo.8

OF SUBSTITUTE GOODS OR SERVICES; LOSS OF USE, DATA, OR PROFITS; OR BUSINESS INTERRUPTION) HOWEVER CAUSED AND ON ANY THEORY OF LIABILITY, WHETHER IN CONTRACT, STRICT LIABILITY, OR TORT (INCLUDING NEGLIGENCE OR OTHERWISE) ARISING IN ANY WAY OUT OF THE USE OF THIS SOFTWARE, EVEN IF ADVISED OF THE POSSIBILITY OF SUCH DAMAGE.

mrouted.8

Copyright © 1989, 2002 The Board of Trustees of the Leland Stanford Junior University

Permission is hereby granted to STANFORD's rights, free of charge, to any person obtaining a copy of this Software and associated documentation files ("MROUTED"), to deal in MROUTED without restriction, including without limitation the rights to use, copy, modify, merge, publish, distribute, sublicense, and/or sell copies of MROUTED , and to permit persons to whom MROUTED is furnished to do so, subject to the following conditions: 1) The above copyright notice and this permission notice shall be included in all copies or substantial portions of the MROUTED . 2) Neither the STANFORD name nor the names of its contributors may be used in any promotional advertising or other promotional materials to be disseminated to the public or any portion thereof nor to use the name of any STANFORD faculty member, employee, or student, or any trademark, service mark, trade name, or symbol of STANFORD or Stanford Hospitals and Clinics, nor any that is associated with any of them, without STANFORD's prior written consent. Any use of STANFORD's name shall be limited to statements of fact and shall not imply endorsement of any products or services.

3) MROUTED IS PROVIDED "AS IS", WITHOUT WARRANTY OF ANY KIND, EXPRESS OR IMPLIED, INCLUDING BUT NOT LIMITED TO THE WARRANTIES OF MERCHANTABILITY, FITNESS FOR A PARTICULAR PURPOSE AND NONINFRINGEMENT. IN NO EVENT SHALL THE AUTHORS OR COPYRIGHT HOLDERS BE LIABLE FOR ANY CLAIM, DAMAGES OR OTHER LIABILITY, WHETHER IN AN ACTION OF CONTRACT, TORT OR OTHER-WISE, ARISING FROM, OUT OF OR IN CONNECTION WITH MROUTED OR THE USE OR OTHER DEALINGS IN THE MROUTED .

mtrace.8

Copyright (c) 1995 by the University of Southern California All rights reserved.

Copyright (c) 1988 The Regents of the University of California. All rights reserved.

Permission to use, copy, modify, and distribute this software and its documentation in source and binary forms for non-commercial purposes and without fee is hereby granted, provided that the above copyright notice appear in all copies and that both the copyright notice and this permission notice appear in supporting documentation, and that any documentation, advertising materials, and other materials related to such distribution and use acknowledge that the software was developed by the University of Southern California, Information Sciences Institute. The name of the University may not be used to endorse or promote products derived from this software without specific prior written permission.

THE UNIVERSITY OF SOUTHERN CALIFORNIA makes no representations about the suitability of this software for any purpose. THIS SOFTWARE IS PROVIDED "AS IS" AND WITHOUT ANY EXPRESS OR IMPLIED WARRANTIES, INCLUDING, WITHOUT LIMITATION, THE IMPLIED WARRANTIES OF MERCHANTABILITY AND FITNESS FOR A PARTICULAR PURPOSE.

Other copyrights might apply to parts of this software and are so noted when applicable.

mtree.8

Copyright (c) 1989, 1990, 1993 The Regents of the University of California. All rights reserved.

Copyright (c) 2001-2004 The NetBSD Foundation, Inc. All rights reserved.

Redistribution and use in source and binary forms, with or without modification, are permitted provided that the following conditions are met: 1. Redistributions of source code must retain the above copyright notice, this list of conditions and the following disclaimer. 2. Redistributions in binary form must reproduce the above copyright notice, this list of conditions and the following disclaimer in the documentation and/or other materials provided with the distribution. 3. Neither the name of the University nor the names of its contributors may be used to endorse or promote products derived from this software without specific prior written permission.

THIS SOFTWARE IS PROVIDED BY THE REGENTS AND CONTRIBUTORS "AS IS" AND ANY EXPRESS OR IMPLIED WARRANTIES, INCLUDING, BUT NOT LIMITED TO, THE IMPLIED WARRANTIES OF MERCHANTABILITY AND FITNESS FOR A PARTICULAR PURPOSE ARE DISCLAIMED. IN NO EVENT SHALL THE REGENTS OR CONTRIBUTORS BE LIABLE FOR ANY DIRECT, INDIRECT, INCIDENTAL, SPECIAL, EXEMPLARY, OR CONSEQUENTIAL DAMAGES (INCLUDING, BUT NOT LIMITED TO, PROCUREMENT OF SUBSTITUTE GOODS OR SERVICES; LOSS OF USE, DATA, OR PROFITS; OR BUSINESS INTERRUPTION) HOWEVER CAUSED AND ON ANY THEORY OF LIABILITY, WHETHER IN CONTRACT, STRICT LIABILITY, OR TORT (INCLUDING NEGLIGENCE OR OTHERWISE) ARISING IN ANY WAY OUT OF THE USE OF THIS SOFTWARE, EVEN IF ADVISED OF THE POSSIBILITY OF SUCH DAMAGE.

ncdcs.8

ndbootd.8

i386/ndiscvt.8

wiconfig.8

newbtconf.8

---

x68k/newdisk.8

x68k/rtcalarm.8

---

newsyslog.8

Copyright 2005 Tyler C. Sarna <tsarna@netbsd.org>

wsmoused.8

Copyright (c) 2002, 2003 The NetBSD Foundation, Inc. All rights reserved.

pam_chroot.8

Copyright (c) 2003 Networks Associates Technology, Inc. All rights reserved.

pam_echo.8

Copyright (c) 2001,2003 Networks Associates Technology, Inc. All rights reserved.

pam_exec.8

Copyright (c) 2001,2003 Networks Associates Technology, Inc. All rights reserved.

pam_ftpusers.8

Copyright (c) 2001 Mark R V Murray All rights reserved.

Copyright (c) 2002 Networks Associates Technology, Inc. All rights reserved.

pam_group.8

Copyright (c) 2003 Networks Associates Technology, Inc. All rights reserved.

pam_guest.8

Copyright (c) 2003 Networks Associates Technology, Inc. All rights reserved.

pam_lastlog.8

Copyright (c) 2001 Mark R V Murray All rights reserved.

Copyright (c) 2001 Networks Associates Technology, Inc. All rights reserved.

pam_login_access.8

Copyright (c) 2001 Mark R V Murray All rights reserved.

Copyright (c) 2001 Networks Associates Technology, Inc. All rights reserved.

pam_rhosts.8

Copyright (c) 2001 Mark R V Murray All rights reserved.

Copyright (c) 2001 Networks Associates Technology, Inc. All rights reserved.

pam_securetty.8

Copyright (c) 2001 Mark R V Murray All rights reserved.

Copyright (c) 2002 Networks Associates Technology, Inc. All rights reserved.

pam_self.8

Copyright (c) 2001 Mark R V Murray All rights reserved.

Copyright (c) 2001 Networks Associates Technology, Inc. All rights reserved.

Portions of this software were developed for the FreeBSD Project by ThinkSec AS and NAI Labs, the Security Research Division of Network Associates, Inc. under DARPA/SPAWAR contract N66001-01-C-8035 ("CBOSS"), as part of the DARPA CHATS research program.

---

pam_krb5.8

---

pam_ksu.8

pam_ssh.8

pam_unix.8

pam_radius.8

paxctl.8

pkg_add.1

pkg_create.1

pkg_delete.1

pkg_info.1

pkg_admin.1

pppd.8

quotaon.8

raidctl.8

rarpd.8

rbootd.8

rcorder.8

revnetgroup.8

route6d.8

rpc.lockd.8

rpc.statd.8

rump_cd9660.8

rump_efs.8

rump_ext2fs.8

rump_ffs.8

rump_hfs.8

rump_lfs.8

rump_msdos.8

rump_nfs.8

rump_ntfs.8

rump_smbfs.8

rump_syspuffs.8

rump_sysvbfs.8

rump_tmpfs.8

rump_udf.8

sntp.1

spray.8

srtconfig.1

zdump.8

zic.8

This file is in the public domain.

---

tcpdrop.8

tcpdump.8

tftp-proxy.8

traceroute.8

veriexecctl.8

vnconfig.8

---

wdogctl.8

---

wlanctl.8

---

zdb.8

zfs.8

zpool.8

COMMON DEVELOPMENT AND DISTRIBUTION LICENSE Version 1.0

1. Definitions.

1.1. "Contributor" means each individual or entity that creates or contributes to the creation of Modifications.

1.2. "Contributor Version" means the combination of the Original Software, prior Modifications used by a Contributor (if any), and the Modifications made by that particular Contributor.

1.3. "Covered Software" means (a) the Original Software, or (b) Modifications, or (c) the combination of files containing Original Software with files containing Modifications, in each case including portions thereof.

1.4. "Executable" means the Covered Software in any form other than Source Code.

1.5. "Initial Developer" means the individual or entity that first makes Original Software available under this License.

1.6. "Larger Work" means a work which combines Covered Software or portions thereof with code not governed by the terms of this License.

1.7. "License" means this document.

1.8. "Licensable" means having the right to grant, to the maximum extent possible, whether at the time of the initial grant or subsequently acquired, any and all of the rights conveyed herein.

1.9. "Modifications" means the Source Code and Executable form of any of the following:

A. Any file that results from an addition to, deletion from or modification of the contents of a file containing Original Software or previous Modifications;

B. Any new file that contains any part of the Original Software or previous Modifications; or

C. Any new file that is contributed or otherwise made available under the terms of this License.

1.10. "Original Software" means the Source Code and Executable form of computer software code that is originally released under this License.

1.11. "Patent Claims" means any patent claim(s), now owned or hereafter acquired, including without limitation, method, process, and apparatus claims, in any patent Licensable by grantor.

1.12. "Source Code" means (a) the common form of computer software code in which modifications are made and (b) associated documentation included in or with such code.

1.13. "You" (or "Your") means an individual or a legal entity exercising rights under, and complying with all of the terms of, this License. For legal entities, "You" includes any entity which controls, is controlled by, or is under common control with You. For purposes of this definition, "control" means (a) the power, direct or indirect, to cause the direction or management of such entity, whether by contract or otherwise, or (b) ownership of more than fifty percent (50%) of the outstanding shares or beneficial ownership of such entity.

2. License Grants.

2.1. The Initial Developer Grant.

Conditioned upon Your compliance with Section 3.1 below and subject to third party intellectual property claims, the Initial Developer hereby grants You a world-wide, royalty-free, non-exclusive license:

(a) under intellectual property rights (other than patent or trademark) Licensable by Initial Developer, to use, reproduce, modify, display, perform, sublicense and distribute the Original Software (or portions thereof), with or without Modifications, and/or as part of a Larger Work; and

(b) under Patent Claims infringed by the making, using or selling of Original Software, to make, have made, use, practice, sell, and offer for sale, and/or otherwise dispose of the Original Software (or portions thereof).

(c) The licenses granted in Sections 2.1(a) and (b) are effective on the date Initial Developer first distributes or otherwise makes the Original Software available to a third party under the terms of this License.

(d) Notwithstanding Section 2.1(b) above, no patent license is granted: (1) for code that You delete from the Original Software, or (2) for infringements caused by: (i) the modification of the Original Software, or (ii) the combination of the Original Software with other software or devices.

2.2. Contributor Grant.

Conditioned upon Your compliance with Section 3.1 below and subject to third party intellectual property claims, each Contributor hereby grants You a world-wide, royalty-free, non-exclusive license:

(a) under intellectual property rights (other than patent or trademark) Licensable by Contributor to use, reproduce, modify, display, perform, sublicense and distribute the Modifications created by such Contributor (or portions thereof), either on an unmodified basis, with other Modifications, as Covered Software and/or as part of a Larger Work; and

(b) under Patent Claims infringed by the making, using, or selling of Modifications made by that Contributor either alone and/or in combination with its Contributor Version (or portions of such combination), to make, use, sell, offer for sale, have made, and/or otherwise dispose of: (1) Modifications made by that Contributor (or portions thereof); and (2) the combination of Modifications made by that Contributor with its Contributor Version (or portions of such combination).

(c) The licenses granted in Sections 2.2(a) and 2.2(b) are effective on the date Contributor first distributes or otherwise makes the Modifications available to a third party.

(d) Notwithstanding Section 2.2(b) above, no patent license is granted: (1) for any code that Contributor has deleted from the Contributor Version; (2) for infringements caused by: (i) third party modifications of Contributor Version, or (ii) the combination of Modifications made by that Contributor with other software (except as part of the Contributor Version) or other devices; or (3) under Patent Claims infringed by Covered Software in the absence of Modifications made by that Contributor.

3. Distribution Obligations.

3.1. Availability of Source Code.

Any Covered Software that You distribute or otherwise make available in Executable form must also be made available in Source Code form and that Source Code form must be distributed only under the terms of this License. You must include a copy of this License with every copy of the Source Code form of the Covered Software You distribute or otherwise make available. You must inform recipients of any such Covered Software in Executable form as to how they can obtain such Covered Software in Source Code form in a reasonable manner on or through a medium customarily used for software exchange.

3.2. Modifications.

The Modifications that You create or to which You contribute are governed by the terms of this License. You represent that You believe Your Modifications are Your original creation(s) and/or You have sufficient rights to grant the rights conveyed by this License.

3.3. Required Notices.

You must include a notice in each of Your Modifications that identifies You as the Contributor of the Modification. You may not remove or alter any copyright, patent or trademark notices contained within the Covered Software, or any notices of licensing or any descriptive text giving attribution to any Contributor or the Initial Developer.

3.4. Application of Additional Terms.

You may not offer or impose any terms on any Covered Software in Source Code form that alters or restricts the applicable version of this License or the recipients' rights hereunder. You may choose to offer, and to charge a fee for, warranty, support, indemnity or liability obligations to one or more recipients of Covered Software. However, you may do so only on Your own behalf, and not on behalf of the Initial Developer or any Contributor. You must make it absolutely clear that any such warranty, support, indemnity or liability obligation is offered by You alone, and You hereby agree to indemnify the Initial Developer and every Contributor for any liability incurred by the Initial Developer or such Contributor as a result of warranty, support, indemnity or liability terms You offer.

3.5. Distribution of Executable Versions.

You may distribute the Executable form of the Covered Software under the terms of this License or under the terms of a license of Your choice, which may contain terms different from this License, provided that You are in compliance with the terms of this License and that the license for the Executable form does not attempt to limit or alter the recipient's rights in the Source Code form from the rights set forth in this License. If You distribute the Covered Software in Executable form under a different license, You must make it absolutely clear that any terms which differ from this License are offered by You alone, not by the Initial Developer or Contributor. You hereby agree to indemnify the Initial Developer and every Contributor for any liability incurred by the Initial Developer or such Contributor as a result of any such terms You offer.

3.6. Larger Works.

You may create a Larger Work by combining Covered Software with other code not governed by the terms of this License and distribute the Larger Work as a single product. In such a case, You must make sure the requirements of this License are fulfilled for the Covered Software.

4. Versions of the License.

4.1. New Versions.

Sun Microsystems, Inc. is the initial license steward and may publish revised and/or new versions of this License from time to time. Each version will be given a distinguishing version number. Except as provided in Section 4.3, no one other than the license steward has the right to modify this License.

4.2. Effect of New Versions.

You may always continue to use, distribute or otherwise make the Covered Software available under the terms of the version of the License under which You originally received the Covered Software. If the Initial Developer includes a notice in the Original Software prohibiting it from being distributed or otherwise made available under any subsequent version of the License, You must distribute and make the Covered Software available under the terms of the version of the License under which You originally received the Covered Software. Otherwise, You may also choose to use, distribute or otherwise make the Covered Software available under the terms of any subsequent version of the License published by the license steward.

4.3. Modified Versions.

When You are an Initial Developer and You want to create a new license for Your Original Software, You may create and use a modified version of this License if You: (a) rename the license and remove any references to the name of the license steward (except to note that the license differs from this License); and (b) otherwise make it clear that the license contains terms which differ from this License.

5. DISCLAIMER OF WARRANTY.

COVERED SOFTWARE IS PROVIDED UNDER THIS LICENSE ON AN "AS IS" BASIS, WITHOUT WARRANTY OF ANY KIND, EITHER EXPRESSED OR IMPLIED, INCLUDING, WITHOUT LIMITATION, WARRANTIES THAT THE COVERED SOFTWARE IS FREE OF DEFECTS, MERCHANTABLE, FIT FOR A PARTICULAR PURPOSE OR NON-INFRINGING. THE ENTIRE RISK AS TO THE QUALITY AND PERFORMANCE OF THE COVERED SOFTWARE IS WITH YOU. SHOULD ANY COVERED SOFTWARE PROVE DEFECTIVE IN ANY RESPECT, YOU (NOT THE INITIAL DEVELOPER OR ANY OTHER CONTRIBUTOR) ASSUME THE COST OF ANY NECESSARY SERVICING, REPAIR OR CORRECTION. THIS DISCLAIMER OF WARRANTY CONSTITUTES AN ESSENTIAL PART OF THIS LICENSE. NO USE OF ANY COVERED SOFTWARE IS AUTHORIZED HEREUNDER EXCEPT UNDER THIS DISCLAIMER.

6. TERMINATION.

6.1. This License and the rights granted hereunder will terminate automatically if You fail to comply with terms herein and fail to cure such breach within 30 days of becoming aware of the breach. Provisions which, by their nature, must remain in effect beyond the termination of this License shall survive.

6.2. If You assert a patent infringement claim (excluding declaratory judgment actions) against Initial Developer or a Contributor (the Initial Developer or Contributor against whom You assert such claim is referred to as "Participant") alleging that the Participant Software (meaning the Contributor Version where the Participant is a Contributor or the Original Software where the Participant is the Initial Developer) directly or indirectly infringes any patent, then any and all rights granted directly or indirectly to You by such Participant, the Initial Developer (if the Initial Developer is not the Participant) and all Contributors under Sections 2.1 and/or 2.2 of this License shall, upon 60 days notice from Participant terminate prospectively and automatically at the expiration of such 60 day notice period, unless if within such 60 day period You withdraw Your claim with respect to the Participant Software against such Participant either unilaterally or pursuant to a written agreement with Participant.

6.3. In the event of termination under Sections 6.1 or 6.2 above, all end user licenses that have been validly granted by You or any distributor hereunder prior to termination (excluding licenses granted to You by any distributor) shall survive termination.

7. LIMITATION OF LIABILITY.

UNDER NO CIRCUMSTANCES AND UNDER NO LEGAL THEORY, WHETHER TORT (INCLUDING NEGLIGENCE), CONTRACT, OR OTHERWISE, SHALL YOU, THE INITIAL DEVELOPER, ANY OTHER CONTRIBUTOR, OR ANY DISTRIBUTOR OF COVERED SOFTWARE, OR ANY SUPPLIER OF ANY OF SUCH PARTIES, BE LIABLE TO ANY PERSON FOR ANY INDIRECT, SPECIAL, INCIDENTAL, OR CONSEQUENTIAL DAMAGES OF ANY CHARACTER INCLUDING, WITHOUT LIMITATION, DAMAGES FOR LOST PROFITS, LOSS OF GOODWILL, WORK STOPPAGE, COMPUTER FAILURE OR MALFUNCTION, OR ANY AND ALL OTHER COMMERCIAL DAMAGES OR LOSSES, EVEN IF SUCH PARTY SHALL HAVE BEEN INFORMED OF THE POSSIBILITY OF SUCH DAMAGES. THIS LIMITATION OF LIABILITY SHALL NOT APPLY TO LIABILITY FOR DEATH OR PERSONAL INJURY RESULTING FROM SUCH PARTY'S NEGLIGENCE TO THE EXTENT APPLICABLE LAW PROHIBITS SUCH LIMITATION. SOME JURISDICTIONS DO NOT ALLOW THE EXCLUSION OR LIMITATION OF INCIDENTAL OR CONSEQUENTIAL DAMAGES, SO THIS EXCLUSION AND LIMITATION MAY NOT APPLY TO YOU.

8. U.S. GOVERNMENT END USERS.

The Covered Software is a "commercial item," as that term is defined in 48 C.F.R. 2.101 (Oct. 1995), consisting of "commercial computer software" (as that term is defined at 48 C.F.R. 252.227-7014(a)(1)) and "commercial computer software documentation" as such terms are used in 48 C.F.R. 12.212 (Sept. 1995). Consistent with 48 C.F.R. 12.212 and 48 C.F.R. 227.7202-1 through 227.7202-4 (June 1995), all U.S. Government End Users acquire Covered Software with only those rights set forth herein. This U.S. Government Rights clause is in lieu of, and supersedes, any other FAR, DFAR, or other clause or provision that addresses Government rights in computer software under this License.

9. MISCELLANEOUS.

This License represents the complete agreement concerning subject matter hereof. If any provision of this License is held to be unenforceable, such provision shall be reformed only to the extent necessary to make it enforceable. This License shall be governed by the law of the jurisdiction specified in a notice contained within the Original Software (except to the extent applicable law, if any, provides otherwise), excluding such jurisdiction's conflict-of-law provisions. Any litigation relating to this License shall be subject to the jurisdiction of the courts located in the jurisdiction and venue specified in a notice contained within the Original Software, with the losing party responsible for costs, including, without limitation, court costs and reasonable attorneys' fees and expenses. The application of the United Nations Convention on Contracts for the International Sale of Goods is expressly excluded. Any law or regulation which provides that the language of a contract shall be construed against the drafter shall not apply to this License. You agree that You alone are responsible for compliance with the United States export administration regulations (and the export control laws and regulation of any other countries) when You use, distribute or otherwise make available any Covered Software.

10. RESPONSIBILITY FOR CLAIMS.

As between Initial Developer and the Contributors, each party is responsible for claims and damages arising, directly or indirectly, out of its utilization of rights under this License and You agree to work with Initial Developer and Contributors to distribute such responsibility on an equitable basis. Nothing herein is intended or shall be deemed to constitute any admission of liability.

www.ingramcontent.com/pod-product-compliance
Lightning Source LLC
Chambersburg PA
CBHW080128060326
40689CB00018B/3712